Research Anthology on Usage, Identity, and Impact of Social Media on Society and Culture

Information Resources Management Association
USA

Volume I

IGI Global
PUBLISHER of TIMELY KNOWLEDGE

Published in the United States of America by
IGI Global
Information Science Reference (an imprint of IGI Global)
701 E. Chocolate Avenue
Hershey PA, USA 17033
Tel: 717-533-8845
Fax: 717-533-8661
E-mail: cust@igi-global.com
Web site: http://www.igi-global.com

Library of Congress Cataloging-in-Publication Data

Names: Information Resources Management Association, editor.
Title: Research anthology on usage, identity, and impact of social media on
   society and culture / Information Resources Management Association,
   editor.
Description: Hershey, PA : Information Science Reference, [2022] | Includes
   bibliographical references and index. | Summary: "This reference set
   discusses the impact social media has on an individuals' identity
   formation as well as its usage within society and cultures, exploring
   new research methodologies and findings into the behavior of users on
   social media as well as the effects of social media on society and
   culture as a whole"-- Provided by publisher.
Identifiers: LCCN 2022016910 (print) | LCCN 2022016911 (ebook) | ISBN
   9781668463079 (hardcover) | ISBN 9781668463086 (ebook)
Subjects: LCSH: Social media--Psychological aspects. | Identity
   (Psychology) | Social media and society.
Classification: LCC HM742 .R46783 2022 (print) | LCC HM742 (ebook) | DDC
   302.23--dc23/eng/20220509
LC record available at https://lccn.loc.gov/2022016910
LC ebook record available at https://lccn.loc.gov/2022016911

British Cataloguing in Publication Data
A Cataloguing in Publication record for this book is available from the British Library.

For electronic access to this publication, please contact: eresources@igi-global.com.

List of Contributors

Table of Contents

Section 2
Development and Design Methodologies

Volume II

Section 3
Tools and Technologies

Section 4
Utilization and Applications

Volume III

Section 5
Organizational and Social Implications

Preface

Over the years, social media has blossomed from a leisure tool used by a select pool of younger individuals to an essential form of communication for everyone. It has connected individuals globally and has become an essential practice in marketing, advertising, broadcasting news stories, conducting research, and more. The internet has quickly become a new hub for communication and community development. In most communities, people develop new cultural norms and identity through social media usage. However, while these new lines of communication are helpful to many, challenges such as social media addiction, cyberbullying, and misinformation lurk on the internet and threaten forces both within and beyond the internet.

Staying informed of the most up-to-date research trends and findings is of the utmost importance. That is why IGI Global is pleased to offer this three-volume reference collection of reprinted IGI Global book chapters and journal articles that have been handpicked by senior editorial staff. This collection will shed light on critical issues related to the trends, techniques, and uses of various applications by providing both broad and detailed perspectives on cutting-edge theories and developments. This collection is designed to act as a single reference source on conceptual, methodological, technical, and managerial issues, as well as to provide insight into emerging trends and future opportunities within the field.

The *Research Anthology on Usage, Identity, and Impact of Social Media on Society and Culture* is organized into six distinct sections that provide comprehensive coverage of important topics. The sections are:

1. Fundamental Concepts and Theories;
2. Development and Design Methodologies;
3. Tools and Technologies;
4. Utilization and Applications;
5. Organizational and Social Implications; and
6. Critical Issues and Challenges.

The following paragraphs provide a summary of what to expect from this invaluable reference tool.

Section 1, "Fundamental Concepts and Theories," serves as a foundation for this extensive reference tool by addressing crucial theories essential to understanding the usage, identity, and impact of social media. The first chapter of this section, "The Dark Side of Engaging With Social Networking Sites (SNS)," by Profs. Eileen O'Donnell and Liam O'Donnell of Technological University Dublin, Ireland, explores the dark side of social networking sites. The final chapter of this section, "The Facebook Me: Gender, Self-Esteem, and Personality on Social Media," by Profs. Robert Andrew Dunn and Heng Zhang of East Tennessee State University, USA, examines the influence of gender, personality, and self-esteem on social media presentation.

Section 2, "Development and Design Methodologies," presents in-depth coverage of the design and development of social media assessment and research. The first chapter of this section, "Psychological Impact and Assessment of Youth for the Use of Social Network," by Profs. Sapna Jain and M. Afshar Alam of Jamia Hamdard, India and Prof. Niloufer Adil Kazmi of Independent Researcher, India, dissects the effect of online life on each youngster in both the negative and positive bearing of their development utilizing the social impact hypothesis. The final chapter of this section, "At the Mercy of Facebook: A Meta-Analysis on Impact of Social Networking Sites, Teen Brain on Teenage Pregnancies," by Prof. Nirupama R. Akella of Wichita State University, USA, is a meta-analysis of teen brain research and social media technology such as Facebook that could result in spiraling rates of teenage pregnancy. The author discusses contemporary theories of brain circuitry including teen brain structure and function as one of the plausible reasons for rising teenage pregnancy rates.

Section 3, "Tools and Technologies," explores the various tools and technologies used in communications and research on social media. The first chapter of this section, "Collaborative Social Networks: Effect of User Motivation, Cognition, and Behavior on User Participation," by Prof. Yulin Chen of Tamkang University, New Taipei City, Taiwan, investigates the relationships between the motivation, cognition, and behavior of knowledge management. It analyzes university students preparing to share content on the Tamshui Humanities Knowledge Collaboration System to determine whether different participation motivation dimensions (community motivation and personal motivation) affected their knowledge management cognition and behavior. The final chapter of this section, "The Important Role of the Blogosphere as a Communication Tool in Social Media Among Polish Young Millennials: A Fact or a Myth?" by Profs. Sylwia Kuczamer-Kłopotowska and Anna Kalinowska-Żeleźnik of University of Gdańsk, Poland, proposes and discusses the hypothesis that the blogosphere is a relatively well-developed and independent social media communication tool used by millennials.

Section 4, "Utilization and Applications," describes the interactions between users on social media. The first chapter of this section, "Adolescents, Third-Person Perception, and Facebook," by Prof. John Chapin of Pennsylvania State University, USA, documents the extent of Facebook use and cyberbullying among adolescents. It is based on a study theoretically grounded in third-person perception (TPP), the belief that media messages affect other people more than oneself. The final chapter of this section, "Facebook Communities of African Diasporas and Their U.S. Embassies: A Content Analysis Study," by Prof. Hesham Mesbah of Rollins College, USA and Prof. Lauren Cooper of Florida House of Representatives, USA, explores how the Nigerian, Ethiopian, and Egyptian diasporas in the United States use their Facebook groups to create their imagined communities. It also draws a parallel between their use of Facebook and how the embassies of their countries of origin use the same platform in performing their official duties.

Section 5, "Organizational and Social Implications," includes chapters discussing the impact of social media usage and interpersonal interaction on society. The first chapter of this section, "Understanding Social Media Addiction Through Personal, Social, and Situational Factors," by Prof. Asli Elif Aydin of Istanbul Bilgi University, Turkey and Prof. Ozge Kirezli of Yeditepe University, Turkey, gains an in-depth understanding of the social media addiction construct. The final chapter of this section, "Transformation of China's Most Popular Dating App, Momo, and Its Impact on Young Adult Sexuality: A Critical Social Construction of Technology Analysis," by Prof. Weishan Miao of Chinese Academy of Social Sciences, China and Prof. Jian Xu of Deakin University, Australia, explores China's most popular dating app 'Momo' and its impact on young adult sexuality.

Section 6, "Critical Issues and Challenges," presents coverage of academic and research perspectives on the critical issues imposed by social media on its users, communities, and society. The first chapter of this section, "Positive vs. Negative Emotions and Network Size: An Exploratory Study of Twitter Users," by Prof. Yeslam Al-Saggaf of Charles Sturt University, Australia, examines the relationship between the expression of positive and negative emotions in Twitter and users' network size. The final chapter of this section, "The Tipping Point: A Comparative Study of U.S. and Korean Users on Decisions to Switch Social Media Platforms," by Prof. Soo Kwang Oh of Pepperdine University, USA; Prof. Seoyeon Hong of Rowan University, USA; and Prof. Hee Sun Park of Korea University, South Korea, focuses on why users quit certain social media and change their favorite platforms, such as the current shift from Facebook to Twitter to Instagram and Snapchat. Furthermore, this exploratory study builds an understanding of social media usage and motivations for switching from a cross-cultural perspective by comparing findings from Korean and U.S. users.

Although the primary organization of the contents in this multi-volume work is based on its six sections, offering a progression of coverage of the important concepts, methodologies, technologies, applications, social issues, and emerging trends, the reader can also identify specific contents by utilizing the extensive indexing system listed at the end of each volume. As a comprehensive collection of research on the latest findings related to social media, the *Research Anthology on Usage, Identity, and Impact of Social Media on Society and Culture* provides social media analysts, communications specialists, computer scientists, online community moderators, sociologists, psychologists, business leaders and managers, marketers, advertising agencies, government officials, libraries, students and faculty of higher education, researchers, and academicians with a complete understanding of the applications and impacts of social media. Given the vast number of issues concerning usage, failure, success, strategies, and applications of social media, the *Research Anthology on Usage, Identity, and Impact of Social Media on Society and Culture* encompasses the most pertinent research on the applications, impacts, uses, and research strategies of social media.

Section 1
Fundamental Concepts and Theories

Chapter 1
The Dark Side of Engaging With Social Networking Sites (SNS)

Eileen O'Donnell
Technological University Dublin, Ireland

Liam O'Donnell
Technological University Dublin, Ireland

ABSTRACT

Although social networking sites (SNS) may have some positive aspects, for example, connecting family members and friends who no longer live close enough to each other to meet in person, or for connecting people with similar health conditions who may need the support of others who understand and can manage the condition, or for groups of people with similar interests to engage and plan events and activities, there are also some possible negative aspects of engaging with SNS, for example, addiction or addictive behaviour, child pornography, cyberbullying, fake news, fear of missing out (FOMO), social comparisons, stalking, amongst many others, which can all lead to neglect of other duties, sleep deprivation, loneliness, isolation, depression, and so forth. The possible negative effects of engaging with SNS on the surface web will perhaps be also relevant to users of the deep and dark web. This article explores the dark side of social networking sites.

INTRODUCTION

Although engagement with the deep or dark web may seem to some to be intimating or possibly threatening, the surface web similarly presents users with challenges which may also be detrimental to one's peace of mind or health. This paper reviews the dark side of engaging with the surface web through the use of Social Networking Sites (SNS), the issues discussed in this paper will also be relevant to users' engagement with the deep and dark web. While SNS have the potential to impact positively on adolescent's health and well-being, the use of SNS has the potential for exposure to possible risks (Guinta & John, 2018). SNS include: Facebook (2018), QZone (2018), YouTube (2018), Twitter (2018), Reddit (2018), Pinterest (2018), Tumblr (2018), Flickr (2018), Whatsapp (2018), Snapchat (2018), Viber

DOI: 10.4018/978-1-6684-6307-9.ch001

(2018), Google+ (2018), Instagram (2018), LinkedIn (2018), Skype (2018), Tinder (2018), Grindr (2018), amongst many others used around the world. Computer algorithms are used to draw people in to frequent use of SNS. Once someone is online and engaging with SNS, more computer algorithms are used to keep the persons attention and hence increase the amount of time spent online. Recommender systems are used to enhance collaborative filtering algorithms which encourage users engagement with Social Networking Sites (Eirinaki, Gao, Varlamis, & Tserpes, 2018; Liu & Lee, 2010). The dark side of engaging with SNS includes: addiction or addictive behavior, child pornography, cyberbullying, fake news, Fear Of Missing Out (FOMO), social comparisons, stalking, amongst many others, which can all lead to neglect of other duties, sleep deprivation, loneliness, isolation, depression, and so forth. The aim of this chapter is to review the negative effects of engaging with SNS and consider what solutions can be proposed to alleviate the damage caused by engagement with SNS.

BACKGROUND

"It is increasingly observable that social media present enormous risks for individuals, communities, firms, and even for society as a whole" (Baccarella, Wagner, Kietzmann, & McCarthy, 2018, p. 431). Now that we as a society are aware of the possible dangers posed by social media, it is time to address all of these potential risks with individuals, communities, organisations, and so forth. By identifying and highlighting these risks and through ensuring that individuals, communities, and organisations are made aware of these risks, only then will it be possible to successfully deal with such risks. "Even with social media executives admitting that their platforms have deleterious impacts, users tend not to question the short- and long-term implications and potential risks of their choices" (Baccarella et al., 2018, p. 432). Users should be encouraged to question the short and long term risks of engaging with SNS. This is a discussion in which all members of society should engage, not just parents and school teachers. Many adults are experiencing problems as a result of excessive engagement with SNS. This paper reviews some of the negative effects of engaging with SNS on the habits (addiction and addictive behaviour, exposure to child pornography, cyberbullying) and mental health (fake news, fear of missing out, social comparisons, stalking) of users. In addition, users are encouraged to consider how their use of SNS may be impacting the lives of others (family members, work colleagues, and other online users).

The Dark Web

The dark web represents a number of anonymously created websites which are hosted on the deep web. The dark web is intentionally hidden (Paul, 2018), the content is not indexed for search engines to find, unlike the surface web where the content is indexed and accessible to standard web browsers, for example, Google Chrome (Google, 2019), Mozilla Firefox (Firefox, 2019), or Microsoft Internet Explorer (Microsoft, 2019). The surface web is the opposite of the deep web (also known as the invisible web and the hidden web). The surface web is easily accessible to all using standard web browsers on the internet. The deep web and the dark web are not accessible through standard web search engines and web crawlers.

In a research study conducted by Dalins, Wilson & Carman (2018) the findings suggest that "criminality on this 'dark web' is based more upon greed and desire, rather than any particular political motivations" (Dalins et al., 2018, p. 62). The dark web refers to a number of anonymously hosted websites on the deep web which are accessible by using specialized software to hide the Internet Protocol (IP) address. IP addresses are assigned to every device that connects to the internet. A Public IP address can be accessed over the internet, a Private IP address cannot be accessed over the internet but are used in internal networks. A Global IP address is specific to a particular network and all devices using that network. Internet Service Providers (ISP) assign Global IP addresses.

The dark web is part of the World Wide Web (WWW) that is only accessible through the use of specialized software (Monk, Mitchell, Frank, & Davies, 2018). The dark web is an encrypted network (to enforce anonymity) that exists predominantly between The Onion Routing (TOR) encryption tools, servers, and their users (Monk et al., 2018). Users of the dark web have the option to remain anonymous and untraceable. Methods employed to access the dark web are quite involved therefore the dark web is not used by the average user. "The globalization of technology and rise of popularity in cryptocurrencies has changed the face of black-market trade and the actors that carry out these crimes" (Paul, 2018, p. 1). Law enforcement agencies and Government Departments are continuously playing catch up in trying to deal with innovations adopted by black market traders to conceal the money trail. "The internet provides an ever-growing number of ways to hide, launder money and pursue a vast range of criminal activities in ways that are difficult to detect or deter" (Slaughter, 2018, p. 118). The handling of criminal activities conducted online is challenging, expensive and requires sufficient quantities of technical resources. The dark web can be used for illegal activities, such as: the sale of drugs (Mackey, 2018; Norbutas, 2018; Porter, 2018), firearms (Porter, 2018), untraceable cryptocurrencies such as Bitcoin (Paul, 2018), child pornography (Dalins et al., 2018), trade in exotic animals (Paul, 2018), sale and purchase of credit card details (Hayes, Cappa, & Cardon, 2018), identify theft (Hayes et al., 2018), money laundering (Dalins et al., 2018; Wegberg, Oerlemans, & Deventer, 2018), amongst others. The monetary cost alone of trying to monitor criminal activities that are conducted online puts a burden on law enforcement agencies and Governments. The Silk Road is a dark net market or an online black market known for the sale of illegal drugs (Dalins et al., 2018; Hayes et al., 2018). It is illegal to use websites that engage with illegal activities. Due to the ubiquitous nature of the WWW and the anonymity provided, the dark web poses serious challenges to law enforcement agencies around the world. Law enforcement agencies can only achieve so much, members of society must be vigilant and mindful of the legality of the interactions and transactions that they conduct online. It is not only on the deep dark web that illegal activities take place, they are also conducted on the surface web, for example, sale of contraband goods, sale of replicas of branded products, sale of government services with an additional administration charge included, and so forth.

Traditional search engines or web browsers cannot access content available on the dark web. This paper reviews SNS that are accessible through the use of traditional search engines on the surface web where the content is indexed and accessible to standard web browsers. The negative effects of engaging with SNS on the surface web also relate to users engagement with the deep and dark web.

Virtual Private Network (VPN)

VPNs can be used covertly to obscure a users' browsing and online activities from prying eyes. Therefore, illegal activities and transactions can be hidden by using VPN transactions. A Virtual Private Network (VPN) enables the user to send and receive data across a public network, as if it were a private network. A Virtual Private Network (VPN) provides a means of connection to a network within an organisation (as if you were inside the organisation) even though you are not physically present. During the online session the connection is made to the remote network (within the organisation) through the VPN therefore none of the devices (printers, shared disks, and so forth) connected to the local network are available for use to the user as long as the user is remotely connected to the network within the organisation.

Figure 1 illustrates a standard connection to a network within an organisation where there is no need for a Virtual Private Network. The users' remote connection to the network of the business or organisation can be diagrammatically represented as a bubble linked to the target network working within the organization as illustrated in Figure 2.

VPNs' are used legitimately by business users to connect remotely and securely to the companies/organisations network.

Figure 1. Connection to a network within an organization

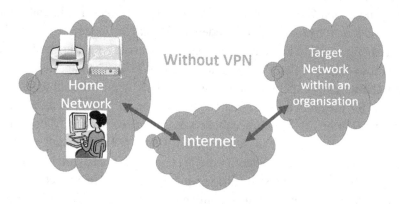

Figure 2. Connection to a network within an organisation using a VPN

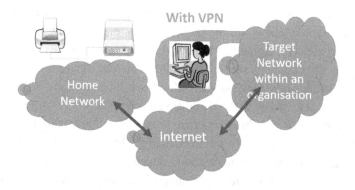

THE DARK SIDE OF ENGAGING WITH SOCIAL NETWORKING SITES (SNS)

The massive diffusion of SNS has led to some adverse and undesirable societal consequences (Salo, Mantymaki, & Islam, 2018). SNS both on the surface web and the deep web can have a dark negative side. This chapter focuses on the dark side of engaging with SNS on the surface web. Some of the negative effects include: addiction or addictive behaviour, child pornography, cyberbullying, fake news, Fear Of Missing Out (FOMO), social comparisons, stalking, amongst many others.

Addiction or Addictive Behaviour

"The powerful and addictive sharing functionality of social media presents risks to those who share content and those who consume the content that is shared" (Baccarella et al., 2018, p. 433). Once content is shared through the use of social media, there is no knowing how many people around the world will see, download, or save the content. Shared information, pictures and videos can go viral very quickly, once this content is made publically available there is no way that anyone can delete every instance or trace of the content. In a study conducted by Wang et al. (2018) the findings suggest that addiction to SNS could potentially be a risk factor for the onset of depression in teenagers. The suggestion that addiction to social networking sites could trigger depression in teenagers is a serious issue that deserves further research. Addiction to SNS could also be a risk factor for the onset of depression in adults.

Kanat-Maymon, Almog, Cohen, & Amichai-Hamburger (2018) suggest that the roles of self-esteem and contingent self-worth (CSW) may possibly be associated with excessive and inappropriate use of SNS. It is impossible to know the extent to which users are involved with or subjected to inappropriate use of SNS. In a study conducted by (Atroszko et al., 2018) the findings suggest that "When suggested tentative personality risk factors model were investigated, addictive Facebook use was related to being female, being older, extraverted, narcissistic, having low self-efficacy as well as feeling loneliness and social anxiety" (Atroszko et al., 2018, p. 335). Unfortunately, some users do not realise the negative effects that addictive use of SNS can have on their lives and the lives of others. The findings of Casale & Fioravanti (2018) suggest that there is "a positive association between grandiose narcissism and problematic SNS use" (p. 317). SNS are a recent phenomenon in the history of mankind, further research is needed to ascertain the influence of addictive use of SNS on personal relationships and general well-being.

Excessive use of modern technological devices for social networking can have negative consequences on the following: quality time spent engaging with friends and family (Osatuyi & Turel, 2018), work environment and performance (Moqbel & Kock, 2018; Osatuyi & Turel, 2018), exercising, involvement with many other activities that are good for both physical and mental welfare, and a reduction in positive emotions (Moqbel & Kock, 2018). "Facebook addiction is related to higher stress, lower general health and lower sleep quality" (Atroszko et al., 2018, p. 335). These negative effects need to be taken seriously and appropriately addressed.

Internet addiction is a recent and changing phenomenon (Mubarak & Quinn, 2017), which has not previously affected society as other addictions have done, therefore, further research is required to promote official recognition of this problem and possibly identify suitable treatments to resolve this problem before social engagement is negatively affected by obsessive use of the internet and SNS. Mubarak & Quinn (2017) suggest that "it is likely that individuals experiencing internet addiction may engage in problem behaviours in cyberspace and create social and psychological problems to other internet users" (p. 9).

Child Pornography

Dalins, Wilson & Carman (2018) suggest that law enforcement agencies show more concern for sites hosting Child Exploitation Materials (CEM) than sites hosting child pornography in the form of cartoons. The sharing of content depicting the exploitation of children for the gratification of others poses a serious challenge to law enforcement agencies. Child pornography and exploitation occurs almost 25% more often than adult pornography (Dalins et al., 2018).

"One site advertised itself as a 'support' forum, though in terms of supporting and normalizing pae-dophilia rather than aiding persons avoid such behavior and actions" (Dalins et al., 2018, p. 71), whilst other sites offered education and training on grooming vulnerable children (Dalins et al., 2018). SNS within the deep and dark web require policing by government supported agencies to infiltrate such sites and monitor the activities of people engaging with these sites.

Cyberbullying

In a study conducted by Mc Hugh, Wisniewski, Rosson, & Carroll (2018) the findings were that "cyber-bullying, sexual solicitations, and exposure to explicit content (but not information breaches) can cause symptoms of PTSD" (p. 1182). Post-Traumatic Stress Disorder (PTSD) is a mental health disorder that effects some people who have been exposed to or have personally experienced some horrifying event, or others who have witnessed such events. Experiencing PTSD as a result of engaging with SNS indicates that there is a dark side to SNS. The Health Service Executive (HSE) have provided on their website some helpful advice and who to contact regarding online bullying (HSE, 2018a). "Cyberbullying may be a way to intentionally harm individuals, while oversharing photos of positive experiences unintention-ally causes anxiety among those who live lives less glamorous" (Baccarella et al., 2018, p. 432). Some users may not intentionally aim to harm other users by oversharing, not all users will be harmed by the positive posts of others, but some users may through social comparison feel that their lot in life is not as glamorous or successful as others.

Fake News

Fake news is the spreading of untrue facts online or through SNS that may influence readers' opinions, voting choices, or even, election outcomes. SNS can be used to spread fake news (Baccarella et al., 2018). Users need to be discerning about what they read and what they believe. "Although the actual effect of fake news online on voters' decisions is still unknown, concerns over the perceived effect of fake news online have prevailed in the US and other countries" (Jang & Kim, 2018, p. 295). Throughout history there has always been concerns with fake news, alternatively known as propaganda. "The unprecedented popularity of social media for gathering news raises a number of critical questions regarding who trusts news in social media and what sites we trust" (Warner-Soderholm et al., 2018, p. 309). Fake news could have the potential to influence political appointments and could possibly even destroy lives. Some people may not know what or who to believe anymore which may lead to mental stress.

Fear of Missing Out (FOMO)

Fear of Missing Out (FOMO) has the greatest impact on the level of fatigue experienced by users of social media (Bright & Logan, 2018). Lack of sleep can lead to various different mental health disorders. FOMO can have an adverse effect on people's lives, as an obsession with wanting to keep up with what everyone else is doing, can lead to user fatigue and other adverse consequences. Nicholar Carr (2010) argued the point that people's attention span has diminished as a result of engaging with the internet and all it offers. "The Shallows: what the internet is doing to our brains" by Nicholar Carr (2010) is an insightful, inspirational, and influential book. After reading this book, one reader selected to "unsubscribe" from numerous e-mail lists, while others deactivated a number of SNS accounts. "The Circle" by Dave

Eggers (2013) is another book that would really make the reader consider the amount of information that is shared online, and how all the data mining conducted by organisations is affecting our privacy.

The data mining conducted by some SNS can also affect the privacy of owners and employees of these organisations. Hackers over the years have gained access to information from many organisations around the world proving that there is no way to safely protect one's privacy. Should an organization which runs a SNS be fined by the European Union for breach of privacy rights, this fine will not bring back the privacy that has been lost to all the users.

Even if an individual is extremely cautious about their own personal information and mindful of every piece of data they share online, others, can upload personal information and images of that person without their explicit permission. This happens all the time and the effort it takes for an individual to get this content taken back down from SNSs is extensive.

In life, it is so easy to go with the flow, without even considering what effects our actions are having on our daily lives and the daily lives of loved ones. It is so easy to get drawn into engaging with online activities, that hours can pass and be lost to the user, which could have been spent engaging with friends, doing productive work, getting exercise, or focusing on things that really matter in life. Some people are so busy recording every meal and experience to post pictures online, that they are not really focusing on the moment, relaxing, and enjoying the time spent with friends. Man has inhabited this earth for years without the need for all this connectivity and lack of privacy. Perhaps one of the reasons obesity and diabetes are on the increase is because mankind now devotes so much time online due to FOMO. If only people would consider what they are missing out by spending so much time online they might then start to relax and enjoy their own life instead of trying to imitate the lives of others as portrayed online.

Social Comparisons

As a result of using SNS some people may get the impression that others posting to the same SNS are leading better lives in comparison to their own. A survey among Korean females found that social comparison was positively associated with the use of blogs, Instagram, and LinkedIn (Chae, 2018). Engagement with SNS can produce social comparison with others (Wang et al., 2018) which may result in feelings of loneliness in others (Sutcliffe, Binder, & Dunbar, 2018), isolation, anxiety and possibly depression. Online users tend to share the highlights of their lives which may not be representative of the real lives that they are living on a day to day basis. "Those with a high social comparison orientation should limit their use of social media to avoid emotional stress" (Chae, 2018, p. 1663). One's self esteem can be adversely affected through social comparison with others. As long as people do not realise the potential damage of engaging with SNS they may continue to suffer from social comparisons with others which could lead to mental health issues.

Stalking

Some SNS have the ability to capture a person's current location through Internet Protocol (IP) address information, this functionality can be used to track or monitor the whereabouts of others (Baccarella et al., 2018). The fact that the location of a person can be tracked may possibly be reassuring to some, for example, parents who have given a mobile phone to a child may then be able to obtain knowledge of their whereabouts at all times. Alternatively, a person's location may be tracked without their knowledge or permission through the use of technology, by someone who is interested in their whereabouts or someone who holds a grudge, therefore, it is an invasion of personal privacy, ethically unacceptable, and potentially a safety threat. "Studies indicate a strong correlation between high Facebook usage and jealousy in relationships; in other words, as Facebook usage increases, so does jealousy" (Warner-Soderholm et al., 2018, p. 306). Some users may get unrealistic expectations of what life should be like, based on how others portray their lives to be online, this can lead to feelings of jealousy. Some may suffer from negative body image if they compare their body to those of others as they are depicted online. Some images available online may have been photo shopped to make them appear more appealing. Jealously in relationships can lead to serious mental problems which can only get worse if one continues to stalk others and compare themselves to others as portrayed online.

SOLUTIONS AND RECOMMENDATIONS

The dark side of engaging with SNS will continue to pose problems to society in general as long as people allow SNS to take up too much of their valuable time and influence how they feel about themselves and others. To avoid undue emotional stress, users who are susceptible to a high social comparison orientation should reduce the time spent engaging with SNS (Chae, 2018), or cease to engage with SNS altogether.

Cyberbullying has the potential for serious consequences, for example, someone may feel so bad from being a victim of cyberbullying that they may consider taking their own life by committing suicide (Cohen-Almagor, 2018), or doing something else extreme. "Suicide is a major public health problem and is the second leading cause of death in young people worldwide. Indicating a lack of adequate treatment approaches, recent data suggest a rising suicide rate" (Bailey, Rice, Robinson, Nedeljkovic, & Alvarez-Jimenez, 2018, p. 499). Government funded supports are available, for example a helpline to listen to victims and help them to deal effectively with the problem (HSE, 2018a, 2018b). Unfortunately, not all victims of online bullying are aware of these services. People of all ages can be victims of cyberbullying and government provided supports should be available to help and guide all victims about the best ways to deal with the online persecution.

SNS can be used to advertise and sell all sorts of goods, including drugs and other illegal products. Concerted efforts by law enforcement agencies, the public, public health authorities, government administrators, and technology companies will be required to successfully combat the sale of illegal drugs online (Mackey, 2018). Due to the complexities involved in dealing with cybercrimes "too few appear currently willing or able to grapple with the issues, let alone provide satisfying answers" (Slaughter, 2018, p. 118). Further research is required to determine the most productive and cost effective methods to combat cybercrimes.

Organisations' should leverage their information security policies based on the perceived threats and benefits of employees engaging with SNS (Silic & Back, 2016). Should an employee be addicted to engaging with SNS and possibly engage during working hours, then the work that they are supposed to be doing may be neglected. Organisations' should be aware of the perceived threats and benefits of SNS, so that they can effectively deal with these by taking appropriate action. "Fake news is a critical major issue that social networking websites can ameliorate with vigilance and skillful use of technology" (Morales, Sosa-Fey, & Farias, 2017, p. 87). Fake news poses a real challenge to society and requires further investigation.

FUTURE RESEARCH DIRECTIONS

Further research is required to determine the most productive and cost effective methods to combat cybercrimes. Law enforcement agencies and Governments have numerous challenges ahead in dealing with the dark side of SNS and cybercrime on the surface web. This is only scratching the surface as the deep and dark web are more embedded in areas where users want to hide their identity, therefore, it is much more difficult to trace the online actions of users.

Fake news has the potential to influence politics and also to destroy lives. Fake news poses a real challenge to society and requires further investigation. Members of society deserve to know the truth so that they can make informed decisions based on honest facts.

The suggestion that addiction to SNS could trigger depression in teenagers is a serious issue that deserves further research. Internet addiction is a recent and changing phenomenon (Mubarak & Quinn, 2017), which has not previously impacted on society as other addictions have done, therefore, further research is required to promote official recognition of this problem. SNS are a recent phenomenon in the history of mankind, further research is needed to ascertain the influence of addictive use of SNS on personal relationships and general well-being.

CONCLUSION

Although SNS are used by many people all around the world to connect with loved ones and friends in a positive context, alas, SNS are also used by many people in a negative context, including some of the topics discussed in this chapter. There are some dark sides or negative aspects to human engagement with SNS which may include the following: exposure to possible risks, spending too much time online, deleterious impacts, access to black market traders, untraceable cryptocurrencies, sale of drugs and firearms, child pornography, trade in exotic animals, identity theft, and money laundering.

Some concerns with users' engagement with SNS are as follows: images going viral, internet addiction, depression in teenagers, lack of quality time to spend with friends and family, impact on work performance, physical and mental welfare, higher stress levels, lack of sleep, loneliness, isolation, anxiety, and jealousy, amongst many others.

These negative effects need to be taken seriously and appropriately addressed. Users should be encouraged to question the short and long term risks of engaging with SNS. Users of Social Networking Sites within the surface web and the deep and dark web require the support of government agencies in dealing with the inappropriate activities of other people engaging with these sites. The monetary cost of dealing with cybercrime puts a burden on Law Enforcement Agencies and Governments.

Society as a whole needs to consciously consider all of the negative effects of engagement with SNS, discuss these with friends, family, and work colleagues then try to reach a consensus on how best to address all of these issues.

REFERENCES

Atroszko, P., Balcerowska, J., Bereznowski, P., Biernatowska, A., Pallesen, S., & Andressen, C. (2018). Facebook addiction among Polish undergraduate students: Validity of measurement and relationship with personality and well-being. *Computers in Human Behavior, 85*, 329–338. doi:10.1016/j.chb.2018.04.001

Baccarella, C., Wagner, T., Kietzmann, J., & McCarthy, I. (2018). Social media? It's serious! Understanding the dark side of social media. *European Management Journal, 36*(4), 431–438. doi:10.1016/j.emj.2018.07.002

Bailey, E., Rice, S., Robinson, J., Nedeljkovic, M., & Alvarez-Jimenez, M. (2018). Theoretical and empirical foundations of a novel online social networking intervention for youth suicide prevention: A conceptual review. *Journal of Affective Disorders, 238*, 499–505. doi:10.1016/j.jad.2018.06.028 PMID:29936387

Bright, L., & Logan, K. (2018). Is my fear of missing out (FOMO) causing fatigue? Advertising, social media fatigue, and the implications for consumers and brands. *Internet Research, 28*(5), 1213–1227. doi:10.1108/IntR-03-2017-0112

Carr, N. (2010). *The Shallows: what the internet is doing to our brains*. New York, NY: W. W. Norton & Company.

Casale, S., & Fioravanti, G. (2018). Why narcissists are at risk for developing Facebook addiction: The need to be admired and the need to belong. *Addictive Behaviors, 76*, 312–318. doi:10.1016/j.addbeh.2017.08.038 PMID:28889060

Chae, J. (2018). Reexamining the relationship between social media and happiness: The effect of various social media platforms on reconceptualized happiness. *Telematics and Informatics, 35*(6), 1656–1664. doi:10.1016/j.tele.2018.04.011

Cohen-Almagor, R. (2018). Social responsibility on the Internet: Addressing the challenge of cyberbullying. *Aggression and Violent Behavior, 39*, 42–52. doi:10.1016/j.avb.2018.01.001

Dalins, J., Wilson, C., & Carman, M. (2018). Criminal motivation on the dark web: A categorisation model for law enforcement. *Digital Investigation, 24*, 62–71. doi:10.1016/j.diin.2017.12.003

Eggers, D. (2013). *The Circle*. McSweeney's Books.

Eirinaki, M., Gao, J., Varlamis, I., & Tserpes, K. (2018). Recommender systems for large-scale social networks: A review of challenges and solutions. *Future Generation Computer Systems, 78*, 413–418. doi:10.1016/j.future.2017.09.015

Facebook. (2018). *Connect with friends and the world around you on Facebook*. Retrieved from https://www.facebook.com/

Firefox. (2019). *Mozilla Firefox*. Retrieved from https://www.mozilla.org/en-US/firefox/new/

Flickr. (2018). *Flickr at its best is a place to connect, to discover, and to evolve as photographers and lovers of photography*. Retrieved from https://www.flickr.com/

Google+. (2018). *Collections*. Retrieved from https://plus.google.com/discover

Google. (2019). *Google Chrome*. Retrieved from https://www.google.com/chrome/?brand=CHBD& gclid=EAIaIQobChMI1L2JsqmB4AIVqrXtCh226QumEAAYASAAEgLzZvD_BwE&gclsrc=aw.ds

Grindr. (2018). *The World's largest social networking app for gay, bi, trans, and queer people*. Retrieved from https://www.grindr.com/

Guinta, M., & John, R. (2018). Social media and adolescent health. *Pediatric Nursing, 44*, 196–201.

Hayes, D., Cappa, F., & Cardon, J. (2018). A framework for more effective dark web marketplace investigations. *Information, 9*(186), 1–17.

HSE. (2018a). *Bullying and harassment Bullying can affect anyone. It isn't always easy to deal with a bully, no matter your age*. Retrieved from https://www2.hse.ie/wellbeing/mental-health/bullying-and-harassment.html?gclid=EAIaIQobChMIoaX58ZfA4QIVz53tCh1GSQDPEAAYASAAEgLU7 fD_BwE&gclsrc=aw.ds

HSE. (2018b). *Cyberbullying is a new form of bullying, but it can be even more harmful than one might think*. Retrieved from https://www2.hse.ie/wellbeing/mental-health/cyberbullying.html

Instagram. (2018). *Sign up to see photos and videos from your friends*. Retrieved from https://www.instagram.com/

Jang, S., & Kim, J. (2018). Third person effects of fake news: Fake news regulation and media literacy interventions. *Computers in Human Behavior, 80*, 295–302. doi:10.1016/j.chb.2017.11.034

Kanat-Maymon, Y., Almog, L., Cohen, R., & Amichai-Hamburger, Y. (2018). Contingent self-worth and Facebook addiction. *Computers in Human Behavior, 88*, 227–235. doi:10.1016/j.chb.2018.07.011

LinkedIn. (2018). *Your dream job is closer than you think*. Retrieved from https://www.linkedin.com

Liu, F., & Lee, H. (2010). Use of social network information to enhance collaborative filtering performance. *Expert Systems with Applications, 37*(7), 4772–4778. doi:10.1016/j.eswa.2009.12.061

Mackey, T. (2018). Opioids and the Internet: Convergence of technology and policy to address the illicit online sales of opioids. *Health Services Insights, 11*, 1–6. doi:10.1177/1178632918800995 PMID:30245569

McHugh, B., Wisniewski, P., Rosson, M., & Carroll, J. (2018). When social media traumatizes teens: The roles of online risk exposure, coping, and post-traumatic stress. *Internet Research, 28*(5), 1169–1188. doi:10.1108/IntR-02-2017-0077

Microsoft. (2019). *Windows Internet Explorer*. Retrieved from https://www.microsoft.com/en-us/download/internet-explorer.aspx

Monk, B., Mitchell, J., Frank, R., & Davies, G. (2018). Uncovering Tor: An examination of the network structure. *Security and Communication Networks, 2018*, 1–12. doi:10.1155/2018/4231326

Moqbel, M., & Kock, N. (2018). Unveiling the dark side of social networking sites: Personal and work-related consequences of social networking site addiction. *Information & Management, 55*(1), 109–119. doi:10.1016/j.im.2017.05.001

Morales, K., Sosa-Fey, J., & Farias, J. (2017). Social Media: Are the benefits worth the risks for business? *International Journal of Business and Public Administration, 14*(1), 87–97.

Mubarak, A., & Quinn, S. (2017). General strain theory of Internet addiction and deviant behaviour in social networking sites (SNS). *Journal of Information, Communication and Ethics in Society*. doi:10.1108/JICES-08-2016-0024

Norbutas, L. (2018). Offline constraints in online drug marketplaces: An exploratory analysis of a cryptomarket trade network. *The International Journal on Drug Policy, 56,* 92–100. doi:10.1016/j.drugpo.2018.03.016 PMID:29621742

Osatuyi, B., & Turel, O. (2018). Tug of war between social self-regulation and habit: Explaining the experience of momentary social media addiction symptons. *Computers in Human Behavior, 85,* 95–105. doi:10.1016/j.chb.2018.03.037

Paul, K. (2018). Ancient artifacts vs. digital artifacts: New tools for unmasking the sale of illicit antiquities on the Dark Web. *Arts, 7*(12), 1–19.

Pinterest. (2018). *Pinterest helps you find ideas to try.* Retrieved from https://www.pinterest.ie/

Porter, K. (2018). Analyzing the DarkNetMarkets subreddit for evolutions of tools and trends using LDA topic modeling. *Digital Investigation, 26,* S87–S97. doi:10.1016/j.diin.2018.04.023

QZone. (2018). Retrieved from https://qzone.qq.com/

Reddit. (2018). *Reddit: the front page of the internet.* Retrieved from https://www.reddit.com/

Salo, J., Mantymaki, M., & Islam, A. (2018). The dark side of social media - and Fifty Shades of Grey introduction to the special issue: The dark side of social media. *Internet Research, 28*(5), 1166–1168. doi:10.1108/IntR-10-2018-442

Silic, M., & Back, A. (2016). The dark side of social networking sites: Understanding phishing risks. *Computers in Human Behavior, 60,* 35–43. doi:10.1016/j.chb.2016.02.050

Skype. (2018). *Skype makes it easy to stay in touch.* Retrieved from https://www.skype.com

Slaughter, R. (2018). The IT revolution reassessed part one: Literature review and key issues. *Futures, 96,* 115–123. doi:10.1016/j.futures.2017.12.006

Snapchat. (2018). *A new way to look.* Retrieved from https://www.snapchat.com/

Sutcliffe, A., Binder, J., & Dunbar, R. (2018). Activity in social media and intimacy in social relationships. *Computers in Human Behavior, 85,* 227–235. doi:10.1016/j.chb.2018.03.050

Tinder. (2018). *Match. Chat. Date.* Retrieved from https://tinder.com

Tumblr. (2018). Come for what you love. Stay for what you discover. Retrieved from https://www.tumblr.com/

Twitter. (2018). *See what's happening in the world right now.* Retrieved from https://twitter.com

Viber. (2018). *Free and secure calls and messages to anyone, anywhere.* Retrieved from https://www.viber.com/

Wang, P., Wang, X., Wu, Y., Xie, X., Wang, X., Zhao, F., ... Lei, L. (2018). Social networking sites addiction and adolescent depression: A moderated mediation model of rumination and self-esteem. *Personality and Individual Differences, 127*, 162–167. doi:10.1016/j.paid.2018.02.008

Warner-Soderholm, G., Bertsch, A., Sawe, E., Lee, D., Wolfe, T., Meyer, J., ... Fatilua, U. (2018). Who trusts social media? *Computers in Human Behavior, 81*, 303–315. doi:10.1016/j.chb.2017.12.026

Wegberg, R., Oerlemans, J., & Deventer, O. (2018). Bitcoin money laundering: Mixed results? An explorative study on money laundering of cybercrime proceeds using bitcoin. *Journal of Financial Crime, 25*(2), 419–435.

WhatsApp. (2018). *Simple. Secure. Reliable messaging.* Retrieved from https://www.whatsapp.com/

YouTube. (2018). *Best of YouTube.* Retrieved from https://www.youtube.com/

ADDITIONAL READING

Ampong, G., Mensah, A., Adu, A., Addae, J., Omoregie, O., & Ofori, K. (2018). Examining self-disclosure on social networking sites: A flow theory and privacy perspective. *Behavioral Science, 8*(58), 1–17. PMID:29882801

Errasti, J., Amigo, I., & Villadangos, M. (2017). Emotional uses of Facebook and Twitter: Its relation with empathy, narcissism, and self-esteem in adolescence. *Psychological Reports, 120*(6), 997–1018. doi:10.1177/0033294117713496

Fox, J., & Moreland, J. (2015). The dark side of social networking sites: An exploration of the relational and psychological stressors associated with Facebook use and affordances. *Computers in Human Behavior, 45*, 168–176. doi:10.1016/j.chb.2014.11.083

Parks, R., Lowry, P., Wigand, R., Agarwal, N., & Williams, T. (2018). Why students engage in cyber-cheating through a collective movement: A case of deviance and collusion. *Computers & Education, 125*, 308–326. doi:10.1016/j.compedu.2018.04.003

Quach, S., & Thaichon, P. (2018). Dark motives-counterfeit selling framework: An investigate on the supply side of the non-deceptive market. *Marketing Intelligence & Planning, 36*(2), 245–259. doi:10.1108/MIP-04-2017-0069

Sapountzi, A., & Psannis, K. (2018). Social networking data analysis tools & challenges. *Future Generation Computer Systems, 86*, 893–913. doi:10.1016/j.future.2016.10.019

Topaloglu, M., Caldibi, E., & Oge, G. (2016). The scale for the individual and social impact of students' social network use: The validity and reliability studies. *Computers in Human Behavior, 61*, 350–356. doi:10.1016/j.chb.2016.03.036

Zhang, X., Shan, L., Chen, X., Wang, L., Gao, B., & Zhu, Q. (2018). Health information privacy concerns, antecedents, and information disclosure intention in online health communities. *Information & Management*, 55(4), 482–493. doi:10.1016/j.im.2017.11.003

KEY TERMS AND DEFINITIONS

Addiction or Addictive Behaviour: Actions which a person can no longer control. Someone may go online to send an e-mail, get distracted and remain online for several hours, and possibly forget to send the e-mail.

Child Pornography: Online sharing of content which shows the sexual exploitation of children.

Cyberbullying: A form of bullying that occurs online.

Dark Web: The dark web refers to a number of anonymously hosted websites on the deep web which are accessible by using specialized software to hide the internet protocol (IP) address.

Fear of Missing Out (FOMO): Some people are afraid to go offline in case they miss out on some exciting piece of news.

Fake News: The spreading of untrue facts online or through Social Networking Sites that may influence readers' opinions, voting choices, and election outcomes.

IP Address: IP addresses are assigned to every device that connects to the internet.

Social Comparisons: As a result of using social networking sites some people may get the impression that other users are leading better lives in comparison to their own.

Social Networking Sites: Social networking sites (SNS) enable users to interact with other people online; similar to how people may socially interact offline by sharing personal experiences, images, making plans, and so forth.

Stalking: A person's location may be tracked without their knowledge or permission through the use of technology, by someone who is interested in their whereabouts or someone who holds a grudge; therefore, it is an invasion of personal privacy, ethically unacceptable, and potentially a safety threat.

Virtual Private Network (VPN): A virtual private network (VPN) provides a means of connecting to a network within an organisation (as if you were inside the organisation) even though you are not physically present.

Chapter 2
The Impact of Social Media on Children

Tuncay Dilci
Cumhuriyet University, Turkey

Anıl Kadir Eranıl
Karacaşar Primary School, Turkey

ABSTRACT

This chapter examines the impacts of social media on children. Advantages and disadvantages of social media are always available. Positive aspects of social media include allowing children to be brought up as multicultural individuals, enabling education and training environments to design for purposes, using as the main or supplementary source of education, a great power in creating and sharing information. Its negative aspects include leading to a reduction of their academic, social, and cognitive skills in the early periods when children were exposed to the social media, causing the children to develop obesity, mostly bringing up as consumption-centered individuals, perceive the world as a screenshot, and have low critical, creative, and reflective thinking skills. Therefore, one of the most important tasks undertaken to reduce or eliminate the negative effects is to raise and educate media-literate individuals.

INTRODUCTION

Social media undoubtedly ranks first when considered how people spend their time today. People always carry small-sized technological devices, especially smart phones, that provide practical use for and solution to them. These tools have today become his organ like human being's arm, leg, feet. Human being did not know any of these tools fifteen to twenty years ago, but now these increasingly globalized tools have become an indispensable part of our lives. Some commonly used social applications are blog blogging, gaming, video and picture-sharing, iPods, iPhones, iPads, YouTube, Twitter, Facebook, LinkedIn, etc. Many of us have known the name of few or all of these off by heart. So to say, their names were imprinted on our memories. Well, are these applications that have come into our life changing our life too? In other words, what kind of changes are they causing in our lives? The answer of this questions

DOI: 10.4018/978-1-6684-6307-9.ch002

undoubtedly yes. We should allow them to use these applications in a controlled manner when considered that they would mostly influence our children. This research focuses mainly on impacts of social media applications on the children and addresses how the likely consequences of these impacts will interpret.

Media

Media is a communication channel that provides news and information for the public. In other words, they are technical tools that provide verbal or written communication for the society (TDK, 2017). As its definition also implies, the media can be thought of as a channel of communication. Any disruption which would occur in this channel or unreasonably reporting the news during the communication process may lead to lack of communication or misuse of the news, which also brings about undesirable results on a large or small scale.

The social media plays an educational and didactical role, as well as a communication tool. When performing this role, it is very important to be known that it includes what kind of data, originates from which source, and is presented for what purpose. Biased presentations out of objective situations are highly influential in leading the individuals biasedly or in the fact that the society holds a biased opinion or belief. It can be said that this impact is strong and prominent on especially children. Cartoons, virtual games and their derivatives, to which children are exposed, have a profound impact on the development of children's world of thought. In a study by Funk, Brouwer, Curtiss, and McBroom (2009), when asked parents their beliefs about the influence of the social media exposure on their children, 99% of them expressed that popular media could have either a short-term impact of 43% or a long-term impact of 56%. Electronic media, especially television, have been criticized for their possible effect on children for a long time (Kirkorian, Wartella & Anderson, 2008). They emphasized that their cognitive development and academic success negatively affected in the early periods when children were uncontrollably exposed to the social media. Therefore, it is extremely important for us to question the contents of the social media tools where they spend time if one wants the children to have a healthy world of thought.

The social network, blog blogging, gaming, video and picture-sharing, iPods, iPhones, iPads, YouTube, Twitter, Facebook, LinkedIn, so on and so forth have become a part of today's common words. It would be hard to believe that many of these devices and networks were unavailable ten years ago (Graber & Mendoza, 2012). Social media, a type of digital media, is a system that is based on the content production and consumption of the participants and has different digital contents via links and content (Andersson, 2016). Although such a definition offers for social media, it is a growing phenomenon with various definitions since it gains popularity in the academic community as well. Its well-known definition refers to the social media used to provide social interaction since social media technology means web-based content in the digital environment through multi-way communications (Alzouebi & Isakovic, 2014). Social media is a key channel of communication in the society today and enables people worldwide to interact with each other with just the click of a mouse (Lofgren, 2014). Furthermore, smartphones and computers have so dramatically altered the manner in which people communicate around the world with ease of use that increases the amount of online interaction. Kahveci (2015) indicated that this change has also been penetrating into the educational environments.

Research on groups using social media applications and having mobile devices revealed that roughly one out of ten children by 5 age get a mobile device, such as a smartphone. Therefore, youths define as the new digital natives in the modern age (Dotterer, Hedges & Parker, 2016). Social media networks such as Facebook and Twitter have the considerable potential to teach and learn in Higher Education through their main functions based on encouraging people to generate and share information and connecting groups of people worldwide (Graham, 2014; Kumi-Yeboah & Smith, 2016). Other social media applications like YouTube, Pinterest, and Glogster make it possible to upload and share various media such as video, animation, and photo. They are also usually used in education as a supplementary rather than the main source (Kilis, Gülbahar & Rapp, 2016). Kothari and Hickerson (2016) found that 70% of students and 65% of faculty members used some social media tools including Facebook, Twitter, and LinkedIn in their courses as the primary or supplementary source for educational purposes.

Smart phones and social media are used as the main popular sources of entertainment and communication for many of students both inside and outside of school (Palekahelu, Hunt, Thrupp & Relmasira, 2016). Many people from all age groups, especially teenagers, take part in online sites to make friends, make themselves known, and express their opinion in a large international audience (Georgakainas & Zaharias, 2016). It is very important for educational practitioners and researchers, and they should successfully use it for their own social practices (Albert, 2015; Pavlik, 2015; Greenhow & Askari, 2017; Georgakainas& Zaharias, 2016; Burbules, 2016; El Bialy & Ayoub, 2017). Teaching and learning processes are not only performed in classrooms but they are combined with the use of electronic environments called e-learning as well (Oktavia, Warnars & Adi, 2017). In addition, social media helps deep learning both directly and indirectly, facilitates learning, promotes long-term retention of content, and fosters a more pleasant, attractive and enjoyable learning environment (Samuels-Peretz, Dvorkin Camiel, Teeley & Banerjee, 2017). All of these stresses the place and importance of social media in the education. Social media applications whose content and use had determined properly could be highly beneficial to both educators and learners. Palvik (2015) reported that technology has at least four key impacts on education. Firstly, technology has almost revolutionized the methods of teaching and learning over time. Secondly, it has reshaped the content of what is taught and learned. Thirdly, it has significantly changed educational institutions, structures, and costs. Lastly, it has redefined the relationships between educational institutions, teachers, and students. Furthermore, the use of social media also varies according to the level of education and training environment. Entertaining and didactical practices should be more preferred for children at primary school level. As the level of the classroom progresses, classroom use of social media tools also varies according to the way students will use them for what purpose. Smith (2017) has recently reported that undergraduates are generally used social media for the purpose of collaborating to create documents online, sharing information online, managing and following academicals schedules, forging closer relationships with peers, posting information found online, creating social media to share online and making comment about social media or information found online.

Burbules (2016) describes the social media as a powerful tool, which is not just a valuable tool in reading and writing, but it also changes our reading and writing activities. In other words, the incorporation of social media into the education and training process has also caused the educational environments to evolve. This evolution continues mutually. Social media education enables itself to shape in education.

In sum, it is not possible that we deny the existence of social media and its effects on our lives. These effects of social media can consider to be either positive or negative. We need to decide the direction of change as a part of this process rather than track how social media is changing people, especially children. In other words *"if we cannot govern events/things, they will manage us"*. This uncontrolled management may not be in favorable of us. Better detecting the impacts of social media and keeping them under control are extremely important for both adults and children.

Positive and Negative Impacts of Social Media on Children

There are the pros and cons of social media. Greenhow and Askari (2017) have recently reported that social network sites are both advantage and disadvantage to teaching and learning. When its positive aspects are examined, Rosenberg, Terry, Bell, Hiltz and Russo (2016) reached three general conclusions regarding the likely advantageous role of social media. Social media can facilitate the development of community, support curriculum advancement and promote networking and collaboration. In parallel with factors, social media may contribute to the knowledge sharing process from e-learning to social learning within the organization (Oktavia, Warnars, & Adi, 2017). Moreover, social media components may help students learn to critically think about the media they use (Dotterer, Hedges & Parker, 2016), and may positively affect the relationship between teachers and students. Thought-out integration of social media through tasks that require involvement in higher-level cognitive activities, such as synthesis and evaluation, can improve a child's educational experience using technology with which he/she may already get acquainted (Albert, 2015).

Social media offers the advantage to students to increase collaboration and interaction with their peers and provides immediate responses to individual's inquiries with the richness of resources (El Bialy & Ayoub, 2017). Additionally, it helps to strengthen collaboration, critical thinking, and reflection, which are among the activities related to deep learning (Samuels-Peretz, Dvorkin Camiel, Teeley & Banerjee, 2017) and builds a bridge between formal and informal learning through participatory digital cultures (Greenhow & Lewin, 2016). Efficient and proper use of technology and social media also serves participants to heighten the awareness and knowledge of multicultural citizenship education (Kumi-Yeboah & Smith, 2016). Students recognize that they do not need to rely on teachers and schools to be independent and control their communication and for learning (Palekahelu, Hunt, Thrupp & Relmasira, 2016).

When looked at positive aspects of social media according to age groups, Khan, Kend and Robertson (2016) pointed out that the use of social media such as Facebook and Twitter has became more widespread among university students. Authors also added that many universities provide students with resources in formats appropriate for iPad, laptop, and mobile phone and that there has been a marked increase in the amount of social media they use while performing university academic activities. Krikorian, Wartella and Anderson (2008) found there is strong evidence that children older than two years learn from educational media and there is moderate evidence that this is positively associated with various measures of academic achievement even ten years later. However their moderate evidence has emphasized that early exposure to the social media containing merely entertainment and violence is negatively linked with cognitive skills and academic success. All of these situations may lead us to the conclusion that social media would be useful or useless for the intended use. Children are not at the level where they can determine the contents that will be useful to them in the social media. Thus, it has also fallen to teachers, especially to parents, to follow this situation closely. Otherwise, unconsciously used social media may result in the deterioration of children's frame of mind and moral fiber. Negative consequences that may arise are the following:

1. Inactive children tend to face the multitude of health problems like obesity,
2. They are brought up as consumption-centered individuals,
3. They isolate themselves from the nature and people/society since they frequently spend more time in indoor environments,
4. The manner in which they perceive the world is just a screenshot,

5.   They demand and use the offering advertising products unconsciously.

6.   They have low ability to manage their environment, especially themselves.

7.   They cannot develop their thinking skills enough.

Resultant negative consequences can also be considered as factors that trigger each other. A negative consequence we have foreseen may also be the cause of another negative outcome we have not foreseen. Positive consequences may emerge as a result of this process, but which should not be left to a chance application.

Studies carried out to prevent or lessen the harmful effects of social media showed that early exposure to television may result in the poor cognitive development (Kirkorian, Wartella & Anderson, 2008). Measures should be taken to reduce the harmful use of social media in a classroom environment. It should be well clarified how and for what purpose social media will be used in the schools. Instructors and educators should be ready to reap more benefits by effectively combining technologies such as social media that prepares the way for long-life learning (Chawinga, 2017). Greenhow and Askari (2017) have indicated more recently that online social networks may impede teaching practices when teachers and students do not see their instructional value or cannot use some social networks to improve learning and teaching goals.

Teachers may want to dissuade pupils from using social media in class. However, they can use social media and technology to teach self-regulation by inviting children to recognize themselves when children experience attention deficit (Dotterer, Hedges & Parker, 2016). Although there is a general negative opinion about the didactic quality of social media, teachers believe that learning and teaching environments combined with social media will enhance both the communication of the students and the whole educational process (Georgakainas & Zaharias, 2016). To put it another way, awareness of the values reflected in virtual settings and utilizing social media consciously would be remarkable with a view to respecting outstanding contributions of social media to social life (Karaduman, Köse & Eryılmaz, 2017). All these results demonstrate the importance of being an excellent media user, in other words, of being a media literate.

Media literacy education teaches to critically examine media messages (Draper, Appregilio, Kramer, Ketcherside, Campbell, Stewart & Cox, 2015). The researchers emphasized that media literacy can be crucial in modifying learners' behavior and that media literacy education should be improved so as to build a conscious society (Nupairoj, 2016). To that end, it should assist individuals from all ages to gain the necessary competences through the media literacy education movement that will be continued (Schmidt,2012). When the importance of being media literate is examined, it is seen that media literacy is the keystone of academic discipline learning and effective teaching, and that instructional and assessment practices are crucial in thoroughly grasping the subject matter (Fedorov, Levitskaya & Camarero, 2016). Media literacy education and media criticism make a significant contribution to the development of analytical thinking. Indeed, one of the most important tasks of media literacy education is not only to understand the mechanisms that function and create in the society, but also to fully analyze media texts of any kinds and types (Levitskaya, 2015). Recently, media literacy of young children has started to be noticed because of the expanding media environment, particularly the increased use of the internet among preschoolers in most Western countries. Additionally, it has been stressed that it is necessary to strengthen them as media literate actors for it seems impossible to guard only children in today's social media environment (Rantala, 2011). It is important that they are raised as media literacy as it is not possible to become aware of everything that children encounter. Media literate children themselves should possess the ability to identify harmful contents and to keep away from them.

Suggestions for Social Media Users and Politicians

There is a need for individual awareness and government policies so that the use of social media can develop for both children and adults. However Rantala (2011) expressed that practices should also be performed without underestimating the effects of raising awareness of and inspiration for media education. When also examined the tasks that the teachers should undertake, the entire incoming media should be approved by the teacher before being released to the designated audience. In other words, all these media should be screened by the teacher (Exley, Willis & McCosker, 2017). School districts should be reviewed, and it should be understood the policies that govern each digital platform whereby educators use in the classroom (Shear, 2016).

It seems that today students are addicted heavily to technology. Therefore, educators need to bring these technologies to their classroom (Chawinga, 2017). Moreover, educators encourage their students to practice as a part of their teaching. They have to find the ways to increase their students' attendance to lesson. They must provide them with the materials that will meet their expectations and contribute to their learning (El Bialy & Ayoub, 2017). In other words, educators should always pay regard to the areas of interest of their students in different settings, and, when necessary, change their methods depending on the learning style, prior knowledge, and a total number of students taking a class (Tucker, 2016).

Experiences should be shared, which improve both formal and informal media education at the schools and during lifelong learning, and further research is urgently needed to identify the possible ways of international collaboration (Mikhaleva, 2015). By using the social media portion in the classrooms which are well equipped with the technology, social media can use more effectively so as to allow students and instructors to create the more useful connections between the course material and classroom experience (Lofgren, 2014). Social media tools have the potential to foster and support out-of-class participation through carefully planned tasks via social media platforms (Graham, 2014). Social media applications can use as a means to bolster support for the education of disabled students by circulating within the undergraduate culture (Hartley, Mapes, Taylor & Bourgeois, 2016). Information, communication, and technologies may play a key role in boosting rural development and in relieving the poverty by presenting equal access opportunities to knowledge and market information, basic public (health, education) and financial services (Rad, Kurt & Polatöz, 2013). Additionally, social media serves an important function in order that each group is able to develop its own objectives (Smedescu, 2014).

As a result, the social media and the applications which are its extensions are nowadays snowballing. When the expanding social media cannot be prevented, we may face the unpredictable negative consequences. It is necessary to create a media-literate society in order not to be negatively affected by this situation. It would undoubtedly be more beneficial to children just as the media-literate society would benefit many areas. In addition, social media are shaping the education, which is one of the important means of raising a society. It is absolutely clear that this shaping that is willingly performed by the media-literate educators will contribute to the students in every stage of education and, in particular, to children.

FUTURE RESEARCH DIRECTIONS

Future social media research can be carried out to examine the effects of social media on age groups. The social media applications whereby each age group is interested in and the effects of these applications may vary. Furthermore, one should be focused on the studies that predict the likely consequences of these effects by being thoroughly analyzed the social media contents. Studies to be conducted within the scope of education and training can be diversified according to the socio-economic levels of the students and their family education level. When considered that the time spent using the social media is a very intensive period of time and is too precious, it is also all important that we should pertinaciously and meticulously conduct this research without loss of time.

CONCLUSION

This study discusses the effects of social media on children. In this context, firstly, it is dealt with what media and social media concepts are meant. Thus, it has been concluded that the social media has not only a communication tool but it undertakes a didactical and educational task as well. Within the educational and didactical context of the media, entertaining and didactical practices should be more preferred for children at primary school level. As students move up to upper levels, classroom use of social media tools also varies according to the way students will use them for what purpose. Educators should be able to control this variability. Therefore, it is important to raise and educate the media-literate educators. Otherwise, students may be confronted with the undesirable consequences of the media. These undesirable consequences may cause children to develop obesity, mostly bring up as consumption-centered individuals, perceive the world as just a screenshot and have low critical, creative and reflective thinking skills.

REFERENCES

Albert, D. J. (2015). Social Media in Music Education: Extending Learning to Where Students "Live". *Music Educators Journal, 102*(2), 31–38. doi:10.1177/0027432115606976

Alzouebi, K., & Isakovic, A. A. (2014). Exploring the Learner Perspective of Social Media in Higher Education in the United Arab Emirates. *Global Education Journal, 2014*(2).

Andersson, E. (2016). Producing and Consuming the Controversial–A Social Media Perspective on Political Conversations in the Social Science Classroom. *JSSE-Journal of Social Science Education, 15*(1), 6–16.

Burbules, N. C. (2016). How We Use and Are Used by Social Media in Education. *Educational Theory, 66*(4), 551–565. doi:10.1111/edth.12188

Chawinga, W. D. (2017). Taking social media to a university classroom: Teaching and learning using Twitter and blogs. *International Journal of Educational Technology in Higher Education, 14*(1), 3. doi:10.118641239-017-0041-6

Dotterer, G., Hedges, A., & Parker, H. (2016). Fostering Digital Citizenship in the Classroom. *Education Digest, 82*(3), 58.

Draper, M., Appregilio, S., Kramer, A., Ketcherside, M., Campbell, S., Stewart, B., & Cox, C. (2015). Educational Intervention/Case Study: Implementing an Elementary-Level, Classroom-Based Media Literacy Education Program for Academically At-Risk Middle-School Students in the Non-Classroom Setting. *Journal of Alcohol and Drug Education, 59*(2), 12.

El Bialy, S., & Ayoub, A. R. (2017). The Trends of Use of Social Media by Medical Students. *Education in Medicine Journal, 9*(1).

Exley, B., Willis, L. D., & McCosker, M. (2017). Children as advocates-The potential of using social media in the early and primary years. *Practical Literacy: The Early and Primary Years, 22*(2), 9.

Fedorov, A., Levitskaya, A., & Camarero, E. (2016). Curricula for Media Literacy Education According to International Experts. *European Journal of Contemporary Education, 17*(3), 324–334.

Funk, J. B., Brouwer, J., Curtiss, K., & McBroom, E. (2009). Parents of preschoolers: Expert media recommendations and ratings knowledge, media-effects beliefs, and monitoring practices. *Pediatrics, 123*(3), 981–988. doi:10.1542/peds.2008-1543 PMID:19255029

Georgakainas, B., & Zaharias, P. (2016). Social Media in Greek K-12 education: A research model that explores teachers' behavioral intention. *Ανοικτή Εκπαίδευση: το περιοδικό για την Ανοικτή και εξ Αποστάσεως Εκπαίδευση και την Εκπαιδευτική Τεχνολογία, 12*(2), 90-102.

Graber, D., & Mendoza, K. (2012). New media literacy education (NMLE): A developmental approach. *The Journal of Media Literacy Education, 4*(1), 8.

Graham, M. (2014). Social media as a tool for increased student participation and engagement outside the classroom in higher education. *Journal of Perspectives in Applied Academic Practice, 2*(3). doi:10.14297/jpaap.v2i3.113

Greenhow, C., & Askari, E. (2017). Learning and teaching with social network sites: A decade of research in K-12 related education. *Education and Information Technologies, 22*(2), 623–645. doi:10.100710639-015-9446-9

Greenhow, C., & Lewin, C. (2016). Social media and education: Reconceptualizing the boundaries of formal and informal learning. *Learning, Media and Technology, 41*(1), 6–30. doi:10.1080/17439884.2015.1064954

Hartley, M. T., Mapes, A. C., Taylor, A., & Bourgeois, P. J. (2016). Digital Media Education and Advocacy: Addressing Attitudes toward Disability on College Campuses. *Journal of Postsecondary Education and Disability, 29*(3), 239–247.

Kahveci, N. G. (2015). Pre-service teachers' conceptions on use of social media in social studies education. *International Journal of Progressive Education, 11*(1).

Karaduman, H., Köse, T. Ç., & Eryılmaz, Ö. (2017). Values in Social Media from the Viewpoint of Social Studies Teacher Candidates. *Turkish Online Journal of Qualitative Inquiry, 9*(2).

Khan, T., Kend, M., & Robertson, S. (2016). Use of social media by university accounting students and its impact on learning outcomes. *Accounting Education, 25*(6), 534–567. doi:10.1080/09639284.2016.1230880

Kilis, S., Gülbahar, Y., & Rapp, C. (2016). Exploration of Teaching Preferences of Instructors' use of Social Media. *European Journal of Open, Distance and E-learning, 19*(1), 1–18. doi:10.1515/eurodl-2016-0001

Kirkorian, H. L., Wartella, E. A., & Anderson, D. R. (2008). Media and young children's learning. *The Future of Children, 18*(1), 39–61. doi:10.1353/foc.0.0002 PMID:21338005

Kothari, A., & Hickerson, A. (2016). Social media use in journalism education: Faculty and student expectations. *Journalism & Mass Communication Educator, 71*(4), 413–424. doi:10.1177/1077695815622112

Kumi-Yeboah, A., & Smith, P. (2016). Critical multicultural citizenship education among black immigrant youth: Factors and challenges. *International Journal of Multicultural Education, 18*(1), 158–182. doi:10.18251/ijme.v18i1.1079

Levitskaya, A. (2015). The Potential of an Alliance of Media Literacy Education and Media Criticism in Russia. *European Journal of Contemporary Education*, (4), 223-231.

Lofgren, E. A. (2014). *Social media and equine science: The effect of LinkedIn on class engagement of equine higher education students* (Doctoral dissertation). Murray State University.

Mikhaleva, G. V. (2015). Impact of European Media Education Strategies on Russian Media Education Development. *European Journal of Contemporary Education*, (4), 239-244.

Nupairoj, N. (2016). The Ecosystem of Media Literacy: A Holistic Approach to Media Education/El ecosistema de la alfabetización mediática: Un enfoque integral y sistemático para divulgar la educomunicación. [English edition]. *Comunicar, 24*(49), 29–37. doi:10.3916/C49-2016-03

Oktavia, T., Warnars, S., Hendric, H. L., & Adi, S. (2017). Integration Model of Knowledge Management and Social Media for Higher Education. *Telkomnika, 15*(2).

Palekahelu, D. T., Hunt, J., Thrupp, R. M., & Relmasira, S. (2016). The Use of Smartphones and Social Media in Schools of Kota Salatiga, Central Java. In *Proceedings of the 2016 International Conference on Information Communication Technologies in Education* (pp. 102-111). International Conference on Information Communication Technologies in Education (ICICTE).

Pavlik, J. V. (2015). Fueling a third paradigm of education: The pedagogical implications of digital, social and mobile media. *Contemporary Educational Technology, 6*(2), 113–125.

Rad, S. T., Kurt, S., & Polatöz, S. (2013). Use of information and communication technologies in rural Mersin (Turkey); Prospects for rural development. *JOTAF/Tekirdağ Ziraat Fakültesi Dergisi, 10*(3), 97-106.

Rantala, L. (2011). Finnish media literacy education policies and best practices in early childhood education and care since 2004. *The Journal of Media Literacy Education, 3*(2), 7.

Rosenberg, J. M., Terry, C. A., Bell, J., Hiltz, V., & Russo, T. E. (2016). Design Guidelines for Graduate Program Social Media Use. *TechTrends, 60*(2), 167–175. doi:10.100711528-016-0023-x

Samuels-Peretz, D., Dvorkin Camiel, L., Teeley, K., & Banerjee, G. (2017). Digitally Inspired Thinking: Can Social Media Lead to Deep Learning in Higher Education? *College Teaching, 65*(1), 32–39. doi: 10.1080/87567555.2016.1225663

Schmidt, H. (2012). Media Literacy Education at the University Level. *Journal of Effective Teaching, 12*(1), 64–77.

Shear, B. (2016). Five Ways to Keep Social Media From Being a Legal Headache. *Education Digest, 81*(5), 54.

Smedescu, D. A. (2014). Using social media marketing in higher education. *Romanian Journal of Marketing*, (1).

Smith, E. E. (2017). Social media in undergraduate learning: Categories and characteristics. *International Journal of Educational Technology in Higher Education, 14*(1), 12. doi:10.118641239-017-0049-y

TDK. (2017). Retrieved from http://tdk.gov.tr/?option=com_karsilik&view=karsilik&kategori1=abec esel&kelime2=M

Tucker, F. T. (2016). Sociological media: maximizing student interest in quantitative methods via collaborative use of digital media. *Problems of Education in the 21st Century, 73*.

KEY TERMS AND DEFINITIONS

Impact of Social Media on Children: The impact of communication, information, and entertainment sharing and e-learning environment on children.

Media: Communication, information, and entertainment sharing and e-learning environment.

Power of Social Media in Education: Use of communication, information, and entertainment sharing and e-learning environment for educational purposes.

Chapter 3
Social Media and Children

Mustafa Ersoy
Cumhuriyet Universitesi, Turkey

ABSTRACT

As a result of high-tech developments and the increase in the importance of the global communication, social media websites and applications have occurred as a new way of communication and self-expression in the contemporary world. Globalization has forced people to obtain and spread the necessary information quickly, and due to this requirement, people of all ages have had to acquire digital skills which they utilize to meet their need of learning and being informed about the issues happening around the world. Social media tools and applications are being highly and commonly used all round the world by all kinds of people from all ages in order to express themselves, get to know other people, share their opinions and learn others' opinions on the world issues, socialize, and have fun. Regarding its effects on children, social media has both advantages and disadvantages.

INTRODUCTION

Social media refers to the environments that change the way people communicate, interact and socialize and, in the meantime, allow people to express themselves as they want, using internet infrastructure.

Social Media is a platform that enables its users to participate in activities and events identified as its content as a way of communicating with their social circles including other users in the system and society, to share their own opinions by bringing them together to create their own content (Cohen, 2011). Although interaction and communication between social media users are emphasized in this definition, Fredman (2013) divides social media platforms into two different groups as interactive and non-interactive social media environments.

According to the way Fredman (2013) distinguishes social media platforms, interactive social media environments provide a way for users to communicate. Outputs of the software programs that make this communication among users possible depend on input from registered users in these environments to the system. In other words, all kinds of information and interpretation that users share in the system directly affect the output of the programs. Digital and electronic devices, software, touch tablets, applications, video games, interactive screen-based media such as Facebook, MySpace, game play sites, club penguins,

DOI: 10.4018/978-1-6684-6307-9.ch003

blogs and YouTube are directly influenced by the output of virtual site programs and they are designed according to these outputs. Non-interactive social media platforms, on the other hand, do not provide an interactive experience. These environments consist of content that electronic devices cannot change, such as songs, movies, photographs, news articles, online images, and ads that appear on sites. These include digital copies of television programs, DVDs and CDs that have been shipped to the market. In summary, interactive social media environments are social media sites where users interact with each other and create their own content through their sharings and comments, while non-interactive social media platforms are the social media sites where users listen to music files and watch the video files that are added to the content without communicating with each other and sharing their own content.

Whether it is interactive or noninteractive social media environment, it is an undeniable fact that social media tools exist and occupy a huge part of modern life. Therefore, it is important that their uses and effects be searched in detail and people, especially parents, be aware of their both positive and negative effects on children and behave accordingly.

BACKGROUND

Increasing Trends About Social Media and Its Uses

In the 21st century, the breathtaking pace of the developments and innovations occurred in the field of high-tech and the increased networking and communication means as a result of these advancements have made people develop digital skills in order to keep track of this rapidly changing information era. Especially, the Z generation have found themselves in a highly digital world in which they have to acquire the digital skills. In today's world, there are children who actively use all the social media websites through the applications in their mobile phones. The fact that communication technologies and the internet are getting more and more accessible from every other day has made it possible to spread the so-called social media tools, applications and services (Boyd, 2008: 92). The fact that people can perform activities such as introducing yourself, getting to know others, sharing and spreading their own opinions and ideas, learning others' ideas and information, having fun, playing games, advertising and organizing events quickly and economically makes social media highly widespread all around the world. When compared to the real life, the cost of doing all the aforementioned activities in the virtual world seems to be quite economical in terms of business, time and other costs. It is also seen that the conditions of competition and business union in the real world change in virtual environment.

It can be said that the increasing trend of the internet which started to be used in the 1990s is continuing and social media is one of the important driving forces in this trend. The fact that naturally, human beings are in the effort of socialization and the decrease of the resources that he has to spend for this effort contributes to the continuation of this upward tendency in internet use. Nearly all Internet sites, such as shopping sites, training and research sites, news sites, forum sites, etc., have social media links in the Internet.

According to the 2017 We Are Social data (We Are Social, 2017), 3.77 billion people, which is equal to almost 50% of the world's whole population, use the internet while 2.8 billion people, which corresponds to 37% of all the people living in the world, use social media. 4.92 billion mobile users make up 66% of the world's population and 2.56 million are social media users.

If these data are compared with that of the year 2016, it can be seen that the number of internet users increased by 10%, social media users by 21%, mobile social media users by 30% and mobile phone users by 5%. (We Are Social, 2017)

The most noticeable increase is seen in mobile social media users. This shows that social media users are willing to make their interactions faster, share instantly, and make comments.

The number of social media users and the attention-grabbing increase in their numbers have made social media sites an invaluable space for advertisers, especially since ads can be shown based on the user's profile, internet searches, age, and gender.

The readers, who can share their own opinions and discuss about the newspaper columns they read in the real world only with their friends around, can interact with many people who write their opinions under the related texts, read others' opinions, suggestions and comments and share their own thoughts with these other people thanks to social media tools.

Through social media, it is possible to reach a lot of information such as culture, art, entertainment, sports, news, weather, etc. in a very fast manner. Moreover, this situation is not only limited to reaching the information, but it also enables to follow the opinions, thoughts and shares of the other social media users regarding these issues and to have an influence on the decisions made upon these issues. In other words, the interaction among people can happen at an unprecedented pace and easiness. This quick interaction can produce many good or bad results for people, depending on what ideas are shared and disseminated. Communication has become faster and easier thanks to the benefits and opportunities offered by social media, but the negative effects and harms of social media are also increasing day by day. In other words, it is obvious that social media, which has high impact and thus can bring positive and negative effects when used, needs to be controlled. Every place where communication and interaction occur among people causes them to experience social, cultural, emotional and cognitive changes. This will inevitably have an impact on social, cultural and political transformations of societies. Trying to ensure that these transformations occur in a positive and intended way should be one of the priority tasks of the governments.

In addition to these aforementioned issues, many families are wondering who their children are interacting with, how their children interact with these other people and what content their children see and share in social media websites and want to control their interactions to protect their children. However, the nature of the social media it seems to be very difficult to control what their children do in these websites owing to the nature of these social media websites. Assuming that parents are one step ahead of their children in using technology, it is the first step towards protecting them. For this reason, professional supervision may be required to ensure that the inspection and control are healthy and safe. However, it is clear that the healthy communication and interaction between the family, in order to ensure that their children do not undergo any dangerous or harmful interactions and content in these social media websites, are a must and cannot be replaced with any technological tools or professional support.

The natural learning style for children is learning through observation; therefore, the forms, amount and purpose of the social media use of the significant others in the children's family and environment will serve as a model for children. In cases where the way parents, grandparents, and others benefit from social media is a positive example, the time spent by children in the virtual environment can be withdrawn at normal levels, and the unwanted content and the children's interaction with dangerous people can be avoided. If the family is a conscious user, the child may also be positively affected. Especially when used for entertainment, games and friendship, it is important to take into consideration that risks may increase; thus, children should be directed to real, physical environments instead of social media or internet which is difficult to control. However, it may be efficient to ensure that this is done through being a good model for children in this issue rather than limiting or forbidding social media use of the children. Otherwise, the children's secretly using a false profile on social media or having a secret social media account with fake identities may make the problem even more intractable.

In the contemporary world, individuals should be raised and educated according to the modern requirements and in today's world, the structure and the content of the information, skills, values, competencies and all the other proficiencies that individuals are asked to possess are changing rapidly. Therefore, in such an environment where the requirements are changing at a high speed, it is necessary to be able to benefit from the social media platforms as a learning tool in order to help individuals obtain intended qualifications. At this point, the fact that there is a natural motivation for students to use social media websites can make these social media platforms a valuable educational tool. Through social media facilities, it can be quite easy to provide feedback, discuss ideas in a variety of dimensions, suggest solutions for problems individually or in groups, work part-time and track tasks. The use of this structure, which offers communication between individuals and groups in a bidirectional way, can be used by the educators, and the communication and interaction between the educators and the students can be rescued from the walls of the class and spread throughout the life.

Chau (2010) expressed that there are five main aspects of the use of social media. The first aspect is that people can express themselves creatively on social networking websites or applications since there are not many restrictions. Almost all the audiovisual elements can be used to express whatever it is in people's minds freely. The second aspect is that social media provides an easy way to share information. It is extremely easy to share ideas, opinions, thoughts, criticism, emotions and so to the world at an instant with only several clicks of the buttons on computers, tablets or smartphones no matter where people are. Social media provides quick and easy way to share anything people want with other users on the social networking applications and websites. The third aspect is that social media provides informal support of other's work because people can learn about what is going on in the world through others' sharings on the social media facilities. Another aspect of the use of social media is that people acquire general understanding and respect of other people's forms of expressions and the last aspect is that social media provides an alternative way of socializing. From these aspects, it can be understood that social media is used in three main ways by its users, which are for communication, entertainment and learning.

Social Media as a Means of Communication

The fact that access to internet via mobile devices has become a popular habit has required the development of web pages designed for big screen devices such as computers to be compatible with small screen devices. Many social networking sites have developed applications for use on mobile devices and have benefited from the location and time advantages of interacting with mobile devices. However, this also necessitated ways for people to write their messages shorter. It is seen as a habit in social media to be able to express oneself by sharing pictures or videos using shorter sentences, few words, abbreviated sentences and words.

People who use social media to make new friendships and to communicate more with their existing friends are also following the frequent brands and the celebrities they like. Their shares usually include their families, friends, places they go on holidays, their excursions, even what they eat and drink, others' shares they like and activities that they do.

At present, it is observed that the vast majority of young and middle-aged populations are connected to social networks via mobile devices. It is not surprising that these people, who have discovered the existence of a large virtual world with the increased ease of access to the internet, go online and use the online websites as their initial and primary resources to find the necessary information no matter what the problems they face. Taking recommendations using social media even for shopping can be given as an example of the increased communication purpose among users.

Social Media as a Portal for Entertainment

Social media is used by children as a gaming tool. This can also cause unique problems, apart from internet and computer-based problems in general. Children find the games including no human interaction boring after a certain period of time. However, the online games played with other children are played a lot and for hours in a non-stop way with the same enthusiasm at the very beginning due to the social characteristics such as competition, business association, cooperation, and the desire to prove themselves these online games have. In addition to being just a way to have fun, these games have become a new way of making new friends and killing time. Considering the fact that a lot of advertisements are being displayed during these games, it is possible for children to encounter inappropriate contents, sexuality, violence, abusive speech and other undesirable situations. The worse is the fact that some games spread rapidly because people earn money through these games and the fact that many of these games include violence, killing, crime, torture and even rape and thus they pose serious threats for children.

It is important to use the games played on social media for educational purposes, besides as a way to find entertainment and friends. In other words, helping children acquire the desired knowledge, skills, attitudes and values through these online games children play should be accepted as an important objective. This objective cannot be reached by increasing the control and developing new control mechanisms. Families should be a part of the games designed for educational purposes and allowing for social interactions in order to achieve this desired objective.

Social Media as a Learning Tool

In today's world, children are required to have the ability to use modern technology and they are expected to be able to conduct research, possess problem solving skills and own creative and critical thinking skills and therefore, it is imperative that children be conscious in the issue of social media use. In this regard, parent and teachers have great responsibilities. In order to fulfill these responsibilities, parents and teachers must have the skills to use social media and internet. Families should be informed about the risks caused by social media and internet use.

As a general view, face-to-face education can be considered to be more effective than virtual environments in terms of developing healthy human relationships. As one of the important reasons causing this situation, it is observed that due to the fact that more than one sensory organ is active during face-to-face communication and the communication is made more versatile, learning is much easier. However, education technologies can also be effective in increasing academic success, where they can attract students' attention and influence their motivation. One of the natural characteristics of technologies such as computers and the internet is that users can achieve attention without any extra effort. This natural state of involvement can be used by teachers to increase students' use of educational technologies.

It can be said that smart board, computer, projection, internet and social media technologies have the desired educational benefits such as hosting and presenting educational content, increasing interactions between students and content, enabling cooperation among students, providing collective or independent research and discussion opportunities.

Many video sharing sites, especially YouTube, offer a rich archive of content. These contents, which are used for fun, learning and communication with other people, bring with it a lot of problems due to being prepared for income generation. Content rating appropriate to the age of the users is inadequate, especially when it is necessary to verify the age of videos that contain violence and sexuality.

Factors That Affect the Use of Social Media

The main reasons for the widespread use of social media are the development of technologies for the computer, internet and mobile devices and their pricing at the affordable level. However, social media has become that much widespread because the infrastructure variables mentioned can be used to meet some of the basic human needs. Social media, through which people can quickly meet their needs like researching, recognizing, discussing and sharing the values of the society they live in, continue to increase their influence because these humanly needs are far from being met by the family and the environment that the city life shapes. The fact that both parents work, the number of siblings' people have is small or the increased number of only children, and the disconnected relations among family members reduce and inactivate communication in the family. If the children in the family are a bit lucky, one of the parents may spend time with them at least in the evening, chatting with them, observing their mysterious worlds, their curiosity, and their development. Otherwise, they may be drawn to their worlds, which they built for themselves with their tablet computers in their hands after dinner. It would have been unnecessary to worry anyhow if they could build that world in the direction of their own beautiful thoughts. However, internet and social media interactions, messages given through games, images and messages engraved with advertisements into tiny minds are very effective in shaping them. Along with their own worlds, their minds will grow unhealthy, full of the ideas and emotions imposed by the internet world broken from the family and society they live in.

For children who have difficulty expressing themselves and feeling constantly alone, the internet creates an escape environment and detaches them from the living reality. In addition, the need to surf and find friends in the social media makes the children addicted to the internet environment. Their exposure to unwanted content and interaction by hiding their age and identity can pose great danger for them (Kırık, 2014). As the social media begins to fill the large gap created by the parents, the amount of time parents spend with their children has begun to decrease more. This can result in a loss of communication in the family and thus a weakening of family ties. Individuals with low self-confidence, poor communications in their surroundings, and no suitable social environments can try to make themselves more visible on social media. Poor communication and interaction among family members together with loneliness, which is mostly felt during adolescence, can leave children unguarded and thus they can be affected more easily by the people or groups they interact with on the social media websites.

Risks and Benefits of Social Media

Risks of Social Media

It is seen that the use of the internet is increasing day by day and social media is used not only by adults and young people but also by children. Thanks to the devices that have a touch screen, even children who are illiterate have become internet users. What children can encounter on the Internet, where they are left alone for playing games and watching videos, should be regarded as an important problem by adults.

Children discovering the virtual world via game applications and video sites also become active social media users after learning to read and write. It is quite easy to get the attention of the children by evoking their senses of curiosity. Especially if the advertisements can be watched by the content providers without considering the age of the users, it should be seen as a serious problem. In addition to this, the fact that some ill-minded adults can show themselves as children by giving misinformation about their real age and try to interact with real children users in social media sites should be considered as a danger, as well.

One of the major threats on the internet was pornography via text, pictures, audio and video, but it seems difficult to prevent the spread of these contents through social media, while the sources of these contents can be identified and closed down. Moreover, the work of those who want to attract children to themselves by creating false profiles through social media seems fairly easy.

In addition to these harmful and unwanted contents, due to the social media contents highlighting the promotion of the substances and drugs potentially hazardous to human health, and attempts of the seemingly friendly terrorists organizations to deceive people and increase their popularity among young people and the similar troublesome sharings directly related to human factors that can be encountered on social media platforms can influence children negatively, cause the problems of sexual exploitation of children, expose children to the recognition of deviant thoughts and heresies that can lead them to commit suicide and even cause them to confront unwanted situations like obscenity and prostitution which may derange their mental health. It is a well-known phenomenon that unsafe and unconscious use of the internet may cause long-term negative effects on children and adolescents and result in social and psychological problems (Bayzan & Özbilen, 2011).

Owing to their inherent desire to share, people can share a lot of things such as their writings, photos, videos and links of commercial goods on their social media accounts. However, in these sharings, people are expected to behave as carefully and meticulously as they do in their daily life while choosing their clothes, eating, talking to others around, and even walking. Responsible people need to think about how people can see what they share, how they can be seen, and how the shared message is meant to be understood. Benefits like expressing yourself easily, sharing information quickly, helping others to share their own experiences and ideas, and discussing a variety of topics are expected to result in unintended consequences when the expected social media is not used carefully and consciously. Among these negative consequences are the uncontrolled display of private life in front of many other users' eyes, exposure to violence and sexuality, dissemination of information that may be dangerous to humans and nature, confrontation with targeted content disregarding social order and rules, misleading product advertising, and exposure to advertisements.

In short, it can be said that if parents and educators are not aware of the potential risks and threats that social media pose for children, it may be dangerous for children more than it is realized. Undiyaundeye (2014), in her study in which she discussed the benefits and risks of the use of social media by children and adolescents, put the aforementioned negative aspects of social media on children into following categories:

- **Cyberbullying and Online Harassment:** It can be said that this is the most dangerous risk that social media pose for children and it is the most common one. Through social media, cyberbullying or online harassment can be realized as "from an adult to children" or" from peers to peers/ from children to children". Social media is an easy and potential platform to spread fake, artificial, embarrassing and hostile information about others, which may affect children profoundly and cause depression, anxiety, isolation and suicide as a result.
- **Sexting:** Social media provides an easy platform to share any kinds of content for its users and some people can use the social media facilities to spread their own sexual messages, videos, photos or information and children users may see these sexually explicit sharings of others or even children may make such sharings and become targets of child pornography. Sexting can be used as a way of cyberbullying as well.
- **Facebook Depression:** Hankings and Jia (1999) expressed a new phenomenon called Facebook depression, which can be defined as the negative emotional mood or situation that occur when children spend too much time on social media websites. Especially, adolescents who feel lonely and have trouble making friends and becoming a part of social peer groups in their environment can use social media websites to avoid this loneliness and may start to use these websites more than enough and thus suffer from a more severe social isolation that may cause them to develop addiction.
- **Defective Social Relationship:** Directly related to the aforementioned item "Facebook depression", children who spend too much time on social media platforms may lose wonderful opportunities of real conversations and face-to-face sharings in their real lives because they spend little time with their families and actual friends, which weakens the family bond and limit interaction with actual people. Real conversations and face-to-face communication make people happier and help them avoid depression, loneliness and any kind of negative emotional mood.
- **Distorted Senescence of Reality:** In today's world, children are extremely active in social networking websites and they may get a different kind of sense of reality in these virtual environments. Children may think that every relationship they make on these websites and every contact they have through these websites are real and totally harmless. They may not be aware of the others that try to contact with them and give harm to them through these websites. Making virtual friends are not always safe. Children may make online friends and start to share their privacy with these friends without noticing that these sharings may be harmful in the future. In addition to these, due to the harmful content of the advertisements seen on social media websites may affect children negatively and change their understanding of what is normal and abnormal.

Benefits of Social Media

According to Chau (2010), social media applications and social networking websites can also be effectively used for the benefits of children, as well. Chau (2010) states that social media is a great platform for children to socialize, increase their creativity, interact and learn. Rosen (2011) put forwards that social media websites can be utilized as an alternative way to increase student motivation and participation in educational activities. Clark-Pearson and O'Keeffe (2011) suggest that social media facilities can help students with their assignments and group projects.

In addition to these educational benefits of the use of social media, it also provides a good platform for children to stay connected with their peers and ease their communication with all the people around who they get to know in their social environments such as family circle, school and gyms (Ito, 2008). Rosen (2011) stresses the importance of social networking websites in that these websites help shy children interact with others in a safe and virtual environment so that their shyness does not occur as a problem that blocks their communication. Ito (2008) suggests that social media websites and applications can be used as a platform for children to find new friends who share the same tastes in different walks of life and these websites are also great avenues where children share their interests in everything and everybody with other users (Clark-Pearson & O'Keeffe, 2011). Social media facilities can be used as social platforms to find self-help suggestions from experts in different problem areas when needed, especially when children go through hard times (Nielsen Online, 2009).

In addition to these social benefits, another advantage of social media is that children can make friends from diverse backgrounds and different cultures from all over the world so that they can develop a cultural awareness (Clark-Pearson & O'Keeffe, 2011), which may lead them to organize social events highlighting cultural awareness in order to make good impacts on policymakers while making decisions on important issues about the services provided to the youth all around the world.

In short, social media websites and their applications on smart devices can serve as great platforms for children to increase their learning experiences by participating in different and effective educational activities; to look for social, medical, and professional advice from the experts who have their accounts on these websites especially when children experience difficult times; to socialize and interact without feeling the stress of face-to-face interactions with new people and to increase their cultural competence by making new friends from different backgrounds and countries. Through social media, children can play an active role in policymaking process.

Undiyaundeye (2014) discusses the benefits of the use of social media by children and adolescents in her study and categories these benefits as follows:

- **Literacy Skills:** Children can be provided with excellent social media applications to help them learn to read and write and improve their skills in digital reading and writing.
- **Numeracy Skills:** Children can learn how to count through the games presented in the social media websites and applications on smartphones and tablet Pcs.
- **Social Skills:** Social media means a great amount of easiness in communicating and interacting with different people from all around world, which directly improve their social skills in the most positive ways. In social media, children are observed to show cooperative and helping behaviours. Furthermore, children may follow their role models through social media and if these role models are chosen correctly, this may affect their development positively. Children can also increase their awareness about what is happening in the world and this may enable them to become more responsible human beings who always try to act upon human rights and protection of the nature. In addition to these social benefits, children may relax as they use social media just for fun, which help them relieve boredom. Furthermore, with their increased motivation and skills, as they grow older and become more mature, they may start use social media to create global contacts to get career information and contact with important figures in the business, political and art world.

- **Intellectual Skills:** Children can improve their problem solving and critical thinking skills through their sharings and comments on others' sharing and they can learn to respect others' points of view and start paying more attention to universal morals and values as they interact with people from all over the world.
- **Creative Skills:** Children try to show themselves in an interesting and different way to attract others' attention and obtain social acceptance. They can cut and design their photos and videos into the applications included in the social media websites so that they may develop new digital skills to promote themselves as true friends and good people who care others.

Table 1. The positive and negative effects of social media on children

The Positive and Negative Effects of Social Media on Children	
Positive Effects	**Negative Effects**
Social Media as a platform to communicate: • To make new friends and expand social circles • To get to know people from different backgrounds and countries and thus improve cultural awareness • To seek for educational, relational, vocational and medical advice • To become a part of the global world in different walks of life • To come together with the related people to organize social events and try to persuade policymakers	*Cyberbullying or Online Harassment:* • To suffer from the release of private/secret personal information by ill-willed users • To suffer from the spread of fake and offending gossips about oneself • To feel humiliated and embarrassed by other users in an unfair way Sexting: To share audiovisual files including sexual content and suffer from negative reputations and not being able to avoid being contacted with other users on this issue
Social Media as a platform to have fun: • To spend fun time and relax • To overcome loneliness and boredom • To play games and increase digital skills • To increase their rivalry skills	*Facebook Depression:* • To spend too much time on social networking websites and lose track of the relationships among family members and friends • To be afraid of not having enough likes and losing the perceived online support
Social Media as a platform to learn: • To develop literacy and numeracy skills with the help of related and intended applications • To increase motivation in educational activities • To increase creative thinking and critical thinking skills • To ease assignments and group projects • To make educational activities more interesting and accessible	*Defective social relationship:* • To get stressed while making face to face contacts with the people around and be addicted to social media to communicate with others *Distorted Senescence of reality:* • To fail in distinguishing what is normal and what is not normal or what friendships are real and what friendships are fake

FUTURE RESEARCH DIRECTIONS

In the presence of the qualifications that the 21st century information age forces people to obtain, no one can deny the importance of the digital literacy. Children of this age should acquire the digital skills that they are going to need in the rest of their life to be able to meet the needs of the information age they live in. Therefore, parents cannot prevent their children from using social media tools. However, children of this age should be led to obtain digital literacy and in addition to these high-tech requirements, they should be taught to possess media literacy. Social media tools are excellent platforms for the children of this age to obtain the 21st century skills and practice them to deal with the requirements of the information age. Considering the risks of social media tools that can be detrimental to children's psychological, mental and physical health, one of the most important 21st century skills gain increasing importance. This skill is the media literacy.

Today, people reach information through an interwoven system of media technologies. Media literacy is an essential skill which means the ability to access, analyze, evaluate and create media. With the help of this skill, children get the necessary competence to understand what information they share or reach on their social media accounts is safe and what information is hazardous. Therefore, prospective educational research on social media and children should focus on how media literacy skills can be taught to children effectively.

Another important point that should be given importance in future research on this issue is about the preventive guidance studies. Preventive guidance services should be provided to children, teachers and parents at school so that they can become informed about the risks of social media. Therefore, future research should focus on how schools, families, police and related authorities can work together to create psychoeducational programmes through which children can be taught to protect themselves against any kind of threats on social media.

CONCLUSION

In the 21st century, the era people live in are called "information era" and this era is marked with high-tech developments that change the way people live in every part of their daily lives. Among these high-tech developments, social media tools seem to be an indispensable occurrence in people's daily routines owing to the increase in access to the Internet and smart phones. Although most adults use social media at high amounts, the real users of these social media tools are the children of this age and thus the benefits and risks of these tools are hold under the microscope meticulously by educators and parents. At this point, what educators and parents should do become significant. Table 2 shows some suggestions for them.

Table 2. What should be done by parents and educators

WHAT SHOULD BE DONE?	
Suggestions for Parents (Ehmke, 2017):	*Suggestions for Educators (Clarke-Pearson & O'Keeffe, 2011):*
1. Parents should curtail their consumption of social media use first and set a good model for their children. **2.** Technology-free zones inside the houses where family members are not allowed to use any kinds of technological devices or gadgets and technology free hours during the day when family members stop using their electronic and technological devices and share these moments by talking and doing activities together instead should be established as a strict family rule. **3.** Children should be ensured that their parents are always willing and ready to help them with their problems; spend time together with them and talk to them about their days, schools, hobbies and interests. **4.** Parents should ensure that they trust their children no matter what happens by letting them know they are good kids. Children should know that they can consult their parents about anything doubtful on their social media accounts. **5.** Parents should establish direct communication with their children rather than distant monitoring in terms of checking and controlling their children's social media sharings. They should never act like spies. Instead, they should talk to their children if they doubt that something is wrong.	**1.** Educators should advise parents to talk to their children about their online use and be in an open conversation with their children on important issues related to the risks of social media. **2.** Educators should recommend parents to be more technologically competent than their children, especially on social media websites. **3.** Educators should inform parents about the correct use of social media for learning, communicating and entertaining purposes and train them about how to set a good example for their children in these beneficial uses. **4.** Educators should train parents on the risks that social media can pose to their children.

REFERENCES

Bayzan, Ş., & Özbilen, A. (2011). Application Examples of Safer Use of The Internet in The World and Investigation of Awareness Activities in Turkey and Suggestions for Turkey. In *5th International Computer & Instructional Technologies Symposium*. Fırat University.

Boyd, D. M. (2008). *American Teen Sociality in Networked Publics* (Ph.D. Thesis). University of California-Berkeley.

Carroll, J. A., & Kirkpatrick, R. L. (2011). *Impact of social media on adolescent behavioral health.* Oakland, CA: California Adolescent Health Collaborative.

Chau, C. (2010). You Tube as a participatory culture. Wiley Periodicals. *Inc., 128,* 65–74.

Clarke-Pearson, K., & O'Keeffe, G. (2011). *The Impact of Social Media on Children, Adolescents, and Families.* Retrieved from http://pediatrics.aappublications.org

Cohen, H. (2011). *30 Social media definitions.* Retrieved from http://heidicohen. com/social-media-definition/

Ehmke, R. (2017). *How Using Social Media Affects Teenagers.* Retrieved from: https://childmind.org/article/how-using-social-media-affects-teenagers/

Fredman, J. (2013). *Definition of non-interactive multimedia.* Retrieved from http://www.ehow.com/info_12211830_ definition-noninteractivemultimedia.html

Hankins & Jiao, K. (1999). Constructing Sexuality and Identity in an online teen chat room. *Journal of Applied Developmental Psychology, 25,* 651–666.

Ito, M. (2008). *Engineering play: A cultural history of children's software.* London: The MIT Press Cambridge.

Kırık, A. M. (2014). Aile ve Çocuk İlişkisinde İnternetin Yeri: Nitel Bir Araştırma. *Eğitim ve Öğretim Araştırmaları Dergisi, 3,* 337–347.

Nielsen Online. (2009). *Global faces and networked places: A Nielsen report on social networking's new global footprint.* Retrieved from http://www.nielsen-online.com

Rosen, L. D. (2011). *Social Networking's Good and Bad Impacts on Kids.* Retrieved from http://www.apa.org

Undiyaundeye, F. (2014). *Impact of social media on children, adolescents and families.* Retrieved from http://www.gifre.org

We Are Social. (2017). *Digital in 2017: Global Overview.* Retrieved from https://wearesocial.com/special-reports/digital-in-2017-global-overview

ADDITIONAL READING

Boyd, D. (2014). *It's complicated: The social lives of networked teens.* Yale University Press.

Calvert, S. L., & Wilson, B. J. (Eds.). (2009). *The handbook of children, media and development*. John Wiley & Sons.

Frith, E. (June, 2017). Social Media and Children's Mental Health: A Review of the Evidence. Education Policy Institute. London, UK. (https://epi.org.uk/wp-content/uploads/2017/06/Social-Media_Mental-Health_EPI-Report.pdf)

Jordan, A. B., & Romer, D. (Eds.). (2014). *Media and the Well-being of Children and Adolescents*. Oxford University Press.

Kross, E., Verduyn, P., Demiralp, E., Park, J., Lee, D. S., Lin, N., ... Ybarra, O. (2013). Facebook Use Predicts Declines in Subjective Well-Being in Young Adults. *PLoS One*, *8*(8), e69841. doi:10.1371/journal.pone.0069841 PMID:23967061

Lemish, D. (2015). *Children and media: A global perspective*. John Wiley & Sons.

McKee, J. (2017). *The Teen's Guide to Social Media... and Mobile Devices: 21 Tips to Wise Posting in an Insecure World*. Shiloh Run Press.

Schlegel, S. (2016). Screen-Smart Parenting: How to Find Balance and Benefit in Your Child's Use of Social Media, Apps, and Digital Devices. *Journal of Developmental and Behavioral Pediatrics*, *37*(7), 600. doi:10.1097/DBP.0000000000000328

Smith, S. J. (2017). Social Media: Your Child's Digital Tattoo: Understanding & Managing Your Child's Digital Footprint. A Wired Family LLC, New York, the USA.

Strasburger, V. C., Wilson, B. J., & Jordan, A. B. (2009). Children, adolescents, and the media. *Sage (Atlanta, Ga.)*. PMID:19465581

KEY TERMS AND DEFINITIONS

Cyberbullying: The act of spreading fake, artificial, embarrassing, and hostile information about others, which may affect children profoundly and cause depression, anxiety, isolation and suicide as a result.

Digital Literacy: The ability to use information and communication technologies to find, evaluate, create, and communicate information, requiring both cognitive and technical skills.

Facebook Depression: The negative emotional mood or situation that occur when children spend too much time on social media websites

Media Literacy: The ability to access, analyze, evaluate, and create media.

Sexting: The act of spreading one's own sexual messages, videos, photos, or information through social media.

Social Media: Websites and internet-based applications which enable users to create and share content or participate in social networking.

This research was previously published in the Handbook of Research on Children's Consumption of Digital Media; pages 11-23, copyright year 2019 by Information Science Reference (an imprint of IGI Global).

Chapter 4
Psychological Benefits and Detrimental Effects of Online Social Networking

Irem Metin Orta
Atilim University, Turkey

Müge Çelik Örücü
TED University, Turkey

ABSTRACT

With the growing prevalence of wireless communication technologies, social networking sites (SNSs) such as Facebook, Twitter, etc. have become an important venues for interpersonal communication. This chapter provides a detailed overview of the current literature on online social networking with respect to its beneficial and detrimental effects on psychological wellbeing. In particular, it provides empirical evidence for the associations of SNS use with depression, self-esteem, loneliness, subjective wellbeing, social anxiety, attachment, personality traits, and addiction. Furthermore, it identifies the characteristics of individuals who are more prone to social networking, and presents possible mediators and moderators playing a role in the relationship between social networking and mental health. The chapter overall provides a comprehensive guideline to parents, researchers, educators, healthcare, and communication professionals to the issue of online social networking from a psychological perspective.

INTRODUCTION

Online social networking plays an important role in the way people communicate and interact. It has benefits for children and adolescents such as socialization, communication, increased learning opportunities, and assessing health information, however it has also some detrimental effects such as cyberbullying, online harassment, and sexting (O'Keefe & Clark-Pearson, 2011). The statistics show that there were 2.34 billion social network users worldwide in 2016 and the number is expected to reach to 2.95 billion by 2020 (Statista Facts on Social Networks, 2017). The average social media user spent 1.7 h per day

DOI: 10.4018/978-1-6684-6307-9.ch004

on social media in the USA and 1.5 h in the UK, with social media users in the Philippines having the highest daily use at 3.7 h. (Statista, 2017).

The growing popularity of online social network sites such as Facebook, MySpace, Twitter has attracted the attention of many scholars, and they have shown particular interest in understanding the psychological correlates of SNS use. Accordingly, this chapter aims to provide a detailed overview of the current literature with respect to the benefits and detrimental effects of online social networking on psychological well-being. To do so, it reviews current empirical evidence for the associations of SNS use with various mental health outcomes including depression, self-esteem, loneliness, subjective well-being, social anxiety, attachment, personality traits and addiction. Furthermore, it identifies the intrapersonal characteristics of individuals who show more tendency to use SNSs. Thus, this chapter would contribute to parents, researchers, educators, healthcare and communication professionals in providing theoretical information and practical implications of online social networking.

Throughout this chapter, several issues are addressed. First, a general introduction to the definition and history of online social networking is given and the emergent interest in this concept is discussed. Second, the empirical research focusing on the relationship between online social networking and psychological variables are systematically reviewed. A comprehensive search is conducted to gain understanding of the existing literature about the benefits and detrimental consequences of online social networking. For this purpose, SSCI, EBSCOhost, Psych ARTICLES, Scopus, and ProQuest electronic databases are consulted for the literature search using several keywords such as *social networking, psychological well-being, mental health, self-esteem, depression, anxiety, loneliness, personality, addiction, attachment etc*. The priority is given to the articles published in the last decade. Finally, practical implications and suggestions for future research are proposed through addressing plausible moderators and mediators in relation to social networking.

BACKGROUND

Social networking websites (SNSs) have become important venues for interpersonal communication and relationships. SNSs are virtual groups where personal information via profiles are shared, meet with other people based on common interests, and contact with people by writing messages or adding them as friends (Krämer & Winter, 2008; Kuss & Griffiths, 2011). The history of social networking sites dates back to 1997, when individuals are linked via six degrees of separation (Boyd & Ellison, 2007), then, the society is viewed as becoming increasingly inter-connected. Without considering time and space, individuals connect with one another online and SNSs have become an important leisure activity for many people (Kuss & Griffiths, 2017).

The sites may have different orientations related with work (i.e. LinkedIn), romantic relationship (i.e. Friendster), sharing interests (i. e. Myspace) or social connection (i.e. Facebook) (Ellison, Steinfield, & Lampe, 2007). The most popular networking sites are respectively Facebook, Whatsapp, Youtube, Facebook Messenger, WeChat, QQ, Instagram, Qzone, Tumble, Twitter, etc (Statista Facts on Social Networks, 2017). In 2004, Facebook was launched as an online community for students at Harvard University (Byod & Ellison, 2007) and has since become the world's most popular SNS. Currently, Facebook is the most dominant SNS in the U.S with 1.97 billion registered users (Statista Facts on Social Networks, 2017). One reason Facebook is the most popular social networking site is the convenience it provides for users (Kuss& Griffiths, 2017). Social information is easily shared and can be stored among members, therefore comments and feedbacks are given.

Social networking is considered as a way of being and relating with others (Kuss & Griffiths, 2017). Especially for young adults, technology is an essential part of their lives. It is such a lifestyle that necessitates them to connect everytime. This has two important consequences. First one is the maintenance of the status quo and second one is the need not to miss out and to stay up to date (Kuss & Griffiths, 2017). Given the substantial importance and prevalence of SNSs in the lives of young people today, it is of crucial importance to understand the psychological correlates of SNS use. Thus, the following section of the chapter reviews the empirical research focusing on the psychological benefits and detrimental effects of online social networking.

MAIN FOCUS OF THE CHAPTER

The popularity of SNSs has raised questions among scholars about their potential impact on mental health (O'Keefe & Clark-Pearson, 2011). Research on social media typically focuses on its benefits; considerably less is known about the dark side of social networking sites. Social networking and online communication in general is linked to psychological well-being such as increase in self-esteem, sense of belongingness, self-disclosure, and emotional supportas well as decreases in social anxiety and social isolation (see Best, Manktelow, & Taylor, 2014 for a review). On the other side, the frequent use of social media is linked to unmet need for mental health support, poor mental health, higher levels of psychological distress and suicidal ideation (Sampasa-Kanyinga & Lewis, 2015; Kim, 2016).

Accordingly, there is an increased interest in the well-being of students at school and potential problems related with students' use of socio-digital technologies (i.e.,the mobile devices, computers, social media, and the internet). In addition to the contribution of social activities to the creativity of individuals, there is a threat of being addicted to or having compulsive behavior which may result in general and school-related mental health problems. To illustrate, researchers have revealed that there is a reciprocal relationship between excessive use of digital technologies and school burnout among adolescent groups (Salmela-Aro, Upadyaya, Hakkarainen, Lonka & Alho, 2016). That is, school burnout is associated with later excessive online social activities, which in turn is related with later school burnout.

Social Networking and Depression

The majority of empirical studies have linked the prolonged use of SNS with higher levels of depression (see Pantic, 2014 for a review). As defined by American Academy of Pediatrics (2011), "Facebook depression" is a phenomena in which teens spend frequent time on SNSs and exhibit symptoms of depression (Jelenchick, Eickhoff, & Moreno, 2013; O'Keefe & Clarke-Pearson, 2011). Thus, the existing research provide promoting evidence for Facebook depression. For instance, research has shown that the time spent on social networking is positively correlated with depressive symptoms among high school students (Pantic, Damjanovic, Todorovic, Topalovic, Bojovic-Jovic, Ristic, & Pantic, 2012) and young adults (Rosen, Whaling, Rab, Carrier, & Cheever, 2013). Several mechanisms might underlie the relationship between social networking and depression.

First, individual's less social engagement and less interaction with others as a result of internet use might explain this relationship (Kraut, Patterson, Lundmark, Kiesler, Mukopadhyay, & Scherlis, 1998).

As stated previously, the time spent on internet has considerably increased with the technological advances, which in turn influences the quality of interpersonal communication and interaction within the family and social environment (Pantic, 2014). A longitudinal study by Kraut and his colleagues (1998) has shown that as the time spent online increases, the communication with family members and the size of local social circle decreases. This situation further leads to feelings of depression and loneliness. Indeed, the online communication is shallower than everyday face-to-face communications (Pantic, 2014) and internet use replaces stronger ties with weaker ties in social relationships (Kraut, Patterson, Lundmark, Kiesler, Mukopadhyay, & Scherlis, 1998). This might explain the negative impact of internet use, in particular, social networking on psychological well-being.

Second, increased levels of screen viewing and decreased levels of outdoor physical activities might explain the link between online social networking and depression (Pantic, Damjanovic, Todorovic, Topalovic, Bojovic-Jovic, Ristic, & Pantic, 2012). For instance, a longitudinal study with a 10-year follow up (Lucas, Mekary, Pan, Mirzaei, O'Reilly, Willett, ... & Ascherio, 2011) has shown that older adults who are most physically active (more than 90 min/a day) and spend less time on TV (0-5 hours/a week) report lowest level of depression than those who are less physically active (less than 10 min/ a day) and spend more time on TV (more than 21 hours/ a week). From this finding, it can be argued that as the time spent on physical activity decreases and/or the time spent on watching TV increases, the risk of developing depression increases (Lucas, Mekary, Pan, Mirzaei, O'Reilly, Willett, ... & Ascherio, 2011).

Third, individuals' incorrect perceptions regarding the lives of online friends might account for the relationship between online social networking and depressive symptoms. For instance, Chou and Edge (2012) have shown that people who spend more time on Facebook are more likely to perceive others as happier and having better lives than themselves. In constrast, people who spend more time on going out with friends are less likely to have these perceptions. Furthermore, people who have more friends on Facebook tend to more perceive the life as fair and less perceive others as happier; however, people who have personally unknown Facebook friends tend to have more perceptions of others having better lives than themselves. It is argued that with a greater extent of social networks, Facebook users tend to employ heuristics (i.e. availability heuristic) when they make judgments or form impressions about others (Chou & Edge, 2012). In addition, they tend to attribute others' actions more to stable personal disposition than situational factors (i.e. correspondence bias) especially when they do not know the person well. These distorted perceptions, in turn, might increase people's vulnerability for developing depression (Pantic, Damjanovic, Todorovic, Topalovic, Bojovic-Jovic, Ristic, & Pantic, 2012).

The existing research also point that the type of use and the quality of social interactions are important determinants for developing depression. For instance, Davila and his colleagues (2012) have shown that depression is not associated with the quantity (frequency) but the quality of online social interactions (how positive or negative it is). In particular, people with less positive and more negative interactions in social networking report more depressive symptoms over time. Furthermore, greater use of Facebook activities for impression management and less online friends are linked to more depressive symptoms (Rosen, Whaling, Rab, Carrier, & Cheever, 2013).

Some of the studies however reveal no significant relationship between SNS use and depression among older adolescents and young adults (Jelenchick, Eickhoff, & Moreno, 2013; Kross, Verduyn, Demiralp, Park, & Lee, 2013; Simoncic, Kuhlman, Vargas, Houchins, & Lopez-Duran, 2014). Interestingly, in one study, the relationship becomes significant when it is moderated by sex and personality trait (Simoncic, Kuhlman, Vargas, Houchins, & Lopez-Duran, 2014). That is, increased Facebook activity is linked to lower levels of depressive symptoms only among young female adults with high neuroticism scores. It is argued that SNS use may be beneficial for vulnerable individuals, in particular, for females high in neuroticismin terms of promoting adaptive social interactions (Simoncic, Kuhlman, Vargas, Houchins, & Lopez-Duran, 2014). The negative association between online communication and depression is also supported by a study conducted by Bessiere, Pressman, Kiesler and Kraut (2010). In their study, researchers reveal that people who use the internet for health-related purposes show small increase in depression whereas those who use the internet for the purpose of communication with family and friends show declines in depression. It is argued that the use of SNSs not extensively may strengthen social ties with family members and close friends, and thus contributes to individual's mental health (Bessiere, Pressman, Kiesler,& Kraut, 2010).

Besides, SNSs, specifically Facebook, can be used for early detection and assessment of depression (Park, Lee, Kwak, Cha & Jeong, 2013). Since depressive prone individuals are more likely to use depression related Facebook activities, the identification of early symptoms may predict future depression. In a study, researchers have examined the social network determinants of depressive symptoms which distinguish depressed individuals from those who are not depressed (Park, Lee, Kwak, Cha, & Jeong, 2013). As a result, depressive symptoms are positively correlated with individuals' Facebook activities such as accumulated app points and number of viewed tips, and negatively correlated with the number of friends and location tags. Supporting findings of other studies (Chou & Edge, 2012; Rosen, Whaling, Rab, Carrier, & Cheever, 2013), having more online friends might protect individuals from developing depression.

In addition to Facebook, depression is found to be common among users of Tumble, which is also a widely used SNS (Cavazos-Rehg, Krauss, Sowles, Connolly, Rosas, Bharadwaj, ... & Bierut, 2017). Popular depression-related Tumblr accounts are monitored in order to gain a better understanding of the depression, self-harm, and suicidal content that is being shared on Tumblr. Posts are randomly selected by the research team and coded based on predetermined topics. Common themes are found as self-loathing, loneliness/feeling unloved, self-harm and suicide. Cavazos-Rehg's study (2017) is an important first step at better understanding the displayed depression-related references on Tumblr. Considering the depression and suicidal content observed on Tumblr, the findings suggest a need for suicide prevention efforts to intervene on Tumblr and this platform can be used in a strategic way (Cavazos-Rehg, Krauss, Sowles, Connolly, Rosas, Bharadwaj, ... & Bierut, 2017).

Social Networking and Self-Esteem

The relationship between online social networking and signs and symptoms of depression might also be explained by changes in self-esteem (Pantic, Damjanovic, Todorovic, Topalovic, Bojovic-Jovic, Ristic, & Pantic, 2012). Self-esteem, the evaluative aspect of the self, is a belief in one's capacity, worth and significance (Coopersmith, 1981). The systematic review of recent research shows mixed findings about the relationship between SNS use and self-esteem (see Pantic, 2014 for a review). In particular, Gonzales and Hancock (2011) propose two different theoretical explanations for the possible impact of social networking on individual's self-esteem. First, based on *objective self-awareness theory* (Duval & Wicklund, 1972), researchers suggest that conscious awareness of one's self (i.e. through mirror, photoor autobiographical information) influences impressions of the self negatively. Extending this rationale to SNSs, viewing one's personal profile containing self-descriptions and pictures may increase self-awareness, thus diminish one's self-esteem.

Second, based on *the hyperpersonal model* (Walther, 1996), researchers state that online communication enables individuals present one's positive (or preferred) aspects of personality which in turn may enhance one's self-esteem (Gonzales & Hancock, 2011). Supporting the process of *selective self-presentation*, researchers have shown that attention to one's own profile (i.e. viewing and updating information) influences impressions of the self positively (Gonzales & Hancock, 2011). As Krämer and Winter (2008) state, SNSs are ideal venues for managing self-presentation, andaccordingly, the modifiable nature of self-presentation in computer-mediated communication enhances one's self-esteem (Gonzales & Hancock, 2011).

In a related vein, a group of researchers has shown that positive feedback on the profiles of networking sites enhances adolescents' social self-esteem (Valkenburg, Peter, & Schouten, 2006). That is, adolescents who receive positive feedback on their profiles report more positive evaluations for their physical appearance, romantic attractiveness and for their ability to form close relationships. However, adolescents who receive negative feedback on their profiles report more negative self-evaluations on these dimensions. These findings can be explained by adolescents engagement of *imaginative audience behavior* (Elkind & Bowen,1979). In general, adolescents think that they are watched and evaluated by others, thus they are overly concerned with their self-presentations. Accordingly, as shown by researchers (Valkenburg, Peter, & Schouten, 2006), the feedback received on profiles in SNSs may affect individual'slevel ofself-esteem either positively or negatively.

Even though a few studies have revealed no relationship between self-esteem and SNS use (Krämer &Winter, 2008; Wilson, Fornasier, & White, 2010), other studies have demonstrated that people with low self-esteem tend to spend more time online (Joinson, 2004; Mehdizadeh, 2010). For instance, those individuals prefer online communication more than face-to-face communication (Joinson, 2004). In addition, people's level of self-esteem is negatively correlated with time spent on online ('Facebook') activities and their narcissism scores are positively correlated with self-promotion content of these activities (Mehdizadeh, 2010). From these findings, it can be argued that lower levels of self-esteem predicts more social networking since it provides benefits to individuals in terms of enhancing their psychological well-being (Ellison, Steinfield, & Lampe, 2007).

Besides, a study conducted by Fioravanti, Dettore, and Casale (2012) show that female adolescents' preferences for an online social interaction (POSI) partially mediates the relationship between self-esteem and internet addiction. That is, low levels of esteem predicts internet addiction directly and indirectly through higher levels of POSI. More interestingly, *the opportunity to escape from the real world* appears as an important characteristics of computer-mediated communication in the relation between self-esteem and POSI. Even though the findings of aforementioned studies link low self-esteem to higher frequency of SNS use, given the cross-sectional nature of thestudies, no causal inferences can be drawn with regard to these relationships.

Social Networking and Subjective Well-Being

Subjective well-being (SWB) in general is comprised of affective (i.e. positive and negative affect) and cognitive components (i.e. satisfaction with life) (Pavot & Diener, 2004). The existing literature has yielded mixed results for the relationship between social networking and subjective well-being. For instance, a study has shown that as the use of Facebook increases, people report more negative feelings and less satisfaction with their lives over time even when the level of loneliness is controlled (Kross, Verduyn, Demiralp, Park, & Lee, 2013). Similarly, Bevan, Gomez, and Sparks (2014) also reveal that the time spent on SNSs is negatively correlated with the quality of life. In contrast, direct interaction with others (face-to-face or phone) is associated with increases in affective well-being (Kross, Verduyn, Demiralp, Park, & Lee, 2013).

On the other side, researchers have shown that the intensity of Facebook use among young adults is correlated with increased life satisfaction scores (Valenzuela, Park, & Kee, 2009), and positive feedback on the profiles of friend networking sites enhances adolescents' life satisfaction via social self-esteem (Valkenburg, Peter, & Schouten, 2006). From these finding, it can be argued that positive evaluations received on a SNS profile enhances individual's self-esteem, which in turn reflects upon on subjective well-being. Supporting this notion, researchers has shown that the Facebook use provides benefits especially for individuals with lower levels of self-esteem and life satisfaction (Ellison, Steinfield, & Lampe, 2007).

In another study, Fox and Moreland (2015) have formed a focus group from Facebook users to understand individuals' negative psychological and relational experiences tied to the SNSs and their utilization (e.g., connectivity, visibility, accessibility, persistence, and social feedback). As a result, five themes related to Facebook stressors have emerged as managing inappropriate or annoying content, being attached, lack of privacy and control, social comparison and jealousy, and relationship tension and conflict. Results also demonstrate that despite having experiences of negative emotions, Facebook users still feel pressured to connect the site frequently due to the fear of missing out and to keep up with relationships. Even though users state that Facebook is unimportant, they later report significant unpleasant events associated with Facebook (Fox & Moreland, 2015).

Considering psychological well-being, scholars have introduced new concepts in relation to social networking. For instance, recent research (Oberst, Wegmann, Stodt, Brand & Chamarro, 2017; Buglass, Binder, Betts & Underwood, 2017) suggests that high engagement in social networking is partially due to what has been named the *fear of missing out* (FOMO). FOMO is a pervasive apprehension that others might be having rewarding experiences from which one is absent (Przybylski, Murayama, DeHaan & Gladwell, 2013). Researchers have shown that higher levels of FOMO is related with greater engagement with Facebook and decreases in mood, well-being, and life satisfaction as well as inappropriate social networking (Przybylski, Murayama, DeHaan, & Gladwell, 2013).

Furthermore, '*nomophobia*' has been defined as no mobile phone phobia, i.e., *the fear of being without one's mobile phone* (Bragazzi & Del Puente, 2014). Researchers have called for nomophobia to be included in the DSM-5, and the following criteria have been outlined to contribute to this problem constellation:

... regular and time-consuming use, feelings of anxiety when the phone is not available, 'ringxiety' (repeatedly checking one's phone for messages, sometimes leading to phantom ring tones), constant availability, preference for mobile communication over face to face communication, and financial problems as a consequence of use (Bragazzi & Del Puente, 2014).

Another presentation of ringxiety is '*phantom vibration syndrome*', defined as *perceived vibration from a cellphone that is not vibrating (Drouin, Kaiser, & Miller, 2012).*

Social Networking, Loneliness, Social Anxiety, and Attachment

Researchers have proposed that feelings of loneliness increases people's tendency to use Facebook (Clayton, Osborne, Miller, & Oberle, 2013; Kross Verduyn, Demiralp, Park, & Lee, 2013). In particular, individuals who perceive themselves lonely tend to use SNSs to connect with others. In a study by Bonetti, Campbell and Gilmore (2010), researchers examined how much time children and adolescents with and without feelings of loneliness and/or social anxiety spend communicating online, the topics they choose, the purpose of communication and the partners they engage with. The results show that as the feelings of loneliness increases, the frequency of online communication about personal and intimate topics increases. In addition, the most common motives for online communication reported by lonely and socially anxious people appears to be social compensation, meeting new people, belonging to a group and relaxing. Supporting the previous findings (i.e. Caplan, 2003; 2007), lonely and socially anxious people prefer online communication more since it provides them an opportunity to compensate for their poorer social skillsto meet new people (Bonetti, Campbell, & Gilmore, 2010). In particular, they state that they do not feel as shy, feel more relaxed and venture more in online communication.

Accordingly, direct interaction with others using Facebook is associated with lower levels of loneliness and greater feelings of social capital (Burke, Marlow & Lento, 2010; Lou, Yan, Nickerson, & McMorris, 2012). In contrast, spending time passively in SNS such as viewing friends' content is correlated with higher levels of loneliness and lower feelings of social capital. Nevertheless, there are mixed findings regarding the causality of the relationships in the related literature. Kraut and his colleagues (1998) suggest that initial levels of loneliness may not predict changes in internet use and the direction of causality may be from the use of internet to declines in psychological well-being. Thus, the directionality of the relationship between loneliness and social networking remains unclear.

Research suggests that online communication may be beneficial for those who have high social anxiety. Accordingly, a number of scholars have shown that social anxiety predicts individual's emotional attachment to Facebook and their connections with others using Facebook (Clayton, Osborne, Miller, & Oberle, 2013). It indicates that socially anxious people prefer to use Facebook for social interaction, and integrate the social network site into their daily lives. Based on past findings (Caplan, 2007; Ebeling-Witte, Frank & Lester, 2007; Kim, LaRose & Peng, 2009), it can be argued that individuals with social anxiety and perceived loneliness have deficient social skills, and since they perceive greater control over self-presentation online, they feel more comfortable in online communication than face-to-facecommunication. Accordingly, it is shown that a person's preference for online social interaction (POSI) mediates the relationship between level of loneliness or social anxiety and negative outcomes resulting from internet use (Caplan, 2003; 2007).

In a related vein, for individuals high in attachment anxiety and/or avoidance, Facebook offers advantages over face-to-face interactions. By managing their self-presentation, anxious individuals may feel more confident in maintaining interpersonal relationships. For people who desire closeness but anticipate and fear rejection, being able to carefully manage self-presentation could be a particularly attractive feature of Facebook (Buote, Wood, & Pratt, 2009). The relationships between attachment anxiety and avoidance and Facebook use are examined by researchers (Oldmeadow, Quinn & Kowert, 2013). When adults feel negative emotions and have high attachment anxiety, it is found that they use Facebook more frequently, as they are more worried about how others see them on Facebook. In contrast, high attachment avoidance is related to less Facebook use, less openness and less positive attitudes towards Facebook. When social skills are controlled, the relationships remain the same. Findings make the scholars consider that Facebook may serve attachment functions and provide a basis for understanding how online communication be related to attachment styles (Oldmeadow, Quinn, & Kowert, 2013). Another way in which Facebook may appeal to individuals with attachment issues is by providing a sense of belonging to a social network. SNSa are also found to increase belongingness among adults (Oldmeadow, Quinn, & Kowert, 2013).

In a study by Gentzler, Oberhauser, Westerman and Nadorff (2011), college students are asked to report on their use of electronic communication with a parent whom they stated as their closest family member. Results indicate that students who report more frequent phone conversations with parents also report more satisfying, intimate, and supportive parental relationships, but those students who use a SNS to communicate with parents report higher levels of loneliness, anxious attachment, as well as conflict within the parental relationship. The findings offer new evidence on how electronic communication technology with parents is related to adjustment in college students. To better understand the young adults' use of technology to communicate in today's society, further research with longitudinal designs is needed (Gentzler Oberhauser, Westerman, & Nadorff, 2011).

Social Networking and Cyberbullying

Another dark side of SNS is that, it can have harmful consequences for users such as cyberbullying, stalking, and online harassment. Cyberbullying refers to:

… the transmission by electronic means of demeaning, distressing, threatening and abusive messages and images which target a particular individual or a group of individuals (Kyriacou, 2017).

Messages, images, recordings which can be sent directly or indirectly to the victim and to the cyberbully's peer group, are forms of cyberbullying. It is an electronic or internet bullying in which individuals intentionally harm a victim via electronic means (Bonanno & Hymel, 2013). A range of other terms has been used to describe the phenomenon including: cyberharassment, cybervictimisation, online harassment and electronic bullying (Beran, Rinaldi, Bickham & Rich, 2012; Brown, Demaray& Secord, 2014).

Unlike traditional or face-to-face forms of bullying, anonymity and invisibility of the perpetrators are important characteristics of cyberbullying (Bonanno & Hymel, 2013). According to Dempsey, Sulkowski, Nichols and Storch (2009), cyberbullying may be particularly harmful to victims for several reasons. First, cyberbullying is hard to escape, as it can occur across settings. Second, the aggressors remain anonymous. As the aggressors do not have direct contact with the victim, feeling empathy or remorse is rare among them. Third, in a short time frame due to the use of technology, the aggressor reaches large audiences. Finally, chances of intervention is reduced due to less adult supervision.

Cyberbullying is related to various mental health outcomes. For instance, Bonanno and Hymel (2013) have shown cyber victimization to be related to depression and suicidal ideation in a sample of 8th to 10th grade students. Similarly, Olenik-Shemesh, Heiman and Eden(2012) have found that cyber victimization is related to both loneliness and depressive mood among young adults. These studies indicate that cyberbullying puts young individuals at risk for internalizing problems. Weight-based cyberbullying is also prevalent among youth and adolescents, and may have lasting negative psychological effects on the victims (Anderson, Bresnahan, & Musatics, 2014). Furthermore, cyberbullying may have physical effects on victims such as weight loss or gain, substance abuse, headache, abdominal pain and sleeping problems. In the related literature, there is not a clear understanding considering gender and developmental differences in experiences of cyber victimization. Inconsistent findings related with gender may result from a number of factors, including researchers examining different age groups, in different countries, and at different reference time periods in the assessments (Brown, Demaray, & Secord, 2014).

Social Networking and Addiction

People engage in a variety of activities in SNS, some of which may potentially be addictive. Rather than becoming addicted to a substance, some users may develop an addiction to some specific online activities. There are five different types of internet addiction, namely computer addiction (i.e., computer game addiction), information overload (i.e., web surfing addiction), net compulsions (i.e., online gambling or online shopping addiction), cybersexual addiction (i.e., online pornography or online sex addiction), and cyber-relationship addiction (i.e., an addiction to online relationships)(Kuss & Griffiths, 2011). SNS addiction falls in the last category since the individuals are motivated to use SNSs to establish and maintain online relationships. Even though some scholars (i.e. Griffiths, 2012) argue that they are not synonymous, the term SNS addiction is sometimes used interchangebly with "Facebook addiction".

Research into social networking addiction fall into one of four types:

1. Self-perception studies of social networking addiction,
2. Studies of social networking addiction utilizing a social networking addiction scale,
3. Studies examining the relationship between social networking and other online addictions, and
4. Studies examining social networking addiction and interpersonal relationships (Griffiths, Kuss & Demetrovics, 2014).

Although the concept of social networking addiction is controversial, some people may experience addiction-like symptoms as a result of excessive use.

Besides, social media supported gambling activities has been found to increase recently. The particular concern is with respect to the possible potential of early age gambling involvement, and development of positive attitudes and/or behavioral intentions toward gambling. In their study, King, Delfabbro, Kaptsis and Zwaans (2014) have examined adolescents' involvement in gambling activities on social media, and tried to find out the indicators of pathological gambling risk. Results have shown that a significant proportion of young people engage in a range of gambling activities in social media. Having a history of engagement in gambling activities, adolescents seem to be at greater risk of pathological gambling. Need for regulation and monitoring of gambling activity are highlighted with the findings. There is also a need for further research on the potential risks of early exposure to gambling activities (King, Delfabbro, Kaptsis, & Zwaans, 2014).

Social Networking, Personality, and Gender Differences

As studies are conducted for understanding the benefits and negative consequences of SNS usage, personality types, traits or disorders have also become the center of attention. Rosen and his colleagues (2013) have examined the impact of the use of specific technologies and media on clinical symptoms of mood disorders and personality disorders. Among these disorders, greater facebook use and using it for impression management motivation and larger number of online friends are found to be related with narcissism and histrionic disorder. Furthermore, Weisskirch and Delevi (2011) have introduced the term sexting, sending text messages with sexual content, as one of the diagnostic criterion for histrionic personality disorder.

Carpenter (2012) has investigated the effect of Facebook activity on antisocial personality behaviors and identified certain antisocial behaviors including taking revenge on negative remarks around oneself, carefully reading others' announcements to check whether they are discussing them, and looking for more social bolster than one gives to others. In the increasing use of SNSs, users' personality traits may be important factors leading them to engage in social media. The related literature in particular suggests that BigFive factors such as extraversion, emotional stability and openness to experience are related to SNS use. In a study done by Correa, Hinsley and De Zuniga (2010) when socio-demographics and life satisfaction variables are controlled, extraversion and openness to experiences are positively whereas emotional stability is negatively related to social media use. These findings differ by gender and age. Extraverted men and women are both likely to be more frequent users of social media tools, while only men with greater degrees of emotional instability are more regular users. The relationship between extraversion and social media use is particularly important among young adults. Conversely, openness to new experiences emerges as an important personality factor in relation with social media use for olderadults (Correa, Hinsley, & De Zuniga, 2010).

Another personality trait, conscientiousness, refers to a person's work ethic, orderliness and thoroughness (Costa & McCrae, 1992), and scholars has suggested that conscientious individuals are inclined to avoid SNS as they promote procrastination and serve as a distraction from more important tasks (Butt & Phillips, 2008). In contrast, people who are high in sociability have positive attitudes towards SNS and show willingness to join SNS (Hughes, Rowe, Batey & Lee, 2012). Agreeableness has been included in several studies relating to internet and social media usage, and has generally been found to be unrelated (Correa, Hinsley, & De Zuniga, 2010; Amichai-Hamburger, & Vinitzky, 2010)

Researchers have also investigated gender differences with regard to the frequency of and motivations for SNS use. Despite a study showing more positive attitudes toward and more use of SNSs at workplace among males (Andreassen, Torscheim, & Pallesen, 2014), considerable research has shown greater social networking among females (Barker, 2009; Bonetti, Campbell, & Gilmore, 2010; Simoncic, Kuhlman, Vargas, Houchins, & Lopez-Duran, 2014; Fioravanti, Dettore, & Casale, 2012; Hargittai, 2008). For instance, Barker (2009) reports that teenage girls show higher overall use of SNSs than boys, and mostly use SNSs for relational purposes (i.e. communication with peers). However, teenage boys mostly use SNSs for social compensation and learning purposesas well as for social identity gratifications. It is argued that social networking may provide social support and peer group belongingness that teenage boys especially need in periods of life transition (Barker, 2009).

In accordance with gender role expectations, researchers have shown that men are more likely to use SNSs for networking, making new friends and finding potential dates, whereas women use them for relationship maintenance (Muscanell & Guadagno, 2012). Similarly, Bonetti and his colleagues (2010) reveal that girls are more involved in online communication for relational purposes than boys. Besides, researchers report more risk taking attitudes among men as compared to women in social networking (Fogel & Nehmad, 2008). That is, men display more private information (telephone number, home address, etc.), and women show greater concern for privacy and less identity information disclosure than men in social networking websites.

CONCLUSION

General Practical Implications

This chapter explains the benefits and detrimental consequences of online social networking from a psychological perspective. To do so, it reviews a growing body of research about online social networking and various indicators of psychological well-being. Overall, the findings show mixed evidence of the links between SNS use and mental health outcomes. While some studies have revealed the beneficial impact of SNS use on mental health including enhanced self-esteem, life satisfaction, sense of belongingness, and reduced social anxiety and loneliness, considerable research has shown its detrimental impact including increased depression, addiction, cyberbullying as well as reduced self-esteem and subjective well-being. Besides, higher engagement in social networking is linked to various types of phobias including FOMO and nomophobia.

Even though this chapter focuses on only certain areas of mental health, the findings presented above provide several implications for research and practice on the impact of SNS use. Taken together, existing findings support that online social networking undermines psychological well-being of adolescents and young adults. Given the prevalence of social media use among this population, it is imperative for scholars to take necessary steps to prevent possible negative consequences of social networking. One way to reduce the potential risk of developing addiction especially among lonely and socially anxious teenagers is monitoring and educating them on appropriate use of online communication tools (O'Keeffe, & Clarke-Pearson, 2011; Subrahmanyam & Lin, 2007). Future studies may wish to include preventive efforts for adolescents and young adults. Scholars may also focus in their future research on identifying signs of possible psychopathological behaviors related of abuse of SNSs (Barbera, Paglia & Valsavoia, 2009).

Limitations and Avenues for Future Research

This chapter concentrates on the psychological correlates of the use of different online SNSs which has a *different patterns of use, user characteristics and social functions* (Wilson, Gosling, & Graham, 2012). To illustrate, Facebook is based on creating and updating personal profiles, while Twitter is based on posting and reading short-messages (Pantic, 2014). Given the variability of SNSs, it is important for scholars to question the generalizability of their findings (Kross Verduyn, Demiralp, Park, & Lee, 2013). Since the research field is relatively young, studies investigating social networking unsurprisingly suffer from a number of methodological problems (Kuss & Griffiths, 2011; Pantic, 2014). For instance, most studies comprise small and unrepresentative samples. For future studies, researchers should select larger samples which represent broader populations across cultures and especially in SNS research, scholars should focus on populations at risk for developing SNS addiction. In current literature, studies use several different psychometric scales (Pantic, 2014). By using more reliable and valid measures in future research, it would be more possible to make generalizations (Griffiths, Kuss, & Demetrovics, 2014).

The vast majority of previous research on social networking and mental health outcomes are cross-sectional in nature, which does not allow for causal inferences. Therefore, it remains unclear whether social networking or mental health outcome is the cause or the effect (Pantic, 2014). To illustrate, it is possible that individuals using SNSs show poor psychological well-being or those individuals with poor psychological well-being show more tendency to use SNSs. Given the cross-sectional nature of past research, it is imperative for scholars to continue with longitudinal studies to identify the temporality and causality of these relationships (Pantic, 2014).Besides, there are limited studies that examine the possible mediators or moderators that play role in the relationship between online social networking and mental health (i.e. Kim, 2016; Simoncic, Kuhlman, Vargas, Houchins, & Lopez-Duran, 2014). Future studies would therefore do well to investigate the differential role of certain factors such as family or school atmosphere or social support on various mental health issues.

In summary, this chapter basically is just a starting point for future studies on social networking by reviewing the current literature with respect to the benefits and detrimental effects of online social networking. Taken all together, the findings suggest that the associations among social networking and psychological well-being are complex and warrant in-depth consideration by scholars and practitioners.

REFERENCES

Amichai-Hamburger, Y., & Vinitzky, G. (2010). Social network use and personality. *Computers in Human Behavior*, 26(6), 1289–1295. doi:10.1016/j.chb.2010.03.018

Anderson, J., Bresnahan, M., & Musatics, C. (2014). Combating weight-based cyberbullying on Facebook with the dissenter effect. *Cyberpsychology, Behavior, and Social Networking*, 17(5), 281–286. doi:10.1089/cyber.2013.0370 PMID:24690025

Andreassen, S. C., Torscheim, T., & Pallesen, S. (2014). Predictors of use of social network sites at work: A specific type of cyberloafing. *Journal of Computer-Mediated Communication*, 19(4), 906–921. doi:10.1111/jcc4.12085

Barbera, L. D., Paglia, L. F., & Valsavoia, R. (2009). Social network and addiction. *Studies in Health Technology and Informatics*, 144, 33–36. PMID:19592725

Barker, V. (2009). Older adolescents' motivations for social network site use: The influence of gender, group identity, and collective self-esteem. *Cyberpsychology & Behavior*, 12(2), 209–213. doi:10.1089/cpb.2008.0228 PMID:19250021

Beran, T. N., Rinaldi, C., Bickham, D. S., & Rich, M. (2012). Evidence for the need to support adolescents dealing with harassment and cyber-harassment: Prevalence, progression, and impact. *School Psychology International*, 33(5), 562–576. doi:10.1177/0143034312446976

Bessiere, K., Pressman, S., Kiesler, S., & Kraut, R. (2010). Effects of internet use on health and depression: A longitudinal study. *Journal of Medical Internet Research*, 12(1), e6. doi:10.2196/jmir.1149 PMID:20228047

Best, P., Manktelow, R., & Taylor, B. (2014). Online communication, social media and adolescent wellbeing:A systematic narrative review. *Children and Youth Services Review*, 41, 27–36. doi:10.1016/j.childyouth.2014.03.001

Bevan, J. L., Gomez, R., & Sparks, L. (2014). Disclosures about important life events on Facebook: Relationships with stress and quality of life. *Computers in Human Behavior*, 39, 246–253. 246-253.doi.org/10.1016/j.chb.2014.07.021. doi:10.1016/j.chb.2014.07.021

Bonanno, R. A., & Hymel, S. (2013). Cyber bullying and internalizing difficulties: Above and beyond the impact of traditional forms of bullying. *Journal of Youth and Adolescence, 42*(5), 685–697. doi:10.100710964-013-9937-1 PMID:23512485

Bonetti, L., Campbell, M. A., & Gilmore, L. (2010). The Relationship of loneliness and social anxiety with children's and adolescents' online communication. *Cyberpsychology, Behavior, and Social Networking, 13*(3), 279-285. doi: 10.1089=cyber.2009.0215

Boyd, D. M. &Ellison, N. B. (2007). Social network sites: Definition, history, and scholarship. *Journal of Computer-Mediated Communication, 13*(1), 210-230. doi: 6101.2007.00393.x doi:10.1111/j.1083

Bragazzi, N. L., & Del Puente, G. (2014). A proposal for including nomophobia in the new DSM-V. *Psychology Research and Behavior Management, 7*, 155. doi:10.2147/PRBM.S41386 PMID:24876797

Brown, C. F., Demaray, M. K., & Secord, S. M. (2014). Cyber victimization in middle school and relations to social emotional outcomes. *Computers in Human Behavior, 35*, 12–21. doi:10.1016/j.chb.2014.02.014

Buglass, S. L., Binder, J. F., Betts, L. R., & Underwood, J. D. (2017). Motivators of online vulnerability: The impact of social network site use and FOMO. *Computers in Human Behavior, 66*, 248–255. doi:10.1016/j.chb.2016.09.055

Buote, V. M., Wood, E., & Pratt, M. (2009). Exploring similarities and differences between online and offline friendships: The role of attachment style. *Computers in Human Behavior, 25*(2), 560–567. doi:10.1016/j.chb.2008.12.022

Burke, M., Marlow, C., & Lento, T. (2010). Social network activity and social well-being. *Postgraduate Medical Journal, 85*, 455–459.

Butt, S., & Phillips, J. G. (2008). Personality and self reported mobile phone use. *Computers in Human Behavior, 24*(2), 346–360. doi:10.1016/j.chb.2007.01.019

Caplan, S. E. (2003). Preference for online social interaction: A theory of problematic Internet useand psychosocial well-being. *Communication Research, 30*(6), 625–648. doi:10.1177/0093650203257842

Caplan, S. E. (2007). Relation among loneliness, social anxiety, andproblematic internet use. *Cyberpsychology & Behavior, 10*(2), 234–242. doi:10.1089/cpb.2006.9963 PMID:17474841

Carpenter, C. J. (2012). Narcissism on Facebook: Self-promotional and anti-social behavior. *Personality and Individual Differences, 52*(4), 482–486. doi:10.1016/j.paid.2011.11.011

Cavazos-Rehg, P. A., Krauss, M. J., Sowles, S. J., Connolly, S., Rosas, C., Bharadwaj, M., ... Bierut, L. J. (2016). An analysis of depression, self-harm, and suicidal ideation content on Tumblr. *Crisis, 38*(1), 44–52. doi:10.1027/0227-5910/a000409 PMID:27445014

Chou, H. G., & Edge, N. (2012). "They are happier and having better lives than i am": The impact of using Facebook on perceptions of others' lives. *Cyberpsychology, Behavior, and Social Networking, 15*(2), 117–122. doi:10.1089/cyber.2011.0324 PMID:22165917

Clayton, R. B., Osborne, R. E., Miller, B. K., & Oberle, C. D. (2013). Loneliness, anxiousness, and substance use as predictors of Facebook use. *Computers in Human Behavior*, *29*(3), 687–693. doi:10.1016/j.chb.2012.12.002

Coopersmith, S. (1981). *Self-esteem inventories*. Palo Alto, CA: Consulting Psychologists Press.

Correa, T., Hinsley, A. W., & De Zuniga, H. G. (2010). Who interacts on the Web?: The intersection of users' personality and social media use. *Computers in Human Behavior*, *26*(2), 247–253. doi:10.1016/j.chb.2009.09.003

Costa, P. T., & McCrae, R. R. (1992). *NEO PI-R professional manual*. Odessa, FL: Psychological Assessment Resources.

Davila, J., Hershenberg, R., Feinstein, B. A., Gorman, K., Bhatia, V., & Starr, L. R. (2012). Frequency and quality of social networking among young adults: Associations with depressive symptoms, rumination, and corumination. *Psychology of Popular Media Culture*, *1*(2), 72–86. doi:10.1037/a0027512 PMID:24490122

Dempsey, A. G., Sulkowski, M. L., Nichols, R., & Storch, E. A. (2009). Differences between peer victimization in cyber and physical settings and associated psychosocial adjustment in early adolescence. *Psychology in the Schools*, *46*(10), 962–972. doi:10.1002/pits.20437

Drouin, M., Kaiser, D. H., & Miller, D. A. (2012). Phantom vibrations among undergraduates: Prevalence and associated psychological characteristics. *Computers in Human Behavior*, *28*(4), 1490–1496. doi:10.1016/j.chb.2012.03.013

Duval, S., & Wicklund, R. A. (1972). *A theory of objective self awareness*. Oxford, UK: Academic Press.

Ebeling-Witte, S., Frank, M. L., & Lester, D. (2007). Shyness, internet use, andpersonality. *Cyberpsychology & Behavior*, *10*(5), 713–716. doi:10.1089/cpb.2007.9964 PMID:17927542

Elkind, D., & Bowen, R. (1979). Imaginary audience behavior in children and adolescents. *Developmental Psychology*, *15*(1), 38–44. doi:10.1037/0012-1649.15.1.38

Ellison, N. B., Steinfield, C., & Lampe, C. (2007). The benefits of Facebook "friends": Social capital and college students' use of online social network sites. *Journal of Computer-Mediated Communication*, *12*(4), 1143–1168. doi:10.1111/j.1083-6101.2007.00367.x

Fioravanti, G., Dettore, D., & Casale, S. (2012). Adolescent internet addiction: Testing the association between self-esteem, the perception of internet attributes, and preference for online social interactions. *Cyberpsychology, Behavior, and Social Networking*, *15*(6), 318–323. doi:10.1089/cyber.2011.0358 PMID:22703038

Fogel, J., & Nehmad, E. (2009). Internet social network communities: Risk taking, trust, and privacy concerns. *Computers in Human Behavior*, *25*(1), 153–160. doi:10.1016/j.chb.2008.08.006

Fox, J., & Moreland, J. J. (2015). The dark side of social networking sites: An exploration of the relational and psychological stressors associated with Facebook use and affordances. *Computers in Human Behavior*, *45*, 168–176. doi:10.1016/j.chb.2014.11.083

Gentzler, A. L., Oberhauser, A. M., Westerman, D., & Nadorff, D. K. (2011). College students' use of electronic communication with parents: Links to loneliness, attachment, and relationship quality. *Cyberpsychology, Behavior, and Social Networking, 14*(1-2), 71–74. doi:10.1089/cyber.2009.0409 PMID:20973676

Gonzales, A. L., & Hancock, J. T. (2011). Mirror, mirror on my Facebook wall: Effects of exposure to Facebook on self-esteem. *Cyberpsychology, Behavior, and Social Networking, 14*(1-2), 79–83. doi:10.1089/cyber.2009.0411 PMID:21329447

Griffiths, M. D. (2012). Facebook addiction: Concerns, criticisms and recommendations. *Psychological Reports, 110*(2), 518–520. doi:10.2466/01.07.18.PR0.110.2.518-520 PMID:22662405

Griffiths, M. D., Kuss, D. J., & Demetrovics, Z. (2014). Social networking addiction: An overview of preliminary findings. *Behavioral addictions: Criteria, evidence and treatment*, 119-141. doi:10.1016/B978-0-12-407724-9.00006-9

Hargittai, E. (2008). Whose space? Differences among users and non-users of social netwrok sites. *Journal of Computer-Mediated Communication, 13*(1), 276–297. doi:10.1111/j.1083-6101.2007.00396.x

Hughes, D. J., Rowe, M., Batey, M., & Lee, A. (2012). A tale of two sites: Twitter vs. Facebook and the personality predictors of social media usage. *Computers in Human Behavior, 28*(2), 561–569. doi:10.1016/j.chb.2011.11.001

Jelenchick, L. A., Eickhoff, J. C., & Moreno, M. A. (2013). Facebook depression?"Social networking site use and depression in older adolescents. *The Journal of Adolescent Health, 52*(1), 128–130. doi:10.1016/j.jadohealth.2012.05.008 PMID:23260846

Joinson, A. N. (2004). Self-esteem, interpersonal risk, and preference for e-mail to face-to-face communication. *Cyberpsychology & Behavior, 7*(4), 472–478. doi:10.1089/cpb.2004.7.472 PMID:15331035

Kim, H. H. (2016). The impact of online social networking on adolescent psychological well-being (WB): A population-level analysis of Korean school aged-children. *International Journal of Adolescence and Youth*, 1–13. doi:10.1080/02673843.2016.1197135

Kim, J., LaRose, R., & Peng, W. (2009). Loneliness as the cause and the effect of problematic internet use: The relationship between internet use and psychological well-being. *CyberPsychology & Behavior, 12*(4), 451-455. doi: 10.1089=cpb.2008.0327

King, D. L., Delfabbro, P. H., Kaptsis, D., & Zwaans, T. (2014). Adolescent simulated gambling via digital and social media: An emerging problem. *Computers in Human Behavior, 31*, 305–313. doi:10.1016/j.chb.2013.10.048

Krämer, N. C., & Winter, S. (2008). Impression management 2.0: The relationship of self-esteem, extroversion, self-efficacy, and self-presentation within social networking sites. *Journal of Media Psychology, 20*(3), 106–116. doi:10.1027/1864-1105.20.3.106

Kraut, R., Patterson, M., Lundmark, V., Kiesler, S., Mukopadhyay, T., & Scherlis, W. (1998). Internet Paradox: A social technology that reduces social involvement and psychological well-being? *The American Psychologist, 53*(9), 1017–1031. doi:10.1037/0003-066X.53.9.1017 PMID:9841579

Kross, E., Verduyn, P., Demiralp, E., Park, J., Lee, S. D., Lin, N., ... Ybarra, O. (2013). Facebook use predicts declines in subjective well-being in young adults. *PLoS One, 8*(8), e69841. doi:10.1371/journal. pone.0069841 PMID:23967061

Kuss, D. J., & Griffiths, M. D. (2011). Online social networking and addiction: A review of the psychological literature. *International Journal of Environmental Research and Public Health, 8*(12), 3528–3552. doi:10.3390/ijerph8093528 PMID:22016701

Kuss, D. J., & Griffiths, M. D. (2017). Social networking sites and addiction: Ten lessons learned. *International Journal of Environmental Research and Public Health, 14*(3), 311. doi:10.3390/ijerph14030311 PMID:28304359

Kyriacou, C. (2017). Dealing with cyberbullying by pupils. In All Party Parliamentary Group on Bullying (Ed.), *Evidence presented at meetings of the All Party Parliamentary Group on Bullying 2011-2016* (pp. 21-22). London: All Party Parliamentary Group on Bullying.

Lou, L. L., Yan, Z., Nickerson, A., & McMorris, R. (2012). An examination of the reciprocal relationship of loneliness and Facebook use among first-year college students. *Journal of Educational Computing Research, 46*(1), 105–117. doi:10.2190/EC.46.1.e

Lucas, M., Mekary, R., Pan, A., Mirzaei, F., O'Reilly, É. J., Willett, W. C., ... Ascherio, A. (2011). Relation between clinical depression risk and physical activity and time spent watching television in older women: A 10-year prospective follow-up study. *American Journal of Epidemiology, 174*(9), 1017–1027. doi:10.1093/aje/kwr218 PMID:21984659

Mehdizadeh, S. (2010). Self-presentation 2.0: Narcissism and self-esteem on Facebook. *CyberPsychology, Behavior, and Social Networking, 13*(4), 357-364. doi: 10.1089=cyber.2009.0257

Muscanell, N. L., & Guadagno, R. E. (2012). Make new friends or keep the old: Gender and personality differences in social networking use. *Computers in Human Behavior, 28*(1), 107–112. doi:10.1016/j. chb.2011.08.016

O'Keeffe, G. S., & Clarke-Pearson, K. (2011). The impact of social media on children, adolescents, and families. *Pediatrics, 127*(4), 800–804. doi:10.1542/peds.2011-0054 PMID:21444588

Oberst, U., Wegmann, E., Stodt, B., Brand, M., & Chamarro, A. (2017). Negative consequences from heavy social networking in adolescents: The mediating role of fear of missing out. *Journal of Adolescence, 55*, 51–60. doi:10.1016/j.adolescence.2016.12.008 PMID:28033503

Oldmeadow, J. A., Quinn, S., & Kowert, R. (2013). Attachment style, social skills, and Facebook use amongst adults. *Computers in Human Behavior, 29*(3), 1142–1149. doi:10.1016/j.chb.2012.10.006

Olenik-Shemesh, D., Heiman, T., & Eden, S. (2012). Cyberbullying victimisation in adolescence: Relationships with loneliness and depressive mood. *Emotional & Behavioural Difficulties, 17*(3-4), 361–374. doi:10.1080/13632752.2012.704227

Pantic, I. (2014). Online social networking and mental health. *Cyberpsychology, Behavior, and Social Networking, 17*(10), 652–657. doi:10.1089/cyber.2014.0070 PMID:25192305

Pantic, I., Damjanovic, A., Todorovic, J., Topalovic, D., Bojovic-Jovic, D., Ristic, S., & Pantic, S. (2012). Association between online social networking and depression in high-school students: Behavioral physiology viewpoint. *Psychiatria Danubina, 24*, 90–93. PMID:22447092

Park, S., Lee, S. W., Kwak, J., Cha, M., & Jeong, B. (2013). Activities on Facebook reveal the depressive state of users. *Journal of Medical Internet Research, 15*(10), 1–15. doi:10.2196/jmir.2718 PMID:24084314

Pavot, W., & Diener, E. (2004). The subjective evaluation of well-being in adulthood: Findings and implications. *Ageing International, 29*(2), 113–135. doi:10.100712126-004-1013-4

Przybylski, A. K., Murayama, K., DeHaan, C. R., & Gladwell, V. (2013). Motivational, emotional, and behavioral correlates of fear of missing out. *Computers in Human Behavior, 29*(4), 1841–1848. doi:10.1016/j.chb.2013.02.014

Rosen, L. D., Whaling, K., Rab, S., Carrier, L. M., & Cheever, N. A. (2013). Is Facebook creating "iDisorders"? The link between clinical symptoms of psychiatric disorders and technology use, attitudes and anxiety. *Computers in Human Behavior, 29*(3), 1243–1254. doi:10.1016/j.chb.2012.11.012

Salmela-Aro, K., Upadyaya, K., Hakkarainen, K., Lonka, K., & Alho, K. (2017). The dark side of Internet use: Two longitudinal studies of excessive Internet use, depressive symptoms, school burnout and engagement among Finnish early and late adolescents. *Journal of Youth and Adolescence, 46*(2), 343–357. doi:10.100710964-016-0494-2 PMID:27138172

Sampasa-Kanyinga, H., & Lewis, R. F. (2015). Frequent use of social network sites is associated with poor psychological functioning among children and adolescents. *Cyberpsychology, Behavior, and Social Networking, 18*(7), 380–385. doi:10.1089/cyber.2015.0055 PMID:26167836

Simoncic, T. E., Kuhlman, K. R., Vargas, I., Houchins, S., & Lopez-Duran, N. L. (2014). Facebook use and depressive symptomatology: Investigating the role of neuroticism and extraversion in youth. *Computers in Human Behavior, 40*, 1–5. doi:10.1016/j.chb.2014.07.039 PMID:25861155

Statista. Average Numbers of Hours Per Day Spent by Social Media Users on all Social Media Channels as of 4th Quarter 2015, by Country. (n.d.). Available online: https://www.statista.com/statistics/270229/usage-duration-of-social-networks-by-country/

Statista Facts on Social Networks. (n.d.). Available online: https://www.statista.com/topics/1164/social-networks/

Subrahmanyam, K., & Lin, G. (2007). Adolescents on the net: Internet use and well-being. *Adolescence, 42*(168), 659–677. PMID:18229503

Valenzuela, S., Park, N., & Kee, K. F. (2009). Is there social capital in a social network site? Facebook use and college students' life satisfaction, trust and participation. *Journal of Computer-Mediated Communication, 14*(4), 875–901. doi:10.1111/j.1083-6101.2009.01474.x

Valkenburg, P. M., Peter, J., & Schouten, A. P. (2006). Friend networking sites and their relationship to adolescents' well-being and social self-esteem. *Cyberpsychology & Behavior, 9*(5), 584–590. doi:10.1089/cpb.2006.9.584 PMID:17034326

Walther, J. B. (1996). Computer-mediated communication: Impersonal, interpersonal, and hyperpersonal interaction. *Communication Research, 23*(1), 3–43. doi:10.1177/009365096023001001

Weisskirch, R. S., & Delevi, R. (2011). 'Sexting' and adult romantic attachment. *Computers in Human Behavior, 27*(5), 1697–1701. doi:10.1016/j.chb.2011.02.008

Wilson, K., Fornasier, S., & White, K. M. (2010). Psychological predictors of young adults' use of social networking sites. *CyberPsychology, Behavior, and Social Networking, 13*(2), 173-177. doi: 10.1089=cyber.2009.0094

Wilson, R. E., Gosling, S. D., & Graham, L. T. (2012). A review of Facebook research in the social sciences. *Perspectives on Psychological Science, 7*(3), 203–220. doi:10.1177/1745691612442904 PMID:26168459

KEY TERMS AND DEFINITIONS

Addiction: A chronic disorder with biological, psychological, social, and environmental factors influencing its development and maintenance.

Attachment: Emotional bond or connectedness between two people, especially child and the caregiver.

Cyberbullying: A kind of harassment that occurs on the internet or either by cell phones or other devices.

Depression: A mood disorder marked by emotional, mental, and physical symptoms such as feelings of sadness, hopelessness, or pessimism, lowered self-esteem, reduced energy and vitality, slowness of thought.

Loneliness: An unpleasant emotional response to isolation.

Personality: Individual differences in characteristic patterns of thinking, feeling, and behaving.

Self-Esteem: A person's overall sense of self-worth or personal value.

Social Anxiety: Nervousness in social situations.

Social Networking Site: An online platform that allows users to create a public profile and interact with other users on the website.

Subjective Well-Being: A term used for people's own judgements over the quality of their lives and includes both emotional and cognitive aspects.

This research was previously published in Intimacy and Developing Personal Relationships in the Virtual World; pages 21-39, copyright year 2019 by Information Science Reference (an imprint of IGI Global).

Chapter 5

Reappraising Social Media:
The Rise of the Global Digital Family

Friedrich H. Kohle

NHTV Breda University of Applied Sciences, The Netherlands

ABSTRACT

This chapter reappraises social media. The corporate perspective promises a growth market based on user data exploitation. On the other hand, users expect emotional contagion and authenticity from their social media experience. They want to connect to friends and family. As a consequence, users accept corporate exploitation of their data. Users see social media as a human right. To users, the technology is key to global knowledge dissemination, with the potential to challenge traditional power structures resisting change. Building on Obar and Wildman, the chapter concludes with an improved definition of social media suggesting that user data tagged to user accounts, user generated content (UGC), and user behavior in the multi-device universe is the lifeblood of social media. Research suggests that social media has propelled mankind beyond McLuhan's global village into the global digital family.

INTRODUCTION

Without a doubt, social media has penetrated our daily lives deeply, influencing the way people connect to friends and family. Research shows that user data tagged to user accounts, UGC and user behaviour is the life blood of social media, making it possible for SNS-owners to generate profits and for users to connect to social media at home, at work and while travelling.

User data makes it possible for Elisabeth Beck-Gernsheim' 'post-familial-family' (Beck-Gernsheim, 1998, p. 68), which is no longer limited by class and ethnic origin, to be extended into the virtual domain, giving rise to the metaphorical Global Digital Family beyond McLuhan's 'Global Village' (McLuhan, 1962, p. 31).

Early during the evolution of the Internet critics argued that "social systems do not work with machine-like precision; human beings have the capacity to interpret and respond to ambiguity" (Daft & Lengel, 1986, p. 569). Back then, the emerging Internet was considered a medium low in richness unlike face-to-face communication. Yet, by 2015, Dunaetz et al find that:

DOI: 10.4018/978-1-6684-6307-9.ch005

Building relationships through lean media has become common and many people find it more effective than face-to-face communication for developing relationships. (Dunaetz, Lisk, & Shin, 2015, p. 3)

Considering definitions proposed by Professor Nicole Ellison, Professor Andreas Kaplan and Assistant Professor Jonathan Obar even communication software Skype can be considered social media, just as crowdfunding platforms Indiegogo and Kickstarter would qualify. All of those feature Web 2.0 technology, user accounts, UGC can be disseminated, and interaction is possible on blogs and threads.

According to scholar Jose van Dijk Wikipedia too can be considered social media (Dijk, 2013a), yet is this perception shared by users? This research highlights the important role of emotional contagion for social media. Kramer et al (2014) investigated emotional contagion in social networks, reaffirming the importance of emotional contagion. Emotional contagion is crucial, just as the extension of a credible and authentic personality. Kaplan understands the need for authenticity and advises marketing experts to be "unprofessional" (Kaplan & Haenlein, 2010, p. 61). But pretending to be unprofessional merely creates the illusion of a real personality with all its faults and weaknesses: it is more likely to be perceived as fake.

What makes the online experience authentic is explored in more detail by Robert Kozinet (Kozinets, 2015), quoting Toennie's idea of Gesellschafts- versus a Gemeinschafts type interaction (Tönnies, 1887). This model explains why for example crowdfunding can be considered a Gesellschafts-type transaction, whereas social media, as understood by users, is a Gemeinschafts-type transaction, shedding light on why users do not perceive crowdfunding sites themselves as social media.

Social media is not just a technology platform that makes it possible for users to connect and companies to exploit user data. Social media is a platform facilitating emotional contagion and the extension of a credible and authentic personality into the virtual social media world, which helps to explain the social media explosion during the last decade. Today, algorithms interpret user data and social media has become ubiquitous, for example:

- By the end of 2016 Facebook exceeded 1.75 billion members (Statista, 2017): a quarter of the world's population has joined Facebook to interact with other humans;
- 310 million users are active on Twitter (Statista, 2017a) and Tweets by President Donald Trump "stoke anxiety" and "move markets" according to the Washington Post (Rucker & Paquette, 2017), evidence how emotionally engaging social media is;
- 467 million people are subscribed to LinkedIn (Statista, 2017b) using the platform to promote their work and career profile;
- Mobile devices have reached 6.9 billion subscriptions worldwide and Ericson predicts that 9.5 billion users will have a mobile device by 2020 with access to social media networking sites (Ericson Mobility Report, 2014). In other words: by 2020 there will be more mobile devices online than there are humans currently living on Earth (Geohive, 2015);
- Google's Loon project aims to provide Internet access anywhere in the world via balloons positioned in the earth's stratosphere (Google, 2013);
- YouTube was acquired by Google in 2006 (Monica, 2006), and streamed its first video on April 23, 2005 (Karim, 2005) featuring over one billion users worldwide in 2015 (Youtube, 2017e).

Social media and networking monoliths Facebook, Twitter, WhatsApp and LinkedIn offer the opportunity to tap into or create communities to and connect to like-minded people, not only changing the way people learn and work (Cuevas & Author, 2012), but also how people choose elective family relationships.

In doing so users establish new transnational boundaries with the potential to discuss issues of global concern. From the environment to human rights issues, social media offers the potential to challenge traditional structures establishing new norms in the form of a global collective consciousness[1].

BACKGROUND

In 2007 Professor Nicole Ellison of the University of Michigan determined social network criteria in the Journal of Computer Mediated Communication as follows:

We define social network sites as web-based services that allow individuals to (1) construct a public or semi-public profile within a bounded system, (2) articulate a list of other users with whom they share a connection, and (3) view and traverse their list of connections and those made by others within the system. The nature and nomenclature of these connections may vary from site to site. (Ellison, 2007, p. 211)

Ellison continues to provide an overview of the history of social media beginning with sites such as sixdegrees.com, she also addresses crucial matters regarding privacy, but the actual user experience on social media is not discussed in detail. Three years later marketing experts Professors Kaplan and Haenlein of the ESCP-business school realise that:

Firms can make profitable use of applications such as Wikipedia, Youtube, Facebook, Second Life and Twitter. Yet despite this interest, there seems to be very limited understanding of what the term 'Social Media' exactly means. (Kaplan & Haenlein, 2010, p. 59)

As a result, Kaplan and Haenlein emerge from their research proposing the following definition of social media:

Social Media is a group of Internet-based applications that build on the ideological and technological foundations of Web 2.0, and that allow the creation and exchange of User Generated Content. (Kaplan & Haenlein, 2010, p. 61)

Their article, published in the journal Business Horizons, advises companies wishing to use social media, to "be active", "be interesting", "be humble", "be unprofessional[2]" and "to be honest" (2010, pp. 66-67). Kaplan and Haenlein's marketing approach is based on reviewed literature and observation of professional practices but we learn little how users experience the same. The definition also does not make any provisions for a time when Web 2.0 technologies will have evolved into the next generation.

More recently Assistant Professor Obar of York University and Professor Wildman at Michigan State University offered another social media definition, this time in the introduction article for the Journal of Telecommunications Policy:

1) Social media services are (currently) Web 2.0 Internet based applications, 2) User generated content is the lifeblood of social media, 3) Individuals and groups create user-specific profiles for a site or app designed and maintained by a social media service, 4) Social media services facilitate the development of social networks online by connecting a profile with those of other individuals and/or groups. (Obar & Wildman, 2015, p. 2)

Obar and Wildman acknowledge the evolving nature of web technologies, recognise Haenlein and Kaplan's work by further highlighting the importance of User Generated Content (UGC) and discuss the criteria for user profiles.

All definitions are based on an exploration of the phenomenon from an observational perspective: users are identified, studied and observed, literature is reviewed, theories are discussed but the qualities of social media from the perspective of the user and how the user experience differs from the corporate perspective are not examined. For that reason, this research examines the corporate perspective and the user position on social media.

METHODOLOGY

To understand the different perceptions of social media, I begin by reviewing contemporary definitions. This is followed by contrasting industry data from sources such as Nielsen (2014), Ooyala (2015)[3], the UK Office for National Statistics (2015), the US Census Bureau (1999), with the user perspective sourced from Pew Research (2015), the Internet Society (ISOC) and surveys[4] as well as focus groups[5] conducted by the author, revealing stark differences not reflected in social media definitions to date.

Participants were able to answer multiple-choice questions which provided a qualitative response to their social media experience. Results gave an indication on research direction. Considering the small sample size of the survey, focus groups provided an opportunity to explore the research topic in more detail. Mcnaghten and Myers make a strong argument for focus groups. Researchers are able to explore a proposed topic's "ambivalences instead of concealing them under yes and no answers" (Macnaghten & Myers, 2015, p. 66). Each group was divided into sub-groups of four to five participants. Each sub-group was then asked to debate the topic and deliver a summary via a Google form.

After completion, results of the debate were retrieved from Google Drive and displayed to the entire group using a projector. Each sub-group was given the opportunity to discuss their findings in more detail in class and, if necessary amend their summary. Planning for digital immigrants followed the same pattern. Findings were analysed by coding and identifying common themes. This made it possible to reveal qualitative aspects of social media like: "a platform to connect you with the rest of the world" (F. Kohle, 2015).

Rosaline Barbour's ideas regarding social media as a research tool itself also proved useful. Instead of following the typical transcription method, data was gathered using Web 2.0 technologies, i.e. Google Forms, which is considered a "new approach" by Barbour (2013, p. 324). Barbour goes on to describe how computerised data analysis "offers the possibility of counting word frequency" (p.324). Data was collected in this way over period of two years.

For the purpose of this study, I considered the advantages of action and cooperative research. Reason and Torbert allow participants to be "co-researchers" in order to make "sense of their experience" (Reason & Torbert, 2001, p. 22) together. Allowing focus group participants to discuss their experience and formulate their own definition elevates them to co-discoverers, rather than being observed and studied focus group participants. It is a form of inquiry embracing "multiple ways of understanding" as Donna Ladkin proposes (2004, p. 480).

LIMITATIONS

The majority of survey participants are residents of the Netherlands, though residents in other countries also participated. Nevertheless, the survey can be considered indicative and appropriate regarding gender and age representation.

USER DATA MANAGEMENT AND EXPLOITATION

The Life Blood of Social Media

Obar & Wildman (Obar & Wildman, 2015, p. 2) consider User Generated Content (UGC) as the life blood of social media. In this article I am going to demonstrate that user data and not UGC is the life blood that makes social media possible. For example, capturing data from stakeholders and audiences makes it possible to:

- Identify strong network partners in the real- and virtual world;
- Build communities;
- Assess the projects viability based on social media activity.

To begin capturing data a database is needed. Without a database, valuable user data is not captured but lost. A good way to begin this activity is to set up a database capable of storing data extracted from the real- and the virtual world.

Customer Relationship Management (CRM) software solutions make it possible to stay on top of that task. The CRM database captures all the details of all the projects stakeholders. This includes but is not limited to, all the players in the value chain. CRM software allows users and companies to:

- Capture stakeholder details on- and offline. This includes contact details, a history of contact points with the stakeholder, a record of promotional materials sent out, even personal preferences that can be relevant to a project;
- Automate communication and marketing activities for a project. A CRM consolidates data and allows makes it possible to target all stakeholders, a specific group or an individual based on preference and background. Automation saves time and still address stakeholders personally. This is important: no one wants to be addressed as just another 'Dear Stakeholder'. CRM tools target stakeholders individually;
- CRM systems ensure that all team-members dealing with external stakeholders are up to date. A complete stakeholder history helps avoids confusion. CRM database makes internal and external communication transparent to the campaign management team;
- Geolocation features are important. Geotagging stakeholders gives an overview of where they are. This helps in a number of ways. Is the company looking for partners in a particular region?

Is the outreach team targeting an area that is underrepresented? Is the team providing an online-overview to the stakeholders of all community screenings to date and where they take place?

There are a number of CRM tools, some of them free, others will charge a fee. Consider the following when planning to set up a CRM database:

- Does the company actually own the data? Some CRM software providers entice users to sign up for their services for free, but migrating to another CRM-system later is impossible if captured data cannot be exported.
- Does the CRM system allow integration with other data management tools? For example, can the CRM access and retrieve data from Mailchimp?
- Is the CRM system cloud-based? If so then the risk of a data breach is higher. Take appropriate steps to keep all data safe. Nothing is more damaging to the stakeholder relationship than their personal data and preferences being leaked into the public domain.
- Let stakeholders know that their data is stored in a database and get their consent.
- Make the way user data is exploited transparent. Stakeholders want to know what happens to their data. Clear Terms of Services (ToS) are a legal requirement in Europe.

Data entry is tedious. It is not an exciting task – but essential to a social media strategy. It needs to be accurate and comprehensive. This can make the difference between finding the needed funds or falling short of that goal.

User Data Application in Practice

Social media from an SNS owner perspective requires access to sensitive user data for appropriation and exploitation. This data can be obtained in a number of ways and users become the target for automated Web 3.0 technology, or the semantic web[6].

At IBC 2017, Web 3.0 technologies revealed new ways of engaging audiences (Kohle F. H., 2017). I reported for Moving Docs on the 2017 IBC panel on audiences as follows:

Owen Geddes of Devicescape (2018)[7] was excited about the potential to track audiences, made possible by software embedded in mobile phones. (He) revealed to the audience that we now know cinemagoers drinking in a pub after the film are 64% more likely to have seen an action movie, for instance. To Ben Johnson of Gruvi (2018)[8], user data is key to understanding audiences. He discussed how capturing user data can identify a digitally-active family on the move simply by cross-referencing the screening times of a movie against location of devices. The family is tracked shopping for food and clothes in town after a screening – with kids getting to buy their fashion items and games as a reward for good behaviour. This way, audiences can be specifically targeted in certain locations and certain times, and this knowledge provides valuable Intel on potential social media partners exhibitors may want to partner with. Geddes claims that making use of this information results in staggering click-through rates (CTR) of 14-20% instead of the more typical CTR rate of 0.1% for media rich ads (Chaffey, 2018). It is not surprising that proposed data protection laws by the EU General Data Protection Regulation (2018) are seen as a threat to user data exploitation. Making money this way is a threat to privacy.

Producers can have apps developed and distributed to their communities that not only track personal user details. The app will also track geographic movement of the consumer. This makes it possible to draw conclusions on the behaviour of the mobile audience, which can be exploited to form new strategic partnerships as Owen Geddes explained. This raises ethical issues. Who owns the data? What is the documentary producer allowed to do with this data?

The user needs to give permission to make these kinds of connections. Having clear Terms of Services (ToS) delineating how user data will be exploited by the company are crucial. The EU General Data Protection Regulation came into effect on May 25, 2018 and seeks to protect user data exploitation:

The conditions for consent have been strengthened, and companies will no longer be able to use long illegible terms and conditions full of legalese, as the request for consent must be given in an intelligible and easily accessible form, with the purpose for data processing to that consent. Consent must be clear and distinguishable from other matters and provided in an intelligible and easily accessible form, using clear and plain language. It must be as easy to withdraw consent as it is to give it. (The EU General Data Protection Regulation, 2018)[9]

Consent must include giving the user the possibility to opt-out of any user-data sharing in an *easy fashion*. Opt-out options should not be hidden in the small print of your email blast. Critics might argue that this way too many users are tempted to unsubscribe. I argue that exciting online content makes it less likely for users to opt-out. If a site needs to make opting-out difficult to retain users, then the company needs to look at the quality of the offered content instead.

The regulation also makes it a legal requirement for companies to delete user data upon request. The right to be forgotten, privacy for the individual and family outweigh commercial concerns. Clear ToS matter if the company wants to establish a relationship with stakeholders that is based on mutual trust.

Maintaining User Data Value Through Open and Transparent Dialogue

Protecting and maintaining user data integrity is the key priority to establishing and maintaining user trust[10]. To the user, online sociality outweighs user data exploitation. To commerce, exploitation of user data is key to building communities and creating new value.

The Center for Social Media and Impact (CMSI) offers insight into how social media technology offers new ways of obtaining user data during the development and design stage (Clark & Abrash, 2011):

- Design the project collaborating with users via surveys, interviews and observations on social media;
- Strategically connect to stakeholders, researchers and developers to "build the production team";
- Road test story boards, short videos and campaigns with users;
- Continuously evaluate audience and stakeholder feedback.

This shows how real- and virtual world activities support each other. Intelligence gathered in each world creates value that can be captured. Based on the analysis of user data, expected outputs during development and pre-production are likely to include:

- Beta/soft/hard launch of the project's website;

- Identification of strong network partnerships;
- Maintenance of ongoing network partnerships;
- Set-up of social media sites strategically built around the project's identity, stakeholders and audiences;
- Publication of SNS and website content: articles, blogs, video clips;
- Ensure effective partnerships are established to strategically position the project in the real and virtual world.

CMSI recognises the importance of social media evaluation based on user data and social media metrics. This includes websites and SNS record visits per week, number of unique visitors and visits from new versus returning visitors. Penetration provides the context of the audience reached[11].

Engagement is a key indicator highlighting how often and how intense visitors' interaction with project websites and SNS is[12]. Website and SNS metrics are part of the user data a documentary production is expected to manage. Surveys provide an excellent source of pre- and post-event qualitative data influencing:

- The design of a transmedia narrative;
- Supervision of a social media production team gathering audio-visual content throughout the entire production;
- Timing the release of any social media content to maximize impact.

Apart from gathering data via site metrics and surveys, evaluation of the project's or companies network performance within its eco-system is crucial.

THE CORPORATE PERSPECTIVE ON SOCIAL MEDIA

This section illustrates the importance to user data exploitation to industry and how and on which social media platforms users are participating in. Drawing from a number of sources such as Nielsen (2014), Ooyala (2015) the Pew Research Centre (2015), the UK Office for National Statistics (2015) and the US Census Bureau (1999) this section illustrates the image of social media and users from a business viewpoint[13]. Drawing from all these sources an overview is established on how users access social media and which platform and SNS they use.

In a 2014 report, Nielsen describes the digital consumer as follows:

Today's consumer is more connected than ever, with more access to and deeper engagement with content and brands, thanks to the proliferation of digital devices and platforms. (Nielsen, 2014, p. 2)

Studying consumer behaviour, the perspective taken by Nielsen is one suitable for companies and organizations with an interest in selling and marketing their products on the Internet. Accordingly, Nielsen claims that the growing number of mobile device owners revolutionizes the shopping experience of the digital consumer. Furthermore, Nielsen states that the ability to deliver content via multiple devices and across platforms is the driving force for the on-going media revolution. (Nielsen, 2014).

Who Is Online?

Pew research reveals relevant demographic consumer details in the US (Duggan, Ellison, Lampe, Lenhart, & Madden, 2015). Though the US differs regarding the demographic composition in Europe, Pew offers relevant insight how people connect via social media:

- Facebook:
- 71% of adult internet users or 58% of the entire US population uses Facebook;
- 93% say they are FB-friends with family other than parents and children;
- 91% are FB friends with current real-world friends;
- 87% state that they are connected to friends from the past;
- 58% say they are FB friends with colleagues;
- 39% are friends with people they have never met;
- 36% are FB friends with their neighbours.
- Twitter:
- 23% of all online users are on Twitter;
- Twitter is more popular with those under 50 years old.
- Instagram:
- 26% of online adults are on Instagram;
- 53% of adults aged 18-29 use Instagram;
- Women are more likely to use Instagram.
- LinkedIn:
- 28% of online adults have a LinkedIn account;
- LinkedIn is popular among college graduates, higher income households and users currently employed;
- College graduates continue to dominate LinkedIn: LinkedIn is the only SNS dominated by users aged 30-64.
- Pinterest (owned by Google):
- 28% of online adults use Pinterest;
- 42% of online women use Pinterest;
- Only 13% of online (who) use Pinterest.

According to Pew more people in 2014 used more than one SNS compared to 2013. For example:

- 24% of all online adults made use of two sites in 2014, an increase of 1% from 2013;
- 16% used three SNS, an increase of 4% from 2013 and 8% used four sites, 3% more than 2013;
- 52% of all online adults use two or more social media sites.

Pew research sheds light on who is online and on which platform, while Nielson provides more detail on the consumer.

The Multi-Device and Mobile Consumer

Data provided by Nielsen reveals that users increasingly access social media while on the move:

- A second screen is already a norm in 2013;
- Multiple devices ensure that 64% of social media users access SNS at least once a day from their computer; and
- 47% via their smart phone.

All population segments see mobile devices as the most important gadget to be upgraded: mobility is a key factor to the digital consumer. In addition to accessing video content and social media via multiple and mobile devices, digital consumers access the Internet while watching TV:

- 60% surf the web on a tablet, 49% on a smartphone;
- 41% look up info on actors and plotlines on a tablet, 29% on a smart phone;
- 23% interact with friends about the TV programme on a tablet, 29% on a smart phone;
- 18% discuss the programme on SNS on a tablet, 12% on a smart phone;
- 17% watch a programme because they read about it on social media on their tablet, 10% because they read about it on their smart phone;
- 64% of all users claim that they visit a SNS at least once a day and again mobility plays a significant role;
- 39% of all adults and 56% of adults aged between 25-34 in the US access social media at work;
- 21% of all adults and 40% of adults aged 25-34 log into social media in the bathroom - an indication that digital natives and 1st degree digital immigrants continue the trend for more connectivity anywhere and anytime.

The multi-device consumer has become the target for advertising via SNS: the next section highlights the most popular SNS according to Nielsen.

Popular SNS From a Corporate Perspective

An overview of the most popular SNS per device, as researched by Nielsen, reveals that more users access SNS on a desktop computer, though smartphones are fast catching up and users already spend more time viewing Facebook and Instagram on a Smartphone when compared to a desktop computer. Mobile apps provided the largest growth for SNS and social media access via smartphone browsers saw significant growth reaffirming the rise of the mobile user. The Pew Research Centre corroborates these findings. According to their 2015 Social Media Update (Duggan, Ellison, Lampe, Lenhart, & Madden, 2015), Facebook remains the most popular site, though other SNS have seen higher growth rates. The above data reveals that mobile devices have become the most important access point for digital consumers in the US for social media sites.

The Mobile Consumer

But is this all we need to know? A question to consider is when these sites are being accessed. Exactly when are users accessing social media? And from where? Streaming provider Ooyala sheds light on these questions[14]. Ooyala is the strongest example of how user data is extrapolated and interpreted to improve OTT-services[15] and target consumers. Without user data, SNS-owners and OTT-service providers have no viable business model. For example, user data makes it possible for Ooyala to track and examine consumer movement: (Q2 2013 Video Index):

- During the workweek, PC video views rise during office hours, peaking at noon. This coincides with a dip in mobile and tablet video plays during working hours;
- Between 5-7pm, PC video views decline during the workweek while mobile and tablet video plays increase;
- On weekends users view more media on phones and tablets when compared to PC views;
- Mobile video views increased a staggering 161% since 2012 representing 45% of all video views globally;
- 88% of views were on smartphones and only 12% on tablets;
- 71% of viewing takes place on connected TVs (CTV) if programmes are longer than 10 minutes: users prefer larger screens for longer content;
- 20% of viewing takes place on tablets for content between 10-30 minutes;
- The UK and Ireland lead in the mobile curve: mobile and tablet viewing make up two-thirds (67%) of all online video plays when compared to a global average of 45%;
- 46% of video adverts are delivered to mobile platforms;
- Smartphone and tablet video plays rose from just under 20% in July 2013 to almost 50% in July 2015;
- Expanding 4G networks worldwide facilitate continued growth for SNS and mobile streaming.

There is a clear pattern emerging:

- Users view video on mobile devices to and from work during commuting hours during the week; this is the time of the weekday when they view a trailer, short-form video content, and share their viewing experience with others on social media networks;
- At work users continue to view video content via their work PC and continue to do so at night on their home PC;
- As described by Ooyala, mobile devices such as smartphones and tablets are more in use in the hours before and after work, while PCs are used at work and again later in the evening at home;
- Mobile devices record a higher peak after work on a Friday, with mobile device use continuing over the weekend, whereas PC use is at its lowest on the weekend.

It is evident that users access social media and the global network anywhere and anytime. These above figures demonstrate that social media continues to grow in the US. The UK's Office for National Statistics reports equally strong growth (2015):

- 86% of adults use the Internet; and
- 99% of 16-24 year olds are online.

At face value these figures are impressive, promising a Golden Age for SNS – and user data exploitation. User data, tagged to UGC, PGC (Professionally Generated Content), user devices and accounts, is crucial to SNS-owners and without the exploitation of the same, SNS owners can not generate needed revenues. But is the Internet really just another platform on which to run a SNS and sell products to the digital consumer? Is growth really driven by content, as stated by Nielsen, Pew and Ooyala? How are users perceiving and experiencing social media?

THE USER PERSPECTIVE ON SOCIAL MEDIA

User data is essential to SNS owners, but what role does user data play for social media users? Previous scholars such as Ellison, Kaplan, Haenlein, Obar and Wildman offered various social media definition, but the user perspective was not included. How do users experience the Internet? What are their expectations?

Representative data can be obtained from the Internet Society (ISOC), which surveyed 10,000 Internet users in 20 countries to reveal how users perceive social media[16]. According to the Internet Society 2012 survey (ISOC, 2012):

- 90% of internet users use social media;
- 98% of users consider the internet essential for their knowledge and education;
- 80% see the internet playing a positive role for their individual lives and society as a whole;
- 75% see the internet as an important source of information;
- Two-thirds think the internet plays a significant role in solving global problems, e.g. child-mortality, improving mental health, eliminating extreme poverty and hunger, prevention of trafficking of women and children;
- 83% consider access to the internet a Human Right;
- 83% strongly agree that freedom of expression should be guaranteed on the internet;
- 70% do not want more government involvement;
- 84% of respondents state that they restrict access to websites and apps regarding their location data, indicating that users are aware of privacy issues on the Internet.

Human Rights, Tackling Poverty and Education

ISOC findings reveal that users do not perceive the Internet as a marketplace to be exploited by companies and organizations. Instead non-commercial values take priority: users clearly see social media as an opportunity to contribute to a global collective consciousness. To users, social media means:

- Access to the Internet is considered a Human Right;
- Social Media is an essential tool to tackle pressing global issues from poverty to improving mental health;
- 98% perceive the Internet as critical to knowledge development and education;
- More importantly, 84% of respondents are concerned that owners of SNS appropriate and exploit user data thus risking a breach of user privacy: another indication of the fragile and uneasy balance between open user sociality and clandestine corporate exploitation.

Users clearly care about social issues, a perspective corporate surveys, such as that of Nielsen and Ooyala, neglect to provide. Without user data, tagged to UGC, PGC and user accounts, users would not be able to find old and new friends and family sharing these values.

Social Media Is More About Free Sharing and Less About Commerce

In addition, I designed surveys (Survey User Experience, 2015)[17] and focus groups (Focus group Social Media, 2015) to further explore what users expect of social media and to gain primary source insight into user expectations. Participants were able to answer multiple-choice questions and provide a qualitative response regarding their social media experience:

- 65% of participants perceive the Internet as more about free sharing and less about buying and selling;
- 26% consider free sharing and commerce to be equally important; and
- Only 4% think of commerce as more important.

Taking into account the growth that online commerce enjoys, it is interesting to note that users do not perceive social media as mainly commercial, reaffirming ISOC findings: free sharing clearly dominates user perception.

User Concerns About Social Media

Qualitative analysis of the survey data also highlights that users are aware of social media weaknesses. Key themes frequently recurring are:

- Privacy and abuse of user data;
- Social Media is too superficial;
- Too much commerce, i.e. adverts;
- Inability of user to deal with the amount of information available online;
- Copyright issues;
- Addiction to being online;
- Extension of exaggerated and fake persona.

Half of Users Are Three Hours or More Online

Participants of this survey were recruited via social media such as Facebook groups and blogs - 65% are considered digital immigrants, 35% are digital natives. Survey results suggest that both groups spent a significant amount of time online, highlighting once again how much social media has penetrated our daily lives:

- 54% of users surveyed claim to be online between 1-3 hours per day;
- 11% state that they were online an average of 4-5 hours;
- 14% claim that they are online 6-8 hours per day;
- 17% say that they are online 9-10 hours per day; and
- 2.8% state that they are online more than 10 online hours every day.

Overall, users claim to spend a great deal more time online when compared with Nielsen's survey participants. Because requests for survey participants were published and promoted via Facebook and the Breda University of Applied Sciences, Netherlands, most participants were Dutch residents; but other nationalities also became aware of the survey and participated.

Qualitative Survey Insight

Participants were also given the opportunity to answer open-ended questions, such as this 21-year-old female German student survey participant:

I think social media is a place where you can communicate with everyone you know or don't know. It is a place where you can choose who you want to be. You can show what you like and dislike and thus you can find people who like the same things or more things that you could probably like. It is also something that takes more time of our private lives than we think. Plus, I think social media makes us less social and sometimes you could get an overload of social media; it becomes very exhausting to always be present and nice. (Survey User Experience, 2015)

This student's experience underscores how difficult it can be to navigate social media, for example in relation to the projection of a 'nice' social media image and social media overload. The comment also raises concerns about the representation of identity and personality online ("choose who you want to be") and the time-consuming nature of social media.

Fake news is a concern, for example this 31-year-old male German working professional survey participant had the following comment: "There is too much bullshit and not a lot of people take time to verify the information." (Survey User Experience, 2015).

The importance of sharing, interacting and communicating with 'friends, family' and 'people with 'common interests' is underscored by this comment, reaffirming the extension of the 'post-familial family' (Beck-Gernsheim, 1998, p. 68) into the virtual domain: "Social media is a communication medium where friends, family or strangers share information or opinion", according to this 21-year-old male Dutch student survey participant. (Survey User Experience, 2015).

Users also had clear expectations on how social media will develop over the next five years, though not every one was as positive about business opportunities on social media like this 20-year-old male Dutch undergraduate survey participant:

Social media will continue to dominate the market even more. Everything will go through it. Without having social media, you wouldn't probably know what's going on in the world (concerning friends, news). I expect social media to get some kind of a monopoly over everybody's life. (Survey User Experience, 2015)

This survey participant anticipated more government control over social media: "Social media may soon be controlled at some point as many governments see this as a way to be against them." (Survey User Experience, 2015). These comments show that users are very well aware of the threat social media poses to governments.

Privacy, and exploitation of user data for business and political reasons are reflected in this statement by a 35-year-old female Dutch working professional survey participant:" Privacy, hard to control, uncurated. Can be exploited for marketing purposes or political purposes" (Survey User Experience, 2015).

Digging Deeper

Understanding what users expect and when users are accessing social media are important pieces of the puzzle, but what can we learn from those users who are online? How do users value the Internet? We have learned that user priorities are to connect with friends and family. Focus group participants were given the opportunity to express their experiences qualitatively as well. While a survey is limited in the expression of qualitative data, a focus group provides an opportunity for participants to express and discuss their views.

I had the opportunity to discuss the nature of social media in three different group settings over a period of two years. The February 2015 focus group consisted of a communication undergraduate student class at Northern Arizona University (NAU, 2016), Flagstaff, USA and at NHTV, University of Applied Sciences in Breda, Netherlands[18]. This presented an opportunity to compare findings and reveal any differences between surveys and focus groups.

Undergraduate groups can be considered digital natives, whereas the third focus group consisted of 1st and 2nd degree digital immigrants. Undergraduate media management students at NHTV, University of Applied sciences, Breda, Netherlands and mass communication students NAU, Flagstaff Arizona were asked to form teams, discuss the topic and then upload their conclusions to Google docs (F. Kohle, 2015)[19].

Comments of digital natives and immigrants were themed as shown in Table 1.

Table 1.

Sample Comment	Theme/Category
"A platform to connect with the rest of the world and share your thoughts."	*Global*
"Social media is a collective term for online platforms where users, without or with minimal intervention from a professional editor, take care of the content."	*Creative*
"The means of sharing information and connecting with others around the world using the Internet."	*Sharing*
"It's a way of sharing information in a fast pace and is also a means of promotion"	*Promotion*
"It connects you to people on the Internet, but it disconnects you to people in real-life."	*Escape*
"Yesterday, we just lost the Internet for 6 hrs., which makes me so anxious and can find nothing to do without Internet."	*Addictive**
"Social media is destroying our country, kids so young seeing stuff a lot more easily and it is making it easier to get into bad stuff"	*Destructive**

*Addictive and destructive were not considered a single category, as a distinction was made between the compulsion of being online as being addictive versus anonymous online bullying as being destructive. Sample comments have been edited for length and/or clarity.

The focus group sessions opened with an explanation as to the purpose of the study. Participants were free to pick one or more partners to form smaller groups to discuss how social media should be defined.

Next, participants logged into Google docs and entered their summary. The session continued and results were revealed to all teams, providing the opportunity to further discuss and revise findings as co-discovers.

Finally, I categorized and coded answers then grouped the emerging pattern into themes (Barbour, 2013). When asked how users experience social media, a dominant view was to connect with friends, family, peers and colleagues.

Themes contain both positive and negative experiences, as shown in Table 2.

Table 2.

Examples of:	Positive Experience	Negative Experience
Interaction (I)	Catching up with friends	Online bullying
News (N)	Staying up to date	Too much fake news
Entertainment (E)	Funny Videos	Too many choices
Marketing (M)	Company promotion	Clickbait
Persona (P)	Self-expression	Misrepresentation of Identity
Security (S)	Feeling safe	Invasion of privacy
Health (H)	Real life/social media balance	Addiction

One participant stated "social media is a great way to keep in touch with friends, but also for school related matters." (Focus group Social Media, 2015). Participants interacting in this way with friends, family, colleagues, peers or strangers online were added to the Interaction category.

Participants who stated that social media are "a great way of remaining up to date" were added to the News category. Avoiding "boredom" and watching "funny" videos are views that were classified in the Entertainment category.

Views describing social media as a platform for "click bait" were added to the Marketing category. Participants who experience social media as a platform to "showcase the best version of them" and for "self-expression" were classified under the Persona category.

Users describing more than one theme were added to more than one category. For example, not everyone perceives social media as entertaining alone, but rather as both entertaining and useful for news updates.

Unsurprisingly Focus group results revealed that 68% consider interaction a top priority, reaffirming survey results regarding interactivity of 73%. Yet, qualitative feedback from focus groups was more critical compared to surveys:

Social media is taken over as the main mode of communication. It can connect or isolate, be funny or sad, present justice or shame. It's the way that the world communicates their ideas be it good or bad. (Focus group Social Media, 2015)

The interactive qualities of social media, being able to share information with people, friends and family, express one's self, clearly take priority over entertainment or health concerns. Nevertheless, one focus group saw social media as a danger to their children:

Social media is destroying our country, kids so young, seeing stuff a lot easier and easier and get into bad stuff because it easier to find it. (Focus group Social Media, 2015)

What Users Think Is Wrong With Social Media

Interacting with friends, family, peers and colleagues dominates the social media experience for all participants, closely followed by presenting an online-persona and self-expression. This matches the outcome of the surveys. It explains why Facebook with its befriending tools has become the most popular SNS to date. Entertainment and Marketing were considered the least important.

But how are social media users experiencing the weaknesses of social media? The above comment shows that not everyone experiences social media as positive[20]. Interaction clearly dominates the positive experience in social media.

Negative comments reflecting the weakness of social media included fake identities. This was a concern to this 22-year-old Dutch student: "Cat video's, wrong information can be perceived as real information, and everyone can create a false identity." (Survey User Experience, 2015).

This 25-year-old male Dutch working professional feared to miss out on something important online: "Feel the need to always check what is going on and afraid to miss something" (Survey User Experience, 2015), (Form responses, line 23).

The effort needed to stay online and user data exploitation were a concern to this 21-year-old female German student:

It is hard and nice to be online 24/7. In addition to that it could be kind of dangerous that a company knows so much about us by looking at our contacts or profiles. (Survey User Experience, 2015)

Compared to the overall experience or strength of social media, social media weaknesses are perceived markedly different:

- 37.8% of survey participants are concerned about negative interaction experiences, followed closely by security concerns;
- 35.1% considers privacy and data abuse a social media weakness. News manipulation ranks in third position, a dishonest online persona fourth, and health in the form of online addiction last.

Participants are aware of the benefits of social media. But they also understand the negative influence social media can have on user data integrity and privacy, as well as the forms of online abuse such as online bullying. According to this 26-year-old male Dutch working professional "the weakness is that it's hard to get things off of social media. Once it's out there it is out there." (Survey User Experience, 2015), (Form responses, line 37).

It is interesting to note that despite this awareness, the overall experience is not diminished. When asked how participants see social media in 5 years, positive predictions included:

- More growth worldwide for social media platforms;
- 24/7 online social media access;
- Highly integrated apps;
- Better-streamlined social media platforms such as Facebook and Twitter.

Negative predictions included:

- Too much advertising;
- Corporations taking over;
- More abuse of privacy.

Users think that more government regulations are needed to protect user data because: "I think that social media content will get even more advertisements." (Survey User Experience, 2015).

Despite differences regarding the perception of social media in news, persona or health, all surveys (74%) and focus groups (76%) feature a majority that considers social media a platform for interactivity, regardless of whether or not users have positive or negative experiences in that category.

User Data Exploitation From a User Perspective

Data suggests that social media is the interactive platform on which to connect to the Global Digital Family, which I explore in more detail below. Just as in real life, friends and family take priority in the virtual world. This is strongly valued by users.

Findings also indicate that survey and focus group participants are aware of the disadvantages of user data appropriation via social media and accept it as a necessity in order to maintain their online sociality experience. To an SNS user data means revenues. To users, data makes it possible to engage with friends and family.

The Global Digital Family and User Data Exploitation From a User Perspective

Research shows that users are well aware of SNS user data exploitation, informing themselves about world issues and connecting to friends and family who share these values. Survey and focus group participants are aware of the disadvantages of user data appropriation and exploitation via social media, but accept it as a necessity in order to maintain their online sociality experience.

To an SNS user data means revenues, and to users data makes it possible to engage with friends and family. It is user data tagged to UGC, PGC, user devices and accounts, data extrapolated from user behaviour, i.e. the mobile consumer, which is the life blood of the social media ecology.

Who Is Not Online?

Students and professionals dominate the statistics, begging the question of how equal the Internet and social media is to other demographic groups, which do not have the average education or professional history recorded in the above statistics. Who is not part of the new Global Digital Family and cannot be reached via social media was explored by Kathryn Zickuhr of Pew Research in detail (Zickuhr, 2013). Her findings reveal that:

- 15% of all Americans are not online;
- 41% of those did not obtain a high school diploma;
- 44% were above the age of 65;
- 24% earned 30,000 USD or less.

Campaigners and businesses intending to reach this target group need to consider a strategy not based on social media. Instead they should engage this target audience via traditional media, press- and outdoor media campaigns. Data suggests a correlation between the level of education, age and income, and interest in accessing the Internet.

SOLUTIONS AND RECOMMENDATIONS

The New 'Global Digital Family'

Connecting Directly to Friends and Family

Research so far suggests that connecting to friends and family is a key priority to users. It is reasonable to argue that McLuhan's Global Village has evolved into the Global Digital Family. Social media and the way user data is exploited makes it possible for SNS to generate revenues and for users to connect to new and old friends and family across the world.

39% of users claim that they are connecting to virtual friends they have never met (Duggan, Ellison, Lampe, Lenhart, & Madden, 2015), reaffirming how users extend their 'post-familial family' into the virtual domain (Beck-Gernsheim, 1998, p. 68).

But what does this new-found family connectedness look like in the social media ecology? Drawing from Westaby et al (2014) Dynamic Network Theory (DNT), we learn that high density networks are more likely to have a higher flow of information: "density represents the number of observed linkages divided by the number of total possible linkages" (Westaby, Pfaff, & Redding, 2014, p. 270). Based on the observations of Westaby et al., a low-density network compares to a high-density network as shown in Figure 1.

Figure 1.

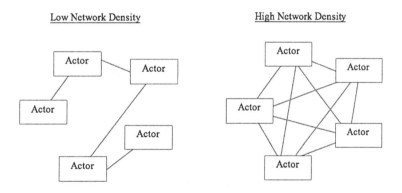

In a high-density network, every network actor is connected directly to every other network actor, making it possible to share information with strong cross-connection influences. A high-density network, however, is not a new phenomenon; one of, if not the oldest, high-density and dynamic network is the family (see Figure 2).

Figure 2.

Family

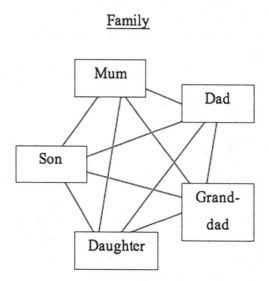

DEFINING THE GLOBAL DIGITAL FAMILY

Any member of a family or tribal network can connect directly to any member of their family and tribal network, though it is important to make a clear distinction between the small network of a family and that of a tribe.

In her article "A Normal Family" (2016) Lisa Belkin discusses the results of a survey by the Pew Centre of Research (Taylor, Morin, & Wang, 2011), highlighting the changing demographics in the contemporary post-familial-family, i.e. emergence of elective family relationships such as the 'patch-work' or 'blended' families not connected by blood relations[21].

Extending our blended post-familial family into the virtual domain is a natural next step. Critics might argue that we are dealing with the digital tribe, rather than the digital family. For example, Paul James, Professor of Globalization and Cultural Diversity at Western Sydney University, explains that the concept of 'tribe', is:

Derived from the traditional Latin term tribus, names real, self-reproducing and changing communities framed by the social dominance of face-to-face integration and living in the world today. (James, 2006, p. 26)

Just as the family, tribal structures facilitate direct face-to-face interaction, which is important in order to maintain a high-density network structure within the tribe.

During the evolution of our species, we connected to each other in this way in families and tribes during the Palaeolithic period, which spanned 3.5 million years (Darvill, 2009). However, for Homo Habilis and Homo Erectus (Gibbons, 2011) emerging in the Lower Palaeolithic period, the number of network actors that could effectively communicated with in a direct fashion was limited to an estimated 300 tribal members (Dunbar, 2003).

Direct connections in a network of 300 tribal network actors or more required the establishment of hierarchies, making it less likely for all tribe members to maintain a highly dense network when compared to a family: the family unit continued to facilitate a highly dense network the Lower Palaeolithic, connecting all family members directly.

For that reason, it is appropriate to use the term Global Digital Family, rather than global digital tribe. Indirect hierarchical connections removed the size limitation of 300 tribe members, enabling mankind to establish larger communities during the Neolithic period. With the arrival of social media, connectedness has reached full circle.

By removing the limitations of indirect hierarchical connections, social media is connecting individuals again directly but on a global scale, as anticipated in McLuhan's metaphorical 'Global Village'. Social media enables users worldwide to reach out directly to any other user participating in the global, digital family network of Humankind. According to a survey conducted by the Pew Research Center (Duggan, Ellison, Lampe, Lenhart, & Madden, 2015):

- 93% of participants stated that they are connected via social media to friends and family, other than parents and children; and
- 91% are connected with current friends reaffirming survey and focus group findings.

Connecting to the post-familial family is key to social media users: therefor it is reasonable to say that social media and user data also facilitates the return of family values, changing the outlook digital natives. This is reflected in the way university graduates carry these expectations into their future workplace.

Social Media, Family and the Workplace

Examining the influence of the Baby Boomers, Generation X[22] and the millennial generation, Anick Tolbize at the University of Minnesota identifies four generational types influencing the work environment (Tolbize, 2016):

- 46% of Traditionals[23] and 45% of Baby Boomers consider family a top priority;
- 67% of Generation X and 73% of Generation Y view family as a top priority[24].

This reaffirms findings from surveys and focus groups, underscoring how direct connectedness via social media facilitates the return of the family. Tolbize's study confirms the importance of family to digital immigrants, who are members of Generation X and Generation Y.

Millenials expect transparent production processes and equal treatment in a work environment connecting everyone and in this section we learn that along with the rise of social media, family and associated values have become more important to digital natives.

FUTURE RESEARCH DIRECTIONS

Without an authentic online experience, it is unlikely that social media can fulfill its potential as a facilitator of a global collective consciousness and research underscored that users expect a real and credible social media experience. Social media makes emotional contagion possible, which plays a strong part in an authentic social media experience.

In addition to emotional contagion research suggested that social media facilitates the projection of personality: i.e. the persona and the shadow as discussed by C.G. Jung (1958/1975). Findings indicate that emotional contagion and an authentic personality are critical social media elements, but what exactly an authentic online personality is, remains unclear and further research into this is warranted.

Synthesizing Jung´s ideas on personality with Kozinet and Toennie shed additional light on the problem of authenticity, but exactly when something is perceived authentic on social media is still not entirely clear.

CONCLUSION

Reappraising Social Media and the Rise of The Global Digital Family

Scholars Kapp (1877)[25], McLuhan (1962)[26] and Kittler (1986/1999)[27] theorised on a global network originating from our collective unconscious[28] and contributing towards a global collective consciousness[29]. Critics suggested that media technology such as the internet lacked the richness needed for real human interaction (Daft & Lengel, 1986), yet we have seen how emotionally contagious tweets by Donald Trump "stoke anxiety" (Rucker & Paquette, 2017) among his followers.

The role of emotional contagion is not included in previous social media definitions. In addition, industry data, surveys and focus groups as part of this study suggest that user expectations significantly differ from the corporate perspective. These fundamental characteristics are not reflected in previous definitions of social media. We recall Nicole Ellison's definition:

We define social network sites as web-based services that allow individuals to (1) construct a public or semi-public profile within a bounded system, (2) articulate a list of other users with whom they share a connection, and (3) view and traverse their list of connections and those made by others within the system. The nature and nomenclature of these connections may vary from site to site. (Ellison, 2007, p. 211)

While Ellison considers user profiles and sharing of crucial importance, her definition does not provide details on the importance of a qualitative authentic and emotional user experience. Nor does it address how the user perspective differs from corporate expectations. Kaplan and Haenlein on the other hand approach their definition from a marketing position:

Social Media is a group of Internet-based applications that build on the ideological and technological foundations of Web 2.0, and that allow the creation and exchange of User Generated Content. (Kaplan & Haenlein, 2010, p. 61)

Kaplan and Haenlein introduced the topic of UGC into their definition and their article raises the topic of authenticity: being 'unprofessional' is recognised as a social media hallmark, but Kaplan and Haenlein do not explore this at a deeper level.

Considering surveys and focus groups, the act of sharing and interacting in an authentic fashion is more relevant than UGC on its own. Users not only share UGC, they also share PGC[30], with friends and family. Obar and Wildman's perspective represents communication theory:

1) Social media services are (currently) Web 2.0 Internet based applications, 2) User generated content is the lifeblood of social media, 3) Individuals and groups create user-specific profiles for a site or app designed and maintained by a social media service, 4) Social media services facilitate the development of social networks online by connecting a profile with those of other individuals and/or groups. (Obar & Wildman, 2015, p. 2)

While Obar and Wildman acknowledge the evolving nature of social media, they also claim that UGC is the lifeblood of social media. Considering what we have learned from the industry and user perspective, it is reasonable to argue that UGC is an important user contribution to social media, but it is not the lifeblood, as users are also sharing PGC.

User data on the other hand can be considered the lifeblood of social media: it allows users to connect with others online according to shared and common interests and it enables SNS to generate revenues by exploiting user data openly – or in a clandestine fashion. However, without user data, SNS have no business model or revenues and users are unable to connect the way they do online.

Additionally, none of the definitions above take into account the potential of social media to contribute towards a global collective consciousness. Kapp and McLuhan as well as Kittler discussed the idea of a global collective consciousness and as we have seen, users are interested in global topics transforming the way we live together on this planet.

From climate change to animal welfare, political activism to human rights: social media offers the potential to users to discuss and even force change to redefine conventions and guidelines governing our global conduct. It is this collective consciousness which will establish global norms of conduct enabling the Global Digital Family to take the necessary steps needed to deal with climate change and inequality.

Findings in this paper suggest that Social Media is more accurately defined as follows:

- Social media makes it possible for users to create specific SNS-profiles and project an authentic online personality as members of the Global Digital Family;
- Social media facilitates emotional contagion;
- On social media users contribute to the digital global collective consciousness;
- The lifeblood for Social Network Sites is user data: it allows users to connect and share content with others and makes it possible for SNS to generate revenues;
- As long as SNS meet user needs, users accept corporate exploitation of their data.

Facebook was launched on February 4, 2004 (Phillips, 2007) and since then social media has disrupted power structures (Kohle F., 2012) forcing industry and governments to adapt.

Considering the global challenges our planet is facing this research suggests that social media is now evolving into a global network facilitating the rise of the Global Digital Family and the establishment of a global collective consciousness needed to face and resolve these challenges.

REFERENCES

Barbour, R. (2013). Analysing Focus Groups. In U. Flick (Ed.), *The SAGE Handbook of Qualitative Data Analysis* (pp. 313–327). London: SAGE.

Beck-Gernsheim, E. (1998). 8 1). On the Way to a Post-Familial Family. *Theory, Culture & Society*, *1*(15), 53–70. doi:10.1177/0263276498015003004

Belkin, L. (2016). *A Normal Family?* Retrieved 2 23, 2011, from New York Times: http://parenting.blogs.nytimes.com/2011/02/23/a-normal-family/

BFI. (2018). *BFI*. Retrieved from http://www.bfi.org.uk/

Britdoc. (2012). *Britdoc Impact*. Britdoc.

Chaffey, D. (2018). *Smart Insights*. Retrieved 2 25, 2018, from Average display advertising clickthrough rates: https://www.smartinsights.com/internet-advertising/internet-advertising-analytics/display-advertising-clickthrough-rates/

Clark, J., & Abrash, B. (2011). *Social Justice Documentary: Designing For Impact*. Retrieved 2 8, 2016, from Center for Media & Social Impact: http://cmsimpact.org/resource/social-justice-documentary-designing-for-impact/

Cuevas, A. (2012). Social media: Changing the way we teach and changing the way we learn. In *INTED* (pp. 221-226). INTED.

Daft, R., & Lengel, R. (1986). Organisational Information requirements, Media Richness and Structural Design'. *Management Science*, *32*(5), 554–571. doi:10.1287/mnsc.32.5.554

Darvill, T. (2009). *The Concise Oxford Dictionary of Archaeology$ The Concise Oxford Dictionary of Archaeology*. Oxford, UK: Oxford University Press.

Devicescape. (2018). Retrieved 1 31, 2018, from Devicescape: http://www.devicescape.com/

Dijk, J. v. (2013a). *Culture of Connectivity: A critical History of Social Media*. Oxford University Press. doi:10.1093/acprof:oso/9780199970773.001.0001

Docsociety. (2018). Retrieved from https://docsociety.org/

Dolan, M. (2010). Children thrive equally with same-sex, heterosexual parents, psychologist testifies at Prop. 8 trial. *L.A.Now*.

Duggan, M., Ellison, N., Lampe, C., Lenhart, A., & Madden, M. (2015). *Social Media Update 2014*. Pew Research Center.

Dunaetz, D. R., Lisk, T. C., & Shin, M. (2015). Personality, Gender, and Age as Predictors of Media Richness Preference. *Advances in Multimedia*, *2015*, 9. doi:10.1155/2015/243980

Dunbar, R. (2003). The Social Brain: Mind, Language, and Society in Evolutionary Perspective. *Annual Review of Anthropology*, *32*(1), 163–181. doi:10.1146/annurev.anthro.32.061002.093158

Durkheim, E. (1893). *De la division du travail social: étude sur l'organisation des sociétés supérieures.* Paris: ALCAN.

Durkheim, E. (1893). *The Divisions of Labour in Society.* University Press.

Ellison, N. (2007, October). Social Network Sites: Definition, History, and Scholarship. *Journal of Computer-Mediated Communication, 13*(1), 210–230. doi:10.1111/j.1083-6101.2007.00393.x

Geohive. (2015). Retrieved 8 10, 2015r, from Geohive - Projected World Population by year 1950-2100: http://www.geohive.com/earth/his_history3.aspx

Gibbons, A. (2011). Who Was Homo Habilis - And Was It Really Home? *Science, 332*(6036), 1370–1371. doi:10.1126cience.332.6036.1370 PMID:21680822

Google. (2013). *Project Loon.* Retrieved 3 6, 2017, from Google: http://www.google.com/loon/

Gruvi. (2018). Retrieved 1 31, 2018, from Gruvi: https://gruvi.tv/

Impact Guide. (2012). *The Invisible War.* Retrieved 1 16, 2018, from Impact Guide: https://impactguide.org/static/library/InvisibleWar.pdf

ISOC. (2012). *Global Internet User Survey 2012 Key Findings.* ISOC.

James, P. (2006). Chapter Two: Social Relations in Tension. In Globalism, Nationalism, Tribalism: Bringing Theory Back in. Academic Press.

Jonsson, P. (2014). *Ericson Mobility Report.* Ericsson. Ericsson.

Jung, C. G. (1958/1975). The Collected Works of C.G. Jung Volume I: Psychology and Religion: West and East. Princeton University Press.

Kaplan, & Haenlein. (2010). Users of the world, unite! The challenges and opportunities of Social Media. *Science Direct, 53*, 59-68.

Kapp, E. (1877). *Grundlinien einer Philosophie der Technik.* Braunschweig: Westermann.

Karim, J. (2005). *Me at the Zoo.* Retrieved 7 31, 2015, from Youtube: https://www.youtube.com/watch?v=jNQXAC9IVRw

Kittler, F. (1986/1999). *Grammophon, Film, Typewriter* (G. Winthrop & M. Wutz, Trans.). Berlin: Brinkmann & Bose, Stanford University Press.

Kittler, F. (2000). *Eine Kulturgeschichte der Kulturwissenschaft.* Muenchen: Wilhelm Fink Verlag.

Kohle. (2015). *Focus group Social Media.* Academic Press.

Kohle, F. (2012). The Social Media "Information Explosion" Spectacle. In J. P. Slain (Ed.), *Social Media and the Transformation of Interaction in Society* (p. 173). Hershey, PA: IGI Global.

Kohle, F. (2015). Survey User Experience. *Survey (London, England).*

Kohle, F. H. (2017, Oct. 23). *The Cinema Audience in 2017.* Retrieved Oct. 23, 2017, from Moving Docs: http://www.movingdocs.org/cinema_audience_2017?recruiter_id=1191

Kozinets, R. (2015). *Netnography: Redefined*. London: SAGE. doi:10.1002/9781118767771.wbiedcs067

Kramer, A., Guillory, J., & Hancock, T. (2014). 7). Experimental evidence of massive-scale emotional contagion through social networks. *Proceedings of the National Academy of Sciences of the United States of America*, *111*(24), 8788–8790. doi:10.1073/pnas.1320040111 PMID:24889601

Ladkin, D. (2004). Action Research. In C. S. Silverman (Ed.), *Qualitative Research Practice* (pp. 478–491). London: SAGE. doi:10.4135/9781848608191.d39

Macnaghten, P., & Myers, G. (2015). Focus Groups. In C. Seale, G. Gobo, J. Gubrium, & D. Silverman (Eds.), *Qualitative Research Practice* (pp. 66–81). London: SAGE.

Mailchimp. (2017). Retrieved 1 26, 2017, from Mailchimp - Benchmark: https://mailchimp.com/resources/research/email-marketing-benchmarks/

McLuhan, M. (1962). *The Gutenberg Galaxy: The Making of Typographic Man*. Toronto: University of Toronto Press.

Monica, P. L. (2006). *Google to buy YouTube for $1.65 billion*. Retrieved 7 31, 2015, from CNN Money: http://money.cnn.com/2006/10/09/technology/googleyoutube_deal/index.htm?cnn=yes

NAU. (2016). *Northern Arizona University*. Retrieved 6 28, 2016, from Northern Arizona University: https://nau.edu/

Nielsen. (2014). *The Digital Consumer, February 2014*. Retrieved 1 13, 2016, from Nielsen: http://www.nielsen.com/us/en/insights/reports/2014/the-us-digital-consumer-report.html

Obar, J., & Wildman, S. (2015). Social Media Definition and the Governance Challenge: An Introduction to the Special Issue. *Telecommunications Policy*, *39*(9), 745–750. doi:10.1016/j.telpol.2015.07.014

Office for National Statistics. (2015). *Internet Users, 2015*. Office for National Statistics.

Ooyala. (2013). *Q2 2013 Video Index*. Retrieved 1 13, 2016, from Q2 2013 Video Index: http://go.ooyala.com/wf-video-index-q2-2013

Ooyala. (2015). *Ooyala*. Retrieved 1 13, 2016, from Ooyala Q3 2015 Video Index: go.ooyala.com/wf-video-index-q3-2015

Phillips, S. (2007). *A brief hisgtory of Facebook*. Retrieved 8 22, 2017, from The Guardian: https://www.theguardian.com/technology/2007/jul/25/media.newmedia

Reason, P., & Torbert, W. (2001). The action turn: Toward a transformational action science. *Concepts and Transformation*, *6*(1), 1–37. doi:10.1075/cat.6.1.02rea

Rucker, P., & Paquette, D. (2017). *How a week of Trump tweets stoked anxiety, moved markets and altered plans*. Retrieved 2 2, 2017, from Washington Post: https://www.washingtonpost.com/graphics/politics/week-of-trump-tweets/

Statista. (2017). *Number of monthly active Facebook users worldwide as of 3rd quarter 2016 (in millions)*. Retrieved 1 11, 2017, from Statista: http://www.statista.com/statistics/264810/number-of-monthly-active-facebook-users-worldwide/

Statista. (2017a). *Number of monthly active Twitter users worldwide from 1st quarter 2010 to 3rd quarter 2016 (in millions)*. Retrieved 1 11, 2017a, from Statista: http://www.statista.com/statistics/282087/number-of-monthly-active-twitter-users/

Statista. (2017b). *Numbers of LinkedIn members active LinkedIn*. Retrieved 1 11, 2017b, from LinkedIn: https://www.statista.com/statistics/274050/quarterly-numbers-of-linkedin-members/

Taylor, P., Morin, R., & Wang, W. (2011). *The Public Renders a Split Verdict On Changes in Family Structure*. Pew Research.

The EU General Data Protection Regulation. (2018). *The EU General Data Protection Regulation*. Retrieved 1 31, 2018, from The EU General Data Protection Regulation: https://www.eugdpr.org/

Tolbize, A. (2016). *Generational differences in the Workplace*. University of Minnesota. University of Minnesota.

Tönnies, F. (1887). Gemeinschaft und Gesellschaft. Leipzig: Fues' Verlag.

Tufekci, Z., & Wilson, C. (2012). Social Media and the Decision to Participate in Political Protest: Observations From Tahrir Square. *Journal of Communication*, *62*(2), 363–379. doi:10.1111/j.1460-2466.2012.01629.x

US Census Bureau, 20th Century Statistics. (1999). Statistical Abstract of the United States. US Census Bureau.

Westaby, J., Pfaff, D., & Redding, N. (2014, April). A Dynamic Network Theory Perspective. *The American Psychologist*, *69*(3), 269–284. doi:10.1037/a0036106 PMID:24750076

YouTube. (2017). *Statistics*. Retrieved 3 6, 2017, from Youtube: https://www.youtube.com/yt/press/statistics.html

Zickuhr, K. (2013). *Who's not online and why*. Washington, DC: Pew Research Center. Retrieved from http://www.pewinternet.org/2013/09/25/whos-not-online-and-why/

ENDNOTES

[1] French sociologist Emile Durkheim developed the idea that societies have a set of shared beliefs, ideas and moral attitudes in the form of a collective consciousness (Durkheim, The Divisions of Labour in Society, 1893). Social media makes it possible for users to contribute towards a global collective consciousness.

[2] 'Unprofessional' is an interesting criterion and I will return to this in more detail chapter 5 when discussing authenticity and personality online.

[3] Ooyala's data analysis features data from than 200 million users in 130 different countries.

[4] Survey participants were recruited via the NHTV, University of Applied Sciences University Breda, NL, network but also included participants from other countries who became aware of the survey via NHTV students. The sample size of 35 participants for a survey is not considered representative but indicative.

5   The February Flagstaff 2015 focus group at NAU consisted of 12 males and 14 female undergraduate students, aged between 19-25. The June 2015 focus group at NHTV, University of Applied Sciences, Breda, in the Netherlands consisted of 10 males and 12 female undergraduate students aged 19-25, and the November 2015 focus group consisted of 6 male and 8 female NHTV lecturers aged 28-50.

6   In the past Humans discuss media, for example a book they read, a film they have seen, with other Humans. In the semantic web, it is the Human who has become object of that conversion: algorithm observe user behaviour, collect user data and then decide which content should be presented. This can be perceived as Kittler's autonomous technology (2000).

7   Devicescape crowd-sources 300 million Wi-Fi access points to build apps for companies reaching out to the mobile consumer.

8   Gruvi offers a specialised marketing service to production companies wishing to reach out to the mobile audience.

9   The EU GDPR is not likely to be in effect in the UK after the UK leaves the European Union.

10   In the section investigating the user perspective I demonstrated that users accept exploitation, provided the balance is maintained between their online experiences versus corporate needs. But without exploitable user data SNS have no business model and no revenues, nor can users cannot connect with other users or explore relevant content.

11   For example, if a documentary about refugee children is aimed at an audience consisting of 10,000 local school children and teachers and 1,000 school children and teachers are reached, then the project's penetration is 10%.

12   For example, metrics include page views per visit and the percentage of visits that complete viewing a video clip and total time spent on the site.

13   Nielsen studies consumer behaviour and provides valuable statistical information about user behaviour in social media. Ooyala is a private and venture capital backed video technology and streaming service provider claiming to have more than 220 million unique viewers, serving over 1.2 billion video ads per month. The US Pew Research Centre provides information on demographic trends in the US and worldwide, the UK Office for National Statistics maintains records and statistics on Internet users and so does the US Census Bureau.

14   With 220 million users as a base, Ooyala data can certainly be interpreted as representative, providing excellent insight into the behaviour of digital consumers accessing video content (Ooyala, 2015). Social media is not part of their statistics, but as we have seen with Nielsen, video content and social media are closely linked.

15   OTT stands for Over-The-Top operators such as Netflix, Spotify or Google Play.

16   ISOC does not investigate from a corporate perspective: its mission is to strive to "promote the open development, evolution, and use of the Internet for the benefit of all people throughout the world".

17   The sample size of 35 participants should be not considered representative but indicative.

18   The February Flagstaff 2015 focus group at NAU consisted of 12 males and 14 female undergraduate students, aged between 19-25. The June 2015 focus group at NHTV, University of Applied Sciences, Breda, in the Netherlands consisted of 10 males and 12 female undergraduate students aged 19-25, and the November 2015 focus group consisted of 6 male and 8 female NHTV lecturers aged 28-50.

[19]   Within the context of this qualitative research, the results are not considered representative regarding the general population, but indicative of students and future media professionals, professional practitioners and faculty.

[20]   To determine this I coded positive experiences with a "+" and negative ones with a "-" for example a positive interaction such as interaction with friends is marked I+, whereas a negative interaction experience such as online-bullying is marked I-. The positive survey group experiences, or strengths, are represented in the below figures.

[21]   How functional 'blended' families are was highlighted in a 2010 court case in the US when Michael Lamb, head of the Cambridge Department of Social and Development Psychology testified that "children do not require both a male and female parent" (Dolan, 2010).

[22]   Digital natives that are undergraduates are considered Generation Z and Y, also known as Millennials.

[23]   Traditionals are also referred to as the Greatest Generation and describes people born between 1922 and 1943 (Value Options, 2017).

[24]   Pew research further illustrates how generations differ from one another.

[25]   In the chapter entitled 'Der Elektromagnetische Telegraph' of 'Die Grundlinien einer Philosophie der Technik' Kapp refers to the telegraph as an extension of the human central nervous system (Kapp, 1877). Preceding McLuhan by almost a century, Kapp remained relatively unknown for his ideas, while McLuhan is largely credited with popularising the idea that technology is an extension of man.

[26]   McLuhan's 'Global Village' (1962, p. 209).

[27]   Kittler realizes that digital media technologies conflate all previous forms of media realities into Leibnitz' single binary system, encompassing all content and information in a global network (Kittler, 1986/1999).

[28]   The idea of the collective unconsciousness is C.G. Jung's unique contribution to Psychology (Jung C. G, 1995/2011).

[29]   French sociologist Emile Durkheim developed the idea that societies have a set of shared beliefs, ideas and moral attitudes in the form of a collective consciousness (Durkheim, De la division du travail social: étude sur l'organisation des sociétés supérieures, 1893). Social media makes it possible for users to contribute towards a global collective consciousness.

[30]   PGC stands for Professionally Generated Content (ComScore, Inc., 2012).

This research was previously published in the Handbook of Research on Examining Cultural Policies Through Digital Communication; pages 362-390, copyright year 2019 by Information Science Reference (an imprint of IGI Global).

Chapter 6
Facebook and Google as Regrettable Necessities

Pietro Frigato
Scuola Professionale Provinciale Luigi Einaudi, Bolzano, Italy

Francisco J. Santos-Arteaga
https://orcid.org/0000-0003-2385-4781
Free University of Bolzano, Bolzano, Italy

ABSTRACT

The following article considers the results from two different studies, a European one involving over 20,000 respondents and an American one closing on 1,000, to illustrate how online platforms such as Facebook and Google can be defined as regrettable necessities. We define regrettable necessities as those whose consumption provides a direct disutility to consumers. That is, other than the standard utility derived from the access to a given service, a direct disutility in terms of privacy losses and preference manipulation results from their use. In addition, users acknowledge this fact and are aware of the disutility suffered, though not necessarily of its intensity, highlighting the fundamental strategic role played by these platforms in current voting environments.

1. Introduction

The capacity of online information providers to manipulate the preferences and decisions of Internet users has recently become a trendy topic given the social emphasis placed on fake news and the increasing interest in big data analysis (Schneier, 2018). This has been the case despite the fact that the Internet was initially considered by its most radical supporters as a free and frictionless information allocation mechanism matching perfectly suppliers with demanders (Golumbia, 2016). Its capacity to process enormous amounts of information and freely distribute it across users led the most optimistic of them to expect a virtually perfect exchange of information. However, it was the extraction of information from the users what became one of the main pillars of the resulting online market in such a way that "by the mid-2010s

DOI: 10.4018/978-1-6684-6307-9.ch006

the average reader on news sites like Boston Globe's bostom.com would be subjected to extraordinary surveillance methods, with only the barest degree of consent" Wu (2016, p. 321).

The online interactions taking place between information providers and Internet users has generated a substantial amount of empirical literature illustrating that "the rankings of search results provided by search engine companies have a dramatic impact on consumer attitudes, preferences, and behavior" (Epstein and Robertson 2015, p. E4512). These biases are seemly due to the trust with which users endow the companies in charge of the search engines to rank the results according to their subjective preferences. This is the case despite the fact that "users generally have no idea how results get ranked" (Epstein and Robertson 2015, p. E4512). The trust placed on an abstract algorithm – designed and updated by human engineers – applies also to Facebook, despite the decrease in satisfaction levels experienced by its users (Kourouthanassis et al., 2015).

One of the main consequences derived from the strategic process of information collection (and transmission) has been the emergence of the Facebook-Google duopoly of information providers, whose dominance over the market is expected to continue increasing

Google and Facebook are set to attract 84 per cent of global spending on digital advertising, excluding China, in 2017, underscoring concerns that the two technology companies have become a digital duopoly (Garrahan, 2017).

The use of Facebook and Google is so widespread and routinized that the data retrieved from their users is being used to generate increasingly accurate profiles of the population (Schneier, 2014). This fact is generally acknowledged by the users – particularly when dealing with privacy concerns (De Wolf et al., 2017) –, who nevertheless continue to use social network sites and search engines on a regular basis. In evolutionary theory, a routine arises whenever a given behavioral pattern is socially accepted among the population.[1] In the current context, such a definition implies that whenever the use of an online platform becomes widespread and accepted as part of the standard behavior to follow, the costs arising in terms of privacy losses and potential manipulability are accepted and assimilated by the population. That is, users are willing to provide online platforms with the information required on a daily basis despite knowing that it can be exploited in a nontransparent way.

Among the theories proposed to justify such a behavior, the scopophilia approach of David Lyon (2006) has gained considerable momentum. The willingness to compete by displaying private information could be considered one of the main incentives driving users to share preference-related data in exchange for free access to the different products of online platforms. This feature links the behavior of users to the positional competition concept developed by Fred Hirsch (1977), where individuals compete within the social spectrum for increased, though marginal, recognition. Within such a framework, "potential customers are choosing to enter into these quasi-feudal user relationships because of the enormous value they receive from them" (Schneier 2014, p. 60), since the services provided by online platforms constitute "the tools of modern life"

they're necessary to a career and a social life. Opting out isn't a viable choice for most of us, most of the time; (…) and choosing among providers is not a choice between surveillance or no surveillance, but only a choice of which feudal lords get to spy on you. (Schneier 2014, pp. 60-61).

A similar conceptual path is followed by Ward (2014), who describes how online interactions can lead to situations of social tyranny where the beliefs and interests of a group of virtual community members are imposed on the other members of the community. In this regard, it has also been empirically illustrated that online platforms, namely, search engines (Epstein and Robertson, 2015) and social network sites (Liberini et al., 2018), are able to manipulate the preferences and, therefore, the subsequent behavior of users. Kosinski et al. (2013) utilized the information available online to predict with considerable precision the main psychological attributes of users. Cambridge Analytica applied their findings to generate psychograms of the whole adult population of U.S. citizens, as its CEO boasted

We're able to identify clusters of people who care about a particular issue, pro-life or gun rights, and to then create an advert on that issue, and we can nuance the messaging of that advert according to how people see the world, according to their personalities. (Burleigh, 2017)

The direct consequences derived from the strategic use of online platforms have been analyzed by Liberini et al. (2018), who estimated that the political advertising of Facebook increased Trump turnout by almost ten per cent in the elections of 2016. Moreover, Epstein and Robertson (2015) illustrated empirically the capacity of online information providers to manipulate the preferences of users in voting environments. A fundamental implication that follows from the ability of suppliers to manipulate information is the fact that users do not generally acknowledge the severity of the effects that may arise from any potential manipulation of their preferences and choices

Psychological manipulation – based both on personal information and control of the underlying systems – will get better and better. Even worse, it will become so good that we won't know we're being manipulated (Schneier 2014, p. 85)

Such a drastic consequence is the result of "living in the golden age of (…) electronic surveillance", which is "efficient beyond Bentham's wildest dreams" (Schneier 2014, pp. 4, 32). The resulting information extraction network has evolved into a complex web of relations that remain for the most part undefined and unquantified

There is no definitive map of network spying services. The allegiances and roles are multifarious and complex. No one really knows the score, though a common opinion is that Goggle has historically been at the top of the heap for collecting spy data about you on the open Internet, while Facebook has mastered a way to corral people under an exclusive microscope (Lanier 2014, p. 109).

We will argue – based on the intuition following from the literature – that the free services provided by online platforms such as Facebook and Google have been transformed into regrettable necessities. Our definition of this latter concept will be stricter than the one generally considered by economists and political scientists. Intuitively, users employ their time (which could be applied to perform alternative productive activities) to disclose private information in exchange for a service deemed to be necessary. They do so while being aware of the fact that the information provided can be used to manipulate their preferences and decisions, decreasing their respective utilities and generating regret. These services are therefore regrettable necessities.

2. DEFINING REGRETTABLE NECESSITIES

The definition of regrettable necessities constitutes a cornerstone of the current paper. As stated in the previous section, we will consider a stricter definition than the one generally applied by economists and political scientists. The former refers to the use of resources to finance an activity or part of a production process that does not provide a direct utility to the decision maker but either reverts some positive social utility or is required for the consumption or availability of a product. Taxes and transportation costs constitute standard examples.

Taxes are always a regrettable necessity, but some are less regrettable than others (Financial times, 2013).

In other words, economic agents give an unwanted use to their money knowing that a positive outcome will result from it and that such outcome would somehow (indirectly or maybe even directly) revert to them. The same intuition applies to the intermediate sections of the production process that are necessary to generate the final product but do not provide any utility to consumers. A couple of examples are given by congestion and screening processes that "absorb real resources and involve a lengthening in the production chain, an increase in intermediate output" (Hirsch 1977, p. 31).

Political scientists follow a similar though stricter approach. The opportunity cost paid by decision makers (DMs) – in terms of the resources allocated to the necessity – has a direct negative effect on a third party. The army and preemptive attacks provide examples of this stricter definition according to which a negative outcome, regrettable but necessary, is delivered to a third party. On the other hand, similarly to taxes, a positive outcome is obtained by the DMs in the form of increased security. Political scientists are therefore stricter than economists, since resources are allocated to deliver morally regrettable outcomes that have a negative effect on others. In the words of Perkins (2009).

The language of regrettable necessities emerges frequently when groups vie against one another. It appears on the home front around such practices as rationing goods and drafting people into the military. It applies to invaded territories in such forms as travel restrictions, curfews and internment camps. And it figures in the conduct of war itself, in such forms as preemptive armament and pre-emptive attack. Again, no one views any of these moves as healthy steps in themselves but simply regrettable necessities (Perkins 2009, p. 179).

Our definition of regrettable necessities will be stricter than the previous ones, with negative outcomes affecting directly the DMs facing the opportunity costs. More importantly, a fundamental characteristic of a regrettable necessity is the fact that DMs acknowledge the negative consequences derived from their actions. Note that this type of regret differs from the one identified by Schwartz (2004) in his paradox of choice, where a substantial amount of information and the limited capacity of DMs to assimilate it lead to purchases that are lately regretted. In the current setting, DMs regret exposing private information online that can be potentially used to manipulate their preferences and, eventually, their behavior. DMs are aware of the drawbacks following from their decisions, but lack knowledge regarding their intensity.

The regrettable quality of the necessities considered in the current paper follows from the bargain inherent to the free access enjoyed by DMs, where privacy violations are traded in exchange for software applications or uses. This type of market transaction implies that "Internet companies can improve their product offerings to their actual customers by reducing user privacy" (Schneier 2014, p. 50). Users are allowed to access free "surveillance-based services" that "are useful and valuable" at the cost of largely accepted data extortions (Schneier 2014, p. 51).

We analyze data retrieved from different surveys performed in Europe and the United States so as to validate the characterization of Facebook and Google as regrettable necessities. The European case corresponds to a study presented by the European Commission while the American one is taken from a Statista report (https://www.statista.com/). Without being explicitly asked about regrettable necessities or stating that they regret the use of online platforms, DMs declare that despite the continuous use they make of both platforms, they do not consider them to be transparent or respectful with their privacy. Explicit concerns are raised regarding the use of their private information and, in the European case, the possibility of public regulation is openly advocated.

3. THE EUROPEAN CASE

The European Commission is sufficiently concerned regarding the attitudes of the European population towards Internet interactions so as to have performed several studies on the subject when designing its Digital Single Market strategy (https://ec.europa.eu/digital-single-market/). The most useful one for the current analysis relates to the attitudes of users towards online platforms (European Commission, 2016). As will be highlighted in the next section, what emerges from the answers provided is strikingly similar to the American case. Users of search engines and social media utilize their services almost on a daily basis while being aware of the lack of transparency exhibited by the corresponding companies regarding the use of the personal information provided. This awareness concerns the European users to the point of agreeing to the supervision of these companies by a public agency. This latter statement is complemented by their lack of interest on the terms and conditions of use, being already aware – to some extent – of the implicit costs faced in terms of information disclosure.

The data described throughout this section correspond to a study that took place from April 9 to April 18, 2016, encompassing more than 21,000 respondents who were 15 years and older.[2] It should be emphasized that the study aimed at illustrating the attitude of the users towards Internet platforms not to describe them as regrettable necessities, though this is indeed one of the main results that arises from the answers received. For instance, Figure 1(a) illustrates how the use of online platforms to retrieve information has become routinized among the European population. The scopophilia inherent to the display of information at the (online) social level (Lyon, 2006) can be observed in Figure 1(b).

Base: Internet and online platforms users (n = 21,776)

Moreover, as the answer to the first question of Figure 2 illustrates, users are aware of the existence of the filter bubble, namely, the fact that online interactions are customized to fit their opinions and preferences (Pariser, 2012). More interesting, however, is the concern raised regarding the use of their personal data and the subsequent agreement on the public regulation of online platforms described in Figure 2. The generality of such statements is then focused on search engines and social networks in Figure 3, where users express specific discomfort regarding the collection and use of personal data by both types of online platforms.

Base: Internet and online platforms users (n=21,550)

Base: Internet and online platforms users (n=21,550)

Finally, Figure 4 confirms the fact that the retrieval and nontransparent use of private information by these platforms is generally accepted and its consequences ignored or omitted by their users. The consumption of both services is routinized and the resulting regrettable consequences assimilated as part of their features, with most DMs ignoring the terms and conditions of use defined by the corresponding companies. All in all, DMs acknowledge the use of their personal information for purposes that may lead to the manipulation of their preferences but fail to recognize the actual capacity of private businesses to do so without them realizing (Lanier, 2014; Schneider, 2014).

Base: Internet and online platforms users (n=21,550)

Figure 1. For each of the following activities, please tell me if it is an activity that you do, or not, on the Internet

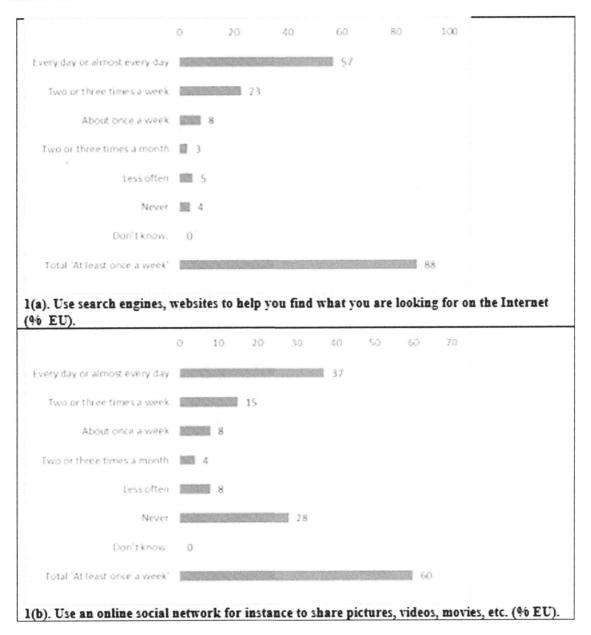

1(a). Use search engines, websites to help you find what you are looking for on the Internet (% EU).

1(b). Use an online social network for instance to share pictures, videos, movies, etc. (% EU).

4. THE AMERICAN CASE

The data described throughout this section correspond to an online study published by Statista (2017) on the use and impact of online platforms in the United States. The survey was conducted from March 22 to March 27, 2017, and consisted of about 1,000 respondents who were 18 years and older. We should note that the American case is almost identical to the European one, the only notable difference being the question about the supervision of online platforms by a public agency.

Figure 2. Please tell me to what extent you agree or disagree with the following statements on the collection and use of these personal data by online platforms (% EU)

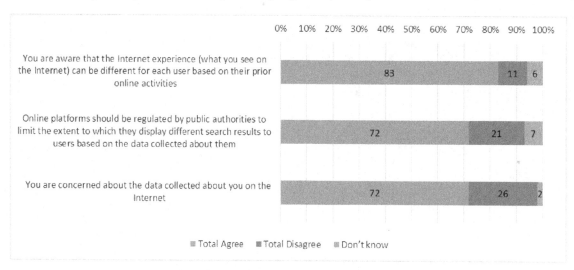

Figure 3. To what extent are you comfortable or not with the fact that (insert item) use information about your online activity and personal data to tailor advertisements or content to what interests you? (% EU)

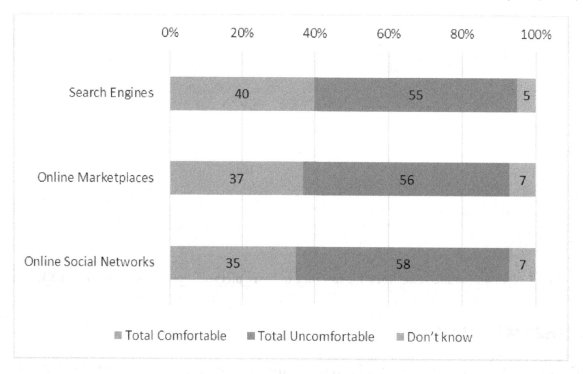

Figure 4. Most online platforms have terms and conditions which explain how you may use the website as well as the various legal requirements that websites must comply with. These include: privacy policy, cookie policy, and intellectual property rights such as copyright terms. Thinking about the terms and conditions on online platforms, which of the following best describes your situation? (% EU).

In sum, the results obtained regarding Google and Facebook are quite similar and validate the routinized use of their services while acknowledging their lack of transparency and the existence of trust concerns among their users. The scores attained by Facebook in this latter fields are lower than those of Google, a result that does not follow from the Cambridge Analytica scandal, which was reported in March 2018.

The routinized use of both platforms is illustrated in Figure 5, with a substantial proportion of respondents recognizing their daily use. At the same time, Figure 6 describes the concern of users regarding their personal information and the care they take to disclose just some basic details when registering data in their platform accounts. That is, the main services provided by both companies are consumed daily, with users trying to limit their exposure and the amount of information revealed. However, user do not seem to consider the substantial amount of information generated through the intensive use of both platforms. Thus, even though users recognize the privacy and trust drawbacks inherent to the use of these platforms, their substantial and widespread magnitude remains unaddressed.

The absence of transparency is emphasized in Figure 7, while privacy concerns arise in Figure 8. Interestingly enough, as Figure 8 illustrates, users acknowledge the existence of alternatives to Facebook and Google. Despite this fact, both platforms continue to be widely used on a daily basis. As can be inferred from the texts of Lanier (2014) and Schneier (2018), this behavior represents the acknowledgement of the fact that the information extraction (and preference manipulation) problem is widespread through the online platforms market, an expected consequence according to the theory of social costs developed by Kapp (1950) and extended by Frigato and Santos Arteaga (2019).

Figure 5. U.S. usage frequency of Google and Facebook services and products 2017

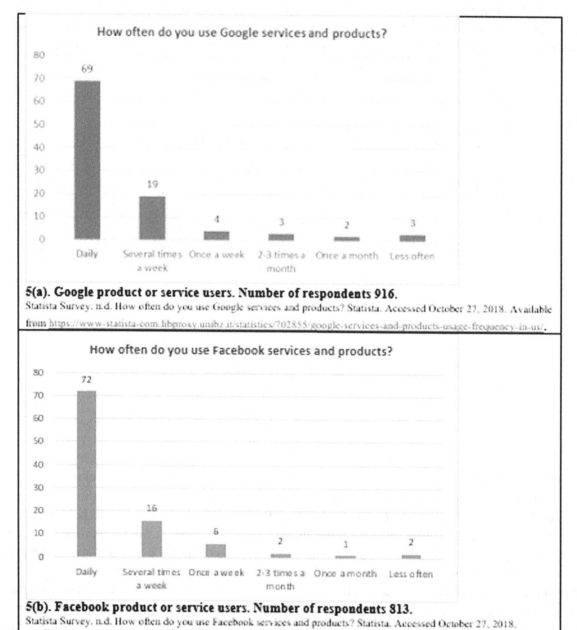

5(a). Google product or service users. Number of respondents 916.
Statista Survey. n.d. How often do you use Google services and products? Statista. Accessed October 27, 2018. Available from https://www-statista-com.libproxy.unibz.it/statistics/702855/google-services-and-products-usage-frequency-in-us/.

5(b). Facebook product or service users. Number of respondents 813.
Statista Survey. n.d. How often do you use Facebook services and products? Statista. Accessed October 27, 2018. Available from https://www-statista-com.libproxy.unibz.it/statistics/703901/facebook-services-and-products-usage-frequency-in-us/.

Figure 6. U.S. consumer personal data sharing within a Google or Facebook user account 2017

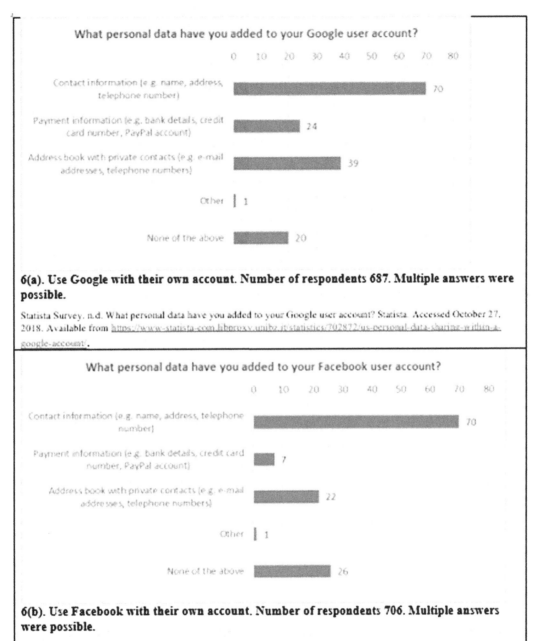

6(a). Use Google with their own account. Number of respondents 687. Multiple answers were possible.

Statista Survey. n.d. What personal data have you added to your Google user account? Statista. Accessed October 27, 2018. Available from https://www-statista-com.libproxy.unibz.it/statistics/702872/us-personal-data-sharing-within-a-google-account/.

6(b). Use Facebook with their own account. Number of respondents 706. Multiple answers were possible.

Statista Survey. n.d. What personal data have you added to your Facebook user account? Statista. Accessed October 27, 2018. Available from https://www-statista-com.libproxy.unibz.it/statistics/703905/us-personal-data-sharing-within-a-facebook-account/.

Figure 7. U.S. consumer opinion on Google and Facebook as a company 2017

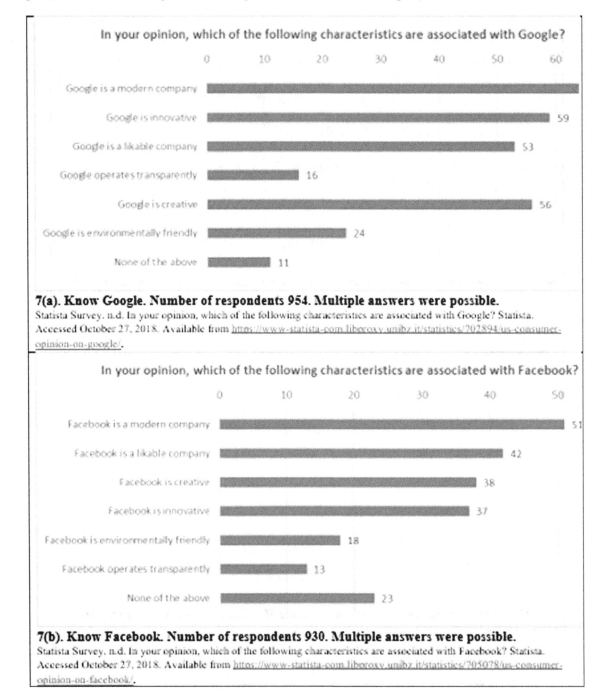

7(a). Know Google. Number of respondents 954. Multiple answers were possible.
Statista Survey. n.d. In your opinion, which of the following characteristics are associated with Google? Statista. Accessed October 27, 2018. Available from https://www-statista-com.liberoxy.unibz.it/statistics/702894/us-consumer-opinion-on-google/.

7(b). Know Facebook. Number of respondents 930. Multiple answers were possible.
Statista Survey. n.d. In your opinion, which of the following characteristics are associated with Facebook? Statista. Accessed October 27, 2018. Available from https://www-statista-com.liberoxy.unibz.it/statistics/705078/us-consumer-opinion-on-facebook/.

Figure 8. U.S. consumer perception of Google and Facebook as a company 2017

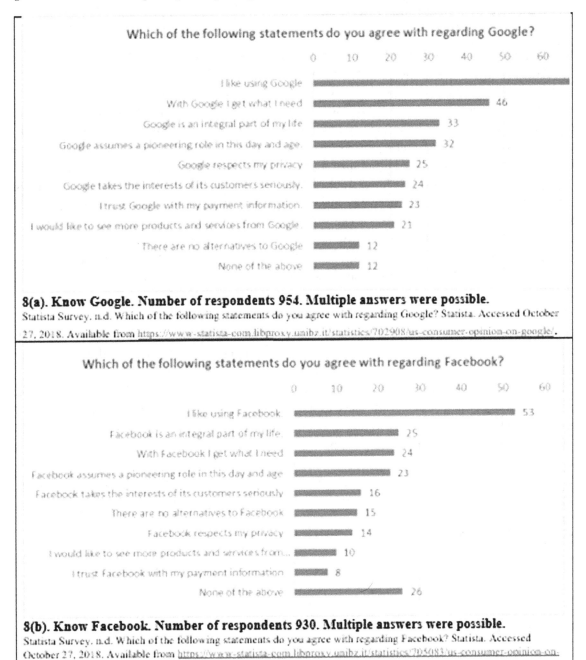

8(a). Know Google. Number of respondents 954. Multiple answers were possible.
Statista Survey. n.d. Which of the following statements do you agree with regarding Google? Statista. Accessed October 27, 2018. Available from https://www-statista-com.libproxy.unibz.it/statistics/702908/us-consumer-opinion-on-google/.

8(b). Know Facebook. Number of respondents 930. Multiple answers were possible.
Statista Survey. n.d. Which of the following statements do you agree with regarding Facebook? Statista. Accessed October 27, 2018. Available from https://www-statista-com.libproxy.unibz.it/statistics/705083/us-consumer-opinion-on-facebook/.

5. CONCLUSION: REGRETTABLE NECESSITIES AND PREFERENCE MANIPULATION

The main purpose of the current paper has been to illustrate how the capacity of two of the main online platforms (and information trading businesses) to retrieve and process information has been acknowledged and routinized across the European and U.S. populations. In this regard, the use of personal data to manipulate the preferences and decisions of DMs according to the interests of private businesses delivers a negative outcome to the users of these platforms, identifying them as regrettable necessities. One of the most problematic consequences arising from these facts is that once users understand the information extraction process and routinize it, they could agree to willingly provide the information required by online platforms, as is for example the case of Amazon highlighted by Bauman and Lyon

Amazon.com, however, also cheerfully makes consumers aware of how they are surveilled by others, through their Wish List feature (…) The Wish List also reminds us of how much people like to be watched; there is a kind of shoppers' scopophilia working here (Bauman and Lyon, 2013, 104).

It therefore follows that, while constituting an information processing and trading duopoly, Facebook and Google are far from being the only companies aiming at controlling information flows and the decisions of users

Surveillance is the business model of the Internet. It's not just the big companies like Facebook and Google watching everything we do online and selling advertising based on our behaviors; there's also a large and largely unregulated industry of data brokers that collect, correlate and then sell intimate personal data about our behaviors (Schneier 2018).

The influence of political technologies on voting environments – such as the 2008 U.S. presidential election – highlights their strategic relevance as information and motivation tools (Khansa et al., 2010). The academic literature has already warned about the capacity of online platforms to modify the preferences and attitudes of users within these settings (Epstein and Robertson, 2015; Liberini et al., 2018). In this regard, Marchal et al. (2018) analyzed 2.5 million tweets and 6,986 Facebook pages over a 30-day period leading up to the 2018 U.S. midterms. They found that the amount of junk news circulating in social media was actually greater than during the 2016 U.S. presidential election and that these news were being consumed by more mainstream conservative users. That is, while being fully aware of the capacity of online platforms to trade the personal information retrieved so as to modify their preferences and behavior, users continued to consume these regrettable necessities and share an increasing amount of information online.

REFERENCES

Bauman, Z., & Lyon, D. (2013). *Liquid Surveillance. A Conversation*. Cambridge, UK: Polity Press.

Burleigh, N. (2017, June 8). How Big Data mines personal info to craft fake news and manipulate voters. *Newsweek Magazine*. Retrieved from http://www.newsweek.com/2017/06/16/big-data-mines-personal-info-manipulate-voters-623131.html

De Wolf, R., Vanderhoven, E., Berendt, B., Pierson, J., & Schellens, T. (2017). Self-reflection on privacy research in social networking sites. *Behaviour & Information Technology*, *36*(5), 459–469. doi:10.1080/0144929X.2016.1242653

Epstein, R., & Robertson, R. E. (2015). The search engine manipulation effect (SEME) and its possible impact on the outcomes of elections. *Proceedings of the National Academy of Sciences of the United States of America, 112*(33), E4512–E4521. doi:10.1073/pnas.1419828112 PMID:26243876

European Commission (2016). Online Platforms. Special Eurobarometer 447, April 2016.

Financial times. (2013, March 15). A least-worst tax.

Frigato, P., & Santos Arteaga, F. J. (2019). *The Dark Places of Business Enterprise. Reinstating Social Costs in Institutional Economics*. London: Routledge. doi:10.4324/9781315208367

Garrahan, M. (2017, December 4). Google and Facebook dominance forecast to rise. Financial Times. Retrieved from https://www.ft.com/content/cf362186-d840-11e7-a039-c64b1c09b482

Golumbia, D. (2016). *The Politics of Bitcoin. Software as Right-Wing Extremism*. Minneapolis: University of Minnesota Press.

Hirsch, F. (1977). *Social Limits to Growth*. London: Routledge and Kegan Paul.

Kapp, K. W. (1950). *The Social Costs of Private Enterprise*. Cambridge, MA: Harvard University Press.

Khansa, L., James, T., & Cook, D. F. (2010). Acceptance, use, and influence of political technologies among youth voters in the 2008 US presidential election. *International Journal of E-Politics, 1*(4), 1–21. doi:10.4018/jep.2010100101

Kosinski, M., Stillwell, D., & Graepel, T. (2013). Private traits and attributes are predictable from digital records of human behavior. *Proceedings of the National Academy of Sciences of the United States of America, 110*(15), 5802–5805. doi:10.1073/pnas.1218772110 PMID:23479631

Kourouthanassis, P., Lekakos, G., & Gerakis, V. (2015). Should I stay or should I go? The moderating effect of self-image congruity and trust on social networking continued use. *Behaviour & Information Technology, 34*(2), 190–203. doi:10.1080/0144929X.2014.948489

Lanier, J. (2014). *Who Owns the Future?* Simon & Schuster.

Lazaric, N. (2000). The role of routines, rules and habits in collective learning: Some epistemological and ontological considerations. *European Journal of Economic and Social Systems, 14*(2), 157–171. doi:10.1051/ejess:2000115

Liberini, F., Redoano, M., Russo, A., Cuevas, A., & Cuevas, R. (2018). Politics in the Facebook era: Evidence from the 2016 US presidential elections. University of Warwick Centre for Competitive Advantage in the Global Economy.

Lyon, D. (2006). 9 / 11, Synopticon, and Scopophilia: Watching and Being Watched. In K. D. Haggerty & R. Ericson (Eds.), *The new Politics of Surveillance and Visibility* (pp. 35–54). Toronto, London: University of Toronto Press.

Marchal, N., Neudert, L. M., Kollanyi, B., Howard, P. N., & Kelly, J. (2018). *Polarization, partisanship and junk news consumption on social media during the 2018 US midterm elections*. Oxford, UK: Project on Computational Propaganda.

Pariser, E. (2012). *The Filter Bubble: What The Internet Is Hiding From You*. London: Penguin. doi:10.3139/9783446431164

Perkins, D. N. (2009). The five languages of war. In D. C. Berliner & H. Kupermintz (Eds.), *Fostering Change in Institutions, Environments, and People: A festschrift in Honor of Gavriel Salomon* (pp. 171–192). New York: Routledge.

Schneier, B. (2014). *Data and Goliath: The Hidden Battles to Collect your Data and Control Your World*. New York: W. W. Norton & Company.

Schneier, B. (2018, June 1). Data protection laws are shining a needed light on a secretive industry. The Guardian. Retrieved from https://www.theguardian.com/commentisfree/2018/jun/01/gdpr-data-protection-laws-shine-light-industry

Schwartz, B. (2004). *The paradox of choice: Why more is less*. New York: Ecco Press.

Statista. (2017). Dossier: Google, Apple, Facebook, and Amazon (GAFA).

Ward, A. (2014). Social tyranny and democratic governance in the information age. *International Journal of E-Politics*, *5*(2), 32–52. doi:10.4018/ijep.2014040103

Wu, T. (2016). *The Attention Merchants: The Epic Scramble to Get Inside Our Heads*. Knopf.

ENDNOTES

[1] The relationship between routines, rules and habits is not straightforward and differs depending on the formal approach considered (Lazaric, 2000). We focus here on Veblen's evolutionary approach to routines and their relationship with habits. In particular, "'habits' are individual bents based on larger institutions that partly determine the individual cognitive schemes and routines at a given moment. These habits are transformed and evolve through a range of historic events that change them. Consequently, for Veblen, routines are defined between instinct and tradition and are a certain way of doing things at a given time. For Veblen, both the cognitive aspect and the dynamic nature of 'habits' are important. This enables habits to be distinguished from a purely sociological approach, describing the social structures of society" (Lazaric 2000, pp. 159-160).

[2] The list of countries included in the study follows: Austria, Belgium, Bulgaria, Croatia, Republic of Cyprus, Czech Republic, Denmark, Estonia, France, Finland, Germany, Greece, Hungary, Ireland, Italy, Latvia, Lithuania, Luxembourg, Malta, The Netherlands, Poland, Portugal, Romania, Slovakia, Slovenia, Spain, Sweden, United Kingdom.

This research was previously published in the International Journal of Strategic Decision Sciences (IJSDS), 11(1); pages 21-34, copyright year 2020 by IGI Publishing (an imprint of IGI Global).

Chapter 7
The Effects of Virtual Likes on Self–Esteem:
A Discussion of Receiving and Viewing Likes on Social Media

Malinda Desjarlais
Mount Royal University, Canada

ABSTRACT

Social networking sites offer opportunities for users to express themselves and receive immediate feedback in the form of virtual likes. Adolescents place a great deal of value on the number of likes, regarding them as indicators of peer acceptance and support. Since peer feedback and social comparison are integral to adolescents' self-evaluations, the aim of the current chapter is to determine whether self-esteem is sensitive to the number of likes associated with their own (peer feedback) and others' posts (social comparison). The synthesis of literature indicates that self-esteem is responsive to indicators of one's value to others as well as the value of others, supporting the sociometer and social comparison theories. Indications of liking online serve to enhance self-esteem, whereas rejection deflates it. In addition, seeing others get many likes negatively impacts viewers' self-esteem. The gaps in the literature are discussed and future research is suggested.

INTRODUCTION

Social media has become ubiquitous in the daily life of adolescents and young adults, providing a forum for youths to interact and make connections with peers, practice social skills, observe others, and to provide and receive feedback (Boyd & Ellison, 2007). Facebook, Instagram, and Snapchat are consistently among the top social networking sites in North America (Greenwood, Perrin, & Duggan, 2016; McKinnon, 2015; Smith, & Anderson, 2018). Users create online profiles containing personal information about the self, in the form of images and/or textual content, that are broadcasted to other social networking members. Not only do users share information with a much larger audience compared to interactions in real life,

DOI: 10.4018/978-1-6684-6307-9.ch007

but they also are open to immediate feedback from the larger audience in the form of quantitative (virtual likes which are represented as a thumbs up symbol or heart) and qualitative (comments) remarks. Overall, social networking sites have the potential to influence psychosocial functioning.

As adolescence is characterized as a developmental period of increased focus on the self, peer feedback and social comparison become integral to adolescents' self-evaluations (Harter, 1999). In effect, adolescents' self-esteem may be sensitive to the number of likes they get in response to their social media posts as well as the number of likes that their peers may acquire. Therefore, the primary objective of the current chapter is to outline research regarding the potential enhancing and adverse effects one's own virtual likes as well as other posters' virtual likes may have on users' self-esteem. First, the chapter will describe theoretical perspectives of self-esteem to support the potential influence of liking indicators on self-esteem. Second, a description of the virtual like is provided, including what likes may stand for, and the types of images that are most likely to elicit a greater number of likes. Third, the author will synthesize the literature that examines (1) the relationship between self-esteem and the number of likes users receive for their information shared on social networking sites, and then (ii) the relationship between self-esteem and seeing how many responses others have received for their posts. Finally, the gaps in the literature will be discussed and future research suggested. Overall, this chapter may aid in the advancement of research, increase public awareness, facilitate policy development, and expand clinical applications related to protecting or enhancing self-esteem among social media users.

SELF-ESTEEM BACKGROUND

Self-esteem can be conceptualized as the extent to which individuals accept, approve of, or value themselves. While state self-esteem represents the momentary fluctuations in one's feelings about him/herself, trait self-esteem captures one's global appraisal of his/her value (Leary, 1999). Researchers agree that low self-esteem is associated with a variety of psychological challenges, including depression, loneliness, substance abuse, and academic failure (Henriksen, Ranøyen, Indredavik & Stenseng, 2017; Leary, 1999; Rosenberg, Schooler, & Schoenbach, 1989; Silverstone & Salsali, 2003). According to Argyle (2008), the following four major factors influence self-esteem: the reactions of others, comparison with others, one's social roles, and one's identification with social roles. The current chapter focuses on the first two factors, which are most relevant for the effect of virtual likes on self-esteem.

One theoretical perspective that highlights the importance of others' evaluations for self-esteem is the sociometer theory (Leary & Baumeister, 2000). According to the sociometer theory, humans have a natural drive to maintain significant interpersonal relationships, which stems from the species survival being dependent on individuals belonging to groups. To facilitate knowledge of group belongingness, humans may have evolved to develop a psychological mechanism that would continuously monitor the social environment for cues regarding the degree to which they were valued and accepted by others. Thus, self-esteem is a psychological meter that monitors the quality of one's relationships with others. Individuals tend to feel good about themselves when experiencing acceptance and conversely feel negative about themselves when experiencing rejection. The sociometer is particularly sensitive to changes in the social environment so that individuals can react to improve situations in their favor. While state self-esteem captures the momentary fluctuations in perceived social inclusion based on others' evaluations, trait self-esteem is an overall appraisal of value, or the degree to which the individual views oneself as a sort of person who is accepted by others (Leary, 1999; Leary & Baumeister, 2000).

In addition to others' evaluations, individuals base judgements about themselves on how they compare to those deemed similar to themselves (Festinger, 1954). When there is no objective measure available, social comparison helps to establish one's standing, and reduce ambiguity about what is considered successful, acceptable, beautiful, and so on (Brown, Ferris, Heller, & Keeping, 2007; Verduyn, Ybarra, Résibois, Jonides, & Kross, 2017). Social comparison provides individuals with the ability to gather information to evaluate their own capacities and characteristics, so they can develop stable and accurate evaluations about the self. Self-evaluation depends on how an individual compares oneself with other people, with a distinction made between upward and downward comparisons (Suls, Martin, & Wheeler, 2002). Upward social comparison refers to instances where the target(s) of social comparison is perceived as doing better than oneself on some dimension. Upward comparisons may serve to enhance the self by eliciting behaviours to improve oneself, such that people are motivated to change the self to be more like the comparison standard (Higgins, 1987; Lockwood & Kunda, 1997). However, upward comparisons more often lead to feelings of inadequacy, jealousy, or negative affect, the development of a negative self-image, and decreases in well-being (Michalos, 1985; Pyszczynski, Greenberg, & LaPrelle, 1985). On the other hand, downward social comparison refers to the situation where the individual perceives the self as more fortunate than the target(s) of social comparison, which is typically associated with a more positive self-image, as well as enhanced well-being and feelings of self-worth (Suls et al., 2002).

Within the following sections, a discussion of the link between self-esteem and both social networking members' responses and social comparison in the context of virtual likes is presented.

AN INTRODUCTION TO VIRTUAL LIKES

Social networking sites offer opportunities for users to express to viewers who one is, including their likes and dislikes, values and opinions, and receive immediate feedback from friends, acquaintances, and strangers (Niera & Barber 2014; Spies Shapiro & Margolin, 2014). When viewing others' shared information on social media, such as images, status updates, or tweets, users can respond to the post through comments or can provide, with the push of a single button, a virtual like (symbolized by the thumbs up emoticon on Facebook or a heart on Instagram). As studies show, liking is popular on social networking sites with adolescents on average clicking the like button several times a week (Utz, 2015) or an average of 2.3 likes per day, a function used more than leaving comments (Wenninger, Krasnova, & Buxmann, 2014). Users are even more likely to receive than give likes (Hampton, Goulet, Marlow, & Rainie, 2012).

What does a virtual like convey? Virtual likes represent a "mixture of active participation and passive following" (Wenninger et al., 2014, p. 6). On the one hand, likes may simply provide the poster with an acknowledgement that someone has read or seen the post (Bosch, 2013 as cited in Wenninger et al., 2014). Users click the like button for entertaining posts just as often as they do for boring posts (Barash, Ducheneaut, Isaacs, & Bellotti, 2010). On the other hand, adolescents appear to place much value on likes (Sarita & Suleeman, 2017), and thus despite their effortless nature to give and get, likes can mean something to users (Wohn, Carr, & Hayes, 2016). Across 24 in-depth interviews with adolescent girls in Singapore, all participants counted their number of likes and believed that the number of likes acquired provided informative feedback from peers, regarding them as more important than the comments they received (Chua & Chang, 2016). Youth seem to actively seek this type of feedback (Valkenburg, Schouten, & Peter, 2005).

Researchers also argue that likes are a method of showcasing one's affirmation and support for one another (Metzler & Scheithauer, 2017; Scissors, Burke, & Wengrovitz, 2016; Zhang, 2017). Through likes, users acquire an understanding of the type of posts that are accepted by their social network (Jong & Drummond, 2013). There is strong evidence that the number of likes is perceived as an indicator of a person's popularity (Fox & Moreland, 2015; Marshall, Lefringhausen, & Ferenczi, 2015; Tajuddin, Hassan, Ahmad, 2013). For example, in a qualitative study of 28 middle school aged girls, there was consensus that likes represent an expression of personal approval for the shared information, and that the number of likes was a direct indicator of popularity (Jong & Drummond, 2016). One participant even claimed that over a hundred likes signifies that the poster is popular among his/her peers. In addition, getting likes or comments from social networking members can translate into perceived social support (Zhang, 2017). Cotten (2008) claimed that the positive feelings associated with receiving likes reinforce a positive relationship between the giver and receiver of the likes. In support of this claim, the earning of likes has been positively linked to building social capital and bonding (Lee, Kim, & Ahn, 2014).

Which social media posts elicit more virtual likes? Some of the factors that influence the number of likes received include image type, number of likes already received and valence of the post. First, images with faces are more attention-grabbing. A recent study demonstrated that individuals were more likely to like a post containing photos, whereas they were more likely to comment on posts containing text (Kim & Yang, 2017). Among photos, ones that contain faces were more popular. After controlling for amount of activity on social networking sites and number of followers, images with faces were 38% more likely to receive likes and 32% more likely to receive comments than photos depicting other types of content (Bakhshi, Shamma, & Gilbert, 2014). Second, people in general conform to their peers, and this is no different on social media. Adolescents were more likely to endorse a photo they believed was posted on a social media site if that photo already received a high number of likes in comparison to posts with a lower number of likes (Sherman, Payton, Hernandez, Greenfield, & Dapretto, 2016).

Finally, most social networking users share positive rather than negative information about themselves (Bazarova, Choi, Sosik, Cosley, & Whitlock, 2015; Utz, 2015). Positive information has been found to elicit likes rather than comments or getting shared on Facebook (Kim & Yang, 2017). While there is evidence that positive posts receive more likes than negative posts (Burke & Develin, 2016; Forest & Wood, 2012), the relationship between valence of posts and likes depends on one's level of self-esteem. Specifically, for users with low self-esteem, greater positivity of status updates was associated with greater social reward (i.e., combined number of likes and comments from friends); however, users with high self-esteem received greater social reward for their more negative status updates than for their less negative posts (Forest & Wood, 2012). The researchers suggested that friends of participants with low self-esteem rewarded positive posts with more validation and attention to encourage this atypical behavior (Forest & Wood, 2012).

In sum, virtual likes may be associated with a variety of meanings, some more significant than the next. However, adolescents tend to agree that likes provide valuable information regarding social status and social support. Therefore, it is conceivable that a simple click could have important implications for self-esteem.

VIRTUAL LIKES AND SELF-ESTEEM

Taking into account the rate at which individuals are exposed to feedback online from friends and strangers, and that adolescents (who are the heaviest users of social media) are most susceptible to positive and negative feedback, the effect of adolescents' interactions on social networking sites on their self-esteem demands attention. The following synthesizes relevant literature pertaining to the effects on self-esteem as a function of (1) the number of likes received, and then (2) the number of likes others have received. The aforementioned theoretical perspectives regarding self-esteem will be applied in each context.

The Number of Likes Users Themselves Receive

As discussed earlier, sociometer theory indicates that one of the primary determinants of self-esteem involves the perceived reactions of other people. On social networking sites, the perceived reactions can be captured through the number of likes received on one's posts. As an indicator of peer attention and one's position in their peer group, there are standards regarding the number of likes adolescents should receive to demonstrate their above-average status (Chua & Chang, 2016). Therefore, the sociometer theory predicts that a large number likes (a situation involving positive feedback) would increase self-esteem, whereas little or no likes (considered as negative feedback) would decrease self-esteem.

A few studies have reported findings counter to the predictions based on sociometer theory. Null and negative relationships between the number of likes acquired and psychological outcomes were found (Burke & Kraut, 2016; Coulthard & Ogden, 2018; Metzler & Scheithauer, 2017). For example, in order to examine the effects of social media activity, number of likes received in relation to activity and the combination of these factors for changes in loneliness, Deters and Mehl (2013) asked some participants to post more status updates than they usually do for one week. Compared to the control group (who did not adjust their status update frequency), participants who increased posting behaviour reported significantly lower loneliness regardless of the number of likes and comments received. These findings suggest a lack of effect for the number of likes received for psychosocial outcomes over and above active participation online.

However, the majority of research does support the number of likes as having esteem-enhancing effects. Both correlational studies (Burrow & Rainone, 2017; Gallagher, 2017; Lup, Trub, & Rosenthal, 2015) and experimental studies (Burrow & Rainone, 2017) support a positive association between the number likes received and increases in self-esteem. People with high self-esteem get a momentary boost in esteem every time they receive likes for their posts (Rutledge, 2013). Narcissists also get self-verified from the likes and positive comments they receive when posting selfies to social media (Barry, Doucette, Loflin, Rivera-Hudson, & Herrington, 2017). Receiving likes for social networking site posts results in increases in feelings of social acceptance (e.g., having opinions respected by others, feeling understood, and feeling accepted), which in turn is related to increased levels of self-esteem (Wang, Nie, Li, & Zhou, 2018).

The esteem-enhancing effects are also recognized by users themselves. Radovic, Gmelin, Stein, and Miller (2017) interviewed 23 adolescents regarding their social media use and how this may influence psychological distress. One particularly evident theme was the use of social media for social approval and social comparison. Adolescents expressed how the number of likes provided information regarding level of popularity, such that getting more likes increases self-esteem and conversely not getting likes decreases self-esteem. This resulted in some adolescents posting images they were not comfortable with, but that typically get likes, in order to obtain recognition. Similar themes were evident in Jong and Drummond's (2016) interviews with middle school aged girls, with likes also regarded as an indicator of popularity and having esteem-enhancing potential.

Similar conclusions regarding the link between feedback and self-esteem have been formed among researchers who examined qualitative instead of quantitative feedback. Similar to likes, positive comments have an esteem-enhancing effect (Frison & Eggermont, 2015; Greitemeyer, Mügge, & Bollermann 2014; Thomaes et al., 2010; Valkenburg, Peter, & Schouten, 2006; Yang & Brown 2016). These effects stand for comments from both friends and acquaintances (Valkenburg, Koutamanis, & Vossen, 2017). Negative comments, in contrast, result in decreases in self-esteem (Thomaes et al., 2010; Valkenburg et al., 2006). According to Valkenburg and colleagues (2006), valence of comments was more important for self-esteem than the simple frequency of comments. Although about three-quarters of adolescent participants reported always or predominantly receiving positive feedback on their profiles, a small percentage (7%) did predominately or always receive negative feedback (Valkenburg et al., 2006). Therefore, while most users may fair well from social media use, there appears to be a small group of users who may experience aversive effects on their self-esteem from posting on social networking sites.

Overall, the aforementioned literature indicates that feedback from peers on social media is influential to self-evaluations. However, receiving likes from peers may not be equally important across users. Findings from both a correlational and an experimental study indicated that the impact of the number of likes received for a post on self-esteem was dependent on one's sense of purpose (Burrow & Rainone, 2017). In their experiment, undergraduate students took a photograph of themselves and were told that the experimenter uploaded their image to a social networking site for other users to view and have a chance to like their image. Participants were given randomized feedback. They were told that compared to pilot testing, they received an average number of likes, above the average number or below the average number. For those low in purpose, receiving a greater number of likes was associated with enhanced self-esteem, but had no effect on self-esteem for those high in purpose. Results were identical for their correlational study, where participants self-reported the average number of likes received on their profile pictures. Burrow and Rainone (2017) suggested that having a high sense of purpose inhibits activation of neural regions involved in reward processing, and thus, sense of purpose lessens responsiveness to likes as social rewards.

While getting many likes may enhance self-esteem, conversely, failing to acquire likes may have aversive effects on self-esteem. Correlational research has supported the negative effects of not receiving any feedback. Failing to get responses such as likes and comments from Facebook friends increased feelings of stress among adolescents (Park et al., 2015), and slightly decreased feelings of connectedness (Utz, 2015). Self-esteem was also adversely affected when participants were bothered if they did not receive as many likes as they thought they were going to on their posts (Gallagher, 2017) and when they did not receive replies in a timely fashion (Taylor & Harper, 2003). Users themselves also acknowledge the negative effects of not accruing likes. It was evident among interviews with middle school aged girls that the lack of feedback from other social networking site users could have a negative impact on self-esteem (Jong & Drummond, 2016). Specifically, likes served as an indicator of popularity, and girls had a tendency to feel disheartened if they received no feedback at all. Some mentioned feeling, or potentially feeling, that they were not liked, upset, depressed, or insecure. Girls also expressed how the need for responses to their posts and validation through likes was relatively immediate, and that they would take down posts that did not receive any likes after a short period of time, as this was perceived as negative feedback. These results resemble findings regarding offline interactions, where the ostracism people experienced after not receiving any feedback led to a decrease in one's sense of belonging and self-esteem (Smith & Williams, 2004).

In sum, there is much empirical support for the esteem-enhancing and esteem-reducing effects of virtual likes on social media. While a high number of likes received on one's social media posts increases feelings of acceptance and self-esteem, esteem-decreasing effects result from a lack of peer feedback.

The Number of Likes Peers Receive

According to social comparison theory, comparing oneself with others provides individuals with information to evaluate their own capacities and characteristics in order to evaluate oneself. The outcomes of self-evaluation depend on whether individuals compare themselves with others who fair better (upward social comparison) or fair worse (downward social comparison). Social networking users share information with one another via pictures and text-based posts, which can make them an upward or downward comparison target to other users (Vogel, Rose, Roberts, & Eckles, 2014). This information is also paired with information about their social network, including comments, replies, likes, and approval of their shared content. Feedback on others' posts can provide viewers with information about what is accepted by the social group and act as a point of reference to evaluate oneself. In line with social comparison theory, seeing others obtain a large number of likes would likely result in upward social comparison and thus decreases in self-esteem. Whereas, others' posts that receive a small number of likes may result in downward social comparison and thus increases in self-esteem.

Within the literature, much attention has been devoted to examining the relationship between two broad categories of activities on social networking sites (passive and active usage) and subjective well-being (see Verduyn et al., 2017 for a critical review). Associated with enhanced self-esteem (Schimmack & Diener, 2003), subjective well-being involves an evaluation of one's life and is partially contingent on life circumstances and activities (Diener, 2009; Lyubomirsky, Sheldon, & Schkade, 2005). Passive usage refers to the browsing of social networking members' posts without direct engagement with the posters (Verduyn et al., 2017). During passive usage, individuals are exposed to both personal attributes conveyed within profiles, pictures, and status updates as well as the corresponding comments and virtual likes. Although research involving the broad category of passive usage does not tease apart the differential effects of social comparison for personal and social content, it does shed like on the prevalence of upward social comparison taking place in the virtual world and its effects. Several studies, including cross-sectional, longitudinal and experimental, have linked passive usage of social networking sites with decreases in subjective well-being (Fardouly, Diedrichs, Vartanian, & Halliwell, 2015; Tandoc, Ferrucci, & Duffy, 2015), regardless of level of self-esteem (Verduyn et al., 2015). This relationship is explained by upward comparisons and increases in envy (Muise, Christofides, & Desmarais, 2009; Tandoc et al., 2015; Verduyn et al., 2015; Vogel et al., 2014). Surprisingly, downward comparisons on social media are not associated with any changes to self-esteem (Vogel et al., 2014).

Focusing on virtual likes, a person who has an active social network (receiving numerous likes and comments) may be an upward comparison target in terms of popularity (Kim & Lee, 2011; Vitak & Ellison, 2013). Peer competition regarding who has the most likes can ensue, which has the potential for important implications on self-esteem. In support of these claims, adolescents admit to feeling worse about themselves when seeing others getting many likes on their post or picture (Radovic et al., 2017). Furthermore, participants report lower self-esteem after viewing a target's profile that contains a larger number of likes, regardless of the content of the profiles (Vogel et al., 2014). Specifically, whether the target's profile showcased engagement in healthy behaviors (a potential upward comparison) or unhealthy behaviours (a potential downward comparison), a large number of likes on the profile was associated with lower self-esteem ratings among participants compared to those who saw the same profiles but with a small number of likes. Moreover, participants also reported a greater discrepancy between the target person and themselves on a variety of positive attributes when the target received a high number of likes for the posted content. In contrast, when the target person had few likes, participants viewed themselves and the target person relatively similar.

Not only does social endorsement lead to behavioral responses, but the number of likes also influences neural responses. Adolescents underwent fMRI while viewing photographs ostensibly submitted to Instagram, which depicted few or many likes. When high likes were presented with a photo, there was greater brain activity in areas that implicated attention, social cognition and social memories. Increased activation suggests that adolescents may have scanned images more attentively, with popular photos resulting in qualitatively different responses compared to less popular images (Sherman et al., 2016).

Collectively, empirical findings indicate that when people receive greater response from social media members, viewers perceive them as doing better on some domain, such as social acceptance, which typically leads to feelings of inferiority. The upward comparisons when attending to others' virtual likes on social media result in decreases in self-esteem, supporting the predictions based on social comparison theory. On the other hand, when others receive few likes, the viewers perceive the target as similar to themselves rather than inferior, and thus self-esteem is not affected.

FUTURE RESEARCH DIRECTIONS

Social media has altered the way in which peers interact with one another. Although offline interactions provided opportunities for social comparison and feedback, social networking sites have increased these opportunities enormously. While attention has been devoted to understanding the link between social media and psychosocial outcomes, the research is still in its infancy. Some of the next steps required to advance knowledge include a consideration of more complex relationships between social media activity and self-esteem, as well as an exploration of the longitudinal implications of posting optimized or false information in order to receive likes.

First, when examining the link between number of likes and self-esteem, most researchers have explored whether the number of likes people receive in response to their social media posts influences self-esteem. All of research in this area has examined momentary fluctuations in state self-esteem, and thus is unknown whether these changes have more long-term effects. Furthermore, it is conceivable that the relationship between feedback and self-esteem is cyclical. Forest and Wood (2012) found that young adults with lower levels of self-esteem express less positively and more negativity in their social media posts compared to peers with higher levels of self-esteem. These negative posts received less social reward (number of likes and comments from social networks) compared to their positive posts. Furthermore, individuals with lower levels of self-esteem are more likely to think that likes are meaningful and consequently feel upset with they do not receive an appropriate number (Scissors et al., 2016). Taking these findings together, it is plausible that the posts from individuals with low levels of self-esteem may elicit fewer likes due to their negativity, which in turn may further decrease (or at least not improve) their self-esteem. As such, they may continue to post more negativity, and continue to receive a small number of likes. Additional research is necessary to examine the validity of this proposed cyclical relationship between self-esteem and the number of likes received.

Second, the anonymity of social media makes it particularly attractive for selective self-presentation (Valkenburg & Peter, 2011). On the Internet, adolescents have control over the information they wish to present - controlling what they want others to know about them and creating opportunities to present themselves in the best light possible. In order to elicit esteem-enhancing reactions, social networking users may attempt to manage the impressions others form and their evaluations by presenting oneself to others in a positive and socially desirable way online (Hart, 2017). Some users do engage in like-seeking behaviours, including using filters or hashtags, buying likes, changing one's appearance completely (Duman, Maxwell-Smith, Davis, & Giulietti, 2017), or posting semi-naked selfies (Mascheroni, Vincent, & Jimenez, 2015). In a qualitative study of social media use, adolescent girls indicated that editing photographs and making oneself look good on social media has become a necessity (Chua & Chang, 2016). All girls admitted to using filters and editing photos with software to, for example, brighten the skin, conceal facial imperfections, and enhance colours. One-third of the girls went so far as to change their facial features, including modifying their face line, and altering the size of their eyes and noses. According to one teen, the purpose of putting so much effort into perfecting their image is so posters can share pictures that meet the standard and to impress their friends (Chua & Chang, 2016). On the one hand, researchers have argued that frequent likes may affirm the ideal self that one presented online and make an individual feel good about him/herself, thereby increasing self-esteem (Bazarova & Choi, 2014; Shin, Kim, Im, & Chong, 2017). In contrast, others have reported that it is the honest self-presentation that enhances perceived social support and thereby has positive implications for subjective well-being (Kim & Lee, 2011). Moreover, high levels of self-discrepancy have been linked to low self-esteem (Moretti & Higgins, 1990). The question that arises then is, how do the likes received for optimized or deceptive information and uncomfortable images impact self-esteem and identity development for adolescents? While receiving many likes signals popularity and social acceptance, the person who is deemed popular in the photo may not be an accurate depiction of the poster in real life. When the online self may not be attainable in real life the receipt of many likes may have detrimental rather than enhancing effects on self-esteem. Moreover, greater discrepancies between the real self and the well-liked virtual self may be especially detrimental to adolescents, who are amid exploring their identities and forming a self-concept - a hypothesis that warrants testing.

RECOMMENDATIONS

As social media users become younger and younger, it is important to provide youth with education about the potential consequences of social media. Policy makers, parents, educators, clinicians and social media providers themselves should educate the public on how to use social media to protect self-esteem. According to Bos, Muris, Mulkens, and Schaalma (2006), "self-esteem enhancement requires the formation and acceptance of realistic goals in domains that are personally relevant, and a supportive social environment" (p. 11). Based on this view and the literature discussed in the current chapter, the following should be considered in educational communication on adaptive social media usage:

1. A virtual like is not always a message about likeability. Although often interpreted as a sign of affirmation for the poster, a virtual like can stand for an acknowledgement of viewed content and

can be easily manipulated by valence or type of post, for instance. With the like button being pressed as often for boring as interesting posts, the credibility of a like should be questioned. Even if virtual likes provide some information regarding popularity, self-worth should never be defined by a single factor. Instead, users should consider more important domains, including their positive interpersonal relationships, and emphasize domains in which they are competent and skillful. It should be noted, however, that enhancing perceptions of one's competence comes with challenges, as those with low self-worth tend to focus on failures and attribute them to internal factors, and they tend to be resistant to feedback that goes against their self-concept (Harter, 1999).

2. A vast majority of American youths (88% of 18- to 29-years-old) surveyed in 2018 indicated that they use some form of social media (Smith & Anderson, 2018). Although taking a break from social media, even for just a week, is associated with enhanced well-being (Tromholt, 2016), given its prevalent use, it is impractical to suggest that adolescents quit social media entirely. Instead, a more practical solution would be to have children and adolescents filter particular content that make them feel particularly upset or threatened. Facebook currently offers users the option to "snooze posts for 30 days", which provides opportunities for youth to temporary hide content without breaking ties with social networking members completely. In addition, adolescents should monitor their social media usage in order to avoid excessive passive usage in general.

3. Social support is a key factor for improving self-esteem (Harter, 1999). If adolescents do interpret a low number likes for their social media content as an indication of low social support, loved ones can help the youth focus on contexts where social support is strong.

CONCLUSION

Despite being an effortless gesture from social networking members, likes are perceived as being meaningful, especially for adolescents. It is clear across the current social media literature that individuals' self-esteem is responsive to indicators of one's value to others as well as the value of others, supporting the sociometer and social comparison theories in virtual environments. With few exceptions, indications of liking online serve to enhance self-esteem, whereas rejection deflates it. In addition, seeing others get a large number of likes negatively impacts viewers' self-esteem, while little likes have no effect. Taking into account the potential rate at which adolescents receive (or do not receive) such feedback from peers and the importance of high self-esteem to psychosocial outcomes, researchers, clinicians, educators, and parents should not regard likes as just a number.

ACKNOWLEDGMENT

This research received no specific grant from any funding agency in the public, commercial, or not-for-profit sectors.

REFERENCES

Argyle, M. (2008). *Social encounters: Contributions to social interaction.* Piscataway, NJ: Aldine Transaction.

Bakhshi, S., Shamma, D. A., & Gilbert, E. (2014, April). Faces engage us: photos with faces attract more likes and comments on Instagram. *Proceedings of the SIGCHI Conference on Human Factors in Computing Systems*, 965-974. 10.1145/2556288.2557403

Barash, V., Ducheneaut, N., Isaacs, E., & Bellotti, V. (2010). Faceplant: Impression (mis)management in Facebook status updates. *Proceedings of the Fourth International AAAI Conference on Weblogs and Social Media*, 207-210. Retrieved from https://www.aaai.org/ocs/index.php/ICWSM/ ICWSM10/ paper/ viewFile/1465/1858/

Barry, C. T., Doucette, H., Loflin, D. C., Rivera-Hudson, N., & Herrington, L. L. (2017). "Let me take a selfie": Associations between self-photography, narcissism, and self-esteem. *Psychology of Popular Media Culture*, *6*(1), 48–60. doi:10.1037/ppm0000089

Bazarova, N. N., & Choi, Y. H. (2014). Self-disclosure in social media: Extending the functional approach to disclosure motivations and characteristics on social network sites. *Journal of Communication*, *64*(4), 635–657. doi:10.1111/jcom.12106

Bazarova, N. N., Choi, Y. H., Sosik, V. S., Cosley, D., & Whitlock, J. (2015, February). Social sharing of emotions on Facebook: Channel differences, satisfaction, and replies. In *Proceedings of the 18th ACM conference on computer supported cooperative work & social computing*, (pp. 154-164). ACM. Retrieved from https://dl.acm.org/citation.cfm?id=2675297

Boyd, D. M., & Ellison, N. B. (2007). Social network sites: Definition, history, and scholarship. *Journal of computer-mediated Communication, 13*(1), 210-230. doi:10.1111/j.1083-6101.2007.00393.x

Brown, D. J., Ferris, D. L., Heller, D., & Keeping, L. M. (2007). Antecedents and consequences of the frequency of upward and downward social comparisons at work. *Organizational Behavior and Human Decision Processes*, *102*(1), 59–75. doi:10.1016/j.obhdp.2006.10.003

Burke, M., & Develin, M. (2016, February). Once more with feeling: Supportive responses to social sharing on Facebook. In *Proceedings of the 19th ACM Conference on Computer-Supported Cooperative Work & Social Computing* (pp. 1462-1474). ACM. Retrieved from https://dl.acm.org/citation.cfm?id=2835199

Burke, M., & Kraut, R. E. (2016). The relationship between Facebook use and well-being depends on communication type and tie strength. *Journal of Computer-Mediated Communication*, *21*(4), 265–281. doi:10.1111/jcc4.12162

Burrow, A. L., & Rainone, N. (2017). How many likes did I get?: Purpose moderates links between positive social media feedback and self-esteem. *Journal of Experimental Social Psychology*, *69*, 232–236. doi:10.1016/j.jesp.2016.09.005

Chua, T. H. H., & Chang, L. (2016). Follow me and like my beautiful selfies: Singapore teenage girls' engagement in self-presentation and peer comparison on social media. *Computers in Human Behavior*, *55*, 190–197. doi:10.1016/j.chb.2015.09.011

Cotten, S. R. (2008). Students' technology use and the impacts on well-being. *New Directions for Student Services*, *124*(124), 55–70. doi:10.1002s.295

Coulthard, N., & Ogden, J. (2018). The impact of posting selfies and gaining feedback ('likes') on the psychological wellbeing of 16-25 year olds: An experimental study. *Cyberpsychology (Brno)*, *12*(2), 4. doi:10.5817/CP2018-2-4

Deters, F. G., & Mehl, M. R. (2013). Does posting Facebook status updates increase or decrease loneliness? An online social networking experiment. *Social Psychological & Personality Science*, *4*(5), 579–586. doi:10.1177/1948550612469233 PMID:24224070

Diener, E. (2009). Happiness. In M. R. Leary, & R. H. Hoyle (Eds.), *Handbook of individual differences in social behavior* (pp. 147–160). New York, NY: Guilford.

Duman, T. M., Maxwell-Smith, M., Davis, J. P., & Giulietti, P. A. (2017). Lying or longing for likes? Narcissism, peer belonging, loneliness and normative versus deceptive like-seeking on Instagram in emerging adulthood. *Computers in Human Behavior*, *71*, 1–10. doi:10.1016/j.chb.2017.01.037

Fardouly, J., Diedrichs, P. C., Vartanian, L. R., & Halliwell, E. (2015). Social comparisons on social media: The impact of Facebook on young women's body image concerns and mood. *Body Image*, *13*, 38–45. doi:10.1016/j.bodyim.2014.12.002 PMID:25615425

Festinger, L. (1954). A theory of social comparison processes. *Human Relations*, *7*(2), 117–140. doi:10.1177/001872675400700202

Forest, A. L., & Wood, J. V. (2012). When social networking is not working: Individuals with low self-esteem recognize but do not reap the benefits of self-disclosure on Facebook. *Psychological Science*, *23*(3), 295–302. doi:10.1177/0956797611429709 PMID:22318997

Fox, J., & Moreland, J. J. (2015). The dark side of social networking sites: An exploration of the relational and psychological stressors associated with Facebook use and affordances. *Computers in Human Behavior*, *45*, 168–176. doi:10.1016/j.chb.2014.11.083

Frison, E., & Eggermont, S. (2015). The impact of daily stress on adolescents' depressed mood: The role of social support seeking through Facebook. *Computers in Human Behavior*, *44*, 315–325. doi:10.1016/j.chb.2014.11.070

Gallagher, S. M. (2017). *The influence of social media on teens' self-esteem* (MA Thesis). Stratford, NJ: Department of Psychology, College of Science and Mathematics, Rowan University. Retrieved from http://rdw.rowan.edu/etd/2438

Greenwood, S., Perrin, A., & Duggan, M. (2016). Social media update 2016: Facebook usage and engagement is on the rise, while adoption of other platforms holds steady. *Pew Research Center*. Retrieved from http://www.pewinternet.org/2016/ 11/11/social-media-update-2016/

Greitemeyer, T., Mügge, D. O., & Bollermann, I. (2014). Having responsive Facebook friends affects the satisfaction of psychological needs more than having many Facebook friends. *Basic and Applied Social Psychology*, *36*(3), 252–258. doi:10.1080/01973533.2014.900619

Hampton, K. N., Goulet, L., Marlow, C., & Rainie, L. (2012). Why most Facebook users get more than they give: The effect of Facebook 'power users' on everybody else. *Pew Research Center.* Retrieved from http://pewinternet.org/Reports/ 2012/Facebook-users.aspx

Hart, M. (2017). Being naked on the Internet: Young people's selfies as intimate edgework. *Journal of Youth Studies, 20*(3), 301–315. doi:10.1080/13676261.2016.1212164

Harter, S. (1999). *The construction of the self: A developmental perspective.* New York, NY: Guilford Press.

Henriksen, I. O., Rановyen, I., Indredavik, M. S., & Stenseng, F. (2017). The role of self-esteem in the development of psychiatric problems: A three-year prospective study in a clinical sample of adolescents. *Child and Adolescent Psychiatry and Mental Health, 11*(1), 68. doi:10.118613034-017-0207-y PMID:29299058

Higgins, E. T. (1987). Self-discrepancy: A theory relating self and affect. *Psychological Review, 94,* 319-340.

Jong, S. T., & Drummond, M. J. (2016). Hurry up and 'like' me: Immediate feedback on social networking sites and the impact on adolescent girls. *Asia-Pacific Journal of Health, Sport and Physical Education, 7*(3), 251–267. doi:10.1080/18377122.2016.1222647

Kim, C., & Yang, S. U. (2017). Like, comment, and share on Facebook: How each behavior differs from the other. *Public Relations Review, 43*(2), 441–449. doi:10.1016/j.pubrev.2017.02.006

Kim, J., & Lee, J. R. (2011). The Facebook paths to happiness: Effects of the number of Facebook friends and self-presentation on subjective well-being. *Cyberpsychology, Behavior, and Social Networking, 14*(6), 359–364. doi:10.1089/cyber.2010.0374 PMID:21117983

Leary, M. R. (1999). Making sense of self-esteem. *Current Directions in Psychological Science, 8*(1), 32–35. doi:10.1111/1467-8721.00008

Leary, M. R., & Baumeister, R. F. (2000). The nature and function of self-esteem: Sociometer theory. In M. P. Zanna (Ed.), Advances in experimental social psychology (Vol. 32, pp. 1–62). San Diego, CA: Academic Press. doi:10.1016/S0065-2601(00)80003-9

Lee, E., Kim, Y. J., & Ahn, J. (2014). How do people use Facebook features to manage social capital? *Computers in Human Behavior, 36,* 440–445. doi:10.1016/j.chb.2014.04.007

Lockwood, P., & Kunda, Z. (1997). Superstars and me: Predicting the impact of role models on the self. *Journal of Personality and Social Psychology, 73,* 91-103.

Lup, K., Trub, L., & Rosenthal, L. (2015). Instagram# instasad? Exploring associations among Instagram use, depressive symptoms, negative social comparison, and strangers followed. *Cyberpsychology, Behavior, and Social Networking, 18*(5), 247–252. doi:10.1089/cyber.2014.0560 PMID:25965859

Lyubomirsky, S., Sheldon, K. M., & Schkade, D. (2005). Pursuing happiness: The architecture of sustainable change. *Review of General Psychology, 9*(2), 111–131. doi:10.1037/1089-2680.9.2.111

Marshall, T. C., Lefringhausen, K., & Ferenczi, N. (2015). The Big Five, self-esteem, and narcissism as predictors of the topics people write about in Facebook status updates. *Personality and Individual Differences, 85*, 35–40. doi:10.1016/j.paid.2015.04.039

Mascheroni, G., Vincent, J., & Jimenez, E. (2015). Girls are addicted to likes so they post semi-naked selfies: Peer mediation, normativity and the construction of identity online. *Journal of Psychological Research on Cyberspace, 9*, 5. doi:10.5817/CP2015-1-5

McKinnon, M. (2015, Jan. 12). 2015 Canadian social media usage statistics. *Canadian Internet Business.* Retrieved from https://canadiansinternet.com/2015-canadian-social-media-usage-statistics/

Metzler, A., & Scheithauer, H. (2017). The long-term benefits of positive self-presentation via profile pictures, number of friends and the initiation of relationships on Facebook for adolescents' self-esteem and the initiation of offline relationships. *Frontiers in Psychology, 8*, 1–15. doi:10.3389/fpsyg.2017.01981 PMID:29187827

Michalos, A. C. (1985). Multiple discrepancies theory (MDT). *Social Indicators Research, 16*(4), 347–413. doi:10.1007/BF00333288

Moretti, M. M., & Higgins, E. T. (1990). Relating self-discrepancy to self-esteem: The contribution of discrepancy beyond actual-self ratings. *Journal of Experimental Social Psychology, 26*(2), 108–123. doi:10.1016/0022-1031(90)90071-S

Muise, A., Christofides, E., & Desmarais, S. (2009). More information than you ever wanted: Does Facebook bring out the green-eyed monster of jealousy? *Cyberpsychology & Behavior: The Impact of the Internet. Multimedia and Virtual Reality on Behavior and Society, 12*(4), 441–444. doi:10.1089/cpb.2008.0263

Niera, C. J. B., & Barber, B. L. (2013). Social networking site use: Linked to adolescents' social self-concept, self-esteem, and depressed mood. *Australian Journal of Psychology, 66*, 56–64. doi:10.1111/ajpy.12034

Park, S., Kim, I., Lee, S. W., Yoo, J., Jeong, B., & Cha, M. (2015, February). Manifestation of depression and loneliness on social networks: A case study of young adults on Facebook. In *Proceedings of the 18th ACM conference on computer supported cooperative work & social computing* (pp. 557-570). ACM. Retrieved from https://dl.acm.org/citation.cfm?id=2675139

Pyszczynski, T., Greenberg, J. L., & LaPrelle, J. (1985). Social comparison after success and failure: Biased search for information consistent with a self-serving conclusion. *Journal of Experimental Social Psychology, 21*(2), 195–211. doi:10.1016/0022-1031(85)90015-0

Radovic, A., Gmelin, T., Stein, B. D., & Miller, E. (2017). Depressed adolescents' positive and negative use of social media. *Journal of Adolescence, 55*, 5–15. doi:10.1016/j.adolescence.2016.12.002 PMID:27997851

Rosenberg, M., Schooler, C., & Schoenbach, C. (1989). Self-esteem and adolescent problems: Modeling reciprocal effects. *American Sociological Review, 54*(6), 1004–1018. doi:10.2307/2095720

Rutledge, P. (2013). *Making sense of selfies.* Retrieved from https://www.psychologytoday.com/blog/positively-media/201307/making-senseselfies\

Sarita, S., & Suleeman, J. (2017). The relationship between the need to belong and Instagram self-presentation among adolescents. *UI Proceedings on Social Science and Humanities*, 1. Retrieved from http://scholarsmepub.com/wp-content/uploads/2018/01/SJHSS-31B-91-103-c.pdf

Schimmack, U., & Diener, E. (2003). Predictive validity of explicit and implicit self-esteem for subjective well-being. *Journal of Research in Personality*, *37*(2), 100–106. doi:10.1016/S0092-6566(02)00532-9

Scissors, L., Burke, M., & Wengrovitz, S. (2016). What's in a like?: Attitudes and behaviors around receiving likes on Facebook. In *Proceedings of the 19th ACM Conference on Computer-Supported Cooperative Work & Social Computing* (pp. 1501–1510). New York, NY: ACM. doi:10.1145/2818048.2820066

Sherman, L. E., Payton, A. A., Hernandez, L. M., Greenfield, P. M., & Dapretto, M. (2016). The power of the like in adolescence effects of peer influence on neural and behavioral responses to social media. *Psychological Science*, *27*(7), 1027–1035. doi:10.1177/0956797616645673 PMID:27247125

Shin, Y., Kim, M., Im, C., & Chong, S. C. (2017). Selfie and self: The effect of selfies on self-esteem and social sensitivity. *Personality and Individual Differences*, *111*, 139–145. doi:10.1016/j.paid.2017.02.004

Silverston, P. H., & Salsali, M. (2003). Low self-esteem and psychiatric patients: Part I - The relationship between low self-esteem and psychiatric diagnosis. *Annals of General Hospital Psychiatry*, *2*(1), 2. doi:10.1186/1475-2832-2-2 PMID:12620127

Smith, A., & Anderson, M. (2018). Social media use in 2018: A majority of Americans use Facebook and YouTube, but young adults are especially heavy users of Snapchat and Instagram. *Pew Research Center.* Retrieved from http://www.pewinternet.org/wp-content/uploads/sites/9/2018/02/PI_2018.03.01_Social-Media_FINAL.pdf

Smith, A., & Williams, K. D. (2004). RU there? Ostracism by cell phone text messages. *Group Dynamics*, *8*(4), 291–301. doi:10.1037/1089-2699.8.4.291

Spies Shapiro, L. A. S., & Margolin, G. (2014). Growing up wired: Social networking sites and adolescent psychosocial development. *Clinical Child and Family Psychology Review*, *17*(1), 1–18. doi:10.100710567-013-0135-1 PMID:23645343

Suls, J., Martin, R., & Wheeler, L. (2002). Social comparison: Why, with whom, and with what effect? *Current Directions in Psychological Science*, *11*(5), 159–163. doi:10.1111/1467-8721.00191

Tajuddin, J. M., Hassan, N. A., & Ahmad, R. (2013). Social media usage among university students: A study on selfie and its impacts. *Global Journal of Business and Social Science Review*, *1*(1), 124–132.

Tandoc, E. C. Jr, Ferrucci, P., & Duffy, M. (2015). Facebook use, envy, and depression among college students: Is facebooking depressing? *Computers in Human Behavior*, *43*, 139–146. doi:10.1016/j.chb.2014.10.053

Taylor, A. S., & Harper, R. (2003). The gift of the gab?: A design oriented sociology of young people's use of mobiles. *Computer Supported Cooperative Work*, *12*(3), 267–296. doi:10.1023/A:1025091532662

Thomaes, S., Reijntjes, A., Orobio de Castro, B., Bushman, B. J., Poorthuis, A., & Telch, M. J. (2010). I like me if you like me: On the interpersonal modulation and regulation of preadolescents' state self-esteem. *Child Development*, *81*(3), 811–825. doi:10.1111/j.1467-8624.2010.01435.x PMID:20573106

Tromholt, M. (2016). The Facebook experiment: Quitting Facebook leads to higher levels of well-being. *Cyberpsychology, Behavior, and Social Networking*, *19*(11), 661–666. doi:10.1089/cyber.2016.0259 PMID:27831756

Utz, S. (2015). The function of self-disclosure on social network sites: Not only intimate, but also positive and entertaining self-disclosures increase the feeling of connection. *Computers in Human Behavior*, *45*, 1–10. doi:10.1016/j.chb.2014.11.076

Valkenburg, P. M., Koutamanis, M., & Vossen, H. G. (2017). The concurrent and longitudinal relationships between adolescents' use of social network sites and their social self-esteem. *Computers in Human Behavior*, *76*, 35–41. doi:10.1016/j.chb.2017.07.008 PMID:29104364

Valkenburg, P. M., & Peter, J. (2011). Online communication among adolescents: An integrated model of its attraction, opportunities, and risks. *The Journal of Adolescent Health*, *48*(2), 121–127. doi:10.1016/j.jadohealth.2010.08.020 PMID:21257109

Valkenburg, P. M., Peter, J., & Schouten, A. P. (2006). Friend networking sites and their relationship to adolescents' well-being and social self-esteem. *Cyberpsychology & Behavior*, *9*(5), 584–590. doi:10.1089/cpb.2006.9.584 PMID:17034326

Valkenburg, P. M., Schouten, A. P., & Peter, J. (2005). Adolescents' identity experiments on the Internet. *New Media & Society*, *7*(3), 383–402. doi:10.1177/1461444805052282

Verduyn, P., Lee, D. S., Park, J., Shablack, H., Orvell, A., Bayer, J., ... Kross, E. (2015). Passive Facebook usage undermines affective well-being: Experimental and longitudinal evidence. *Journal of Experimental Psychology. General*, *144*(2), 480–488. doi:10.1037/xge0000057 PMID:25706656

Verduyn, P., Ybarra, O., Résibois, M., Jonides, J., & Kross, E. (2017). Do social network sites enhance or undermine subjective well-being? A critical review. *Social Issues and Policy Review*, *11*(1), 274–302. doi:10.1111ipr.12033

Vitak, J., & Ellison, N. B. (2013). 'There's a network out there you might as well tap': Exploring the benefits of and barriers to exchanging informational and support-based resources on Facebook. *New Media & Society*, *15*(2), 243–259. doi:10.1177/1461444812451566

Vogel, E. A., Rose, J. P., Roberts, L. R., & Eckles, K. (2014). Social comparison, social media, and self-esteem. *Psychology of Popular Media Culture*, *3*(4), 206–222. doi:10.1037/ppm0000047

Wang, Y., Nie, R., Li, Z., & Zhou, N. (2018). WeChat Moments use and self-esteem among Chinese adults: The mediating roles of personal power and social acceptance and the moderating roles of gender and age. *Personality and Individual Differences*, *131*, 31–37. doi:10.1016/j.paid.2018.04.012

Wenninger, H., Krasnova, H., & Buxmann, P. (2014). Activity matters: Investigating the influence of Facebook on life satisfaction of teenage users. In *Twenty Second European Conference on Information Systems* (pp. 1–18). Academic Press. Retrieved from https://aisel.aisnet.org/ecis2014/proceedings/track01/13/

Wohn, D. Y., Carr, C. T., & Hayes, R. A. (2016). How affective is a "Like"?: The effect of paralinguistic digital affordances on perceived social support. *Cyberpsychology, Behavior, and Social Networking*, *19*(9), 562–566. doi:10.1089/cyber.2016.0162 PMID:27635443

Yang, C. C., & Brown, B. B. (2016). Online self-presentation on Facebook and self development during the college transition. *Journal of Youth and Adolescence*, *45*(2), 402–416. doi:10.100710964-015-0385-y PMID:26534776

Zhang, R. (2017). The stress-buffering effect of self-disclosure on Facebook: An examination of stressful life events, social support, and mental health among college students. *Computers in Human Behavior*, *75*, 527–537. doi:10.1016/j.chb.2017.05.043

ADDITIONAL READING

Burrow, A. L., & Rainone, N. (2017). How many likes did I get?: Purpose moderates links between positive social media feedback and self-esteem. *Journal of Experimental Social Psychology*, *69*, 232–236. doi:10.1016/j.jesp.2016.09.005

Chua, T. H. H., & Chang, L. (2016). Follow me and like my beautiful selfies: Singapore teenage girls' engagement in self-presentation and peer comparison on social media. *Computers in Human Behavior*, *55*, 190–197. doi:10.1016/j.chb.2015.09.011

Festinger, L. (1954). A theory of social comparison processes. *Human Relations*, *7*(2), 117–140. doi:10.1177/001872675400700202

Forest, A. L., & Wood, J. V. (2012). When social networking is not working: Individuals with low self-esteem recognize but do not reap the benefits of self-disclosure on Facebook. *Psychological Science*, *23*(3), 295–302. doi:10.1177/0956797611429709 PMID:22318997

Jong, S. T., & Drummond, M. J. (2016). Hurry up and 'like' me: Immediate feedback on social networking sites and the impact on adolescent girls. *Asia-Pacific Journal of Health, Sport and Physical Education*, *7*(3), 251–267. doi:10.1080/18377122.2016.1222647

Joseph, J. J., Desjarlais, M., & Herceg, L. (2019). Facebook depression or Facebook contentment: The relation between Facebook use and well-Being. In R. T. Gopalan (Ed.), Intimacy and Developing Personal Relationships in the Virtual World (pp. 104–125). Hershey, PA: IGI Global. doi:10.4018/978-1-5225-4047-2.ch007

Leary, M. R. (1999). Making sense of self-esteem. *Current Directions in Psychological Science*, *8*(1), 32–35. doi:10.1111/1467-8721.00008

Radovic, A., Gmelin, T., Stein, B. D., & Miller, E. (2017). Depressed adolescents' positive and negative use of social media. *Journal of Adolescence*, *55*, 5–15. doi:10.1016/j.adolescence.2016.12.002 PMID:27997851

Valkenburg, P. M., Koutamanis, M., & Vossen, H. G. (2017). The concurrent and longitudinal relationships between adolescents' use of social network sites and their social self-esteem. *Computers in Human Behavior*, *76*, 35–41. doi:10.1016/j.chb.2017.07.008 PMID:29104364

Vogel, E. A., Rose, J. P., Roberts, L. R., & Eckles, K. (2014). Social comparison, social media, and self-esteem. *Psychology of Popular Media Culture*, *3*(4), 206–222. doi:10.1037/ppm0000047

KEY TERMS AND DEFINITIONS

Downward Social Comparison: Instances where the target of social comparison is perceived as doing worse than oneself on some dimension.

Passive Social Networking Usage: consumption of social networking content without direct engagement with the information owner (e.g., browsing news feeds or looking at profiles, pictures, and status updates posted by other social network users).

Qualitative Feedback: Responses on social media from friends and followers consisting of written text (i.e., comments).

Quantitative Feedback: Responses on social media from friends and followers consisting of numbers (i.e., number of likes).

Self-Esteem: The extent to which individuals accept, approve of, or value themselves.

Social Media: Online platforms that permit users to create a profile, as well as connect and exchange information about oneself with other members. Examples include social networking sites, instant messaging services, blogging sites, and multiplayer online games.

Status Update: A feature on social networking sites which allows users to share their thoughts, feelings, experiences, whereabouts, and so on. A status is often short and posted on the user's profile page, as well as in the new feeds of friends and followers.

Upward Social Comparison: Instances where the target of social comparison is perceived as doing better than oneself on some dimension.

Virtual Like: Also referred to as a like, this is a symbol, such as thumbs up or heart, viewers on social media can select to provide feedback or acknowledgement to posts on social media.

This research was previously published in The Psychology and Dynamics Behind Social Media Interactions; pages 289-312, copyright year 2020 by Information Science Reference (an imprint of IGI Global).

Chapter 8
Clinical Topics in Social Media:
The Role of Self-Disclosing on Social Media for Friendship and Identity in Specialized Populations

Jessica J. Joseph
Mount Royal University, Canada

Diana Florea
Alberta Health Services, Canada

ABSTRACT

The overall objective of the proposed chapter is to increase the reader's understanding of the role that social media plays in self-disclosing information about ourselves in the development of friendships and identity, as well as explore these themes in a clinical context. As such, readers will gain knowledge regarding the relations between self-disclosing on social media sites and the ensuing friendship and identity development that occurs, the extension of the research findings to clinical populations, and the questions that still remain unanswered. This information may be useful for the advancement of research, policy development, mental health programs, parenting, and education.

INTRODUCTION

Social media is a rapidly growing enterprise that has become pervasive in society today. In fact, internationally, billions of people log onto social media sites such as Facebook, Instagram, SnapChat, and YouTube every single day (Gramlich, 2018). In order to understand the outcomes associated with this modern, innovative, and evolving form of communicating with friends, researchers have examined the role that social media plays in social development. More specifically, this research has led investigators to suggest that when users log on to social media sites they are effectively using the media site as a vehicle to disclose information about the self (Verduyn et al., 2017), gain information about others (Feinstein

DOI: 10.4018/978-1-6684-6307-9.ch008

et al., 2013; Vogel et al., 2014), and ultimately develop closer friendships (Desjarlais & Joseph, 2017) as a result. In addition, investigators have found that disclosing on social media sites also plays a role in our identity formation (Valkenburg, Schouten, & Peter, 2005). As such, the first purpose of the current chapter is to present and discuss the literature pertaining to self disclosing online and its relationship to friendship and identity development in general. The second objective of the current chapter is to uncover how these processes work in populations where self-disclosing, social engagements, and identity development are hindered as part of a clinical diagnoses such as autism, psychosis, schizophrenia, depression, and anxiety; or due to social marginalization as present in the LGBT+ community.

Therefore, the overall objective of this chapter is to increase understanding of the role that social media plays in self-disclosing information in the development of friendships and identity, as well as explore these themes in a clinical context. This information may be useful for the advancement of research, policy development, mental health programs, parenting, and education.

WHAT IS SOCIAL MEDIA

Social media is a term that can be extended to any form of technology that aids in our communication with others. This includes text messaging, instant (or direct) messaging, online gaming, social networking sites, video sharing sites, and e-mail. All of these have one major theme in common: They are intended to be social environments that allow for quick and easy connections to be made among existing and new friends (Smith & Anderson, 2018). While there are a number of different types of social media, social networking sites, video sharing sites, gaming and direct messaging will be the focus of the current chapter.

Social media has become ubiquitous with daily life. Internationally, billions of people log onto social media sites every single day (Stats, 2018). In fact, the Pew Research Centre estimates that roughly 70% of the American public uses some form of social media, with the majority of logins occurring daily (Factsheet, 2018). According to Smith and Anderson (2018), the most popular social media sites include the video sharing site YouTube (73% of American adults), and social networking sites such as Facebook (68% of American adults), Instagram (35% of American adults), or SnapChat (27% of American Adults). On average, social media users are comprised of young adults between the ages of 18 and 29 years, with female users being slightly more common than male users (Factsheet, 2018; Greenwood et al., 2016). It should also be noted that there is a growing number of adolescent social media users, roughly 85% of American adolescents (Anderson & Jiang, 2018). Adolescents generally follow the same social media use patterns as young adults, where the video sharing site YouTube (85% of American adolescents) was among the most popular, followed by the social networking sites Instagram (72%), SnapChat (69%), and Facebook (51%).

Generally speaking, social media websites are set up so that the user is able to create a personal profile where they are able to share an amalgamation of text, picture, and video content about themselves (Ellison, Steinfield, & Lampe, 2007). This often includes some combination of personal information, photographs, videos, memes, and/or ideas that the user identifies with. In addition, users are typically given the ability to 'follow' or 'friend' other users, becoming, in a sense, enrolled to see the information these users have posted about themselves online (Ellison et al., 2007). These websites then allow for instantaneous connections to be made, and provide a plethora of information about other users--all at the click of a mouse. Users typically turn to social media sites to aid in the maintenance of their relationships (e.g., to post or send messages, stay in touch with friends), to pass time, or for entertainment purposes (e.g., to see other people's pictures and read their profiles; Davis, 2012; Sheldon 2008; Smith, 2011).

The types of social features offered on social media sites are somewhat dependent on the specific site. For instance, the video-sharing site YouTube allows users, both professional and amateur, to create a profile where they can upload and share videos (Xu, Park, Kim, & Park, 2016). This includes either personal videos, videos the profile owner finds entertaining, or some combination thereof. Once a video is shared on YouTube, it is typically broadcasted to a combination of friends and strangers.

Similarly, social networking sites such as Facebook, Instagram, and SnapChat enable users to create personal profiles and broadcast information online. These sites differ from YouTube in the sense that (1) the audience of the information shared on social networking sites is typically comprised of friends made previously offline (Ellison, et al., 2007); and (2) social networking sites offer opportunities more geared toward text and photo based interactions. For example, Facebook allows users to create a personal 'timeline' where the user is able to share information about themselves in the form of directly messaging friends, posting status updates, sharing memories, posting on timelines, or reacting to others' posts. Similarly, Instagram is a photo based social networking site, where users share photos of themselves, or things they find cute, attractive, or inspirational (Hu, Manikonda, & Kambhampati, 2014). These photos are often filtered, or manipulated, to present the most attractive version of the users' photos (Hu et al., 2014). SnapChat shares the same features as Instagram, although users are able to directly select the people who view their posts, and the photos that are shared are only temporarily broadcasted (within 10 seconds of being opened by the recipient) before automatically being deleted (Kotfila, 2014). Although these sites may differ among specific features, a common theme among them is being able to instantaneously share, or self-disclose, information about oneself to others.

SELF-DISCLOSURE AND SOCIAL MEDIA

Self-disclosure is defined as the act of purposefully sharing intimate or personal information about oneself to others (Collins & Miller, 1994). Self-disclosure is integral to several aspects of psychosocial development, including building friendships and navigating one's identity. Altman and Taylor (1973) proposed the social penetration theory, which postulates that the development of interpersonal relationships follows a systematic and stable course from shallow and superficial connections to increasingly deeper and more intimate connections. Further, the mechanism by which these relationships evolve from superficial to intimate is through self-disclosure. According to Altman and Taylor (1973), self-disclosure follows a similar trajectory to that of the developing relationship, starting with the sharing of relatively impersonal information, which becomes increasingly intimate as the relationship grows (see also Davis, 2013; Greene, Derlega, & Mathews, 2006).

Considering the types of activities associated with social media use (e.g., sharing photos, videos, memories, personal information), a common theme among them is self-disclosure. Active engagement while on social media has been conceptualized as actively disclosing personal information in the form on photos, videos, status updates, and messages (Verdyun et al., 2017). It is plausible then that social media platforms provide an additional (and pervasive) venue for individuals to disclose information about themselves, and in turn experience increases in the quality of their friendships (Desjarlais, Gilmour, Sinclair, Howell & West, 2015; Valkenburg & Peter, 2009). Indeed, self disclosing online has resulted in increases in friendship quality (Valkenburg & Peter, 2007), social connectedness (Burke, Kraut, &

Marlow, 2011), and social support (Wright et al., 2012). Further, there are instances where disclosing online may be preferred over face-to-face disclosures, such as during sensitive or embarrassing conversations (Yang, Yang, & Chiou, 2010). These findings provide support for the increases in friendship quality that accompany self-disclosure, as well as suggest that the themes observed in the creation of the social penetration theory extend to social media.

Self-disclosure also plays a role in identity development, that is the development of a specific set of goals, values, morals, and personal beliefs that encompass the way an individual views, and acts in, day to day life (Marcia, 1966). One perspective on identity development suggests that social environments are essential for creating, understanding and interpreting an individual's identity (Goffman, 1959). This is potentially because social environments offer individuals the opportunity for self expression, where individuals are able to present themselves, or present who they wish to be, through sharing personal information with those around them (Goffman, 1959; Walther, 2007). Self-disclosure then could be viewed as the mechanism for said self expression. In fact, Mclean (2005) found that sharing personal information that is pertinent to one's identity, such as sharing an experience that represents who one is, helps individuals develop their own personal narratives, which ultimately then shapes identity. It is also believed that sharing information, gaining feedback, and comparing oneself to others is a means by which individuals explore, alter, and develop their identity (Festinger, 1954; Turner, 1975).

While there is evidence to suggest that an individual's identity is impacted by disclosing while face-to-face (e.g., Mclean, 2005), social media sites offer additional social environments for individuals to share personal information that can impact identity (Code, 2013; Katz & Rice, 2002; Valkenburg, Shouten, & Peter, 2005; Zhao, Grasmuck, & Martin, 2008). While on social media, users are able to actively engage in disclosing personal information in the form of photo uploads, video uploads, updating statuses (sharing what is on one's mind), as well as sharing links, memories, or memes that one identifies with (Ellison et al., 2007). Thus, while on social media, the sharing of personal information is typically in the form of showing oneself as opposed to directly telling others about oneself (Zhao, Grasmuck, & Martin, 2008). The content shared on social media is also fully controlled by the user, such that the poster has the ability to modify or conceal parts of themselves, as well as chose to only present the most socially attractive and desirable information about themselves (selective self presentation; Walther, 2007). Social media environments then offer a more controlled and safer environment for users to disclose information about themselves, allowing for more control when engaging in identity experiments (McKenna & Bargh, 2000). Valkenburg, Shouten, and Peter (2005) also found that adolescents who use social media report having engaged in identity experiments while online. These adolescents reported that they were motivated to disclose online as a means of self exploration, as well as gaining others' reactions to their identity related posts (Valkenburg, Shouten, & Peter, 2005).

CLINICAL APPLICATIONS

It is long standing wisdom that humans possess a fundamental need for friendship and belonging (Altman & Taylor, 1974). These friendships are imperative for an individual's well-being (Diener et al., 1999). It is also clear that the mechanism by which people build friendships and meaningful relationships is through self-disclosure (Altman & Taylor, 1974). Self-disclosure also plays an important role in identity development, both online and offline (Valkenburg, Shouten, & Peter, 2005). What about the instances however, when developing social relationships, or self disclosing in general, becomes hindered as part of a clinical diagnosis or social marginalization? Could social media offer a venue for more comfortable and safe disclosures for these populations?

According to Valkenburg and Peter's (2009) social compensation hypothesis, the anonymity, reduced audio/visual cues, and expected delayed response time that are associated with social media provide a comfortable environment for shy, and/or socially anxious individuals to take part in meaningful conversations that may have been too difficult when face-to-face (see also Desjarlais & Willoughby, 2010). Thus, social media may provide a safe and comfortable environment for users to share and connect with friends, and perhaps be used as a compensatory resource for individuals whose social skills/comfort are either lacking or underdeveloped.

While there is a growing body of literature that suggests that social media offers a comfortable environment for socially anxious users to disclose and build friendships, the literature focuses on the general population. This typically includes high, or average, functioning young adults with no qualms or issues with developing friendships or identity; or individuals with higher levels of social anxiety relative to a sample as opposed to meeting clinical criteria. The question that arises then is, could the findings regarding social media being used as a facilitatory resource for comfortable disclosure extend to clinical populations? More specifically, and in line with the social compensation hypothesis, could social media provide a venue for individuals coping with severe social afflictions as part of a clinical diagnosis, such as in autism, depression and anxiety, schizophrenia and psychosis, or due to social marginalization such as in the LGBT+ community to more comfortably self disclose?

The objective of the remainder of the chapter is to synthesize the current literature regarding how disclosing on social media impacts populations of people with the aforementioned social limitations. Each topic will be presented separately and include brief discussions regarding (1) how socialization is hindered for the specific population; and (2) highlight current findings regarding self-disclosure on social media for these populations, and whether social media disclosures impact friendship and/or identity for them.

SOCIAL MEDIA AND AUTISM SPECTRUM DISORDER

Autism spectrum disorder (ASD) is a clinical term that is used in the classification of a neurodevelopmental disorder that includes pervasive developmental delays and significant impairments in interpreting, understanding, and engaging in social situations (American Psychiatric Association, 2013; World Health Organization, 2018). The social challenges that are paramount to ASD typically include difficulty making and understanding eye contact (Senju, & Johnson, 2009), as well as an inability to decode complex social information such as body language or facial cues (Frith, 2003; Sainsbury, 2000). This then results in an inability to initiate and/or engage in social conversations (Bauminger & Shulman, 2003). As such, individuals coping with ASD diagnoses have limited social exchanges with peers and lack the social skills to be able to build closer relationships (Lawson, 2001). It should be noted however, that individuals on the autism spectrum do report feelings of loneliness (Sainsbury, 2000), and a desire to gain friendships (Rowley et al., 2012). Given that social media offers more structure and control, and includes less reliance on interpreting non-verbal information such as body language or changing facial expressions (Burke et al., 2010; Valkenburg & Peter, 2009), social media may provide a more comfortable venue for individuals on the autism spectrum to engage in social exchanges, share and interpret personal information, and ultimately build social relationships.

The current literature on social media and ASD highlights that, in general, individuals on the autism spectrum typically prefer screen time when compared to their average functioning counterparts; this has been observed in both adolescents (eight-18 years; Mazurek, Shattuck, Wagner, & Cooper, 2012; Mazurek & Wenstrup, 2012; van Schalwyk et al., 2017), and adults (Mazurek, 2013). During screen time, these individuals do report using social media (Mazurek, 2013). Their preferences for social engagements while on social media typically reside in online gaming as opposed to social networking sites (Mazurek et al., 2012; Mazurek & Engelhardt, 2013). Individuals with ASD who do choose to engage in social activity while gaming (i.e., online chatting or messaging during gameplay), do exhibit increases in social interactions and social connectedness (Cole & Griffiths, 2007; Sunsberg, 2018), and decreases in loneliness (Sunsberg, 2018).

It should also be noted that although individuals with ASD are not necessarily motivated to use social networking over gaming, their social media consumption does include social networking sites. In fact, one study by Mazurek (2013) indicated that nearly 80% of young adult participants with ASD reported using social networking sites. Further, the most common motivation for using these sites included gaining social connections (Mazurek, 2013). Perhaps most importantly, individuals with ASD who do choose to gain connections via social networking sites report increases in social interactions and thus increases in social connections (Mazurek, 2013), as well as significant decreases in loneliness (Ward, Dill-Shackleford, & Mazurek, 2018).

Taken together, the current literature then suggests that, consistent with the social compensation hypothesis, the features of social media (particularly in gaming and social networking environments) may offer the structure, control, and simplicity necessary for individuals with ASD to be comfortable socializing. Social media then may provide a compensatory resource for these individuals to engage in more social exchanges with peers and ultimately gain friendships that may not have been possible offline.

SOCIAL MEDIA, SOCIAL ANXIETY, AND MAJOR DEPRESSIVE DISORDER

Major depressive disorder and social anxiety are also clinical diagnoses that include a lack of social exchanges, and deficits in developing close friendships. These disorders are also highly prevalent throughout the world. The World Health Organization (2017) estimates that, internationally, over 300 million people suffer from depression, anxiety, or some combination thereof (aka comorbidity). For the following discussion regarding major depressive disorder, social anxiety, and social media, the two diagnoses will be discussed concurrently for two reasons. First, comorbidity of these diagnoses is exceptionally common, such that the vast majority of people suffering from major depressive disorder (approximately 85%) also suffer from clinical anxiety (Gorman, 1996). The comorbidity of these disorders is also stable across various life stages (Essau et al., 2018). Second, behaviourally, social inhibitions present similarly across both diagnoses in that, in both cases, social withdrawal and isolation tends to be the major contributing factor for lacking social exchanges and deficits in friendships among these populations. For instance, individuals with major depressive disorder tend to exhibit decreased interest in social activities and engaging with others (Saunders & Roy, 1999), often resulting in avoiding social interactions altogether (Coyne et al., 1987). Similarly, individuals with anxiety, especially social anxiety and/or social phobias, also tend to engage in severe social avoidance (Watson & Friend 1969). Individuals with anxiety also present a preoccupation with hiding imperfections and fears of being judged by others or viewed as inadequate (Clarke & Wells, 1995; Hewitt et al., 2003; Watson & Friend, 1969). Given that, in both cases, social avoidance and/or withdrawal is a factor, individuals with either, or a combination, of these diagnoses are at risk for social isolation and loneliness (Weiss, 1973).

Considering the increased control over the personal information shared and the lack of engagement expectations associated with social media platforms, these environments may provide avenues for individuals with depression and/or anxiety to engage in social situations and reduce their risk of loneliness and social isolation. The vast majority of the literature highlighting social media use among depressed and/or anxious populations, however, is speculative. This is because research in this area typically measures relative levels of depressive symptoms (e.g., Tandoc, Ferrucci, & Duffy 2015), or relative social anxiety (e.g., Desjarlais & Willoughby, 2012) while on social media, as opposed to clinical levels.

What can be derived from the studies that have measured relative levels of depression is that (1) the majority of studies, including the studies highlighted in this section, have focused on social networking sites as the social media platform of interest in these samples; and (2) how social networking sites influence depression, anxiety, and social connections depends on how an individual uses the social networking site. If users are passively engaged while on social media, such that they are scrolling through their social media news feeds with no posting or interacting (aka *passive* Facebook use), it is typically associated with increases in depressive symptoms for young adults (Kraut et al., 1998; Tandoc, Ferrucci, & Duffy, 2015; Verduyn et al., 2015). The underlying mechanisms responsible for these increases in depressive symptoms while browsing social media are negative social comparison and envy (see Joseph, Desjarlais, & Herceg, 2019 for review). In this context, users are effectively comparing themselves to the information their friends post about themselves, and feeling as though their friends are happier and better of than they are (Chou & Edge, 2012). For example, Tandoc, Ferrucci, and Duffy (2015) found that when users passively engage on Facebook, they then negatively compare themselves to the information their friends have posted about themselves, feel envious of the attractiveness, power, and popularity exemplified by their friends' posts, and thus exhibit increases in depressive symptoms. Conversely, when users more actively engage while on social media, such that they are actively sharing personal information via posting photos, status updates, sending messages, or sharing links, memes, or memories they affiliate with (aka *active* Facebook use), they exhibit decreases in depression. Here, social media use is associated with increases in young adults' social connectedness (große Deters & Mehl, 2013) and decreases in depressive symptoms (Grieve, Indian, Witteveen, Tolan, & Marrington, 2013). Furthermore, a longitudinal study by große Deters and Mehl (2013) indicated that higher levels of status updates on social media negatively predicted loneliness one week later, through feelings of social connectedness.

Similarly, research examining social media as a compensatory resource for individuals with social anxiety has also largely been based on relative levels of social anxiety. This research has demonstrated that individuals with relatively high anxiety do exhibit increases in friendship quality from actively sharing and/or chatting online (Kraut et al., 2002; Valkenburg & Peter, 2009). For example, Desjarlais and Willoughby (2010) found that, among adolescent boys with relatively higher levels of social anxiety, those who reported more instances of chatting online reported greater friendship quality than those who chat online less frequently.

While research on social media use among individuals with clinical depression or anxiety is sparse, the studies that have been conducted are consistent with the preceding findings. Studies show that clinically depressed individuals exhibit envy while browsing on social media, even more so than their non-depressed counterparts (Appel, Crusius, & Gerlach, 2015). Additionally, clinically depressed individuals tend to perceive that social media only provides them with social support when they actively share, or post, information about themselves that is positive (Park et al., 2016). This may be of particular interest given that individuals with clinical depression tend to post more negative information than non-depressed people, and thus feel more depressed after posting (Moreno et al., 2012).

Insofar as social media being used as a compensatory resource for individuals with clinical depression and/or social anxiety to gain close friendships, it appears to be a double-edged sword. On one hand, and consistent with the social compensation hypothesis, social media may provide the opportunity for clinically depressed and/or anxious individuals to engage in social situations, and gain closer friendships, provided that they are actively posting, sharing, and chatting while on social media. On the other hand, if clinically depressed or anxious individuals passively browse social media, it could lead to feelings of envy and thus be detrimental to their friendships and their clinical symptoms.

SOCIAL MEDIA, SCHIZOPHRENIA, AND PSYCHOSIS

Schizophrenia Spectrum Disorder is classified as a pervasive psychotic disorder that includes significant social, emotional, and daily life impairments (American Psychiatric Association, 2013). Deficits in social functioning have been paramount in the diagnosis of schizophrenia since the DSM III (American Psychiatric Association, 1987; Bellack, Morrison, Wixted, & Mueser, 1990). The social impairments associated with schizophrenia typically stem from two general origins: (1) negative symptoms such as flat affect and disorganized speaking, thinking, and interpreting (Andreasen, 1982; Bellack et al., 1990); and (2) behavioural symptoms such as deficits in verbal communication (Lavelle, Healey, & McCabe, 2013), and underdeveloped social skills, including difficulties sharing appropriately and understanding social situations in general (Bellack et al., 1990). This is important because the deficits in social functioning that are attributed to schizophrenia often result in diminished social networks (Erickson, Beiser, Iacono, Fleming, & Lin, 1989; Giacco, 2013). This then leaves these individuals at risk for social isolation (Kohn & Clausen, 1955) and loneliness (Neeleman, & Power, 1994).

Given that social media platforms require less decoding of audio and visual cues, less reliance on speaking and speech interpretation, and offer users the ability to take time to formulate appropriate responses, social media may provide an avenue for individuals coping with schizophrenia, or symptoms of psychosis, to increase social connections. Indeed, both adolescents (Mittal, Tessner, & Walker, 2007), and adults (18-65 years; Schrank, Sibitz, Unger, & Amering, 2010) with schizophrenia do report frequently using social networking sites, as well as video sharing sites (Naslund, Grande, Aschbrenner, & Elwyn, 2014). Adolescents with schizophrenia typically report that they are motivated to use social media to maintain the offline friendships that they do have (Mittal et al., 2007), as well as establish and maintain new friendships (Daley et al., 2005). Further, both adolescents and young adults with schizophrenia who do use social media report feelings of social support, reduced isolation, and the ability to learn from others (Naslund et al., 2014), as well as report closer friendships and the desire to include texting, chatting, and social networking into their treatment plans (Miller et al., 2015).

These self-report findings are also supported by empirical evidence. Studies show that chatting and direct/text messaging increases socialization among these populations (Alvarez-Jimenez et al., 2014; Alvarez-Jimenez et al., 2018; Granholm, Ben-Zeev, Link, Bradshaw, & Holden, 2011). In an experimental study by Alvarez-Jimenez and colleagues (2018), a social networking site was created by the researchers, and changes in social functioning, life satisfaction, and social support among users with schizophrenia were observed. The results demonstrated that participants exhibited increases in social functioning, social support, and life satisfaction after using the social networking site, both immediately and after a two-month follow-up (Alvarez-Jimenez et al., 2018). It should be noted however, that some of the social challenges that individuals on the schizophrenia spectrum experience offline may also transfer online. For instance, over-sharing or sharing socially inappropriate information is prominent among YouTube users with schizophrenia (Naslund et al., 2014). In addition, social media users with schizophrenia also tend to consistently post more negative information than control users, especially when sharing information about depression and anxiety while online (Hswen, Naslund, Brownstein, & Hawkins, 2018). This is important considering self-indulgent and/or negative posts tend to get fewer acknowledgements from other social media users (Burke & Develin, 2016) and thus may hinder making social connections via social media.

The research highlighted in this section indicates that there may be some benefits for social media users coping with schizophrenia and psychosis, especially surrounding increased socialization and social functioning. Although, more social coaching surrounding what is most appropriate to share online may be needed in tandem with encouraging these users to engage in social networking, chatting, and video sharing to help with social connections.

SOCIAL MEDIA AND SOCIAL MARGINALIZATION

In addition to social connections being hindered as part of clinical diagnoses, there are instances where typically functioning individuals are socially marginalized to the point where both social connections and identity development may be at risk. These risks are particularly prominent among members of the lesbian, gay, bisexual, and transgender (LGBT+) community. This is because of the stigma attached to the sexual orientation, expression, and identity of these individuals, whose sexual narratives fall outside the expected heterosexual, bi-gender norms that are pervasive in society today (Subhrajit, 2014). As such, members of the LGBT+ community experience significant social marginalization and isolation (Hillier et al., 2010; Hiller, Mitchell, & Ybarra, 2012; Ryan & Rivers, 2003), as well as become victims of bullying and/or physical abuse for their sexual differences (D'Augelli, 2002). The effects of the marginalization, isolation, and victimization then leading to long-term mental health concerns, including depleting social networks, and an increased likelihood of depression (D'Augelli, 2002).

Research examining social media use among members of the LGBT+ community, and how it relates to friendship and identity, have found that adolescent members of this community do report feeling as though social media are safe places to share personal information and receive social support from friends (Hiller, Horsely, & Kurdas, 2004), some reporting that they are a safer place to socialize than traditional face-to-face environments (Hiller & Harrison, 2007). As such, researchers have found that members of this community turn to social media to express their marginalized identities, gain social support and social connections, and promote social understanding and social change (Mehra, Merkel, & Bishop, 2004). This then results in LGBT+ youth gaining support and understanding for their marginalized experiences (Ybarral Mitchell, Palmer, & Reiser, 2015), and creating friendships that may not have been possible otherwise (Pullen & Cooper, 2010). In addition, the anonymity and control offered by social media environments allows LGBT+ users to more safely experiment with, and learn about, their own identities (Pullen & Cooper, 2010). For instance, Fox and Ralston (2016) found that LGBT+ adolescent social media users report turning to social media for resources to learn about their emerging identity, experiment with their identity, and teach others about their identity while online (see also DeHaan et al., 2013).

Taken together, and consistent with social compensation hypothesis, social media environments provide the opportunity for LGBT+ community members to engage in identity experiments, and build friendships and support networks that may not have been possible offline. Where social compensation hypothesis has typically presented social media as a means of socially anxious, or socially inept, individuals to gain connections online, these themes may also transfer to the socially marginalized and isolated members of the LGBT+ community.

RECOMMENDATIONS FOR FUTURE PROGRAM DEVELOPMENT

Moving forward, support networks such as clinicians, educators, and parents should be aware of the potential for social media to be used as a compensatory resource for individuals struggling with severe and/or clinical social deficits—perhaps especially in the development of treatment plans, education, or social remediation programs. When working to develop this type of programming for these populations, there are a few key points to bear in mind. First, there is evidence to suggest that these specialized populations do exhibit benefits in friendship quality and well-being from using social media platforms. These platforms could then, at the very least, be considered as a tool or resource for these individuals to engage in social exchanges that may not have existed otherwise (aka social compensation).

Second, the benefits for friendships and well-being that are associated with social media use among clinical and/or marginalized populations are consistent across a variety of age categories. This suggests that the inclusion of social media platforms in social remediation programming may be beneficial for both adolescents and adults. Further, given that adolescence is a period where social skills, identity, and friendships are rapidly developing (Choudhury, Blakemore, & Charman, 2006), and that social media may be viewed as a compensatory resource for adolescents who are struggling with social development and friendships (in both clinical and general populations), adolescents may benefit the most from social interventions that include a social media component. It may be particularly beneficial to then target adolescents with deficits in social functioning when developing future programming.

Finally, clinical support networks should consider whether using social media benefits everyone, and whether promoting social media use among clinical populations needs to be treated differently from promotion in the general population. It should be noted that although the majority of the research presented in this chapter highlights the potential for social media to be used as a positive resource to engage in personal self-disclosure and gain social connections, social media sites could have negative consequences—perhaps especially for clinical or marginalized populations. In addition to the negative social comparison and increases in clinical symptoms that can accompany passively browsing social media (e.g., Verdyun et al., 2015), there are other factors that can negatively impact social media use that are outside the scope of the present chapter (e.g., cyberbullying, social media addiction). Individuals with clinical or marginalized social disadvantages may particularly be at risk for these negative consequences (e.g., Mazurek & Engelhardt, 2013). As such, future program development may need to consider including a component that helps these individuals not only use social media, but encourage ways for them to effectively, actively, and appropriately engage (van Schalkwyk et al., 2017).

LIMITATIONS AND DIRECTIONS FOR FUTURE RESEARCH

This chapter highlighted the current literature pertaining to the use of social media among clinical and socially marginalized populations, exploring the idea that social media may be used as a compensatory mechanism for the social disadvantages experienced by these populations. For knowledge advancement, future researchers will need to assess the long-term effects and magnitude of the effects, as well as develop ways to test whether the use of social media is beneficial for the specific social disadvantages posed by each of the preceding diagnoses.

The vast majority of research highlighted in the current chapter is cross-sectional and correlational. While this research can reveal the relationship between variables (e.g., social media use is associated with increases in social connectedness and/or social skills), the directionality and causal links among variables are currently speculative. The research suggests that individuals with social disadvantages exhibit benefits from using social media, however, it is equally plausible that individuals who have higher levels of social functioning are the ones turning to social media to utilize and rehearse the social skills that they already possess, and thus gaining additional social benefits. Although there are a few experimental studies that have examined the causality of these effects (e.g., schizophrenia and social media; Alvarez-Jimenez et al., 2018; Granholm, Ben-Zeev, Link, Bradshaw, & Holden, 2011), they are limited and do not exist across all the diagnoses discussed in the present chapter. Future research will need to include experimental manipulations of social media use across ASD, major depressive disorder, social anxiety, schizophrenia, and social marginalization to truly justify whether the use of social media does have a positive social impact for these populations.

Longitudinal studies are also necessary to evaluate the practical significance of the relationship between social media use and friendships among clinical and/or marginalized populations. Although using social networking sites, video gaming, and video sharing platforms are positively correlated with increases in social activity, social skills, and friendship development, how meaningful these increases are over time is largely unexplored. On one hand, it may be that social media use produces additive effects over time, such that the more these individuals use these platforms to gain social skills and social support, the more significant and meaningful the effects are for the users' psychosocial functioning. On the other hand, it may be that the benefits associated with social media use are more immediate, making the individual feel more connected in the moments that they are using the social media sites, but may not facilitate the long-term social skills development needed by these populations. Therefore, longitudinal research would be valuable for understanding any reciprocal relationships between use and psychosocial functioning as well as additive effects.

Lastly, perhaps particularly among clinically depressed or socially anxious individuals, the proposed social benefits for these populations are derived from speculating that the benefits associated from social media use among typical users with relatively higher levels of depression or anxiety symptoms will extend to clinical populations. Further, although there are studies that do consider clinical populations, the scales used to assess the social media benefits are largely those developed for average functioning individuals that are being used in a clinical context. To gain insight as to whether using social media is truly beneficial for specialized populations, future researchers will need to develop measurement strategies that assess the specific social disadvantages characterized by each of the clinical diagnoses discussed in the present chapter, and whether social media may compensate for the specific, respective social impairments therein (e.g., Mazurek et al., 2012; van Schalkwyk, 2017).

CONCLUSION

There are common themes detected among the studies highlighted in this chapter. First, social penetration theory offers an appropriate theoretical framework to describe that individuals gain closer friendships via sharing increasingly more personal and intimate about themselves (Altman & Taylor, 1975). Further, this framework can be extended to social media, such that when social media users engage in active, positive, and personal disclosures while online, they too exhibit increases in the quality of close friendships (Desjarlais et al., 2015). Perhaps most importantly, the benefits for friendships that occur from disclosing on social media may extend to populations of people with significant social disturbances, such as in the diagnosis of autism, anxiety, depression, and schizophrenia, or in cases of social marginalization as found in the LGBT+ community.

In addition, Valkenburg and Peter's (2009) social compensation hypothesis may also extend to clinical and/or marginalized populations. Although the social compensation hypothesis was initially created to suggest that individuals with relatively higher levels of social anxiety, or shyness, may use social media platforms as compensatory resources for their lack of social interactions, the findings highlighted in the current chapter suggest that this theoretical framework may extend farther. More specifically, individuals struggling with severe social impairments such as in autism and schizophrenia spectrum disorders, clinical depression, and/or clinical anxiety may also benefit from social media interactions for increasing social skills and social connections, and be able to compensate for some of their social difficulties offline. Further, individuals struggling with social marginalization, and the ensuing deficits for friendships and identity development, may also experience compensatory benefits for sharing on social media. Ultimately then, the social compensation hypothesis may be extended to clinical and marginalized populations, suggesting that these individuals could also benefit from the structure and functions of online social environments, and compensate for their offline social struggles. Moving forward, support networks such as clinicians, educators, and parents should be aware of the potential for social media to be used as a compensatory resource for individuals struggling with severe and/or clinical social deficits—perhaps especially in the development of treatment plans, or social remediation programs.

ACKNOWLEDGMENT

This research received no specific grant from any funding agency in the public, commercial, or not-for-profit sectors.

REFERENCES

Altman, I., & Taylor, D. A. (1973). *Social Penetration: The Development of Interpersonal Relationships.* New York, NY: Holt, Rinehart & Winston.

Alvarez-Jimenez, M., Alcazar-Corcoles, M. A., Gonzalez-Blanch, C., Bendall, S., McGorry, P. D., & Gleeson, J. F. (2014). Online, social media and mobile technologies for psychosis treatment: A systematic review on novel user-led interventions. *Schizophrenia Research, 156*(1), 96–106. doi:10.1016/j.schres.2014.03.021 PMID:24746468

Alvarez-Jimenez, M., Gleeson, J. F., Rice, S., Bendall, S., D'alfonso, S., Eleftheriadis, D., ... Nelson, B. (2018). 4.3 Enhancing Social Functioning And Long-term Recovery In Young People With First Episode Psychosis (fep) And Young People At Ultra High Risk (uhr) For Psychosis: A Novel Online Social Therapy Approach. *Schizophrenia Bulletin*, *44*(suppl_1), S4–S5. doi:10.1093chbulby014.010

American Psychiatric Association. (1987). *Diagnostic and statistical manual of mental disorders* (3rd ed.). Washington, DC: APA.

American Psychiatric Association. (2013). *Diagnostic and statistical manual of mental disorders* (5th ed.). Arlington, VA: APA.

Anderson, M., & Jiang, J. (2018, May 31). Teens, social media & technology 2018. *Pew Research Center*. Retrieved from http://www.pewinternet.org/2018/05/31/teens-social-media-technology-2018/

Andreasen, N. C. (1982). Negative symptoms in schizophrenia: Definition and reliability. *Archives of General Psychiatry*, *39*(7), 784–788. doi:10.1001/archpsyc.1982.04290070020005 PMID:7165477

Appel, H., Crusius, J., & Gerlach, A. L. (2015). Social comparison, envy, and depression on Facebook: A study looking at the effects of high comparison standards on depressed individuals. *Journal of Social and Clinical Psychology*, *34*(4), 277–289. doi:10.1521/jscp.2015.34.4.277

Bauminger, N., & Shulman, C. (2003). The development and maintenance of friendship in high-functioning children with autism: Maternal perceptions. *Autism*, *7*(1), 81–97. doi:10.1177/1362361303007001007 PMID:12638766

Bellack, A. S., Morrison, R. L., Wixted, J. T., & Mueser, K. T. (1990). An analysis of social competence in schizophrenia. *The British Journal of Psychiatry*, *156*(06), 809–818. doi:10.1192/bjp.156.6.809 PMID:2207511

Burke, M., & Develin, M. (2016, February). Once more with feeling: Supportive responses to social sharing on Facebook. In *Proceedings of the 19th ACM Conference on Computer-Supported Cooperative Work & Social Computing* (pp. 1462-1474). ACM. Retrieved from https://dl.acm.org/citation.cfm?id=2835199.

Burke, M., Kraut, R., & Marlow, C. (2011, May). Social capital on Facebook: Differentiating uses and users. In *Proceedings of the SIGCHI conference on human factors in computing systems* (pp. 571-580). ACM. 10.1145/1978942.1979023

Burke, M., Kraut, R., & Williams, D. (2010, February). Social use of computer-mediated communication by adults on the autism spectrum. In *Proceedings of the 2010 ACM conference on Computer supported cooperative work* (pp. 425-434). ACM. 10.1145/1718918.1718991

Chou, H. T. G., & Edge, N. (2012). "They are happier and having better lives than I am": The impact of using Facebook on perceptions of others' lives. *Cyberpsychology, Behavior, and Social Networking*, *15*(2), 117–121. doi:10.1089/cyber.2011.0324 PMID:22165917

Choudhury, S., Blakemore, S. J., & Charman, T. (2006). Social cognitive development during adolescence. *Social Cognitive and Affective Neuroscience*, *1*(3), 165–174. doi:10.1093can/nsl024 PMID:18985103

Clark, D. M., & Wells, A. (1995). A cognitive model of social phobia. In M. Liebowitz, & R. G. Heimberg (Eds.), *Social phobia: Diagnosis, assessment, and treatment* (pp. 69–93). New York, NY: Guilford Press.

Code, J. (2013). Agency and identity in social media. In Digital identity and social media (pp. 37–57). Hershey, PA: IGI Global. doi:10.4018/978-1-4666-1915-9.ch004

Cole, H., & Griffiths, M. D. (2007). Social interactions in massively multiplayer online role-playing gamers. *Cyberpsychology & Behavior, 10*(4), 575–583. doi:10.1089/cpb.2007.9988 PMID:17711367

Collins, N. L., & Miller, L. C. (1994). Self-disclosure and liking: A meta-analytic review. *Psychological Bulletin, 116*(3), 457–475. doi:10.1037/0033-2909.116.3.457 PMID:7809308

Coyne, J. C., Kessler, R. C., Tal, M., Turnbull, J., Wortman, C. B., & Greden, J. F. (1987). Living with a depressed person. *Journal of Consulting and Clinical Psychology, 55*(3), 347–352. doi:10.1037/0022-006X.55.3.347 PMID:3597947

D'Augelli, A. R. (2002). Mental health problems among lesbian, gay, and bisexual youths ages 14 to 21. *Clinical Child Psychology and Psychiatry, 7*(3), 433–456. doi:10.1177/1359104502007003039

Daley, M. L., Becker, D. F., Flaherty, L. T., Harper, G., King, R. A., Lester, P., ... Schwab-Stone, M. (2005). Case study: The Internet as a developmental tool in an adolescent boy with psychosis. *Journal of the American Academy of Child and Adolescent Psychiatry, 44*(2), 187–190. doi:10.1097/00004583-200502000-00011 PMID:15689732

Davis, K. (2012). Friendship 2.0: Adolescents' experiences of belonging and self-disclosure online. *Journal of Adolescence, 35*(6), 1527–1536. doi:10.1016/j.adolescence.2012.02.013 PMID:22475444

Davis, K. (2013). Young people's digital lives: The impact of interpersonal relationships and digital media use on adolescents' sense of identity. *Computers in Human Behavior, 29*(6), 2281–2293. doi:10.1016/j.chb.2013.05.022

DeHaan, S., Kuper, L. E., Magee, J. C., Bigelow, L., & Mustanski, B. S. (2013). The interplay between online and offline explorations of identity, relationships, and sex: A mixed-methods study with LGBT youth. *Journal of Sex Research, 50*(5), 421–434. doi:10.1080/00224499.2012.661489 PMID:22489658

Desjarlais, M., Gilmour, J., Sinclair, J., Howell, K. B., & West, A. (2015). Predictors and social consequences of online interactive self-disclosure: A literature review from 2002 to 2014. *Cyberpsychology, Behavior, and Social Networking, 18*(12), 718–725. doi:10.1089/cyber.2015.0109 PMID:26652672

Desjarlais, M., & Joseph, J. J. (2017). Socially interactive and passive technologies enhance friendship quality: An investigation of the mediating roles of online and offline self-disclosure. *Cyberpsychology, Behavior, and Social Networking, 20*(5), 286–291. doi:10.1089/cyber.2016.0363 PMID:28418718

Desjarlais, M., & Willoughby, T. (2010). A longitudinal study of the relation between adolescent boys and girls' computer use with friends and friendship quality: Support for the social compensation or the rich-get-richer hypothesis? *Computers in Human Behavior, 26*(5), 896–905. doi:10.1016/j.chb.2010.02.004

Deters, F. G., & Mehl, M. R. (2012). Does posting Facebook status updates increase or decrease loneliness? An online social networking experiment. *Social Psychological and Personality Science, 4,* 579-586. doi:10.1177/1948550612469233

Diener, E., Suh, E. M., Lucas, R. E., & Smith, H. L. (1999). Subjective well-being: Three decades of progress. *Psychological Bulletin, 125*(2), 276–302. doi:10.1037/0033-2909.125.2.276

Ellison, N. B., Steinfield, C., & Lampe, C. (2007). The benefits of Facebook "friends:" Social capital and college students' use of online social network sites. *Journal of Computer-Mediated Communication*, *12*(4), 1143–1168. doi:10.1111/j.1083-6101.2007.00367.x

Essau, C. A., Lewinsohn, P. M., Lim, J. X., Moon-ho, R. H., & Rohde, P. (2018). Incidence, recurrence and comorbidity of anxiety disorders in four major developmental stages. *Journal of Affective Disorders*, *228*, 248–253. doi:10.1016/j.jad.2017.12.014 PMID:29304469

Fact Sheet. (2018, Feb. 5). Social media fact sheet. *Pew Research Centre*. Retrieved from http://www.pewinternet.org/fact-sheet/social-media/

Feinstein, B. A., Hershenberg, R., Bhatia, V., Latack, J. A., Meuwly, N., & Davila, J. (2013). Negative social comparison on Facebook and depressive symptoms: Rumination as a mechanism. *Psychology of Popular Media Culture*, *2*(3), 161–170. doi:10.1037/a0033111

Festinger, L. (1954). A theory of social comparison processes. *Human Relations*, *7*(2), 117–140. doi:10.1177/001872675400700202

Fox, J., & Ralston, R. (2016). Queer identity online: Informal learning and teaching experiences of LGBTQ individuals on social media. *Computers in Human Behavior*, *65*, 635–642. doi:10.1016/j.chb.2016.06.009

Frith, U. (1989). *Autism: Explaining the enigma*. Hoboken, NJ: Blackwell Publishing.

Giacco, D., McCabe, R., Kallert, T., Hansson, L., Fiorillo, A., & Priebe, S. (2012). Friends and symptom dimensions in patients with psychosis: A Pooled Analysis. *PLoS One*, *7*(11), e50119. doi:10.1371/journal.pone.0050119 PMID:23185552

Goffman, E. (1959). *The presentation of self in everyday life*. Oxford, UK: Doubleday. Retrieved from books.google.com

Gorman, J. M. (1996). Comorbid depression and anxiety spectrum disorders. *Depression and Anxiety*, *4*(4), 160–168. doi:10.1002/(SICI)1520-6394(1996)4:4<160::AID-DA2>3.0.CO;2-J PMID:9166648

Gramlich, J. (2018, Oct. 24). 8 facts about Americans and Facebook. *Pew Research Centre*. Retrieved from http://www.pewresearch.org/fact-tank/2018/10/24/facts-about-americans-and-facebook/

Granholm, E., Ben-Zeev, D., Link, P. C., Bradshaw, K. R., & Holden, J. L. (2011). Mobile Assessment and Treatment for Schizophrenia (MATS): A pilot trial of an interactive text-messaging intervention for medication adherence, socialization, and auditory hallucinations. *Schizophrenia Bulletin*, *38*(3), 414–425. doi:10.1093chbulbr155 PMID:22080492

Greene, K., Derlega, V. J., & Mathews, A. (2006). Self-disclosure in personal relationships. The Cambridge Handbook of Personal Relationships, 409-427.

Greenwood, S., Perrin, A., & Duggan, M. (2016, Nov. 11). Social media update 2016: Facebook usage and engagement is on the rise, while adoption of other platforms holds steady. *Pew Research Center*. Retrieved from http://www.pewinternet.org/2016/11/11/social-media-update-2016/

Grieve, R., Indian, M., Witteveen, L., Tolan, G. A., & Marrington, J. (2013). Face-to-face or Facebook: Can social connectedness be derived online? *Computers in Human Behavior*, *29*(3), 604–609. doi:10.1016/j.chb.2012.11.017

Hewitt, P. L., Flett, G. L., Sherry, S. B., Habke, M., Parkin, M., Lam, R. W., ... Stein, M. B. (2003). The interpersonal expression of perfection: Perfectionistic self-presentation and psychological distress. *Journal of Personality and Social Psychology*, *84*(6), 1303–1325. doi:10.1037/0022-3514.84.6.1303 PMID:12793591

Hillier, L., & Harrison, L. (2007). Building realities less limited than their own: Young people practising same-sex attraction on the Internet. *Sexualities*, *10*(1), 82–100. doi:10.1177/1363460707072956

Hillier, L., Horsely, P., & Kurdas, C. (2004). It made me feel braver, I was no longer alone: Same sex attracted young people negotiating the pleasures and pitfalls of the Internet. In J. A. Nieto (Ed.), Sexuality in the Pacific. Madrid: AECI (Asociación Española de Coperación Internacional) and the AEEP (Asociación Española de Estudios del Pacífico).

Hillier, L., Jones, T., Monagle, M., Overton, N., Gahan, L., Blackman, J., & Mitchell, A. (2010). *Writing themselves in 3: The third national study on the sexual health and wellbeing of same sex attracted and gender questioning young people*. Melbourne, Australia: Australian Research Centre in Sex, Heath, and Society, La Trobe University.

Hillier, L., Mitchell, K. J., & Ybarra, M. L. (2012). The Internet as a safety net: Findings from a series of online focus groups with LGB and non-LGB young people in the U.S. *Journal of LGBT Youth*, *9*(3), 225–246. doi:10.1080/19361653.2012.684642

Hswen, Y., Naslund, J. A., Brownstein, J. S., & Hawkins, J. B. (2018). Online Communication about Depression and Anxiety among Twitter Users with Schizophrenia: Preliminary Findings to Inform a Digital Phenotype Using Social Media. *The Psychiatric Quarterly*, 1–12. PMID:29327218

Hu, Y., Manikonda, L., & Kambhampati, S. (2014, May). What we Instagram: A first analysis of Instagram photo content and user types. *Eighth International AAAI conference on weblogs and social media*.

Joseph, J. J., Desjarlais, M., & Herceg, L. (2019). Facebook depression or Facebook contentment: The relation between Facebook use and subjective well-being. In R. Gopalan (Ed.), Intimacy and Developing Personal Relationships in the Virtual World (pp. 104–125). Hershey, PA: IGI Global. doi:10.4018/978-1-5225-4047-2.ch007

Katz, J. E., & Rice, R. E. (2002). *Social consequences of Internet use: Access, Involvement, and Interaction*. MIT Press. doi:10.7551/mitpress/6292.001.0001

Kohn, M. L., & Clausen, J. A. (1955). Social isolation and schizophrenia. *American Sociological Review*, *20*(3), 265–273. doi:10.2307/2087384

Kotfila, C. (2014). This message will self-destruct: The growing role of obscurity and self-destruct- ing data in digital communication. *Bulletin of the American Society for Information Science and Technology*, *40*(2), 12–16. doi:10.1002/bult.2014.1720400206

Kraut, R., Kiesler, S., Boneva, B., Cummings, J., Helgeson, V., & Crawford, A. (2002). Internet paradox revisited. *The Journal of Social Issues*, *58*(1), 49–74. doi:10.1111/1540-4560.00248

Kraut, R., Patterson, V., Lundmark, M., Kiesler, S., Mukophadhyay, T., & Scherlis, W. (1998). Internet paradox: A social technology that reduces social involvement and psychological well-being? *The American Psychologist*, *53*(9), 1017–1031. doi:10.1037/0003-066X.53.9.1017 PMID:9841579

Lavelle, M., Healey, P. G., & McCabe, R. (2013). Is nonverbal communication disrupted in interactions involving patients with schizophrenia? *Schizophrenia Bulletin*, *39*(5), 1150–1158. doi:10.1093chbulbs091 PMID:22941744

Lawson, W. (2001). *Understanding and working with the spectrum of autism: An insider's view*. London, UK: Jessica Kingsley.

Marcia, J. E. (1966). Development and validation of ego-identity status. *Journal of Personality and Social Psychology*, *3*(5), 551–558. doi:10.1037/h0023281 PMID:5939604

Mazurek, M. O. (2013). Social media use among adults with autism spectrum disorders. *Computers in Human Behavior*, *29*(4), 1709–1714. doi:10.1016/j.chb.2013.02.004

Mazurek, M. O., & Engelhardt, C. R. (2013). Video game use in boys with autism spectrum disorder, ADHD, or typical development. *Pediatrics*, *132*(2), 260–266. doi:10.1542/peds.2012-3956 PMID:23897915

Mazurek, M. O., Shattuck, P. T., Wagner, M., & Cooper, B. P. (2012). Prevalence and correlates of screen-based media use among youths with autism spectrum disorders. *Journal of Autism and Developmental Disorders*, *42*(8), 1757–1767. doi:10.100710803-011-1413-8 PMID:22160370

Mazurek, M. O., & Wenstrup, C. (2013). Television, video game and social media use among children with ASD and typically developing siblings. *Journal of Autism and Developmental Disorders*, *43*(6), 1258–1271. doi:10.100710803-012-1659-9 PMID:23001767

McKenna, K. Y. A., & Bargh, J. A. (2000). Plan 9 from Cyberspace: The Implications of the Internet for Personality and Social Psychology. *Personality and Social Psychology Review*, *4*(1), 57–75. doi:10.1207/S15327957PSPR0401_6

McLean, K. C. (2005). Late adolescent identity development: Narrative meaning-making and memory telling. *Developmental Psychology*, *41*(4), 683–691. doi:10.1037/0012-1649.41.4.683 PMID:16060814

Mehra, B., Merkel, C., & Bishop, A. P. (2004). The Internet for empowerment of minority and marginalized users. *New Media & Society*, *6*(6), 781–802. doi:10.1177/146144804047513

Miller, B. J., Stewart, A., Schrimsher, J., Peeples, D., & Buckley, P. F. (2015). How connected are people with schizophrenia? Cell phone, computer, email, and social media use. *Psychiatry Research*, *225*(3), 458–463. doi:10.1016/j.psychres.2014.11.067 PMID:25563669

Mittal, V. A., Tessner, K. D., & Walker, E. F. (2007). Elevated social Internet use and schizotypal personality disorder in adolescents. *Schizophrenia Research*, *94*(1-3), 50–57. doi:10.1016/j.schres.2007.04.009 PMID:17532188

Moreno, M. A., Christakis, D. A., Egan, K. G., Jelenchick, L. A., Cox, E., Young, H., ... Becker, T. (2012). A pilot evaluation of associations between displayed depression references on Facebook and self-reported depression using a clinical scale. *The Journal of Behavioral Health Services & Research*, *39*(3), 295–304. doi:10.100711414-011-9258-7 PMID:21863354

Naslund, J. A., Grande, S. W., Aschbrenner, K. A., & Elwyn, G. (2014). Naturally occurring peer support through social media: The experiences of individuals with severe mental illness using YouTube. *PLoS One*, *9*(10), e110171. doi:10.1371/journal.pone.0110171 PMID:25333470

Neeleman, J., & Power, M. J. (1994). Social support and depression in three groups of psychiatric patients and a group of medical controls. *Social Psychiatry and Psychiatric Epidemiology*, *29*, 46–51. PMID:8178222

Park, J., Lee, D. S., Shablack, H., Verduyn, P., Deldin, P., Ybarra, O., ... Kross, E. (2016). When perceptions defy reality: The relationships between depression and actual and perceived Facebook social support. *Journal of Affective Disorders*, *200*, 37–44. doi:10.1016/j.jad.2016.01.048 PMID:27126138

Pullen, C., & Cooper, M. (Eds.). (2010). *LGBT identity and online new media*. New York, NY: Routledge. doi:10.4324/9780203855430

Rowley, E., Chandler, S., Baird, G., Simono, E., Pickles, A., Loucas, T., & Charman, T. (2012). The experience of friendship, victimization and bullying in children with an autism spectrum disorder: Associations with child characteristics and school placement. *Research in Autism Spectrum Disorders*, *6*(3), 1126–1134. doi:10.1016/j.rasd.2012.03.004

Ryan, C., & Rivers, I. (2003). Lesbian, gay, bisexual, and transgender youth: Victimization and its correlates in the USA and UK. *Culture, Health & Sexuality*, *5*(2), 103–119. doi:10.1080/1369105011000012883

Sainsbury, C. (2000). *Martian in the playground: Understanding the schoolchild with Asperger Syndrome*. Bristol, UK: Lucky Duck Publishers.

Saunders, S. A., & Roy, C. (1999). The relationship between depression, satisfaction with life, and social interest. *South Pacific Journal of Psychology*, *11*(1), 9–15. doi:10.1017/S0257543400000717

Schrank, B., Sibitz, I., Unger, A., & Amering, M. (2010). How patients with schizophrenia use the Internet: Qualitative study. *Journal of Medical Internet Research*, *12*(5), e70. doi:10.2196/jmir.1550 PMID:21169176

Sheldon, P., & Bryant, K. (2016). Instagram: Motives for its use and relationship to narcissism and contextual age. *Computers in Human Behavior*, *58*, 89–97. doi:10.1016/j.chb.2015.12.059

Smith, A. (2011, Nov. 15). Why Americans use social media friends. *Pew Research Center*. Retrieved from http://www.pewinternet.org/2011/11/15/why-americans-use-social-media/

Smith, A., & Anderson, M. (2018, March 1). Social media use in 2018. *Pew Research Centre*. Retrieved from http://www.pewinternet.org/2018/03/01/social-media-use-in-2018/

Stats. (2018, Sept. 30). Retrieved from https://newsroom.fb.com/company-info/

Subhrajit, C. (2014). Problems faced by LGBT people in the mainstream society: Some recommendations. *International Journal of Interdisciplinary and Multidisciplinary Studies, 1*, 317–331.

Sundberg, M. (2018). Online gaming, loneliness and friendships among adolescents and adults with ASD. *Computers in Human Behavior, 79*, 105–110. doi:10.1016/j.chb.2017.10.020

Tandoc, E. C. Jr, Ferrucci, P., & Duffy, M. (2015). Facebook use, envy, and depression among college students: Is facebooking depressing? *Computers in Human Behavior, 43*, 139–146. doi:10.1016/j.chb.2014.10.053

Turner, J. C. (1975). Social comparison and social identity: Some prospects for intergroup behaviour. *European Journal of Social Psychology, 5*(1), 1–34. doi:10.1002/ejsp.2420050102

Valkenburg, P. M., & Peter, J. (2007). Preadolescents' and adolescents' online communication and their closeness to friends. *Developmental Psychology, 43*(2), 267–277. doi:10.1037/0012-1649.43.2.267 PMID:17352538

Valkenburg, P. M., & Peter, J. (2009). Social consequences of the Internet for adolescents a decade of research. *Current Directions in Psychological Science, 18*(1), 1–5. doi:10.1111/j.1467-8721.2009.01595.x

Valkenburg, P. M., Schouten, A. P., & Peter, J. (2005). Adolescents' identity experiments on the Internet. *New Media & Society, 7*(3), 383–402. doi:10.1177/1461444805052282

van Schalkwyk, G. I., Marin, C. E., Ortiz, M., Rolison, M., Qayyum, Z., McPartland, J. C., ... Silverman, W. K. (2017). Social media use, friendship quality, and the moderating role of anxiety in adolescents with autism spectrum disorder. *Journal of Autism and Developmental Disorders, 47*(9), 2805–2813. doi:10.100710803-017-3201-6 PMID:28616856

Verduyn, P., Lee, D. S., Park, J., Shablack, H., Orvell, A., Bayer, J., & Kross, E. (2015). Passive Facebook usage undermines affective well-being: Experimental and longitudinal evidence. *Journal of Experimental Psychology: General, 144*, 480-488. doi:2062/ doi:10.1037/xge0000057

Verduyn, P., Ybarra, O., Résibois, M., Jonides, J., & Kross, E. (2017). Do social network sites enhance or undermine subjective well-being: A critical review. *Social Issues and Policy Review, 11*(1), 274–302. doi:10.1111ipr.12033

Vogel, E. A., Rose, J. P., Roberts, L. R., & Eckles, K. (2014). Social comparison, social media, and self-esteem. *Psychology of Popular Media Culture, 3*(4), 206–222. doi:10.1037/ppm0000047

Walther, J. B. (2007). Selective self-presentation in computer-mediated communication: Hyperpersonal dimensions of technology, language, and cognition. *Computers in Human Behavior, 23*(5), 2538–2557. doi:10.1016/j.chb.2006.05.002

Ward, D. M., Dill-Shackleford, K. E., & Mazurek, M. O. (2018). Social Media Use and Happiness in Adults with Autism Spectrum Disorder. *Cyberpsychology, Behavior, and Social Networking, 21*(3), 205–209. doi:10.1089/cyber.2017.0331 PMID:29485900

Watson, D., & Friend, R. (1969). Measurement of social-evaluative anxiety. *Journal of Consulting and Clinical Psychology, 33*(4), 448–457. doi:10.1037/h0027806 PMID:5810590

Weiss, R. S. (1973). *Loneliness: The experience of emotional and social isolation*. Cambridge, MA: MIT Press.

World Health Organization. (2017). Depression and other common mental disorders: Global health estimates. *World Health Organization*. Retrieved from https://apps.who.int/iris/bitstream/handle/10665/254610/WHO-MSD-MER-2017.2-eng.pdf?sequence=1

World Health Organization. (2018). *International statistical classification of diseases and related health problems*. Retrieved from https://icd.who.int/browse11/l-m/en

Wright, K. B., Rosenberg, J., Egbert, N., Ploeger, N. A., Bernard, D. R., & King, S. (2012). Communication competence, social support, and depression among college students: A model of Facebook and face-to-face support network influence. *Journal of Health Communication, 18*(1), 41–57. doi:10.1080/10810730.2012.688250 PMID:23030518

Xu, W. W., Park, J. Y., Kim, J. Y., & Park, H. W. (2016). Networked cultural diffusion and creation on YouTube: An analysis of YouTube memes. *Journal of Broadcasting & Electronic Media, 60*, 104-122.

Yang, M. L., Yang, C. C., & Chiou, W. B. (2010). Differences in engaging in sexual disclosure between real life and cyberspace among adolescents: Social penetration model revisited. *Current Psychology (New Brunswick, N.J.), 29*(2), 144–154. doi:10.100712144-010-9078-6

Ybarra, M. L., Mitchell, K. J., Palmer, N. A., & Reisner, S. L. (2015). Online social support as a buffer against online and offline peer and sexual victimization among US LGBT and non-LGBT youth. *Child Abuse & Neglect, 39*, 123–136. doi:10.1016/j.chiabu.2014.08.006 PMID:25192961

Zhao, S., Grasmuck, S., & Martin, J. (2008). Identity construction on Facebook: Digital empowerment in anchored relationships. *Computers in Human Behavior, 24*(5), 1816–1836. doi:10.1016/j.chb.2008.02.012

KEY TERMS AND DEFINITIONS

Anxiety: A clinical term used to define a state of fear, worry, and stress. Anxiety is also a cluster of a variety of fear and stressed based symptoms that often result in social avoidance.

Autism Spectrum Disorder: A clinical term used to classify symptoms of a disorder that includes pervasive developmental delays and severely impaired social functioning.

Depression: Clinically referred to as Major Depressive Disorder, a clinical categorization for a disorder containing extreme sadness, hopelessness, and decreased interest in social engagements.

Friendship: An interpersonal bond between two or more people that includes a level of emotional attachment.

Identity: A specific set of principles, morals, and values by which an individual views, and acts in, the world around them.

Schizophrenia Spectrum Disorder: A clinical term used in the classification of symptoms including psychosis, hallucinations, delusions, disorganization, and marked social impairments.

Social Compensation Hypothesis: A hypothesis that postulates that individuals with social challenges may be able to use social media to compensate for their limited social exchanges.

Social Media: A term that extends to any technological medium that helps facilitate communication and connections.

Social Networking Sites: A specific form of social media that includes creating an online profile to share photos, videos, and text based personal information that is broadcasted to friends on the internet.

Social Penetration Theory: A theory developed to demonstrate the mechanism by which individuals develop close relationships is through increasingly personal self-disclosure.

Video Sharing Sites: A specific form of social media that includes uploading or sharing videos and broadcasting them to some combination of friends and/or strangers.

This research was previously published in The Psychology and Dynamics Behind Social Media Interactions; pages 28-56, copyright year 2020 by Information Science Reference (an imprint of IGI Global).

Chapter 9
The Facebook Me:
Gender, Self–Esteem, and Personality on Social Media

Heng Zhang
East Tennessee State University, USA

Robert Andrew Dunn
iD https://orcid.org/0000-0003-0415-6662
East Tennessee State University, USA

ABSTRACT

For a better understanding of social networking site usage, the present study examines the influence of gender, personality, and self-esteem on social media presentation. The researchers found that extroverted women posted more Facebook pictures than extroverted men did. Neuroticism was related to self-presentation, and agreeableness is related to Facebook friends. Lower self-esteem was related to more self-presentation on Facebook. Women were more likely to post gender role expressions than men were. And higher levels of neuroticism were related to greater gender role expressions.

INTRODUCTION

Millions of people are living part of their lives on social networking sites. Social networking sites are places where users present themselves to the world. Individuals have the opportunity to mold their images for social purposes online by using social networking sites like Facebook and Twitter (Rosenberg & Egbert, 2011). Social networking sites permit users to create unique profiles to influence how others see them in order to build up the images they desire.

Individuals communicate and engage with others through social networking sites by using the images they created online, revealing personal details and insights into their lives. Personalities and self-esteem are both influential factors of how individuals communicate with others (Hamburger & Ben-Artzi, 2000; MacIntyre, Babin, & Clément, 1999). Many social networking sites allow users to post status updates to express emotions. The posts reflect the ways they present themselves, which can be used to examine

DOI: 10.4018/978-1-6684-6307-9.ch009

their personality and self-esteem in online environments. To understand the relationships between these factors better, the current study assesses how individuals' personality traits and self-esteem impact self-presentation on Facebook. Gender differences in communication have been discussed in many aspects, and personality has been shown to be relevant to many types of interactions (Adrianson, 2001; Muscanell & Guadagno, 2012; Simpson & Stroh, 2004). In online communication, people form and manage their online image and interact with each other using different tactics (Aronson, Wilson, Timothy, Akert, & Robin, 2009).

This study explores the relationship between personality and social media usage to provide a better understanding of the differences in social media usage among men and women based on their personality and self-esteem. The purpose of this study is to determine if there is a connection among gender and personalities in terms of the use of social media. The participants in this study are undergraduate students. The results of this study could be used to gain a deeper understanding of the link between social media usage and personality among young adults. The body of literature on engaging through social media is limited; this research will gain a greater understanding of social trends as well as a better understanding of college students' social media usage by gender, self-esteem, and personality traits.

GENDER STEREOTYPES

The distinction between men and women is a basic organization principle for every society. Men and women identify their gender during their childhood and continue to behave in ways following prescribed gender role stereotypes (Bem, 1981). Gender role stereotypes are also displayed in the way men and women communicate. Researchers have spent considerable energy examining gender differences in face-to-face (FtF) communication (Simpson & Stroh, 2004).

Simpson and Stroh (2004) found that men and women have different ways to display emotions in FtF communication. Women more often tend to follow feminine expression rules, which require the suppression of negative emotions such as anger and frustration. Feminine expression rules also support the simulation of positive emotions such as enthusiasm, warmth, and love. Conversely, men more often adopt masculine expression rules, which dictate the subdual of positive emotions and encourage the expression of negative ones. The researchers also found that emotions that contribute to the maintenance of social relationships, such as warmth and cheerfulness, tend to be regarded as more appropriate for women, but the expression of positive emotions is generally found to be less desirable for men. The results suggest emotional display patterns in FtF communication are different between men and women.

Crick (1997) indicated that in communication, the expression of anger and aggression are generally seen as acceptable for men but not for women. This is in line with Adrianson's (2001) idea that social judgments were more positive from women than from men, and that women expressed more opinions and agreements in communication than men did.

Gender role stereotypes in communication have been examined in both FtF and computer-mediated communication (CMC) environments. There have been many studies conducted about trends based on gender in social media use (Adrianson, 2001; Muscanell & Guadagno, 2012; Simpson & Stroh, 2004). Men and women use different amounts of time and have different motivations for using social networking sites (Sheldon, 2008).

Men and women use social networking sites in different ways and for different purposes. In general, researchers have found that women generally use social networking services more often than men and for distinctive social purposes (Simpson & Stroh, 2004). For women, their online behavior tends to be interpersonal in nature, while men are considered to be more task-and information-oriented (Jackson, Ervin, Gardner, & Schmitt, 2001).

Women use many tactics to build their images in computer-mediated communication to elicit more socially favorable impressions. Previous studies showed that women spend more time on Facebook (Sheldon, 2008) and use social networking sites more frequently to compare themselves with others. Conversely men are more likely to view other people's profiles and find friends (Haferkamp, Eimler, Papadakis, & Kruck, 2012). These tendencies not only indicate dissimilarities in the way men and women use social media, but also suggest fundamental differences in the underlying reasons for engaging in social media.

Recent research indicates that the amount of time spent online and the motivations for Internet use are different between men and women (Muscanell & Guadagno, 2012). For example, compared with men, women use the Internet more frequently to moderate social interaction and behave in ways that are consistent with feminine stereotypes that promote relationship maintenance. Men are more likely to engaging in more task-focused activities online, such as reading the news and obtaining financial information. Additionally, men have been found to be more likely to behave in ways consistent with masculine stereotypes that promote an achievement-orientation (Adrianson, 2001).

GENDER ROLE EXPRESSION ON SOCIAL MEDIA

With the increasing presence of social media in the average person's life, gender role expectations for online behavior often shape the way people choose to represent themselves online. Research on how gender role stereotypes work in social media often amount to the expression of those roles by the author. Research has argued that women are more likely than men to portray themselves as attractive and as wanting or needing social connectivity (Haferkamp et al., 2012; Manago, Graham, Greenfield, & Salimkhan, 2008). That is not to say that presentation of gender is inherently problematic. On the contrary, the expression of femininity including feminine sexuality by women on social media can be quite liberating and empowering (Dobson, 2015), even though such expressions can then be redistributed and repurposed by men in objectifying ways (Davis, 2018). Steeves (2015) wrote about the very complex balancing act girls and women must maintain to follow the unwritten rules of social media.

They described social media as a place where they faced an incredible amount of judgment and pressure, especially about their bodies: a place where girls are open to criticism because they are too fat, too made up, not made up enough, expose too much cleavage (and are therefore sluts), don't expose enough cleavage, have too many friends (and are therefore desperate), and/or don't have enough friends (and are therefore losers). The oppressive need for attention to detail, to present that just right image, was often exhausting, especially for high school students. (p. 163)

SELF-PRESENTATION AND IMPRESSION MANAGEMENT

Desired impressions are impressions a person wants to display (Leary, 1996). Making desired impressions is a goal both males and females attempt to achieve (Leary, 1996). Desired impressions are manipulated more easily in an online environment than in FtF interactions. Goffman (1959), though writing in a time long before computer-mediated communication, offered insight for understanding the functions and meaning of women's communication in online environments. Before engaging in self-presentation and impression management tactics, people first must decide what impression they hope to make. In this context, developing a favorable impression is thought to be the primary goal. Once the primary goal has been identified, individuals will use self-presentation and the management of impressions to reach the goal.

Self-presentation is a type of communication behavior used to create an image of oneself to present to others (Lee, Quigley, Nesler, Corbett, & Tedeschi, 1999). Individuals design an image of themselves to exert their personal identity and present themselves in a way that is consistent with that desired image (Schlenker, 1980). Through communication, people identify the image they want to present to the public then constantly use many tactics to present themselves to the public in order to build up their desired image. Self-presentation researchers have provided a great deal of support for the existence and use of many self-presentation tactics (Jones & Pittman, 1982; Lee et al., 1999). Self-presentation is an important aspect of daily life, and people use self-presentation to lead others to perceive them positively, such as being trustworthy, competent, friendly, and caring. Individuals often employ multiple self-presentation tactics to create a favorable image (as cited in Rosenberg & Egbert, 2011).

Impression management theory states that an individual or organization must create and maintain impressions that correspond with the perceptions they wish to convey to the public (Goffman, 1959). Goffman asserted that people engage in strategic actions to establish and sustain a desired image. He also wrote that people not only try to convince others to view them as just, respectable, and moral people, but also that people want to maintain the positive impressions they have already established (as cited in Rosenberg & Egbert, 2011). People adopt many different impression management strategies. According to experts (Aronson et al., 2009; Goffman, 1959; Schlenker, 1980), the strategies can be divided into three categories. The first is ingratiation, where people use flattery or praise to increase their interpersonal attractiveness by emphasizing their best traits so that others will like them (Schlenker, 1980). Intimidation is another impression management strategy, and it involves aggressively showing anger to get others to listen and obey. The third one is self-handicapping (Aronson et al., 2009). Individuals use self-handicapping when they generate "obstacles" and "excuses" (Aronson et al., 2009, p. 174) for themselves so they can avoid accountability when they fail to succeed. People who self-handicap elect to blame their failures on external causes rather than internal causes, such as their own lack of ability.

Both self-presentation and impression management are tactics used to achieve socially favorable impressions. Most of these tactics fall into two major categories: one is self-enhancement, which means efforts to increase one's appeal to others, which includes self-handicapping. The other is other-enhancement, which indicates efforts to make other people feel good, which includes ingratiation and intimidation (as cited in Pandey, Singh, & Singh, 1987). Self-presentation and impression management are both efforts people make consciously to present and display certain behaviors and traits in order to make a desired and designed impression on a target audience (Leary, 1996; Schlenker, & Pontari, 2000).

Impression management and self-presentation are applicable not only to FtF interactions, but also online (Zhao, Grasmuck, & Martin, 2008). When considering online environments, such as social networking sites, a great deal of convenience is provided for users to interact with each other and maintain relationships. The ease of online communication allows people to interact with more people with less effort expended, which results in individuals maintaining relationships they would be unable to manage face to face.

According to Leary (1996), there are two motivations for the management of impression in online environments. The first is publicity, and the second is the likelihood of future interactions. The public nature of the individual's impression encourages him or her to manage impressions more carefully. In addition, future interactions with a person's social media connections are highly likely to occur, perhaps both FtF and online, which contributes to individuals' motivation to manage their impressions closely.

Social media is used as a public social setting, and users perceive social networking sites as social settings because much information is disclosed on the platform. However, social media also blurs these lines because people are alone when they use it. This may affect the users' expressions on social networking sites. Buck, Losow, Murphy, and Costanzo (1992) presented evidence that the expressions and communication of emotion can be "either facilitated or inhibited by the presence of others, depending on the nature of the emotional stimulus and of the personal or social relationship with the other or others" (p. 967). According to Buck et al. (1992), people's behavior and responses vary depending on if they are alone or in a perceived social environment; when a subject is alone the spontaneous response to emotional stimuli is relatively clear, but in a social setting the response is relatively complicated.

The nature of impression management in general is socially favorable. According to Walther (1996), "people expend considerable social energy attempting to get others to like and to appreciate them" (p. 91). Walther (2007) also mentioned the hyperpersonal model of CMC, which involves people using CMC to judiciously craft messages in order to manage impressions and build relationships. Messages on CMC are editable, a unique feature not available in FtF communication. Users can revise and refine their content before they publish it with less social awkwardness (Walther, 2007). Manago et al. (2008) suggested that college students use social media to explore their identities, engage in social comparison, and express idealized aspects of themselves that they wish to become. The study also suggested that social networking sites provide meaningful opportunities for emerging adults to explore potential versions of themselves and form desirable impressions. Procuring a desired socially favorable impression is one reason for people's self-presentation on social networking sites. To achieve the desired impressions, different users with different personalities would present themselves and manage impressions through different ways.

PERSONALITY

The "Big Five" (Benet-Martínez & John, 1998) model of personality traits has been widely used by many researchers in recent years (Amichai-Hamburger & Ben-Artzi, 2003; Golbeck, Robles, & Turner 2011; Qiu, Lin, Ramsay, & Yang, 2012). Many researchers have discussed the relationship between social media usage and personality traits (Hughes, Rowe, Batey, & Lee, 2012; Schrammel, Köffel, & Tscheligi, 2009). The "Big Five" model has become a major personality measurement. The "Big Five" personality dimensions include openness to new experiences, conscientiousness, extraversion, agreeableness, and neuroticism. Golbeck et al. (2011) argued that these personality traits come with their own attributes. Openness to new experiences is a personality trait that relates to being positively receptive to a diversity of personal experiences and is characterized by being curious, intelligent, and imaginative. Conscientiousness is a personality trait that relates to the responsibility one feels toward goals, being organized, and persevering. Extraversion is a personality trait that relates to socialization, being amicable, and being assertive. Agreeableness is a personality trait that relates to a prosocial proclivity, being cooperative, being helpful, and being nurturing. Neuroticism is a personality trait that relates to emotional reactivity, anxiety, insecurity, and sensitivity. Specifically, the researchers for the present study were interested in the personality traits of extraversion, agreeableness, and neuroticism.

Social media is a place where users present themselves to the public and reveal personal details. Users with different personality tendencies use Internet services differently (Hamburger & Ben-Artzi, 2000). Social networking sites are becoming increasingly popular in peoples' lives. People often use microblogs, such as Twitter, in order to express their opinions and activities; it is reasonable to expect that an individual's microblog will also contain his or her personality-related residue (Qiu et al., 2012). Social networking sites can be used to predict and present users' personality, and there are several studies that attempt to find the relationship between social media and personality. Golbeck et al. (2011) wrote about how social media users' "Big Five" personality traits could be predicted from the information they shared on social media. Social media can also be used to examine personality expressions occurring in writings (Qiu et al., 2012). In this case, many social networking sites allow users to post status updates to express emotions, which can be used to examine personality and also see if the posts actually reflect users' personalities.

In recent years, many researchers have found that men and women belong to different patterns in the relationship between personality factors and Internet use. Men's use of social networking sites is not related to loneliness, neuroticism, or extraversion; however, in comparison with men, women who are lonely prefer to use the Internet mostly to avoid loneliness and find group belonging (Amichai-Hamburger & Ben-Artzi, 2003). According to Correa, Hinsley and De Zuniga (2010), extraverted men and women were both likely to be more frequent users of social networking sites. Women who are more extraverted and open to new experiences are more likely to engage in online interactions. Men who are high in extraversion use social media more often and are more likely to engage in social interaction (Correa, et al., 2010). Generally, gender differences are vaguely present among personalities' differences in social media usage, but there are still slight differences between them.

SELF-ESTEEM

Self-esteem is a self-valuation; it is how people perceive their own value and how valuable they think they are to others (MacIntyre et al., 1999). Many scholars have discussed the relationship between self-esteem and communication behaviors. MacIntyre et al. (1999) indicated that people who are lower in self-esteem are less likely to engage in communication than those who are higher in self-esteem, because they think they may have less to contribute to the conversation and are likely to receive negative feedback from others. Individuals with lower self-esteem are less likely to be involved in FtF communication. Research indicates that individuals with lower self-esteem spend increased time using instant messaging instead of FtF communication because they find communicating with others via technology easier than FtF (Ehrenberg, Juckes, White, & Walsh, 2008). Therefore, individuals with lower self-esteem are less likely to take part in FtF communication. However, research is unclear about how lower self-esteem individuals act online compared with those who have greater self-esteem.

FACEBOOK

By 2018, Facebook remains the No. 2 most popular social media site, just behind YouTube (Murnane, 2018). Even though the overall growth has decelerated, Facebook acts as the home base for most social media users and overlaps with other social media sites (Duggan, Ellison, Lampe, Lenhart, & Mardden,

2015). Facebook is a flexible and versatile social networking site; users can upload pictures, videos, games, and many other social activities to their profiles, implant information from other social networking sites, and post calendar events among other socialization activities.

Facebook, like many other social networking sites, provides a setting for people to communicate with other individuals. Facebook is specifically known as a friend-networking site, the main purpose of using Facebook is to maintain relationships. Facebook also provides a space for people to communicate with others, present themselves in the way they want, and share selected personal information. Many researchers have already conducted studies on Facebook and self-presentation. Research has shown that the number of Facebook friends have a positive relationship with individuals' social attractiveness (Walther, Van Der Heide, Kim, Westerman, & Tong, 2008). According to Caers and Castelyns (2010), individuals usually believe Facebook profile pictures are providing accurate signals on the profile owner's level of extraversion and maturity, which indicated individuals consider their profile pictures as an important way of self-presentation (Zarghooni, 2007).

SOCIAL MEDIA COMMUNICATION BY GENDER

Gender stereotypes appear both in FtF communication and in online communication. Men and women use self-presentation and impression management tactics to present themselves to the public (Aronson et al., 2009; Goffman, 1959; Schlenker, 1980). According to the literature, individuals with different personalities presented themselves in different ways and also have different social networking site use habits (Amichai-Hamburger & Ben-Artzi, 2003; Golbeck et al., 2011; Qiu et al., 2012; Schrammel et al., 2009). Self-esteem is also a factor, which influences how individuals use social networking sites (Ehrenberg et al., 2008). Despite extensive research on social media use related to gender, impression management, personality, and self-esteem, the nature of young adults' social media expressions' relationship with personalities and self-esteem is still unknown. Furthermore, the gender differences in self-presentation based on social media expression and personality require further research.

According to the literature above, men and women have different patterns in communication and Internet-based communication on social media. Women's Internet-based communication on social media usually exposes their emotions more often than compared with men. In addition, women disclosed more detailed information on their social media sites than men do (Jackson et al., 2001). The goal of the present study is to examine the relationship between social media expressions and personality for men and women. Personality traits and self-esteem are related to users' expression on social media.

Previous reviews of related literature show that men and women have different patterns in FtF communication and CMC on social media (Adrianson, 2001; Muscanell & Guadagno, 2012; Simpson & Stroh, 2004). Women's CMC on social networking sites more often expose their emotions when compared with men's communication, and women reveal more personal information and details on their social networking sites than men do. According to Schrammel et al. (2009) there are no significant relations between personality traits and information disclosure on social media. There are several aspects connected to the personality and social media usage patterns. For example, individuals who are highly extraverted are more sociable and have more online friends than individuals with lower scores on extraversion (Schrammel et al., 2009). According to recent research, men and women tend to have different communication patterns, so the relationship between personality and social media use may differ by gender. Social media allows individuals to display every aspect of their lives, and it can also allow someone to portray himself or herself with a different persona (Correa et al., 2010).

Extraversion is related to being sociable and outgoing. According to Schrammel et al. (2009), individuals high in extraversion have more friends on social networking sites than individuals in low extraversion. Simpson and Stroh (2004) indicated that women who are extraverted prefer to use social networking sites more than men and for more social purposes. Profile pictures are a way to build individuals' physical attractiveness, and women try to receive positive evaluations on social networking sites in comparison with men. In this case, women may try to disclose their appearance by posting more photos then men. Thus, the following hypothesis was posed.

H1: Women who are high in extraversion will post more Facebook profile pictures than men who are high in extraversion.

Agreeableness relates to trusting, cooperative, helpful, and tender-minded people who prefer to maintain positive relations (Jensen & Graziano, 2001). Thus, it stands to reason that there will be a relationship between agreeableness and online connections. So a second hypothesis is posed.

H2: Individuals who are high in agreeableness will have more Facebook friends than individuals who are high in other personality traits.

Neuroticism relates to emotional reactivity, anxiousness, insecurity, and sensitivity. Research has found individuals who are highly neurotic are highly interested in using the Internet for communication (Amichai-Hamburger, Wainapel, & Fox, 2002). In order to examine the relationship between neuroticism and self-presentation online, Hypothesis 3 is posed.

H3: Individuals who are high in neuroticism will do more self-presentation on Facebook.

According to research reviewed, gender accounts for differences in CMC communication and self-presentation. Many studies have shown that the effect of gender may be influenced by personality (Correa et al., 2010; Schrammel et al., 2009). Thus, it is necessary to examine the relationships that gender, personality, and self-esteem have on social media presentation. Research indicates that individuals with lower self-esteem spend more time using instant messaging instead of FtF communication because they find communicating with others via technology easier than FtF (Ehrenberg et al., 2008). Therefore, individuals with lower self-esteem are less likely to take part in FtF communication. Therefore, the first research question is posed.

RQ1: What is the relationship between self-esteem and self-presentation on Facebook?

Muscanell and Guadagno (2012) wrote about how women are more likely to use the Internet to maintain social interaction and engage in behavior consistent with feminine stereotypes to maintain relationships compared with men. However, recent research suggests that both men and women might be less inclined to express stereotypical gender roles on Facebook profiles (Oberst, Renau, Chamarro, & Carbonell, 2016). So the frequency of women who express gender roles compared to men is still unknown. Also, research has suggested there is a relationship between gender roles and neuroticism (Davis, Dionne, & Lazarus, 1996; Tokar, Fischer, Schaub, & Moradi, 2000). Thus, the following research questions are posed.

RQ2: Will women present more gender role expressions than men do on Facebook?
RQ3: What is the relationship between neuroticism and gender-role expression?

METHOD

In order to examine the personality and social media use habits between genders, an online questionnaire to investigate participants' social media use habits was devised. In this study, participants took a survey to indicate their social media use habits, personality characteristics, and self-esteem levels. The participants were asked to provide their Facebook user names so that the researchers could follow them and see their posts and subsequently code them.

Participants and Procedure

This research was conducted at a mid-sized regional university in Appalachia. The experiment was administered to participants through an online survey tool. A total of 459 participants took the online survey. That included 314 women (68.41%) and 143 men (31.15%). Participants ranged in age from 18 to 58 years old. However, the sample consisted mostly of female college students between the ages 18 and 24. Participants answered a survey questionnaire that included four parts. The first part was demographic questions concerning age, gender, education, and employment information. The second part featured social media usage questions concerning participants' social networking sites use and online activities. The third part was the 44-item inventory that measures an individual on the Big Five Factors of personality (Benet-Martinez & John, 1998). The last part was levels of self-esteem questions, which were derived from the Rosenberg Self-Esteem Scale (Rosenberg, 1965).

At the end of the survey, participants were asked to provide their Facebook user names. The researchers created a Facebook account related to the project so that the researchers were able to follow participants for one month. Data was then collected including every Facebook post made by participants; this information was coded for self-presentation expression. The participants' profiles were coded based on a coding sheet. The researchers chose the month of February to code, as it was after the New Year and after the start of school but prior to spring break and any major disruption of normal collegiate life. Participants' status updates on Facebook were coded based on a coding sheet. Only the participants' initial posts were recorded. Any comments or responses from anyone other than participants were not recorded. No personal information from the posts in the research was used; participants are identified only by their codes.

Measures of the Online Survey

A self-developed scale was used to gather demographic questions concerning age, sex, and employment status; and measure Facebook usage. The Big Five personality measures (Benet-Martinez & John, 1998), and the self-esteem Likert scale (Rosenberg, 1965) were collated into a single online questionnaire.

Social Media Usage

The social media usage portion of the survey contained multiple-choice questions and a 7-point frequency scale. The multiple-choice questions examined participants' preferred social networking sites by asking, "Which of the following social networking websites do you currently have an account with?" and "In a typical week, which of the following social networking websites do you use most often?" Participants were also asked to respond questions about the frequency of their use of social media. For example, participants will be asked to report, "How often do you update your status on social media?" and "How often do you check your social media feed?" Participants answered based on a 7-point scale from 1 = Less than once a month to 7 = Many times a day.

Personality Traits

Extraversion, agreeableness, and neuroticism were assessed using the 44-item Big Five Inventory (Benet-Martinez & John, 1998). Openness and conscientiousness data were collected but not used for this study. The 44 items include participants' responses to self-examination questions such as, "I see myself as someone who is relaxed and handles stress well." The Likert-scale answers are based on participants' self-examination of feelings about themselves from Disagree Strongly = 1 to Agree Strongly = 5.

Self-Esteem

A ten-item survey derived from Rosenberg (1965) answered on a 4-point Likert-scale was used to measure self-esteem. The scale had five positive statements and five negative statements, for example, "On the whole, I am satisfied with myself, " and "All in all, I am inclined to feel that I am a failure." Participants chose from a scale of Strongly Agree = 3 to Strongly Disagree = 0.

Coding

Profile Coding

Participants' basic information from the questionnaire and profile information from social media was coded using a profile-coding sheet and its corresponding answer sheet. The profile-coding sheet categorizes the demographics, personalities, and self-esteem of participants. The corresponding answer sheet identifies the number of friends, schools, and companies shown in a Facebook profile. The number of albums and profile pictures is counted.

Post Coding

To address the concerns of the research questions and hypotheses for this study, a Facebook posts coding sheet and its corresponding answer sheet were developed. The coding sheet's content was influenced by past researchers, which included some but not all of the aspects of this study, such as Capwell (1997) and Kane (2008). On the post-coding sheet, self-presentation and impression management tactics were evaluated (Goffman, 1959). These tactics include how participants use self-presentation and impression management in posts on Facebook, such as ingratiation, self-handicapping, intimidation, exemplification, and supplication. Each tactic on the coding sheet has a detailed explanation. The coders, who were both women, determined gender role expressions by selecting from expressions of gender role, such as marriage/family roles (references to being a wife/husband, a mother/father, a daughter/son, a sister/brother), or overt expressions about femininity (a selfie or post featuring relationships, cooking, home décor, or fashion and/or jewelry typically associated with women) or masculinity (a selfie or post featuring sports, cars, tools, or references to toughness, manliness/machismo, hypermasculinity). Expressions of self-attractiveness related to pictures of beauty, romance/sex (specifically pictures that demonstrate physical attractiveness), and social life are coded. Other pictures that do not fit in these categories are coded as "Other" with explanations. Expressions of social status, social relationships, inner thoughts and feelings, and mundane experiences were coded in the final section.

For self-presentation and impression management tactics, and gender role expressions, 1 represented "Present", 0 represented "Not present", and 99 represented "Cannot tell." Expressions of personal life were participants' ways of choosing to display aspects of themselves, such as social life, family roles, etc., as presented in Facebook posts. The code for expression of personal life was, 1 represented "Yes", 0 represented "No", and 99 represented "Cannot tell."

Coder Training and Intercoder Reliability

Two coders coded participants' Facebook profile information and each post participants shared for the month. An intercoder reliability analysis using the Cohen's (1960, 1968) Kappa statistic was executed to define the consistency among coders. A 10% random subsample of coding sheets was used to evaluate the extent to which there was intercoder reliability. The results of the intercoder analysis were Kappa=0.869 with $p < 0.001$. This measure of agreement is statistically significant.

Content Analysis

Variables

In this study, gender was the primary independent variable. This study also relied on Rosenberg's (1965) Self-Esteem Scale and Benet-Martinez and John's (1998) Big Five Personality Scale to determine the covariates such as the self-esteem score, extraversion, agreeableness, and neuroticism.

The dependent variables of this study were the tactics of self-presentation and impression management, gender role expression, and personal life expressions on Facebook. The number of Facebook friends also acted as a dependent variable in this study. The coders rated these metrics according to the post-coding sheet. Self-presentation and impression management on Facebook were measured by what tactics were used to establish online identity. Gender role expressions on Facebook were measured by the public image of being masculine or feminine that participants present online.

Cronbach's alpha (1951) was used to evaluate the reliability of all scales. The gender role expression on Facebook had a reliability coefficient of $\alpha= .90$. The five items of Facebook self-presentation tactics were reliable measure with a reliability coefficient of $\alpha= .649$, which is acceptable because the sample distribution is uneven among men and women in this research.

There were 129 (28%) participants that offered their Facebook account in the online survey. And two of them declined to answer personality and self-esteem questions. The number of Facebook friends, Facebook self-expression and Facebook gender role expressions are used as variables in data analyses.

RESULTS

This study was aimed to examine the internal relationship of gender, social media usage, self-esteem, and personality. Of the 459 participants who took part in the online survey, 314 (68.41%) of them were women and 143 (31.15%) of them were men. Facebook account information was offered by 131 participants (28.54%), 101 (77.1%) of which were women and 30 (22. 9%) were men.

Extraversion

H1 predicted that women who scored high in extraversion would have more Facebook profile pictures than men who scored high in extraversion. No significant relationships were found among gender, extraversion, and number of Facebook profile pictures (F (1, 127) = .11, p = .74). In order to examine the relationship between gender and number of Facebook profile pictures, a t test was conducted but no significant relationship was found (t (129) = -2. 50, p = .01). There was a statistically significant relationship between gender and the number of Facebook profile pictures. The number of profile pictures provided by women (M=34.06, S.D.=43.22) was significantly higher than the number of profile pictures provided by men (M=19.37, S.D. = 21.82), therefore women tended to post more Facebook profile pictures than men did. A regression test also did not reveal significant relationships between extraversion and the number of Facebook profile pictures (F (1, 129) = .82, p = .78). Therefore, H1 was not supported. However, the data does indicate that women do post more Facebook profile pictures than men do.

Agreeableness

A regression test was conducted to examine H2, the relationship between agreeableness and the number of Facebook friends (F (1, 129) = 4.81, p= .03), with an R^2 of 0.36. A β of .19 shows a positive relationship. Thus, H2 is supported; the individuals who scored higher in agreeableness tended to have more friends on Facebook.

Neuroticism

H3 predicted individuals who scored high in neuroticism would make more self-presentation posts on Facebook. The researchers conducted a regression test to examine the relationship between neuroticism and Facebook self-presentation (F (1, 129) = 4.43, p = .04), with an R^2 of .03. A β of .18 shows a positive relationship. H3 is supported; individuals who are higher in neuroticism tended to have more self-presentation posts on Facebook.

The research questions in the study sought to explore the relationships between gender and a number of other variables: self-presentation, profile pictures, and gender role expressions.

Self-Esteem

RQ1 examined the relationship between self-esteem and self-presentation on social networking sites, a regression test was conducted to examine the relationship (F (1, 129) = 4.86, p= .029), with an R^2 of 0.36. A β of -.19 indicated a negative relationship between self-esteem and Facebook self-presentation; the lower a person's self-esteem, the more self-presentation individuals did on Facebook.

Gender Role Expressions

RQ2 was posed to find the differences between men and women in expression of gender roles on Facebook. A *t* test was conducted to examine the relationship (t (129) = - 2.34, p = .021). Posts that fit gender role expectation for women (M =2.79, S.D.=4.92) were significantly higher than gender role expectation posts for men (M=1.23, S.D.=2.47). The results show that women post more gender role expressions on Facebook than men do.

RQ3 was posed to examine the relationships between gender role expressions on Facebook and neuroticism. The researchers conducted a regression test and found a significant relationship between neuroticism and Facebook gender role expressions (F (1, 129), p =. 02), with an R^2 = .04, and a β of .20. The positive relationship indicates that individuals who are higher in neuroticism expressed more gender role traits on Facebook than did those who were lower in neuroticism.

DISCUSSION

The body of literature on engaging through social media is limited; the goal of this research project was to study individuals' expressions through social media with consideration of their gender. The study explores the relationship between personality and gender differences in online communication to gain a better understanding of young adult men and women's self-presentation on social networking sites.

The results of H1 indicated women post more Facebook profile pictures than men do. However, no significant differences between genders were found in terms of extraversion. This result is in line with Schrammel et al.'s (2009) research where women revealed more detailed personal information on their social media sites than men did. No significant relations between personality traits and information disclosure on social media were found.

H2 results indicated that individuals who were higher in agreeableness had more friends on Facebook. People may be more likely to be friends with other people who exhibit traits of agreeableness in FtF communication and in online communication. And this makes sense given that the agreeableness personality trait is one that is marked by friendly connections to others.

H3 results indicated that individuals who scored high in neuroticism would engage in more self-presentation on Facebook. Finding a relationship between neuroticism and self-presentation is supported by some research (Dunn & Guadagno, 2012) and would tend to be in line with the idea that neurotic people may tweak their self-presentations out of insecurities.

RQ1 investigated the relationship between self-esteem and self-presentation on social networking sites. The results indicated a negative relationship between self-esteem and Facebook self-presentation; the lower self-esteem is, the more self-presentation individuals did on Facebook. People with lower self-esteem obviously did more self-presenting online than people with higher self-esteem. These results may be affected due to the date during which social media data were gathered. The data were collected during February, a time period that includes Valentine's Day. During this holiday, people tend to be concerned about their relationships and self-present more around Valentine's Day than other times of the year. Due to the tendency of people to be especially sensitive to relationship status, activities, and gifts at this time, participants may have posted more during this time than during other months.

This study explored whether women present more gender role expressions than men do on Facebook in RQ2. The results indicated that women posted more gender role expressions, those that are stereotypical expectations of femininity, such as relationships, beauty, fashion, cosmetics, on Facebook than men did. This finding supports Muscanell and Guadagno's (2012) study that found women were more likely to engage in behavior in line with feminine gender role expectations that foster relationship maintenance compared with men. Based on the results from this study, women tended post more gender role expressions than men did and engaged in feminine gender role norms. Based on RQ3, this study also found a positive relationship between neuroticism and Facebook gender role expression. Individuals who scored high in neuroticism expressed more about gender roles on Facebook. The findings could suggest that women might post more gender role expressions due to the high gender role conformity expectations for women in society, particularly as one considers the growth in beauty influencers. Moreover, because of the pressure to conform to gender role expectations, women might post more about their gender role norms. A positive relationship between neuroticism and gender role expressions was also found in this study, which is logical because individuals who worry a great deal and tend to be more anxious, insecure, and sensitive might try harder to present themselves in an acceptable way on social media by posting more gender role congruent expressions to avoid conflict and receive positive feedback.

The goal of this study was to investigate individuals' expressions through social media with consideration of their personalities, and levels of self-esteem. The results of the study indicated women post more Facebook profile pictures than men do. This result is in line with Haferkamp et al.'s study (2012); the choice of photographs used in social networking sites is related to women's need for self-presentation. Profile pictures are particularly attractive because pictures provide people with the measures to present themselves in a way to obtain valuable social image or social capital. Women tend to show more physical attractiveness as one aspect of self-presentation in comparison with men; in this case, women try to disclose their appearance in detail by photos.

Women posted more gender role expressions on Facebook than men. The gender differences found in this study included the number of Facebook profile pictures and the frequency of gender role expressions. The results indicated women might try to receive positive evaluations on social networking sites by disclosing their appearance and meeting gender role expectations.

Individuals who are higher in agreeableness have more friends on Facebook. Among the more common motivations for social media use, particularly among women, is communication, interaction, and maintaining relationships. Facebook allows individuals to feel informed and involved with others and maintain relationships. People who are more agreeable tend to be cooperative, helpful, and nurturing, they tend to maintain their relationships online, and they might be more interested in developing a larger number of online friendships.

The research has two findings related to neuroticism. Individuals who are high in neuroticism expressed more about gender roles and did more self-presentation on Facebook. Neuroticism relates to emotional reactivity, anxiety insecurity, and sensitivity. Research has found individuals who are highly neurotic are primarily interested in using the Internet for communication and presenting their real identity (Amichai-Hamburger et al., 2002). So the results of this study are supported by literature, individuals who scored high in neuroticism tended to present themselves more and tried to build up a desirable image for themselves online to meet the models provided by peer groups because they may be insecure and want to act acceptable online.

The study found the lower individuals' self-esteem, the more self-presentation individuals did on Facebook. People who are lower in self-esteem tend to be less confident; they may not want to take part in FtF communications because they think they are less valuable to others (MacIntyre et al., 1999). The results of the current study are in line with previous research that has shown individuals with lower self-esteem spend increased time communicating with others via technology instead of FtF communication because they find CMC easier than FtF (Ehrenberg et al., 2008). Individuals with lower self-esteem tend to present themselves in CMC rather than FtF communication, because in CMC they may feel more comfortable doing self-presentation.

The results of this study show that the self-expressions through social media do not actually reflect individuals' personalities and levels of self-esteem. CMC is different than FtF communication; individuals with neurotic personality traits and individuals with a lower level of self-esteem may present themselves online in a way that is contrary to the way they behave in real life.

REFERENCES

Adrianson, L. (2001). Gender and computer-mediated communication: Group processes in problem solving. *Computers in Human Behavior*, *17*(1), 71–94. doi:10.1016/S0747-5632(00)00033-9

Amichai-Hamburger, Y., & Ben-Artzi, E. (2003). Loneliness and Internet use. *Computers in Human Behavior*, *19*(1), 71–80. doi:10.1016/S0747-5632(02)00014-6

Amichai-Hamburger, Y., Wainapel, G., & Fox, S. (2002). "On the Internet No One Knows I'm an Introvert": Extroversion, Neuroticism, and Internet Interaction. *Cyberpsychology & Behavior*, *5*(2), 125–128. doi:10.1089/109493102753770507 PMID:12025878

Aronson, E., Wilson, D., Timothy, D., Akert, M., & Robin, M. (2009). *Social Psychology* (7th ed.). Prentice Hall.

Bem, S. L. (1981). Gender schema theory: A cognitive account of sex typing. *Psychological Review*, *88*(4), 354–364. doi:10.1037/0033-295X.88.4.354

Benet-Martinez, V., & John, O. P. (1998). Los Cinco Grandes across cultures and ethnic groups: Multitrait multimethod analyses of the Big Five in Spanish and English. *Journal of Personality and Social Psychology*, *75*(3), 729–750. doi:10.1037/0022-3514.75.3.729 PMID:9781409

Caers, R., & Castelyns, V. (2010). LinkedIn and Facebook in Belgium: The influences and biases of social network sites in recruitment and selection procedures. *Social Science Computer Review*, *29*(4), 437–448. doi:10.1177/0894439310386567

Capwell, A. (1997). *Chick flicks: An analysis of self-disclosure in friendships* (Unpublished master's thesis). Cleveland State University, Cleveland, OH.

Cohen, J. (1960). A coefficient of agreement for nominal scales. *Educational and Psychological Measurement*, *20*(1), 37–46. doi:10.1177/001316446002000104

Cohen, J. (1968). Weighted kappa: Nominal scale agreement with provision for scaled disagreement or partial credit. *Psychological Bulletin*, *70*(4), 213–220. doi:10.1037/h0026256 PMID:19673146

Correa, T., Hinsley, A. W., & De Zuniga, H. G. (2010). Who interacts on the Web?: The intersection of users' personality and social media use. *Computers in Human Behavior*, *26*(2), 247–253. doi:10.1016/j.chb.2009.09.003

Cronbach, L. J. (1951). Coefficient alpha and the internal structure of tests. *Psychometrika*, *16*(3), 297–334. doi:10.1007/BF02310555

Davis, C., Dionne, M., & Lazarus, L. (1996). Gender-role orientation and body image in women and men: The moderating influence of neuroticism. *Sex Roles*, *34*(7-8), 493–505. doi:10.1007/BF01545028

Davis, S. E. (2018). Objectification, Sexualization, and Misrepresentation: *Social Media and the College Experience. Social Media + Society, 4*(3). doi:10.1177/2056305118786727

Dobson, A. S. (2016). *Postfeminist Digital Cultures: Femininity, Social Media, and Self-Representation*. Springer.

Duggan, M., Ellison, N., Lampe, C., Lenhart, A., & Mardden, M. (2015, January 9). Social media update 2014. *Pew Research Internet Project*, Retrieved February 3, 2015 from https://www.pewinternet. org/2015/01/09/social-media-update-2014/

Dunn, R. A., & Guadagno, R. E. (2012). My avatar and me – gender and personality predictors of avatar-self discrepancy. *Computers in Human Behavior*, *28*(1), 97–106. doi:10.1016/j.chb.2011.08.015

Ehrenberg, A., Juckes, S., White, K. M., & Walsh, S. P. (2008). Personality and self-esteem as predictors of young people's technology use. *Cyberpsychology & Behavior*, *11*(6), 739–741. doi:10.1089/ cpb.2008.0030 PMID:18991531

Goffman, E. (1959). *The presentation of self in everyday life*. New York: Anchor Books.

Golbeck, J., Robles, C., & Turner, K. (2011, May). Predicting personality with social media. In *CHI'11 Extended Abstracts on Human Factors in Computing Systems* (pp. 253–262). ACM.

Haferkamp, N., Eimler, S. C., Papadakis, A. M., & Kruck, J. V. (2012). Men are from Mars, women are from Venus? Examining gender differences in self-presentation on social networking sites. *Cyberpsychology, Behavior, and Social Networking*, *15*(2), 91–98. doi:10.1089/cyber.2011.0151 PMID:22132897

Hamburger, Y. A., & Ben-Artzi, E. (2000). The relationship between extraversion and neuroticism and the different uses of the Internet. *Computers in Human Behavior*, *16*(4), 441–449. doi:10.1016/S0747-5632(00)00017-0

Hughes, D. J., Rowe, M., Batey, M., & Lee, A. (2012). A tale of two sites: Twitter vs. Facebook and the personality predictors of social media usage. *Computers in Human Behavior*, *28*(2), 561–569. doi:10.1016/j.chb.2011.11.001

Jackson, L. A., Ervin, K. S., Gardner, P. D., & Schmitt, N. (2001). Gender and the Internet: Women communicating and men searching. *Sex Roles*, *44*(5-6), 363–379. doi:10.1023/A:1010937901821

Jensen-Campbell, L. A., & Graziano, W. G. (2001). Agreeableness as a moderator of interpersonal conflict. *Journal of Personality*, *69*(2), 323–362. doi:10.1111/1467-6494.00148 PMID:11339802

Kane, C. (2008). *See you on Myspace: Self-presentation in a social network website* (Unpublished master's thesis). Cleveland State University, Cleveland, OH.

Leary, M. R. (1996). *Self-presentation: Impression management and interpersonal behavior*. Boulder, CO: Westview Press.

MacIntyre, P. D., Babin, P. A., & Clément, R. (1999). Willingness to communicate: Antecedents & consequences. *Communication Quarterly, 47*(2), 215–229. doi:10.1080/01463379909370135

Manago, A. M., Graham, M. B., Greenfield, P. M., & Salimkhan, G. (2008). Self-presentation and gender on MySpace. *Journal of Applied Developmental Psychology, 29*(6), 446–458. doi:10.1016/j.appdev.2008.07.001

Murnane, K. (2018, March 3). *Which Social Media Platform Is The Most Popular In The US?* Retrieved November 7, 2018, from https://www.forbes.com/sites/kevinmurnane/2018/03/03/which-social-media-platform-is-the-most-popular-in-the-us/

Muscanell, N. L., & Guadagno, R. E. (2012). Make new friends or keep the old: Gender and personality differences in social networking use. *Computers in Human Behavior, 28*(1), 107–112. doi:10.1016/j.chb.2011.08.016

Oberst, U., Renau, V., Chamarro, A., & Carbonell, X. (2016). Gender stereotypes in Facebook profiles: Are women more female online? *Computers in Human Behavior, 60*, 559–564. doi:10.1016/j.chb.2016.02.085

Pandey, J., Singh, P., & Singh, P. (1987). Effects of Machiavellianism, other-enhancement, and power-position on affect, power feeling, and evaluation of the ingratiator. *The Journal of Psychology, 121*(3), 287–300. doi:10.1080/00223980.1987.9712669

Qiu, L., Lin, H., Ramsay, J., & Yang, F. (2012). You are what you tweet: Personality expression and perception on twitter. *Journal of Research in Personality, 46*(6), 710–718. doi:10.1016/j.jrp.2012.08.008

Rosenberg, J., & Egbert, N. (2011). Online impression management: Personality traits and concerns for secondary goals as predictors of self-presentation tactics on Facebook. *Journal of Computer-Mediated Communication, 17*(1), 1–18. doi:10.1111/j.1083-6101.2011.01560.x

Rosenberg, M. (1965). *Society and the adolescent self-image*. Princeton, NJ: Princeton University Press. doi:10.1515/9781400876136

Schlenker, B. R. (1980). *Impression management: The self-concept, social identity, and interpersonal relations* (pp. 21–43). Monterey, CA: Brooks/Cole Publishing Company.

Schlenker, B. R., & Pontari, B. A. (2000). The strategic control of information: Impression management and self-presentation in daily life. In A. Tesser, R. B. Felson, & J. M. Suls (Eds.), *Psychological perspectives on self and identity* (pp. 199–232). Washington, DC: American Psychological Association. doi:10.1037/10357-008

Schrammel, J., Köffel, C., & Tscheligi, M. (2009, September). Personality traits, usage patterns and information disclosure in online communities. In *Proceedings of the 23rd British HCI Group Annual Conference on People and Computers: Celebrating People and Technology* (pp. 169-174). British Computer Society. 10.14236/ewic/HCI2009.19

Sheldon, P. (2008). The relationship between unwillingness-to-communicate and students' Facebook use. *Journal of Media Psychology, 20*(2), 67–75. doi:10.1027/1864-1105.20.2.67

Simpson, P. A., & Stroh, L. K. (2004). Gender differences: Emotional expression and feelings of personal inauthenticity. *The Journal of Applied Psychology*, *89*(4), 715–721. doi:10.1037/0021-9010.89.4.715 PMID:15327356

Steeves, V. (2015). "Pretty and Just a Little Bit Sexy, I Guess": Publicity, Privacy, and the Pressure to Perform "Appropriate" Femininity on Social Media (SSRN Scholarly Paper ID 2714723). *Social Science Research Network*. https://papers.ssrn.com/abstract=2714723

Tokar, D. M., Fischer, A. R., Schaub, M., & Moradi, B. (2000). Masculine gender roles and counseling-related variables: Links with and mediation by personality. *Journal of Counseling Psychology*, *47*(3), 380–393. doi:10.1037/0022-0167.47.3.380

Walther, J. B. (1996). Computer-mediated communication impersonal, interpersonal, and hyperpersonal interaction. *Communication Research*, *23*(1), 3–43. doi:10.1177/009365096023001001

Walther, J. B. (2007). Selective self-presentation in computer-mediated communication: Hyperpersonal dimensions of technology, language, and cognition. *Computers in Human Behavior*, *23*(5), 2538–2557. doi:10.1016/j.chb.2006.05.002

Walther, J. B., Van Der Heide, B., Kim, S., Westerman, D., & Tong, S. T. (2008). The role of friends' appearance and behavior on evaluations of individuals on Facebook: Are we known by the company we keep? *Human Communication Research*, *34*(1), 28–49. doi:10.1111/j.1468-2958.2007.00312.x

Zarghooni, S. (2007). *A study of self-presentation in light of Facebook*. Institute of Psychology, University of Oslo.

Zhao, S., Grasmuck, S., & Martin, J. (2008). Identity construction on Facebook: Digital empowerment in anchored relationships. *Computers in Human Behavior*, *24*(5), 1816–1836. doi:10.1016/j.chb.2008.02.012

This research was previously published in Young Adult Sexuality in the Digital Age; pages 176-193, copyright year 2020 by Information Science Reference (an imprint of IGI Global).

Section 2
Development and Design Methodologies

Chapter 10
Psychological Impact and Assessment of Youth for the Use of Social Network

Sapna Jain

https://orcid.org/0000-0002-5659-1941

Jamia Hamdard, India

M. Afshar Alam

Jamia Hamdard, India

Niloufer Adil Kazmi

Independent Researcher, India

ABSTRACT

This chapter dissects the effect of online life on each youngster in both the negative and positive bearing of their development utilizing the social impact hypothesis. Reliance of youth via web-based networking media has both negative and beneficial outcomes. This hypothesis portrays social effect concerning social power handle that encroach upon us, pushing us to think or keep thinking about a specific goal. These social powers have been stood out from physical powers that control the transmission of light, solid, gravity, interest, and so forth. The discoveries uncovered that the utilization of internet-based life impacts adolescent conduct when contrasted with positive aspects. This study shows a connection among contradictory and imaginative qualities of online life and displays roads for future investigations by encouraging a superior comprehension of electronic interpersonal organization use. In the chapter, the social effect felt by a person as a component of the quality, instantaneousness, and number of source people is exhibited and examined.

DOI: 10.4018/978-1-6684-6307-9.ch010

INTRODUCTION

This section gives an understanding how web based life has turned out to be interlinking into the material of most recent youth. Youth trust vigorously via web-based networking media for correspondence, cooperation, and subsequently the dispersal of information. Web based life could be a territory that is supercharged by people, and can, in this way, reverberation individuals' best aims, yet as their awfully most exceedingly terrible; those that search for to hurt others region unit strong by the web, by indistinguishable will be aforementioned for those that search for exclusively to help others. Online life makes our social relationship inside the feeling that, being on field we'd not be prepared to manufacture a great deal of companions. The reliance of young people on the online life has come to at such dimension that, while not web based life, every adolescent can't depend on the course of their development. Reliance of youth via web-based networking media has each negative and positive effect .

Researchers have discovered that abuse of innovation ordinarily, and web based life most importantly, makes an incitement design equivalent to the example made by various propensity shaping practices. a fresh out of the plastic new investigation demonstrates that getting "likes" via web-based networking media actuates indistinguishable circuits inside the youthful mind that territory unit enacted by nourishing chocolate or winning money. The pros and cons of social network affects the psychological behaviour of youth when interacting on a social network. It is basic for teenagers to check sources and truth, rather than taking all that youth should see as truth. They tend to wish to be "pulled over the coals" as a result of a wrong move that they tend to work by posting one thing that is inadequately investigated and eventually exposed. The technique by which the youth convey their contemplations when online defines the impact of the features and facilities on the social network.

BACKGROUND

Online Social Networks (OSNs) area unit seen because the pay attention of framework resource for affiliations that association key regard and business execution (Zhou, Wu, and Luo, 2007). On bigger casual network areas, people area unit commonly not eager to meet new individuals however rather area unit logically enthused regarding supervision associations by maintaining contacts with recent mates WHO area unit beginning at currently a part of their wide comprehensive relative association (Boyd and Ralph Waldo Ellison, 2007). To total up, casual association goals will be seen as elective specific mechanical assemblies that support existing associations and activities during a fun and hanging method that may build up the customers' experiences several relative association destinations have risen; actuation specifically get-togethers of consumers subject to their economic science and a few be careful for systems with unequivocal shared interests (Palmer and Koenig-Lewis, 2009). there's nowadays a good deal of affirmation that easy going affiliation zones have pushed toward obtaining the prospect to be normal and it's been spoken to it all around, these objectives address one in at traditional intervals spent on the net (Jones, 2009). fifty four % of internet shoppers some spot within the extent of sixteen and twenty four have created their terribly own exceptional page or profile on someone to singular correspondence website page (Palmer and Koenig-Lewis, 2009). Social affiliation locales have party of individuals quite another on-line life these days. Facebook accomplishes 710 million customers (H. Hanafizadeh and Behboudi, 2012). Meanwhile, if Facebook were a rustic, it'd be the third greatest nation on earth, waiting behind simply China and Asian country. half those "locals" check in faithfully and victimization the positioning once per day (Zarrella and Zarrella, 2011). the standard client has one hundred thirty partners and is expounded with eighty system pages, social affairs, and events each pay a normal of forty six minutes out of systematically on Facebook (Facebook.com, 2011). Moreover, one hundred million individuals build a social proceed onward YouTube faithfully and 800 million distinctive customers visit this website every month (Youtube.com). Casual association districts provide opportunities to attach with these arduous to-contact social affairs of people sailplaning faraway from normal media. it would be deduced that utilization of relative association is extending at Associate in Nursing large speed, and it's influencing however individuals share information over the world. SNS may be a crisp out of the plastic new purpose for authorities thanks to its relative peculiarity, and one or two of researchers in numerous settings tried to contemplate this new phonemena. The impact of casual associations is logically bound, with activities running from the financial e.g., shopping and advancing e.g. complete building, advertising) to the social (e.g., social and physiological impacts) and enlightening (e.g., separate preparing) (for instance mangold-wurzel and Smith, 2011; golf player and Koenig-Lewis, 2009; S. Pookulangara and K. Koesler, 2011; Teo, Chan, Weib, and Zhang, 2003). In any case, paying very little mind to its noteworthiness within the new info time, no total composition review has been driven within the field of casual networks beside a review paper coordinated by Hanafizadeh, et al. (2012) on casual correspondence business effects composing. Everything thought of, there's a necessity for driving this type of analysis works, since it'll fill in as a guide for the 2 scholastics and specialists. it'll in like manner show the lilting movement state and course of analysis subjects, and will be of interest. a web relative association (OSN) may be a growth of the quality casual association on the web, that is very internet based mostly programming that individuals use to develop social affiliations. OSN fuses numerous online headways, for example, blog, Twitter, Facebook, Mashup, content, video gathering, virtual world, linguistics destinations, . (S. M. Lee and subgenus Chen, 2011). OSNs use computer support because the reason of correspondence among its individuals (Andrews, Preece, and Turoff, 2001). Drawing on Boyd and Ralph Waldo Ellison (2007), OSNs area unit represented as on-line associations that (1) have interaction individuals to create Associate in Nursing open or semi-open profile for themselves within Associate in Nursing obligated framework, (2) show a fast summary of various shoppers with whom they're connected, and (3) see and investigate their summation of affiliations and people created out by totally different shoppers within the structure. In express settings, as an example, the propellant structure, the terms 'online social affiliation' and 'virtual framework' area unit frequently utilised synonymously. Virtual society area unit seen as consumer parties of adjusting sizes that expire habitually and for a few zero in a managed manner over the web through a typical zone or fragment to accomplish individual additionally as shared focuses of their kin (Dholakia, Bagozzi, and Pearo, 2004; Ridings, Gefen, and Arinze, 2002). the $64000 nice position of OSN is its capability to grant a lot of important long vary easygoing correspondence openings than the quality social affiliation transversally over numerous geographical, social, social, or institutional settings. OSN doesn't uproot the quality easygoing affiliation, rather supplements it and starts new social affiliations. The affront of OSN is that people have low trust and faithfully feel nervous or unsure within the virtual condition (S. M. Lee and subgenus Chen, 2011).

WHAT IS A SOCIAL NETWORK?

Social network is online unit organizations that helps people to build up an and open profile, to develop an online posting platform of different users with whom they share an affiliation and read their once-over of affiliations and people made by others users on the network.

CHARACTERISTICS OF SOCIAL NETWORKS

Interpersonal interaction Sites like Facebook and Linkedin are the most prevalent web goals today . They give a stage to individuals to interface with companions, relatives and colleagues over the world. They have basic characteristics that make them well known and utilized by today's youth.

Core Characteristics of Social Networks.

Those characteristics are as follows.

1.   User-based: Before online social network like Facebook or twitter turned into the standard, sites depended on substance that was refreshed by all youth age group users. The progression of data was in a solitary bearing, and the course of future updates was dictated by the website admin, or author. Online social organizations, then again, are manufactured and coordinated by users them-selves. Without the users, the system would be an unfilled space loaded up with void discussions, applications, and talk rooms. Clients populate the system with discussions and substance .

2.   Interactive: In the present day informal communities is the way that they are so intuitive that an informal community isn't only a gathering of chatrooms and discussions any longer for youth. Sites like Facebook are loaded up with system based gaming applications, where you can play poker together or challenge a companion to a chess competition.

3.   Community-driven: Social systems are fabricated and flourish from network ideas. This implies simply like networks or social gatherings around the globe are established on the way that indi-viduals hold basic convictions or leisure activities, interpersonal organizations depend on a similar standard.

4.   Relationships: The ability to viably utilize web search tools and see has been contemplated by United Nations office or what associations made or support the information; wherever the data originates from and its believability . Join that have some expertise in morals, style and cooperation make a significant commitment to discussions round the job of internet based life in scholarly settings, giving numerous chances to inventive reasoning and articulation, while maintaining a strategic distance from the over-disentangled investigation that might be identified with sane evaluate of online networking writings. In any case, while concurring that such open doors should be important elements of online networking in scholastic settings, we will in general contend that there's as yet a need for reflexive scrutinize.

5.   Emotion over content: Another one of a kind normal for social network is the passionate factor. While sites of the past were focused essentially around giving data to a guest, the online community really furnishes young users with enthusiastic security and a feeling that regardless of what occurs, their companions are inside simple reach.

6. Persistence: Unlike the fleeting nature of discourse in unmediated publics, arranged interchanges are recorded for descendants. This empowers offbeat correspondence however it likewise expands the time of presence of any discourse demonstration. Accessibility can be improved in light of the fact that articulations are recorded and character is set up through content, hunt and disclosure devices help individuals discover like personalities. While individuals can't at present procure the geological directions of any individual in unmediated spaces, discovering one's computerized body online is simply an issue of keystrokes. While we can outwardly identify a great many people who can catch our discourse in unmediated spaces, it is for all intents and purposes difficult to discover each one of the individuals who may keep running over our appearances in arranged publics.

Emprical Characteristics of Social Network

Unlike the fleeting nature of discourse in unmediated publics, arranged interchanges are recorded for descendants. This empowers offbeat correspondence however it likewise expands the time of presence of any discourse demonstration. Accessibility can be improved in light of the fact that articulations are recorded and character is set up through content, hunt and disclosure devices help individuals discover like personalities. While individuals can't at present procure the geological directions of any individual in unmediated spaces, discovering one's computerized body online is simply an issue of keystrokes. While we can outwardly identify a great many people who can catch our discourse in unmediated spaces, it is for all intents and purposes difficult to discover each one of the individuals who may keep running over our appearances in arranged public.

Facebook

Facebook is an Internet-based administration going for interfacing individuals, sharing substance and transferring photographs among companions and relationship. Facebook cases to have in excess of 55 million clients and a normal of 250,000 new enrolled clients every day (by April 2008), consequently being one of the world most prevalent administrations. Usefulness and configuration show an emphasis on private use and contacts are alluded to as "companions". The framework is created and kept up by the proprietors yet the substance, similar to pictures, diversions and connections, are transferred and kept up by the clients. Each client creates and keeps up their very own online profile, which should concur with their disconnected character, yet no genuine control is made (or is conceivable). Users are urged to create applications inside the structure of the site, bringing about in excess of 20,000 one of a kind applications. Facebook has progressively grown new highlights, as Facebook Notes and news channels showing the ongoing exercises of part's companions. The organic reach for pages has nearly flatlined, it is popularly utilised by seventy two of all adult net users in America as shown in Figure 1 . More women users: seventy seven of on-line female users area unit on Facebook. The Younger audience: eighty 2 of all on-line users between 18-29 area unit on Facebook. The Facebook Demographics analysis results show as USA (14%), Republic of India (9%) and Brazil (7%) kind the three largest markets.

Figure 1. Facebook demographics usage

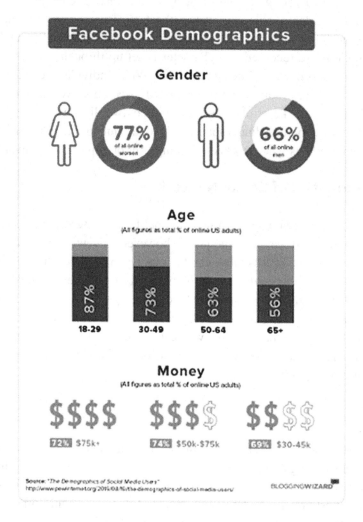

Twitter

Twitter, propelled in 2006, is an on-line application planned around the idea of smaller scale blogging. The on-line stage enables clients to send open updates ("tweets") about themselves as short content based presents available on different clients who have joined to get them. Presents are constrained on 140 characters, which make them reasonable for conveyance through texting administrations, (e.g.: MSN Messenger), or short message benefits on cell phones. Twitter is likewise intended to coordinate inside outsider informal communication programming, for example, Facebook. Facebook clients can buy in to Twitter and control it's administrations through Facebook. Clients who become companions, can peruse each other's posts on either the Twitter site, a cell phone, another SNS stage, or a texting administration. Clients can control which companions get their updates, and confine the updates got from others: for example, short message administration on cell phones can be turned off around evening time, or unde- sired clients' updates can be won't. The product permits the expansion of client made applications, for example, realistic representation of the systems made by client memberships to individual miniaturized scale postings. Twitter's snappy streaming 'data stream' pulls in A crowd of people that swings more youthful and is normally urban and semi-urban. The Youngers utilized it by thirty seventh of all on-line clients somewhere in the range of eighteen and twenty-nine. The Educated community has fifty-four of users have either graduated faculty or have some faculty experience. The Richer square measure fifty-four of on-line adults World Health Organization produce over $50,000 and have area unit on Twitter (Figure 2). Overall, twenty third of on-line adult's area unit on Twitter.

Figure 2. Twitter demographics usage

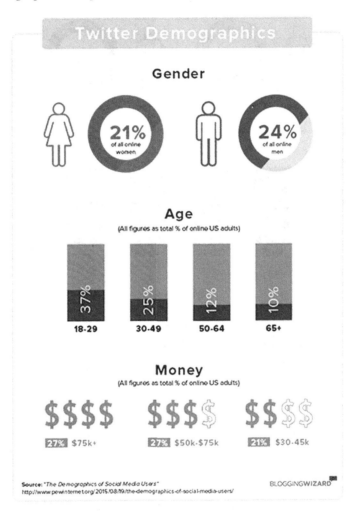

Instagram

Instagram recently overtook Twitter to become the second largest social network. bench estimates that twenty sixth of all on-line adults unit on Instagram inside the USA as shown in figure 5.There are a lot of women victimisation than, twenty ninth of all on-line women unit on Instagram, vs. alone twenty second of all men. fifty 3 of all 18 to 29 year olds unit on Instagram in figure 3. The Less educated on

Instagram users unit college graduates, whereas thirty initial have some college experience that is fitting as primarily younger audience.

Figure 3. Instagram demographics usage

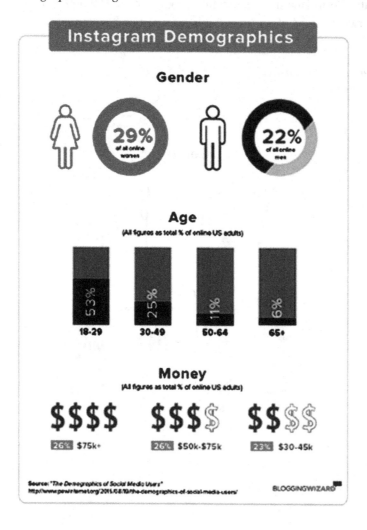

LinkedIn

Linkedin is an Internet-based virtual world propelled in 2003, created by Linden Research, Inc. A downloadable customer program called the Second Life Viewer empowers its clients (occupants) to cooperate with one another's symbols, giving a propelled long range informal communication administration. Linden Labs guarantees more than 6,000,000 occupants from 106 nations. Occupants can investigate, meet different inhabitants, mingle, take an interest in individual and gathering exercises, and make and exchange things (virtual property) and administrations. Second Life has its own in-world monetary market and money (Linden dollar - replaceable for genuine monetary forms). Though the geo-spatial foundation is overseen by the proprietors, the destinations (islands) are principally worked by inhabitants in-world, utilizing three-dimensional graphical control and scripting. Organizations, intrigue gatherings and NGOs are generally spoken to, as are government offices and ideological groups. Second Life's computerized world has numerous associations with the outside world. The more seasoned network has only twenty third of clients unit between 18-29 years later. Twenty first percent were more than sixty five years, and thirty one percent somewhere in the range of thirty and forty nine years versed people as appeared in figure 4.The Urban individuals truly limited differ of provincial clients – solely 14 July. sixty one unit either urban or regional territory. The Wealthier people square measure seventy fifth of clients acquire over $50,000.The incredibly instructed contribute 5 hundredth of LinkedIn clients unit personnel graduates. An additional twenty second have some workforce understudies.

Figure 4. LinkedIn demographics usage

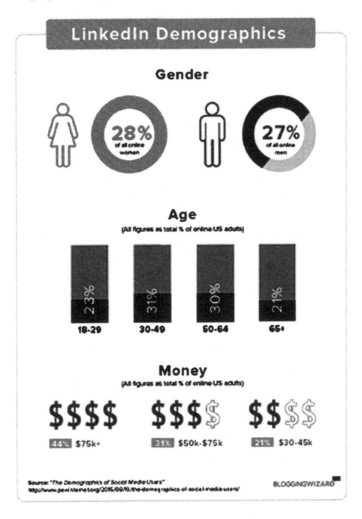

SOCIAL NETWORK PSCHYCOLOGY

An social network is comprised of people or associations who impart and connect with one another. Long range informal communication destinations for example, Facebook, Twitter, and LinkedIn – are characterized as innovation empowered instruments that help clients with making and keeping up their connections. The users identified with long range interpersonal communication is affected by real individual contrasts. The individuals contrast methodically in the amount and nature of their social connections. Two of the principle character attributes that are in charge of this fluctuation are the characteristics of extraversion and introspection. Extraversion alludes to the inclination to be socially prevailing, apply authority, and impact on others. Contrastingly, introspection alludes to the propensity of an individual to have an air of modesty, social fear, or even maintain a strategic distance from social circumstances through and through, which could prompt a decrease in the quantity of potential contacts that individual may have. These individual contrasts may result in various long range interpersonal communication results. Other mental variables identified with internet based life are: melancholy, uneasiness, connection, self-character, and the need to have a place. Internet based life and mind capacity go connected at the hip. Our cerebrum is the 'social organ' of our bodies and the maker of online networking itself. The mind needs to associate with other individuals, to submerge and comprehend other individuals' encounters through correspondence, regardless of whether that be up close and personal or through broad communications. Internet based life requires a lot of self-referential idea. Individuals utilize internet based life as a stage to express their suppositions and hotshot their over a wide span of time selves. Self-referential idea includes movement in the average prefrontal cortex and the back cingulate cortex. The cerebrum utilizes these specific frameworks when considering oneself. The information encased in a profile shifts by interpersonal organization, anyway some of the time incorporates a picture of the client and a client name, also as information in regards to socioeconomics and demeanour, similar to sexual orientation, dates of birth, training, business, and interests. Facebook is by and by the premier wide utilized on-line interpersonal organization, with 1.5 billion ordinary clients on various informal communities spend significant time in explicit employments. LinkedIn, Twitter with a microblogging centre, and Instagram with a photograph partaking in various significant classes of informal organization . System sharing stages, as twitter and Instagram, give people a field to share system like recordings or photographs. This class normally covers with informal communities, because of system sharing stages commonly give profiles, remarks, or input on indicate content. for example, Instagram has been classified as each an informal organization focused on sharing, also as a system sharing stage. Social news stages, as Reddit and Digg, give people with a field to share and talk about news. The users will create, alter, and erase content, anyway ordinarily don't move as socially as in various platforms.

The online users give a stage for people to fulfil these rudimentary social drives. In particular, interpersonal organization license youth to join with others and husband to be our name through at least 5 key practices (Figure 5)- *Social network users can:*

1. Broadcast information;
2. Receive feedback on this information;
3. Observe the broadcasts of others;
4. Provide feedback on the broadcasts of others;
5. Compare themselves with others.

Figure 5. Five key social network behaviours

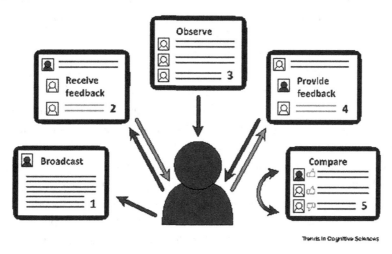

For instance, an online user may require photographs of an excursion that she might truly want to impart to other people. The online user photographs to informal community so various users give criticism by remarking on the pictures and additionally giving an image of endorsement (e.g., a 'like' or 'top choice', looking on the interpersonal organization stage). This correspondence works inside the other route also: (iii)users watch information communicated by others; and (iv) users give criticism on others' posts. for example, a user would conceivably observe a picture of a companion's get-away, 'similar to' the picture on Facebook, so address what amount fun the occasion looked. Input is here and there noticeable to the client's system or, at times, people in general. In either case, (v) user communicate in social correlation, by various their very own communicates and input to other people, similar to the amount of preferences got.

Web-based social networking has turned out to be interlaced into the texture of most recent youthfulness. Youth trust vigorously web-based networking media for correspondence, association, and consequently the scattering of data. Web based life may be a space that is supercharged by individuals, and can, accordingly, reverberation individuals' best goals, in any case as their most noticeably terrible; individuals who scrounge around for to hurt others square measure brave by the net, still indistinguishable are previously mentioned for individuals who scavenge around for just to help other people. Web based life shapes social relationship inside the feeling that, being on field online who are capable not have the option to construct huge amounts of companions.

Web based life may be a stage in making new companions. It causes the young to frame relationship by knowing ourselves higher and apparently inside the more drawn out term, we'd end up serving to ourselves. Our reality isn't planning to alteration, and innovation will at present infiltrate society much more profound exertion next to zero opportunity to respond to the clearly day by day augmentations to our lives. Utilization of online long range interpersonal communication is accomplice principal a region of Indian youth today. Over utilization of web based life, has gotten the thought of youth completely. The dependence of youngsters on the online life has come to at such measurement that, while not web based life, each juvenile can't recognize the course of their advancement. Dependence of youth by means of online systems administration media has each negative and constructive outcome. Specialists have found that maltreatment of advancement unremarkably, and electronic long range informal communication exceptionally, makes a prompting structure unclear in light of the way that the model made by absolutely novel addictive lead. The points of interest and drawbacks of electronic life through and through depend on yet we tend to use it. regardless, it's as one essential to expect the opposite side thusly on keep up a key separation from any sort of complexities. it's central for U.S. to check sources and truth, instead of taking all that we should constantly see as truth. we tend to should be "pulled over the coals" inferable from a wrong move that we tend to make by posting one factor that is deficiently researched and finally uncovered! the framework by that we will when all is said in done pass on our thoughts to our gathering of spectators might be raised to quality on condition that those contemplations zone unit a unit particularly contained with checked convictions and sources.

It has right now turned into a clear and normal sight to face individuals being unfeeling toward talk in revering places, homes once relatives and visitors square measure around, expressways, schools, schools and parties whereby youth is so distracted and charmed into their telephones that they are doing not bother to appear up on wherever they're which finishes in their failure to put on what's fundamental and what isn't. The essential target of this section is to toss light on anyway viably has the use of person to person communication destinations influenced the young by assessing every one of its positive and negative angles.

With connection to the discoveries it completely was obviously confounded out anyway reasonable, insightful, humorous and mindful the young is inside the present time. Through the help of the data that was gathered and examined very couple of ends have been drawn down which might be explained and intricate as pursues .The young now a days isn't exclusively mindful to what fits in best for them in any case, are sharp and ardent to draw their own needs and fix on to which of them square measure most critical and the way. similarly these destinations fill to their need of associating them with people the whole way across the globe by not hampering their work hours and timetables. Be that as it may, interpersonal interaction destinations supply them a stage to append with new individuals, share encounters and increase presentation. With connection to the normal result the investigation has delighted to an unmistakable edge whereby not exclusively negative effects have well-endeavoured to exist through the utilization of long range informal communication locales be that as it may likewise the presence of positive effects have involved a zone in one's life. The teenagers have decided their own limits and have set their possess restrains on be that as it may and once to utilize online networking paying little respect to the positive and negative impacts .

SOCIAL NETWORK ACTIONS

Why We've Got an Inclination to Post on Social Network

People dedicate concerning thirty to four-hundredth ever talking concerning themselves. be that as it may, on-line that determination bounces to concerning eightieth of interpersonal organization posts. Talking eye to eye is chaotic and genuinely is concerned. We don't have sufficient energy to acknowledge what to state, we must peruse facial prompts and correspondence on-line. We have time to develop and refine clinicians call of self-introduction, situating yourself the way you'd like to be seen. The inclination we have a tendency to prompt from self-introduction is seeing your own Facebook profile has been appeared to expand your vainness. What's together captivating for advertisers is that the preeminent extraordinary proposes that we have a tendency to will in general work on self-introduction is through things, purchasing things and stress things that mean UN office we have a tendency to demonstrate.

Why We've a Bent to Share on Social Network

On the off chance that we have a bowed to love talking concerning ourselves such loads, what might create our picture to share one issue of somebody else's. It encourages for Self-introduction and reinforcing connections that help to make our own self-esteem. As indicated by review directed sixty eight of individuals state they offer to oversee others the following feeling of United Nations organization they are and what they care concerning. But the chief fundamental reason we've a twisted to share is concerning different people: seventy eight folks} state they share as a consequences of it causes them to remain associated with individuals. various investigations have demonstrated that the preeminent powerful indicators of infectious ideas among the cerebrum square measure related with the components that attention on contemplations concerning people. this suggests substance intended for informal community doesn't need to be constrained to appeal to A curiously large bunch or a mean group. it only should appeal to a chose individual. Informal community Currency is by having one issue captivating to state.

Why We've Got a Bent to Like on Social Network

Facebook, with over an attempt of billion month to month dynamic clients could likewise be a wonderful case of a stage where individuals wish to like. Truth be told, since Facebook implemented the "Like" catch, it has been utilized over one.13 multiple times, therewith choice developing by the day. We do this as a consequences of we will in general need to require care of connections. when we watch out for most loved and like each other's posts. Teenagers got a bowed to highlight an incentive to the connection, and strengthen that closeness. we will in general set up together turn out a correspondence result. We have a bowed to feel committed to oversee back to the individuals who have given to North American nation to redesign the scales. A man of science sent Christmas cards to 600 arbitrary outsiders and got two hundred equally. That is the intensity of correspondence. Youth can correspondence on Instagram in like manner, where getting a tag or direct message makes you feel constrained to send one back. What's more, whenever anyone get a like on your profile, they potentially feel scarcely dismantle to respond in be that as it may, regardless of whether or not by sharing one factor proportionally, language up upgrades out social connections.

Why We've Got a Bent to Comment

The selling organizations will in general guess discussions with clients region unit massively significant. The commitment, cooperation with the most clients the greatest sum as potential forms long help. An overview of over seven thousand clients found that only twenty third percent people did that what they did, solely 13 referred to visit associations with the whole as an explanation behind having a relationship. The customers same shared qualities were a so a lot bigger driver for a relationship than unnumbered cooperation with a whole clients. this can be to not say that remarks aren't amazing. Indeed, they will be unrealistically so there's an advancement alluded to as shared reality that claims our entire experience of 1 issue is stricken by if and in this manner the way we have a twisted to impart it to others.85% various individuals' reactions on an issue helps U.S.A. comprehend and approach data and occasions. This implies remarks even have the ability to change our psyches, and science backs this up. An investigation on news destinations demonstrated that remarks that simply assault the creator, without any realities the littlest sum bit, are sufficient to shift our impression of an issue. On the elective hand, well-mannered audits – even once they're negative – cause a whole to be viewed as a lot of legitimate and healthy. Clients were truly ready to pay concerning $41 a lot of for a watch once they saw courteous negative audits than once the surveys were evacuated. Essentially, any remark concerning you, anyplace on-line, is to a customer an impression of what very organization you are. It's not explicitly coherent, yet that is nevertheless our cerebrums work. This implies being effectively connected inside the remarks area of your diary and with the customer audits of your item is critical, not such a lot to the individual you're reacting to beside everybody taking an interest inside the mutual truth of remarks and surveys.

Selfie Craze

Historically, portraits are relating to standing, and dominant the means that our image is perceived.

Today, they're the thanks to estimate for the tendency WHO we tend to are . The "looking-glass self" could also be a psychological thought that claims that we can, we will, we are able to ne'er be really see ourselves. We would really like our reflection from others therefore on grasp who we have an inclination to are. Selfies put together work as a results of we have an inclination to pay loads of attention to faces than we've an inclination to try and do to the remainder. The profile image is that the first place the eye is drawn to on Facebook and different social network sites. On Instagram, footage with human faces are thirty eight percent loads of in all probability to receive likes and thirty 2% that is loads of in all probability to attract comments. Eye-tracking studies show that on-line, we've an inclination to follow the eyes of the oldsters we've an inclination to check on screen.

Emoji Power on Social Network

Most people have a bent to mimic each other's expressions in face-to-face spoken communication. In on-line arena, we have a bent to recreate that crucial a part of sympathy using emoticons and emoji. Today, ninety 2 of people out hundreds of times use stickers, emoticons or emojis in their on-line communication, and 10 billion emoji are sent around the world every day. Emoji may be a powerful link between emoji use and social network power. it's Associate in Nursing analysis of over 5 years in social network found that emoji were a customary issue among important and customary social network sharers. A study that had participants chat on-line with various forms of specialists found that participants rated the specialists friendlier and tons of competent once they used emoticons in their communication. There are several fun ways that during which to incorporate emoji into your merchandising campaigns. Brands like Ikea, Coca-Cola, Burger King and Comedy Central have even created their own branded emoji for their popularity.

Network Nostalgia

Sometimes the network and life moves thus fast that we have a tendency to would like things to dam. This is where craving comes in, and this longing for the past is an unbelievable strategy for modern social network selling. yearning is universal across all cultures and it provides U.S. the way of social connectedness, feelings of being favourite and protected.

CONCEPTUAL FRAMEWORK

See Figure 6.

Figure 6. Conceptual framework

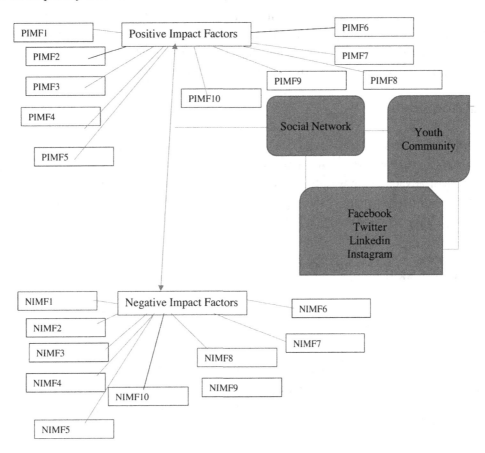

POSITIVE SOCIAL NETWORK PSYCHOLOGY

Web-based social networking is progressively turning into a basic component of human culture by changing our social standards, qualities, and culture. Data sharing and the conveyance of substance are getting to be significant social wants . Web based life has changed how individuals, including college understudies impart, cooperate, and associate through the span of their learning forms at instructive establishments. This new type of media is assuming an imperative job in substance sharing among colleges understudies and the remainder of society. Understudies currently have the chance to partake in social talk by sharing pictures and pictures, posting their remarks, scattering thoughts, . . Advanced media and person to person communication are altering strategies for ordinary correspondence, coordinated effort, data sharing, and data utilization .

Media Skill

The ability to viably utilize web search tools and see has been contemplated by United Nations office or what associations made or support the information; wherever the data originates from and its believability . Join that have some expertise in morals, style and cooperation make a significant commitment to discussions round the job of internet based life in scholarly settings, giving numerous chances to inventive reasoning and articulation, while maintaining a strategic distance from the over-disentangled investigation that might be identified with sane evaluate of online networking writings. In any case, while concurring that such open doors should be important elements of online networking in scholastic settings, we will in general contend that there's as yet a need for reflexive scrutinize.

Technical Acquirement

The information and skills needed to use a laptop, application or specific package program or application. company learners World Health Organization have a high degree of technical acquirement acumen to use technology to their advantage. they will realize all the knowledge they have by looking out the net and exploitation the tech-based resources that square measure out there. These people even have the ability to beat everyday challenges and reach their goals with the assistance of their mobile devices. Technical acquirement is important in our tech-centric society.

Critical Content Skill

The ability to viably utilize web search tools and see has been contemplated by United Nations office or what associations made or support the information; wherever the data originates from and its believability . Join that have some expertise in morals, style and cooperation make a significant commitment to discussions round the job of internet based life in scholarly settings, giving numerous chances to inventive reasoning and articulation, while maintaining a strategic distance from the over-disentangled investigation that might be identified with sane evaluate of online networking writings. In any case, while concurring that such open doors should be important elements of online networking in scholastic settings, we will in general contend that there's as yet a need for reflexive scrutinize.

Communicative and Social Networking Literacy

Open partner studied informal communication process in different totally various zones of correspondence on the online web. The formal standards that administer guide the material conduct, dimension of protection to influence undesirable or unseemly correspondence through them; creative substance and visual securing furthermore to the capacities to shape and exchange picture and video content this incorporates seeing how on-line visual substance is adjusted and developed, what sensibly substance is satisfactory and the manner in which copyright applies to their exercises. Research shows that the work of long range interpersonal communication administrations will bolster the occasion of media procurement. The creation and sharing of substance on administrations like Myspace has been believed to expand every youthful people groups specialized education, as they figure out how to utilize code to frame their profiles, and inventive substance and visual literacy.

Formal Education Outcome

The potential of public SNS and social media like blogs to helps to conduct formal tutorial activities and enhance learning outcomes. whereas e-learning frameworks square measure presently integrated into most tutorial settings, the use of SNS could be a smaller quantity comprehensively used. The SNS varies in keeping with state and there's inadequacy of proof on the impact of SNS on young people's formal education . SNS is in addition obtaining accustomed increase opportunities for formal learning across geographical contexts. Using SNS, youngsters from the two schools act with learners from over forty various SNS use between lecturers and students can improve rapport and motivation and engagement with education .Studies conducted inside the point on the role of ICT in learning and development .

On-line forums and SNS can support the continuation and extension of learning and discussion outside formal as Peer based learning can be a key characteristic of the strategy throughout that teenagers direct their own learning outside school & formal organisations .Evaluations of e-learning ways that have found SNS platforms enable the extension of learning discussion outside the formal area setting, therefore promoting deeper learning as teenagers not exclusively interact with the material for extended but square measure further apparently to relate thereto and incorporate it into their everyday lives. Finally, studies conducted on the use of hand-held devices to deliver point learning demonstrable that regular accessibility suggests that children can access resources in a very technique that is every convenient and relevant to them. The elearning tutorials have positive impact on learners and help socio-economic backgrounds and folks living in remote areas, face persistent challenges of internet access and skill . Increasing the benefits of SNS for these groups specifically wants addressing access and digital skill.

Creativity

Rapid uptake of digital technologies have displayed unexampled prospects for amateur users to make and distribute content specified media users became producers. User-generated content describes each the generation of „original" inventive content and „remixed" content that creatively reworks or repurposes existing content. The interrelatedness between SNS and social media has provided a key impetus (via platforms like youtube.com and flickr.com) for the sharing of this self-generated content with broader networks. teens particularly area unit additional immersed during this democratic media surroundings than the other age-group. They currently produce and share their own 'small media' in their everyday communicative, inventive and social activities.

Creative content sharing practices such as blogs, animations, videos, photos associate degreed digital collages . It plays a big role in young people developing sense of identity and community. inventive content production and sharing empowers individual teens through the subsequent incontestable benefits. Developing a way of aspiration, personal action and self-worth, and fostering additional creative thinking and self-Notley of all of that area unit key predictors of wellbeing.

Individual Identity and Self-Expression

Individual Identity SNS area necessary for the expression of identity. This articulation is not simply egotistic, but supports essential peer-based nature. As a results of SNS area unit essentially versatile and designed to push individual customisation youngsters use SNS to experiment nonetheless as notice legitimacy for his or her political, ethnic, cultural or sexual identity .

SNS can offer youngsters with a part to work out identity and standing, add from cultural cues and discuss public life. Free from adult regulation young people's articulation and expression of assorted components of their identity to their friends et al. supports essential peer-based nature . Such processes of socialisation area unit essential for psychosocial development at a time once many youngsters are consolidating their identities, propulsion up roots from their family, pains for independence and developing new sorts of relationships, yet as intimate ones .

Strengthening Existing Relationships

Having positive social relationships in web use, generally, has been found to strengthen young people's existing social relationships Most analysis has centered on the role SNS play within the maintaining and strengthening of existing offline relationships. However, for a few teenagers, notably those that area unit marginalised or otherwise socially isolated, on line relationships provided a major, and generally the sole, chance for such socialisation. As a study of SNS for teenagers that suffer chronic sickness and/ or incapacity demonstrates, not solely did it offer the chance to develop such friendships however participants represented these friendships as "true friends" that were amongst their most dependable and enduring . Another study incontestable however Facebook helped teenagers with lower levels of social skills develop friendships on-line that then translated offline .Indeed, teenagers area unit more and more partaking at the same time in on-line and offline social networking. As an example, multi-player gambling includes a long tradition of mixing on-line and offline interactions of players with web cafes and computer network parties providing such areas .whereas there has been very little analysis it seems that teenagers typically work collaboratively within the on-line area through SNS, making and commenting on YouTube videos or different such activities, whereas physically co-located. teenagers not solely can take into account their on-line and offline worlds together however truly mix the two during a physical and temporal sense. This insight is additional emphatic by analysis demonstrating that the potential of SNS for promoting social inclusion depends upon finding ways that of bridging online communication .

Belonging and Collective Identity

SNS facilitates people, children, kids, youngsters, teenagers, teens, adolescents, youth . The sexually and gender varied to meet folks and learn from each other, creating the sense of happiness to a broader community . This sense of happiness and acceptance can mean that youth United Nations agency might even be tons of in danger of isolation like those with chronic malady or a incapacity usually keep members of an online community long once their initial impetus is content sharing plays a major role in cultivating happiness and some way of collective identity. Sharing written, visual or audio content on SNS that represents or portrays a private or community experience invites others to act and relate. This phenomenon is associated with current visual access to a small-scale communication cluster or community via spontaneous and everyday photos uploaded to a cooperative media space. Such a mode of sharing and connection does not want of time communication and will to boot mitigate feelings of social isolation.

Civic and Political Participation

SNS speak to new territories for municipal commitment and political cooperation just as information sharing and transferral along new systems for activity using email, client produced substance and distinctive systems administration rehearses. Concentrates inside the U.S. understand that thirty seventh of eighteen – twenty multi year olds use online journals and SNS for political or community commitment. Political competitors zone unit increasingly using SNS and online life, as territory unit backing and issue-situated groups. SNS zone unit getting utilized for dialog, association and assembly as a piece of rising political talk in youthful people groups presence . despite the fact that focused on balloting, efforts like Rock the Vote, The Hip Hop Summit Action Network, subject adjustment and Voces del Pueblo zone unit tests of the technique that long range informal communication is inserted in new assortments of network and political sorting out and electioneering . For youth United Nations organization don't consider their investment in community or issue-based exercises as inside the old or institutional sense, SNS region unit thought of a great deal of fundamental than „civic locales. Person to person communication administrations, as <u>web.myspace.com</u> region unit acclimated choose what individuals do by associating with individuals with comparable interests, existing efforts or distributive data in regards to their own comes.

NEGATIVE SOCIAL NETWORK PSYCHOLOGY

The threatening effects of these individual to individual correspondence goals surpass the helpful ones. The study suggests that electronic life is an engaging way for understudies to keep up a vital separation from weariness while they are thinking about or glancing through their course material web, diverting their thought from their work . The online network filling has a net-negative effect on one life. For instance, the going with electronic life stages have been situated from the most to the least negative reliant on customer evaluations: Twitter, Facebook, linkedin, and Instagram.

Sedentary Behaviour

Inactive practices square measure exercises that include sitting or resting and square measure described by an espresso Metabolic Equivalent Total (MET) vitality use. Inert practices square measure performed at or somewhat over the resting rate go 1 to 1.5 METS and grasp an assortment of exercises like television seeing, PC use, appreciating computer games, and latent diversion These dormant practices square measure unavoidable in our general public, grown-ups pay a middle of twenty eight hours out of each week recognition . Internet based life more supports these sorts of dormant practices. Commonly, an individual uses web based life on their workstation or cell phone while hanging loose all through a dormant movement: sitting on the train or transport, holding up in line, and so on. In any case, very that, internet based life commonly works as Associate in Nursing movement amid and of itself – as in an individual will plunk down all through relaxation time explicitly to imagine their web-based social networking destinations, making idle conduct rather than only exploiting it. Inactive practices, similar to those propelled by web based life use, are joined to physical wellbeing dangers. The raised danger of kind polygenic infection lard, issue, high weight level, and metabolic disorder square measure all identified with idle conduct. Be that as it may, less is thought in regards to the consequences of idle conduct on the peril of mental state issues.

Displaced Behaviour

As per uprooting hypothesis, it isn't simply the web based life use all by itself that effects affects emotional wellness, but instead the nonattendance of different exercises. One idea may put forth a defense for anyway the dormant practices motivated by web based life influence mental state is that of uprooting. people that compensation longer in inert practices like web based life use possess less energy for up close and personal social association and physical movement, both of that are attempted to ensure against mental issue. In accordance with removal hypothesis, it's not simply the online networking use all by itself that affects mental state, anyway rather the nonattendance of various exercises. As per Open Thinking Exchange (2013), Americans matured 18-64 United Nations office utilize informal communities report that they pay a mean of three.2 hours every day doing in this manner. This range is significantly higher for youthful grown-ups: 18-34-year-olds report abuse internet based life a mean of three.8 hours out of every day, with one out of five clients matured 18-34 reportage that they're on interpersonal interaction destinations six or a great deal of hours out of each day. NBC News reports that in July 2012 alone, Americans went through a joined 230,060 years via web-based networking media destinations. concerning hundredth of the time Americans utilize their PCs, they are via web-based networking media; half-hour of the time region on their cell phones they're completing a proportional. Whatever the reason, work up is all around archived to support mental state. The dangers of supplanting physical exercises with an inert conduct, together with web based life use, must be thought of as an achievable issue once talking about the outcomes of web based life use on mental health. Face-to-confront social cooperation conjointly plays an occupation in uprooted conduct hypothesis. Like work out, it diminishes the opportunity of creating mental state issues and eases mental state issues that exist as of now. The uprooted conduct hypothesis contends that dormant practices like web-based social networking use could be dislodging this vis-à-vis cooperation and along these lines the edges it offers. The social withdrawal theory is one system of clarifying the relationship between expanding latent practices and expanding danger of despondency. This speculation recommends that the a ton of generally people stare at the TV or utilize the PC/web, the any they expel themselves from social collaboration, that progressively will build their danger of despondency. Krout (2002) expanded this hypothesis alongside his social confinement speculation, recommending that drawn out commitment in latent practices, similar to TV survey or pc use, not just expels the client from social connection, anyway conjointly results in the breakdown of social help or correspondence systems which can result in expanded danger of mental sick wellbeing.

Sleep Interruption Due to Blue Light-Weight

Wright. (2013) found that individuals United Nations association went through consistently spot to remain inside the Rocky Mountains, displayed to solely ordinary light-weight and no electronic contraptions, had their unit of time tickers synchronized with the development and fall of the sun. Regardless, these normal unit of time rhythms are not by any means the standard in the present snappy and involved world. Our typical rest cycles are being meddled with .An Associate in Nursing said our workstations, cell phones what's more, cell phones and pc screens wont to peruse internet based life destinations all share one issue practically speaking. The concealed interims their which sparkle, they emanate abnormal amounts of blue light-weight. This fake light-weight upsets sound rest cycles demonstrated that evening time introduction to fake light-weight disturbs the body's organic time, or the 24-hour system that controls our rest cycle. In what capacity will this counterfeit light-weight disturb rest per Holzman

(2010), the blue light-weight encased in fake light-weight is that the most destructive to people. Blue light-weight smothers inner discharge, or the mind's "sluggish compound," creation extra keenly than various wavelengths. Blue light-weight stifles inner discharge through one in every one of the sensors in our eye: the essentially light-delicate retinal neural structure cells, or RGCs. The RGCs are most delicate to blue light; in this way, it exclusively takes alittle amount of blue light-weight for the mind to flag the ductless organ to forestall causation out interior discharge, making it problematic to desire to rest. This inside discharge smothering blue light-weight is blessing in our TVs, pc screens and cell phones. Perusing internet based life before bed isn't just diverting from rest, it will for all intents and purposes prevent you from being drowsy peered toward in any regard.

Rapid Task Switch

Fast errand change (additionally alluded to as performing various tasks), propelled by online life, could likewise be one root clarification for wretchedness. Rosen et al. (2013) states that "while performing various tasks is innately a character's property, innovation has possibly excessively roused and advanced it by our multi-window workstation situations, multi-application cell phone screens and furthermore the wide-going tangible incitement (and diversion) offered by top notch, adjustable visual and methodology flag also material incitement through vibration.

Cybersickness

Cybersickness is tantamount to kinetosis and for the most part occurs all through or once drenching in an exceedingly virtual climate. Cybersickness is accepted to happen essentially as an aftereffects of contentions between 3 tangible frameworks: visual, proprioception and interoception. therefore, the eyes comprehend a development that is out of alter by a few milliseconds with what's apparent by the vestibular device, while the remainder of the body remains for all intents and purposes unmoving . Cybersickness might be brought about by elements related with the work of video game instrumentation (for example largeness of the head protector, closeness of screen to the eyes. As per Kennedy, Lane, Berbaum and Lilienthal (1993), the transitory feature impacts related to cybersickness will be isolated into 3 classes of indications related with the tactile clashes and to the work of computer game gear: (1) visual side effects (eyestrains, obscured vision, cerebral pains), (2) confusion (vertigo, unevenness) and (3) sickness (regurgitating, tipsiness). Visual side effects normally happen as an aftereffects of closeness of the screen and square measure limited fundamentally to the work of a virtual protective cap. The sickness and bewilderment extreme square measure brief, like perusing in an exceedingly moving vehicle and square measure caused essentially as an after-effects of tactile clash.

In any event hour of computer game climate clients report having felt side effects of cybersickness all through an essential session. The extent of individual who feel extra serious and long-run auxiliary impacts is like the extent of individuals who are experiencing an affectability to kinetosis. around five-hitter of clients really feel no feature impacts of any sort as an after-effects of being drenched inside the computer game air.

Cyberbullying

Cyberbullying is harassing that happens over computerized gadgets like phones, PCs, and tablets. Cyberbullying will happen through SMS, Text, and applications, or on-line in online life, gatherings, or redirection wherever people will peruse, take an interest in, or offer substance. Cyberbullying incorporates causation, posting, or sharing negative, unsafe, false, or mean substance with respect to another person. It will grasp sharing individual or non-open data in regards to another person perpetrating shame or embarrassment. Some cyberbullying crosses the street into unlawful or criminal conduct. The most widely recognized places wherever cyberbullying happens are: Online life, as Facebook, Instagram, Snapchat, and Twitter, SMS (Short Message Service) moreover alluded to as Text Message sent through gadgets Text (by means of gadgets, email provider administrations, applications, and online networking electronic informing highlights) email. With the predominance of internet based life and computerized gatherings, remarks, photographs, posts, and substance shared by individuals will ordinarily be seen by outsiders besides as associates. The substance an individual offers on-line – each their own substance moreover as any negative, mean, or pernicious substance – makes a type of lasting open record of their perspectives, exercises, and conduct. This open record will be thought of as a web name, which can be available to universities, businesses, schools. UN organization is likewise exploring an individual right now or inside what's to come. Cyberbullying will hurt the net notorieties of everyone concerned isn't just the individual being scared, anyway those doing the harassing or partaking in it .

Cyberaddiction

Internet addiction is represented as an impulse management disorder, that doesn't involve use of an intoxicating drug and is extremely the same as pathological gambling. Some web users could develop AN emotional attachment to on-line friends and activities they produce on their laptop screens. web users could get pleasure from aspects of the web that enable them to satisfy, socialize, and exchange concepts through the utilization of chat rooms, social networking websites, or "virtual communities." different web users pay endless hours researching topics of interest on-line or "blogging". Blogging may be a contraction of the term "Web log", within which a private can post commentaries and keep regular chronicle of events. It may be viewed as journaling and also the entries area unit primarily matter. Similar to different addictions, those full of web addiction use the virtual phantasy to attach with real individuals through the web, as a substitution for real-life human association, that they're unable to realize ordinarily.Internet addiction leads to personal, family, academic, financial, and activity issues that area unit characteristic of different addictions. Impairments of real world relationships area unit non continuous as a results of excessive use of the web. people full of web addiction pay longer in solitary seclusion, pay less time with real individuals in their lives, and area unit usually viewed as socially awkward. Arguments could result thanks to the degree of your time spent on-line. Those full of web addiction could conceive to conceal the quantity of your time spent on-line, which ends in distrust and also the disturbance of quality in once stable relationships. Some full of web addiction could produce on-line personas or profiles wherever they're ready to alter their identities and fake to be somebody apart from himself or herself. Those at highest risk for creation of a secret life area unit those that suffer from low-self esteem feelings of inadequacy, and concern of disapproval. Such negative self-concepts result in clinical issues of depression and anxiety.

Many persons United Nations agency conceive to quit their web use expertise withdrawal including: anger, depression, relief, mood swings, anxiety, fear, irritability, sadness, loneliness, boredom, restlessness, procrastination, and dyspepsia. Being captivated with the web may also cause physical discomfort or medical issues such as: Carpal Tunnel Syndrome, dry eyes, backaches, severe headaches, consumption irregularities such as skipping meals, failure to attend to non-public hygiene, and sleep disturbance.

Cyber Depression

Another research presumes that there's if in all honesty a causative connection between the use of online networking and negative impacts on prosperity, basically despondency and dejection. The investigation was uncovered inside the Journal of Social and psychotherapeutics. "What we tend to establish by and large is that in the event that you utilize less web based life, you're extremely less discouraged and less forlorn, which implies that the decreased internet based life use is the thing that causes that subjective move in your prosperity," previously mentioned Jordyn Young, a creator of the paper and a senior at the University of Pennsylvania. The scientists state this is frequently the essential time a causative connection has ever been built up in research venture. The examination encased 143 understudies from the University of Pennsylvania. They were helter and skelter named 2groups: one that may proceed with their online networking propensities as was normal or one that may significantly restrain access to internet based life. For three weeks, the exploratory group had their web based life utilize decreased to half-hour of the day for ten minutes on 3 entirely using Facebook, Instagram, and Twitter.In request to remain these trial conditions, the specialists looked at telephone use data, that reported what amount time was spent exploitation each application every day. The majority of the examination members needed to utilize iPhones. The outcomes were clear: The bunch that utilized less web-based social networking, despite the fact that it wasn't completely disposed of, had higher mental state results. Gauge readings for members were taken toward the beginning of the preliminary in numerous zones of prosperity: social help, stress of passing up a great opportunity, forlornness, tension, dejection, vanity, independence, and self-acknowledgment. At the tip of the preliminary, those inside the test group saw every forlornness and burdensome side effects decay, with the most significant changes occurring in those that revealed greater dimensions of melancholy.

Eating Disorders

"Selfies, self-image, vanity and therefore the "self" is incredibly abundant at the guts of socialmedia these days. It pay loads of your time urging folks with ingestion disorders to be additional crucial of the bloggers they give the impression of being at, as a result they're promoting their lifestyles on social media . Whether clean ingestion, fitspiration or the virtues of veganism, several celebrities and "vloggers" use social media sites to push their food decisions, exercise regimes and toned bodies. For folks fighting low vanity and body confidence, the constant timeline of body and food-related posts could cause heightened levels of stress and anxiety around what they understand because the perfect lifestyle.

Attention Deficit Upset Disorder

Teens diagnosed having Attention Deficit Disorder Disorder (ADD) expertise identical core symptoms as younger youngsters with the disorder, including: basic cognitive process, impulsivity, and, in some cases, disorder. Teens conjointly face exaggerated expectations socially and academically throughout this point, which may work to accentuate some symptoms of attention deficit disorder. Developmentally, teenagers may be characterised by higher educational and social expectations. Teens have additional autonomy and fewer structure each in school and reception, and fewer teacher oversight once it involves finishing assignments and maintaining with work. For teens with minimal brain dysfunction which is new independence will backfire.

Many youngsters with minimal brain dysfunction exhibit difficulties in peer relationships thanks to impulsivity, hyperactivity, and aggression. Frequent interruptions, issue dealing with frustration, and poor social skills will negatively impact early friendships, which pattern will continue into adolescence. The importance of peer relationships will increase throughout adolescence, as teens pay additional of their time engaged with peers. Lack of follow with social skills within the early years will build it troublesome to ascertain new friendships throughout the teenager years. Many teens with minimal brain dysfunction expertise alternative difficulties. analysis shows high levels of comorbidity between minimal brain dysfunction and mood disorders, anxiety disorders, and conduct disorder.4 One study found that adolescent females with minimal brain dysfunction have a a pair of 0.5 times higher risk of major depression than feminine adolescents while not minimal brain dysfunction.

Teens with minimal brain dysfunction want further emotional support from their folks and lecturers. The behaviours that folks and lecturers take for frustrating or annoying are the terribly behaviours that trigger anxiety and low vanity in teens with minimal brain dysfunction. Left uncurbed, these behaviours will intensify and end in symptoms of tension depressive disorders. Due to impulsivity, emotional regulation may be a struggle for teens with minimal brain dysfunction. mix exaggerated pressure, high educational demands, low social interaction skills with low emotional regulation skills and it all adds up to teens with minimal brain dysfunction combating varied social-emotional struggles day after day.

SOCIAL IMPACT THEORY

Social Impact Theory become created turned into by Bibb Latane in 1981 as a shape for comprehension the general regulations that guide the association of networks and connections. Social effect alludes to, as Latane noticed, "the pleasant form of adjustments in physiological states and abstract sentiments, thought tactics and feelings, perceptions and convictions, qualities and conduct, that manifest in an individual as an aftereffects of the large, inferred, or whimsical nearness or activities of non-compulsory people. Latane stated that take a seat wasn't produced for its explicitness or its ability to explain the exact methodologies by using that social effect is exchanged from person to an change. sit down just shows that social effect is a part into 'social powers' along with high-quality, instantaneousness, and quantity, which the impact of every social strength are regularly spoken to numerically. Latane(1981) displays each social power and its essential examination, regardless of the fact that he concedes that most of his related statistics alludes to his third social electricity. run as an detail of social effect alludes, most sensibly, to the amount of humans that shape up an impacting supply. Latane contends that enthusiastic or intellectual element sway on an man or woman will increment in light of the reality that the affecting institution develops in length. however, the impact of each affecting individual is a littler sum than that of the individual that preceded. Latane clarifies the idea through a similarity: while price of a person's first dollar is as much as the unique estimation in their one centesimal dollar, the impact of the one hundredth greenback is a littler sum than the effect of the important. eventually, the social impact of quite a few 100 humans is not a couple of times as massive in mild of the truth that the effect of 1 character. Latane communicates the instance part of team spirit thru a situation, wherever "I" is social impact, "s" could be a scaling regular, "N" is that the scope of resources, and "t" will be a value but one: $I = sNt$. research that, Latane closes, is confirmative of sit down and typically confirmative of his clinical articulation of bunch size consists of an expansion of each human and non-human practices, collectively with ingesting spot tip estimate in regard to bolstering gathering size, situation in guinea pigs, and similarity amongst understudies. The social powers, great and quickness, are not any reduced, Latane (1981) states, however he exhibits this kind of terrific deal much less confirmative examination. every quality (i.e. the standing or depth of an affecting source) and quickness, or "the closeness in house or time and nonappearance of interceding hindrances or channels," are represented as Latane reviews the outcomes of news events. Latane alludes to his own exam with Bassett, gave in 1976, that researched every of the 3 social powers with the aid of displaying numerous fake functions and test information memories to technology understudies. Understudies have been entrusted with deciding on what quantity article inches each story ought to be relegated. The status (or strength) of the issues concerned in each story perceived to haven't any have an impact on at the users choices, but the quantity of subjects concerned and also the space of the occasion (Columbus, close to; Phoenix, some distance) did. Fewer column inches had been committed to occasions in Phoenix, and even though the amount of topics worried collected column inches for each near and far off occasions, the gap among the 2 sets widened as cluster size collected. Latane concludes that distance would not boom impact logarithmically, and later is going on to specify that impact, "might be an mathematical feature of the sq. of the space among people.The result would possibly, perhaps, be extra associated with strength than Latané supposes. Latane in 1996 redeveloped sit as dynamic Social impact idea. Dynamic Social Impact Theory conceives of social effect as an repetitious approach inside which probably haphazardly distributed attributes cluster over the years supported, in part, physical distance through immediacy. Latane shows that much less well favored attributes persist thru minority subgroups. therefore, dynamic take a seat proposes that these social forces are responsible for a backside-up formation of culture thru communication. As a consequences of Latane development, this principle will become in general concerning styles and social groupings, cultural shifts and social commonalities.

Legal Guidelines of Conduct

Latané contends that every individual is conceivably a "source" or an "objective" of social impact now and then each on the double. He supposes there are three recommendations or legal guidelines at paintings.

Social Pressure

Social force is made by impact, danger, amusingness, disgrace and diverse consequences that is contained power, Immediacy and Numbers:

1. Power: that is how a whole lot strength you believe the man or woman influencing you has. for example, if the man or woman has rank in an association, their solicitations could have extra fine.
2. Immediacy: that is the methods via which later the effect is and the way close you, from a solicitation a minute again out of your leader standing suitable with the aid of you (fast) to an electronic mail you obtain out of your director seven days prior (now not fast)

3. Numbers: The extra people placing weight on you to attain something, the extra social power they'll have

The Psychosocial Law

The Psychosocial law in social impact will occur within the advancement from 0 to one source .the amount of assets are manufactures. The condition Latané uses for this regulation is impact = s.Nt. The electricity (t) of the quantity of people (N) copied with the aid of the scaling unfaltering (s) chooses social impact. Asch's stated of congruity in understudies denies the psychosocial law, displaying up or three wellsprings of social impact have little impact. Regardless, Gerard, Wilhelmy, and Conolley drove a practically equal document on closeness testing from auxiliary school understudies. The Auxiliary school understudies were regarded as greater against be impenetrable to likeness than college students. Latane explained his law to pantomime likewise, the use of Milgram's sizeable check. in this exam diverse amounts of confederates stayed on a road nook in new york expanding and expanding on the sky. The outcomes showed that greater confederates inferred greater spectators, and the trade ended up being logically beside the point as more confederates were available. In an exam Latane and Harkins proved before a set of human beings warning and shame, the effects in like manner renowned the psychosocial law seeming moreover assembling of individuals human beings inferred steadily great uneasiness and that the pleasant distinction existed some location within the scope of 0 and 1 swarm human beings.

Divisions of Effect

The regulation of division impact communicates that the exceptional, immediacy, and wide variety of targets take delivery of an occupation . The more pleasant and immediacy and the more essential quantity of centers in a social scenario reasons the social effect to be apportioned amongst maximum of the destinations. The condition that addresses this division is affect = f(SIN) .The social effect hypothesis is each a generalizable and a particular hypothesis. It uses one parcel of conditions, that are cloth to diverse social situations. for instance, the psychosocial regulation may be used to ascertain times of comparability, pantomime and shame. in any case, it's miles in like way unequivocal in light of the truth that the gauges that it makes are express and can be associated with and noticed on earth. The concept is falsifiable furthermore. It makes dreams making use of conditions; in any case, the conditions could be undeserving to correctly predict the consequence of social situations. Social impact principle is in like way accommodating. It might be used to fathom which social situations result in the exceptional impact and which conditions gift exceptions to the gauges. Even as Social effect hypothesis explores social conditions and can assist count on the consequences of social situations, it moreover has multiple inadequacies and questions which might be left uncertain. The regulations coordinating the idea depict human beings as recipients that latently understand social effect and do not take into account the social impact that human beings may accurately hunt out. The model is in like manner static, and does no longer completely compensate for the additives drew in with social participations. The principle is tolerably new and fails to address some pertinent problems. those issues consolidate finding dynamically genuine approaches to address degree social results, know-how the "t" type in psychosocial law, considering, perceiving how flashing results can shape into steady outcomes, utility to accumulate affiliations, know-how the version's inclination .

APPLYING SOCIAL IMPACT THEORY

Survey Approach

Social impact theory facilities around the non-separate social powers, which might be the span of the affecting accumulating and the influencer's high-quality popularity or intensity of the influencer. This exploration turned into meant to restrict or dispense with impedance from those social powers. right off the bat, it turned into clarified to participants that their mission companion turned into someone. This element was communicated whilst booking project aid and amid project hobby in some exceptional ways. to begin with, the challenge companion changed into continuously alluded to as a specific detail. second, a particular separation become given to each member to their errand partner. ultimately, amid challenge funding, the elements included had been recorded within the "Babbles on-line" place of the speak application, and the main names recorded had been the member, the expert, and the gazing scientist. exceptional as a social strength became an increasing number of muddled to represent. Conversationalists are in all likelihood going to border conclusions approximately the status in their cooperating accomplices dependent on subsequent to no facts. because of the want of giving the equivalent printed contributions to every member, it turned into considered as full-size that the pre-composed reactions suggest subsequent to no approximately the mission partner/specialist. Reactions have been composed with insignificant slang and internet-specific expressing or truncations, general spelling, popular accentuation and capitalization, and negligible but responsive utilization of emoticons. This changed into finished to restriction the opportunity that members would create suppositions about the age, instructive status, or sexual orientation of their undertaking accomplice (Marwick, 2013). In light of time limitations, reactions sent amid undertaking interest should have been brisk. Hence, the pre-composed reactions were sent, reliably crosswise over errand cooperation, as fast as it was esteemed conceivable to have kept in touch with them at a sensible speed in order to keep away from suggestions that may have identified with age or capacity. At last, on the grounds that an enormous concern in regards to much past SIT research is that members may have predispositions about specific places, this investigation tried member conduct and observation utilizing a separation and not a spot.

Data was collected from University Students of Jamia Hamdard through survey. A self administered questionnaire was used for data collection. In the survey the data was collected from students (n = 560) to examine the validity and reliability of the adapted scales. The questionnaire pattern for the study was prepared in two portions to examine the opinions of the respondents. This investigation additionally incorporated an open-finished inquiry to assemble data about the view of understudies' learning conduct through web based life. The study asked college understudies to answer inquiries dependent on positive and negative elements, demonstrating how such components influenced their every day lives, particularly regarding maintainable instructive learning. The study depended on a five-point Likert scale to survey the level of understanding. The information of study one was incorporated into the complete information to keep up the consistency in the information gathered from arbitrary example of understudies. Total 560 questionnaires were distributed online using google forms among the randomly chosen students and the response rate was 83%. The age ranges of the sample students were as follows. The sample students were enrolled in undergraduate degree programs, graduate degree programs, and postgraduate degree programs respectively. The result analysis shown in figure 7 analysed that facebook has strength 60%, immediacy as 48% with approx. 200 users,twitter has strength 51%, immediacy as 50% with 240 users, Instagram has strength 93%, immediacy 50% with 120 users, linkden has strength 51%, immediacy 20% with 100 users.

The Psychosocial Law Impact for the survey is calculated as Impact which is 224 people per transcation can be used to understand which social situations and behaviour. The division of impact for all the users has impact of diffusion of responsibility refers to the decreased responsibility of action each member of a group feels when she or he is part of a group. As per the diffusion of responsibility, people feel that their need to intervene in a situation decreases as the number of other (perceived) witnesses increases which has both negative and positive effect on the behaviour of the user. Group size significantly influenced the likelihood of helping behaviour in a staged emergency: 85% of participants responded with intervention when alone, 62% of participants took action when with one other person, and only 31% did when there were four other bystanders. Figure 8 shows the behaviour impact analysis on the user according to the age groups. The analysis resulted that >21 age group have most changing behaviour on online networks, age group between 21-29 shows steady change in behaviour analysis as compared to age group > 31.

Figure 7. SIT survey analysis

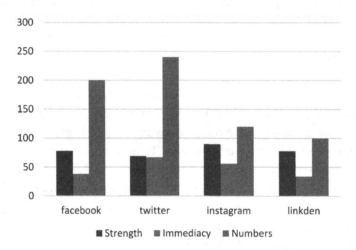

Figure 8. Behaviour impact analysis

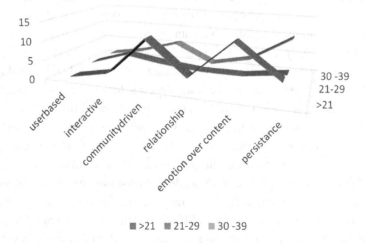

Psychological Impact Factors List

The data we gathered from the surveys from the users through google forms, the information was checked, sent into the SPSS programming variant 25. Next, expressive measurements, recurrence investigation, dependability, graphic insights examination, ANOVA, and a t-test were performed on the legitimate information of the 560 respondents. The reaction rate resulted to be 87.033%, which is an incredible reaction rate. Our discoveries demonstrate that 53.08% of the respondents hold a graduate degree; 36.02% of the respondents hold a four year certification, and 10.90% of the understudy respondents hold an expert degree. Table 1 presents 10 chose web-based social networking factors. The estimation of Cronbach's alpha for the positive web based life elements estimated was agreeable ($\alpha = 0.7$), and the negative web based life factors likewise introduced a palatable Cronbach's alpha esteem ($\alpha = 0.9$). Information consistency mirrors the information source, and it requires data about the respondents' comprehension of the chose survey. This investigation connected Cronbach's alpha (α) to evaluate the dependability of the got information, and the ascertaining instrument was SPSS rendition 25. Accordingly, the unwavering quality of the overview poll uncovered a satisfactory estimation of Cronbach's alpha ($\alpha = 0.762$, $\alpha = 0.815$) for both the positive and negative internet based life factors, and these outcomes demonstrate that the respondents had a full hold and comprehension of the data incorporated into the study and great nature with the effect of the positive and negative components of web based life use on the online network.

Figure 9. Positive and negative psychological impact factors

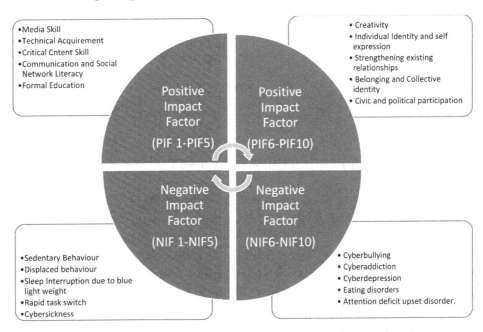

Table 1. Cronbach's alpha values for psychological impact positive and negative factors

Reliability Test -Positive factors	
Scale Items No of Items -10 Positive Psychological Impact Factors of Social Network	Data Reliability 0.862 Crobach's alpha values
Scale Items No of Items -10 Negative Psychological Impact Factors of Social Network	Data Reliability 0.715 Crobach's alpha values

Data Processing

In the data processing the primary challenge of this specific study was to explore and determine the most influential social media factors and their ultimate impact on the students' communities. These factors were identified from the previous literature after an in-depth investigation, and each element was analysed independently. Table 2 displays the mean score (M) and standard deviation (SD) of the selected positive social media factors.

Table 2. Participants using various applications of social media

Social Network Types	Frequency	Percent	Valid Percent	Cumulative Percent (%)
Facebook	*280*	*41*	*41*	*41*
Twitter	*160*	*11.6*	*11.6*	*52.6*
Instagram	*100*	*7.8*	*7.8*	*60.4*
Linkedin	*120*	*31.6*	*31.6*	*92.1*
All	*66*	*7.9*	*7.9*	*100*

Positive Psychological Impact Positive Factor Social Network Analysis

Table 3 describes the mean scores (M) and standard deviations (SD) of selected positive social media factors. The results of all the positively related factors are close to each other. The most significant impacts of social media include the following: Media Skill (M = 4.0241, SD = 1.3566), Technical Acquirement (M = 4.0144, SD = 1.3298), Critical Content Skill (M = 4.0903, SD = 1.1955), Communication and Social network literacy (M = 4.0542, SD = 1.3101), Formal education outcome (M = 4.0830, SD = 1.3431), and Strengthening existing relationship (M = 4.0457, SD = 1.3282).

Negative Psychological Impact positive Factor Social Network Analysis

Table 4 shows the antagonistic effects of the unreasonable utilization of web based life and nine basic variables chose from the writing. Figure 12 demonstrates the most significant negative factors, the particular mean score (M) and standard deviation (SD), and the situating of the components of this gathering dependent on the respondents' perspectives: Sedentary Behaviour (M = 4.0975, SD = 1.3076),

Cyberbullying (M= 3.2058, SD = 1.0664), Cyberdepression (M = 4.0241, SD = 1.3566), Cybersickness (M = 4.0878, SD = 1.3374), Cyberaddiction (M = 4.0866, SD = 1.3207), and Attention deficit upset disorder (M = 4.0710, SD = 1.3285). The mean scores of the selected factors are shown respectively.

Table 3. Mean scores and standard deviations of positive psychological impact positive factors

PIF	Positive Psychological Impact Positive Factor	M	SD
PIF1	Media Skill	4.0241	1.355
PIF2	Technical Acquirement	4.0144	1.3101
PIF3	Critical Content Skill	4.0903	1.3566
PIF4	Communication and Social network literacy	4.0542	1.3101
PIF5	Formal education outcome	4.0830	1.3431
PIF6	Creativity	3.042	0.342
PIF7	Individual Identity and self-expression	3.219	0.231
PIF8	Strengthening existing relationship	4.0557	1.3282
PIF9	Belonging and collective identity	4.001	1.562
PIF10	Civic and Political Participation	3.780	1.674

Table 4. Mean scores and standard deviations of negative psychological impact positive factors

NIF	Negative Psychological Impact Positive Factor	M	SD
NIF1	Sedentary Behaviour	4.0975	1.3076
NIF2	Displaced Behaviour	4.0144	1.3101
NIF3	Sleep Interruption due to blue light	4.0903	1.3566
NIF4	Rapid Task switch	4.0542	1.3101
NIF5	Cybersickness	4.0878	1.3374
NIF6	Cyberbullying	3.2058	1.0664
NIF7	Cyberaddiction	4.0866	1.3566
NIF8	Cyberdepression	4.0241	1.3566
NIF9	Eating Disorders	4.001	1.562
NIF10	Attention deficit upset disorder	4.0710	1.3285

CONCLUSION AND RECOMMENDATIONS

Web-based social networking has a few advantages, it is a spot to make associations, for private and gifted work. Anyway there are standard issues with web-based social networking, especially on the long range informal communication destinations, there are some elective online life issues which establish that the Update Syndrome issue delineates the extra you keep and take a gander at what others have shared, or see the welcome to make diversions, or visit unnecessary pages, the more you squander subsequently ignoring family and duties. Today's youth assemble associations with on-line companions, check their profiles before making companions with them and depend on-line companions rather than physical companions. This survey shows new exact discoveries with respect to internet based life utilization, and it expected to look at the impacts of online networking on college understudies learning conduct and social change . The point of this investigation is bolstered by the earlier writing, as online life has turned into a fundamental component of training, and it has turned out to be progressively significant in both course conveyance and course appraisals. Crafted by Stathopoulou et al. (2019) uncovered that consolidating internet based life in training positively affects understudies' profound learning knowledge. Internet based life is a supporting device for understudies amid the learning procedure, and it is useful for teachers also. Be that as it may, instructors and guardians have been encouraged to keep up a sound equalization when permitting the utilization of web-based social networking, as inordinate use may result in unfavourable consequences for understudies . These examination discoveries uncovered that internet based life has both positive and negative effects on understudies' learning forms, and a fair methodology is suggested while utilizing online networking applications .The social effect hypothesis indicates the impacts of social factors quality, quickness, and number of sources . In this way, in the use of the social impact theory to instigate somebody with a restricting position to change, and strength, the capacity to enable the individuals who to concur with somebody's perspective to oppose the impact of others, is presented. Eventually, a person's probability of progress and being affected is an immediate capacity influence, promptness and the quantity of promoters and is an immediate opposite capacity of solidarity steadiness, instantaneousness and number of target people.

DISCUSSION QUESTIONS

1. Define the Social Networking.
2. What are the advantages and disadvantages of social networking?
3. Do you think that excessive social networking affects lifestyle and food habits? Do teenagers get influenced with the popular trends going online?
4. What is Social Impact theory.
5. Today's youth has knowledge of the contrasts between who you appear to be and who you think you are. Does spending pretending to be someone you are in deepest darkest fear for teenagers? What do you think Attention Syndrome is responsible for Cyber Crimes ?
6. How can Strength factor of social impact theory help to improve the psychological analysis of behaviour on social network websites?
7. What are characteristics of social network?
8. Communication may be evolving but being a quality communicator will remain a critical success factor. What are the implications for building effective lines of communication with different generation?
9. Teasing, lying, gossiping, threatening, spreading rumours, and harassing are all forms of bullying. If these things occur online, are they perceived as harming? How these actions can be prevented?
10. The usage of social media on youth affects the physical, social emotional, and psychological feature development. Does the problems concerning body image, educational action, and behaviour interrelated? Does it affect social relationships?

11. Social networks have failed to tackle cyber-bullying which results in affecting the mental health of young people. The teenagers just delete your account to stop the bullying, but that's taking something away from that young person's life for something that's not their fault. Do you think it is best way to avoid it?
12. What is Cyberaddiction?
13. What is Social Network literacy?
14. What is cyberdepression?
15. What is division of impact?

REFERENCES

Abbas, J., Aman, J., Nurunnabi, M., & Bano, S. (2019). The Impact of Social Media on Learning Behavior for Sustainable Education: *Evidence of Students from Selected Universities in Pakistan. Sustainability, 11*(6), 1683. doi:10.3390u11061683

Aravindh & Baratwaj. (2016). Examining the Regularity and consistency level of profile updation in social media applications by active users in Tamil Nadu. *International Journal for Innovative Research in Multidisciplinary Field, 2*(11).

Pink, B. (n.d.). *Australian Social Trends*. Australian Bureau of Statistics Catalogue no. 4102.

Baumeister, R.F., & Leary, M.R. (1995). The need to belong, desire for interpersonal attachments as a fundamental human motivation. *Psychological Bull., 117*, 497–529.

Bazarova, N. N. (2015). Online disclosure. In C. R. Berger & M. E. Roloff (Eds.), *The International Encyclopedia of Interpersonal Communication*. Hoboken, NJ: Wiley-Blackwell. doi:10.1002/9781118540190.wbeic251

Berson. (2003). Grooming cybervictims: The psychosocial effects of online exploitation for youth. *Journal of School Violence, 2*(1), 5-18.

Besley. (2008). Cyberbullying: An Emerging Threat to the always on Generation. *Canadian Teacher Magazine*, 18-20.

Blanchard, M., Metcalf, A., & Burns, J. M. (2007). *Bridging the digital divide: creating opportunities for marginalised young people to get connected. Report for the Inspire Foundation & Orygen Youth Health Research Centre*. Melbourne: University of Melbourne.

Blanchard, M., Metcalf, A., Degney, J., Hermann, H. & Burns, J.M. (2008). Rethinking the digital divide: findings from a study of marginalised young people's information communication technology (ICT) use. *Youth Studies Australia*.

Boase, J., Horrigan, J. B., Wellman, B., & Raine, L. (2006). *The Strength of Internet Ties: The Internet and email aid users in maintaining their social networks and provide pathways to help when people face big decisions*. Washington, DC: Pew Internet & American Life Project.

Dahl, S. (2018). Social Media Marketing: Theories and Applications. Thousand Oaks, CA: SAGE Publications.

Ding, C., Cheng, H. K., Duan, Y., & Jin, Y. (2017). The power of the "like" button: *The impact of social media on box office. Decision Support Systems, 94,* 77–84. doi:10.1016/j.dss.2016.11.002

Dunbar, R. I. M. (2012). Social cognition on the Internet: Testing constraints on social network size. *Philosophical Transactions of the Royal Society of London. Series B, Biological Sciences, 367*(1599), 2192–2201. doi:10.1098/rstb.2012.0121 PMID:22734062

Haferkamp, N., & Krämer, N. C. (2011). Social comparison 2.0: Examining the effects of online profiles on social-networking sites. *Cyberpsychology, Behavior, and Social Networking, 14*(5), 309–314. doi:10.1089/cyber.2010.0120 PMID:21117976

Harton, H., Green, L., Jackson, C., & Latane, B. (1998). Demonstrating Dynamic Social Impact: Consolidation, Clustering, Correlation, and (Sometimes) the Correct Answer. *Teaching of Psychology, 25*(1), 31–35. doi:10.120715328023top2501_9

Hawk, S. T., van den Eijnden, R. J., van Lissa, C. J., & ter Bogt, T. F. M. (2019). Narcissistic adolescents' attention-seeking following social rejection: Links with social media disclosure, problematic social media use, and smartphone stress. *Computers in Human Behavior, 92,* 65–75. doi:10.1016/j.chb.2018.10.032

Helliwell, J. F., & Putnam, R. D. (2004). *The social context of well-being.* Philos. doi:10.1098/rstb.2004.1522

Hogg & Tindale. (n.d.). *Blackwell Handbook of Social Psychology: Group Processes.* John Wiley.

Holt-Lunstad, J., Smith, T. B., & Layton, J. B. (2010). Social relationships and mortality risk: A meta-analytic review. *PLoS Medicine, 7*(7), e1000316. doi:10.1371/journal.pmed.1000316 PMID:20668659

Issa, T., Isaias, P., & Kommers, P. (2016). *Social Networking and Education: Global Perspectives.* Cham, Switzerland: Springer International Publishing. doi:10.1007/978-3-319-17716-8

Jošanov, Pucihar, & Vrgović. (2016). Opinions and behavior of students about abuse of internet in social involvements: Gender analysis. *Business School.*

Karau, S., & Williams, K. (1995). Social Loafing: Research Findings, Implications, and Future Directions. *Current Directions in Psychological Science, 4*(5), 135. doi:10.1111/1467-8721.ep10772570

Kwahk, G. (2012). Social impact theory: An examination of how immediacy operates as an influence upon social media interaction in Facebook fan pages. *The Marketing Review.*

Luck, B. (2007). *Cyberbullying: an emerging issue bernadette luck, record of the communications policy & research forum.* Retrieved from https://apo.org.au/sites/default/files/resource-files/2007/10/apo-nid69033-1106296.pdf

Meshi, Tamir, & Heekeren. (2015). The Emerging Neuroscience, Trends in Cognitive Science. *Trends in Cognitive Sciences, 19*(12), 771–782.

Osatuyi, B., & Passerini, K. (n.d.). Twittermania: Understanding how social media technologies impact engagement and academic performance of a new generation of learners, *Communications of the AIS.*

Radovic, A., Gmelin, T., Stein, B.D., & Miller, E. J. (2017). *Depressed adolescents' positive and negative use of social media.* Academic Press.

Ravasan, A. Z., Rouhani, S., & Asgary, S. (2013). A Review for the Online Social Networks Literature (2005-2011). *European Journal of Business and Management, 6*(4).

Shabir, Hameed, Safdar, & Gilani. (2014). The impact of social media on Youth: A case study of Bahawalpur City. *Asian Journal of Social Sciences & Humanities, 3*(4).

Siddiqui, S., & Singh, T. (2016). Social Media its Impact with Positive and Negative Aspects. *International Journal of Computer Applications Technology and Research, 5*(2), 71 - 75. Retrieved from http://www.ijcat.com/archives/volume5/issue2/ijcatr05021006.pdf

Tamir, D. I., & Ward, A. F. (2015). Old desires, new media. In The Psychology of Desire (pp. 432–455). Guilford Press.

Van Schaik, C. P. (1983). Why are diurnal primates living in groups? *Behaviour, 87*(1-2), 120–144. doi:10.1163/156853983X00147

Ward, M. L. (2003). *Understanding the role of entertainment media in the sexual socialization of American youth: A review of empirical research.* Academic Press.

KEY TERMS AND DEFINITIONS

Brain Science: It is the logical investigation of the human personality and its capacities, particularly those influencing conduct in a given setting.

Cyberbullying: Cyberbullying is tormenting that happens over computerized gadgets like mobile phones, PCs, and tablets.

Cybersickness: Cybersickness for the most part occurs all through or once submersion in an exceedingly virtual air.

Digital Laws: Cyber law is the piece of the generally lawful framework that manages the Internet, the internet, and their particular lawful issues.

Dispersion of Responsibility: Being a piece of a huge gathering makes individuals feel mysterious and this lessens their sentiments of obligation. It may make them less inclined to obey orders.

Informal Organization: The stage online unit that administers the license individuals to develop an open or open profile and construct a posting of various clients with whom they share an association and read their rundown of associations and individuals made by others among the framework.

Media Skill: It is the capacity to. get to, dissect, assess, make, and act utilizing all types of correspondence.

This research was previously published in the Handbook of Research on Social and Organizational Dynamics in the Digital Era; pages 344-382, copyright year 2020 by Business Science Reference (an imprint of IGI Global).

APPENDIX

Research Into Social Impact Theory

Latané (1981) discusses various instances of Social Impact with an intriguing findings with US Christian TV minister Billy Graham (see left). The theory was that Billy Graham would make more believers before little gatherings of people. Latané looked into the quantities of individuals who reacted to Graham's intrigue for proselytes and found that when the groups of onlookers were little, individuals were all the more ready to sign cards enabling nearby vicars to reach them later. This exhibits divisions of effect (otherwise called dispersion of duty). Sedikides and Jackson (1990) did a field try in the perch room at a zoo. A confederate advised gatherings of guests not to incline toward the railings close to the winged creature confines.

Applying Social Impact Theory (Ao2)

With regards to submission, a ton relies upon whether you see the individual giving the requests to be an expert figure or not. Various types of Power helps to provide details of applying the theory-
    French and Raven (1959) distinguished various sorts of power:

1.   Genuine power which expert figures with high status
2.   Remunerate influence with the individuals who have cash or who can perform favors
3.   Coercive power with individuals who can rebuff others
4.   Master control individuals which are proficient), and
5.   Referent power with individuals users have a place with gatherings you regard.

    This fits in well with Social Impact Theory since it clarifies the various reasons why an individual's requests may have Social Force. "Referent Power" likewise applies to Tajfel's Social Identity Theory since it demonstrates that requests originating from an individual from our ingroup convey more Social Force than requests originating from an outgroup part. This is the reason a group part may have more specialist over a young man than an instructor: the educator has authentic expert however the posse part may have reward control, coercive power and referent power since he can give the teenager favors, they will hurt you in the event that him cross him and the teenager sees him as his ingroup.

Dispersion of Responsibility

Being a piece of a huge gathering makes individuals feel unknown and this diminishes their sentiments of duty. It may make them less inclined to obey orders. Latané and Darley (1968) completed a celebrated analysis into this. Members sat in corners examining medical problems over a radio. One of the speakers was a confederate who might profess to show at least a bit of kindness assault. In the event that there was just a single other member, they went for assistance 85% of the time; this dropped to 62% if there were two different members and 31% if there were 4+. Nobody was giving requests in this investigation, however the standard "proceed to get help when somebody breakdown" is a kind of request that is available all the time in the public eye. Following these kind of social guidelines is called prosocial conduct and defying the norms is standoffish conduct. Social Impact Theory clarifies prosocial conduct just as dutifulness.

There's a developing assemblage of research supporting Social Impact Theory. What's more, the hypothesis likewise comprehends a ton of Classic investigations from the '60s and '70s that used to appear irrelevant – like Latané and Darley (1968) into dispersion of duty, Tajfel (1970) into intergroup separation also, Milgram (1963) into compliance. Looking back, these investigations can be viewed as taking a gander at various viewpoints of Social Impact. There have been later augmentations to Social Impact Theory. Lateen et al. (1996)developed Dynamic Social Impact Theory to focus on how minorities and larger parts impact one another, for example, how individuals will in general change their perspectives to coordinate the gathering they are in yet why they now and then "adhere to their weapons".

Protests

Social Impact gives a ton of consideration to the attributes of the individual giving the requests however very little to the individual accepting them. For instance, there might be character types that are especially consistent (oblige anything) or defiant. An individual might be glad to oblige a few sorts of requests yet adhere to a meaningful boundary at others –, for example, arranges that annoy them ethically or humiliate them socially. A comparative issue is that Social Impact Theory treats individuals as latent. It suggests that anyone will do anything if the appropriate measure of Social Force is applied as a powerful influence for them. In any case, individuals here and there obey orders while in the meantime subverting them. A model may be Oskar Schindler who given Jewish representatives over to the Nazis amid WWII while covertly helping numerous others to get away.

Contrasts

Milgram's Agency Theory is oversimplified contrasted with Social Impact Theory. Milgram recommends we have advanced to go into a respectful mental state around anybody we perceive as an expert. There's very little proof for this by and large. Social Impact Theory recommends numerous highlights of Agency Theory are valid – that the quality (S) of the expert figure is a significant indicator of how devoted somebody will be – yet there are other situational factors too, similar to the quantities of individuals included (N) and the instantaneousness (I) of the requests. In any case, Agency Theory clarifies a few things superior to Social Impact Theory. For instance, in Variation #10, compliance was let in a summary office contrasted with Yale University. Milgram clarifies this through the eminence of the setting adding to the expert figure's status, yet this is hard for Latane to give a scientific incentive to. Also, Milgram has a clarification for the shaking and sobbing his members occupied with – moral strain. There's no discourse of good strain in Social Impact Theory, which perspectives individuals as either obeying or ignoring and nothing in the middle.

Applications

The possibility of a numerical equation to compute Social Impact is valuable. Lateen trusts that, in the event that you know the number (N) of individuals included and the instantaneousness (I) of the request and the quality (S) of the expert figure, you can ascertain precisely that somebody is so liable to comply

(I) utilizing the recipe I = f (SIN). This implies you can anticipate whether laws will be pursued, regardless of whether mobs will break out and whether 9B will get their work done.

The hypothesis proposes in the event that you need to get individuals to comply, you have to coordinate Social Force at them when they are in little gatherings and in a perfect world stop them getting together into enormous gatherings. This is the reason some oppressive governments endeavour to stop individuals utilizing internet based life and social occasion for open gatherings. Since requests should be prompt it is essential to rehash them frequently and put them on signs, TV adverts and customary declarations.

Dynamic Social Impact Theory

The Dynamic Social Impact Theory by Bibb Latane and his associates has great impact of individuals among dominant part and minority gatherings. Dynamic social effect hypothesis recommends that culture is made and moulded by neighbourhood social impact as characterized by four wonders:

1. Clustering, or provincial contrasts in social components;
2. Relationship, or rising relationship between components;
3. Combination, or a decrease in fluctuation; and (iv) proceeding with assorted variety.

The hypothesis fills in as expansion of the beginning Social Impact Theory (i.e., impact is controlled by the quality, quickness, and number of sources present) as it clarifies how gatherings, as intricate frameworks, change and create after some time. Gatherings are always sorting out and re-arranging into four essential examples: combination, grouping, relationship, and proceeding with decent variety. These examples are predictable with gatherings that are spatially appropriated and interfacing more than once after some time.

1. **Union**: As people communicate with one another normally, their activities, demeanours, and suppositions become increasingly uniform. The assessments done have good effect all through the gathering and the minority diminishes in size.
    a. E.g., Individuals who live in a similar school residence will, after some time, create comparable demeanors on an assortment of subjects.
2. **Bunching**: Happens when gathering individuals convey all the more as often as possible as an outcome of closeness. As the law of social effect recommends, people are defenseless to impact by their nearest individuals, thus bunches of gathering individuals with comparative suppositions rise in gatherings. Minority bunch individuals are regularly protected from larger part impact because of grouping. In this manner, subgroups can develop which may have comparative plans to each other, however hold unexpected convictions in comparison to the greater part populace. E.g., Neighbors on a sub-urban road persuade different neighbors to shape a network watch gathering.
3. **Connection**: After some time, singular gathering individuals' conclusions on an assortment of issues of join, with the goal of suppositions to become associated. E.g., Individuals on an official society, discover they concede to subjects they have talked about all through a gathering -, for example, the best money related arrangement, however that they likewise concur on points which they have not examined.

4. **Proceeding With Diversity**: As referenced beforehand, minority individuals are frequently protected from larger part impact because of bunching. Assorted variety exists if Sedikides and Jackson (1990) did a field try in the perch room at a zoo. The confederate suggested gatherings of guests not to rail close to the winged creature confines. The guests were then seen to check whether they complied.

In the event that the confederate was wearing the uniform of a zookeeper, submission was high, yet on the off chance that he was dressed coolly, it was lower. This shows differing Social Force, specifically S (Strength) due to the apparent expert of the confederate. As time passed, more guests began overlooking the guidance not to incline toward the railing. This likewise indicates Social Force, particularly I (Immediacy), on the grounds that as the guidance gets less prompt it has less effect. Divisions of effect were additionally considered.

Chapter 11
Formation and Control of Identity:
In a Social Media World

Christine Yunn-Yu Sun
eBookDynasty.net, Australia

Steve Goschnick
Swinburne University of Technology, Australia

ABSTRACT

This chapter explores the construction of identity in online communities and websites for social purposes, and its consequences in terms of how one's online identity may be utilized to such an extent that one's real-world identity is either enforced or eroded. It does so by investigating the very nature of identity, coming predominantly from a cultural studies research and philosophical view, although it also cites some related findings and advances in computing and information systems (IS) research. The central argument across the chapter is two-fold: firstly, in promoting an initial shift in focus from the management of online identity to the nature and significance of identity itself whose construction may be conceptualized as a process of sense making and strengthening; and only then, armed with a better understanding of identity, one can focus back upon the management of it more effectively, with a view to the individual taking more control of their own identity within cyberspace, which is increasingly transitioning us all into a functioning global community, in both predictable and unforeseen ways.

INTRODUCTION

This chapter explores the construction of identity in online communities and websites for social purposes, and its consequences in terms of how one's online identity may be utilized to such an extent that one's real-world identity is either enforced or eroded. We also present a case study with the aim of demonstrating that an individual's identity can be methodically represented, so that they may be appropriately notified of information coming in from the online world from multiple sources; and, which may be used as both

DOI: 10.4018/978-1-6684-6307-9.ch011

an aide in taking control of how one is represented in the online world, and in placing information in the context of one's own roles, interests and knowledge generation.

This chapter argues that identity is an imagined "site" the boundaries of which distinguish whoever is assigned within them, from those outside. Identity is flexible and ever-changing in nature, constructed on the needs of an individual to react to the demands of their political, economic, societal and cultural circumstances. As such, the formation, standardization and circulation of one's identity within society affects not only how one understands and represents oneself to others, but is also the basis of how one is recognized and treated by others accordingly. Furthermore, from the individual's point of view, having a model that represents identity, helps them stay orientated on the things that matter to them. In his book *The News: A User's Manual* philosopher Alain de Botton wrote, that immersing ourselves in the daily electronic news feeds and other news sources, is *"to raise a shell to our ears and to be overpowered by the roar of humanity"*. That there is too much of it for our own good, and that we are becoming "news junkies". He suggests that one must know themselves well, to not be left disorientated and distracted by the constant flow of news and information.

To take this argument one step further, unlike the real world, the Internet is capable of enabling one to reach across nearly all political, cultural and sociological traits that are commonly used to construct one's identity as an imagined "site". What's more, the Internet (also known as cyberspace) itself is an imagined "site" whose social functions, capacities and protocols are continually expanding and regularly redefined. The imagined boundaries of the Internet are therefore considerably different from those of the real world, creating the needs, opportunities and means for one to continuously present, reproduce and dynamically manage one's online identity. Most importantly, in the case of online identity, it is more often a matter of one's choice to actively construct a specific identity than being randomly assigned an identity by others. This presents one with ample opportunity and choice not only to represent oneself but also to have a significant bearing on how one is recognized.

As a result, there is a clear and urgent need to examine the formation, standardization and circulation of one's online identity and how it impacts upon the ways in which one interacts with others on the Internet. Because of the social nature of online communities and websites, the imagined "site" that is online identity becomes even more fluid and its boundaries increasingly fragile due to a lack of protection against misrepresentation and privacy violations. At this point it is worth stating that Identity is researched, defined and managed from several different fields of study. The research behind this paper is best described as Cultural in nature. However, given the technological foundation of the Internet that enables cyberspace as we know it, Information Systems (IS) research and development also has a significant interest and research record in Identity, which we draw upon in the case study. While this paper focuses on cultural and even philosophical aspects of identity, papers in other fields including IS are cited from time-to-time as there are some parallel findings and observations across these disparate fields of study.

Additionally, when Facebook, LinkedIn, Google+ and other social network platforms are discussed further down, we will see that there is a continuing push from the technology companies behind the preeminent social networking platforms today, to mesh one's real world identity, with as many of one's online sub-identities as possible, through our various interactions spread across the Internet. Indeed, in February 2017, the Facebook founder outlined what has become known in the tech industry as the Facebook Manifesto (Zuckerberg, 2017) in an article titled – Building Global Community – in which he puts heavy emphasis on Facebook supporting (by evolving Facebook tools) real world traditional community groups, and in doing so, wooing them to come online if such groups do not already have a representation on Facebook. Zuckerberg expresses the eventual goal of forming a functioning worldwide community of sub-communities, with media, safety and recovery mechanisms, voting on community standards (initially, but later global governance), and other functionality.

At this point a useful paper from IS research by Roussos et al. (2003), titled 'Mobile Identity Management: An Enacted View', suggests three principles regarding Identity. The first two are of some use in clarifying the discussion here:

- **The Locality Principle:** Identities are situated within particular contexts, roles, relationships and communities. People will have multiple different and overlapping identities in (these) different contexts, and each of these should be respected.
- **The Understanding Principle:** In human relationships, knowledge of identities is negotiated and both sides in a relationship should know how properties that characterize identity are exchanged and used. Relationships should be symmetrical and reciprocal.

The third principle, not repeated here, is really a restatement of the second with emphasis upon mutual understanding by those in a relationship. Much of the technology and management issues around identity focus on the Locality Principle (e.g. identifiers and how they are used for particular services, while in specific contexts), whereas, the Understanding Principle as given by Roussos et al., leans much more towards a Cultural Studies approach to identity, such as the emphasis in this paper. And yet, both principles involve aspects of identity that we are all interested in, and have a particular view on, no matter what one's outer field of study.

While the technical, legal and security issues have been and will continue to be investigated from IS, sociological and psychological perspectives, this paper argues for two things: a shift in focus from the management of online identity to the nature and significance of identity itself whose construction may be conceptualized as a long process of sense making and strengthening; and then, armed with a better understanding of identity, one can focus back upon the management of it more effectively, with a view to the individual taking more control of their own identity within the technology space.

An inquiry into how one positions oneself on the Internet also helps in the estimation and measurement of the extent to which such positioning, affects what is being said by whom and for what social purposes they are saying it. Finally, we add to the current and future research on the management of one's reputation on the Internet through tactics of online identity disclosure and control. The case study we refer to, models identity and considers technology outside of and apart from the various social networks, to help an individual identify, disclose and control aspects of themselves, and to also aggregate information and assemble knowledge specific to them according to the Locality Principle, with less reliance on external filters

IDENTITY AS A SELF-PRODUCED CONTINUITY AND THE MEDIA

In his essay "Cultural Identity and Cinematic Representation" (Hall, 1989), British cultural theorist Stuart Hall proposed to define identities as being "always constructed through memory, fantasy, narrative and myths". Instead of providing "unifying and unchanging points of reference and meaning", identities are made "within the discourses of history and culture" and are therefore "not an essence but a positioning". This view supports the argument that identity is not and should not be seen as a "given fact", although the persuasiveness of a given representation may lead to this form of essentialization. Instead, it is necessary to conceptualize identity as a constructed, normalized and widely circulated cultural "norm" that has the potential to cause different positive and/or negative effects on different individuals and groups.

Hall's essay mainly deals with cinematic constructions and presentations of national identity in Caribbean countries, where new generations of native artists strove to create and express a "Caribbean uniqueness" in films that may unify their people politically and culturally against a colonized past. However, Hall's conceptualization of identity as a self-produced continuity that designates what is said by whom and for what purposes, is particularly useful for this chapter, as it attempts to understand the formation, standardization and circulation of identity through powerful social channels which includes the Internet. Hall's view is further supported by Graeme Turner who, in his essay "Media Texts and Messages" (Turner, 1997), studies the important role of the media in the promotion of a national identity in the Australian context:

While there have been plenty of nationalist arguments for the media's active collaboration in the preservation of an Australian "identity", most recent accounts accept that such an identity is an invention. By this I mean that there is no "natural" reason why all of us who live on this island continent should share the same government, the same institutions, common values or characteristics. That Australians think of themselves as doing so, "naturally", is a result of the cultural construction of the idea of the nation through language, myths and history. The "national identity" is in a sense of a "national fiction" Australians collaborate in producing everyday.

Turner suggests that the analysis of the media is important because media texts "are among the most important sites for interrogating the work of representing the nation, assessing its effects and interests, and revealing its ideological and political determinants". This is because the texts produced by the media are "crucial components in definitions of the nation which do not simply represent a 'real', national identity, but which selectively construct versions of nationhood which serve some interests, and not others". Yet, if the words "nation" and "national" are omitted from the quotations above, and if one supplants "the media" with one's personal communications via the Internet, then it becomes obvious that Turner's argument is highly relevant to an investigation on how much the construction of one's identity reveals about oneself. In this context, the political, cultural and sociological traits used by the *individual* to establish, maintain and utilize one's identity are the most important sites in which one's perceptions of oneself may be adequately explored. Particularly in communications with others for social purposes, one's identity is a form of "personal fiction" that we and those around us collaborate in producing everyday, with each intercommunication further defining, refining or rebuking minute aspects, bit by bit.

Alain de Botton (ibid) places the role in society of the media, specifically *the news*, at an even higher level of impact. He argues that the news is a major source of authority in modern technological society to the point where it has replaced religion as a dominant source of guidance to many, becoming the "prime creator of political and social reality". Little wonder the turmoil surrounding fake news involving Facebook and Google emanating from the 2016 US election (more on fake news later), where it has been revealed that more than half of the American people receive their news through Facebook. If we take the analogy made in the previous paragraph, i.e. from society to the individual, then the impact of the deluge of news on and through the Internet upon an individual, taking into consideration de Botton's well-argued view, is highly likely to affect the nature of identity further in the more-fluid direction. This may help explain the rise of social networks on the Internet – as something of a refuge from that increasing fluidity, just as they were originally something of a refuge from spam email. In this light, the rise of so-called *filter bubbles* within social networks and search engines, is not surprising. A definition of filter bubbles from Wikipedia (2017):

A filter bubble is a state of intellectual isolation that can result from personalized searches when a website algorithm selectively guesses what information a user would like to see based on information about the user, such as location, past click-behavior and search history. As a result, users become separated from information that disagrees with their viewpoints, effectively isolating them in their own cultural or ideological bubbles. The choices made by these algorithms are not transparent. Prime examples include Google Personalized Search results and Facebook's personalized news-stream.

Many have been concerned about the *political polarization* (a person's view being reinforced by an extreme counter view, without any consideration of other alternative views) and its effect on democracy that can come of filter bubbles, particular since the 2016 US election. It is one of the concerns discussed by the Facebook founder in (Zuckerberg, 2017). Since objections were first raised about personalised news feeds and search results, Facebook and others have conducted research about filter bubbles. E.g. Bleiberg & West (2015) report that "The Facebook study demonstrates that the polarization phenomenon also applies to the social network (even with personalisation filtering turned off). The study finds that roughly speaking a Facebook user has five politically likeminded friends for every one friend on the other side of the spectrum." I.e. According to the Facebook study, even in the absence of filter bubbles, people seek the articles and information that aligns with their interests and views and avoid the others, as evidence that there is nothing unique here regarding social media platforms.

Other researchers are concerned about filter bubbles with regard to the hidden algorithms selecting one's news, search results, and social network experience, and that some individuals may even have their identities socially constructed for them to some degree (Bozdag & Timmerman, 2011). After conceding the need for filtering to manage the information deluge, they state their concern is specifically related to transparency of the filtering used: "Personalized filtering is thus based on an interpretation of a user's identity. Identity refers to people's understanding of who they are over time, embracing both continuity and discontinuity. To a certain extent there is also a discontinuity of identity when a person moves from one context to the other." The filters are generally not aware of the subtleness of changing contexts. They finish with 3 guidelines for those designing personalisation filter algorithms:

1. Make sure different identities are allowed per user, which might differ per context.
2. Design for autonomy, so that the user can customize the filter, and change the identity that is formed on basis of his previous interactions.
3. Design for transparency, so that the user is aware that a filter is taking place. The user must be able to see which criteria is used for filtering, and which identity the system has of the user.

There is conflicting research about the effects of filter bubbles, and de Botton's insight coupled with the fluidity of identity backs up the idea that weighing us the pros and cons of personalised filtering is far from a simple choice situation.

Identity is an invented and/or imagined label that is open to interpretation. Because identity is developed through shared patterns of interaction, one's identity in practice alters depending on the groups of people with whom one regularly and habitually interacts. This is explicitly illustrated by Paul Macgregor as he discusses the limits of geography and ethnicity as determinants of identity:

We are part of a multiplicity of communities, and we interact with different communities on different occasions.

We thus have multiple identities, intrinsically tied to processes of shared communal activity. Depending on which community of people we are with, we change aspects of our speech, mannerisms, even, to an extent, our thoughts, to take part in the shared rituals of behavior which ties us together in temporary, yet continually repeated, gatherings of each community. We temporarily locate in a shared space, read the same newspapers, exchange according to shared patterns, then go off and join with other groups, make other patterns. (Macgregor, 1995)

Figure 1. The ShadowBoard Agent Architecture

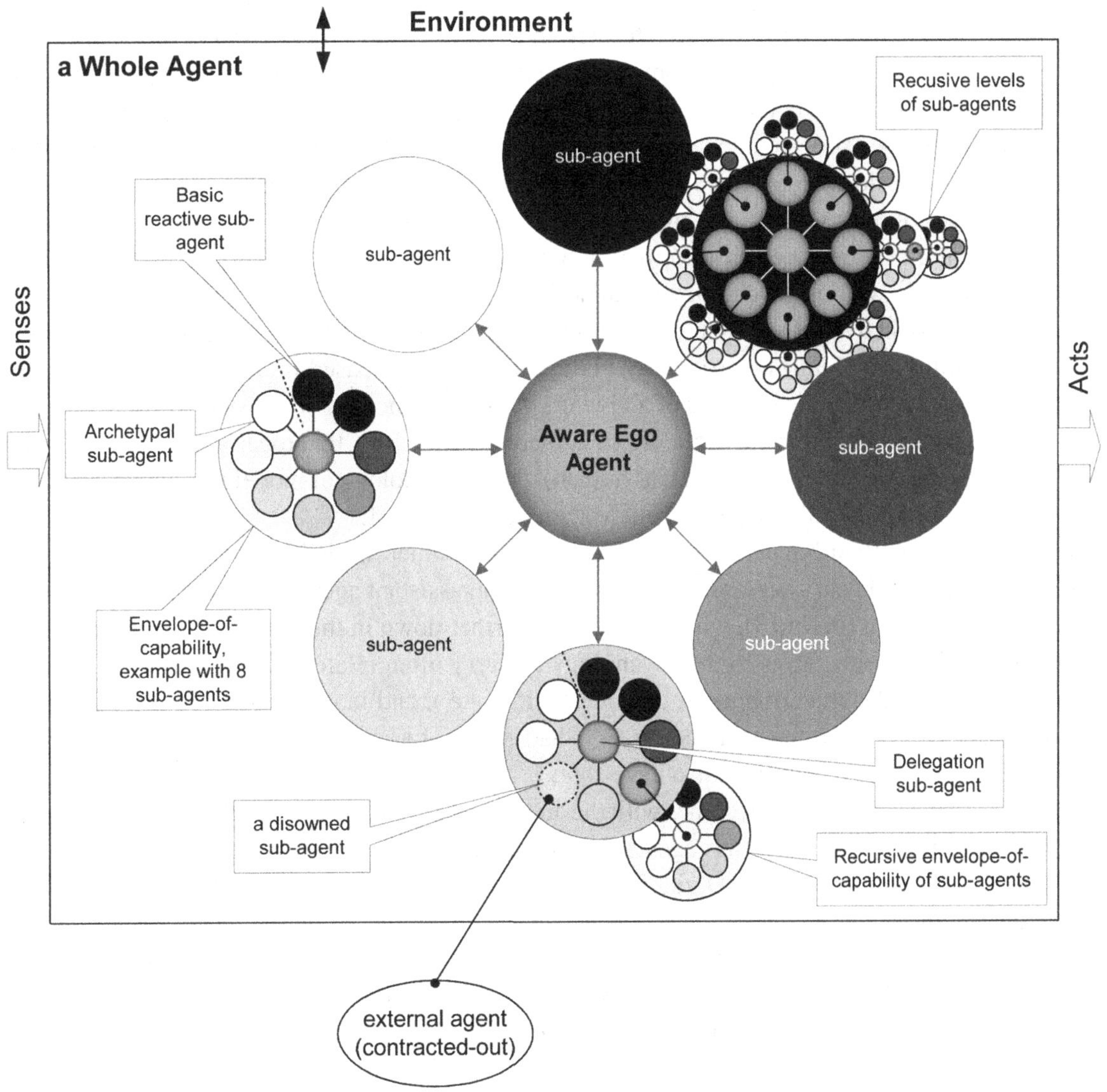

What Macgregor illustrates here is the extremely complex nature of identity as an abstract construct embodied in practice, and thus given to change both historically and when it encounters all kinds of pressure within the context of an individual's or a group's everyday experience. One's identity is exhibited to a certain degree at any given moment, depending on the nature of the people with whom one interacts, the meaning of the occasion, the role one sees oneself in, and the location of the interaction. The result is that various "shared patterns" or "shared rituals of behaviour", which are always subject to change, are what constitute the flexible nature of identity in individual circumstances. This supports Hall's and Turner's conceptualization that identity is a never-ending process of positioning. More importantly, throughout this process, identity is not and should not be seen as something that is based on a mere "recovery" of the past, such as one's cultural roots which is waiting to be found, and when found, will secure one's sense of belonging. Rather, according to Hall, "identities are the names we give to the different ways we are positioned by, and position ourselves within, the narratives of the past" (Hall, 1989). In other words, identity is not only about the past, but also in the naming and the meaning attached to those names; about how one narrates and interprets such a past, in the present and in the future.

At this point some people may object somewhat to Hall's depiction of identity as 'an ongoing positioning', of being quite fluid, an identity that includes deeply held cultural and religious aspects, which they may view as definitely fixed, as 'unchanging points of reference and meaning'. It is certainly true that the majority of people do operate with a set of deeply held *core values*, but equally, most agree that other aspects and values of ones self-identity may well be subject to change, never mind their wider identity.

Helpfully, within Computing and Information Systems research, there are so-named agent-oriented (AO) systems that draw upon psychology for underlying models of the mind when building intelligent support systems (applied AI). One such AO architecture called ShadowBoard (see Figure 1), was created to help augment human abilities, particularly via the Internet. It is based on the *Theory of Sub-selves* from psychology. The theoretical source of a given *sub-agent* (embodied or enlisted software) within it, is the *sub-self*, within a hierarchical grouping of numerous sub-selves, that together make up the whole Agent (the one that augments the individual human). That psychological model fits the description of identify briefed upon in the above quote from Macgregor, quite well.

Note: The ShadowBoard agent architecture is the initial blueprint behind the software developed and used in our case study, a system that combines personal assistant agents. The overarching system is called the *DigitalFriend* (Figure 3), which we turn to, further down in the case study.

Furthermore, these sub-selves in the psychology are very often related to different roles in a given person's life (parent, daughter, manager, defender, critic, etc.), and that is where the overlap with the theory of sub-selves and the agent model in the ShadowBoard architecture, align. I.e. the sub-agents in the human-supporting technology also have *roles* – in turn supporting the roles of the person being augmented - and the *role model* that comes with the architecture, is central to a methodology (of the same name) for collecting and building sub-agents that populate and enhance one's *digital self* (Goschnick & Graham, 2006), enacted via the DigitalFriend software. See the role model in the ShadowBoard methodology in Table 1.

Returning to our discussion on the seemingly *fixed* aspects of identity: even deeply held core values are sometimes subject to change, albeit, at glacial speed or subject to seismic events in one's personal history. Consider this anecdote to underline several related points:

A Western-raised husband and a Chinese-ethnic raised wife have just seen the wife's mother off at the airport, heading home after a 6-week stay with the happy couple and their children. Husband says to wife: "The first 4 weeks was great, but nobody enjoyed the last week or two. Next time you should invite her to come for 4 weeks, it is a much better length of time, where we can focus the proper amount of attention and activity around her visit." To which the wife answers: "I can't suggest to her how long she should stay. There is no way in the world that I could ever say that to my mother! You don't do that in my culture. Its called filial piety - very high respect for ones elders." To which he answers: "I don't see what the problem is? She'd be happier with a shorter stay. You'd be happier with a shorter stay. I'd be happier with a shorter stay. She might even visit more often if that were the case. Where is the disrespect? I can't see the issue?" To which she again replies: "It is just impossible for me to have such a conversation with my mother." To which he replies: "Some years ago now, it was similarly impossible that you could or would marry a foreigner, and yet, here we are."

Table 1. Generic Roles and Sub-roles in the ShadowBoard methodology

Manager Benevolent Manager *(arch.)* Conciliatory Manager Planner Scheduler Coordinator Recycler Controller Decisive Manager *(reactive)*	**Protector** Safety Officer *(archetype)* Defender Risk Analyst Environmentalist Pacifier Doctor Exit Strategist *(reactive)*	**Personal Assistant** Selfless Pleaser *(archetype)* Service Provider Networker Communicator Marketer Teacher Adviser	**Initiator** Inventor *(archetype)* Success Seeker Resource Master Trouble Shooter Pusher Reminder *(reactive)*
Critic Perfectionist *(archetype)* Editor Quality Controller Doubter Cynic *(reactive)*	**Adventurer** Explorer *(archetype)* Risk Taker Traveller Vacationer 2D Situator 3D Situator Lazybones *(reactive)*	**Knowledge Seeker** Knowledge Worker *(arch.)* Concept Learner Learner Information Officer Data Miner Random Generator *(react.)*	**Intuitive** Seer *(archetype)* Mood Senser Pattern Finder Dreamer Profiler Role Keeper Core Value Bearer Affirmation Agent

That they each had a different view of the identity of the other (e.g. her self-identity, versus his idea of her identity), makes the point that identity is not a fixed nor a singular thing. Furthermore, the concept of identity being fluid, a continuing positioning, does not mean all aspects of an identity are fluid to the same degree, all the time. Some aspects might stay as fixed points of reference for very long periods of time, even a lifetime.

To take this argument one step further, not only can one actively form, standardize and circulate an identity for the purpose of distinguishing one from others under all kinds of political, economic, societal and cultural circumstances, but one can also be passively assigned an identity by others for the same reason. This is because one not only positions oneself within, but is also positioned *by*, the numerous narratives and interpretations of one's surroundings that never cease re-producing and re-defining themselves. Therefore, if identity may be conceptualized as an imagined "site", then one can either actively assign oneself or be passively assigned within its boundaries. While both acts of assignment can happen at the same time, they also take place constantly and continuously, in the same way that numerous identities or imagined "sites" are subject to ongoing construction and are continually impacting on how individuals and groups interact with each other, and why for example, democracy can bring about change (hence the concerns raised above with filter bubbles). Ultimately, identity is a construction reified in practice and resembles geo-political entities such as Australia and the United States. It differs from geo-political entities insofar as it is somewhat more open-ended and subject to change.

Unfortunately, precisely because one's identity is constructed for the purpose of differentiating one from others, the boundaries of this imagined "site", though forever fluid and open to interpretation in their nature, are often considered to be as necessary and unalterable as geo-political borders that require safeguarding. Furthermore, such safeguarding is often conducted by those within or outside of the boundaries of an imagined "site" that is identity, or both, by enforcing those political, cultural and sociological traits that were used to construct this "site" in the first place. A risk thus occurs that these traits, or "shared patterns" or "shared rituals of behaviour" as referred to by Macgregor, are perceived by all involved to be as permanent and unchallengeable as the borders of geo-political entities. A highly likely result of such perception, intentional or otherwise, is the invention and prolonged utilization of all kinds of labels, or "norms", that affect the ways in which those both within and outside of the imagined "site" negotiate with each other and among themselves.

Most importantly, in the same way that the subjects of a geo-political entity such as Australia or the United States "naturally" consider themselves as belonging within its boundaries and feeling the need to distinguish themselves against those outside, those who assign themselves or are assigned by others to be within the boundaries of their identity may also feel its "binding power". That is, in spite of the fluid and complex nature of one's identity as an imagined "site", one is likely to do all that is possible to uphold and even strengthen those political, cultural and sociological traits that one considers as being essential to the continued existence of such identity or imagination, which provides one with a sense of belonging. That one "naturally" feels obliged to do so is the consequence of a long process of *sense making*. Instead of embracing all the narratives and interpretations of one's surroundings that can possibly be employed to help one position oneself, one willingly and actively chooses to acknowledge and even advocate a much lesser set that one believes are the "facts". It also involves less intellectual work. Some might call these their core values. To borrow Hall's words, the result of such an "essentialist" approach is to render identity as something concrete and permanent that provides "unifying and unchanging points of reference and meaning", whose existence cannot be neglected and whose omnipresent influence can be felt in one's life at any moment.

Such an "essentialist" approach is in sharp contrast to Turner's "non-essentialist" conceptualization of identity, "a positioning" as a form of "personal fiction" that one and those around one collaborate in producing every day. However, together, they explicitly illustrate the actual dichotomous nature of identity. Although one's identity may be formed, standardized and circulated either by oneself or by those around her for the purpose of differentiating one from others, it can easily become a self-produced continuity that grants value to one's existence and provides one with both a sense of belonging and of an evolving identity. More importantly, although one's identity is constructed using those various political, cultural and sociological traits that one is commonly associated with, these traits, or "shared patterns" or "shared rituals of behaviour", are often employed by both oneself and others as a "definite" and "necessary" means to uphold and even advocate such identity. Finally, although one's identity is flexible and always subject to some degree of change, it does have the potential to become a caricature, an identity made up of just that set of concrete "facts" that one "naturally" considers to being essential to one's existence under all kinds of political, economic, societal and cultural circumstances - something very much like a stereotype.

ONLINE IDENTITY, ITS CONSTRUCTION AND CIRCULATION

The conceptualization of identity as a "personal fiction", a "positioning", an imagined "site" whose boundaries are forever ambiguous and open to definition and interpretation by those assigned both within and outside of them - is a particularly useful idea here, with respect to exploring the construction of identity in online communities and websites for social purposes. Specifically, the formation, standardization and circulation of one's online identity -- the deliberate and active establishment of one's reputation on the Internet and its long-term management -- can have such profound consequences that one's identity in the real world may be either enforced or eroded. Indeed, in the case of online identity, rather than one being randomly assigned a username, it is more often the matter of one's choice to construct and maintain a special identity that well reflects how one positions oneself within the narratives and interpretations of the much larger and complex imagined "site" that is the Internet. Nonetheless, in the same way that identity is established to differentiate one from others under all kinds of political, economic, societal and cultural circumstances, online identity functions as a self-produced continuity that grants certain values to one's existence and provides one with a sense of belonging on the Internet, something that has a global span. Whether online identity is capable of providing one with a sense of security within and outside of the Internet is a separate matter that was discussed in an earlier related paper (Sun, 2012).

In the same way that one's identity is constructed using various political, cultural and sociological traits that one is commonly associated with, an online identity reveals varying amounts of information that help identify the characteristics of one's real-world identity, depending on whom one interacts with and for what purpose. As Dorian Wiszniewski and Richard Coyne propose in their paper 'Mask and Identity: The Hermeneutics of Self-Construction in the Information Age', one portrays a mask of one's real-world identity whenever one interacts online for social purposes. "Identity is clearly related to community. The Enlightenment promoted the concept of the individual, the lone identity, who sets herself apart from the collection of other individuals, or amongst whom she has her place, and with whom she may ultimately identify. In as much as we wear a mask, it is to assume a role in the social sphere." (Wiszniewski & Coyne, 2002). Throughout this process, at least something of the subject behind the mask is revealed by the kind of mask one chooses, whether it is by answering specific questions about one's age, gender, address and so on, in the process of registering as a member of an online community or website, or through the style of writing, vocabulary and topics one frequently uses as one interacts with others. In the words of Wiszniewski and Coyne, "the mask is an artifice, but the face behind it is subject to the same account. The question of what constitutes a mask and what is not is subject to the workings of the practical field of engagement". This observation supports Macgregor's argument that identity as a construction reified in practice is "intrinsically tied to processes of shared communal activity". Just as much online as in the real world, one changes aspects of one's speech, mannerisms and even thoughts in order to take part in the shared rituals of behavior that ties together the members of each community.

Wiszniewski and Coyne further suggest "insofar as it acts as a signifier, the mask deflects the function of the sign away from the object behind the mask to some other object". As a result, attention is deflected "away from the mask to the context, the situation in which the masking takes place". For example, if one chooses to blog about American writer Stephen King, this mask reveals an interest in horror fiction. Even if one chooses to hide behind a completely false online identity, this in itself reveals something about a fear or perhaps a lack of self-esteem behind the false mask.

An online identity is one of the numerous "points of reference and meaning" that helps one position oneself and be positioned by others on the Internet. As one participates in different online communities and websites, one establishes different online identities, each of them being an abstract construct embodied in practice and forever subject to change in nature. It is through the process in which these online identities are formed, standardized and circulated *that glimpses of one's identity in the real world are gained*. The metaphor of "mask", in this case, may signify not only one's online identity but also one's real-world identity, both of which can also be seen as "masks" that reveal something about oneself as an individual among the numerous narratives and interpretations of one's surroundings. While a commonly accepted notion is that there is nothing behind the mask that is online identity (e.g. "On the Internet, nobody knows you're a dog", which is generally perceived as a comment on one's ability to socialize online in general anonymity), others argue there is everything behind such a self-produced mask (e.g. "On the Internet, everybody knows you're a dog", a comment created to illustrate the collective human effort in collaborated exposure and mass distribution of personal information amidst the "human flesh search" phenomenon in China, which an earlier paper discusses (Sun, 2012), strongly related to 'wisdom of the crowd' in the West). Tension inevitably arises between these two views, as the act of "masking" that is the construction and management of online identity, is scrutinized. However, it is the interaction among one's many masks both online and in the real world that is and should always be the focus of attention.

Wiszniewski and Coyne declare in their paper that "it is no longer possible to discuss identity in traditional terms. Identity is constantly in flux, the repetition of the question into identity being the only constant. By its very nature, identity is always elusive, and the notion of community follows suit". Such a view sheds light onto the significance of online identity as a self-produced continuity for social purposes, an abstract construct that grants certain values to one's existence and provides one with a sense of belonging on the Internet. Specifically, while those assigned within an imagined "site" that is identity, are distinguished from those outside of it. The two groups are also intrinsically connected via the boundary of this "site", and neither can exist without the other. This conceptualization is particularly applicable to the case of online identity because, on the Internet, the notion of self cannot make sense without that of community.

One's perception of oneself via the formation, standardization and circulation of online identity very much reflects one's awareness of the other members of the enormous imagined "site" that is the Internet. Note: further down we drawn on the ShadowBoard methodology introduced in Table 1 above, to construct a representation of a digital self on a computer, done so within the DigitalFriend (software based on the ShadowBoard Architecture shown earlier in Figure 1). This example digital self is held outside of all of one's communities on Internet, where an individual can create and 'nurture' a digital representation of their self-identity, from which facets of self (see Figure 1) can be revealed in specific online communities that they choose; but more so, it is used to store and reference information and other resources in a private space, as the individual selects and builds knowledge, through the filter of their own goals, interests, activities, interactions, capabilities and outcomes.

Finally, considering the fact that online identity is more often than not proactively established for social purposes, Coyne (2011) observes in his essay "Profile Yourself (Narcissus online)" that:

Social media encourage personal and private disclosures, or at least, the tools for presenting oneself professionally readily elide into tools for personal presentation. You have to decide whether to let your online professional persona deliver insights into hobbies, holidays and family matters. The scope of identity formation seems to be expanding, or at least changing. There will always be some group or other, no matter how small, amongst whom one can entertain unusual or idiosyncratic interests, and with whom one can readily identify. There is a group out there, possibly not yet formed, and unknown to you, amongst whom you can enjoy a ration of fame if you really want it.

Specifically, in the process of constructing one's online identity, one has "control (or at least the illusion of control)" over how one projects oneself to others (notwithstanding lone trolls and other reputation damaging entities), what one chooses to make public or private, and the extent to which one may reveal different identities in different contexts. This is a significant distinction between one's online identity and real-world identity -- this ability to control, or at least the sense of it, that enables one to choose the extent to which one reveals some characteristics of one's real-world identity to different groups on the Internet. Specifically, the imagined boundaries of one's identity as a series of political, cultural and sociological traits, are often employed by oneself or others as "definite" and "necessary" ways to uphold and even advocate such identity. In sharp contrast, one is free to establish and manage any online identity that one deems as "definite" and "necessary", as ways to uphold and advocate the kinds of political, cultural and sociological traits that one considers as representative of oneself. More importantly, as a result of constant and continuous management, one's online identity has the tendency to become a caricature of a set of concrete "facts" that one considers as being essential to one's existence *on the Internet*, as one interacts with others under all kinds of political, economic, societal and cultural circumstances. This, to a large extent, is distinct from one's real-life identity that is more fluid and subject to change - both one's self-identity and how others identify us: that two-way real-life identity. Think of a well-known author's or celebrity's online profile, maintained over a decade or two, versus their changing real life circumstances over the same time period. For some there is little difference, for others, it is greatly so.

It is this separation between one's online managed identity, and one's real world identity, that the largest social network companies, particularly Facebook, Google and Twitter, want to bring into alignment, for all sorts of reason's but mainly for capturing the advertising dollar, upon which their respective main business models are founded. They want to have the ultimate profile of an individual, all individuals. They want a complete identity, no matter how unrealistic that possibility is (i.e. the myths "We know what you want to buy before you do!" and "We know what you will do before you do?"). We will discuss this further in the next section.

SOCIAL MEDIA IDENTITY AND THE MEANING OF SELF

Since this paper investigates the complex interrelations between oneself and the communities with which one interacts, both online and in the real world, we find Yehudah Mirsky's position in his essay 'Identity = ?' (Mirsky, 2011), to be acutely helpful. Using 'Jewish identity' as an example in his discussion of what it means to be Jewish in contemporary America, Mirsky argues

instead of signifying that individuals are what they are in any fixed sense, as in x = x, 'identity' today is often used to indicate that individuals are what they will themselves to be, over time and in different ways. Resistant to classification by any external standard or institution, one's identity is, rather, a complex truth that emerges from within.

This existentialist notion that "individuals are what they will themselves to be", that identity is something that "emerges within", echoes what Coyne refers to as the decision, and often the determination as well, to "profile yourself" (Coyne, 2011). Coyne declares "part of the definition of identity involves connections with people, associating with the right group of other individuals (identifying with them), and letting it be known with whom you identify". In other words, it is not only the act of "identifying" with a community, but also that of "letting it be known" that such identification is established, that explicitly illustrates the nature and significance of online identity. The social function of online identity is thus self-evident.

Indeed, on today's Internet, particularly in Facebook, LinkedIn, Google+, other online communities, mobile apps and websites with a social aspect - one is increasingly required to "profile" oneself, to provide a series of political, cultural and sociological traits that can be used to not only identify but also verify and even solidify oneself to others, including to marketers and instruments of government. (E.g. Not only do they try to get you to use your 'Google Login' or your 'Facebook Login' on other partnering web-sites, they also try to extract the details of your contacts from your mobile phone, both to grow their membership, and to enhance their knowledge of the social network in your pocket). To make various aspects of one's real-world identity available online is to make even more elastic the boundaries of the imagined "site" that is one's self. Instead of eradicating the abstract line that distinguishes one from others, it allows personal and private disclosures that enable others to cross this line in a way, at a time and/or on an occasion that one determines and makes known. In doing so, *when appropriate safeguards are in place*, one allows such crossings to take place conditionally upon certain political, economic, societal and cultural circumstances. Throughout this process, one's sense of self can be considerably strengthened, and one's awareness of the larger imagined "site" that is the Internet can also be enhanced - *provided that the line crossings abide by one's agreed to conditions*. Unlike one's identity in the real world, which may be either self-produced or assigned by others, one's online identity is almost always proactively formed, standardized and circulated by oneself, in the first instance. However, the amassed identity behind the scenes, built up by the profiling engines behind Facebook, Google and other social network facilitators, is far more complex and detailed than that one initially outlined in the submitted profile. And they work at continually adding detail to it.

Currently, the 2 billion active users of Facebook (Constine, 2017) across the globe are 'required' to provide their true identities in terms of their basic details – name, age, gender, and so. Although there are clear violations of these Facebook designated terms by many, including the 7.5+ million children under the age of 13 with accounts even back in 2011 (Fox, 2011). The popularity and high penetration rate of this social networking platform does indicate the desire of its users to announce, affirm and promote something of their real-world identities on the Internet. This phenomenon is intriguing because it represents a large-scale attempt to merge real-world identity and online identity; or, more specifically, to "borrow" from one's real-world identity and use that as one's online identity in order to enhance one's interactions with communities both online and in the real world.

Particularly with the conceptualization of identity as an imagined "site" in mind, the Facebook phenomenon appears to suggest a tendency (willed or co-erced?) amongst the website's users to combine into one, the many imagined "sites" that they have previously constructed and assigned their identity within, including those much larger "sites" that are the greater Internet and the real world. There is also an apparent attempt by many of those users, to join together, or at least make coexistent, those many real-world and online *communities* with which one associates, which may be readily achieved through various Facebook features such as Messenger, Groups, Events, Like Pages, Share, News Feed, Notifications, Photo and Video Tagging, Status Updates, and even checking-in to Places (i.e. tying one's online Facebook identity, with one's current geographic location in the real world, and with the identities of those who you are with). Mobile social media apps have accelerated this trend, given that one's mobile phone is on or near one's person, for most of the waking hours.

Mark Zuckerberg is famously said to have "emphasized three times in a single interview" with David Kirkpatrick in his book 'The Facebook Effect: The Inside Story of the Company that is Connecting the World' (2010), "you have one identity… The days of you having a different image for your work friends or co-workers and for the other people you know are probably coming to an end pretty quickly". So, it seems safe to suggest that these words, together with Zuckerberg's observation "having two identities for yourself is an example of a lack of integrity" (Culter, Kim-Mai, 2010), explicitly illustrate Facebook's approach to providing what Hall refers to as the "unifying and unchanging points of reference and meaning" among the numerous narratives and interpretations of one's online surroundings.

In other words, in Facebook currently, the identity of each user is "essentialist", rather than one of "positioning". Although it started out with your 'friends' and 'family', it soon appropriated everyone else that it could. As each user is encouraged to allow crossings over the boundaries of the imagined "site" that is his or her self, either by agreeing to accept others as new friends or by requesting to become a friend of others, or to allow public *Follows*, it considerably essentialises one's awareness of self. This process of essentialisation also merges the online and real-world communities with which one interacts, as the "shared patterns" or "shared rituals of behaviour" that connect the members of each community, are no longer distinguished. All communities that one ever had anything to do with, are merged into one that is conceptualized by the user as a larger imagined "site" that is the Facebook universe. The jury is still out on whether Zuckerberg has identified and is servicing some new social trend in this regard for some large percentage of people, or whether his particular 20-something view back then (2010) on identity is yet to embrace the broader complexities of identity as one moves further through other parts of the life-cycle, including having one's own children, as he now has, and holding passionate time-consuming interests beyond ones immediate passion for the work currently being done. Not to mention the security and privacy issues regarding unforeseen crossing of the lines one had hoped to keep control over.

Two other social networking websites/platforms requiring users to provide their true identities are LinkedIn (bought by Microsoft in 2016 for $26 billion) and Google+. Unlike Facebook whose users are encouraged to add anyone and everyone on Facebook to their Friends Lists, to get maximum inclusion on the site, LinkedIn is (currently) mainly used for professional networking, while the 'Circles' feature of Google+ enables users to organize their 'contacts' into different groups as a first-class feature, from the ground up. Whereas *Groups* within the Facebook platform, is a relatively recent addition in its considerable lifeline (inception in 2005) as an evolving technical platform (Chai, 2010), and is currently non-hierarchical (i.e. no sub-groups of groups). It seems reasonable to suggest that in sharp contrast to Facebook's "essentialist" approach, LinkedIn and Google+ attempt to help their users better position themselves among the numerous narratives and interpretations of their surroundings by distinguishing the "professional" and "personal" aspects of their social lives on the Internet. In fact, Jeff Weiner, the Chief Executive Officer (CEO) of LinkedIn (with 7 years prior senior management experience at Yahoo, a company also heavily invested in social media), is on record as saying that he believes there are *at least* three distinct, major, social groupings that Facebook has attempted to merge into one, namely: "Personal, Professional and Family" (Weiner & Battelle, 2010) - while conceding that they overlap, more or less depending on the individual. Accordingly, LinkedIn has differentiated itself from Facebook by going for just the "professional identity".

Figure 2. That part of the Conceptual Data Model dealing with Facebook Groups (from figure 1.6, Goschnick (2014))

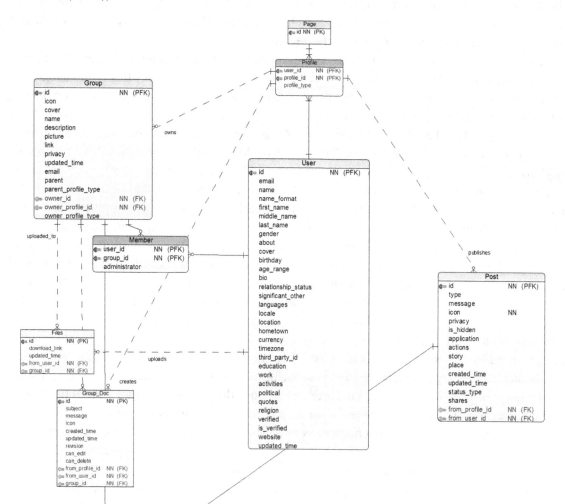

A shift of focus is necessary here, from the notion of disclosure to that of control over disclosure. That is to say, despite the social functions of Facebook, LinkedIn and Google+, the fact that these social networking platforms enable their users to choose their own privacy settings and decide who can see specific parts of their profiles, explicitly demonstrates the resilient nature of the boundaries of the imagined "site" that is one's self. The sense of control (or at least the illusion of it, as Coyne suggests) over how one projects oneself to others, what one chooses to make public or private, and the extent to which one might reveal different aspects of one's online and/or real-world identities in different contexts, is so fundamental that Facebook has met prolonged criticism on numerous related issues since its launch in February 2004 (Wikipedia, 2017). Indeed, the aforementioned later addition of Groups (see Figure

2) to the Facebook technology platform, came about to address users expressed need to differentiate amongst their accumulated Facebook 'Friends'. This addition is expressed in the data model part of the overall Facebook data model, that caters for Groups. Note: a *Group* is expressed as a first-class entity that a number of *Users* can join, represented in the *Member* many-to-many entity (i.e. a Group can have many Users as Members, while a User can also be a Member of many Groups). In addition to sharing general Facebook *Posts* via the *Group-Feed*, these individuals can also share other *Files* and even collaboratively edit shared documents (see the *Group_Doc* entity in Figure 2).

Google+, launched in 2011, which came after the addition of the Groups feature in Facebook (in October, 2010), picked up on that much needed feature, calling their approach 'Circles' and embedding it into the opening user interface in a much more intuitive and usable manner than Facebook did with their Groups feature. Even LinkedIn, which so far has been considered by many as having "a solid track record of taking user privacy seriously", faces questions of how to protect the data of its users from being accessed by third parties (Sampson, 2011). Indeed, some of their business model revolves around providing paid access to various details of people beyond those an individual has listed as their immediate 'Connections', via an annual subscription fee to 'LinkedIn Premium'.

What is worth noting here is the ambiguous nature of the boundaries of the imagined "site" that is one's self on the Internet. On the one hand, one actively forms, standardizes and circulates an online identity by disclosing and distributing one's personal and private information, an act that Yehudah Mirsky and the social network industry in general refers to as 'opting-in' that not only is 'meaningful' but also helps "realize the significance of today's personal freedom" (Mirsky, 2011). On the other hand, one constantly fears the discovery and disclosure of such personal and private information by others without one's permission, and/or in ways not originally foreseen, such as by potential employers far in the future. Consider the following legal terms designated by Google when it launched Google+, with regard to the content one submits, posts or displays on or through its numerous services:

You retain copyright and any other rights you already hold in Content which you submit, post or display on or thorough the Services. By submitting, posting or displaying the content you give Google a perpetual, irrevocable, worldwide, royalty-free, and non-exclusive license to reproduce, adapt, modify, translate, publish, publicly perform, publicly display and distribute any Content which you submit, post or display on or through the Services. This license is for the sole purpose of enabling Google to display, distribute and promote the Services and may be revoked for certain Services as defined in the Additional Terms of those Services. (Google, 2011)

It seems highly unlikely that a sane person would sign a contract giving someone such free range with his or her intellectual property if they consider it to have any value. However, according to Google's then CEO Larry Page, within just three weeks of the launch of Google+ in its invite-only "field testing" phase on June 28, 2011, there were already more than 10 million users sharing and receiving more than a billion items each day (Matthews, 2011). While not all of these items may be of a private nature, and many of these people were probably early-adopters of technology for the sake of evaluation, the need for users of supposedly free social networking websites such as Google+ to disclose and distribute personal information to each other is evidently overwhelming - enough to overcome terse conditions of usage. As one makes these boundaries of the imagined "site" that is one's online identity, extremely flexible, the risk that others can cross these boundaries in ways, at times and/or on occasions that one may not be able to anticipate or control nor even be aware of, apparently becomes an almost insignificant personal consideration to many, when signing on to these so-called 'free' services. This well demonstrates the perceived nature and significance of online identity as a self-produced and community-oriented continuity.

There are earlier precedents of 'service providers' taking many more benefits than their 'users', in such provider-consumer arrangements, that hold forewarnings for both parties in the current use of social networking websites/platforms. In Satchell et al's paper 'Knowing Me, Knowing You: End User Perceptions of Identity Management Systems' (2006), the authors set out in an IS research project, to determine people's views and reactions to, what is called *Federated Identity*. The concept of Federated Identity, although used across inter-related organizations in the past (e.g. using Microsoft Passport), to provide 'one login' (i.e. username and password authentication), has been more recently subscribed to by Facebook and other Internet based companies. E.g. third-party Facebook developers can allow their users to in turn use their Facebook login, to access the 3rd party site in question, and use various services there (such as posting a facebook Like against content on that site, which shows up in the news feeds of the user's friends, etc.). What Satchell et al found with Federated Identity, was that the benefits were very much in the providers favor and not in the end users favor much at all - apart from the convenience of that single login.

However and more importantly, they found that when the "options to control and personalise" ones data was out of the end users hands, and very much in the providers hands, users usually provided as little information about themselves as possible. E.g. one user informated "I separate or compartmentalise my personal information when I don't know the source of who is asking for them." and "if all information is kept under one banner it could be accessed by the wrong person (or people)." Satchell et al concluded: "failure to provide control (to end users) results in the erosion of trust between users and the provider and culminates in a culture of use where the user aims to suppress rather than reveal information." Anecdotally, that is certainly the way that many people have adapted their usage of Facebook, Google+ and other social networking websites in more recent times, as control and disclosure mechanisms are perceived to be further out of users hands than they had thought when they first signed on, not to mention the ramification eminating from the fake news and political polarisation issues for Facebook, Twitter and Google in particular, being researched and examined since the 2016 US election (Allcott & Gentzkow, 2017).

The number of users of these sites is significant. While Facebook has gone on to 2 billion users, Google+ has struggled with 395 million active accounts in 2017, but with only 34 million of them visiting per month (https://www.statisticbrain.com/google-plus-demographics-statistics/). However, Google's YouTube site has 1.5 billion active monthy users, and numerous other social media sites have gained significant numbers, particular via mobile apps (Constine, 2017): WeChat with 890 million (mainly China), Twitter 328 million, SnapChat 255 million, Line 217 million (mainly Japan), KaKaoTalk 43 million (South Korea), and Facebook-owned WhatsApp 2 billion (its not clear how many of these are also Facebook users). LinkedIn has 470 million users with 106 million of the active per month (https://www.linkedin.com/pulse/linkedin-numbers-2017-statistics-meenakshi-chaudhary)

Interestingly, LinkedIn also has 10,000 employees worldwide, which makes it a very significant commercial organisation in scale. For comparison, Facebook had 19,000 employees by March 2017 (https://qz.com/975081/facebook-fb-is-adding-employees-at-a-faster-clip-even-as-revenue-growth-slows/).

Table 2. Action Types that third-party Facebook Developers can use (Facebook, 2017)

Name	Description
apps.saves	An action representing someone saving an app to try later.
books.quotes	An action representing someone quoting from a book.
books.rates	An action representing someone rating a book.
books.reads	An action representing someone reading a book.
books.wants_to_read	An action representing someone wanting to read a book.
fitness.bikes	An action representing someone cycling a course.
fitness.runs	An action representing someone running a course.
fitness.walks	An action representing someone walking a course.
games.achieves	An action representing someone reaching a game achievement.
games.celebrate	An action representing someone celebrating a victory in a game.
games.plays	An action representing someone playing a game. Stories for this action will only appear in the activity log.
games.saves	An action representing someone saving a game.
music.listens	An action representing someone listening to a song, album, radio station, playlist or musician
music.playlists	An action representing someone creating a playlist.
news.publishes	An action representing someone publishing a news article.
news.reads	An action representing someone reading a news article.
og.follows	An action representing someone following a Facebook user
og.likes	An action representing someone liking any object.
pages.saves	An action representing someone saving a place.
restaurant.visited	An action representing someone visiting a restaurant.
restaurant.wants_to_visit	An action representing someone wanting to visit a restaurant
sellers.rates	An action representing a commerce seller has been given a rating.
video.rates	An action representing someone rating a movie, TV show, episode or another piece of video content.
video.wants_to_watch	An action representing someone wanting to watch video content.
video.watches	An action representing someone watching video content.

Also demanding attention is that one's sense of self on the Internet inevitably comes under the influence of the communities with which one *interacts*, both online and in the real world. While LinkedIn may have borrowed that part of our professional identity that was traditionally captured on the 'business cards' that people physically share, now that it is in an electronic and social form, it balloons in scope and blends with other sites, at a scale not before seen in professional identity management. For an example of that increased scope, LinkedIn offers "Hiring Solutions at massive scale" (Weiner & Batelle, 2010). As an example of blending, LinkedIn integrates with Twitter to some degree - the *Comments* in one can be automatically passed on to the other. Similarly, the "Like" button on websites external to Facebook, allows external political, commercial, cultural and sociological promotion, to enter the Facebook universe with ease (Facebook, 2011), in a similar manner to the Federated Identity approach discussed above, in past identity management systems. In linking and blending such websites and the related new functionality, the boundaries of the imagined "site" that is one's online identity are increasingly blurred, causing one to constantly re-define and re-interpret the meaning of privacy. And *Like* is just the first verb that Facebook appropriated for its representation of one's identity through *structured interaction*. It has appropriated other verbs for use on similar buttons and in other ways, to represent other activities such as *Eating, Watching, Reading* and *Running* (Geron, 2011), in what it terms 'frictionless sharing'. See table 2 for the current *Action Types* that Facebook has available to third party developers. Clearly, these verbs were chosen as significant handles that the advertising dollar can use.

Facebook on Building a Global Community in the Near Future

According to the aforementioned Facebook manifesto (Zuckerberg, 2017), Facebook now intends to dramatically expand its Groups feature ("social infrastructure for communities"), towards a platform capable of supporting a Global Community. In what seems to be a new recognition of the need for diversity and multiple identities of individual users, Zuckerberg lays down a blueprint of what Facebook thinks is needed, and what its already doing about it. That is, to turn their platform into one that will support a truly Global Community, effectively etching out a real world global community (connected, voting, caring through action – since global problems require global solutions) in the absence of one that includes the individual participants themselves (i.e. not just one's representative in the UN). In the online article:

- He makes a pitch for traditional communities ("Whether they're *churches, sports teams, unions or other local groups,* they all share important roles as social infrastructure for our communities…") to join up, offering them technology-enabled functionalities that come with the social network platform, to help traditional groups arrest "their declining memberships in recent times". Zuckerberg calls these groups "very meaningful groups". I.e. the sort that Mirsky (ibid) positions one as: "identifying" with a community, and also that of "letting it be known" that is where I stand.
- At the same time he pitches to people to join existing virtual Facebook Groups, and to would-be leaders to create new virtual communities on common interests, that can aspire to the sociability that those real world traditional communities already have: "These communities don't just interact online. They hold get-togethers, organize dinners, and support each other in their daily lives".
- On the Global Community front, he shows a careful eye to the importance of balance in benefits between *service provider* and *user* that Satchell (ibid) highlighted, as he outlines the benefits that a global community in a single social network would reap: "Problems like terrorism, natural disasters, disease, refugee crises, and climate change need coordinated responses from a worldwide vantage point … There is a real opportunity to build global safety infrastructure, … the *Facebook community is in a unique position* to help prevent harm, assist during a crisis, or come together to rebuild afterwards … When a child goes missing, we've built infrastructure to show *Amber Alerts* … To *rebuild* after a crisis, we've built the world's largest social infrastructure for collective action. A few years ago, after an earthquake in Nepal, *the Facebook community raised $15 million to help people recover and rebuild…*"
- He also has an eye on the new revenue stream that would come of it, with those same structured 'actions' in mind as depicted in table 2, coming into play: "We can *look at many activities* through the *lens of building community.* Watching video of *our favorite sports team or TV show, reading our favorite newspaper,* or playing our *favorite game* are not just entertainment or information but *a shared experience …*", but it is a learned eye that concurs with Macgregor's (ibid) argument

discussed earlier, that identity as a construction reified in practice is "intrinsically tied to processes of shared communal activity".

- To counter the *fake news* issues that have dogged Facebook recently, he turns to advancing AI techniques to identify it, and to increasing Facebook's fact checking ability.

- To counter the *filter bubble* concerns of critics outlined above, he discussed the complexity of the issue, then to disarm the polarisation of opinions, he suggests "A more effective approach is to show a range of perspectives, let people see where their views are on a spectrum and come to a conclusion on what they think is right" and to do enable that: "*A strong news industry is also critical to building an informed community.* Giving people a voice is not enough without having people dedicated to uncovering new information and analyzing it". As mentioned above, more than 50% of the US population admit to getting their news through Facebook, and now Facebook looks like doubling-down on traditional/partnered news outlets for more professional collection and analysis of news intermixed within the people's personal news feeds. Interestingly, de Botton (ibid) thinks that "proper" investigative journalism should "start with an all-encompassing interest in the full range of factors that sabotage group and individual existence", including health, family structures, relationships, architecture, leisure time, and so on – all the complexities of modern life. Social media in general and Facebook in particular, are in an excellent position to do that with news if they so wish, beyond just the advertising opportunities.

- A lot of people and companies see a lucrative future for electronic voting systems. Zuckerberg sees that future too. He sees a way that brings cultural diversity into those new 'meaningful groups' (e.g. traditional communities) in Facebook. By allowing them to vote on their own 'community standards'. "The guiding principles are that *the Community Standards should reflect the cultural norms of (the) community,* that each person should see as little objectionable content as possible, and each person should be able to share what they want while being told they cannot share something as little as possible..." In addition to voting, AI will be used to apply the results to the group as a whole, or customised for the individual within that group: "The approach is to combine creating a large-scale democratic process to determine standards with AI to help enforce them. The idea is to give everyone in the community options for how they would like to set the content policy for themselves. Where is your line on nudity? On violence? On graphic content? On profanity? What you decide will be your personal settings... For those who don't make a decision, the default will be whatever the majority of people in your region (sub-community) selected. Of course, you will always be free to update your personal settings". That, becomes a compelling reason to provide even more profile information to Facebook.

- Beyond voting within respective 'meaningful groups' Zuckerberg has a global scale voting technology in mind: "Building an inclusive global community requires establishing a new process for citizens worldwide to participate in community governance. I hope that we can explore examples of how collective decision-making might work at scale."

In other words, in that new future Facebook, the identity of each user will serve as both "essentialist" *and* "positioning". Where he has people "positioning" beyond just family and friends via the melding of Facebook with traditional and other "meaningful" groups; while the "essential" identity of each user, is both centred on an 'authentic' Facebook profile – a much expanded profile via the voting upon numerous community standards options that may be expanded by the service provider into the future - and upon a new Global Citizenship. While Zuckerberg never mentions the UN at any point in the article, his musings are in that same sphere of governance, but the one he envisages involves mass participation, through Facebook technologies.

Zuckerberg's article outlines an audacious plan in a mid-way career built on audacious plans. Given the current 2 billion users of Facebook and a market value hovering around $400 billion in 2017, the article/plan is worth a full read and should not be dismissed lightly in any discussion on the future of identity and the impact upon it by social media.

Echoing Mersky's observation above is Danah Boyd's assertion that "cyberspace is not our utopian fantasy; many of the social constraints that frame physical reality are quickly seeping into the digital realm" (Boyd, 2011). Boyd's observation of the differences between social interaction on the Internet and that in the real world is worth quoting at some length:

The underlying architecture of the digital environment does not provide the forms of feedback and context to which people have become accustomed. The lack of embodiment makes it difficult to present oneself and to perceive the presentation of others. As people operate through digital agents, they are forced to articulate their performance in new ways. Additionally, the contextual information that they draw from does not have the same implications online. Situational context can be collapsed with ease, thereby exposing an individual in an out-of-context manner. Unlike physical architecture, the digital equivalent is composed of bits, which have fundamentally different properties than atoms. The interface to the digital world is explicitly constructed and designed around a user's desires. As with any fundamental differences in architecture, there are resultant differences in paradigms of use, interpersonal expectations, and social norms. Performing online requires that people be aware of and adjust to these differences so as to achieve the same level of social proficiency that they have mastered offline.

That Facebook has invested heavily in Virtual Reality (VR) technology via its Occulus Go technology (ABC, 2017), is an investment in adding embodiment to the virtual world.

The whole approach at Facebook to building global community is often in stark contrast to other existing (potentially) global communities, such as some of the citizen science projects with inclusive social network functionality, as alluded to by Preece (2017) in an article appropriately titled: *How two billion smartphone users can save species*. For example, the iNaturalist.org site. The push in that article is one of global responsibility via local action, in the form of collecting data to be used by scientists to record changes in the population and distribution of species, "enabling us" (global citizens) to take action to help save threatened species in particular (of which is a lot) and maintain biodiversity (of the planet). The biodiversity data is typically "*collected using smartphones can include photos, comments, numerical data, video, and sound, together with metadata (e.g., time, date, and geolocation logging)*". The focus of citizen science is on the real world, using the virtual world in a crowd sourcing manner. These citizen science biodiversity projects are interested in using people's smartphones as information probes to collect data around the individual, while building participant commitment, enthusiasm and community for a cause. While Facebook is more interested in the data from the same devices that can add detail to the profile of the individual. Citizen science projects are happy with a slice of an individual's life and attention, often focusing on pressing issues facing humanity. Facebook wants the lot. Wants to do the lot, global platform wise. However, both Zuckerberg and Preece (ibid) make a play for attracting would-be leaders in creating new 'meaningful groups'. In Preece's case, to members of the HCI community to start new biodiversity maintaining initiatives, lending their unique skillset to make citizen science a more effective vehicle for global health – and making HCI even more relevant. In Facebooks case 'think of a meaning group' – making Facebook even more relevant. Facebook assumes it will gather all of your identity information; citizen science projects just want a slice of your time and resources, and to focus your passion on a particular scientific quest, for humanity – a slice of your identity.

Boyd's study, titled "Faceted Id/entity: Managing representation in a digital world", specifically focuses on one's ability to maintain control of personal representation and identity information. While she too argues for "a design approach that will aid sociable designers in developing human-centred technologies that allow for individual control over personal identity", it is equally important that one is constantly aware of the flexible nature of identity as one interacts online for social purposes, as well as the positive and negative consequences such interaction may have on one's reputation both on the Internet and in the real world. Only a full awareness of identity can empower one with a desire to appropriately control it.

A CASE STUDY IN REPRESENTATION AND CONTROL OF IDENTITY AND PRIVACY

That future Facebook realised, or not, one's sense of community is changing, as a result of different online communities being introduced within the confines of one larger imagined "site" that is the Internet, which increasingly causes the distinct "shared patterns" or "shared rituals of behaviors" of each community to impact upon each other. Empowered individuals are increasingly becoming global citizens at some level of their identity. This forces the commonly accepted notion of privacy to become open to interpretation, depending on the nature of the community with whom one interacts, the meaning of the occasion, and the location of the interaction not only online but also in the real world.

As Mirsky observes, the construction of identity "involves not just trying out, or trying on, a random set of 'shifting, syncretic, and constructed' accoutrements that 'can be re-forged under new circumstances' but assuming real, durable responsibilities" (Mirsky, 2011). In the context of the Internet, where many traditional structures of the real world appear to have dissolved for a time, such "real, durable responsibilities" entail the ability to remain aware of the fact that one's online identity is simply an imagined "site", and then being rather proactive in positioning one's self among the numerous narratives and interpretations of numerous much larger imagined "sites" that are the online communities with which one interacts. The flexibility of the boundaries of these "sites" very much depends on whether a fine balance can be achieved throughout this process of positioning between the disclosure and control of personal and private information for social purposes. However, much like the assumption that people read the legal conditions when signing up to a so-called 'free' service such as Google+ or Facebook, to assume that people will really embrace such a responsibility en mass, is a big and probably unrealistic Ask - or whether they even can if they wished to. This question of balance between disclosure and control - whether it can realistically be achieved within these new overlapping, interrelated technologies - still has a long way to run. At stake is mass trust in the service providers of these new social media and search platforms. Also at stake is the last interior privacy firewall of Self.

A REPRESENTATION OF A DIGITAL SELF IN THE DIGITALFRIEND

Where better to create a digit self, a digital representation of one's self-identity, than on a personal computer (PC)? However, the question then quickly moves to a technical one, of what constitutes one's personal computer these days? Is it a laptop, a desktop, a tablet, a smart phone or some other mobile device? Or a virtualisation that materialises on all of the above, when summoned, as needed? We are going to leave that technical question out of this discussion while we briefly present a working example of a such a digital representation of a self-identity, one that does run on many platforms, but in this case (Figure 3) on a personal desktop computer.

However, before describing what is represented in this figure, we return to Mirsky's notion that "individuals are what they will themselves to be", that identity is "resistant to classification by any external standard or institution, one's identity is, rather, a complex truth that emerges from within". The approach taken in this case study, is that rather than have one's identity either: classified by some external entity, or floating around in mind where it is perhaps stronger on a good day than not, or that can perhaps be somehow gleaned from a super-set of all those on and off-line communities pronouncements and activities – the best thing to do once one knows themselves well, is to build a computer model of it on one's private personal computing device. The DigitalFriend is like a living diary for both building and maintaining such a representation. As Satchell et al (ibid) concluded: "failure to provide control (to end users) results in the erosion of trust between users and the provider and culminates in a culture of use where the user aims to suppress rather than reveal information." We are yet to see an online system or social network where the user is both aware of the full model of themselves that has been built up behind the scenes, nor one where the user can control such a model, in particular, who has access to it, for what purposes, now and in the future. Keeping the most complete model themselves, of themselves, and deciding themselves on which information goes to which provider, is the most obvious solution to having providers get the best reveals of accurate information for the actual service they are providing. It is the individual's Identity, after all. It seems that the citizen science communities assume this, while the large social media platforms, fight it.

Figure 3. Interface of the DigitalFriend representing a Digital Self

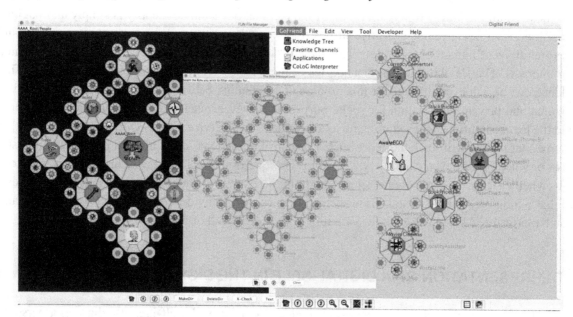

Furthermore, by having a deliberative and reactive system (i.e. applied AI), that can store, retrieve, notify and monitor all sorts of relevant information feeds, makes for a representation of identity that is live, that is running in real time with the user, and even as they sleep, and in many ways, can augment their cognitive functions.

Figure 3 represents a person's digital self, built and maintained in the DigitalFriend system. There are currently 3 windows open in the figure, representing 3 interrelated hierarchies, that are displayed in such a way as to instantiate the underlying architecture represented back in Figure 1. The middle hierarchy instantiates the generic role model represented in Table 1. The initial model in the table is a starting point only, as the individual user then customises it into a role model that matches the actual roles in their life. This live role model alerts and notifies the user about important messages and data feeds, ones that they have prioritised as important to them (Goschnick, 2006).

Figure 4. Meta-model of the DigitalFriend, V1

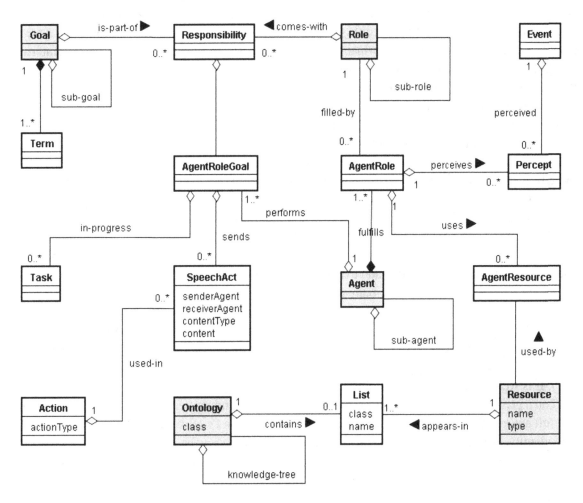

The hierarchy on the left is the user's custom Knowledge Tree, where personal files and all sorts of data is stored. Again, the methodology used with the DigitalFriend provides a starting personal ontology as a default structure (Goschnick, 2005), which the user can modify or completely replace, as their personal ontology deems necessary over time. The user can store their photos, videos, documents and files of all sorts into this hierarchy, where they can easily relocate them any time. Other sorts of data that is deposited into this personal ontology, are the newsfeeds coming from RSS aggregators (news feeds) and various types of web services. Bozdag & Timmerman (2011) argued that the good that comes of having information can only be obtained by individuals if they rely on filtering technology of some sort, due to the enormous increase in the information supply – hence the complexity around the discussion on filter bubbles mentioned above. As de Botton (2014) tells us, the way to deal with the excessive amounts of information available via the Internet, is to 'know yourself well' and use those biases as the filter. By having both a personal role model, a goal model, and a personal ontology structure to receive the information, the individual is in control of what information they gather and store for future use. Bozdag & Timmerman (ibid) also identified three important criteria in the design of personalization systems: autonomy, identity and transparency. The DigitalFriend has all three very well covered.

The hierarchy to the right is the configuration of the user's personal assistant agents. These are running processes, either receiving information from the internet, from sensors in an IoT way (Internet of Things), or using stored data within the Knowledge Tree, or computing new information possibly from those other sources. These running agents are interlinked in such a way that they can achieve user goals (computational plans), and even carry out some of their forward intentions (e.g. sending a message off to the outside world, when a desired condition has been met).

The conceptual model in Figure 4 is a structural model for the first version of the DigitalFriend. We have advanced it considerable since then. The conceptual model in Figure 5, taken from and explained more fully in Goschnick et al. (2015), is the model of the second version of the DigitalFriend, currently in beta. One small detail to note here: the SocialWorld hierarchy in the right middle of the figure -- it enables a structure of sub-communities within communities, to any depth -- the sort that Zuckerberg (2017) alludes to in a future Facebook. Where the V1 model had 4 interrelated hierarchies, the V2 model has 8 interrelated hierarchies. (Note: These extra levels of complexity add to the functionality and sophistication but don't need to add to complexity in the user interface – the reverse is often the case in software. For example, there are many more levels of complexity behind the user interface in an iPad than there are in a Windows XP interface, and there are many more levels of complexity in the Windows XP interface than there are in the harder to use character-based interface of Microsoft DOS)

That is all the explanation of the DigitalFriend we give in this chapter – it is presented here to demonstrate what is possible regarding a self-managed computational representation of identity (a digital self). It is well documented in the references already given above. This example of one's digital self is held on a private personal computer, outside of all of one's communities on the Internet. The individual has full autonomy and control over it, where they can create and evolve a digital representation of their self-identity. From it, sub-sets of information about their identity can be put out into specific online communities. Furthermore, it is used to store and reference information and other resources, as the individual goes about their life building knowledge through the filter of their own interests, activities, interactions, capabilities, goals and their outcomes.

Figure 5. Meta-model of the DigitalFriend, V2

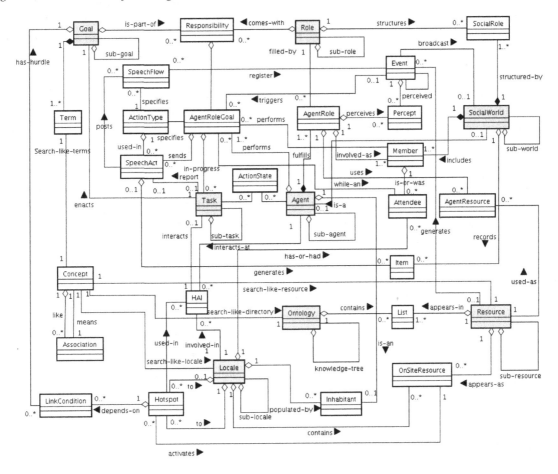

CONCLUSION

This chapter has explored the fundamental nature of identity and how identity can be constructed in online communities, with respect to how one's online identity may reflect and affect one's real-world identity. In summary, in the first section *Identity as a Self-Produced Continuity and the Media* we considered the traditional views of identity in the context of the media, particularly with regard to the News. A dichotomy of 'essence' and 'positioning' within Identity is uncovered and discussed. We considered the new concept of the *filter bubble*, and whether it is a new effect or whether one's daily dose of selective news and views has long been the case. We also briefly introduced a software architecture based on the psychological theory of sub-selves, that closely matches a construct of identity by the cultural theorists introduced. We argued that one's identity is flexible and subject to change in the real, non-Internet world, but that perceived identity by the individual, is often a caricature in the form of a set of concrete "facts" that one considers essential to one's existence there. We point out that even the 'essentialist' core values of an identity, are also subject to change, sometimes.

In section *Online Identity, Its Construction and Circulation*, we note that while identities on the Internet and in the real world are both of a flexible and ever-changing nature, serving as a point of reference among the many narratives and interpretations of one's surroundings, online identity is far more proactively constructed and managed for social purposes. In the same way that one's identity can be conceptualized as an imagined "site" whose boundaries are those political, cultural and sociological traits commonly that one commonly subscribes to, one's online identity also reveals various amounts of information that help identify the characteristics of one's real-world identity, depending on whom one interacts with and on what occasion. There is a clear and present risk that the boundaries of both real-world identity and online identity are perceived to be as permanent and unchallengeable as the borders of geo-political entities, which in turn prompts the invention and prolonged utilization of all kinds of labels, caricatures and "norms", that affect the ways in which those within and outside of these imagined "sites" interact with each other and among themselves, in our daily lives.

In section *Social Media Identity and the Meaning of Self* we outline how one can 'position' oneself in both the online world and in the real world, by identifying with communities, in a 'let it be known' way. In early social media platforms we are free to present and manage what one considers to be the current best representation of oneself if one wills it so (e.g. LinkedIn is for a professional identity) - with better control over the disclosure of personal and private details at a time, in a way and on an occasion that one sees fit.

However, after discussing several different platforms that use the Internet -- namely, Facebook, LinkedIn and Google+ -- it becomes clear that personal control over one's Internet identity has been significantly loosened. The individual needs to be aware and on guard that the timely disclosure and personal control over one's private information used for social purposes in the online communities they interact with, is paramount to being able to manage one's online identity. Platforms such as Facebook have continued to try and meld one's online identity with real world identity, with plans to bring in many more traditional communities, where peoples 'essentialist' identities are likely to reside, together with your 'positioning' identities, such as your professional network. As incentive to get people to meld their identities in Facebook, they make a pitch with their unprecedented infrastructure and toolset to build a truly global community. Meanwhile, certain citizen science communities (e.g. those dedicated to maintaining biodiversity), demonstrate how authentic global communities, are being built through local action for (up to) global responsibilities. We looked at lessons from earlier research on 'federated identity' in IS, and apply them to Social Media ambitions.

Awareness of identity as an imagined "site" helps in managing all crossings over its boundaries, but if one can personally facilitate much of the traffic between this "site" and other larger imagined "sites" that are the communities in which one interacts both online and offline, then one can ensure a balanced control of the fluidity of the borders. If one cannot do so through a lack of proper control over such deliberate disclosures then ones reputation, opportunities and even safety may at times be at risk. Mass erosion of trust in the mainstream service providers may well then follow. People need to be fully aware of what Identity is and the issues that surround it, to be empowered rather than disempowered by these increasingly sophisticated social media platforms.

In *A Case Study in Representation and Control of Identity and Privacy* we present an innovative approach to dealing with the issues and actions that revolve around the control and disclosure of identity, outlined above. Initial emphasis is placed on 'knowing yourself well' through one's interests and roles in life. We present two conceptual models of the technology used to instantiated a digital-self, running on a personal computing device, that helps a person manage and evolve their own identity, as they interact in the online world, both through social media and the greater Internet.

In this chapter we urge a careful re-evaluation of the nature of online identity and a comprehensive comparison between its formation, standardization and circulation and that of identity in general. The central argument that runs across this chapter is two-fold, firstly, we promote and indeed demonstrate an initial shift in focus from the management of online identity to the nature and significance of identity itself, whose construction may be conceptualized as a process of sense making and strengthening. We demonstrate with theory, an example technology and a methodology, how this can be assisted at the individual level. Then, armed with a better understanding of identity, one can focus back upon the management of it more effectively, with a view to the individual taking more control of their own identity, particularly with regard to privacy. We emphasise the importance of this, as the technology space (most notably but not limited to, social media, search engines, and mobile apps) is increasingly transitioning us all into members of a global community, that needs to be functional not dysfunctional. It is important that we are each represented in this community as authentically as possible while also only revealing as much of ourselves that we agree to, in each sub-community in which we have a role. Gaining proper permission from each individual, and revealing transparency (to each person) regarding the storage and usage of identity data by service providers and their communities, is necessary for the sake of both individual privacy and reputation, and for gaining and maintaining trust in service providers, community organisations, and their governance. The larger the community, the more important these issues are.

REFERENCES

Allcott, H., & Gentzkow, M. (2017). Social Media and Fake News in the 2016 Election. *The Journal of Economic Perspectives, 31*(2), 211–236. doi:10.1257/jep.31.2.211

Anderson, B. (2006). *Imagined Communities: Reflections on the Origin and Spread of Nationalism.* London: Verso. (Original work published 1983)

Bleiberg, J., & West, D. M. (2015). *Political Polarization on Facebook.* Retrieved Nov 30, 2017 from https://www.brookings.edu/blog/techtank/2015/05/13/political-polarization-on-facebook

Boyd, D. (2011). *Faceted Id/entity: Managing representations in a digital world* (Master's Thesis). MIT Media Lab's Sociable Media Group. Retrieved on July 17, 2011 from http://smg.media.mit.edu/people/danah/thesis/thesis/

Bozdag, E., & Timmerman, J. (2011). Values in the filter bubble Ethics of Personalization Algorithms in Cloud Computing. In *Proceedings, 1st International Workshop on Values in Design – Building Bridges between RE, HCI and Ethics* (pp. 7-15). Lisbon, Portugal: Academic Press.

Chai, D. (2010). *New Groups: Stay Closer to Groups of People in Your Life.* The Facebook Blog. Retrieved April 2, 2013 from http://blog.facebook.com/blog.php?post=434700832130

Constine, J. (2017). *Facebook now has 2 billion monthly users… and responsibility.* Retrieved on 30 Nov 2017, from https://techcrunch.com/2017/06/27/facebook-2-billion-users/

Coyne, R. (2011). *Profile yourself (Narcissus on line).* Retrieved February 20, 2013, from http://richardcoyne.com/2011/02/12/narcissus-on-line/

Culter, K.-M. (2010). Why Mark Zuckerberg needs to come clean about his views on privacy. *SocialBeat*. Retrieved on July 15, 2011 from http://social.venturebeat.com/2010/05/13/zuckerberg-privacy/

De Botton, A. (2014). *The News, A User's Manual*. Penguin.

Facebook. (2017). *Open Graph Reference Document*. Retrieved from https://developers.facebook.com/docs/reference/opengraph

Fox, J. (2011). *Five million Facebook users are 10 or younger*. ConsumerReports.org. Retrieved on July 15, 2011 from http://news.consumerreports.org/electronics/2011/05/five-million-facebook-users-are-10-or-younger.html

Geron, T. (2011). *Facebook Moves Beyond 'Like'--To Listen, Watch, Eat, Run*. Retrieved on March 20, 2012, from http://www.forbes.com/sites/tomiogeron/2011/09/22/facebook-moves-beyond-like-to-listen-watch-eat-run/

Google. (2011). *Google Terms of Services*. Retrieved from http://www.google.com/accounts/TOS

Goschnick, S. (2005). *The FUN File Manager*. Accessed Nov 30, 2017 from http://digitalfriend.org/knowledge-tree/know.html

Goschnick, S. (2006). *The DigitalFriend: The First End-User Oriented Multi-Agent System*. OSDC 2006, the third Open Source Developers Conference, Melbourne, Australia.

Goschnick, S. (2014). Facebook From Five Thousand Feet: a visual mapping from conceptual model down to ground level graph api data. eBookDynasty.net.

Goschnick, S., & Graham, C. (2006). Augmenting Interaction and Cognition using Agent Architectures and Technology Inspired by Psychology and Social Worlds. *Universal Access in the Information Society*, *4*(3), 204–222. doi:10.100710209-005-0012-x

Goschnick, S., Sterling, L., & Sonenberg, L. (2015). Modelling Human Activity in People-Oriented Programming with Metamodels. International Journal of People-Oriented Programming, 4(2), 1-24. doi:10.4018/IJPOP.2015070101

Kirkpatrick, D. (2010). *The Facebook Effect: The Inside Story of the Company that is Connecting the World*. Simon & Schuster.

Macgregor, P. (1995). Chinese? Australian? the limits of geography and ethnicity as determinants of cultural identity. In J. Ryan (Ed.), *Chinese in Australia and New Zealand: a multidisciplinary approach* (pp. 5–20). New Delhi: New Age International.

Matthews, L. (2011). Google CEO confirms Google+ has more than 10 million users. *International Business Times*. Retrieved from http://www.ibtimes.com/articles/180869/20110715/google-google-google-circles-google-1.htm

Mirsky, Y. (2011). Identity =? *Jewish Ideas Daily*. Retrieved on March 17, 2013 from http://www.jewishideasdaily.com/839/features/identity/

Preece, J. (2017, March-April). How two billion smartphone users can save species! *Interaction*, 24(2), 26–33. doi:10.1145/3043702

Roussos, G., Peterson, D., & Patel, U. (2003). Mobile Identity Management: An Enacted View. *International Journal of E-Commerce, 8*(1), 81–100.

Samson, T. (2011). *Will Linkedin Suffer Facebook's privacy problems?* Retrieved on Nov 30, 2017, from http://www.infoworld.com/t/internet-privacy/will-linkedin-suffer-facebooks-privacy-problems-677

Satchell, C., Shanks, G., Howard, S., & Murphy, J. (2006). Knowing me, knowing you: end user perceptions of identity management systems. *Proceedings of the 14th European Conference on Information System (ECIS 2006)*, 795-806.

Sun, C. Y. (2012). Something Old, Something New, Something Borrowed, Something Blue: The Construction of online Identity and Its Consequences. *International Journal of People-Oriented Programming, 2*(1), 53–73. doi:10.4018/ijpop.2012010103

Weiner, J., & Battelle, J. (2010). A Conversation with Jeff Weiner. *Web 2.0 Summit 2010*. Retrieved from http://www.youtube.com/watch?v=R1yNDDLiHyY&feature=player_embedded

Wikipedia. (2017). *Criticism of Facebook*. Retrieved on Nov 30, 2017 from http://en.wikipedia.org/wiki/Criticism_of_Facebook

Wiszniewski, D., & Coyne, R. (2002). Mask and Identity: The Hermeneutics of Self-Construction in the Information Age. In Building Virtual Communities: Learning and Change in Cyberspace (pp. 191-214). Cambridge University Press.

Zuckerberg, M. (2017). *Building Global Community*. Retrieved on Nov 30, 2017 from https://www.facebook.com/notes/mark-zuckerberg/building-global-community/10154544292806634/

This research was previously published in Innovative Methods, User-Friendly Tools, Coding, and Design Approaches in People-Oriented Programming; pages 286-323, copyright year 2018 by Engineering Science Reference (an imprint of IGI Global).

Chapter 12
Development and Validation of the Social Media Self-Esteem Scale for Adolescents

Devanshi Sudhindar Rao
Christ University (Deemed), India

Aneesh Kumar
ⓘ https://orcid.org/0000-0003-1081-7201
Christ University (Deemed), India

ABSTRACT

Development of the self is a vital aspect during the period of adolescence. Interaction with peers contributes to the development of various aspects of self. Due to the technological advances in today's times, adolescents interact with their peers through social media sites and portals. It is essential to study this development in light of the increasing use of social media by adolescence. Thus, the study aimed at developing an item pool to tap the construct of social media influencing self-esteem of adolescents following the procedure of tool construction. Participants included adolescents ranging between 16 to 18 years of age, who have at least one social media account for personal use. There were 110 participants for the first phase and 397 participants for the second phase of the study. The scale has eight items with the overall reliability of .7. It indicates a fitting measure of self-esteem influenced by social media, with looking-glass self theory, according to which individuals develop their self, based on their perceptions of others responses to their behaviour.

INTRODUCTION

Adolescence is a period where interaction with peers becomes significant for the development of the self (Long & Chen, 2007. The feedback from their peers plays a vital role in the development of the adolescent's identity (Erikson, Theory of identity development, 1959). With society becoming sophisticated and technologically advanced, one must consider the developmental influences these new technologies

DOI: 10.4018/978-1-6684-6307-9.ch012

have on adolescents. Thus interaction with peers has become more influential because of technology (Hawi & Samaha, 2016).

There is widespread use of social media due to increased ownership of Smartphone and tablet ownership and advancement of technologies and substantial applications, to the extent that it often leads to addiction (Hawi & Samaha, 2016). According to a survey conducted by The Associated Chambers of Commerce and Industry of India (ASSOCHAM) Social Development Foundation (ASDF) in 2015 on Indian teenagers found that 95% of teens use the internet, 81% use social media and 72% use social media for more than once a day. Hence the online platforms play a crucial role in the social and emotional development of adolescents (O'Keeffe & Clarke-Pearson, 2011).

The internet has enabled new forms of interactions through uploading content on social media which could be photographs, of themselves or anything they like. The pictures are not only to celebrate the various important events in one's lives but also to record their daily life routines and interactions. Seeing that social media is an essential part of an adolescents' life, it does influence the way they think about themselves. Through posting pictures and other content, communication on social media, affects the adolescent (Stefnone, Lackaff, & Rosen, 2011).

Much of the content to present an online self is posted on social media. This self-presentation may be with a motivation to create a favourable impression on others, which corresponds to one's ideals. Now social media is a space where the teenagers can present themselves and explore the effects of this online self-presentation. The teenagers receive feedback on this self-presentation which may be positive or negative, which in turn affects their self-esteem (Herring & Kapidzic, 2015). When adolescents upload a post on social media, the response to it influences their self-esteem (Pounders, Kowalczyk, & Stowers, 2016). People receive recognition on social media through the number of likes or comments from their 'high-status friends' on the posts they put up, which may boost their self-esteem (Blease, 2015, as cited in Gallagher, 2017). Also, if they do not receive as many likes and comments as they thought they would, it affects their self-esteem. If they receive a large number of negative reactions to their posts, there would be an adverse effect on self-esteem (Gallagher, 2017).

The tone of the feedback received on social media influences adolescents' self-esteem. If they receive positive responses, it enhances their self-esteem, and if they receive negative responses it reduces their self-esteem (Valkenburg, Peter, & Schouten, 2006). Responses through "likes" and "comments", makes individuals aware of their limitations and shortcomings, which could lower their self-esteem or increase their self-esteem depending on the responses and how they have presented themselves (Gonzales & Hancock, 2011).

Enhanced self-esteem due to the responses they receive on their posts could have a detrimental effect on their behaviour. The response they receive on their self-presentation on social media enhances their self-esteem which could lead to a decrease in self-control and being involved in impulsive or indulgent behaviours (Wilcox & Stephen, 2013). Low self-esteem, on the other hand, could lead to the development of poor mental and physical health (Trzesniewski, Donnellan, Moffitt, Robins, Poulton, & Caspi, 2006). Therefore, a scale is developed to determine how social media influences adolescents' self- esteem.

Looking-Glass Theory of Self forms the theoretical background for developing the scale. According to this theory, one's self-concept is developed based on how one believes they appear in front of others. The self being involved in the social environment, must also be influenced by it. Thus, one's ideas about self are affected by how others evaluate us and more importantly, how we view these evaluations (Gecas & Schwalbe, 1983).

The scale would aim to give a view about how responses from social media influence an adolescent's self-esteem. Therefore, the objective of the study is to develop a scale tapping the construct of self-esteem in the context of social media, secure the items based on item analysis and test the psychometric properties of the developed unidimensional scale.

METHOD

Participants

Particpants of the study included 500 high school adolescents from various English medium school in Bengaluru city, India. All participants had a smartphone and at least one social media account. They had their accounts on Whatsapp, Instagram, Facebook and/or Snapchat. Participants age ranged from 16 to 18 years. The item analysis phase included 110 participants and final administration included 397 participants.

Research Design

A tool was developed to determine how social media influences self-esteem in adolescents. Social media self-esteem was defined as positive and negative feelings about the self-developed based on the frequency of the use of various social media platforms and nature of responses received on the posts uploaded (Gonzales & Hancock, 2011).

Materials

Item generation phase included the Rosenberg self-esteem scale which measures both positive and negative feelings about self. The Rosenberg self-esteem scale is a unidimensional scale with a 4-point Likert scale format ranging from strongly agree to strongly disagree. This scale inspired for wording and structuring the items to measure self-esteem. The alpha reliability of Rosenberg Self-Esteem Scale is 0.88 and the concurrent validity of the scale with a single item self-esteem scale is 0.75. The factor analysis of the ten items suggested a single general factor (Robins, Hendin, & Trzesniewski, 2001). Other resources include referring to the existing literature on how social media influences an adolescent's self-esteem. These resources provided an excellent source for the development of items of high quality for the five-point Likert scale. A potential tool to assess social media self-esteem was developed and tested.

Procedure

The researchers scrutinized and filtered the items. Three experts in the field of psychology with a research experience of more than ten years in the area of tool development or adolescent psychology reviewed and validated the tool items. The item pool was pilot tested on a group of six participants. The group rated the items as accept, reject, revise, change or if they were vague. The items that the majority accepted were retained and other items were reviewed based on the suggestions. The developed items were administered on 110 participants for item analysis. All ethical considerations of using human participants in the research were followed. The participants were briefed about their rights, including voluntary participation and informed consent. All participant response sheets were coded, and the participant identity was maintained.

Data Analysis

Item analysis was done to determine the item discrimination index by the point biserial method and Cronbach's alpha. Based on the point bi-serial value, the mean and standard deviation of each item, items were reduced, and the scale was given shape.

The researcher approached 500 participants. Out of which responses of 397 participants were fit for use. The rest of the 103 data were rejected due to the response being incomplete or because they did not fit the inclusion criteria. Exploratory Factor Analysis was run on the data that determined if there were any underlying factors developed. Following this procedure, the items that do fall in factors were eliminated, and the final scale was developed.

RESULTS AND DISCUSSION

Phase 1

Based on the theoretical background, the item pool generation was completed along the dimensions of self-esteem and responses from social media. A total of 80 items were generated. The response pattern that was selected was five-point Likert-scale ranging from strongly agree to strongly disagree. The objective of this phase was to use expert evaluation and statistical analysis to decide between retaining and discarding items.

Expert Evaluation

Three experts from the field of social psychology evaluated the items and provided their expert validation to the items. They assessed the items along with the basis of the context, simplicity of words and how closely it tapped the construct. The items were generated with differently worded items. After expert validation, many items were eliminated based on redundancy in meaning, context and language. The number of items retained was 24. All the items were along the dimensions of self-esteem influenced by social media.

The 24-item scale was administered on a hundred and ten participants. The results were as follows.

Item Analysis

The score of 1-5 was assigned to the responses strongly disagree to strongly agree respectively. Negatively worded items were reverse scored. The mean, standard deviation, correlation and bi-serial correlation values of the items were computed. The items with mean values ranging from 2-4 and standard deviation value of greater than one were retained (Sungoh & Lyngdoh, 2017). Mean and standard deviation values were obtained to compute item difficulty. Items such as 'I feel happy about myself when my post is shared by someone' had a standard deviation value of .975 which indicated low item difficulty. Thus, these items were rejected from the pool.

Table 1. Item analysis of self-esteem influenced by social media scale showing mean, SD, point bi-serial and Cronbach's alpha if the item is deleted

Items	Mean	SD	r_{pbs}	Cronbach's Alpha if Item Deleted
I feel satisfied with myself when I get the expected number of likes on my post.*	3.339	1.155	-0.16	.514
I think I am not good enough to be on social media when I don't get the likes I desire.	3.60	1.080	+0.14	.479
When I get a desired number of likes I think I have qualities that are admirable.	3.17	1.153	-0.18	.477
When I get lesser likes than I expect, I feel like should delete my account.*	4.10	1.055	+0.3	.479
I feel I am not good enough to be on social media.	3.54	1.291	+0.15	.492
I don't feel the need to get a certain number of likes every time I post something on social media.*	3.62	1.043	-0.21	.508
I will remove my post from social media, if I don't get the likes I expected.	4.11	1.040	+0.3	.506
Gaining a particular number of likes on my post is a way gaining approval from my peers.*	2.74	1.144	+0.07	.507
Getting a high number of likes on my post is a matter of recognition for me.*	2.78	1.291	-0.28	.537
I am not affected when I get a low number of likes on my post.*	3.99	1.068	-0.13	.486
When I am complimented on social media, I feel good about myself.*	3.62	1.034	+0.21	.468
I feel bad about myself when I don't get any comments on the post I upload on social media.	3.75	1.150	+0.22	.481
I am not bothered about the comments I receive on my post on social media.*	3.77	1.095	-0.12	.499
Only when I receive good comments on my post I feel good about myself.*	2.49	1.185	-0.12	.535
Whenever I get negative comments on my post, I believe it's true.	3.40	1.181	+0.37	.480
I feel admirable about myself when I gain a follower.*	3.09	1.233	-0.05	.507
Having a certain number of followers is not important for me.	3.84	1.134	+0.28	.516
I feel that I am not good enough to be on social media when I lose some followers.	3.91	1.095	+0.13	.475
Looking at the number of likes on someone else's post, I feel that I can reach that number too.*	2.93	1.308	-0.11	.530
It is very important for me to get more number of likes than others.	3.81	1.183	+0.39	.508
I am satisfied with the number of followers on social media*	3.80	1.077	-0.07	.478
I feel good about myself when I see I have same number of posts as my close friends.*	3.25	1.158	-0.16	.533
I feel happy about myself when my post is shared by someone.*	3.69	.975	-0.12	.490
I feel I am good enough to be on social media.*	3.55	1.118	+0.08	.456

*Indicates rejected items

Point bi-serial correlation value was calculated to compute the item discrimination index. This was done by arranging the values in ascending order. The first thirty responses were assigned with the value of zero and the lower thirty responses with the value of one. The difference between the upper 27% of responses and lower 27% of responses of the total 110 responses shows value of item discrimination. As mentioned in Table 1, the items that showed a point biserial value of or above +0.12were retained and the items which showed a point bi-serial value lesser than +0.12were rejected. Items with point biserial of .012 show acceptable point-biserial values (Varma, 2006). Thus, the items marked '*' were rejected from the scale.

The Cronbach's alpha- score of reliability was .509. Items which showed that upon rejection increased the overall reliability above .509 were rejected. Based on this, the above twenty-five items were rejected and nine items were retained. The revised scale consists of nine items. The reliability of the revised scale was to .780.

Phase 2

Exploratory Factor Analysis (EFA) is a technique for data exploration and to determine the structure of factors to be analysed. This technique is also a data reduction method and it uses several extraction methods for constructing a scale. The objective of this stage was to identify the factors of the scale using principal component analysis. The nine-item scale was administered to 397 adolescents based on purposive sampling. The data obtained was run in SPSS to compute factor analysis. Sample adequacy and Bartlett's test of sphericity and Kaiser-Meyer-Olkin (KMO) were measured first. The results indicated that the KMO value is .841 which indicates the sample size was adequate and significant. Bartlett's test result is also significant ($x^2(36) = 947.720, p < .05$). These results indicated that the data was fit for running the process of factor analysis (Williams, Onsman, & Brown, 2010). Table 2 represents KMO and Bartlett's test results of sampling adequacy.

Table 2. Results of KMO and Bartlett's test

KMO	x^2	df	p
.897	947.720	36	.000

The purpose of exploratory factor analysis is to find the number of factors that explain the correlations. The most commonly used method of factor analysis is the Principal Component Analysis and widely used factor rotation is the Varimax rotation. The standard Varimax factors denote a high possibility of the depiction of corresponding domain factors (Kaiser, 1958). As commonly considered, items attaining the eigenvalue of one or above due to high factor loading were retained (Hayton, Allen, & Scarpello, 2004). This paved the way for two factors. Factor 1 explained 29.762% of the variance, whereas factor 2 explained 10.400%.

Commonalities measure the percent of the variance in a given variable explained by all the factors jointly and may be interpreted as the reliability of the indicator. An item with a commonality of less than .40, may either not be related to the other items or additional factor be explored. A high value of extraction indicates that extracted items represent the variable well (Costello & Osborne, 2005). The range of commonalities obtained was .059 to .609. Table 3 shows the commonalities for each variable.

Now, item 'Having a certain number of followers is not important for me' obtained a commonality of .059, which is less. Thus, this item was removed from the scale. Other items, with commonalities less than .40, such as the item 'I will remove my post from social media if I don't get the likes I expected', 'I feel bad about myself when I don't get any comments on the post I upload on social media' and 'Whenever I get negative comments on my post, I believe it is true' had to be deleted from the present scale, but the statements seem to have potential to gauge more information about the social media self-esteem of the adolescent and thus could have items of the similar nature in further research.

Table 3. Extraction values obtained by principal axis factoring (commonalities)

Items	Extraction
I think that I am not good enough to be on social media when I don't get the likes I desire.	.609
When I get lesser likes than I expect, I feel like I should delete my account.	.507
I feel I am not good enough to be on social media, if I don't get the likes I expected.	.432
I will remove my post from social media if I don't get the likes I expected.	.387
I feel bad about myself when I don't get any comments on the post I upload on social media.	.399
Whenever I get negative comments on my post, I believe it is true.	.186
Having a certain number of followers is not important for me.	.059
I feel that I am not good enough to be on social media when I lose some followers.	.511
It is very important for me to get more number of likes than others.	.526

Table 4. Rotated factor matrix of factor loading

Items	Component	
	1	2
I think that I am not good enough to be on social media when I don't get the likes I desire.	.777	
When I get lesser likes than I expect, I feel like I should delete my account.	.670	
I feel I am not good enough to be on social media, if I don't get the likes I expected.	-.655	
I will remove my post from social media if I don't get the likes I expected.	.532	.322
I feel bad about myself when I don't get any comments on the post I upload on social media.	.502	.384
Whenever I get negative comments on my post, I believe it is true.	.387	
Having a certain number of followers is not important for me.	-	
I feel that I am not good enough to be on social media when I lose some followers.	.596	.395
It is very important for me to get more number of likes than others.	.396	.608

Table 4 represents the rotated factor matrix of factor loading. It indicated how much the item representing the factor it had loaded in. For instance, all the items except item 'Having a certain number of followers is not important for me' had not loaded in either of the factors. Thus, it indicated that the item did not measure anything on the scale or either of the factors.

There were two emerging factors. The first factor threw light on how one feels based on the likes, comments and followers they receive for their posts on social media. The items in this factor indicated the aspect of self-worth, which is a factor under self-esteem. Self-worth is the evaluative experience of oneself as a social object, good or bad person (Tafarodi & Swann, 2001). The items indicated how the individuals ascribe themselves a social value based on the responses they receive on social media. The second factor indicated a comparison of self with others. It showed how one would feel based on comparing their responses to their post on social media with that of the responses on the posts of others.

However, as seen, item 'It is very important for me to get more number of likes than others', is loaded in both the factors. When careful attention to the item was paid it did not stand out significantly from the other items. The item 'It is very important for me to get more number of likes than others' indicated low self-esteem due to low number of likes on the post uploaded on social media, which did not seem to be significantly different from items, 'I think I am not good enough to be on social media when I don't get the likes I desire', 'When I get lesser likes than I expect, I feel like I should delete my account', 'I feel I am not good enough to be on social media, if I don't get the likes I expected' and 'I will remove my post from social media if I don't get the likes I expected'.Therefore, it was not created as a different dimension . The revised scale is a unidimensional scale. The item 'Having a certain number of followers, is not important for me' did not have loadings in either of the factors, so it was removed from the scale. On the whole, the retained items on the scale indicated the influence of social media on the adolescent's self-esteem, for instance, the items tapped on how not receiving a certain number of likes, or how having certain comments on their post would influence how they feel about themselves being on social media.

Looking-Glass Self Theory asserts that one's self-concept is a reflection of one's perceptions about how one appears to others. The self is inseparable from social life and necessarily involves some reference to others. Thus, one's attitudes about the self can be based on the person's observations of his behaviour and the stimulus in which it occurs. These attitudes could be functionally similar to those that an observer would make about the person (Shrauger & Shoeneman, 1979). Thus, using Looking-Glass Self theory as the theoretical base among adolescents, the social media self-esteem scale provided an appropriate measure for self-esteem. The items indicated how one's self-evaluations are affected by the evaluations which others have on us and importantly, how one perceives those evaluations. Items such as 'I think I am not good enough to be on social media when I don't get the likes I desire', 'When I get lesser likes than I expect, I feel like should delete my account', 'I will remove my post from social media, if I don't get the likes I expected', 'I feel bad about myself when I don't get any comments on the post I upload on social media', 'Whenever I get negative comments on my post, I believe it's true' and 'I feel that I am not good enough to be on social media when I lose some followers' indicated adolescents' perception of themselves based on other's responses to their post. The item such as 'I feel I am not good enough to be on social media', signified individuals' overall social media self-esteem, to understand how the individual feels about themself being on social media. The item 'It is very important for me to get more number of likes than others' was added to the scale since comparison of self is another reason why adolescents use social media and which also contributes to their self-esteem (Barker, 2009).

In this stage the reliability of the scale was computed. Cronbach's alpha reliability was 0.653. However, Split-half test of reliability showed reliability was 0.7.

This tool is useful for organisations working with adolescents and adolescents with internet addiction. It helps to determine how self-esteem is related to internet addiction or the use of social media. Individuals with lower self-esteem and traits with neuroticism reported more definite addictive tendencies (Ehrenberg, Juckes, White, & Walsh, 2008). The tool could be used for further research on adolescent's self-development in this growing age technology. There is growing research on how adolescents use social media and how it influences their development of self (Valkenburg & Peter, 2011).

Furthermore, the scale could help as a determinant if adolescents spend more time than required on social media. Parents and teachers could guide them on the use of social media and how adolescents can build their confidence and self-recognition. Adolescents make comparisons of themselves with others on social media which may negatively affect their self-confidence. Increased usage of social media and increased comparisons could indicate low self-esteem (Jan, Soomro, & Ahmad, 2017).

Limitations

There could be more data added for item analysis phase so that it would provide better information about the items to be retained so that more items could be retained. The scale has not been through the process of Confirmatory Factor Analysis (CFA). Thus, the underlying factors weren't confirmed and the Convergent and Divergent Validity of the scale was also not determined.

Implications

Further research may focus on developing more items on the scale. The developed scale could be resourceful in understanding if low self-esteem due to the influence of social media, predicts internet addiction. The scale could also help to determine if low social media self-esteem is related to depression among adolescents, considering the high use of social media among them. The scale could also help to predict the amount of time being spent on the consumption of social media.

CONCLUSION

The present study developed and validated the instrument for measuring how social media influence the self-esteem of adolescents. Social Media Self-Esteem was measured using the definition- the positive and negative feelings about the self, which was developed based on the use of various social media platforms and nature and responses received on the posts uploaded (Gonzales & Hancock, 2011). Looking at adolescents' growing use of social media, during crucial period in life where they are developing their identity and self-image, it essential to understand how social media influenced their self-esteem. Considering how important the development of self-esteem affects their growth, this tool provides much more help to understand this aspect.

REFERENCES

ASSOCHAM. (2015, December 21). *76% minors under age of 13 use Youtube: ASSOCHAM Survey*. Retrieved from Assocham India: http://assocham.org/newsdetail.php?id=5400

Barker, V. (2009). Older adolescents' motivations for social network site use: The influence of gender, group identity, and collective self-esteem. *Cyberpsychology & Behavior*, *12*(2), 209–213. Advance online publication. doi:10.1089/cpb.2008.0228 PMID:19250021

Costello, A. B., & Osborne, J. W. (2005). Best practices in exploratory factor analysis: Four recommendations for getting the most from your analysis. *Practical Assessment, Research & Evaluation*, *10*(7), 1–9. https://www.pareonline.net/pdf/v10n7.pdf

Ehrenberg, A., Juckes, S., White, K. M., & Walsh, S. P. (2008). Personality and self-esteem as predictors of young people's technology use. *Cyberpsychology & Behavior*, *11*(6), 739–741. doi:10.1089/cpb.2008.0030 PMID:18991531

Erikson, E. (1959). *Theory of identity development*. Retrieved from Child Development Psychology: http://childdevpsychology.yolasite.com/resources/theory%20of%20identity%20erikson.pdf

Gallagher, S. M. (2017). The influence of social media on teen's self-esteem. *Rowan Digital Works*. https://rdw.rowan.edu/etd

Gecas, V., & Schwalbe, L. M. (1983). Beyond the looking glass-self: Social structure and efficacy based self-esteem. *Social Psychology Quarterly*, *46*(2), 77–88. doi:10.2307/3033844 PMID:6879222

Gonzales, A. L., & Hancock, J. T. (2011). Mirror, mirror on my facebook wall: Effects of exposure to facebook on self- esteem. *Cyberpsychology, Behavior, and Social Networking*, *14*(1-2), 79–83. Advance online publication. doi:10.1089/cyber.2009.0411 PMID:21329447

Hawi, N. S., & Samaha, M. (2016). The relations among social media addiction, self-esteem and life satisfaction in university students. *Social Science Computer Review*, ●●●, 1–11. doi:10.1177/0894439316660340

Hayton, J. C., Allen, D. G., & Scarpello, V. (2004). Factor retention decisions in exploratory factor analysis: A tutorial on parallel analysis. *Organizational Research Methods*, *7*(2), 191–205. doi:10.1177/1094428104263675

Herring, S. C., & Kapidzic, S. (2015). Teens, gender and self-presentation in social media. *International encyclopedia of social and behavioural sciences*. doi:10.1016/B978-0-08-097086-8.64108-9

Hinduja, S., & Patchhin, J. W. (2008). Personal information of adolescents on the internet: A quantitative analysis of myspace. *Journal of Adolescence*, *31*(1), 125–146. doi:10.1016/j.adolescence.2007.05.004 PMID:17604833

Jan, M., Soomro, A. S., & Ahmad, N. (2017). Impact of social media on self-esteem. *European Scientific Journal*, *13*(23), 329–341. doi:10.19044/esj.2017.v13n23p329

Kaiser, H. (1958). The varimax criterion for analytic rotation in factor analysis. *Pschometrika, 23*, 187-200. https://www.psychometricsociety.org/sites/default/files/kaiser_citation_classic_varimax.pdf

Livsey, B. K. (2013). Self-concept and online social networking in young adolescents: implications for school counsellors. *University of Texas at Austin.* https://repositories.lib.utexas.edu/handle/2152/22468

Long, J. H., & Chen, G.-M. (2007). The impact of internet usage on adolescent self-identity development. *University of Rhode Island.* https://digitalcommons.uri.edu/com_facpubs

O'Keeffe, G. S., & Clarke-Pearson, K. (2011). *Clinical Report- The impact of social media on children, adolescents and families*. American Academy of Pediatrics. doi:10.1542/peds.2011-0054

Pounders, K., Kowalczyk, C., & Stowers, K. (2016). Insight into the motivation of selfie postings: impression management and self-esteem. *European Journal of Marketing, 50*. doi:10.1108/EJM-07-2015-0502

Shrauger, J. S., & Shoeneman, T. J. (1979). Symbolic interactionist view of self-concept: Throough the looking glass darkly. *Psychological Bulletin*, *86*(3), 549–573. doi:10.1037/0033-2909.86.3.549

Stefnone, M. A., Lackaff, D., & Rosen, D. (2011). Contingencies of self-worth and social-networking-site behavior. *Cyber Psychology, Behavior and Social Networking, 14*. doi:10.1108/EJM-07-2015-0502

Sungoh, S., & Lyngdoh, S. (2017). Construction and standardisation of teacher's attitude scale towrds constructivist approach in teaching (TASCAT). *Educational Quest*, *8*, 305–308. doi:10.5958/2230-7311.2017.00068.X

Tafarodi, R., & Swann, W. J. Jr. (2001). Two-dimensional self-esteem: Theory and measurement. *Personality and Individual Differences*, *31*(5), 653–673. doi:10.1016/S0191-8869(00)00169-0

Trzesniewski, K. H., Donnellan, M. B., Moffitt, T. E., Robins, R. W., Poulton, R., & Caspi, A. (2006). Low self-esteem during adolescence predicts poor health, criminal behavior and limited prospects durig adulthood. *Developmental Psychology*, *42*(2), 381–390. doi:10.1037/0012-1649.42.2.381 PMID:16569175

Valkenburg, P. M., & Peter, J. (2011). Online communication among adolescents: An integrated model of its attraction, opportunities and risks. *The Journal of Adolescent Health*, *48*(2), 121–127. doi:10.1016/j.jadohealth.2010.08.020 PMID:21257109

Valkenburg, P. M., Peter, J., & Schouten, A. (2006). Friend networking sites and their relationship to adolescents' well-being and social self-esteem. *Cyberpsychology & Behavior*, *9*(5), 584–590. doi:10.1089/cpb.2006.9.584 PMID:17034326

Varma, S. (2006). Preliminary item statistics using point-biserial correlation and p-values. *Educational Data Systems*, 1-8. https://jcesom.marshall.edu/media/24104/Item-Stats-Point-Biserial.pdf

Wilcox, K., & Stephen, A. T. (2013). Are close friends the enemy? online social networks, self-esteem, and self control. *Journal of Consumer Research*. doi:10.1086/668794

Williams, B., Onsman, A., & Brown, T. (2010). Exploratory factor analysis: A five-step guide for novices. *Journal of Emergency Primary Health Care*, *8*(3). Advance online publication. doi:10.33151/ajp.8.3.93

This research was previously published in the International Journal of Cyber Behavior, Psychology and Learning (IJCBPL), 10(4); pages 1-13, copyright year 2020 by IGI Publishing (an imprint of IGI Global).

Chapter 13
A Study of Networking and Information Exchange Factors Influencing User Participation in Niche Social Networking Sites

Carlos Andres Osorio
https://orcid.org/0000-0002-5562-3868
University of Manizales, Manizales, Colombia

Savvas Papagiannidis
https://orcid.org/0000-0003-0799-491X
Newcastle University Business School, Newcastle upon Tyne, UK

ABSTRACT

This article tests a number of networking and information exchange factors that may influence users' participation in niche social networking sites (SNS). The factors identified in the literature review as influential for participation in social networking sites were implemented in a model tested using quantitative data from 152 users. Gratifications related to socialising, self-status seeking, social support, and learning and innovativeness were identified as significant for participating in niche SNS. As only a subset of the general purpose SNS gratifications were found to be of statistical significance for niche sites, it is suggested that further research that includes a wider set of factors is necessary to determine the similarities and differences between gratifications influencing participation in general purpose and niche SNS.

1. INTRODUCTION

Users are a critical resource for the success of any social networking site (SNS) (Xu et al. 2014). Achieving users' participation in SNS is considered to be one of the main factors in having a sustainable community in which users remain engaged over time. For this reason, researchers and practitioners are interested in finding what the factors influencing the participation in the network are. So far, research has had a

DOI: 10.4018/978-1-6684-6307-9.ch013

strong focus on large SNS, which are mostly associated with general purpose SNS like Facebook and Twitter (Leskovec et al. 2008, Foregger 2008, Goggins et al. 2011, Smock et al. 2011, Tosun 2012, Kourouthanassis et al. 2015, Chen 2014, Yang and Lin 2014) General purpose networks are only part of the SNS world, which also includes niche SNS (Boyd and Ellison 2008). Niche SNS seek to narrow audiences by focusing on characteristics of the population, activities, identity and/or affiliations (Boyd and Ellison, 2008). Examples of niche SNS include Beautifulpeople.com, which is a network oriented to good looking people, Cafemom.com, which is oriented to women who are or who are going to be mothers, and Mychurch.org, which is oriented to Christian people.

One of the most accepted definitions of what a social networking site is was given by Boyd and Ellison (2008), who defined an SNS as "*web-based services that allow individuals to (1) construct a public or semi-public profile within a bounded system, (2) articulate a list of other users with whom they share a connection, and (3) view and traverse their list of connections and those made by others within the system*" (Boyd and Ellison, 2008, p. 2). This definition implies that the scope of the network is defined by the system, which these authors use later to differentiate between general purpose and niche SNS. The main difference relies on the purpose of the SNS, wherein the niche ones focus on characteristics of the population as noted above, narrowing their public to people with those characteristics or people interested in what the network is about. Niche SNS are gaining part of the market due precisely to their private nature (Bhappu and Schultze 2018, Calero-Valdez et al 2018, Crawford et al 2017, Kwon et al 2017, Lim, et al 2018). An additional fact arising is that Facebook, which is the most representative example of a general purpose SNS, has been losing a significant amount of users recently, not only due to privacy issues such as Cambridge Analytica, but also due to generational change (Castillo, 2018; Welch, 2018), which helps to show how people prefer to be with others who are similar to them, known as homophily (Kim, Lee, & Bonn, 2016; Kwon et al., 2017). Since SNS are now part of our everyday routine, if people leave Facebook, they will go to another SNS, and that is where niche SNS become an alternative given the homophilous tendency of SNS users.

A parallel topic that arises with the study of SNS types is the study of SNS user types, which made it possible to discover that not everyone in the network behaves in the same way. Research like that developed by Brandtzæg (2012) proposed the following types of SNS users: Sporadics, Lurkers, Socializers, Debaters, which is similar to Constantinides et al (2010), who identified beginners, habitual Users, outstanding Users and Experts. These typologies contrast with the one proposed by Kilian et al, (2012) who, in their research about millennials, identified three clusters, namely: the restrained millennials, the entertainment-seeking millennials and the highly connected millennials. A similar approach was taken by Bulut and Doğan (2017), who identified advanced users, business-oriented users, communication seekers, and dawdlers. The classifications of SNS users shows a variety of approaches that this topic can take, producing different typologies. However, acknowledging the importance of user typologies, this topic goes beyond the scope of the present research, as we first have to find whether there is a difference between General Purpose and Niche SNS, and then we can start wondering about the types of users and their behaviours on the networks.

Due to the difficulty of accessing niche networks and their participants, it is not surprising that most research related to SNS participation typically revolves around general purpose SNS (Boyd and Ellison, 2008), leaving a gap for research into niche SNS. Given the differences in the nature and objectives of the two types of networks, it cannot be assumed that that the findings obtained for general purpose networks can be generalised for niche SNS. In fact differences in motivations for using SNS may exist even for general-purpose networks (Chung et al 2015, Gan & Wang 2015, Kim and Jiyoung 2017, Phua et al.

2017, Krasnova 2017, Bae 2018, Bulut & Doğan 2017). This paper's objective is to test this assumption, by examining a number of factors related to networking and information exchange identified for general purpose networks in a niche SNS environment. A better understanding of the reasons for using niche SNS and the differences from and similarities to general purpose ones could have significant implications. For example, it can inform the design and promotion of such networks when competing against the general purpose ones for users' attention. Given the above, in this project we adopted the uses and gratifications theory in order to study users' participation and, more specifically, the networking and information exchange factors that affect participation. The section following presents the relevant literature and the hypotheses to be tested. The paper then continues by outlining the methodology followed. In turn, it presents the results and findings of the analysis, which are put in the context of the previous studies. The paper concludes by considering future research avenues.

2. LITERATURE REVIEW

One of the most significant indicators of SNS health is the proportion of active users, showing to what extent people are using the network, which can be complemented by the number of transactions or the amount of bandwidth required. Since the success of the network is mostly associated with participation, this has become the main focus for academics and practitioner research. The most common approaches to studying SNS participation are framed within the Theory of Planned Behaviour (TPB) (Hajli et al. 2015, Huang and Shiau 2015, Chen et al. 2016) and its variation, the Decomposed Theory of Planned Behaviour (Gironda and Korgaonkar 2014).

TPB aims to explain a particular human behaviour based on the intention, which is influenced by attitudinal beliefs and social norms and perceived behaviour control. According to TPB, attitudinal belief is orientated towards the favourability that the user has towards performing certain behaviour. Subjective norm is related to the social pressure to perform the behaviour, and perceived behavioural control (PBC) is related to the resources and opportunities available that may influence the behaviour (Ajzen, 1991). One of the main criticisms of the TPB is the unidimensionality of the factors involved in the standard TPB model for explaining belief formation (Hsu et al., 2006, Taylor and Todd, 1995). Closely related to the TPB, the Technology Acceptance Model has also been used to investigate participation (Shen 2015, Zhu et al. 2014, Xu et al. 2012, Lorenzo-Romero, Constantinides, & Alarcón-del-Amo, 2011), Kwon and Wen 2010). This model, similarly to the TPB, predicts the behaviour based on the intention, considering attitude, perceived usefulness and perceived ease of use as antecedents. The parsimony of TAM is also one of its potential shortcomings as *"it is unreasonable to expect that one model, and one so simple, would explain decisions and behaviour fully across a wide range of technologies, adoption situations, and differences in decision making and decision makers"*. (Bagozzi, 2007, p. 244). These theories find their origins in the Theory of Reasoned Action (Fishbein and Ajzen 1975), and are based on a cognitive/behavioural framework, aimed at predicting a behaviour (in this case SNS participation) based on the intention to perform that behaviour. A second stream of user participation research follows the Uses and Gratifications (U&G) theory (Baek 2011, Giannakos et al. 2013, Yang and Lin 2014, Hsu et al. 2015, Chiu and Huang 2015b, Chiu and Huang 2015a, Wei et al. 2015, Bulut and Doğan 2017, Bae 2018, Gan & Wang, 2015), which is based on psychosocial variables attempting to understand decision making processes about media (Rubin 2002). For this project a flexible approach such as the

U&G theory was better suited to the aims of the project, as it includes a broader variety of constructs to understand users' participation.

The theory of uses and gratifications (U&G) was postulated by Katz et al. (1973), based on sociological and psychological foundations. U&G has been used to explain the reasons for choosing one particular medium over another, suggesting that *"people's needs influence their media selections; by seeking out and using specific media, people can meet these individual needs"* (Foregger 2008, p. 2). The initial aims of U&G theory were "a) to explain how people use media to gratify their needs, b) to understand motives for media behaviour, and c) to identify functions or consequences that follow" (Rubin 2002, p. 166). The original foundations of the model were proposed by Katz (as cited by Forreger 2008, p. 15) in five elements: *"a) the audience is active, b) media choice depends on the audience's link between media and need gratification, c) media compete with other sources, both interpersonal and other media, for need satisfaction, d) audience members can self-report their needs, and e) value judgments of mass media content should be suspended until motives and gratifications are understood"*. These assumptions were revised by Rubin (Rubin 2002), who proposed an updated version based on the evolution of the media. The revised assumptions are: firstly, that communication behaviour is goal-directed, purposive, and motivated; secondly that people select media; thirdly that many factors guide our media selection; fourthly, that media compete with other channels for messages; and finally that people are typically more influential than media (Rubin 2002). The updated version considers the role of the user as a more active element, influenced mainly by needs, social and psychological factors and interpersonal interactions (Rubin 2002), along with the influence of the messages in the selection of the media. These assumptions fit with the aim of the research as people have the choice between general purpose and niche SNS to post what they want to say, as well as where to look for information and where to spend their time. Baek et al. (2011) stated that the main objective of this theory is to examine the motivations for media use, as well as the factors influencing these motivations by the users. Given the above, this paper focuses on the networking and information exchange factors that affect user intentions to participate in niche networks. These are discussed in more detail below.

2.1. Networking and Information Exchange in Niche Networks

2.1.1. Networking and Socialising

Networking and socialising are needs related to building and maintaining a network of contacts, as well as the benefits obtained from the contacts in the network. Bulut and Doğan (2017) studied how social gratifications such as socialisation and status seeking influence not only the usage of the networks, but also how they change according to the type of user present on the networks. The creation and maintenance of contacts in the social network looks to build the network of contacts either with relationships previously created (offline) or with new relationships created online (Cha 2010, Foregger 2008, Kim et al. 2010, Kim et al. 2011, Papacharissi and Rubin 2000, Park et al. 2009, Sangwan 2005, Xu et al. 2012, Hou 2011, Hsu et al. 2015, Bae 2018). Regarding the benefits obtained from the network, the gratifications of this type are related to what can be achieved (and/or offered) through the interaction with the members of the network. Thus, *socialising* is at the core of the gratifications for SNS participation (Goggins et al. 2011, Chen 2014, Cheung et al. 2011, Hsu et al. 2015, Park et al. 2009, Cocosila and Igonor 2015, Bulut and Doğan 2017. Due to the social needs of human beings, SNS have been gaining terrain as a space to develop and enhance the social activities that were held offline previously, hence having a positive influence on SNS participation. Associated to socialisation are the gratifications related to *interconnectedness,* which relates to expanding your network of contacts by finding people through existing contacts, having a direct relation with SNS usage (Foregger 2008, Ali-Hassan et al. 2015, Syn and Oh 2015). Another frequent use of SNS is m*aintaining of old ties* (Foregger 2008, Joinson 2008, Ellison et al. 2007, Raacke and Bonds-Raacke 2008), which is exemplified by bringing friends from offline networks, such as friends from school or former work colleagues, and adding them to your online network. Along with the use of SNS to find their old friends, people are highly motivated to use SNS to find new friends (*seeking friends*) (Kim et al. 2011, Ellison et al. 2007, Huang 2008, Papacharissi and Rubin 2000, Smock et al. 2011).

Based on the presented literature we hypothesise that:

H: (1) Socialising, (2) interconnectedness, (3) maintaining old ties, (4) seeking friends, have a positive and significant effect on the intensity of participation in niche SNS.

Using SNS to share information with your whole network or part of it is a popular gratification. Among the examples are the changes in relationship status such as being in a relationship, break-ups, engagements, etc., or sharing photos from different events. Likewise, the groups are used to arrange events and resolve conflicts in the group (Dimmick et al. 2007, Baek et al. 2011, Ramirez Jr et al. 2008, Hsu et al. 2015).

Interpersonal utility (Cha 2010, Papacharissi and Rubin 2000, Wong 2012), which is related with the information that the user finds important for personal life, such as the opinion that other people have about him or her, information about social events or keeping up to date with what is going on in the user's circles. Following the utility of the SNS, there is an additional gratification related with the image that the user wants to project in the SNS, which is labelled *self-status seeking* (Park et al. 2009, Hsu et al. 2015), which has traditionally been presented as the efforts that people make to present themselves in a particular maner to others. The image that the user portrays in the network can be a real reflection of the user's life, or a desired image that the user wants to project, which is associated with belongingness and narcissistic behaviours (Schau and Gilly 2003, Pugh 2010, Zhao et al. 2008, Mehdizadeh 2010). In this regard, Chung et al (2017) presented the self-image, which is closely related to self-status seeking, as a "constant process of controlling and managing information to continuously deliver one's specific image to others" (p. 82), which can be connected with the finding of Baek et al. (2011), who found the likelihood for people to share information about themselves, with this information sharing having an impact on SNS usage. A final gratification in this group is *seeking social support,* which is very common in networks related with health issues like Ihadcancer.com, in which the members support each other by providing pastoral care as well as sharing treatments and medicines that have helped them to feel better, having a positive effect on network participation (Kim et al. 2011, Shen 2015, Hajli et al. 2015, Ridings and Gefen 2004, Wong 2012, Bae 2018). Chung et al (2017) argue that the more people interact with each other, the more they start creating this attachment to others, which allows them to extend and ask for help given the situation, which in turn strengthens the ties between them.

Based on the above we propose that:

H: (5) interpersonal utility, (6) self-status seeking, and (7) seeking social support have a positive and significant effect on the intensity of participation in niche SNS.

2.1.2. Information Exchange

Information exchange is a key motivation for participating in social networking sites, as studied by Chung et al. (2017), considering the number of members in the network, social interaction helping and self-image as predictors of this factor and Crawford et al. (2017), who focused on the self-status motivation of the user. This information could be about the user (i.e. personal information such as photos, list of contacts, movies, bands, among others) or information about specific interests or purposes, for example photography, astronomy, etc. Information exchange gratifications are related to the second type of information, considering the SNS as a repository of information about specific topics. For the *information exchange*, the user comes to the network either looking for information and the opinions of the members of the networks about topics of interest to them, or looking to acquire deeper knowledge of the topics discussed in the network (Cha 2010, Foregger 2008, Kim et al. 2011, Papacharissi and Rubin 2000, Huang 2008, Chung et al. 2012, Park et al. 2014, Chang and Chen 2014, Hsu et al. 2015, Park et al. 2015, Syn and Oh 2015, Yen 2016, Chung et al. 2015). This *information seeking* and exchange results in a new alternative type of web search known as "*social search*" (Lampe et al. 2006), as well as in a "*social shopping*" process (Kang and Johnson 2015), which is based on the opinions of the network members about specific topics.

Attached to the *information seeking* are the *learning and knowledge gratifications*, whereby it is expected that people will access better or specialised resources that are not usually shared in the general SNS groups, this being an attractive motivation to use the SNS (Cha 2010, Huang 2008, Kim et al. 2011, Papacharissi and Rubin 2000, Park et al. 2009, Chunngam et al. 2014, Lingreen et al. 2013, Syn and Oh 2015, Yen 2016). *Innovativeness* is a popular gratification in SNS (Huang 2008, Sangwan 2005, Park et al. 2015), which is related to the openness to new ideas (Cha 2010, Rogers 2003). The next factor is related to the convenience of the SNS as a tool to conduct specific activities. A representative example is the use of the SNS as a *communication tool*, making it possible to be in touch with other members of the network at a fraction of the cost paid when compared to other means. In addition to the money savings, there are some time and effort savings (Cha 2010, Dimmick et al. 2007, Foregger 2008, Kim et al. 2011, Papacharissi and Rubin 2000, Ramirez Jr et al. 2008, Dimmick et al. 2000, Huang 2008, Nyland 2007, Sangwan 2005).

Given the above, we put forward the following hypotheses:

H: (8) information seeking, (9) learning, (10) innovativeness and (11) communication gratifications have a positive and significant effect on the participation in niche SNS.

3. METHODOLOGY

3.1. Questionnaire design

Studies grounded on U&G are typically based on questionnaires using Likert scales to collect data from primary sources (Lee et al. 2010, Cheung et al. 2011, Kim et al. 2010, Papacharissi and Rubin 2000). Following the example of previous research, a survey was adopted as the instrument for data collection using a Likert scale of five points. Due to the lack of research on niche SNS, this research adopted the constructs identified as influential in general purpose networks, when it came to networking and information seeking to develop the data collection instrument. Using these constructs was considered to be a good first approach to understanding niche SNS. Further research could potentially include new constructs or exclude constructs among those examined by this paper. The model implemented tested the relationship of each item with the user's participation in SNS. The questionnaire was tested in a pilot study and feedback was received about the length of the questionnaire and items with similar wording, with minor adjustments made before finalising the questionnaire. Given the nature of the research, a web-based survey was deemed appropriate for collecting data. Tables 1 and 2 present the constructs and items used in the questionnaire to collect data.

Table 1. Niche SNS participation construct sources

Gratifications	Acronym	Definition	Source	Items	Niche Mean	Niche Std. Dev.
Socialising	SOC	Is based on the need for and interest in meeting and talking with other people	(Park et al. 2009)	4	3.572	0.997
Interconnectedness	IC	Finding connections and information through existing contacts	(Foregger 2008)	7	2.809	0.996
Maintaining old ties	MAT	Keeping the connection online with friends known from before	(Foregger 2008)	5	2.845	1.174
Seeking friends	SFRIE	Finding new friends to exchange information with	(Kim et al. 2011)	2	3.552	0.955
Interpersonal utility	IPU	The utility sought in the interaction with other people at a relational level	(Cha 2010, Papacharissi and Rubin 2000)	8	3.580	0.853
Self-status seeking	STA	Seeking and maintaining the user's personal status through online group participation	(Park et al. 2009)	3	3.747	1.053
Seeking social support	SUP	Obtaining emotional support from their group of contact	(Kim et al. 2011)	3	2.477	1.183
Information seeking	INSK	Searching for information that is of interest to the users, such as activities carried out by their group of contacts	(Papacharissi and Rubin 2000, Park et al. 2009, Kim et al. 2011)	5	3.570	0.898
Learning	LEARN	Obtain information and being educated about a topic, and learning new things	(Cha, 2010)	4	2.618	1.076
Innovativeness	INNOV	Individual's tendency to be more receptive to new ideas	(Cha, 2010)	4	3.281	1.021
Communication convenience	COM-CON	How SNS facilitates the communication process with other people	(Cha 2010)	4	3.290	0.853
Intensity of use	INT-USE	Measures the engagement of the user with the SNS based on the integration of the SNS with the user´s routine	(Ellison et al. 2007)	5	3.411	0.915

Table 2. Items used for each construct

Gratification	Acronym	Items
Socialising	soc1	To stay in touch with people I know
	soc2	To meet interesting people
	soc3	To talk about something with others
	soc4	To get peer support from others
Interconnectedness	ic1	To network with others
	ic2	To see who knows who
	ic3	To look at pictures of my "friends' friends"
	ic4	To see who my contacts and I have in common
	ic5	To see if my contacts and I know the same people
	ic6	To see how everyone is connected
	ic7	To see where people know each other from
Maintain/Establish old ties	mat1	To keep in touch with old friends
	mat2	To contact out-of-state friends
	mat3	To track down old friends
	mat4	To see where people are at now
	mat5	To maintain old friendships
Seeking Friends	sfrie1	To hang out with people I enjoy
	sfrie2	To talk with people with the same interests
Interpersonal utility motive	ipu1	To meet new people
	ipu2	To belong to a group
	ipu3	To express myself freely
	ipu4	Because I wonder what other people said
	ipu5	To keep contact with my contacts
	ipu6	To feel involved with what's going on with other people
	ipu7	To keep my contacts up–to–date
	ipu8	To strengthen my relationships with my contacts
Self-status seeking	sta1	Because it makes myself look cool
	sta2	To develop my career through group participation
	sta3	Because I feel peer pressure to participate
Seeking Social Support	sup1	To let out my emotions easily to others who will understand me
	sup2	To talk out my problems and get advice
	sup3	To let others know I care about their feelings
Information seeking	insk1	To look for information
	insk2	To get information for free
	insk3	Because it is easier to search for information
	insk4	To see what is out there
	insk5	Because it is a new way to do research

continues on following page

Table 2. Continued

Gratification	Acronym	Items
Learning motive	learn1	Because it lets me explore new things
	learn2	Because it extends my mind
	learn3	Because it advances my knowledge
	learn4	Because it opens me up to new ideas
Innovativeness	innov1	Because I am very curious about how things work
	innov2	Because I like to experiment with new ways of doing things
	innov3	Because I like to take a chance
	innov4	Because I like to be around unconventional people who dare to try new things
Communication convenience	com-con1	Using SNS makes me more efficient
	com-con 2	Using SNS helps me accomplish things more quickly
	com-con 3	Using SNS makes my life easier
	com-con 4	Using SNS would be useful in my life
Intensity of use	Int-use1	This niche network is part of my everyday activity
	Int-use2	I am proud to tell people I'm on this niche network
	Int-use3	I feel out of touch when I haven't logged onto this niche network for a while
	Int-use4	I feel I am part of the this niche network community
	Int-use5	I would be sorry if this niche network shut down

3.2. Sampling

Based on the gap and the research question for this study, the initial population framework was users of niche SNS. Following the definition of Boyd and Ellison (2008), a niche SNS is a network with a specific purpose and/or oriented to a specific target of the population. Thus, niche SNS could be networks from LinkedIn, which, despite its size, is oriented to professional purposes, to networks like Little Monsters, oriented to the fans of Lady Gaga. However, the very niche nature of these networks makes it difficult to map the population, as many of them are only known among the group of people who share the same interest. Looking for statistics to define a population framework, it was found that there is a lack of information about how many networks there are or how many users are registered in each of these networks. There are some private initiatives trying to generate network directories, but they are not reliable enough to create a full map of the population. Based on the above, it was deemed appropriate to use a non-probabilistic sampling method. Since the sampling framework was unknown, volunteer opportunity sampling was the most suitable alternative to reach niche network users. The sample was narrowed down to UK residents to ensure a minimum of experiential consistency. The invitations to participate in this research project were posted on different social media accounts as recommended by Hewson and Laurent (2012). In addition, a second strategy to collect data was based on identifying the main niche SNS platforms. From this search, Ning, SocialGo and Elgg were found to be popular options. The first group approached was the developers' community on these platforms, as they are usually the administrators of their own networks. The invitation to complete the questionnaire, including the link, was posted on these forums. Likewise, network administrators were contacted via email, requesting permission to post the invitation on their networks. Posting the invitation on an open forum was found to be a more effective strategy, compared to the option of the administrators, as they were reluctant to promote the questionnaire in their networks.

Of the 203 questionnaires completed over four months in Q3/2012, we filtered out those indicated using an SNS that was not a niche one or were outliers. The final samples used for the analysis had responses from 152 participants. 44% were from women and 56% were from men, so there was a relatively balanced composition of the sample regarding gender. The average age of participants was 29.53 years old (std. dev.=11.01). When it came to the occupation of the participants, 55.26% were students, 23.03% were full time employees, 10.53% were part-time employees and finally 9.21% were self- employed. From the results, LinkedIn was the most popular niche SNS, with 25 cases. This network is followed by QQ from China, with 14 respondents, academia with 10 and VKontackte with 7. These four networks represent 36.84% of the total respondents. Given the nature of niche SNS, there is a wide variety of networks with few cases. Examples of these niche SNS used by the respondents are DevianArt, Path, Naijapals, and Tony Arts. More details about the demographic variables are presented in Table 3.

Table 3. Sample demographics

Characteristic	Frequency	%	Characteristic	Frequency	%
Gender			**Age**		
Male	85	55.92%	Blank	1	0.66%
Female	67	44.08%	< 19	6	3.95%
Total	**152**	**100%**	20-29	89	58.55%
Employment Status			30-39	37	24.34%
Paid full-time employment	35	23.03%	40-49	5	3.29%
Paid part-time employment	16	10.53%	> 50	14	9.21%
Self-employment	14	9.21%	**Total**	**152**	**100%**
Unemployed	3	1.97%	**Educational attainment**		
Student	84	55.26%	Primary School	0	0.00%
Total	**152**	**100%**	High School	13	8.55%
Annual household income			Technical Education	5	3.29%
Less than £10,000	50	32.89%	Undergraduate	53	34.87%
£10,000 to £19,999	21	13.82%	Postgraduate	68	44.74%
£20,000 to £29,999	16	10.53%	Doctorate degree	13	8.55%
£30,000 to £39,999	24	15.79%	**Total**	**152**	**100%**
£40,000 to £49,999	12	7.89%			
£50,000 to £59,999	10	6.58%			
£60,000 or more	19	12.50%			
Total	**152**	**100%**			

3.3. Analysis

The information was cleaned and the constructs were tested regarding validity. The diagonal of Table 3 lists the Cronbach's Alpha for each construct. A Kaiser-Meyer-Olkin (KMO) Test and a factor analysis were also conducted (Table 4 & 5). A multiple regression analysis was used to analyse the data. The regression model was run in SPSS, starting with all the variables proposed above using the stepwise method. The Durbin-Watson coefficient was 2, meaning that there were no autocorrelation issues, and the VIF values for all the significant variables were below 1.55, suggesting that there were no collinearity issues. The residuals showed no evident patterns. All these considerations suggested that the model complied with the assumptions of the regression model.

Table 4. KMO and Bartlett's test

KMO and Bartlett's test		
Kaiser-Meyer-Olkin Measure of Sampling Adequacy		0.865
Bartlett's test of sphericity	Approx. Chi-Square	7802.795
	df	1431
	Sig.	.000

Table 5. Factor analysis

	Component									
	ipu	mat	ic	int use	sta	learn	com-con	sup	innov	soc
Int_use1				0.765						
Int_use2				0.710						
Int_use3				0.769						
Int_use4				0.814						
Int_use5				0.754						
soc1										
soc2										0.724
soc3										
soc4										0.339
ic1			0.261							
ic2			0.769							
ic3			0.322							
ic4			0.797							
ic5			0.819							
ic6			0.785							
ic7			0.746							
mat1		0.866								

continues on following page

Table 5. Continued

	Component									
	ipu	mat	ic	int use	sta	learn	com-con	sup	innov	soc
mat2		0.784								
mat3		0.783								
mat4		0.588								
mat5		0.858								
sfrie1										
sfrie2										
ipu1	0.410									
ipu2	0.734									
ipu3	0.778									
ipu4	0.779									
ipu5	0.755									
ipu6	0.656									
ipu7	0.792									
ipu8	0.755									
sta1					0.718					
sta2					0.803					
sta3					0.580					
sup1								0.786		
sup2								0.748		
sup3								0.739		
insk1										
insk2										
insk3										
insk4										
insk5										
learn1						0.837				
learn2						0.904				
learn3						0.906				
learn4						0.716				
innov1									0.739	
innov2									0.556	
innov3									0.720	
innov4									0.738	
pu1							0.826			
pu2							0.800			
pu3							0.798			
pu4							0.782			

4. RESULTS

Table 6 presents the correlation coefficients of the variables included in the model, as well as its reliability coefficients.

Table 6. Correlation matrix and Cronbach's alpha (diagonal)

	1	2	3	4	5	6	7	8	9	10	11	12
Socialising	0.739											
Interconnectedness	.288**	0.914										
Maintaining old ties	.082	.476**	0.914									
Seeking friends	.165*	.042	-.106	0.608								
Interpersonal utility	.229**	.186*	-.117	.588**	0.900							
Self-status seeking	.429**	.010	-.142	.517**	.422**	0.808						
Seek. social support	.380**	.227**	.375**	-.122	-.063	.001	0.857					
Information seeking	.420**	.104	-.155	.435**	.405**	.504**	-.013	0.760				
Learning	.031	.273**	.259**	.139	.101	.094	.295**	.126	0.934			
Innovativeness	.156	.353**	.415**	-.006	.038	.096	.146	.223**	.363**	0.871		
Com. convenience	.205*	.251**	.197*	.128	.284**	.121	.085	.246**	.158	.332**	0.867	
Intensity of use	.563**	.124	.108	.184*	.234**	.385**	.331**	.297**	-.052	.198*	.175*	0.871

*p<0.05; **p<0.01; ***p<0.001

The value of R^2 for the regression was 41.2%. Based on the results obtained, the significant factors were found to be the socialising, self-status seeking, seeking social support and learning and innovativeness gratifications (Figure 1). These results show that users prefer to use the niche SNS for specific purposes and interact with like-minded people, which is the purpose of the niche SNS. Likewise, the results show that gratifications related with creating/maintaining the network of contacts are not significant for niche SNS, suggesting that these gratifications apply only to general purpose networks.

5. DISCUSSION

The model proposed for testing the motivations for participating in niche SNS aimed to study the direct relationship of each construct with the intensity of use. Out of the 11 gratifications tested, five were found to be significant. Keeping in mind that the model aimed to test whether the gratifications identified for general purpose networks applied to niche ones, it was no surprise that only a few variables were not as relevant and were eventually rejected. This suggests that there is indeed a difference in the motivations to participate in general purpose networks and niche SNS, contrary to the current practice that treats all networks as the same (Wilson et al. 2012) Further research on niche SNS is needed if we are to understand user behaviour in these networks better and more reliably.

Figure 1. The model and results

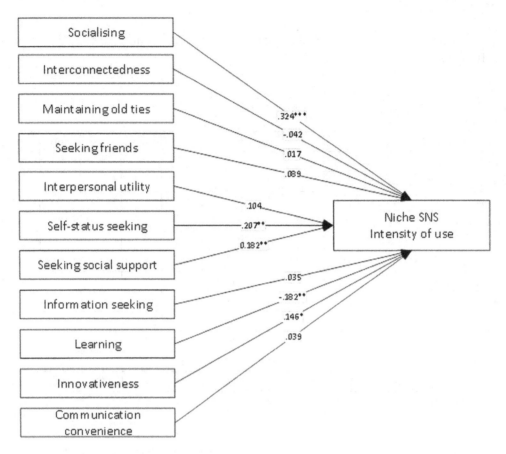

More specifically, the socialising hypothesis related to the social nature of the SNS, which regardless of the type, niche or general purpose, is still a key factor explaining why a user participates in an SNS as Bulut and Doğan (2017) show in their research. This is reflected in the value of its coefficient, which is the largest among the factors tested. Users participate in niche SNS for social reasons, but not the typical reasons such as people looking to connect with old contacts or to meet new people for the sake of it. This argument is supported by the rejection of the interconnectedness and maintaining old ties, which are factors associated with these behaviours. Considering these results, it can be argued that socialising, as presented by Park (2009), is more about sharing time and opinions with like-minded people on topics that they are interested in, which fits with the purpose of a niche SNS.

The second significant factor was support sought and/or provided by people sharing the same issues, interest, goals or tastes (Cha 2010, Foregger 2008, Kim et al. 2011, Li et al. 2015, Hajli et al. 2015, Shen 2015, Wong 2012). As an example, one may consider a health-related network called tudiabetes. org, which is a network oriented to people dealing with diabetes, also providing a platform to share experiences with other people with the same condition. Kim et al. (2011) argue that the social support is rooted in the need to belong to a community of people with similar characteristics to the user created by a sense of identification, and this is supported by Kwon et al (2017), Shen (2015), and by Wong (2012). This identification with the group is reflected in the search for encouragement and companionship from the people in the network (either previous contacts or new contacts made in the network). This identification enables them to express themselves more openly, as people in the group can understand what the person is looking for more easily. Also, sharing the same interest/condition makes it possible for them to be less concerned about being judged or misinterpreted by other people (Chung et al. 2015). A common practice in general purpose networks is to put together all the contacts, mixing family, friends, colleagues, etc. Still, when people need support, they prefer to appeal to those who can understand them better. A niche SNS could potentially be a safe place in which the users can express themselves freely, as these networks consist of people with similar characteristics to the user (from physical condition, to similar interests, etc.).

The third gratification was self-status seeking, which is related to building and maintaining an image through the continuous participation in a group. This participation is based on the identification with the group and the desire to be acknowledged as part of the group (Nadkarni and Hofmann 2011, Kilian et al, 2012). Sangwan (2005) argues that the self-status seeking gratification looks to reaffirm the self-identity by being recognised as the image the user is projecting, as well as interacting with (influential) people in the group that otherwise would be difficult to meet. The identity is reaffirmed by the acknowledgement of one's status as a member of the group, feeding the self-satisfaction need. In this regard, Bulut and Doğan (2017) stressed the importance of status seeking as part of the reinforcement of personal values and the creation of a social identity, which is part of the identification process. This identification process points to belongingness as one of the needs that people look for when participating in SNS (Krasnova et al. 2008, Pai and Arnott 2012, Smock et al. 2011, Zolkepli and Kamarulzaman 2015, Hsu et al. 2015, Nadkarni and Hofmann 2011, Wong 2012). The belongingness is fostered by the interaction with people that otherwise it would be difficult to be in contact with, due to geographical distance, different social circles, etc. The belongingness has been studied by Chung et al (2016) by the attachment that the person has to a group, which makes them share information that they will not share with everybody. This finding is in line with Tan's (Tan et al. 2015) argument about the importance of weak ties over the strong ones regarding trust and identification with a specialised group. It is important to highlight that the identity projected in the network does not necessarily match the identity of the person in real life (Zhao et al. 2008, Wong 2012, Tosun 2012). In fact, a user can have accounts on different networks for different purposes (Mital and Sarkar 2011), having the chance to create a different identity on each one of them, or even create several users in the same network. Each can have a different identity, as in the case of people with different Facebook accounts or the current trend of fake intagram accounts (finstagram) used by people to post their private photos (Carman 2018, The Guardian 2017). This point is important, as when users join due to peer or superior pressure, they may not necessarily project their real self (Tosun 2012). The same may apply to those users participating in niche networks for operational reasons, e.g. trying to get some benefit from the network, such as information, contacts or knowledge. These users will participate in the network just to get what they are looking for. There may exist conditions for admitting new users, like the case of aSmallworld, which is an SNS for millionaires, and the people are accepted only if they are invited by a current member of the network.

The fourth gratification emerging as an important factor for understanding participation in a niche SNS was learning. Contrary to prior research (Cha, 2010, Foregger 2008), the coefficient for this variable was negative. Considering that self-status seeking was found to be a significant factor, one may interpret this as evidence that users on niche networks are more interested in sharing in order to be recognised as experts by their peers, rather than learning. Those who participate in niche SNS may want to position themselves as experts on the topic more than on the learner role. This situation can be seen on LinkedIn, on which users demonstrate their expertise not only using the information presented on their profiles, but also by drawing kudos from the recommendations of other users. Users participate in niche SNS as these networks provide information about a specific topic, as well as access to people who know about the topic (Cha 2010, Huang 2008, Kim et al. 2011, Papacharissi and Rubin, 2000 Park et al. 2009). The resources (people and information) that people perceive they will find in the niche SNS are something that they will rarely find in the general-purpose networks. Posting specialised views on niche networks may have been more appreciated compared to general purpose networks, while the highly focused discussion would help engage more members, encouraging them not only to read, but also to contribute to the conversation.

Finally, innovativeness follows the use of niche SNS for specific purposes, in this case as a source of innovative ideas, alternative points of view, or information that can lead to new developments. Cha (2010) portrays innovativeness as the tendency of the person the be more open or receptive to new ideas. Niche SNS contain information that is interesting for their members, and that users can post and where they can find information that is not easy to find elsewhere. Users participating in these networks are looking for new ideas, to enrich and receive feedback about their ideas, or to propose initiatives that can be found to be interesting for the other members of the network. The information sharing was found important by Baek et al. (2011) to explain the SNS usage, as it allowed information exchange and ideas that could be useful. Niche SNS can offer more opportunities to find specific information, ideas and projects to be noticed by the right audience than when posted on general purpose networks, where they could go under the radar and be ignored along with the other sea of posts presented on the timeline.

6. CONCLUSION

This research has provided evidence that there may be potentially different factors influencing the participation in general purpose networks and niche SNS. In turn, this suggests that general purpose and niche SNS cannot be assumed to be similar in nature or treated in the same manner.

The literature review suggested that socialisation and information exchange gratifications played an important role in user participation. A number of factors related to these gratifications were tested on niche SNS users. Socialising, social support, self-status seeking, learning and innovativeness were the main factors that motivated users to participate in niche SNS. Socialising, social support and self-status seeking gratifications suggested that belongingness was an underlying factor in participating, following the findings of Park et al (2009) about SNS usage and Chung et al (2016) about attachment. Users want to be with people who share the same interest; they want to be part of the groups of like-minded people, which aligns with the concept of homophily (Leskovec et al. 2008, Goggins et al. 2011). In niche SNS, Identity plays an important role as people participate in the SNS as a way of reaffirming their own identity (real or desired) through the participation in the network, which is related with research on self-status seeking (Park et al. 2009, Chung et al 2009) This triggers the identification process, which enables users to share the situation they are going through more easily, looking for support from others in the network. In the same vein, users reaffirm their identity through group validation. The results are related to the self-status seeking and learning gratifications. They suggest that users may participate in niche SNS as an opportunity to demonstrate their knowledge about a specific topic (self-status seeking). Niche SNS present a good opportunity for users not only to access specialised information, but also to interact with other similarly-minded users interested in the same topics, integrating the self-status seeking and social support characteristics in this gratification. These gratifications are complemented by innovativeness. Users may utilise niche SNS as a source for new ideas or as an outlet to present their ideas or projects to a public that has a higher chance of being interested in it or hearing about it, following Baek et al.'s (2011) results.

As it is becoming more frequent for business or interest groups to establish their own social networks, the managerial implications of this research are oriented towards potential ways of designing such SNS and promoting user participation in them. People are present in niche SNS not only because of the socialisation gratifications, but because they want to create links with like-minded people, following the homophily concept, wherein the degree of specialisation of the network, the topics, and/or its members, becomes a differential of the network. In other words, they are networks that are not for everybody, creating a sense of exclusivity. This sense of exclusivity is supported by the self-status seeking gratification, as people search actively to be recognised by the people they try to identify with. A niche SNS makes it possible for users to showcase their expertise, offering users a platform on which to propose new ideas that can be improved by others. Thus, a niche SNS allows the user to establish a reputation among people related to their interest, which could be difficult to reach in general purpose SNS. In the same vein, learning and innovativeness gratifications can be used by niche SNS managers to encourage participation among users, as these networks are places where they can be inspired to do new things or to go for innovative ideas and learn how to do it, which can be exemplified with academic SNS such as academia or research gate, who are niche SNS for academics.

6.1. Research Implications and Further Research

This proposed approach to adopt general purpose constructs and test them in a niche SNS context was able to explain 41.2% of the variance of the dependent variable. Although such a result could be considered as a good starting point, shedding light on the motivations to participate in niche SNS, it also calls for more research to be undertaken in this area. Future efforts can help increase the predictive power of the model by including new variables that could be relevant to niche SNS. Another stream of research is the type of users in niche SNS, which is guided by the research of Constantinides et al, (2010), Constantinides and Stagno (2011), Kilian et al, (2012), Brandtzæg (2012) and Bulut and Dogan (2017), who found that different types of users have different motivations to use SNS. Consequently, it would be interesting to study the type of users and their proportion in niche SNS. Due to the difficulties of accessing primary sources, it is recommended that qualitative research approaches be used in order to gain a deeper understanding of these networks. Such an approach could potentially help identify a wider list of influential factors to test in a quantitative manner, within models like the one adopted for this research. A case study approach may also be useful for gaining insights into specific niche networks considering different types of networks, e.g. based on objectives, audiences, geographical attributes etc.

REFERENCES

Ajzen, I. (1991). The theory of planned behavior. *Organizational Behavior and Human Decision Processes, 50*(2), 179–211. doi:10.1016/0749-5978(91)90020-T

Ali-Hassan, H., Nevo, D., & Wade, M. (2015). Linking dimensions of social media use to job performance: The role of social capital. *The Journal of Strategic Information Systems*, *24*(2), 65–89. doi:10.1016/j.jsis.2015.03.001

Bae, M. (2018). Understanding the effect of the discrepancy between sought and obtained gratification on social networking site users' satisfaction and continuance intention. *Computers in Human Behavior*, *79*, 137–153. doi:10.1016/j.chb.2017.10.026

Baek, K., Holton, A., Harp, D., & Yaschur, C. (2011). The links that bind: Uncovering novel motivations for linking on Facebook. *Computers in Human Behavior*, *27*(6), 2243–2248. doi:10.1016/j.chb.2011.07.003

Bhappu, A., & Schultze, U. (2018). Implementing an Organization-sponsored Sharing Platform to Build Employee Engagement. *MIS Quarterly Executive*.

Boyd, D. M., & Ellison, N. B. (2008). Social Network Sites: Definition, History, and Scholarship. *Journal of Computer-Mediated Communication*, *13*(1), 210–230. doi:10.1111/j.1083-6101.2007.00393.x

Brandtzæg, P. B. (2012). Social networking sites: Their users and social implications - A longitudinal study. *Journal of Computer-Mediated Communication*, *17*(4), 467–488. doi:10.1111/j.1083-6101.2012.01580.x

Bulut, Z. A., & Doğan, O. (2016, January). The ABCD typology: Profile and motivations of Turkish social network sites users. *Computers in Human Behavior*, *67*, 73–83. doi:10.1016/j.chb.2016.10.021

Calero Valdez, A., Brell, J., Schaar, A. K., & Ziefle, M. (2018). The diversity of why: A meta-analytical study of usage motivation in enterprise social networks. *Universal Access in the Information Society*, *17*(3), 549–566. doi:10.100710209-017-0561-9

Carman, A. (2018). Fake Instagrams are one of the last refuges of the authentic online self. *The verge*. Retrieved from https://www.theverge.com/2018/4/3/17189912/fake-instagram-finsta-account-whyd-you-push-that-button

Castillo, M. (2018). *Facebook's North American daily active users stay flat after scandals*. Retrieved September 13, 2018, from https://www.cnbc.com/2018/07/25/facebooks-north-american-daily-active-users-after-scandals.html

Cha, J. (2010). Factors affecting the frequency and amount of social networking site use: Motivations, perceptions, and privacy concerns. *First Monday*, 15.

Chang, L., & Chen, J. V. (2014). Aligning principal and agent's incentives: A principal-agent perspective of social networking sites. *Expert Systems with Applications*, *41*(6), 3091–3104. doi:10.1016/j.eswa.2013.10.040

Chen, A., Lu, Y., & Wang, B. (2016). Enhancing perceived enjoyment in social games through social and gaming factors. *Information Technology & People*, *29*(1), 99–119. doi:10.1108/ITP-07-2014-0156

Chen, Y. F. (2014). See you on Facebook: Exploring influences on Facebook continuous usage. *Behaviour & Information Technology*, *33*(11), 1208–1218. doi:10.1080/0144929X.2013.826737

Cheung, C. M. K., Chiu, P.-Y., & Lee, M. K. O. (2011). Online social networks: Why do students use facebook? *Computers in Human Behavior*, *27*(4), 1337–1343. doi:10.1016/j.chb.2010.07.028

Chiu, C.-M., & Huang, H.-Y. (2015a). Examining the antecedents of user gratification and its effects on individuals' social network services usage: The moderating role of habit. *European Journal of Information Systems*, *24*(4), 411–430. doi:10.1057/ejis.2014.9

Chiu, C. M., & Huang, H. Y. (2015b). Examining the antecedents of user gratification and its effects on individuals' social network services usage: The moderating role of habit. *European Journal of Information Systems*, *24*(4), 411–430. doi:10.1057/ejis.2014.9

Chung, N., Koo, C., & Park, S.-B. (2012). Why People Share Information in Social Network Sites? Integrating with Uses and Gratification and Social Identity Theories. In J.-S. Pan, S.-M. Chen, & N. Nguyen (Eds.), *Intelligent Information and Database Systems*. Springer Berlin Heidelberg. doi:10.1007/978-3-642-28490-8_19

Chung, N., Nam, K., & Koo, C. (2015). Examining information sharing in social networking communities: Applying theories of social capital and attachment. *Telematics and Informatics*, *33*(1), 77–91. doi:10.1016/j.tele.2015.05.005

Chunngam, B., Chanchalor, S., & Murphy, E. (2014). Membership, participation and knowledge building in virtual communities for informal learning. *British Journal of Educational Technology*, *45*(5), 863–879. doi:10.1111/bjet.12114

Cocosila, M., & Igonor, A. (2015). How important is the "social" in social networking? A perceived value empirical investigation. *Information Technology & People*, *28*(2), 366–382. doi:10.1108/ITP-03-2014-0055

Constantinides, E., Amo, M., Del C. A., & Romero, C. L. (2010). Profiles of Social Networking Sites Users in the Netherlands. *18th Annual High Technology Small Firms Conference*. Retrieved from http://purl.utwente.nl/publications/73399

Crawford, S., Hall, M., Gray, W., Johnson, B., & Price, R. A. (2017). What motivates buy-side analysts to share recommendations online? *Management Science*, *64*(6), 2473–2972.

Dimmick, J., Kline, S., & Stafford, L. (2000). The Gratification Niches of Personal E-mail and the Telephone Competition, Displacement, and Complementarity. *Communication Research*, *27*(2), 227–248. doi:10.1177/009365000027002005

Dimmick, J., Ramirez, A. Jr, Wang, T., & Lin, S. F. (2007). Extending society: The role of personal networks and gratification-utilities in the use of interactive communication media. *New Media & Society*, *9*(5), 795–810. doi:10.1177/1461444807081225

Ellison, N., Heino, R., & Gibbs, J. (2006). Managing Impressions Online: Self-Presentation Processes in the Online Dating Environment. *Journal of Computer-Mediated Communication*, *11*(2), 415–441. doi:10.1111/j.1083-6101.2006.00020.x

Ellison, N. B., Steinfield, C., & Lampe, C. (2007). The benefits of facebook "friends:" Social capital and college students' use of online social network sites. *Journal of Computer-Mediated Communication*, *12*(4), 1143–1168. doi:10.1111/j.1083-6101.2007.00367.x

Fishbein, M., & Ajzen, I. (1975). *Belief, attitude, intention and behavior: An introduction to theory and research*. Academic Press.

Foregger, S. K. (2008). *Uses and gratifications of Facebook.com*. Michigan State University.

Gan, C., & Wang, W. (2015). Uses and gratifications of social media: A comparison of microblog and WeChat. *Journal of Systems and Information Technology, 17*(4), 351–363. doi:10.1108/JSIT-06-2015-0052

Giannakos, M. N., Chorianopoulos, K., Giotopoulos, K., & Vlamos, P. (2013). Using Facebook out of habit. *Behaviour & Information Technology, 32*(6), 594–602. doi:10.1080/0144929X.2012.659218

Gironda, J. T., & Korgaonkar, P. K. (2014). Understanding consumers' social networking site usage. *Journal of Marketing Management, 30*(5-6), 571–605. doi:10.1080/0267257X.2013.851106

Goggins, S. P., Laffey, J., & Gallagher, M. (2011). Completely online group formation and development: Small groups as socio-technical systems. *Information Technology & People, 24*(2), 104–133. doi:10.1108/09593841111137322

Hajli, N., Shanmugam, M., Powell, P., & Love, P. E. D. (2015). A study on the continuance participation in on-line communities with social commerce perspective. *Technological Forecasting and Social Change, 96*, 232–241. doi:10.1016/j.techfore.2015.03.014

Hewson, C., & Laurent, D. (2012). Research design and tools for internet research. In N. G. Fielding, R. M. Lee, & G. Blank (Eds.), *Sage Internet Research Methods*. SAGE.

Hou, J. (2011). Uses and gratifications of social games: Blending social networking and game play. *First Monday*, 16.

Hsu, M. H., Tien, S. W., Lin, H. C., & Chang, C. M. (2015). Understanding the roles of cultural differences and socio-economic status in social media continuance intention. *Information Technology & People, 28*(1), 224–241. doi:10.1108/ITP-01-2014-0007

Hsu, T.-H., Wang, Y.-S., & Wen, S. (2006). Using the decomposed theory of planning behavioural to analyse consumer behavioural intention towards mobile text message coupons. Journal of Targeting. *Measurement and Analysis for Marketing, 14*(4), 309–324. doi:10.1057/palgrave.jt.5740191

Huang, E. (2008). Use and gratification in e-consumers. *Internet Research, 18*(4), 405–426. doi:10.1108/10662240810897817

Huang, L. C., & Shiau, W. L. (2015). Why do people use microblogs? An empirical study of Plurk. *Information Technology & People, 28*(2), 281–303. doi:10.1108/ITP-07-2012-0067

Joinson, A. N. 2008. Looking at, looking up or keeping up with people?: motives and use of facebook. *Proceeding of the twenty-sixth annual SIGCHI conference on Human factors in computing systems*. Florence, Italy: ACM. 10.1145/1357054.1357213

Kang, J.-Y. M., & Johnson, K. K. (2015). F-Commerce platform for apparel online social shopping: Testing a Mowen's 3M model. *International Journal of Information Management, 35*(6), 691–701. doi:10.1016/j.ijinfomgt.2015.07.004

Katz, E., Blumler, J. G., & Gurevitch, M. (1973). Uses and Gratifications Research. *Public Opinion Quarterly, 37*(4), 509–523. doi:10.1086/268109

Kilian, T., Hennigs, N., & Langner, S. (2012). Do Millennials read books or blogs? Introducing a media usage typology of the internet generation. *Journal of Consumer Marketing, 29*(2), 114–124. doi:10.1108/07363761211206366

Kim, J. H., Kim, M. S., & Nam, Y. (2010). An Analysis of Self-Construals, Motivations, Facebook Use, and User Satisfaction. *International Journal of Human-Computer Interaction, 26*(11-12), 1077–1099. doi:10.1080/10447318.2010.516726

Kim, M., & Cha, J. (2017, October). A comparison of Facebook, Twitter, and LinkedIn: Examining motivations and network externalities for the use of social networking sites. *First Monday.*

Kim, M. J., Lee, C. K., & Bonn, M. (2016). The effect of social capital and altruism on seniors' re-visit intention to social network sites for tourism-related purposes. *Tourism Management, 53*, 96–107. doi:10.1016/j.tourman.2015.09.007

Kim, Y., Sohn, D., & Choi, S. M. (2011). Cultural difference in motivations for using social network sites: A comparative study of American and Korean college students. *Computers in Human Behavior, 27*(1), 365–372. doi:10.1016/j.chb.2010.08.015

Kourouthanassis, P., Lekakos, G., & Gerakis, V. (2015). Should i stay or should i go? the moderating effect of self-image congruity and trust on social networking continued use. *Behaviour & Information Technology, 34*(2), 190–203. doi:10.1080/0144929X.2014.948489

Krasnova, H., Hildebrand, T., Günther, O., Kovrigin, A., & Nowobilska, A. (2008). *Why participate in an online social network: an empirical analysis.* 16th European Conference on Information Systems ECIS, Galway, Ireland.

Krasnova, H., Veltri, N.F., Eling, N., & Buxmann, P. (2017). Why men and women continue to use social networking sites: The role of gender differences. *Journal of Strategic Information Systems, 26*(4), 261-284.

Kwon, H. E., Oh, W., & Kim, T. (2017). Platform Structures, Homing Preferences, and Homophilous Propensities in Online Social Networks. *Journal of Management Information Systems, 34*(3), 768–802. doi:10.1080/07421222.2017.1373008

Kwon, O., & Wen, Y. (2010). An empirical study of the factors affecting social network service use. *Computers in Human Behavior, 26*(2), 254–263. doi:10.1016/j.chb.2009.04.011

Lampe, C., Ellison, N., & Steinfield, C. (2006). *A Face(book) in the crowd: Social searching vs. social browsing.* ACM. doi:10.1145/1180875.1180901

Lee, J. H., Kim, J. H., & Hong, J. H. (2010). A comparison of adoption models for new mobile media services between high- and low-motive groups. *International Journal of Mobile Communications, 8*(5), 487–506. doi:10.1504/IJMC.2010.034934

Leskovec, J., Backstrom, L., Kumar, R., & Tomkins, A. 2008. Microscopic evolution of social networks. In *Proceeding of the 14th ACM SIGKDD international conference on Knowledge discovery and data mining.* Las Vegas, NV: ACM. 10.1145/1401890.1401948

Li, X., Chen, W. & Popiel, P. (2015). What happens on Facebook stays on Facebook? The implications of Facebook interaction for perceived, receiving, and giving social support. *Computers in Human Behavior, 51*(A), 106-113.

Lim, V., Frangakis, N., Tanco, L. M., & Picinali, L. (2018). PLUGGY: A Pluggable Social Platform for Cultural Heritage Awareness and Participation. Lecture Notes in Computer Science, 10754, 117–129. doi:10.1007/978-3-319-75789-6_9

Lingreen, A., Dobele, A., Vanhamme, J., Luís Abrantes, J., Seabra, C., Raquel Lages, C., & Jayawardhena, C. (2013). Drivers of in-group and out-of-group electronic word-of-mouth (eWOM). *European Journal of Marketing, 47*(7), 1067–1088. doi:10.1108/03090561311324219

Lorenzo-Romero, C., Constantinides, E., & Alarcón-Del-Amo, M. (2011). Consumer adoption of social networking sites: Implications for theory and practice. *Journal of Research in Interactive Marketing, 5*(2/3), 170–188. doi:10.1108/17505931111187794

Mehdizadeh, S. (2010). Self-presentation 2.0: Narcissism and self-esteem on Facebook. *Cyberpsychology, Behavior, and Social Networking, 13*(4), 357–364. doi:10.1089/cyber.2009.0257 PMID:20712493

Mital, M., & Sarkar, S. (2011). Multihoming behavior of users in social networking web sites: A theoretical model. *Information Technology & People, 24*(4), 378–392. doi:10.1108/09593841111182250

Nadkarni, A., & Hofmann, S. G. (2011). Why do people use Facebook? *Personality and Individual Differences.* PMID:22544987

Nyland, R. (2007). *The Gratification Niches of Online Social Networking, E-Mail and Face-to-Face Communication* (Master's Thesis). Brigham Young University.

Pai, P., & Arnott, D. C. (2012). User adoption of social networking sites: Eliciting uses and gratifications through a means–end approach. *Computers in Human Behavior.*

Papacharissi, Z., & Rubin, A. M. (2000). Predictors of Internet Use. *Journal of Broadcasting & Electronic Media, 44*(2), 175–196. doi:10.120715506878jobem4402_2

Park, C., Jun, J., & Lee, T. (2015). Consumer characteristics and the use of social networking sites: A comparison between Korea and the US. *International Marketing Review, 32*(3/4), 414–437. doi:10.1108/IMR-09-2013-0213

Park, J. H., Gu, B., Leung, A. C. M., & Konana, P. (2014). An investigation of information sharing and seeking behaviors in online investment communities. *Computers in Human Behavior, 31*, 1–12. doi:10.1016/j.chb.2013.10.002

Park, N., Kee, K. F., & Valenzuela, S. (2009). Being Immersed in Social Networking Environment: Facebook Groups, Uses and Gratifications, and Social Outcomes. *Cyberpsychology & Behavior, 12*(6), 729–733. doi:10.1089/cpb.2009.0003 PMID:19619037

Phua, J., Jin, S. V., & Kim, J. (2017). Uses and gratifications of social networking sites for bridging and bonding social capital: A comparison of Facebook, Twitter, Instagram, and Snapchat. *Computers in Human Behavior, 72*, 115–122. doi:10.1016/j.chb.2017.02.041

Pugh, J. L. (2010). *A Qualitative Study of the Facebook Social Network: the desire to influence, associate, and construct a representative and ideal identity*. College of Business Administration Honors Program at California State University. Long Beach, CA: Mayıs.

Raacke, J., & Bonds-Raacke, J. (2008). MySpace and Facebook: Applying the uses and gratifications theory to exploring friend-networking sites. *Cyberpsychology & Behavior, 11*(2), 169–174. doi:10.1089/cpb.2007.0056 PMID:18422409

Ramirez, A. Jr, Dimmick, J., Feaster, J., & Lin, S. F. (2008). Revisiting Interpersonal Media Competition The Gratification Niches of Instant Messaging, E-Mail, and the Telephone. *Communication Research, 35*(4), 529–547. doi:10.1177/0093650208315979

Ridings, C. M. & Gefen, D. (2004). Virtual Community Attraction: Why People Hang Out Online. *Journal of Computer-Mediated Communication, 10*.

Rogers, E. M. (2003). *Diffusion of Innovations* (5th ed.). Free Press.

Rubin, A. M. (2002). The uses-and-gratifications perspective of media effects. In J. Bryant & M. B. Oliver (Eds.), *Media effects: advances in theory and research*. Routledge.

Sangwan, S. (2005). Virtual Community Success: A Uses and Gratifications Perspective. *System Sciences, 2005. HICSS '05. Proceedings of the 38th Annual Hawaii International Conference on*. 10.1109/HICSS.2005.673

Schau, H. J., & Gilly, M. C. (2003). We are what we post? Self-presentation in personal web space. *The Journal of Consumer Research, 30*(3), 385–404. doi:10.1086/378616

Shen, G. C. (2015). How quality of life affects intention to use social networking sites: Moderating role of self-disclosure. *Journal of Electronic Commerce Research, 16*, 276–289.

Smock, A. D., Ellison, N. B., Lampe, C., & Wohn, D. Y. (2011). Facebook as a toolkit: A uses and gratification approach to unbundling feature use. *Computers in Human Behavior, 27*(6), 2322–2329. doi:10.1016/j.chb.2011.07.011

Syn, S. Y., & Oh, S. (2015). Why do social network site users share information on Facebook and Twitter? *Journal of Information Science, 41*(5), 553–569. doi:10.1177/0165551515585717

Tan, C. H., Sutanto, J., & Tan, B. C. Y. (2015). Empirical investigation on relational social capital in a virtual community for website programming. *The Data Base for Advances in Information Systems, 46*(2), 43–60. doi:10.1145/2795618.2795622

The Guardian. (2017). Finstagram – a secret Instagram account to post ugly selfies. *The Guardian*. Retrieved from https://www.theguardian.com/technology/shortcuts/2017/feb/21/finstagram-secret-instagram-account-post-ugly-selfies

Tosun, L. P. (2012). Motives for Facebook use and expressing "true self" on the Internet. *Computers in Human Behavior, 28*(4), 1510–1517. doi:10.1016/j.chb.2012.03.018

Wei, H. L., Lin, K. Y., Lu, H. P., & Chuang, I. H. (2015). Understanding the intentions of users to 'stick' to social networking sites: A case study in Taiwan. *Behaviour & Information Technology*, *34*(2), 151–162. doi:10.1080/0144929X.2014.928745

Welch, C. (2018). More people are taking Facebook breaks and deleting the app from their phones. *The Verge*. Retrieved September 13, 2018, from https://www.theverge.com/2018/9/5/17822736/facebook-break-delete-app

Wilson, R. E., Gosling, S. D., & Graham, L. T. (2012). A Review of Facebook Research in the Social Sciences. *Perspectives on Psychological Science*, *7*(3), 203–220. doi:10.1177/1745691612442904 PMID:26168459

Wong, W. K.-W. (2012). *Faces on Facebook: A study of self-presentation and social support on Facebook*. Run Run Shaw Library, City University of Hong Kong.

Xu, C., Ryan, S., Prybutok, V., & Wen, C. (2012). It is not for fun: An examination of social network site usage. *Information & Management*, *49*(5), 210–217. doi:10.1016/j.im.2012.05.001

Xu, Y. C., Yang, Y., Cheng, Z., & Lim, J. (2014). Retaining and attracting users in social networking services: An empirical investigation of cyber migration. *The Journal of Strategic Information Systems*, *23*(3), 239–253. doi:10.1016/j.jsis.2014.03.002

Yang, H.-L., & Lin, C.-L. (2014). Why do people stick to Facebook web site? A value theory-based view. *Information Technology & People*, *27*(1), 21–37. doi:10.1108/ITP-11-2012-0130

Yen, C. (2016). How to unite the power of the masses? Exploring collective stickiness intention in social network sites from the perspective of knowledge sharing. *Behaviour & Information Technology*, *35*(2), 118–133. doi:10.1080/0144929X.2015.1105297

Zhao, S., Grasmuck, S., & Martin, J. (2008). Identity construction on Facebook: Digital empowerment in anchored relationships. *Computers in Human Behavior*, *24*(5), 1816–1836. doi:10.1016/j.chb.2008.02.012

Zhu, D. H., Chang, Y. P., Luo, J. J., & Li, X. (2014). Understanding the adoption of location-based recommendation agents among active users of social networking sites. *Information Processing & Management*, *50*(5), 675–682. doi:10.1016/j.ipm.2014.04.010

Zolkepli, I. A., & Kamarulzaman, Y. (2015). Social media adoption: The role of media needs and innovation characteristics. *Computers in Human Behavior*, *43*, 189–209. doi:10.1016/j.chb.2014.10.050

This research was previously published in the International Journal of E-Business Research (IJEBR), 15(2); pages 1-21, copyright year 2019 by IGI Publishing (an imprint of IGI Global).

Chapter 14
Participation in Online Social Networks:
Theories and Models

Giulio Angiani
Department of Information Engineering, University of Parma, Parma, Italy

Paolo Fornacciari
Department of Information Engineering, University of Parma, Parma, Italy

Eleonora Iotti
Department of Information Engineering, University of Parma, Parma, Italy

Monica Mordonini
Department of Information Engineering, University of Parma, Parma, Italy

Michele Tomaiuolo
Department of Information Engineering, University of Parma, Parma, Italy

ABSTRACT

Why and how more and more people get involved and use social networking systems are critical topics in social network analysis (SNA). As a matter of fact, social networking systems bring online a growing number of acquaintances, for many different purposes. Both business interests and personal recreational goals are motivations for using online social networks (OSN) or other social networking systems. The participation in social networks is a phenomenon which has been studied with several theories, and SNA is useful for common business problems, e.g., launching distributed teams, retaining people with vital knowledge for the organization, improving access to knowledge and spreading ideas and innovation. Nevertheless, there are some difficulties, such as anti-social behaviors of participants, lack of incentives, organizational costs and risks. In this article, a survey of the basic features of SNA, participation theories and models are discussed, with emphasis on social capital, information spreading, motivations for participation, and anti-social behaviors of social network users.

DOI: 10.4018/978-1-6684-6307-9.ch014

INTRODUCTION

Widespread participation to online social networks has rapidly become a matter of fact, worldwide. In fact, social networking systems attract billions of people all around the world. Many of them -- from several different social groups, regardless of age, gender, education, or nationality -- participate daily in social online activities. While some systems are dedicated to some specific scope, most of them instead blur the distinction between the private and working spheres, and users are known to use such systems both at home and on the work place both professionally and with recreational goals. For example, the chat systems, that are embedded in social networking platforms and may be used to organize a birthday party, are often the most practical way to contact a colleague to ask an urgent question, to organize a work meeting, or a formal event with colleagues, especially in technologically oriented companies. At the same time, several traditional information systems have been modified in order to include social aspects. Currently, social networking platforms are mostly used without corporate blessing, maintaining their status as feral systems. In fact, the attitude of firms and organizations is quite varied: in some cases, external social networking platforms are tolerated or even encouraged (e.g., Facebook was available for Microsoft and Apple employees before the general public launch), at least for specific purposes (Millen et al., 2006); in other cases, internal tools are promoted or imposed (DiMicco & Millen, 2007).

While the phenomenon of online social networking is relatively new, however to understand some of its dynamics, it is necessary to use analytical models, based on both network topology and users' own interests. For example, according to DiMicco (2008), most users that use social networking platforms for work purposes are mostly interested in accumulating social capital, either for career advancement or to gather support for their own projects inside the company. In fact, in order to understand how a social network could be used to increase interactions, information sharing and benefits in teams and organizations, it is useful to refer to Social Network Analysis, a set of data analysis techniques that focuses on the structural and topological features of the network (Otte, 2002). Also, participation in such networks has long been studied as a social phenomenon according to different theories. Understanding the status of a social network, or the usage pattern of an online social networking platform, requires study of the system according to both static and dynamic models. Moreover, the theories of participation in social networks allow not only to study, but also to guide the dynamics of a given social network.

The review is organized in the following way. First of all, we will describe the different kinds of virtual communities, social media technologies and applications which are available. Then, we will focus on models and theories of participation in social media, discussing also various models of information spreading and the issue of anti-social behaviours. We will then highlight the challenges faced by organizations and firms in adopting social media, either in internal or public way. Finally, we will provide some concluding remarks.

TECHNOLOGIES FOR SOCIAL ONLINE COLLABORATION

In general, Computer-Mediated Communication (CMC) is defined as any human communication that occurs through the use of two or more electronic devices (McQuail, 2005). Through CMC, users are able to create various kinds of virtual communities, i.e., networks of users whose connections mainly exist online. In the following paragraphs we discuss the features of the most typical kinds of virtual communities: (*i*) Virtual Organizations, (*ii*) Virtual Teams, and (*iii*) online Networks of Practice.

Types of Virtual Communities

Although there are several differences that clearly set the concepts apart, different kinds of virtual communities may share some common traits, including (*i*) the lack of central authority, (*ii*) their temporary and impromptu nature, and (*iii*) the importance of reputation and trust as opposed to bureaucracy and law.

According to the definition given by Mowshowitz (1994), a virtual organization is "...a temporary network of autonomous organizations that cooperate based on complementary competencies and connect their information systems to those of their partners via networks aiming at developing, making, and distributing products in cooperation." The term was then popularized by the Grid Computing community, referring to Virtual Organizations as "...flexible, secure, coordinated resource sharing among dynamic collections of individuals, institutions, and resources..." (Foster et al., 2001). The premise of Virtual Organizations is the technical availability of tools for effective collaboration among people located in different places, but their definition also emphasizes the possibility to share a large number of resources, including documents, data, knowledge and tools among interested people (Poggi & Tomaiuolo, 2010; Bergenti et al., 2005). Their importance is sustained by continuing trends in production and social forms, including the growing number of knowledge workers, the emergence of integrated industrial district and other aspects developing at an international level, like dynamic supply chains, just-in-time production, sub-contracting, delocalization, externalization, global logistics and mass migrations which collectively are usually named "globalization."

A virtual team, according to Powell et al. (2004), is a "...group of geographically, organizationally and/or time dispersed workers brought together by information and telecommunication technologies to accomplish one or more organizational tasks." Virtual Teams can represent organizational structures within the context of Virtual Organizations, but they can also come into existence in other situations, where independent people collaborate on a project, for example an open source software.

An online network of practice (or interest) is a group of people who share a profession or a craft, whose main interactions occur through communication networks and tools, including forums and other discussion boards. The creation of the group typically occurs either: (*i*) in a spontaneous and natural way, because of a common interest of its members, or (*ii*) it can be tailored exclusively to actual practitioners, forged specifically with the goal of sharing and increasing their professional skills and knowledge.

Requirements and Features of Online Social Networks

In OSNs there are at least three distinct functional elements: (*i*) profile management, (*ii*) social graph management and (*iii*) content production and discussion. In fact, by definition, a social network cannot lack social graph management and self-presentation, no matter how minimal. On the other hand, virtually no modern OSN lacks the content generation features.

According to these three main functional areas, it is also possible to draw a classification of the OSNs in three main categories: (*i*) systems where the profile and social graph management is prevalent; (*ii*) systems where the content has a prominent role with respect to social networking activities and there are frequent interactions with people not closely related; and (*iii*) systems where the two aspects have roughly the same importance.

The archetypal examples of the first category of systems are business-related and professional OSNs, like Linkedin. People pay a great deal of attention in creating their profile. In this type of systems there are usually various relationships among users, representing the variety of relationships that members may have in real life. Most users do not visit the site daily and do not add content to the system often (Skeels & Grudin, 2008).

The second type includes blogging, micro-blogging and media sharing web sites, like Twitter. The "follow" relationships, which are typical for a system of this kind, are usually not symmetric. The focus is in information transmission; often the system does not support a proper profile and sometimes even the contacts may be hidden. Often weak semantic techniques such as Twitter hash-tags are used, in order to read content by subject instead than by author. Through collaborative tagging, the actors of the system may develop a sort of emergent semantics (Mika, 2007), possibly in the form of so-called "folksonomies." Considering that tags usage is a heavy tailed power-law like distribution, i.e., most people actually uses very few tags, collaborative tagging usually produce a good classification of data (Halpin et al., 2007).

The third category includes the personal OSNs, like Facebook. In this type of systems, users have a profile, partly public and partly confidential. Frequently, there is only one kind of relation, "friendship," which is symmetric and requires approval by both users. These sites have extremely frequent updates: a noticeable percentage of users perform activities on the system at least on a daily basis.

One of the goals motivating the participation in online communities is the benefit of team work over solo work. Various studies (Van de Ven et al., 1976; Malone & Crowstone, 1994) describe the advantages and costs of coordinating team activities. In fact, while an increase in coordination can lead to greater effectiveness, typically it also produces a faster growth of coordination costs. As a consequence, a lot of effort is being devoted in creating tools and technologies that make group work more effective by containing the costs of their coordination. Virtual Teams assembly is another problem that online social platforms can help to solve. In fact, the success of a team depends largely on its assembly process, for identifying the best possible members.

Social collaboration platforms should also help to model and manage multidimensional networks. In fact, apart from direct relationships among people, such platforms should also include other resources. For example, in the area of academic research, a network model could include both people and the events they attend (Wasserman & Faust, 1994), thus creating a bimodal network. Su and Contractor (2011) propose a more complex multi-dimensional network model, including people, documents, data sets, tools, keywords/concepts, etc.

Additionally, in some online communities, participation may also strongly depend on adopted mechanisms and policies for preserving privacy, including confidentiality of messages and identity. For personal identity privacy, stable pseudonyms could be assigned at registration (Andrews, 2002). Moreover, in online communities and Virtual Teams, acquaintance may happen online, without previous connection in real life. In those cases, a member's reputation is directly related to his pseudonym, and ratability of his online activities may be more important than his real-world identity for creating trust (Poggi et al., 2003). Complete anonymity may also have a value in some activities of Virtual Teams, apart from encouraging participation in general. For example, an anonymous brainstorm activity may help opening a conversation about trust and ground rules for online meetings (Young, 2009).

For reaching wider and more effective adoption in open and dynamic online communities, including Virtual Organizations, Virtual Teams and online Networks of Practice, we argue that social networking platforms should embrace an open approach (Franchi et al., 2016a; Poggi & Tomaiuolo, 2013). The model of autonomous software agents has been often used in the development such systems (Poggi & Tomaiuolo, 2010; Poggi & Tomaiuolo, 2013; Bergenti, Poggi & Tomaiuolo, 2014). In fact, many isolated sites could not satisfy the need for an inter-organizational collaborative environment. On the other hand, organizations are not keen to rely on a single centralized site, which may pose risks to privacy and may control published data. Moreover, openness is important for participation, too. In fact, a closed environment can hardly reach the minimal dimension and variety required for activating the typical dynamics at the basis of the different theories taken into consideration by analysts, for explaining participation in OSNs.

Integration of Social Features Into Existing Applications

The trend toward introducing social media systems in the work environment has seen a massive increase in importance in recent years. At their first appearance, without indications from the management and without integration with internal information systems, social media took the form of feral systems. However, organizations and firms are finally becoming to accept this situation as a matter of fact, trying to gain benefits from the same features that drove the introduction of social platforms in the first place. Thus, information systems are moving from the communication level, to the coordination and collaboration levels, increasingly acknowledging and leveraging the various dimensions of social relations among people, both internally and across organization boundaries.

A first strategy, that some organizations and brands are adopting, is to use social media for improving their customer relationship management (CRM). In fact, social media can be a means for firms and organizations to listen to customers and to cope with the difficulties in collecting data through interviews (Murphy et al., 2011). Social media allow the use of online sources of information, sometimes for free. So, firms and organizations are moving to reduce costs and time needed by traditional survey researches. Moreover, in the last years several social media monitoring tools and platforms have been developed to listen to the social media users, analyze and measure their content in relation to a brand or enterprise business and so it is reducing the time necessary for extracting the useful information through the huge data provided by social media (Stavrakantonakis et al., 2012). However, this quite popular trend towards so-called "*Social CRM*" has not always been satisfactory. A study by IBM (2011) shows that there's a quite large gap between the expectations of brand managers and social media users. In fact, only the 23% of users are keen to engage with brands on social media, and only 5% of users declare active participation. The majority, instead, limit their communications and shares with parents and relatives. Among the potentially interested people, many expect tangible benefits, including discounts, services, additional information and reviews about products. The study is in accordance with the difficulties that brands face to engage with users and to launch viral campaigns. Nevertheless, businesses continue to be greatly interested in using social media for rapid distribution of offers and content, reaching new people through trusted introducers, but also for improving customer care and research.

A second type of effort is directed to augment internal tools, in particular knowledge management (KM) systems, with explicit and rich data about relationships among involved people. The long-term goal of KM, in fact, is to let insights and experiences existing in implicit way into an organization emerge and become easily accessible for wider internal adoption. Such knowledge can be either possessed by individuals or embedded into common practices. To provide effective access to valuable internal knowledge and expertise, it is essential to recognize and value the particular knowledge possessed by different persons, and then to have means to contact the relevant persons in a timely manner, thus making information-seeking an easier and more successful experience. In many regards, such a scenario can be fully developed only on the basis of the evolution of existing ICT tools and the creation of new ones, by making some typical features of social networking applications available in tools for daily activities.

This trend regards existing Information Systems and also, for some aspects, platforms for enterprise resource planning (ERP). In fact, some aspects of traditional ERP systems are integrating features of social networking platforms, fostering collaboration among people on the basis of direct interpersonal links and simple knowledge sharing tools. The centralized and inward approach of early systems is being challenged also in the core area of production management software. The drift towards network of integrated enterprises is testified by an increasingly dynamic production environment, arranged in the form of complex Virtual Organizations and Virtual Enterprises. In this context, the tasks of supply chain management, project and activity management, data services and access control management require the participation of actors of different organizations and possibly different places and cultures.

MODELS OF PARTICIPATION

The result of the interactions among the users in a social networking system is an Online Social Network, i.e., a special case of the more general concept of social network. A social network is defined as a set or sets of actors and the relations defined on them (Wasserman & Faust, 1994). Social networks are typically studied using social network analysis, a discipline that focuses on the structural and topological features of the network. More recently, additional dimensions have been added to the traditional social network analytic approach (Monge & Contractor 2003; Borgatti & Foster 2003; Parkhe et al. 2006; Hoang & Antoncic 2003).

Figure 1. A graphical illustration of the IMDb online movie database. The depicted social network consists of 58984 nodes and 295099 edges. Nodes represent actors who starred in at least two movies, in the period 2001 – 2010, and edges connect actors if they starred together in at least 2 movies (undirected graph). Edges colors emphasize subgroups of actors, called communities, found by the PaNDEMON algorithm (Amoretti et al.,2016).

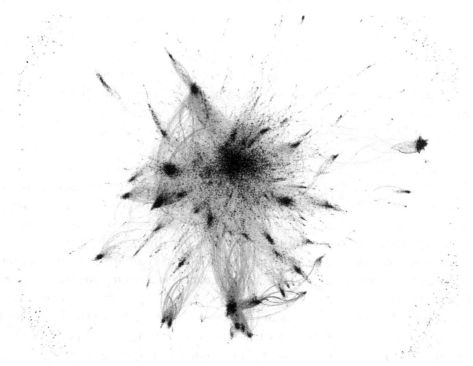

Social Network Analysis

Social network analysis (SNA) is the process of studying social networks and understanding the behaviours of their members (Laumann & Pappi, 2013). Graph theory provides the basic foundations for representing and studying a social network (Wasserman & Faust, 1994). In fact, each member of the social network can be mapped onto a node of the graph and each relationship between two members onto an edge that connects two nodes. An example is shown in Figure 1.

In real life, it is very common to find examples of social networks: groups of friends, a company's employees, contributors with different aims, etc. In fact, SNA is currently used in many research fields including anthropology, biology, economics, geography, information science, organizational studies, political science and social psychology.

The main goals of SNA are:

- To investigate behaviours of some network users;
- To identify users' membership and position into sub-communities;
- To find possible relationships among some users;
- To discover changes in network structure over time.

Different aspects are useful for investigating the behaviours of a participant in a social network: the most relevant are his position in the social network (i.e., which other members it is connected to) and his contributions to discussions or collaborations (knowing which groups he belongs to could be an important information). Another important aspect is the kind of activity performed by a user in his social network (Klein, Ahlf & Sharma, 2015). Mainly, a user can be identified as "active" (when he produces contents, sends videos and photos, comments posts of other users, reports original texts and documents) or "passive" (when he is only a consumer of other users' contents, limiting himself to liking or unliking those contents).

A second aspect, which we want to focus in, is the relationship between two members of the network (Golbeck & Hendler, 2006). Discovering the type of relationship between two members, their reciprocal trust, and their distance in the network, are basic information used by SNA to speculate about information diffusion and users contamination or contagion, i.e., the mechanism of imitation in social contexts (Burt, 1995).

Another significant application of SNA is to find subgroups composed by different users, i.e., to perform community detection (Amoretti et al., 2016), as shown in Figure 1. For example, Fortunato (2010) presents a case study about the Belgian population, which can be split and clustered using phone communication data. Many users can be considered a community if existing connections between them are many more than the number of users (this situation is similar to a dense graph). Detecting the presence of a community allows analysts to recognize the paths followed by information for reaching the network users. According to a user's position, it is possible to identify three main metrics: Degree Centrality, Betweenness Centrality, and Closeness Centrality. Degree Centrality, strictly connected to the concept of graph-node degree, tells us the number of direct connections a node has. The higher the degree, the stronger the capability to spread information to other users is. Instead, Betweenness Centrality is a gauging of how much a user could be able to diffuse information from a community to another, especially if he belongs to many communities. A very interesting approach aims at identifying influential users on the basis of their activity level, comparing it with the activity and reactions of their followers/friends (Klein, Ahlf & Sharma, 2015). Finally, Closeness Centrality is a measurement connected to the concept of graph-path length. It provides information about how far a user is from all the users of his community: the shorter this value is, the greater the possibility to reach all the participants of the network is, when he posts a content.

The last major aspect, which SNA concentrates in, is to discover the changes of a social network structure during time (Barabási et al., 2002). Studying the dynamics of a network allows analysts to detect persistent relationships, if they exist, and also to discover the lead users. Lead users play an important role in the network, since they have the best marks, according to the main centrality metrics mentioned before, and remain stable in the network for a long period. Studying network changes can also be useful in predicting users' real connections (Wang et al., 2011).

Social Capital

An important theoretical foundation for the analysis of participation in social networks is constituted by social capital. Social capital represents a person's benefit due to his relations with other persons, including family, colleagues, friends and generic contacts. The concept originated in studies about communities, to underline the importance of collective actions and the associated enduring relations of trust and cooperation, for the functioning of neighborhoods in large cities (Jacobs, 1961).

Social capital has been studied as a factor providing additional opportunities to some players in a competitive scenario, and, from this point of view, it has been studied in the context of firms (Backer, 1990), nations (Fukuyama, 1995) and geographic regions (Putnam, 1995). In this sense, social capital is defined as a third kind of capital that is brought in the competitive arena, along with financial capital, which includes machinery and raw materials, and human capital, which includes knowledge and skills. Moreover, the role of social capital in the development of human capital has been studied by Loury (1987) and Coleman (1988).

Social capital is typically studied: (*i*) by drawing a graph of connected people and their own resources, creating a connection between each player's resources and those of his closest contacts; or (*ii*) by analyzing social structures in their own right, and supposing that the network structure alone can be used to estimate some player's competitive advantage, at the social stance (Franchi et al., 2016b).

The size of the ego-centered social network is an important factor to estimate the social capital of one individual; however, the size alone does not provide enough information. According to Burt (1992) social capital is related with the number of non-redundant contacts and not directly with the simple number of contacts.

In fact, although information spreads rapidly among homogeneous, richly interconnected groups, Granovetter (1973) argues that new ideas and opportunities are introduced in the groups by contacts with people from outside the group. In order to explain this phenomenon, Granovetter distinguished among three types of ties: (*i*) strong ties, (*ii*) weak ties, and (*iii*) absent ties.

A quantitative distinction between strong and weak ties has been subject of debate, but intuitively weak ties are simple acquaintances, while strong ties are reserved for close friends and family. The "absent ties" indicate missing relations in the network. Burt capitalizes on Granovetter's insight, and emphasizes the importance of absent ties, that create the "structural holes" in the network texture. According to Burt, structural holes allow the individuals that create a weak link among two otherwise separated communities to greatly increase their social capital. A graphical example of structural holes is illustrated in the following figure 2.

Figure 2. The simple social network in the image illustrates the concept of structural hole. In grey, the three different and separated communities are highlighted, and the node with the maximum betweenness centrality score is colored in red. Such a node is also responsible of linking those communities, allowing exchanges among them, which increase significantly its social capital.

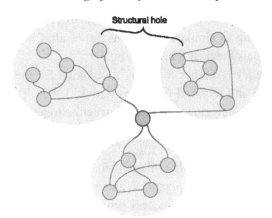

Nahapiet and Goshal (1998) discuss the role of social capital in building intellectual capital inside organizations. The authors distinguish the structural, relational, and cognitive aspects of social networks. The structural properties describe the patterns of connection among actors and regard the social system as a whole, i.e., given an actor, the set of actors it can reach and the way it could relate with them. The relational properties describe the type of ties people have developed during their interactions, including relationships like friendship, trust, and respect. As a concrete example, consider two actors which have similar networks, and that their positions inside such networks could be considered equivalent: their actions may differ significantly, based on their different attachment w.r.t. other members, in emotional and personal extent. The cognitive properties refer to basic knowledge, representations, languages and other systems of meaning, shared among actors, e.g., shared narrative. Moreover, they focus on the development of intellectual capital, which is essentially an aspect of human capital, but may also be owned by a social collectivity. In fact, they classify knowledge as (*i*) either implicit or explicit, and (*ii*) either individual or social. In the case of social knowledge, they argue that social capital facilitates the creation of intellectual capital primarily by creating conditions for exchange and combination of knowledge. Finally, they discuss the features of an organization that are more effective for the development of intellectual capital, including duration of contacts, type and frequency of interactions, interdependence of actors and closure of the community.

Contractor and Monge (2003) proposed a multifaceted approach, with a Multi-theoretical multilevel (MTML) model, for explaining the various motivations for the existence of social connections in a network. Their analysis considers the following theories:

- **Self-interest:** According to the theories of self-interest, people create ties with other people and participate in team activities in order to maximize the satisfaction of their own goals. The most known theories of self-interest are based on the notion of social capital (Burt, 1992). Another foundation of these theories lies on transaction cost economics (Williamson, 1991);

- **Mutual interest and collective action:** These theories study the coordinated action of individuals in a team. They explain collective actions as a mean for reaching outcomes which would be unattainable by individual action (Fulk et al., 2004). Thus, individuals collaborate in a community because they share mutual interests;

- **Homophily and proximity:** The principle at the basis of these theories is that connections are mostly structured according to similarity (McPherson et al., 2001). Moreover, connections between dissimilar individuals break at a higher rate;

- **Exchange and dependency:** Another founding motivation for the emergence of groups can be the exchange of available and required resources (Cook, 1982). Thus, these theories explain the creation of communities by analyzing the network structure together with the distribution and flow of resources in the network. Examples of exchange networks vary from data analysts to bands of musicians;

- **Co-evolution:** The underlying principle of these theories is that evolution based on environmental selection can be applied to whole organizations, and not only to individuals. Thus, they study how organizations compete and cooperate to access limited resources, and how communities of individuals create ties both internally and towards other communities (Campbell, 1985; Baum, 1999);

- **Contagion:** For explaining the spread of innovations, contagion theories study how people are brought in contact trough the social structure (Burt, 1987). Social contagion is described as a sort of interpersonal synapse through which ideas are spread. Conversely, some sort of social inoculations may prevent ideas from spreading to parts of the network;

- **Balance and transitivity:** Since macroscopic patterns originate from local structures of social networks, balance theories (Holland & Leinhardt, 1975) start from the study of triads in a digraph, or a socio-matrix. The typical distributions of triads configurations in real social networks show that individuals' choices have a consistent tendency to be transitive;

- **Cognition:** Finally, another aspect of social network analysis regards the importance of knowledge and semantics in the development of teams and the impact of increasing specialization over collaboration. In this sense, the decision to form a collective depends on what possible members know (Hollingshead et al. 2002). These studies are grounded on the concept of transactive memory.

The study of structure of Online Social Networks, expressed as patterns of links among nodes, can exploit models and ideas from classical sociology and anthropology, with particular attention to contextual and relational approaches. In fact, all the results obtained in decades of studies of human networks are also at the basis of the analysis of Online Social Networks. However, these results cannot be simply applied to the different context of online relations. Instead they have to be evaluated and adapted to the new networks, which may have significantly different structure and dynamics. Moreover, online social networking platforms may greatly vary both technically and in their aims. They may be used by people for organizing quite diverse activities, in different virtual communities.

Information Spreading

In social network analysis, the study of information spreading processes is a critical topic. As a matter of fact, understanding the dynamics of information (or rumor) spread in social networks is very important for many different purposes, such as marketing campaigns, political influence, news diffusion and so on.

The way a piece of information reaches people and how much time it takes to do it are examples of analysis of information spreading processes. They depend mainly on *(i)* network characteristics – topology, dynamism, sparsity, etc. –, *(ii)* the meaning of the information content, and *(iii)* the influence of the source of information.

Several models have been developed in order to study such a phenomenon, but there is no existing unique standard option, due to the heterogeneity of social networks (Moreno, Nekovee & Pacheco, 2004), that range from real-world ones to online social networks, such as micro-blogging services or forums.

Despite those diversities, social networks share common features that are taken as basis for the analysis. First of all, a network is often viewed as a graph $G = (V, E)$, where V is a discrete finite set of nodes (or vertices) that represents the people or users involved, and E is a binary relation on V, that represents relationships among users. The neighborhood of a node is the set of other nodes directly connected to him.

Depending on networks, the topological characteristics of the graph change, and several models have been investigated to match the correct shape of a network. Examples of such models include complete graphs (Pittel, 1987), hypercubes (Feige et al., 1990), random graphs (Erdős & Rényi, 1959) and evolving random graphs (Clementi et al., 2015), preferential attachment graphs (Barabási & Albert, 1999; Doerr, Fouz & Friedrich, 2012), power-law degree graphs (Fountoulakis, Panagiotou & Sauerwald, 2012).

Among these models, there is not a "better" one. Choosing one of them depends on the problem to be addressed. For example, online social networks present often a scale-free structure, which can be successfully modeled by power-law degree graphs. If the focus is the time evolution of such a network, other models can be considered. As a matter of fact, evolving random graphs operates well in analyzing the problem of rumor spreading.

In literature, rumor spreading on a graph (thus, a social network) has been studied by means of two types of distributed mechanisms (Kuhn, Lynch & Oshman, 2010; Kuhn & Oshman, 2011): the push protocol and the flooding protocol. Both protocols are synchronous, i.e., time steps, or rounds, are used to describe the behavior of a node, and the piece of information or rumor originates by a single source node.

In flooding protocol, starting from the source at the first-time step, each node forwards the information to all nodes in its neighborhood. In push protocol, instead, at every time step, each informed node in the social network chooses uniformly at random another node and shares with it the piece of information. Behavior of such protocols are widely investigated for several types of graphs (Karp et al., 2000), and their performance, time of completion (Baumann, Crescenzi & Fraigniaud, 2011; Clementi et al., 2010) or other measures, such as conductance (Giakkoupis, 2011), are well-known.

The actual challenge is to understand when and how such protocols, or their variants, are suitable in order to describe information spreading in a certain social network, with its own topological model. Answers to such problems differ according to social network characteristics and platforms, taking account of communication patterns. For example, for online social networks, the Twitter retweet mechanism (Kwak et al., 2010; Ye & Wu, 2013) or the way Facebook users share posts (Fan & Yeung, 2013; Kee et al., 2016) can be considered as communication patterns.

The study of information diffusion often gives rise to other inherent questions, such as how a topic becomes popular and what mechanisms to make it viral (Zaman et al., 2010). Those matters are analyzed by means of statistical models. Such models aim to predict the future impact of a new information released within the social network.

Currently, "little is known about factors that could affect the dissemination of a single piece of information" (Wang et al., 2011), and several predictive models have been proposed. Each model have to face three main issues: *(i)* the impact of the topology of the underlying social network – with all the related formalizations, *(ii)* the influence of the individual behaviour of users and, finally, *(iii)* the communication patterns of the community (online or not).

A common approach is to assign a score to the characteristic features of the network (Shah & Zaman, 2011; Zhou et al., 2008; Zaman, Fox & Bradlow, 2014). In some networks, the underlying graph model is very important because diffusion is subordinated to connection among users, for example if the piece of information is visible only to a user's neighborhood. In other networks, messages or posts are public, and this fact overcome topological limits, bypassing relationship to address wide audience. Moreover, the propagation speed depends on the context in which the piece of information is introduced.

All those considerations are useful to obtain the correct score of a feature, and then the scores are put together to obtain an estimation of the diffusion probability of a single topic. Such estimations are obtained, for example, by means of statistical methods such as the method of moments or the Maximum Likelihood Estimation (MLE), in which features represent the population of parameters to estimate (Scholz, 2014).

Motivations for Participation

In order to understand the reasons that motivate the users in engaging in online social activities in general, and, more specifically, in sharing their valued knowledge in online communities, it is necessary to analyze *(i)* the nature and the structure of their relationships in the context of a specific community, and *(ii)* their implication over both online and offline reputation. Wasko and Faraj (2005), for example, analyze the motivations for participation in a specific online Network of Practice. In particular, the analyzed network is a public online forum of legal professionals, who participate under their real identities. In Wasko and Faraj (2005) the following features are taken into account, as possible enablers of participation:

- **Individual motivations:** One key aspect of social contribution is an individual's expectation that some new value will be created, as result of his participation in the network. The individual should expect to receive some benefits from his contribution, even in the absence of direct acquaintance with other members of the community and without mechanisms enforcing or encouraging reciprocity. Increasing the reputation is one of the most important forms of return of investment, especially if the online reputation is believed to have a positive impact on the professional reputation;
- **Relational capital:** Another enabling factor for contributions to an online community is represented by the personal relationships among individuals, as members of that community. Relational capital is directly related to the level of an individual's identification with the community, trust with other members (Tomaiuolo, 2013), perception of obligation to participate and reciprocate, acceptance of common norms. In particular, commitment can be associated with a community, apart from individuals;
- **Cognitive capital:** Any meaningful interaction between two members of a community requires some basic shared understanding. All those common semantic resources, including languages, interpretations, narratives, contexts and norms, are usually described as cognitive capital. In fact, an individual can participate in community activities only if he possesses the required knowledge and, more in general, the required cognitive capital;
- **Structural capital:** Communities with dense internal connections show more collective actions than other types of networks. In fact, individuals who are strongly embedded in a social network, have many direct ties with other members and a habit of cooperation. On the other hand, an indi-

vidual's position in the network influences his willingness to contribute, thus increasing both the number and quality of interactions.

Those factors have different weight in different social contexts. In the case study analyzed by Wasko and Faraj (2005), reputation plays a crucial role, since it also affects professional reputation. Other factors, though, also have meaningful relationships with the number and usefulness of contributions in the online community. The final results compare both the level and helpfulness of contributions against the following factors: (*i*) reputation, (*ii*) willingness to help, (*iii*) centrality in the network structure, (*iv*) self-rated expertise, (*v*) tenure in field, (*vi*) commitment, (*vii*) reciprocity.

With regard to individual motivations, results for the case at hand show a stronger influence of reputation over intrinsic motivations, like willingness to help. Social capital, assessed by determining each individual's degree of centrality to the network, is confirmed to play the most significant role in knowledge exchange. Also, cognitive capital, assessed by self-rated expertise and tenure in the field, shows a strong influence over participation, but this is mostly limited to the individual's experience in the field, while self-rated expertise is not quite significant. Finally, in the analyzed Network of Practice, relational capital, assessed by commitment and reciprocity, is not strongly correlated with knowledge contribution, suggesting that these kinds of ties are more difficult to develop in an online network.

The increasingly important role of social media in society makes it clear to both individuals and organizations that they are crucial tools for innovation. In fact, creativity and innovation have long been notable subjects of organizational studies and social network analysis. Fedorowicz et al. (2008) note that creative ideas rarely come from individuals. More often, they come from teams and groups, including those formed through social media. Dwyer (2011) argues that, apart from the number of collaborators, it is also important to measure the quality of collaboration. In fact, various collaborator segments can be identified, with significant differences in the value of contributed ideas and the timing of participation. Thus, new metrics should be used, taking those differences into account and being based on information content. Hayne and Smith (2005) note that groupware performance depends on the fit between the structure and task of the group. However, they argue that an important role may also be played by the cognitive structure, which also maps to the group structure. In fact, collaborative tasks may push human cognitive capabilities to their limits, in terms of perception, attention and memory. Thus, the authors argue for the integration of different areas of study, such as: psychology, especially with regard to abilities and limitations; theories of social interactions, with regard to group communication and motivation; studies of groupware structures and human interactions mediated by artifacts.

Anti-Social Behaviours and Trolling

In Computer-Mediated Communication (CMC), user behavior is very different from a face-to-face communication and every type of communication medium creates its own communication rules. Depending on the kind of CMC, users are allowed to adjust the degree of identity they reveal. The level of anonymity usually guaranteed in online discussions allows users to engage in behaviours they would otherwise be averse to carry out in face-to-face discussion. This lack of identifiability has contributed to the codification of new communication behaviours, like trolling (Morrisey, 2010).

Trolls are often seen as corrupters within an online community. They often share a group's common interests and try to pass as a legitimate member of the group (Donath, 1999). After that, they try to lead the conversation toward pointless discussion (Herring et al., 2002). Morrisey (2010) suggests that "…

trolling is an utterer producing an intentionally false or incorrect utterance with high-order intention to elicit from recipient a particular response, generally negative or violent."

Trolls can damage a group in many ways. They can interrupt discussions, give bad advice, or undermine the mutual confidence of the user community. Trolls usually post a message into different sections (Cross-Posting), by doing this they are able to annoy more groups simultaneously. Nowadays many companies are using tools such as blogs, forums, social media (including self-developed ones) for their own interests. Trolls are therefore a threat to private social platforms as well as for public ones.

The most widely used solution against trolls is to ignore provocations. Some systems provide filters (killfile, blacklist) that allow users to exclude trolls from public discussions. In recent years, many projects have been developed for the automatic detection of trolls in online communities. Some works (Seah et al., 2015) use a supervised learning algorithm, which allows to classify the polarity of posts and identify trolls as users with a high number of negative messages. The classifiers are trained using examples of positive and negative sentences. The polarity classifier is trained on a data set of movie reviews written in standard English. The Support Vector Machine algorithm is used to do binary classification of trolls. Since the data set contains messages from different topics (different forums), some domain adaptation techniques are used to get better results.

Furthermore, the frequency of messages, and possibly also the frequency of generated answers, is another factor for determining the presence of a troll in the network: the higher the frequency, the higher the probability that he is a troll (Buckels, Trapnell & Paulhus, 2014). In Ortega et al. (2012), the authors propose a method to compute a ranking of the users in a social network, regarding their reliability. The goal is to prevent malicious users to gain a good reputation in the network. To achieve this purpose, they create a graph taking the users of the network as the nodes. The edges represent the opinions of some users about others, and the weights of the edges correspond to the intensity of the relationship between the nodes.

In (Galán-García et al., 2015), the authors suppose that "...it is possible to link a trolling account to the corresponding real profile of the user behind the fake account, analysing different features present in the profile, connections data and tweets characteristics, including text, using machine learning algorithms." In fact, machine learning techniques can be used to associate users' posts with various emotions, in addition to generic positive or negative sentiments (Fornacciari, Mordonini & Tomaiuolo, 2015; Angiani et al., 2016).

More recently, researchers from Stanford and Cornell Universities have developed an algorithm that can estimate the need to ban a member of an online community, after observing only five to ten online posts (Cheng et al., 2015). In particular, the authors present a data-driven approach to detect antisocial behavior in online discussion. The data sets are collected from users that have been banned from a community.

RISKS AND CHALLENGES FOR FIRMS AND ORGANIZATIONS

The initial adoption of online collaboration tools and social networking platforms in the work environment has occurred largely on an individual basis. Faced with an increasingly decentralized, expanded and interconnected environment, workers and members of organizations began adopting social networking platforms as better tools for connecting and collaborating with colleagues and partners (Franchi et al., 2016a). Thus, social media made their first appearance in firms and organizations mostly without indications from the management and without integration with internal information systems. In this sense, they took the form of feral systems. In fact, (*i*) they were not "part of the corporation's accepted information technology infrastructure", and (ii) they were "designed to augment" that infrastructure, along with the definition of Feral Information Systems provided by Houghton and Kerr (2006). In a study published by AT&T (2008), ten main challenges are listed for the adoption of social media by businesses. In fact, these challenges can be grouped in three main areas: (*i*) organizational costs, (*ii*) risks of capital loss, and (*iii*) technical challenges.

About organizational costs, the first issue is that social networking has indirect benefits, which often are not fully appreciated. It is probably the main area of resistance, due to the perceived costs of networking time in terms of employees' productivity. The necessity to allow employees to manage their working time with more freedom is restrained by the risk of decreasing the time and attention dedicated to the most cost-effective activities. However, traditional ROI methods make it difficult to incorporate all the benefits of social media, both direct and indirect. Thus, new performance indicators will be needed. Another issue is the definition of an effective plan to reach the critical mass for the social network to be functional. In fact, common figures of users creating content and collaborating through social media are pretty low, typically from 1% to 20%. Resistance to adoption can come from both regular employee and cadres, possibly including managers and executives. Such a plan would also face the problem of timeliness. In fact, developments in the Web 2.0 environment occur very fast: successful applications may reach millions of users in a couple of years, sometimes creating a new market.

Other challenges are related to the risk of loss of capital, faced by organizations in the adoption of social media. The capital at risk can include intellectual property, as well as human and social capital. In fact, organization members may easily and inadvertently leak sensible and protected content on social media, and such content may face rapid diffusion by "word of mouth" mechanisms. An even greater risk, however, may come from the increased mobility of organization members and employees. This risk is increased by the exposure of members' profiles to the outside world, including other organizations and competitors.

Finally, the adoption of Online Social Networks incurs technical costs for creating and maintaining a more complex and open infrastructure. Some important challenges regard security, which is harder to enforce as intranets need to open to the external world, for enabling social collaboration (Franchi et al., 2015). The risks include the malicious behavior of users, as well as the proliferation of viruses and malware. Also, on the technical front, social media applications require increased levels of bandwidth, storage and computational capacity, to support interactions through videos and other form of rich content. Moreover, the increased and differentiated use of social media will pose challenges for the interoperability of different applications, especially with regard to security and authentication schemes.

While AT&T (2008) study was conducted in reference to the business context, it is interesting to notice that similar considerations are also referred to government agencies and other types of organizations. For example, Bev et al. (2008) describe the case of government agencies. Among other issues, the study underlines the problems of (*i*) employees wasting time on social networks, (*ii*) risk of malware and spyware coming from high traffic sites, and (*iii*) bandwidth requirements. About the first issue, that we described as one aspect of the organizational costs, we argue that the problem is not specific to Web 2.0 technologies. In fact, a similar argument was used with respect to mobile phones, emails, etc. For this reason, it is better treated as a management problem instead of a technology problem. About security, efforts should be dedicated to at least mitigate the risks, if they cannot be canceled. Finally, with regard to bandwidth and other technological issues, enough resources should be deployed, to allow at least some selected employees to use rich-content media to communicate with the public, in the most effective way.

To leverage the advantages of social networking, organizations and firms should support their transition from the individual adoption as feral systems to the formal incorporation into existing information systems. To achieve this goal, knowledge management professionals should act as social networking architects, in conjunction with other managers and IT professionals. In fact, social network analysis can highlight the patterns of connection among individuals and the main knowledge flows in a whole organization. Thus, it can be used by managers as a basis for reshaping the organization and advancing towards the business goals. Anklam (2004) describes three main types of intervention, to conduct after a social network analysis: (*i*) structural/organizational, i.e. change the organigrams to improve the knowledge transfer; (*ii*) knowledge-network development, i.e. overcome resistance to action on the basis of evidence, instead of intuition; (*iii*) individual/leadership, i.e. resolve problems with the particular role of individuals, for example acting as factual gatekeepers and resulting in a knowledge bottleneck. More in general, social network analysis can be useful to cope with common business problems, including: launching distributed teams, retention of people with vital knowledge for the organization, improve access to knowledge and increase innovation.

Along the same lines, Roy (2012) discusses the profile of leaders in Virtual Teams. In fact, apart from usual technical and leadership capacities, to work effectively in a virtual environment, they also need abilities to build relationships among participants and to defuse frustrations. In fact, on the one hand, they need particular communication skills, as well as good knowledge for operating video conferencing software and other CSCW tools. On the other hand, they must be able to establish trust, embrace diversity, motivating team members and fostering the team spirit.

CONCLUSION

The theories of participation in social networks and the general results in the field of social network analysis are important for dealing with some crucial issues of modern online social networks. The study of individual motivations in order to belong to an online social network can benefit from classical social networking models, that have been developed in the general context of human sociology. In assessing the performance of a social media, those models are of great importance. Also, it is crucial to find the appropriate parameters for measuring the success factors of online social networks and virtual communities.

In this article, the discourse started with the reasons for and the benefits of belonging to a social network, with particular reference to the theories of social capital. Then, the problem of information spreading (i.e., virality) was analysed, since it is crucial for understanding and improving the diffusion of knowledge and innovation inside and among online communities. One problem that limits the potential of online social networks is their misuse by some participants who, for various reasons, adopt antisocial behaviours. The identification of so-called "trolls" is still an open research topic and, in part, it can be facilitated by an "ad hoc" knowledge on the network. Thus, it is important to join the different competences of computer engineers, data scientists and knowledge management professionals.

To augment the topological analysis of a social graph, a promising research area regards the study of the semantics of links, to refine the models of participation in an online social network. In particular, this kind of knowledge could be used for determining the corrective actions to adopt for improving the success of a certain social media initiative.

REFERENCES

Amoretti, M., Ferrari, A., Fornacciari, P., Mordonini, M., Rosi, F., & Tomaiuolo, M. (2016). Local-first algorithms for community detection. In *CEUR Workshop Proceedings*.

Angiani, G., Cagnoni, S., Chuzhikova, N., Fornacciari, P., Mordonini, M., & Tomaiuolo, M. (2016). Flat and hierarchical classifiers for detecting emotion in tweets. In Conference of the Italian Association for Artificial Intelligence (pp. 51-64). Cham: Springer. doi:10.1007/978-3-319-49130-1_5

Anklam, P. (2004). KM and the Social Network. *Knowledge Management Magazine*, (May), 24-28.

AT&T. (2008). The Business Impacts of Social Networking. Retrieved from http://www.business.att.com/content/whitepaper/WP-soc_17172_v3_11-10-08.pdf

Baker, W. E. (1990). Market networks and corporate behavior. *American Journal of Sociology*, *96*(3), 589–625. doi:10.1086/229573

Barabási, A. L., & Albert, R. (1999). Emergence of scaling in random networks. *Science*, *286*(5439), 509–512. doi:10.1126cience.286.5439.509 PMID:10521342

Barabási, A. L., Jeong, H., Néda, Z., Ravasz, E., Schubert, A., & Vicsek, T. (2002). Evolution of the social network of scientific collaborations. *Physica A*, *311*(3), 590–614. doi:10.1016/S0378-4371(02)00736-7

Baum, J. A. (1999). Whole-part coevolutionary competition in organizations. In *Variations in organization science* (pp. 113-135). Thousand Oaks, CA: Sage Publications

Baumann, H., Crescenzi, P., & Fraigniaud, P. (2011). Parsimonious flooding in dynamic graphs. *Distributed Computing*, *24*(1), 31–44. doi:10.100700446-011-0133-9

Bergenti, F., Iotti, E., Poggi, A., & Tomaiuolo, M. (2016). Concurrent and Distributed Applications with ActoDeS. *MATEC Web of Conferences CSCC 2016*.

Bergenti, F., Poggi, A., & Tomaiuolo, M. (2014). An Actor Based Software Framework for Scalable Applications. In International Conference on Internet and Distributed Computing Systems (pp. 26-35). Cham, Switzerland: Springer. doi:10.1007/978-3-319-11692-1_3

Bergenti, F., Poggi, A., Tomaiuolo, M., & Turci, P. (2005). An Ontology Support for Semantic Aware Agents. In *Proc. Seventh International Bi-Conference Workshop on Agent-Oriented Information Systems (AOIS-2005@ AAMAS), Utrecht, The Netherlands*.

Bev, G., Campbell, S., Levy, J., & Bounds, J. (2008). *Social media and the federal government: Perceived and real barriers and potential solutions*. Federal Web Managers Council.

Borgatti, S. P., & Foster, P. C. (2003). The network paradigm in organizational research: A review and typology. *Journal of Management*, *29*(6), 991–1013. doi:10.1016/S0149-2063(03)00087-4

Buckels, E. E., Trapnell, P. D., & Paulhus, D. L. (2014). Trolls just want to have fun. *Personality and Individual Differences*, *67*, 97–102. doi:10.1016/j.paid.2014.01.016

Burt, R. S. (1987). Social Contagion and Innovation: Cohesion versus Structural Equivalence. *American Journal of Sociology*, *92*(6), 1287–1335. doi:10.1086/228667

Burt, R. S. (1995). *Structural holes: The social structure of competition*. Harvard University Press.

Campbell, J. H. (1985). An organizational interpretation of evolution. In *Evolution at a crossroads*. MIT Press.

Cheng, J., Danescu-Niculescu-Mizil, C., & Leskovec, J. (2015). Antisocial Behavior in Online Discussion Communities. arXiv:1504.00680

Clementi, A., Crescenzi, P., Doerr, C., Fraigniaud, P., Pasquale, F., & Silvestri, R. (2015). Rumor spreading in random evolving graphs. *Random Structures and Algorithms*.

Clementi, A. E., Macci, C., Monti, A., Pasquale, F., & Silvestri, R. (2010). Flooding time of edge-markovian evolving graphs. *SIAM Journal on Discrete Mathematics*, *24*(4), 1694–1712. doi:10.1137/090756053

Coleman, J. S. (1988). Social capital in the creation of human capital. *American Journal of Sociology*, *94*, 95–120. doi:10.1086/228943

DiMicco, J. (2007). Identity management: multiple presentations of self in Facebook. In *6th International Conference on Supporting Group Work (GROUP'07)*, Sanibel Island, FL (pp. 1–4). 10.1145/1316624.1316682

DiMicco, J., Millen, D., & Geyer, W. (2008). Motivations for social networking at work. *Conference on Computer Supported Cooperative Work (CSCW'08)*, San Diego, CA (pp. 711–720).

Doerr, B., Fouz, M., & Friedrich, T. (2012). Why rumors spread so quickly in social networks. *Communications of the ACM*, *55*(6), 70–75. doi:10.1145/2184319.2184338

Donath, J. S. (1999). Identity and deception in the virtual community. *Communities in cyberspace*, 29-59.

Erdős, P., & Rényi, A. (1959). On Random Graphs. *Publ. Math.*, *6*, 290–297.

Fan, W., & Yeung, K. H. (2013). Virus Propagation Modeling in Facebook. In *The Influence of Technology on Social Network Analysis and Mining* (pp. 185–199). Springer Vienna. doi:10.1007/978-3-7091-1346-2_8

Feige, U., Peleg, D., Raghavan, P., & Upfal, E. (1990). Randomized broadcast in networks. *Random Structures and Algorithms*, *1*(4), 447–460. doi:10.1002/rsa.3240010406

Fornacciari, P., Mordonini, M., & Tomaiuolo, M. (2015). A case-study for sentiment analysis on twitter. *CEUR Workshop Proceedings*.

Fornacciari, P., Mordonini, M., & Tomaiuolo, M. (2015). Social network and sentiment analysis on Twitter: Towards a combined approach. *CEUR Workshop Proceedings*.

Fortunato, S. (2010). Community detection in graphs. *Physics Reports*, *486*(3), 75–174. doi:10.1016/j.physrep.2009.11.002

Foster, I., Kesselman, C., & Tuecke, S. (2001). The anatomy of the grid: Enabling scalable virtual organizations. *International Journal of High Performance Computing Applications*, *15*(3), 200–222. doi:10.1177/109434200101500302

Fountoulakis, N., Panagiotou, K., & Sauerwald, T. (2012, January). Ultra-fast rumor spreading in social networks. In *Proceedings of the twenty-third annual ACM-SIAM symposium on Discrete Algorithms* (pp. 1642-1660). SIAM. 10.1137/1.9781611973099.130

Franchi, E., Poggi, A., & Tomaiuolo, M. (2015). Information and password attacks on social networks: An argument for cryptography. *Journal of Information Technology Research, 8*(1), 25–42. doi:10.4018/JITR.2015010103

Franchi, E., Poggi, A., & Tomaiuolo, M. (2016a). Blogracy: A peer-to-peer social network. *International Journal of Distributed Systems and Technologies, 7*(2), 37–56. doi:10.4018/IJDST.2016040103

Franchi, E., Poggi, A., & Tomaiuolo, M. (2016b). Social media for online collaboration in firms and organizations. *International Journal of Information System Modeling and Design, 7*(1), 18–31. doi:10.4018/IJISMD.2016010102

Fukuyama, F. (1995). *Trust: The social virtues and the creation of prosperity*. New York: Free Press.

Fulk, J., Heino, R., Flanagin, A. J., Monge, P. R., & Bar, F. (2004). A test of the individual action model for organizational information commons. *Organization Science, 15*(5), 569–585. doi:10.1287/orsc.1040.0081

Galán-García, P., De La Puerta, J. G., Gómez, C. L., Santos, I., & Bringas, P. G. (2015). Supervised machine learning for the detection of troll profiles in twitter social network: Application to a real case of cyberbullying. *Logic Journal of the IGPL*. doi:10.1093/jigpal/jzv048

Giakkoupis, G. (2011). Tight bounds for rumor spreading in graphs of a given conductance. In *Symposium on Theoretical Aspects of Computer Science (STACS2011)*, Dortmund, Germany (pp. 57-68).

Golbeck, J., & Hendler, J. (2006). Inferring binary trust relationships in web-based social networks. *ACM Transactions on Internet Technology, 6*(4), 497–529. doi:10.1145/1183463.1183470

Goldschlag, D., Reed, M., & Syverson, P. (1999). Onion routing. *Communications of the ACM, 42*(2), 39–41. doi:10.1145/293411.293443

Granovetter, M. S. (1973). The strength of weak ties. *American Journal of Sociology, 78*(6), 1360–1380. doi:10.1086/225469

Herring, S., Job-Sluder, K., Scheckler, R., & Barab, S. (2002). Searching for safety online: Managing "trolling" in a feminist forum. *The Information Society, 18*(5), 371–384. doi:10.1080/01972240290108186

Hoang, H., & Antoncic, B. (2003). Network-based research in entrepreneurship: A critical review. *Journal of Business Venturing, 18*(2), 165–187. doi:10.1016/S0883-9026(02)00081-2

Holland, P., & Leinhardt, S. (1974). The Statistical Analysis of Local Structure in Social Networks. *National Bureau of Economic Research*.

Hollingshead, A. B., Fulk, J., & Monge, P. (2002). Fostering intranet knowledge sharing: An integration of transactive memory and public goods approaches. In *Distributed work* (pp. 335-355).

Houghton, L., & Kerr, D. V. (2006). A study into the creation of feral information systems as a response to an ERP implementation within the supply chain of a large government-owned corporation. *International Journal of Internet and Enterprise Management, 4*(2), 135–147. doi:10.1504/IJIEM.2006.010239

IBM Institute for Business Value. (2011). *From social media to Social CRM*. Retrieved from http://public.dhe.ibm.com/common/ssi/ecm/en/gbe03391usen/GBE03391USEN.PDF

Jacobs, J. (1961). *The death and life of great American cities*. Vintage.

Jones, B. F., Wuchty, S., & Uzzi, B. (2008). Multi-university research teams: Shifting impact, geography, and stratification in science. *Science, 322*(5905), 1259–1262. doi:10.1126cience.1158357 PMID:18845711

Karp, R., Schindelhauer, C., Shenker, S., & Vocking, B. (2000). Randomized rumor spreading. In *Proceedings of the 41st Annual Symposium on Foundations of Computer Science* (pp. 565-574). IEEE. 10.1109/SFCS.2000.892324

Kee, K. F., Sparks, L., Struppa, D. C., Mannucci, M. A., & Damiano, A. (2016). Information diffusion, Facebook clusters, and the simplicial model of social aggregation: A computational simulation of simplicial diffusers for community health interventions. *Health Communication, 31*(4), 385–399. doi:10.1080/10410236.2014.960061 PMID:26362453

Klein, A., Ahlf, H., & Sharma, V. (2015). Social activity and structural centrality in online social networks. *Telematics and Informatics, 32*(2), 321–332. doi:10.1016/j.tele.2014.09.008

Kuhn, F., Lynch, N., & Oshman, R. (2010, June). Distributed computation in dynamic networks. In *Proceedings of the forty-second ACM symposium on Theory of computing* (pp. 513-522). ACM.

Kuhn, F., & Oshman, R. (2011). Dynamic networks: Models and algorithms. *ACM SIGACT News, 42*(1), 82–96. doi:10.1145/1959045.1959064

Kwak, H., Lee, C., Park, H., & Moon, S. (2010, April). What is Twitter, a social network or a news media? In *Proceedings of the 19th international conference on World wide web* (pp. 591-600). ACM. 10.1145/1772690.1772751

Laumann, E. O., & Pappi, F. U. (2013). *Networks of collective action: A perspective on community influence systems*. Elsevier.

Loury, G. C. (1987). Why should we care about group inequality? *Social Philosophy & Policy, 5*(1), 249–271. doi:10.1017/S0265052500001345

Malone, T. W., & Crowstone, K. (1994). The Interdisciplinary Study of Coordination. *ACM Computing Surveys, 26*(1), 87–119. doi:10.1145/174666.174668

McPherson, M., Smith-Lovin, L., & Cook, J. M. (2001). Birds of a Feather: Homophily in Social Networks. *Annual Review of Sociology, 27*(1), 415–444. doi:10.1146/annurev.soc.27.1.415

McQuail, D. (2005). *Processes and models of media effects. In D. McQuail (Ed.), McQuail's mass communication theory* (pp. 455–478). London: Sage.

Millen, D. R., Feinberg, J., Kerr, B., Rogers, O., & Cambridge, S. (2006). Dogear: Social bookmarking in the enterprise. In *Proceedings of the SIGCHI conference on Human Factors in computing systems* (pp. 111-120). ACM.

Monge, P. R., & Contractor, N. (2003). *Theories of communication networks*. USA: Oxford University Press.

Moreno, Y., Nekovee, M., & Pacheco, A. F. (2004). Dynamics of rumor spreading in complex networks. *Physical Review. E, 69*(6), 066130. doi:10.1103/PhysRevE.69.066130 PMID:15244690

Morrissey, L. (2010). Trolling is a art: Towards a schematic classification of intention in internet trolling. *Griffith Working Papers in Pragmatics and Intercultural Communications, 3*(2), 75-82.

Mowshowitz, A. (1994). Virtual organization: A vision of management in the information age. *The Information Society, 10*(4), 267–288. doi:10.1080/01972243.1994.9960172

Murphy, J., Kim, A., Hagood, H., Richards, A., Augustine, C., Kroutil, L., & Sage, A. (2011). Twitter Feeds and Google Search Query Surveillance: Can They Supplement Survey Data Collection?. *Shifting the Boundaries of Research*, 228.

Nahapiet, J., & Ghoshal, S. (1998). Social capital, intellectual capital, and the organizational advantage. *Academy of Management Review, 23*(2), 242–266. doi:10.5465/amr.1998.533225

Ortega, F. J., Troyano, J. A., Cruz, F. L., Vallejo, C. G., & Enríquez, F. (2012). Propagation of trust and distrust for the detection of trolls in a social network. *Computer Networks, 56*(12), 2884–2895. doi:10.1016/j.comnet.2012.05.002

Otte, E., & Rousseau, R. (2002). Social network analysis: A powerful strategy, also for the information sciences. *Journal of Information Science, 28*(6), 441–453. doi:10.1177/016555150202800601

Parkhe, A., Wasserman, S., & Ralston, D. A. (2006). New frontiers in network theory development. *Academy of Management Review, 31*(3), 560–568. doi:10.5465/amr.2006.21318917

Pittel, B. (1987). On spreading a rumor. *SIAM Journal on Applied Mathematics, 47*(1), 213–223. doi:10.1137/0147013

Poggi, A., & Tomaiuolo, M. (2010). Integrating peer-to-peer and multi-agent technologies for the realization of content sharing applications. *Studies in Computational Intelligence, 324*, 93–107. doi:10.1007/978-3-642-16089-9_6

Poggi, A., & Tomaiuolo, M. (2013). A DHT-based multi-agent system for semantic information sharing. In *New Challenges in Distributed Information Filtering and Retrieval* (pp. 197–213). Springer Berlin Heidelberg. doi:10.1007/978-3-642-31546-6_12

Poggi, A., Tomaiuolo, M., & Vitaglione, G. (2003, November). Security and trust in agent-oriented middleware. In *OTM Confederated International Conferences" On the Move to Meaningful Internet Systems"* (pp. 989-1003). Springer Berlin Heidelberg. 10.1007/978-3-540-39962-9_95

Powell, A., Piccoli, G., & Ives, B. (2004). Virtual Teams: A Review of Current Literature and Directions for Future *Research. The Data Base for Advances in Information Systems, 35*(1), 7. doi:10.1145/968464.968467

Putnam, R. D. (1995). Bowling alone: America's declining social capital. *Journal of Democracy, 6*(1), 65–78. doi:10.1353/jod.1995.0002

Roy, S. R. (2012). Digital Mastery: The skills needed for effective virtual leadership. *International Journal of e-Collaboration, 8*(3), 56–66. doi:10.4018/jec.2012070104

Scholz, F. W. (2014). Maximum Likelihood Estimation. In Wiley StatsRef: Statistics Reference Online. doi:10.1002/9781118445112.stat01663

Seah, C. W., Chieu, H. L., Chai, K. M. A., Teow, L. N., & Yeong, L. W. (2015, July). Troll detection by domain-adapting sentiment analysis. In *18th International Conference on Information Fusion (Fusion)* (pp. 792-799). IEEE.

Shah, D., & Zaman, T. (2011). Rumors in a network: Who's the culprit? *IEEE Transactions on Information Theory*, *57*(8), 5163–5181. doi:10.1109/TIT.2011.2158885

Stavrakantonakis, I., Gagiu, A. E., Kasper, H., Toma, I., & Thalhammer, A. (2012). An approach for evaluation of social media monitoring tools. *Common Value Management*, *52*(1), 52-64.

Su, C., & Contractor, N. (2011). A multidimensional network approach to studying team members' information seeking from human and digital knowledge sources in consulting firms. *Journal of the American Society for Information Science and Technology*, *62*(7), 1257–1275. doi:10.1002/asi.21526

Tomaiuolo, M. (2013). dDelega: Trust management for web services. *International Journal of Information Security and Privacy*, *7*(3), 53–67. doi:10.4018/jisp.2013070104

Tomaiuolo, M. (2013). Trust management and delegation for the administration of web services. In Organizational, Legal, and Technological Dimensions of Information System Administration (pp. 18–37). Hershey, PA: IGI Global. doi:10.4018/978-1-4666-4526-4.ch002

Van de Ven, A., Delbecq, A., & Koenig, R. (1976). Determinants of coordination modes within organizations. *American Sociological Review*, *41*(2), 322–338. doi:10.2307/2094477

Wang, D., Pedreschi, D., Song, C., Giannotti, F., & Barabasi, A. L. (2011, August). Human mobility, social ties, and link prediction. In *Proceedings of the 17th ACM SIGKDD international conference on Knowledge discovery and data mining* (pp. 1100-1108). ACM. 10.1145/2020408.2020581

Wang, D., Wen, Z., Tong, H., Lin, C. Y., Song, C., & Barabási, A. L. (2011, March). Information spreading in context. In *Proceedings of the 20th international conference on World wide web* (pp. 735-744). ACM.

Wasko, M. M., & Faraj, S. (2005). Why should i share? examining social capital and knowledge contribution in electronic networks of practice. *Management Information Systems Quarterly*, *29*(1), 35–57. doi:10.2307/25148667

Wasserman, S., & Faust, K. (1994). *Social network analysis: Methods and applications* (Vol. 8). Cambridge University Press. doi:10.1017/CBO9780511815478

Williamson, O. E. (1991). Comparative Economic Organization: The Analysis of Discrete Structural Alternatives. *Administrative Science Quarterly*, *36*(2), 219–244. doi:10.2307/2393356

Wuchty, S., Jones, B. F., & Uzzi, B. (2007). The increasing dominance of teams in production of knowledge. *Science*, *316*(5827), 1036–1039. doi:10.1126cience.1136099 PMID:17431139

Ye, S., & Wu, F. (2013). Measuring message propagation and social influence on Twitter.com. *International Journal of Communication Networks and Distributed Systems*, *11*(1), 59–76. doi:10.1504/IJCNDS.2013.054835

Zaman, T., Fox, E. B., & Bradlow, E. T. (2014). A Bayesian approach for predicting the popularity of tweets. *The Annals of Applied Statistics*, 8(3), 1583–1611. doi:10.1214/14-AOAS741

Zaman, T. R., Herbrich, R., Van Gael, J., & Stern, D. (2010, December). Predicting information spreading in twitter. In *Workshop on computational social science and the wisdom of crowds, NIPS* (Vol. 104, No. 45, pp. 17599-601). Citeseer.

Zhou, Y., Guan, X., Zhang, Z., & Zhang, B. (2008, June). Predicting the tendency of topic discussion on the online social networks using a dynamic probability model. In *Proceedings of the hypertext 2008 workshop on Collaboration and collective intelligence* (pp. 7-11). ACM. 10.1145/1379157.1379160

This research was previously published in the International Journal of Interactive Communication Systems and Technologies (IJICST), 8(2); pages 36-55, copyright year 2018 by IGI Publishing (an imprint of IGI Global).

Chapter 15
An Examination of Factors That Influence Social Networking Community Participation Among Millennials

Celeste See Pui Ng
Yuan Ze University, Taoyuan City, Taiwan

Anita Lee-Post
University of Kentucky, USA

ABSTRACT

This study investigates main and moderating factors that influence Millennials' intention to participate in a social networking community (SNC). The authors modified the unified theory of consumers' acceptance and use of technology (UTAUT2) to incorporate six main and two moderating factors to explain Millennials' SNC participation intention. By considering the implications of the unique characteristics of Millennials on their social networking behavior, the authors' model is better suited to answer what drives these tech-savvy individuals to participate in a SNC via such sites as Facebook. Specifically, the authors find that hedonic motivation, trust in technology, trust in community, and social influence are significant factors in influencing Millennials' SNC participation intention, with hedonic motivation being the most influential factor. In addition, gender and educational background moderate the main effects of these determinants in different manner. Theoretical and practical implications of these findings are discussed.

1. INTRODUCTION

The purpose of this paper is to further our understanding of factors that influence Millennials' participation intention in a social networking community (SNC). Millennials are individuals born between 1981 to 1996 (Dimock, 2018) who grew up in the Internet age and are regarded as the always connected, social and tech-savvy generation (Pew Research Center, 2014). The integral use of information technology

DOI: 10.4018/978-1-6684-6307-9.ch015

(IT) in the Millennials' social lives sets them apart from generations before them (Pew Research Center, 2010). Being digital natives, Millennials belong to a generation in which they have been immersed with everything digital since childhood. It is no surprise that Millennials are the first adopters of emerging technologies like tablets and digital wearables (Fleming et al., 2015). They are also avid producers and consumers of all kinds of digital contents – from blogs to video to photos to music to apps, with 55% of them posted a selfie on a social media (Pew Research Center, 2014). Over 75% of Millennials admit that they cannot live without their laptops or mobile phones (Brown, 2011). Social media defines their lives as 80% of Millennials are on sites like Twitter, Facebook and Weibo to chat, post comments, and send messages (Brown, 2011). Indeed, Millennials named "technology use" as what made their generation unique (Pew Research Center, 2010). Their technology use behavior has transformed social networking sites (where a group of people stay connected via social media) into SNCs (where a group of people interacting in social networking sites to fulfill their social needs and extend relationship building from family and friends to complete strangers), a phenomenon of interest in this paper. Note that unlike the formal-type of SNC such as Enterprise Architecture Group in LinkedIn, SNC here refers to an individual's personal group of friends and connections.

Millennials are also becoming a market segment of growing importance. They represent 25% of the world population, with 77 million in the US, 500 million in India, and 200 million in China (Brown, 2011). Millennials are the most educated generation with 33% of them having a college degree. They are highly optimistic about their financial future, with 53% believe they will have enough income to live the lives they want (Pew Research Center, 2014). Ten percent of them are already successful entrepreneurs and nearly 50% of them want to run their own business in the future (The Nielsen Company, 2014). A better understanding of the opportunities the Millennials present will equip business with effective strategies to reach, connect, and engage with this emerging economic power for long-term growth and success.

While much has been written about Millennials' beliefs, values, attitudes, traits and the like (e.g., they are multitaskers, open to change, adept with social networking, self-expressive, willing to share personal interests, opinion, and behaviors, community-minded, associate IT with information seeking and entertainment) (Moore, 2012; Seppanen and Gualtieri, 2012), there is a dearth of studies on exploring the implications of the unique characteristics of Millennials on their social networking behavior (Bolton et al., 2013). This is especially prudent as extant literature in information systems (IS) today focuses primarily on topics of IT acceptance and adoption from a utilitarian perspective in organizational contexts. We still know little about what drives individuals to SNC in particular, not to mention having to deal with a generation of individuals who are both avid providers and consumers of digital contents on SNCs. In order to fill this gap in literature, we argue for research that reexamines, challenges, and extends existing theories and models to better explain Millennials' participation in SNCs. As such, we develop a model based on Venkatesh et al.'s (2012) unified theory of consumers' acceptance and use of technology (UTAUT2) to do so.

UTAUT2 is an extension of Venkatesh et al.'s (2003) unified theory of technology acceptance and use of technology (UTAUT) to predict behavioral intention and use of a technology in a consumer context. UTAUT2 shares the same impressive explanatory power as UTAUT in accounting for about 70% of the variance in behavioral intention and 50% of the variance in technology use (Venkatesh et al., 2012). We retain relevant factors in UTAUT2 and add new relationships in our model after synthesizing past literature on SNC participation. The resultant model has trust in technology, trust in community, hedonic motivation, effort expectancy, social influence, and facilitating conditions as main factors and gender and educational background as moderating factors. We empirically tested our model from surveys of university students in Taiwan.

This study has both theoretical and practical contributions. Theoretically, we integrate IS technology use with psychological theories on knowledge sharing and intrinsic motivation to advance a model to explain Millennials' SNC participation intention. Practically, our study has managerial implications for SNC service providers, online advertisers, and brand managers.

The rest of the paper is organized as follows. We discuss the relevant theoretical background of this study leading to the development of our research model and hypotheses in the next two sections. The research method and research results are described in sections 4 and 5 respectively. Research findings are presented in section 6. Finally, research implications and future research directions are detailed in section 7.

2. THEORETICAL BACKGROUND AND MODEL DEVELOPMENT

Extant literature has heavily relied on Davis' (1989) technology acceptance model (TAM) and its extension, particularly Venkatesh et al.'s (2003) unified theory of acceptance and use of technology (UTAUT), to explain IS adoption intention and behavior. TAM established perceived usefulness and perceived ease of use as the fundamental determinants of individuals' acceptance and use of IT (Davis, 1989). Since its inception, TAM has undergone validation (e.g., Davis and Venkatesh, 1996; Sambamurthy and Chin, 1994), extension (e.g., Gefen et al., 2003; Venkatesh and Davis, 2000), and unification (e.g., Venkatesh et al., 2003; Venkatesh et al., 2012). These extensions of TAM are reflective of the rapid advancement in IT that requires adapting current understanding of IT acceptance and use to new contexts, e.g., online banking (Chandio et al., 2017), mobile commerce, (Kalinic and Marinkovic, 2016), tablet adoption (Magsamen-Conrad et al., 2015), and social media use (Rauniar et al., 2014).

Of all the extensions of TAM, Venkatesh et al.'s (2012) UTAUT2 is by far the most up-to-date, comprehensive, theoretically-based and empirically-tested model to explain consumers' acceptance and use of IT. UTAUT2 extends Venkatesh et al.'s (2003) UTAUT from an organizational to a consumer context. UTAUT integrates eight theories of technology use into a model that consists of three direct determinants of intention to use IT (performance expectancy, effort expectancy, and social influence), two direct determinants of actual usage of IT (intention and facilitating conditions), and four moderators of key relationships (age, gender, experience, and voluntariness). The eight theories include theory of reasoned action (Fishbein and Ajzen, 1975), technology acceptance model (TAM) (Davis, 1989), PC utilization (Thompson et al., 1991), theory of planned behavior (TPB) (Ajzen, 1991), motivational model (Davis et al., 1992), combined TAM and TPB (Taylor and Todd, 1995), innovation and diffusion theory (Rogers, 1995), and social cognitive theory (Compeau et al., 1999). The determinants of UTAUT are about utilitarian/extrinsic motivation, time and effort, and intentionality. Recognizing that UTAUT is not applicable to a consumer context, Venkatesh et al. (2012) proposed UTAUT2 to incorporate three new constructs: hedonic motivation, price value, and habit as important drivers of consumer use of mobile Internet and drop voluntariness as a moderator. While empirical support of UTAUT2 was reported, Venkatesh et al. (2012) cautioned its generalizability. In particular, our study is about Millennials as participants of SNCs. They are both providers and consumers of digital contents, not simply consumers of IT products and services. As a result, we follow Venkatesh et al.'s (2012) three steps process to develop a new model for our study: (1) identify irrelevant constructs in UTAUT2, (2) identify relevant determinants from extant research, and (3) add new relationships. The way we develop the new model is in line with Venkatesh et al.'s (2016) recommendations for future UTAUT-related research.

2.1. UTAUT2 Adaption

UTAUT2 posits that there are seven direct determinants of consumer technology acceptance and use, namely, performance expectancy, effort expectancy, social influence, facilitating conditions, hedonic motivation, price value, and habit. The effect of these direct determinants is moderated by individual differences in age, gender, and experience (Venkatesh et al., 2012). In adapting UTAUT2 to our context, the unique characteristics of Millennials help simplify the conceptualization of UTAUT2 in our model development by identifying and removing irrelevant constructs from consideration. First, Millennials associate IT with social networking, information sharing and entertainment purposes (Moore, 2012; The Nielsen Company, 2014). Their perceived values/benefits of participation in SNCs are derived from hedonic/intrinsic motivation of fun and social connectivity instead of utilitarian/extrinsic motivation of performance gains and monetary trade-offs. Furthermore, they are both providers and consumers of digital contents and not just consumers of IT products and services. This implies that performance expectancy and price value will no longer be meaningful determinants of Millennials' SNC participation intention and behavior. Second, Millennials are still in their formative stage when learning and experience can play a role in shaping their habitual behavior (Pew Research Center, 2010). Their openness to change means their technology usage behavior is neither automatic yet nor habitual. In fact, it has been speculated that Snapchat may surpass Facebook as the social media of choice for Millennials (Smith and Anderson, 2018; Plank and Shoulak, 2015). Consequently, habit is excluded as a determinant in our context. Third, Millennials are highly experienced with the use of IT and they belong to the below thirty age group. That means age and experience will not be significant individual differentiators among the Millennials. As a result, we drop performance expectancy, price value, habit, age, and experience from consideration in our model.

2.2. Extant Research on SNC Participation

We found support from extant literature in retaining four main determinants (effort expectancy, social influence, facilitating conditions, hedonic motivation) and one moderating factor (gender) from UTAUT2 in our model. Effort expectancy or perceived ease of use is defined as the degree of ease associated with technology usage and has been found to have a significant effect on SNC participation intention (Sledgianowski and Kulviwat, 2009; Wu et al., 2014). Social influence is defined as the perceived social pressure from friends and family on using a particular technology. Since participants of SNCs are affecting and being affected by their circle of influence both before and after they start interacting in SNCs, a positive relationship is found between social influence and SNC participation intention (Al-Debei et al., 2013; Kim, 2011; Lin, 2006; Pelling et al., 2009; Wu et al., 2014). Faciliting conditions refer to the extent in which resources and opportunities are available to enable technology usage. A high level of facilitating conditions is found to increase SNC participation intention (Al-Debei et al., 2013; Lin, 2006; Wu et al., 2014). Hedonic motivation or perceived enjoyment is the extent of pleasure or fun when using a technology. It has been found to be a critical antecedent of users' SNC participation intention (Basak and Calisir, 2015; Gwebu et al., 2014; Sun et al., 2014). Finally, Gefen and Ridings (2005) found that gender differences in communication determined what made a virtual community successful because women communicated to give and get social support and affinity, as oppose to men communicated to maintain and reinforce social standing and independence. As a result, women were more likely than men to participate in a SNC for emotional support than information exchange. Therefore, gender is kept as a moderator in our model.

2.3. New Relationships Incorporated Into UTAUT2

UTAUT2 is proposed to model consumers' technology use intention and behaviors. Its emphasis is on explaining how and why consumers adopt such personal technology as mobile Internet. As mentioned earlier, our interest in this paper is about understanding Millennials' intention to participate in a SNC. It goes beyond studying Millennials' technology use as passive consumers of IT products/services to examining their knowledge-sharing and community building behaviors as active providers and users of digital contents. According to the social exchange theory (Blau, 1964) and social capital theory (Nahapiet and Ghoshal, 1998), two types of trust are pivotal in influencing individuals' knowledge-sharing behaviors – trust in technology and trust in community (Chen, 2012; Chiu et al., 2006; Chow and Chan, 2008; Fang and Chiu, 2010; Hsu and Lin, 2008; Hsu et al., 2007; Lin et al., 2009). Trust in technology refers to the trustworthiness of the technological environment where structural provisions are in place for privacy and security assurance. A trust in technology to provide proper security mechanisms (e.g., authentication, privacy protection, integrity, and reliability) is needed before a user willingly divulges personal opinions, photos, experiences, and the like on a SNC (Obal and Kunz, 2013; Gefen et al., 2003; McKnight et al., 2002). Trust in technology has been demonstrated to have a positive impact on behavioral intention in SNCs (Gwebu et al., 2014; Krasnova et al., 2010; Sledgianowski and Kulviwat, 2009; Sun et al., 2014; Wu et al., 2014).

Trust in community, on the other hand, is the tendency to rely on community participants to behave in a socially acceptable manner (e.g., refrain from opportunistic behavior, exhibit positive reciprocation, provide verified information). A trust in community that everyone behaves in such manner is crucial to establish interpersonal relationship within the SNC. It requires a faith in humanity that others act with integrity, competence, and benevolence. With such trust, one will risk becoming vulnerable and dependable on other community members (McKnight et al., 2002). Trust in community was shown to have an effect on participants' intention to give and get information through the SNC, thus affecting community building (Lin, 2006; Ridings et al., 2003). It is an important consideration for Millennials as well, as only 19% of them say people can be trusted, as opposed to 30 to 40% of generations before them (Pew Research Center, 2014). Following the significance of trust in knowledge sharing and community building, we incorporate trust in technology and trust in community into UTAUT2 as two new determinants in our model.

Recently, the theory of self-determination has been applied in knowledge sharing studies to underscore the importance of intrinsic motivation in driving human behaviors (Yoon and Rolland, 2012; Zhang et al., 2015). Self-determination theory posits that individuals are more inclined to perform intrinsically motivating activities that meet their psychological needs of competence, relatedness, and autonomy (Ryan and Deci, 2000). Yoon and Rolland (2012) showed that individuals' perceived competence and relatedness with a virtual community had a strong impact on their knowledge sharing behaviors in that community. More importantly, they found that familiarity with the virtual community, established through education and trainings, but not repeated interactions, was effective in raising perceptions of competence and relatedness. For example, knowing how to professionally share an article on a SNC shows one's competence in searching and using a technical tool. On the other hand, sharing a relevant popular topic and high quality SNC content indicates one's connectivity to the latest news and happenings online, and relatedness to the community needs. We conceptualize familiarity with SNC participation through learning in our context as educational background of the Millennials. Although Millennials are avid users of technologies, their level of familiarity with SNCs can still be impacted by formal IT education and training. As a result, we add educational background as a new moderator in our model.

3. HYPOTHESIS DEVELOPMENT

Figure 1 shows the modified UTAUT2 model we propose to examine Millennials' intention to participate in a SNC.

Figure 1. Research model

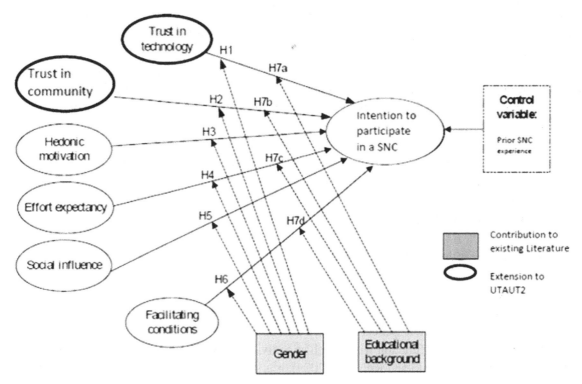

Our proposed model has six main determinants – trust in technology, trust in community, effort expectancy, hedonic motivation, social influence, and facilitating conditions. The main effects of these determinants are moderated by two factors – gender and educational background. A set of seven hypotheses are developed and presented as follows.

3.1. Trust in Technology as Moderated by Gender

Trust in technology as related to SNCs, as explained earlier, is the trustworthiness of the technological environment. It can be considered as an institution-based trust belief that "the needed structural conditions are present (e.g., on the Internet) to enhance the probability of achieving a successful outcome in an endeavor" (McKnight et al., 2002, p.339). These structural conditions include technological and legal safeguards that protect users from cyber-bullies (CBC News, 2007) and cyber-predators (The Canadian Press, 2010). Prior studies show that trust in technology has a direct and positive effect on a user's intention to participate in a SNC (Gwebu et al., 2014; Sledgianowski and Kulviwat, 2009; Sun, 2014; Wu et al., 2014). As such, SNC users who believe a site to be secure and trustworthy will be more willing to enter their personal details, photos, personal experiences, new discoveries and reviews on the site. The opposite is also true: when users feel that sites are vulnerable due to a lack of appropriate security mechanisms such as proper authentication of logon, privacy protection and code of conduct provision, they are less likely to participate. Krasnova et al. (2010) found that users' perception of self-disclosure risk can be mitigated by their trust in the SNC provider and the availability of security and privacy control options.

Previous studies by Chaudhuri et al. (2003) and Buchan et al. (2008) on western countries and by Cho and Koh (2008) on the Asian continent suggest that trust is moderated by gender, such that men have a significantly higher level of trust in online activities than women. Women tend to be more skeptical of online activities (Rodgers and Harris, 2003) and less likely to trust and use online information resources. In contrast, men perceive a higher trustworthiness in online activities than women (Slyke et al., 2002), they are more likely to participate in online activities such as taking part in a SNC. Base on this line of reasoning, we hypothesize:

H1: The positive influence of trust in technology on the intention to participate in a SNC is moderated by gender, such that the effect is stronger for men.

3.2. Trust in Community as Moderated by Gender

Trust in community is the tendency to rely on community participants to behave in a socially acceptable manner. It is a belief that community members will act with integrity, competence, and benevolence (McKnight et al., 2002). The predominant types of interaction for SNC users consist of sent or received messages or feedback from other participants. Users invite friends to be part of their own community through invitations. However, a user can request a connection with any other user. Although a SNC typically provides a permission function with which an individual can allow or prevent access to his or her online content (Sledgianowski and Kulviwat, 2009), it is still cumbersome to set access control to each element each time one shares contents on a SNC. Facebook, the biggest SNC site, continues to encounter photo tagging (for photo sharing) privacy issues (Mui, 2011), and privacy is a major concern for users — especially those who are unfamiliar with or neglectful of how to change the default security and privacy settings. Therefore, the posting of personal details and/or accepting friendship invitations from a person require a fundamental sense of trust regarding other SNC users. This situation can be compared to the level of trust that must exist between a user and a vendor engaging in e-commerce (Wang and Benbasat 2005), or the level of trust required between citizens and the government within an e-government website (Teo et al., 2009). Other studies on virtual communities have found that interpersonal trust significantly influences members' intention to provide or access certain types of information (Lin, 2006; Ridings et al., 2003). As such, if users trust a SNC, they exhibit greater intention to participate.

Foubert and Sholley (1996) found that gender has a significant interaction effect on online self-disclosure. Other researchers have consistently discovered that trust is moderated by gender (Buchan et al., 2008; Chaudhuri and Gangadharn, 2003). Women tend to perceive a much higher risk than males in disclosing details of their private lives online (Mine and Rhom, 2000). They are also more concerned about privacy and disclosure of identifying information when communicating and forming relationships through a SNC than their male counterparts (Fogel and Nehmad, 2009). This is partially driven by the fact that women attempt to process information in a more comprehensive and conscientious manner than men (Kemp and Palan, 2006). As a result, women are more cautious about trusting a SNC. Following this line of argument, we hypothesize:

H2: The positive influence of trust in community on the intention to participate in a SNC is moderated by gender, such that the effect is stronger for men.

3.3. Hedonic Motivation as Moderated by Gender

Hedonic motivation or perceived enjoyment is the extent of pleasure or fun when using a technology. Based on the general motivation theory, Davis et al. (1992), identified perceived enjoyment as a powerful intrinsic motivator for technology adoption and use. It pertains to an individual's perception of pleasure derived from engaging in an activity (Davis et al., 1992), such as using a SNC to maintain and develop interpersonal relationships. Unlike Web usage at work (Cheung et al., 2000), perceived enjoyment is certainly an important SNC participation factor for Millennials, as SNC usage is completely voluntary. Prior studies have found hedonic motivation to be a critical antecedent of users' SNC participation intention (Basak et al., 2015; Gwebu et al., 2014; Hsu and Lin, 2008; Kim et al., 2011; Sun et al., 2014).

A survey of 684 users of mobile chat services finds that enjoyment (as a hedonic motivation) is an important determinant of female users' intention to use SNCs, whereas their male counterparts are more motivated by extrinsic factors such as usefulness (Nysveen et al., 2005). SNCs are usually used for leisure purposes and this suggests that it better fits the desire for hedonic motivation among women. Therefore, we posit that:

H3: The positive influence of hedonic motivation on the intention to participate in a SNC is moderated by gender, such that the effect is stronger for women.

3.4. Effort Expectancy as Moderated by Gender

Effort expectancy or perceived ease of use refers to the degree of ease associated with participating in a SNC. Following TAM's finding that perceived ease of use is a key determinant of intention to use the technology, past research has confirmed that users have a stronger SNC participation intention if they believe that such participation is free of effort (Lin, 2006; Wu et al., 2014).

Bozionelos (1996) suggests that effort expectancy is more salient for women than men. Other studies have found that effort expectancy is a stronger determinant of individual intention for women (Venkatesh and Morris, 2000). This is because men may possess stronger technical oriented skills than women (Friessen, 1992; Trauth et al., 2003) since women conventionally "must accept that science and technology is considered a masculine domain which can easily lead to a scrutinizing of their skills and abilities" (Wilson, 1992, p. 901). In separate studies by Liaw and Huang (2009) in Taiwan and Comber et al. (1997) in the United Kingdom, male students were found to exhibit a more positive attitude toward the use of computers than female students. As a result, we expect that:

H4: The positive influence of effort expectancy on the intention to participate in a SNC is moderated by gender, such that the effect is stronger for women.

3.5. Social Influence as Moderated by Gender

Social influence reflects the degree to which an individual believes that important others think or expect him or her to participate in a SNC. It is a construct integrating the concepts of social norm (Fishbein and Ajzen, 1975) and social factors (Thompson et al., 1991) to explain IT acceptance and use (Venkatesh et al., 2003). SNCs provide a platform for social connections among friends and other like-minded individuals to share knowledge, post comments, share photos, chat, seek information, send/receive messages, etc. It has been estimated that global social network users will increase from 1.47 billion people in 2012 to 2.55 billion people by 2017 (eMarketer, 2013). SNC sites such as Facebook, Twitter, LinkedIn and Weibo offer users a channel for friends or fans to extend their social influence across politics (Lebeaux, 2008), business (Richardson, 2008), knowledge management (Cayzer 2004), social networking and communications (Lin and Anol, 2008). Social influence, clearly, plays a role in influencing individual's SNC participation intention (Wu et al., 2014; Al-Debei et al., 2013; Kim, 2011; Sledgianowski and Kulviwat, 2009; Lin, 2006).

Women have a higher disposition towards interpersonal relationships than men (Venkatesh and Morris, 2000; Venkatesh et al., 2000). This relational disposition tends to motivate women, more so than men, to participate in SNCs for rapport building and social connectivity reasons to maintain and strengthen existing relationships (Foster et al., 2012). Other researchers have found that social influence becomes more salient in terms of forming an intention to use new technology for women than for men (Venkatesh et al., 2000). Rhoades (1981) says that women are easier to be persuaded than men. A similar finding is reported by Carli (2001) and Bae and Lee (2011), stating that women are more easily influenced than men. Based on these findings, we posit:

H5: The positive effect of social influence on the intention to participate in a SNC is moderated by gender, such that the effect is stronger for women.

3.6. Facilitating Conditions as Moderated by Gender

Facilitating conditions refers to the degree to which an individual believes that resources and support are available to enable participations in a SNC. Facilitating conditions, including self-efficacy, resource availability, and objective factors in the environment, affect an individual's perceptions of control over external and internal constraints on his/her behavior (Taylor and Todd, 1995; Thompson et al., 1991). Cheung et al. (2000) confirm that facilitating conditions are one of the most important factors influencing Internet usage. This is substantiated by a recent study showing that students with greater access to required resources (i.e., in the presence of facilitating conditions) spend more time using SNC sites (Hargittai, 2007). Logically, people look for support to resolve problems or difficulties in conducting online activities. A high level of facilitating conditions is found to increase SNC participation intention (Al-Debei et al., 2013; Lin, 2006; Wu et al., 2014).

Slyke et al. (2002) indicate that women rate the complexity of Web activities higher than men and are more likely to require assistance in conducting online activities than their male counterparts. Following this line of reasoning, we hypothesize that:

H6: The positive influence of facilitating conditions on the intention to participate in a SNC is moderated by gender, such that the effect is stronger for women.

3.7. Moderating Effects of Educational Background

Educational background refers to the education and training that influence one's skills, knowledge, confidence, self-efficacy and therefore familiarity with the subject matter. As such, individuals with an IT educational background are expected to have a deep understanding of how to use technology effectively and efficiently. Gefen (2000) finds that familiarity with Web technologies builds trust in technology that promotes online purchasing intention. Similarly, Wang (2002) suggests that familiarity with IT influences one's trust in technology (or perceived credibility) of an electronic tax filing system. This in turn affects the behavioral intention to use the system. Recently, Yoon and Rolland (2012) show that individuals who are more familiar with virtual communities from education and training increase their trust of other people, thus become more active in sharing their knowledge in their virtual communities. Based on this reasoning, individuals with an IT educational background are more familiar with and more likely to trust a SNC because they have a higher level of self-efficacy and relatedness that motivate them to use the SNC, participate in online activities and interact with others in the community. As such, we hypothesize:

H7a: The positive influence of trust in technology on the intention to participate in a SNC is moderated by educational background, such that the effect is stronger for individuals with IT background.
H7b: The positive influence of trust in community on the intention to participate in a SNC is moderated by educational background, such that the effect is stronger for individuals with IT background.

Prior studies (Grant et al., 2009; Wallace and Clariana, 2005) show that individuals without an IT educational background put forth greater effort with SNCs as they perceive more cognitive efforts are required to operate the system and their self-efficacies are lower. They also tend to need help to use the system (Cowan and Jack, 2011). Following this line of argument, we propose:

H7c: The positive influence of effort expectancy on the intention to participate in a SNC is moderated by educational background, such that the effect is stronger for individuals without an IT background.
H7d: The positive influence of facilitating conditions on the intention to participate in a SNC is moderated by educational background, such that the effect is stronger for individuals without an IT background.

3.8. Control Variable

We regard familiarity and experience with SNCs as two related but distinct concepts. Familiarity with SNCs deals with the knowledge of SNCs gained through learning and interactions with them (Gefen, 2000). As such, familiarity is operationalized as educational background, as a moderator, in our model.

Experience, on the other hand, is one's extent of exposure to SNCs and is defined as the passage of time from initial SNC participation (Venkatesh et al., 2012). In order to ensure that the empirical results of this study are not caused by prior SNC experience, it is included as a control variable.

4. RESEARCH METHOD

4.1. Samples

The participants in this study are undergraduate students at a comprehensive university in Taiwan. University students are good representatives of the Millennials as they are the embodiment of a generation that grew up in the Internet age. For example, educated Millennials are more likely to be online, use SNCs, post/read digital contents, use mobile internet, and send/receive text messages (Pew Research Center, 2010). In addition, Millennials in Taiwan share comparable attitudes and behaviors as Millennials in other parts of the world (Brown, 2011). In fact, the pervasiveness of technology in the lives of Millennials has been attributed to the "global homogeneity" of this generation (Moore, 2012). The targeted SNC site is Facebook, as it is the largest and the most popular social networking site. More than 30% of their 1.4 billion monthly active visitors are from Asia-Pacific countries, as compared to 15% in the US (Plank and Tovar, 2015).

4.2. Instrument and Data Analysis Method

A survey research method was adopted for this research. The survey instrument was developed with items validated by prior research, whenever possible, and was adapted to the technologies and individuals considered in the present study. The measurements of the constructs used in this study are provided in Table 1. A paper-based survey was administered to the participating university students in the classroom. Their responses were collected after they completed the survey. The survey questions and their associated references are listed in Appendix A.

A total of 337 students took part in this study. The collected survey data were analyzed using the Partial Least Squares (PLS) method which was applied for testing similar models in the studies by Venkatesh (2008; 2003). PLS is used in this study because it is a preferred method when constructs are measured using reflective scales, and theoretical testing research in the field of SNCs is relatively small (Gefen et al., 2011). The PLS software utilized was SmartPLS (Ringle et al., 2005). The decision rules set by Jarvis et al. (2003) were used to determine whether constructs should be designated as reflective or formative (see Table 1). These decision rules involved considering the direction of causality from construct to indicators/items, interchangeability of the indicators, covariation among the indicators, and the nomological net of the construct indicators (Jarvis et al., 2003). To test the validity of reflective constructs, we examined the construct validity, discriminant validity, and internal reliability (using Cronbach's Alpha) of the constructs. To confirm the convergent and discriminant validity of the collected data, both intra-construct item correlations and inter-construct item correlations were examined (Fornell and Larcker, 1981).

Table 1. Measurement of constructs

Latent Construct	Construct Type	Sub Construct	Sub-Construct Type	Code	No. of Items	Reference
Trust in technology	Reflective	Perceptions of trust in technology	Reflective	TT1-3	3	(McKnight et al. 2002)
Trust in community	Reflective	Perceptions of trust in community	Reflective	TC1-3	3	(McKnight et al. 2002)
Hedonic Motivation	Reflective	Perceived enjoyment	Reflective	HM1-4	4	(Agarwal and Karahanna 2000; Davis et al. 1992)
Effort expectancy	Reflective	Perceived ease of use	Reflective	EE1-5	5	(Davis 1989),
Social influence	Reflective	Subjective norm	Reflective	SI1-2	2	(Ajzen 1991)
		Social factor	Reflective	SI3	1	(Thompson et al. 1991)
Facilitating conditions	Reflective	Perceived Behavioral Control	Reflective	FC1-3	3	(Ajzen 1991)
		Facilitating Conditions	Reflective	FC4	1	(Thompson et al. 1991)
Intention to participate in a SNC	Reflective	Continuance participation intention	Reflective	IP1-3	3	(Agarwal and Karahanna 2000)

Table 2. Gender and SNC experience cross-tabulation

	SNC Experience						Total
	< 1mth	1-3mths	3-6mths	6-9mths	9-12mths	>12mths	
Male	18	14	8	8	9	88	145
Female	12	11	10	4	11	108	156
Total	30	25	18	12	20	196	301

In an effort to rigorously identify the statistical significance of differences across gender groups and educational background groups and to conduct the statistical comparison of paths, the procedures suggested by Chin et al. (1996) was used in this study, similar to Keil et al. (2000) and Ahuja & Thatcher (2005). On the other hand, in evaluating the moderating effects, Kenny (2009) suggests that a complete moderation occurs when the causal effect of a predictor on an outcome variable becomes null as a moderator takes on a particular value. In addition, a discrete variable such as gender has a moderating effect on a causal relationship if "… the results are not strongly consistent within subgroups, or the results are strongly consistent but do not coincide with the overall results obtained after pooling over the subgroups" (Wermuth, 1989): p.82. The R-square statistic produced by the PLS indicates the fit of the research model in terms of explaining the variance in the sample.

5. DATA ANALYSIS AND RESULTS

5.1. Demographic Data

Among the 337 participants, the valid response rate was 89% after discounting the responses of 36 students who did not use a SNC voluntarily. Out of the remaining 301 undergraduate students, 198 of them (65.8%) were IT majors, who had taken quite a number of programming languages (such as Visual Basic, C++, Java, ASP.net), system design and analysis, database management and management information systems courses. The remaining 103 students (34.2%) were non-IT majors, who had taken only one introductory course in management information systems. A detailed cross-tabulation between gender and SNC experience is given in Table 2. Specifically, 48% were male, and 65% had more than 12 months experience using SNCs. Approximately 17% had between 3 and 12 months' experience using SNCs, and the remaining 18% had less than three months experience. It is observed in Figure 2 that the SNC participation rate among IT major students is higher than that of non-IT major students. The distributions of the male and female groups for both IT major and non-IT major undergraduate students are shown in Table 3.

Figure 2. Major and SNC experience (in months)

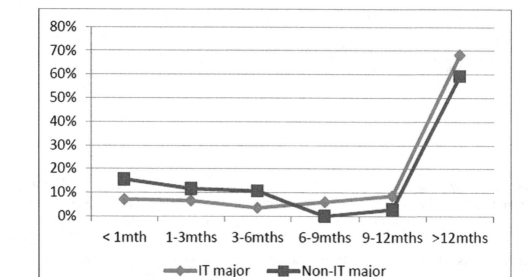

Table 3. Distribution of male and female groups

	IT Major	Non-IT Major
Male	105	40
Female	93	63
Total	198	103

5.2. The Measurement Model

To test for the problem of common method bias in the collected data, Harman's single factor test was conducted (Podsakoff et al., 2003). For this purpose, principle component factor analysis for one extracted factor and none-rotation was run using the SPSS. The result shows that the single factor explains less than 38% of the variation in sample data. Thus, the collected data does not indicate evidence of severe common method bias. Next, to further test the common method bias, the modeling of a latent common factor, as suggested in Liang et al. (2007) is carried out in SmartPLS. The results are shown in Appendix B. The average substantive variance of the indicators is 0.785, whereas the average method-based variance is 0.022. Besides, the ratio of the substantive variance to method variance is about 36:1 and most of the method factor loadings are either insignificant or less significant than the substantive factor loadings. This confirms that common method bias is unlikely to be a serious problem in this study.

Table 4. Factor loadings for the seven constructs

	Factor						
	EE	**FC**	**HM**	**IP**	**TT**	**SI**	**TC**
EE1	.644						
EE2	.741						
EE3	.777						
EE4	.605						
EE5	.781						
FC1		.797					
FC2		.731					
FC3		.892					
HM1			.542				
HM2			.711				
HM3			.701				
IP1				.802			
IP2				.820			
IP3				.789			
TT1					.865		
TT2					.866		
TT3					.909		
SI1						.882	
SI2						.803	
TC1							.557
TC2							.612
TC3							.695

EE= Effort expectancy, FC= Facilitating conditions, HM=Hedonic motivation, IP= Intention to participate in a SNC, TT= Trust in technology, SI= Social influence, TC= Trust in community

In order to confirm the convergent validity of the constructs, the factor loadings of each item on its corresponding construct were examined. Items with loadings less than 0.5 had been dropped, as shown in Table 4. As a result, items FC4, HM4, and SI3 were excluded from further path analysis. The Average Variance Extracted (AVE) for each construct is given in Table 5. All figures exceeded the 0.5 threshold suggested by Fornell and Larcker (1981). Moreover, the composite reliability values were all above 0.7, which was the internal consistency threshold recommended in the literature (Fornell and Larcker 1981; Nunnally 1978). Furthermore, discriminant validity was evident—all items loaded more heavily on their corresponding constructs than on other constructs (Table 4), and the square root of all AVEs exceeded the correlations among constructs (Table 6).

Table 5. Descriptive statistics, average variance extracted and composite reliability

Construct	Mean	Std. Dev.	AVE	Composite Reliability	Cronbach's Alpha
Trust in technology (TT)	4.066	1.344	0.872	0.953	0.927
Trust in community (TC)	4.715	1.027	0.740	0.895	0.825
Hedonic Motivation (HM)	5.112	1.062	0.788	0.918	0.866
Effort expectancy (EE)	4.914	1.031	0.648	0.901	0.865
Social influence (SI)	4.096	1.449	0.872	0.931	0.855
Facilitating conditions (FC)	4.771	1.176	0.822	0.932	0.892
Intention to participate in a SNC (IP)	4.914	1.173	0.863	0.949	0.921

Table 6. Correlation table

	TC	HM	EE	SI	TT	FC	IP
TC	**0.860**						
HM	0.650	**0.888**					
EE	0.471	0.522	**0.805**				
SI	0.296	0.308	0.193	**0.934**			
TT	0.341	0.222	0.051	0.044	**0.934**		
FC	0.401	0.386	0.427	0.196	0.137	**0.907**	
IP	0.526	0.596	0.357	0.309	0.308	0.349	**0.929**

Note: The square root of AVE is shown on the diagonal.

To justify for multi-group analysis, according to Sarstedt and Ringle (2010), an appropriate means of testing measurement model invariance in PLS may build on whether the measurement parameters are the same across all subgroups and whether the same construct is measured in all subgroups. The analysis in Appendix C proves that both the gender subgroups (in Appendix C) and the educational background subgroups (in Appendix C) demonstrate same and adequate construct reliability and discriminant validity within their subgroups. In addition, for analyzing the moderating effect in PLS, Carte and Russell (2003) suggest that item weights (for all constructs) showing that the two subgroups do not vary significantly in construct score weighting are required. This requirement is met, and the results are shown in Appendix D for the gender subgroups and Appendix D for the educational background subgroups. All of the results indicate that items load and cross-load consistently across samples. Appendix D also shows convergent validity in both subgroups of gender and educational background.

5.3. The Structural Model

Based on the PLS analysis, the R-squared for the research model not including any of the moderating effects is 0.429. We found that trust in technology, trust in community, hedonic motivation, and social influence all have significant positive effects on the intention to participate in a SNC. Hedonic motivation (path coefficient = 0.388, t-value = 5.323, $p < 0.001$) is the most significant factor, followed by trust in technology (path coefficient = 0.153, t-value = 3.149, $p < 0.01$), trust in community (path coefficient = 0.140, t-value = 2.130, $p < 0.05$) and social influence (path coefficient = 0.120, t-value = 2.184, $p < 0.05$). Surprisingly, effort expectancy does not exhibit any significant effect on the intention to participate in a SNC (Figure 3). The reason may be that the hedonic factor outweighs the effort expectancy factor, or because the survey respondents do not perceive that an additional cognitive effort is required to participate in a SNC, due to the unique characteristics of early exposure to the digital world for Millennials.

Figure 3. Path analysis results for the entire sample

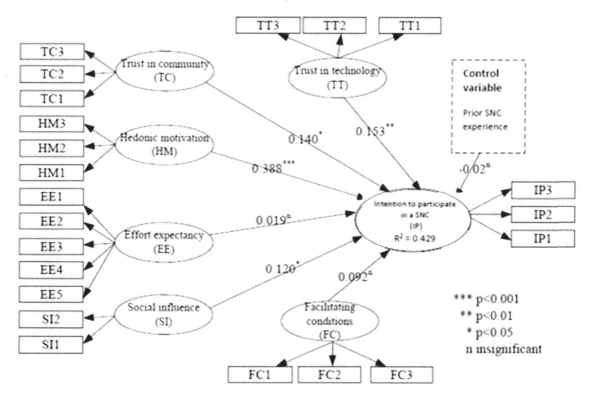

To justify for comparing the structural model results across the gender subgroups in a more rigorous way, t-statistics as suggested by Chin et al. (1996) to evaluate the differences in path coefficients across the model are computed in Appendix E. Following this, we can then make a valid comparison between the path model for the male subgroup (Figure 4-a) and the female subgroup (Figure 4-b). The result shows the significant positive influence of trust in technology (path coefficient = 0.247, t-value = 3.408, $p < 0.001$) and trust in community (path coefficient = 0.156, t-value = 1.983, $p < 0.05$) on the intention to participate in a SNC for male respondents, but not for female respondents. It appears that a complete moderation occurred. The statistical analysis for testing the significance of differences in the corresponding path coefficient between the male and female subgroups in Appendix E shows that the two path coefficients are significantly different. This suggests that the male subgroup in our sample trust in technology and social network community more than the female counterparts.

As such, H1 stating that the positive influence of trust in technology on the intention to participate in a SNC is moderated by gender, such that the effect is stronger for men, is supported. In addition, H2, which states that the positive influence of trust in community on the intention to participate in SNC is moderated by gender, such that the effect is stronger for men, is supported. These are consistent with prior results (Lewis et al. 2008) that suggest women are more protective of their personal information, which in turn implies that women are more cautious with other people than their male counterparts are.

Both the male (path coefficient = 0.363, t-value = 4.185, $p < 0.001$) and female (path coefficient = 0.412, t-value = 3.738, $p < 0.001$) groups exhibited a significant positive influence of hedonic motivation on the intention to participate in a SNC. The path coefficient for the female subgroup is greater than the male subgroup; and this difference is statistically significant (see Appendix E). This provides the support for H3, which states that the influence of hedonic motivation on intention to participate in a SNC is moderated by gender, such that the effect is stronger for women. This result indicates that female perceives relatively more enjoyments in the participation in social networks; and this explains the reason women like SNCs (cf. (Hargittai, 2007)), and are more active in their use of SNCs compared to their male counterparts (Brenner, 2013). In contrast, the motivation for the male group to use SNCs would be something other than enjoyment – a similar situation in the use of other online systems.

Although effort expectancy seemingly has no significant influence on either the male or female subgroup in regards to their intention to participate in a SNC, the path coefficients from effort expectancy on the intention to participate in a SNC for men (path coefficient = -0.001, t-value = 0.016) and women (path coefficient = 0.023, t-value = 0.261) are significantly different from one another (|t-value| = 2.556, see Appendix E). According to Kenny (2007), the difference between the subgroups rather than the path coefficient significance determines the moderation effect. As a result, H4, which states that the positive influence of effort expectancy (i.e., perceived ease of use) on the intention to participate in a SNC is moderated by gender, such that the effect is stronger for women, is supported. This demonstrates that, to some degree, female subgroup thinks that the use of social media networks still requires a bit of related technology skill and familiarity than the male subgroup.

The results in Figures 4a and 4b indicate that social influence had no significant positive effect on the intention to participate in a SNC for both the male subgroup (path coefficient = 0.128, t-value = 1.620, $p > 0.05$) and the female subgroup (path coefficient = 0.123, t-value = 1.375, $p > 0.05$). The comparison test on the path coefficients from social influence to the intention to participate in a SNC conducted for the two subgroups (shown in Appendix E) are also found to be insignificantly different. Therefore, H5, which states that the effect of social influence on the intention to participate in a SNC is moderated by gender, such that the effect is stronger for women, is not supported. This implies that there is no significant difference between men and women on how social influence affects their intention to participate in a SNC. So, in contrast to prior studies, our study does not support the notion that women are more easily persuaded by others than men to participate in a SNC. This finding can be due to differences in different generation group, having different social exposure and mindsets.

Facilitating conditions are found to be insignificant at $p < 0.05$ for both the male subgroup (path coefficient $= 0.058$, t-value $= 0.667$, $p > 0.05$) and female subgroup (path coefficient $= 0.124$, t-value $= 1.488$, $p > 0.05$). However, the statistical comparison test in Appendix E shows that there is a significant difference in the corresponding path coefficient between the male and female subgroups. Therefore, H6, which states that the influence of facilitating conditions on intention to participate in a SNC is moderated by gender, such that the effect is stronger for women, is supported. This finding is related to one's technology self-efficacy, i.e. when one's technology self-efficacy is low than facilitating conditions are needed to provide supports, otherwise it can cause barrier in one's intention to continue to use that technology.

Similar to the subgroup analysis involved in the gender subgroups, to justify for comparing the structural model results across the educational background subgroups in a more rigorous way, t-statistics as suggested by Chin et al. (1996) are computed to evaluate the differences in path coefficients across the models. The multi-group comparison test results, between the two subgroups of students majoring in IT and non-IT, are summarized in Table 7 (see Appendix F for details). We find that the IT major group, which has more of an IT educational background, shows a significantly stronger effect of the positive influence of trust in technology, and trust in community on participants' intention to participate in a SNC than the non-IT major subgroup. However, the t-statistics for testing the differences in the path coefficient, from trust in technology to the intention to participate in a SNC across the models, shows that there is no practical significance in the difference between the IT-major subgroup and non-IT major subgroup. Thus, H7a is partially supported and H7b is supported.

The result for H7a suggests that our survey respondents, regardless of their IT educational background, possess an almost similar level of trust in technology. On the other hand, the result for H7b indicates that IT educational background positively influences one's perceived relatedness, belonging and trust in one's SNC. This could be that trust is transferred from trust in IT/SNC to trust in community (Ng 2013).

Although the t-values are not significant (in Table 7) for the paths from effort expectancy and facilitating conditions on the intention to participate in a SNC, the non-IT major subgroup shows a stronger negative effect of effort expectancy (path coefficient $= -0.122$) as well as a stronger positive effect of facilitation conditions (path coefficient $= 0.121$) on the intention to participate in a SNC, as compared to the IT major group (path coefficient $= 0.110$ and path coefficient $= 0.092$, respectively). In comparing the significance of differences in the corresponding two path coefficients, the multi-group comparisons based on the parametric approach in Table 7 indicate that these two path coefficients are significantly different between the IT major and non-IT major subgroups. Thus, H7c is partially supported and H7d is supported. In general, the non-IT major group shows a stronger effect of the positive influence of facilitating conditions on the intention to participate in a SNC than the IT major group. This is because the availability of facilitating conditions can serve as a stimulus in case one (e.g., the non-IT major group) faces difficulties in using the technology.

Figure 4. (a) Path analysis results for male group; (b) Path analysis results for female group

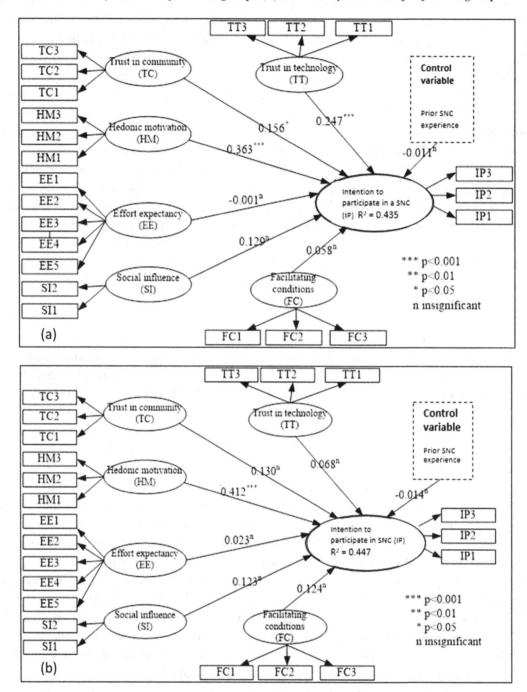

Table 7. PLS results - moderating effect of educational background

	IT Major		Non-IT Major		Statistical Comparison of Path Coefficients[A]
	β	T-Value	β	T-Value	T-Value
Trust in technology (TT)	0.164**	2.857	0.157	1.815	0.827
Trust in community (TC)	0.168*	2.334	0.064	0.634	10.238***
Hedonic Motivation (HM)	0.305***	3.495	0.534***	4.925	-19.820***
Effort expectancy (EP)	0.110	1.422	-0.122	1.532	24.400***
Social influence (SI)	0.161*	2.568	0.049	0.594	13.206***
Facilitating conditions (FC)	0.092	1.246	0.130	1.191	-3.595***
Experience	-0.055	0.930	0.051	0.803	
R-square	0.437		0.469		

$*p < .05; **p < .01; ***p < .001$; A – see Appendix F for details

6. DISCUSSION

In this study, hedonic motivation, trust in technology, trust in community, and social influence are demonstrated to be significant factors in influencing Millennials' intention to participate in a SNC, with hedonic motivation exhibiting the most impact. This is consistent with the results of Gwebu et al. (2014), and Sledgianowski et al. (2009). As such, website designers looking to improve a SNC should consider incorporating enjoyable entertainment applications and interesting user interfaces to maintain and increase the popularity and attractiveness of the SNC. They should also implement privacy and security mechanisms to ensure the trustworthiness of their sites. In addition, ways to increase participants' relatedness by promoting trust and bonding among one another while bridging ties with new participants should be considered.

Our results concerning the influence of effort expectancy on users' intention to participate in a SNC differ from prior studies (Lin, 2006; Sledgianowski and Kulviwat, 2009; Wu et al., 2014) since we do not find this factor to be significant. As the Millennial generation becomes more IT literate and access to the Internet becomes more widespread, the impact of effort expectancy on IT or online systems adoption will continue to diminish over time. Interestingly, in the absence of hedonic motivation, effort expectancy does become a significant determinant of the intention to participate in a SNC, which suggests that a lack of enjoyable applications leads users to focus greater attention on perceived ease of use of the system for social interaction and communication.

A summary of the tested hypotheses is presented in Table 8. Gender exhibits a moderating effect on the intention to participate in a SNC through trust in technology, trust in community, hedonic motivation, effort expectancy and facilitating conditions. However, contrary to previous studies, the impact of social influence is not moderated by gender. This finding is in line with the observation that both male and female Millennials place less trust in people and are less influenced by those who are unrelated to and/or unassociated with them (Pew Research Center, 2014). Furthermore, while men and women may have different goals in participating in a SNC, they are under no obligation to participate in a community that does not meet their needs, no matter who is in that community.

Educational background, operationalized as IT background (as seen in Tables 8), was found to play an important role in moderating the main effect of trust in community, hedonic motivation, effort expectancy, social influence and facilitating conditions. For students who are non-IT majors, social influence has no impact on their behavioral intention to participate in a SNC. We also observe that the negative effects of effort expectancy on the intention to participate in a SNC are indeed stronger for the non-IT major male group than the IT major male group, and likewise for the non-IT major female group versus the IT major female group. The majority of the hypotheses related to the moderator of educational background (as listed in Table 8) is proved to be significant. This indicates that one's choice of major is an important factor that influences behavioral intention to participate in a SNC through factors such as trust in community, facilitating conditions, and effort expectancy.

Table 8. Summary of tests of hypotheses and results

Hypothesis	Test Result
H1: The positive influence of trust in technology on the intention to participate in a SNC is moderated by gender, such that the effect is stronger for men.	Supported
H2: The positive influence of trust in community on intention to participate in a SNC is moderated by gender, such that the effect is stronger for men.	Supported
H3: The positive influence of hedonic motivation on the intention to participate in a SNC is moderated by gender, such that the effect is stronger for women.	Supported
H4: The positive influence of effort expectancy on the intention to participate in a SNC is moderated by gender, such that the effect is stronger for women.	Supported
H5: The positive effect of social influence on the intention to participate in a SNC is moderated by gender, such that the effect is stronger for women.	Not Supported
H6: The positive influence of facilitating conditions on the intention to participate in a SNC is moderated by gender, such that the effect is stronger for women.	Supported
H7a: The positive influence of trust in technology on the intention to participate in a SNC is moderated by educational background, such that the effect is stronger for individuals with IT background.	Partially Supported*
H7b: The positive influence of trust in community on the intention to participate in a SNC is moderated by educational background, such that the effect is stronger for individuals with IT background.	Supported
H7c: The positive influence of effort expectancy on the intention to participate in a SNC is moderated by educational background, such that the effect is stronger for individuals without IT background.	Partially Supported**
H7d: The positive influence of facilitating conditions on the intention to participate in a SNC is moderated by educational background, such that the effect is stronger for individuals without IT background.	Supported

* The positive influence of trust in technology on the intention to participate in a SNC is stronger for individuals with IT educational background; but this relationship is not practically significantly moderated by educational background.

**The positive effect of effort expectancy on the intention to participate in a SNC has not been found to be stronger for individuals without IT training.

7. CONCLUSION

7.1. Theoretical Implications

This study adapts UTAUT2 model to explain Millennials' intention to participate in a SNC by integrating the underlying eight theories of UTAUT with social exchange, social capital, and self-determination theories from psychology. Our resultant model has six determinants (*hedonic motivation, trust in com-*

munity, *trust in technology*, *effort expectancy*, *social influence*, and *facilitating conditions*) and two moderators (*gender* and *educational background*). We provide a better understanding of Millennials' intention to participate in a SNC from an intrinsic motivation of enjoyment and relatedness perspective. This implies that Millennials will participate in a SNC as long as their innate psychological need of pleasure and the desire to be connected to others are met.

7.2. Implications for SNC Service Providers

SNC sites that provide interesting and enjoyable applications are better able to retain and/or increase Millennials' loyalty, and can better manage relationships with these tech savvy users. However, satisfying all Millennials is difficult because of their individual differences. Findings of our study show that individual differences pertaining to gender and IT educational background impose different requirements and standards for facilitating conditions, effort expectancy, trust in technology and trust in community. SNC service providers can consider the feasibility of providing Millennials with customized and dynamic SNC content and functionality tailored to their individual differences. For example, chat support, Q&A forum, or SNC training can be offered to women and individuals with non-IT background to increase their trust in technology, trust in community, facilitating conditions, and effort expectancy. SNC service providers can also develop more mechanisms to improve SNC security and privacy protection to ensure women Millennials feel safe and comfortable in the SNC environment. Trust is an important issue with social networking especially for the future development of social commerce. By properly establishing and maintaining site standards, and by promoting SNC familiarity through education and training, trust in technology and community can be elevated across all Millennials to ensure their SNC participations.

7.3. Implications for Online Advertising

Consumers in general and Millennials in particular are accessing new and existing types of online media, such as SNC, more frequently and for longer periods of time. Enterprises recently allocate greater percentages of their marketing budgets to this channel due to its relatively low costs and its pervasiveness. Although there are research and market reports indicating that many users of Facebook and other SNCs remain dissatisfied with privacy levels (Xu et al., 2013), frequent website changes, and increases in commercialization and advertising (Gaudin, 2010), this does not necessarily mean that online advertising does not have its place within SNCs. The issue simply relates to how and who to target with what types of advertisements.

The findings from this research help to answer these questions. A better understanding of the characteristics and preferences of Millennials enables advertisers to provide target advertising more efficiently, deliver the right content to the right audience, as well as develop a platform for brand management. For example, e-marketers can focus more on advertising male-oriented products as male Millennials have more trust in technology and communities than females. In addition, knowing women Millennials' SNC participations are more intrinsically motivated than men, advertising to women should be more than expressing a brand message. It should provide a platform of two-way communication between women and the brand for relationship building, feedback and/or review solicitation, and electronic word-of-mouth viral marketing (IBM 2012; Tadena 2015).

7.4. Limitations and Future Study

This study focuses on Millennial users of Facebook in Taiwan. As such, the results discussed are only applicable to other SNCs with similar purposes, contents, and user groups. In addition, this study excludes performance expectancy from the research model as Millennials associate IT primarily for fun and enjoyment instead of work-related activities. Some studies, however suggest that perceived usefulness has a significant influence on users' intention to use SNCs (Al-Debei, 2013; Lin and Lu, 2011; Shin, 2010; Wu, 2014) and different countries also present different motivators and barriers for using SNCs (see Chang and Zhu, 2011; Kim et al., 2011). Thus, further studies may examine other motivations behind using a SNC such as the performance expectancy factor especially if job-related SNCs are examined.

Different types of SNCs such as Snapchat (a photo sharing site), Twitter (a microblogging site), LinkedIn (a SNC for professional occupations) and Research Gate (a SNC for researchers and scientists) require additional studies focusing on a different set of factors such as credibility of a user profile, reliability of the data provided, reciprocity/shared values among members, and cultural differences. Moreover, in light of the low R-square value, further study is needed to examine additional factors that may be significant in influencing SNC participations, potentially including webpage design, website navigation style (cf. Nathan and Yeow, 2011), and the impact of online advertising.

ACKNOWLEDGMENT

This study was supported by a National Science Council NSC 99-2410-H-155-031 grant.

REFERENCES

Agarwal, R., & Karahanna, E. (2000). Time files when you're having fun: Cognitive absorption and beliefs about information technology usage. *Management Information Systems Quarterly*, 24(4), 665–694. doi:10.2307/3250951

Ahuja, M. K., & Thatcher, J. B. (2005). Moving beyond intention and toward the theory of trying: effects of work environment and gender on post-adoption information technology use. *Management Information Systems Quarterly*, 29(3), 427–459. doi:10.2307/25148691

Ajzen, I. (1991). The Theory of Planned Behavior. *Organizational Behavior and Human Decision Processes*, 50(2), 179–211. doi:10.1016/0749-5978(91)90020-T

Al-Debei, M., Al-Lozi, E., & Papazafeiropoulou, A. (2013). Why people keep coming back to facebook: Explaining and predicting continuance participation from an extended theory of planned behaviour perspective. *Decision Support Systems*, 55(1), 43–54. doi:10.1016/j.dss.2012.12.032

Bae, S., & Lee, T. (2011). Gender differences in consumers' perception of online consumer reviews. *Electronic Commerce Research*, 11(2), 201–214. doi:10.100710660-010-9072-y

Basak, E., & Calisir, F. (2015). An empirical study on factors affecting continuance intentions of using Facebook. *Computers in Human Behavior*, *48*, 181–189. doi:10.1016/j.chb.2015.01.055

Blau, P. M. (1964). *Exchange and Power in Social Life*. New York: Wiley.

Bolton, R. N., Parasuraman, A., Hoefnagels, A., Migchels, N., Kabadayi, S., Gruber, T., ... Solnet, D. (2013). Understanding Generation Y and their use of social media: A review and research agenda. *Journal of Service Management*, *24*(3), 245–267. doi:10.1108/09564231311326987

Bozionelos, N. (1996). Psychology of Computer Use: Prevalence of Computer Anxiety in British Managers and Professionals. *Psychological Reports*, *78*(3), 995–1002. doi:10.2466/pr0.1996.78.3.995 PMID:8711058

Brenner, J. (2013). *Pew Internet: Social Networking (Full Detail)*. Pew Internet.

Brown, M. (2011). Connecting with the Millennials. *Visa Asia*. Retrieved from http://www.visa-asia.com/ap/sea/mediacenter/pressrelease/includes/uploads/Visa_Gen_Y_Report_2012_LR.pdf

Buchan, N. R., Croson, R. T. A., & Solnick, S. (2008). Trust and Gender: An Examination of Behavior and Beliefs in the Investment Game. *Journal of Economic Behavior & Organization*, *68*(3-4), 466–476. doi:10.1016/j.jebo.2007.10.006

Carli, L. L. (2001). Gender and Social Influence. *The Journal of Social Issues*, *57*(4), 725–741. doi:10.1111/0022-4537.00238

Carte, T. A., & Russell, C. J. (2003). In Pursuit of Moderation: Nine Common Errors and Their Solutions. *Management Information Systems Quarterly*, *27*(3), 479–501. doi:10.2307/30036541

Cayzer, S. (2004). Semantic Blogging and Decentralized Knowledge Management. *Communications of the ACM*, *47*(12), 47–52. doi:10.1145/1035134.1035164

CBC News. (2007). 11 Ontario Students Suspended for "Cyber-Bullying." Retrieved from http://www.cbc.ca/canada/ottawa/story/2007/02/12/school-facebook.html

Chandio, F. H., Irani, Z., Zeki, A. M., Shah, A., & Shah, S. C. (2017). Online banking information systems acceptance: An empirical examination of system characteristics and web security. *Information Systems Management*, *34*(1), 50–64. doi:10.1080/10580530.2017.1254450

Chang, Y. P., & Zhu, D. H. (2011). Understanding Social Networking Sites Adoption in China: A Comparison of Pre-Adoption and Post-Adoption. *Computers in Human Behavior*, *27*(5), 1840–1848. doi:10.1016/j.chb.2011.04.006

Chaudhuri, A., & Gangadharn, L. (2003). Gender differences in trust and reciprocity. The University of Melbourne, Melbourne.

Chen, C. (2012). Motivators, prohibitors and outcomes of social networking site user's behavior. *African Journal of Business Management*, *6*(16), 5657–5670.

Cheung, W., Chang, M. K., & Lai, V. S. (2000). Prediction of Internet and World Wide Web Usage at Work: A Test of an Extended Triandis Model. *Decision Support Systems*, *30*(1), 83–100. doi:10.1016/S0167-9236(00)00125-1

Chin, W. W., Marcolin, B. L., & Newsted, P. R. (1996). A Partial Least Squares Latent Variable Modeling Approach for Measuring Interaction Effects: Results from a Monte Carlo Simulation Study and Voice Mail Emotion/Adoption Study. In J.I. DeGross, S. Jarvenpaa and A. Srinivasan (Eds.), *The 17th International Conference on Information Systems,* Cleveland, OH (pp. 21-41).

Chiu, C., Hsu, M., & Wang, E. (2006). Understanding knowledge sharing in virtual communities: An Integration of social capital and social cognitive theories. *Decision Support Systems*, *42*(3), 1872–1888. doi:10.1016/j.dss.2006.04.001

Cho, H., & Koh, S. J. (2008). Influence of gender on internet commerce: An explorative study in Singapore. *Journal of Internet Commerce*, *7*(1), 95–119. doi:10.1080/15332860802004394

Chow, W. S., & Chan, L. S. (2008). Social network, social trust and shared goals in organizational knowledge sharing. *Information & Management*, *45*(7), 458–465. doi:10.1016/j.im.2008.06.007

Comber, C., Colley, A., Hargreaves, D. J., & Dorn, L. (1997). The effects of age, gender and computer experience upon computer attitudes. *Educational Research*, *39*(2), 123–133. doi:10.1080/0013188970390201

Compeau, D., Higgins, C. A., & Huff, S. (1999). Social cognitive theory and individual reactions to computing technology: A longitudinal study. *Management Information Systems Quarterly*, *23*(2), 145–158. doi:10.2307/249749

Cowan, B. R., & Jack, M. A. (2011). Exploring the Wiki User Experience: The Effects of Training Spaces on Novice User Usability and Anxiety Towards Wiki Editing. *Interacting with Computers*, *23*(2), 117–128. doi:10.1016/j.intcom.2010.11.002

Davis, F., & Venkatesh, V. (1996). A Critical Assessment of Potential Measurement Biases in the Technology Acceptance Model. *International Journal of Human-Computer Studies*, *45*(1), 19–45. doi:10.1006/ijhc.1996.0040

Davis, F. D. (1989). Perceived Usefulness, Perceived Ease of Use, and User Acceptance of Information Technology. *Management Information Systems Quarterly*, *13*(3), 319–340. doi:10.2307/249008

Davis, F. D., Bagozzi, R. P., & Warshaw, P. R. (1992). Extrinsic and Intrinsic Motivation to Use Computers in the Workplace. *Journal of Applied Social Psychology*, *22*(14), 1111–1132. doi:10.1111/j.1559-1816.1992.tb00945.x

Dimock, M. (2018). Defining Generations: Where Millennials End and Post-Millennials Begin. *Pew Research Center*. Retrieved from http://www.pewresearch.org/fact-tank/2018/03/01/defining-generations-where-millennials-end-and-post-millennials-begin/

eMarketer. (2013). Social Networking Reaches Nearly One in Four around the World. Retrieved from http://www.emarketer.com/Article/Social-Networking-Reaches-Nearly-One-Four-Around-World/1009976

Fang, Y. H., & Chiu, C. M. (2010). In Justice We Trust: Exploring Knowledge-Sharing Continuance Intentions in Virtual Communities of Practice. *Computers in Human Behavior*, *26*(2), 235–246. doi:10.1016/j.chb.2009.09.005

Fishbein, M., & Ajzen, I. (1975). *Belief, Attitude, Intention and Behavior: An Introduction to Theory and Research*. Reading, MA: Addison-Wesley.

Fleming, G., Reitsma, R., & Pappafotopoulos, T. (2015). *Millennials: A Demographic Overview*. Cambridge, MA: Forrester Research.

Fogel, J., & Nehmad, E. (2009). Internet Social Network Communities: Risk Taking, Trust and Privacy Concerns. *Computers in Human Behavior*, *25*(1), 153–160. doi:10.1016/j.chb.2008.08.006

Fornell, C., & Larcker, D. F. (1981). Evaluating Structural Equation Models with Unobservable Variables and Measurement Error: Algebra and Statistics. *JMR, Journal of Marketing Research*, *18*(3), 382–388. doi:10.1177/002224378101800313

Foster, M. K., Francescucci, A., & West, B. C. (2010). Why Users Participate in Online Social Networks. *International Journal of Business and Management*, *4*(1), 3–19.

Foubert, J. D., & Sholley, B. K. (1996). Effects of Gender, Gender Role, and Individualized Trust on Self-Disclosure. *Journal of Social Behavior and Personality*, *11*(5), 277–288.

Friessen, V. (1992). Trapped in Electronic Cages? *Media Culture & Society*, *14*, 31–49.

Gaudin, S. (2010). Update: Facebook User Satisfaction "Abysmal." Retrieved from http://www.computerworld.com/s/article/9179378/Update_Facebook_user_satisfaction_abysmal_

Gefen, D. (2000). E-Commerce: The Role of Familiarity and Trust. *Omega: The International Journal of Management Science*, *28*(6), 725–737. doi:10.1016/S0305-0483(00)00021-9

Gefen, D., Karahanna, E., & Straub, D. W. (2003). Trust and TAM in Online Shopping: An Integrated Model. *Management Information Systems Quarterly*, *27*(1), 51–90. doi:10.2307/30036519

Gefen, D., Rigdon, E. E., & Straub, D. W. (2011). An Update and Extension to SEM Guidelines for Administrative and Social Science Research. *Management Information Systems Quarterly*, *35*(2), iii–xiv. doi:10.2307/23044042

Grant, D. M., Malloy, A. D., & Murphy, M. C. (2009). A Comparison of Student Perceptions of Their Computer Skills to Their Actual Abilities. *Journal of Information Technology Education*, *8*, 141–160. doi:10.28945/164

Gwebu, K. L., Wang, J., & Guo, L. (2014). Continued Usage Intention of Multifunctional Friend Networking Services: A Test of a Dual-Process Model Using Facebook. *Decision Support Systems*, *67*, 66–77. doi:10.1016/j.dss.2014.08.004

Hargittai, E. (2007). Whose Space? Differences among Users and Non-Users of Social Network Sites. *Journal of Computer-Mediated Communication*, *13*(1), 276–297. doi:10.1111/j.1083-6101.2007.00396.x

Hsu, C.-L., & Lin, J. C. (2008). Acceptance of Blog Usage: The Roles of Technology Acceptance, Social Influence and Knowledge Sharing Motivation. *Information & Management*, *45*(1), 65–74. doi:10.1016/j.im.2007.11.001

Hsu, M. H., Ju, T. L., Yen, C. H., & Chang, C.-M. (2007). Knowledge sharing behavior in virtual communities: The relationship between trust, self-efficacy, and outcome expectations. *International Journal of Human-Computer Studies*, *65*(2), 153–169. doi:10.1016/j.ijhcs.2006.09.003

IBM. (2012). *Leading through Connections: Insights from the Global Chief Executives Officer Study*. New York: IBM Corporation.

Jarvis, C. B., MacKenzie, S. B., & Podsakoff, P. M. (2003). A critical review of construct indicators and measurement model misspecification in marketing and consumer research. *The Journal of Consumer Research*, *30*(2), 199–218. doi:10.1086/376806

Kalinic, Z., & Marinkovic, V. (2016). Determinants of users' intention to adopt m-commerce: An empirical analysis. *Information Systems and e-Business Management*, *14*(2), 367–387. doi:10.100710257-015-0287-2

Keil, M., Tan, B. C. Y., Wei, K. K., Saarinen, T., Tuunainen, V. K., & Wassenaar, A. (2000). A cross-cultural study on escalation of commitment behavior in software projects. *Management Information Systems Quarterly*, *24*(2), 299–226. doi:10.2307/3250940

Kemp, D. A. S., & Palan, K. M. (2006). The Effects of Gender and Argument Strength on the Processing of Word-of-Mouth Communication. *Academy of Marketing Studies Journal*, *10*(1), 1–18.

Kenny, D. A. (2007). Statistics FAQs. Retrieved from http://www.psy.surrey.ac.uk/cfs/p4.htm

Kenny, D. A. (2009). Moderator Variables. Retrieved from http://davidakenny.net/cm/moderation.htm

Kim, B. (2011). Understanding antecedents of continuance intention in social networking services. *Cyberpsychology, Behavior, and Social Networking*, *14*(4), 199–205. doi:10.1089/cyber.2010.0009 PMID:21192764

Kim, Y., Sohn, D., & Choi, S. M. (2011). Cultural difference in motivations for using social network sites: A comparative study of American and Korean college students. *Computers in Human Behavior*, *27*(1), 365–372. doi:10.1016/j.chb.2010.08.015

Krasnova, H., Spiekermann, S., Koroleva, K., & Hildebrand, T. (2010). Online social networks: Why we disclose. *Journal of Information Technology*, *25*(2), 109–125. doi:10.1057/jit.2010.6

Lebeaux, R. (2008). Democracy via technology: Obama and the power of Web 2.0. *TechTarget*. Retrieved from http://totalcio.blogs.techtarget.com/2008/11/05/democracy-via-technology-obama-and-the-power-of-web-20/

Lewis, K., Kaufman, J., & Christakis, N. (2008). The taste for privacy: An analysis of college student privacy settings in an online social network. *Journal of Computer-Mediated Communication*, *14*(1), 79–100. doi:10.1111/j.1083-6101.2008.01432.x

Liang, H., Saraf, N., Hu, Q., & Xue, Y. (2007). Assimilation of enterprise systems: The effect of institutional pressures and the mediating role of top management. *Management Information Systems Quarterly*, *31*(1), 59–87. doi:10.2307/25148781

Liaw, S., & Huang, H. (2009). Gender Difference, Computer Experience, Self-Efficacy, Motivation and Intention toward E-Learning: A Case Study of the Blackboard System. In T.e.a. Bastiaens (Ed.), *World Conference on E-Learning in Corporate, Government, Healthcare, and Higher Education* (pp. 1762-1770). Chesapeake, VA: AACE.

Lin, C. P., & Anol, B. (2008). Learning Online Social Support: An Investigation of Network Information Technology Based on UTAUT. *Cyberpsychology & Behavior*, *11*(3), 268–272. doi:10.1089/cpb.2007.0057 PMID:18537495

Lin, H. (2006). Understanding behavioral intention to participate in virtual communities. *Cyberpsychology & Behavior*, *9*(5), 540–547. doi:10.1089/cpb.2006.9.540 PMID:17034320

Lin, K. Y., & Lu, H. P. (2011). Why people use social networking sites: An empirical study integrating network externalities and motivation theory. *Computers in Human Behavior*, *27*(3), 1152–1161. doi:10.1016/j.chb.2010.12.009

Lin, M. J. J., Hung, S. W., & Chen, C. J. (2009). Fostering the determinants of knowledge sharing in professional virtual communities. *Computers in Human Behavior*, *25*(4), 929–939. doi:10.1016/j.chb.2009.03.008

Magsamen-Conrad, K., Upadhyaya, S., Joa, C. Y., & Dowd, J. (2015). Bridging the divide: Using UTAUT to predict multigenerational tablet adoption practices. *Computers in Human Behavior*, *50*, 186–196. doi:10.1016/j.chb.2015.03.032 PMID:25937699

McKnight, K. H., Choudhury, V., & Kacmar, C. (2002). Developing and validating trust measures for e-commerce: An integrative typology. *Information Systems Research*, *13*(3), 334–359. doi:10.1287/isre.13.3.334.81

Mine, G. R., & Rhom, A. J. (2000). Consumer privacy and namr removal across direct marketing channels: Exploring opt-in and opt-out alternatives. *Journal of Public Policy & Marketing*, *19*(2), 238–249. doi:10.1509/jppm.19.2.238.17136

Moore, M. (2012). Interactive media usage among millennial consumers. *Journal of Consumer Marketing*, *29*(6), 436–444. doi:10.1108/07363761211259241

Mui, C. (2011). Facebook's Privacy Issues Are Even Deeper Than We Knew. *Forbes*. Retrieved from http://www.forbes.com/sites/chunkamui/2011/08/08/facebooks-privacy-issues-are-even-deeper-than-we-knew/

Nahapiet, J., & Ghoshal, S. (1998). Social capital, intellectual capital, and organizational advantage. *Academy of Management Review*, *23*(2), 242–266. doi:10.5465/amr.1998.533225

Nathan, R. J., & Yeow, P. H. P. (2011). Crucial web usability factors of 36 industries for students: A large-scale empirical study. *Electronic Commerce Research*, *11*(2), 151–180. doi:10.100710660-010-9054-0

Ng, C. S.-P. (2013). Intention to purchase on social commerce websites across cultures: A cross-regional study. *Information & Management*, *50*(8), 609–620. doi:10.1016/j.im.2013.08.002

Nunnally, J. C. (1978). *Psychometric Theory*. New York: McGraw-Hill.

Nysveen, H., Pedersen, P. E., & Thorbjornsen, H. (2005). Explaining intention to use mobile chat services: Moderating effects of gender. *Journal of Consumer Marketing*, 22(5), 247–256. doi:10.1108/07363760510611671

Obal, M., & Kunz, W. (2013). Trust development in e-services: A cohort analysis of millennials and baby boomers. *Journal of Service Management*, 24(1), 45–63. doi:10.1108/09564231311304189

Pelling, E. L., Behav.Sc, B., & White, K. M. (2003). The Theory of planned behavior applied to young people's use of social networking web sites. *Cyberpsychology & Behavior*, 12(6), 755–759. doi:10.1089/cpb.2009.0109 PMID:19788377

Pew Research Center. (2010). Millennials: confident, connected, open to change. Retrieved from http://www.pewsocialtrends.org/files/2010/10/millennials-confident-connected-open-to-change.pdf

Pew Research Center. (2014). Millennials in Adulthood: Detached from Institutions, Networked with Friends. Retrieved from http://www.pewsocialtrends.org/2010/02/24/millennials-confident-connected-open-to-change/

Plank, W., & Shoulak, J. (2015). Millennials, Country Music and Zombies. *The Wall Street Journal*. Retrieved from http://blogs.wsj.com/corporate-intelligence/2015/04/29/millennials-country-music-and-zombies/

Plank, W., & Tovar, C. A. (2015). Who Are Facebook's Biggest Friends? *The Wall Street Journal*. Retrieved from http://blogs.wsj.com/corporate-intelligence/2015/04/08/who-are-facebooks-biggest-friends/

Podsakoff, P. M., MacKenzie, S. B., Lee, J.-Y., & Podsakoff, N. P. (2003). Common Method Biases in Behavioral Research: A Critical Review of the Literature and Recommended Remedies. *The Journal of Applied Psychology*, 88(5), 879–903. doi:10.1037/0021-9010.88.5.879 PMID:14516251

Rauniar, R., Rawski, G., Yang, J., & Johnson, B. (2014). Technology acceptance model and social media usage: An empirical study on Facebook. *Journal of Enterprise Information Management*, 27(1), 6–30. doi:10.1108/JEIM-04-2012-0011

Rhoades, M. J. R. (1981). A Social Psychological Investigation of the Differential Influence of Male and Female Advocates of Nontraditional Sex Roles. *Dissertation Abstracts International*, 41, 4747.

Richardson, B. (2008). Of Salesforce.Com and Amazon, Facebook, Google ... And Workforce.Com. Retrieved from www.amr.com

Ridings, C. M., Gefen, D., & Arinze, B. (2003). Some antecedents and effects of trust in virtual communities. *The Journal of Strategic Information Systems*, 11(3-4), 271–295. doi:10.1016/S0963-8687(02)00021-5

Ringle, C. M., Wende, S., & Will, A. (2005). SmartPLS 2.0 (beta). Retrieved from http://www.smartpls.de

Rodgers, S., & Harris, M. A. (2003). Gender and E-Commerce: An Exploratory Study. *Journal of Advertising Research*, 43(3), 322–329. doi:10.2501/JAR-43-3-322-329

Rogers, E. (1995). *Diffusion of Innovations*. New York: Free Press.

Ryan, R., & Deci, E. L. (2000). Self-determination theory and the facilitation of intrinsic motivation, social development and well-being. *The American Psychologist*, *55*(1), 68–78. doi:10.1037/0003-066X.55.1.68 PMID:11392867

Sambamurthy, V., & Chin, W. (1994). The effects of group attitudes toward alternative Gdss Designs on the decision-making performance of computer-supported groups. *Decision Sciences*, *25*(2), 215–241. doi:10.1111/j.1540-5915.1994.tb01840.x

Sarstedt, M., & Ringle, C. M. (2010). Treating unobserved heterogeneity in PLS path modelling: A comparison of Fimix-Pls with different data analysis strategies. *Journal of Applied Statistics*, *37*(8), 1299–1318. doi:10.1080/02664760903030213

Seppanen, S., & Gualtieri, W. (2012). *The Millennial Generation Research Review. National Chamber Foundation*. Washington, D.C.: U.S. Chamber of Commerce.

Shin, D. H. (2010). Analysis of online social networks: A cross-national study. *Online Information Review*, *34*(3), 473–495. doi:10.1108/14684521011054080

Sledgianowski, D., & Kulviwat, S. (2009). Using social network sites: The effects of playfulness, critical mass and trust in a hedonic context. *Journal of Computer Information Systems*, *49*(4), 74–83.

Slyke, C. V., Comunale, C. L., & Belanger, F. (2002). Gender differences in perceptions of web-based shopping. *Communications of the ACM*, *45*(8), 82–86. doi:10.1145/545151.545155

Smith, A., & Anderson, M. (2018). Social Media Use in 2018. Retrieved from http://www.pewinternet.org/2018/03/01/social-media-use-in-2018/

Sun, Y., Liu, L., Peng, X., Dong, Y., & Barners, S. J. (2014). Understanding Chinese users' continuance intention towards online social networks: an integrative theoretical model. *Electronic Markets*, *24*(1), 57–66. doi:10.100712525-013-0131-9

Tadena, N. (2015). For millennials, use of technology just as important as brand name, study finds. *The Wall Street Journal*. Retrieved from http://blogs.wsj.com/cmo/2015/01/27/for-millennials-use-of-technology-just-as-important-as-brand-name-study-finds/

Taylor, S., & Todd, P. A. (1995). Assessing IT usage: the role of prior experience. *Management Information Systems Quarterly*, *19*(2), 561–570. doi:10.2307/249633

Teo, T. S. H., Srivastava, S. C., & Jiang, L. (2009). Trust and electronic government success: an empirical study. *Journal of Management Information Systems*, *25*(3), 99–131. doi:10.2753/MIS0742-1222250303

The Canadian Press. (2010). Cyber Predator Who Targeted 55 Teen Girls Jailed for 10 Years. Retrieved from http://www.theglobeandmail.com/news/national/cyber-predator-who-targeted-55-teen-girls-jailed-for-10-years/article1661783/

The Nielsen Company. (2014). Millennials - Breaking the Myths. Nielsen Holdings, New York. Retrieved from http://www.nielsen.com/content/dam/corporate/us/en/reports-downloads/2014%20Reports/nielsen-millennial-report-feb-2014.pdf

Thompson, R. L., Higgins, C. A., & Howell, J. M. (1991). Personal Computing: Toward a Conceptual Model of Utilization. *Management Information Systems Quarterly, 15*(1), 124–143. doi:10.2307/249443

Trauth, E. M., Nielsen, S. H., & von Hellens, L. A. (2003). Explaining the It Gender Gap: Australian Stories for the New Millennium. *Journal of Research and Practice in IT, 35*(1), 7–20.

Venkatesh, V., Brown, S. A., Maruping, L. M., & Bala, H. (2008). Predicting Different Conceptualizations of System Use: The Competing Roles of Behavioral Intention, Facilitating Conditions, and Behavioral Expectation. *Management Information Systems Quarterly, 32*(3), 483–502. doi:10.2307/25148853

Venkatesh, V., & Davis, F. D. (2000). A Theoretical Extension of the Technology Acceptance Model: Four Longitudinal Field Studies. *Management Science, 46*(2), 86–204. doi:10.1287/mnsc.46.2.186.11926

Venkatesh, V., & Morris, M. G. (2000). Why don't men ever shop to ask for directions? Gender, social influence, and their role in technology acceptance and usage behavior. *Management Information Systems Quarterly, 24*(1), 15–139. doi:10.2307/3250981

Venkatesh, V., Morris, M. G., & Ackerman, P. L. (2000). A longitudinal field investigation of gender differences in individual technology adoption decision making processes. *Organizational Behavior and Human Decision Processes, 83*(1), 33–60. doi:10.1006/obhd.2000.2896 PMID:10973782

Venkatesh, V., Morris, M. G., Davis, G. B., & Davis, F. D. (2003). User Acceptance of Information Technology: Toward a Unified View. *Management Information Systems Quarterly, 27*(3), 425–478. doi:10.2307/30036540

Venkatesh, V., Thong, J., & Xu, X. (2012). Consumer Acceptance and Use of Information Technology: Extending the Unified Theory of Acceptance and Use of Technology. *Management Information Systems Quarterly, 36*(1), 57–178. doi:10.2307/41410412

Venkatesh, V., Thong, J., & Xu, X. (2016). Unified Theory of Acceptance and Use of Technology: A Synthesis and the Road Ahead. *Journal of the Association for Information Systems, 17*(5), 328–376. doi:10.17705/1jais.00428

Wallace, P., & Clariana, R. B. (2005). Perceptions Versus Reality--Determining Business Students' Computer Literacy Skills and Need for Instruction in Information Concepts and Technology. *Journal of Information Technology Education, 4*, 141–151. doi:10.28945/269

Wang, W., & Benbasat, I. (2005). Trust in and Adoption of Online Recommendation Agents. *Journal of the Association for Information Systems, 6*(3), 72–101. doi:10.17705/1jais.00065

Wang, Y.-S. (2002). The Adoption of Electronic Tax Filing Systems: An Empirical Study. *Government Information Quarterly, 20*(4), 33–352.

Wermuth, N. (1989). Moderating Effects of Subgroups in Linear Models. *Biometrika, 76*(1), 81–92. doi:10.1093/biomet/76.1.81

Wilson, F. (1992). Language, Technology, Gender, and Power. *Human Relations, 45*(9), 883–903. doi:10.1177/001872679204500902

Wu, C., Huang, Y., & Hsu, C. (2014). Benevolence Trust: A Key Determinant of User Continuance Use of Online Social Network. *Information Systems and e-Business Management, 12*(2), 189–211. doi:10.100710257-013-0216-1

Xu, F., Michael, K., & Chen, X. (2013). Factors Affecting Privacy Disclosure on Social Network Sites: An Integrated Model. *Electronic Commerce Research, 13*(2), 151–168. doi:10.100710660-013-9111-6

Yoon, C., & Rolland, E. (2012). Knowledge-Sharing in Virtual Communities: Familiarity, Anonymity and Self-Determination Theory. *Behaviour & Information Technology, 31*(11), 1133–1143. doi:10.10 80/0144929X.2012.702355

Zhang, T., Wang, W. Y. C., Lin, Y. C., & Tai, L.-H. (2015). Understanding User Motivation for Evaluating Online Content: A Self-Determining Theory. *Behaviour & Information Technology, 34*(5), 479–491. doi:10.1080/0144929X.2014.964319

This research was previously published in the International Journal of Technology Diffusion (IJTD), 10(2); pages 34-68, copyright year 2019 by IGI Publishing (an imprint of IGI Global).

APPENDIX A

Table 9. Survey items and associated reference

Construct	Items	Ref.
Trust in technology	1. The Internet has enough safeguards to make me feel comfortable using it. 2. I feel assured that legal and technological structures adequately protect me from problems on the Internet. 3. I feel confident that the encryption and other technological advances on the Internet make it safe for me to transact (i.e., socialize with others) there.	(McKnight et al., 2002)
Trust in community	1. I feel fine interacting with the SNC since it fulfills my needs of interaction efficiently. 2. I always feel confident that I can rely on the responses and feedback from the SNC when I interact with them. 3. I am comfortable relying on the contents of any discussion topic from the SNC.	(McKnight et al., 2002)
Hedonic motivation	1. The actual process of participating in a SNC is pleasant. 2. I have fun participating in a SNC. 3. Participating in a SNC bores me. 4. I enjoy participating in a SNC.	(Agarwal and Karahanna 2000; Davis et al., 1992)
Effort expectancy	Perceived ease of use 1. Learning to operate the system would be easy for me. 2. I would find it easy to get the system to do what I want it to do. 3. I would find the system easy to use. 4. Using Facebook involves too much time doing mechanical operations (e.g. data input). (reversed scale) 5. It takes too long to learn how to use Facebook to make it worth the effort. (reversed scale)	(Davis, 1989)
Social influence	Subjective Norm 1. My friends think that I should use the system. 2. My classmates think that I should use the system.	(Ajzen, 1991)
	Social Factors 3. I use the system because of a proportion of my classmates use it.	(Thompson et al., 1991)
Facilitating conditions	Perceived Behavioral (Control) 1. I have control over using the system. 2. I have the resources necessary to use the system. 3. I have the knowledge necessary to use the system.	(Ajzen, 1991)
	Facilitating Conditions 4. Specialized instruction concerning the system was available to me.	(Thompson et al., 1991)
Intention to participate in a SNC	1. I intend to participate in a SNC in the future. 2. I expect my use of the SNC to continue in the future. 3. I plan to use the SNC in the future.	(Agarwal and Karahanna, 2000)

APPENDIX B

Table 10. Common method bias analysis

Construct	Indicator	Substantive Factor Loading (R1)	R1-Square	Method Factor Loading (R2)	R2-Square
Facilitating conditions	FC1	0.904***	0.818	0.099	0.010
	FC2	0.895***	0.802	0.117	0.014
	FC3	0.920***	0.847	0.076	0.006
Intention to participate in a SNC	IP1	0.938***	0.879	0.088	0.008
	IP2	0.927***	0.860	0.095	0.009
	IP3	0.922***	0.851	0.097	0.009
Hedonic Motivation	HM1	0.864***	0.747	0.117	0.014
	HM2	0.908***	0.825	0.139*	0.019
	HM3	0.891***	0.794	0.203***	0.041
Effort expectancy	EE1	0.793***	0.629	0.077	0.006
	EE2	0.837***	0.700	0.051	0.003
	EE3	0.837***	0.701	0.145*	0.021
	EE4	0.729***	0.531	0.438***	0.192
	EE5	0.835***	0.696	0.280	0.078
Social influence	SI1	0.932***	0.868	0.029	0.001
	SI2	0.938***	0.879	0.059	0.004
Trust in community	TC1	0.855***	0.731	0.163**	0.026
	TC2	0.872***	0.760	0.174**	0.030
	TC3	0.854***	0.730	0.034	0.001
Trust in technology	TT1	0.933***	0.870	0.020	0.000
	TT2	0.922***	0.850	0.003	0.000
	TT3	0.947***	0.897	0.007	0.000
	Average	0.884	0.785	0.114	0.022

*p < .05; **p < .01;***p < .001

APPENDIX C

Table 11. Composite reliabilities and discriminant validity for the two gender and educational background subgroups

3-1: The Gender Subgroups

	Male Subgroup								Female Subgroup							
	CR	Correlation of Constructs							CR	Correlation of Constructs						
		1	2	3	4	5	6	7		1	2	3	4	5	6	7
1. EE	0.90	**0.80**							0.90	**0.81**						
2. FC	0.93	0.43	**0.90**						0.93	0.42	**0.91**					
3. IP	0.94	0.31	0.28	**0.92**					0.96	0.40	0.41	**0.94**				
4. HM	0.90	0.49	0.36	0.58	**0.87**				0.93	0.56	0.42	0.62	**0.91**			
5. SI	0.93	0.21	0.16	0.24	0.23	**0.93**			0.93	0.18	0.22	0.37	0.37	**0.93**		
6. TC	0.90	0.46	0.37	0.51	0.63	0.16	**0.86**		0.90	0.49	0.43	0.55	0.67	0.40	**0.86**	
7. TT	0.96	0.06	0.05	0.40	0.27	-0.04	0.34	**0.95**	0.94	0.05	0.22	0.23	0.17	0.14	0.35	**0.92**

3-2: The Educational Background Subgroups

	IT Major Subgroup								Non-IT Major Subgroup							
	CR	Correlation of constructs							CR	Correlation of constructs						
		1	2	3	4	5	6	7		1	2	3	4	5	6	7
1. EE	0.89	**0.79**							0.92	**0.83**						
2. FC	0.92	0.44	**0.89**						0.95	0.41	**0.93**					
3. IP	0.95	0.42	0.33	**0.93**					0.95	0.27	0.43	**0.92**				
4. HM	0.90	0.55	0.34	0.57	**0.87**				0.95	0.52	0.51	0.64	**0.92**			
5. SI	0.93	0.15	0.14	0.31	0.25	**0.93**			0.93	0.28	0.35	0.29	0.36	**0.93**		
6. TC	0.89	0.47	0.33	0.53	0.64	0.24	**0.94**		0.90	0.48	0.52	0.52	0.68	0.37	**0.87**	
7. TT	0.95	0.02	0.10	0.29	0.18	0.02	0.27	**0.94**	0.95	0.12	0.23	0.36	0.30	0.08	0.47	**0.93**

EE=Effort expectancy, FC= Facilitating conditions, IP= Intention to participate in a SNC, HM= Hedonic motivation, SI= Social influence, TC= Trust in community, TT=Trust in technology.CR= Composite reliability, Note: Diagonal is the square-root of the construct's AVE. For adequate discriminate validity, diagonal elements should be greater than corresponding off-diagonal elements

APPENDIX D

Table 12. Item weights and cross loadings for the two gender subgroups

	Male Subgroup							Female Subgroup						
	EE	**FC**	**IP**	**HM**	**SI**	**TC**	**TT**	**EE**	**FC**	**IP**	**HM**	**SI**	**TC**	**TT**
EE1	**0.77**							**0.84**						
EE2	**0.85**							**0.89**						
EE3	**0.87**							**0.83**						
EE4	**0.69**							**0.66**						
EE5	**0.81**							**0.82**						
FC1	0.39	**0.92**						0.44	**0.93**					
FC2	0.41	**0.88**						0.35	**0.88**					
FC3	0.36	**0.91**						0.33	**0.91**					
IP1	0.37	0.28	**0.93**					0.41	0.36	**0.95**				
IP2	0.26	0.23	**0.93**					0.31	0.37	**0.93**				
IP3	0.23	0.25	**0.89**					0.38	0.41	**0.94**				
HM1	0.47	0.39	0.53	**0.88**				0.49	0.31	0.52	**0.85**			
HM2	0.39	0.28	0.51	**0.88**				0.54	0.43	0.60	**0.95**			
HM3	0.43	0.25	0.45	**0.85**				0.50	0.41	0.57	**0.92**			
SI1	0.22	0.13	0.17	0.17	**0.90**			0.16	0.17	0.33	0.32	**0.93**		
SI2	0.18	0.17	0.26	0.25	**0.96**			0.18	0.24	0.36	0.37	**0.94**		
TC1	0.43	0.38	0.46	0.59	0.17	**0.86**		0.47	0.41	0.53	0.64	0.36	**0.89**	
TC2	0.40	0.32	0.49	0.58	0.16	**0.89**		0.38	0.36	0.44	0.58	0.39	**0.87**	
TC3	0.35	0.23	0.35	0.45	0.07	**0.83**		0.40	0.35	0.44	0.50	0.28	**0.83**	
TT1	0.07	0.03	0.38	0.24	-0.06	0.33	**0.94**	0.04	0.21	0.19	0.17	0.14	0.30	**0.90**
TT2	0.00	0.03	0.33	0.22	-0.06	0.25	**0.94**	0.07	0.18	0.24	0.15	0.14	0.31	**0.92**
TT3	0.09	0.09	0.42	0.31	0.00	0.37	**0.97**	0.03	0.23	0.20	0.15	0.10	0.36	**0.92**

EE=Effort expectancy, FC= Facilitating conditions, IP= Intention to participate in a SNC, HM= Hedonic motivation, SI= Social influence, TC= Trust in community, TT=Trust in technology. Note: Bold are the item weights showing that the two subgroups do not vary significantly in construct score weighting (Carte and Russell 2003).

APPENDIX E

Table 13. Item weights and cross loadings for the two educational background subgroups

	IT Major Subgroup							Non-IT Major Subgroup						
	EE	FC	IP	HM	SI	TC	TT	EE	FC	IP	HM	SI	TC	TT
EE1	**0.78**							**0.86**						
EE2	**0.89**							**0.82**						
EE3	**0.82**							**0.89**						
EE4	**0.62**							**0.78**						
EE5	**0.82**							**0.81**						
FC1	0.42	**0.92**						0.44	**0.94**					
FC2	0.41	**0.85**						0.34	**0.93**					
FC3	0.35	**0.91**						0.34	**0.91**					
IP1	0.46	0.32	**0.94**					0.29	0.38	**0.95**				
IP2	0.33	0.27	**0.92**					0.23	0.42	**0.94**				
IP3	0.37	0.33	**0.93**					0.23	0.39	**0.88**				
HM1	0.54	0.33	0.51	**0.86**				0.44	0.45	0.52	**0.88**			
HM2	0.45	0.30	0.50	**0.88**				0.50	0.48	0.65	**0.96**			
HM3	0.44	0.24	0.46	**0.86**				0.51	0.49	0.61	**0.93**			
SI1	0.12	0.15	0.27	0.21	**0.93**			0.32	0.21	0.19	0.28	**0.89**		
SI2	0.15	0.11	0.31	0.26	**0.94**			0.23	0.39	0.32	0.37	**0.96**		
TC1	0.44	0.34	0.50	0.63	0.18	**0.87**		0.49	0.48	0.50	0.61	0.42	**0.89**	
TC2	0.38	0.31	0.46	0.55	0.24	**0.87**		0.40	0.40	0.47	0.64	0.36	**0.90**	
TC3	0.40	0.19	0.40	0.46	0.20	**0.83**		0.35	0.48	0.39	0.50	0.15	**0.82**	
TT1	0.02	0.08	0.26	0.16	0.02	0.27	**0.93**	0.11	0.20	0.34	0.30	0.07	0.42	**0.93**
TT2	0.01	0.08	0.29	0.17	0.06	0.24	**0.93**	0.08	0.17	0.28	0.21	0.01	0.36	**0.92**
TT3	0.03	0.11	0.26	0.18	-0.01	0.27	**0.95**	0.13	0.26	0.38	0.32	0.12	0.53	**0.94**

EE=Effort expectancy, FC= Facilitating conditions, IP= Intention to participate in a SNC, HM= Hedonic motivation, SI= Social influence, TC= Trust in community, TT=Trust in technology. Note: Bold are the item weights showing that the two subgroups do not vary significantly in construct score weighting (Carte and Russell 2003).

APPENDIX F

Table 14. Model summary – Statistical comparison of paths for the two gender subgroups

Construct	Male (N1=145, R1-Squared=0.435)			Female (N2=156, R-Squared=0.447)			Statistical Comparison of Paths[A]
	Std. Path Coefficient	T-Value	Std. Error	Std. Path Coefficient	T-Value	Std. Error	T-Value
Trust in technology -> Intention to participate in a SNC	0.247***	3.408	0.073	0.068	0.865	0.079	20.459***
Trust in community -> Intention to participate in a SNC	0.156*	1.983	0.078	0.130	1.255	0.104	2.391*
Hedonic motivation -> Intention to participate in a SNC	0.363***	4.185	0.087	0.412***	3.738	0.110	-4.270***
Effort expectancy -> Intention to participate in a SNC	-0.001	0.016	0.074	0.023	0.261	0.087	-2.556*
Social influence -> Intention to participate in a SNC	0.128	1.620	0.079	0.123	1.375	0.089	0.542
Facilitating conditions -> Intention to participate in a SNC	0.058	0.667	0.087	0.124	1.488	0.083	-6.714***

*=0.10 significance **= 0.05 significance, ***= 0.001 significance

[A]The statistical comparison of paths was carried out using the following procedure as suggested byChin et al. (1996) and applied by Keil et al. (2000) and Ahuja & Thatcher (2005):

$S_{pooled} = sqrt\{ [(N_1-1) / (N_1 + N_2 -2)] \times SE_1^2 + [(N_2-1) / (N_1 + N_2 -2)] \times SE_2^2 \}$

$t = (PC_1 - PC_2) / [S_{pooled} \times sqrt(1/N_1 + 1/N_2)]$

APPENDIX G

Table 15. Model summary – Statistical comparison of paths for the two educational background subgroups

Construct	IT Major (N1=198, R1-Squared=0.437)			Non-IT Major (N2=103, R-Squared=0.469)			Statistical Comparison of Paths[A]
	Std. Path Coefficient	T-Value	Std. Error	Std. Path Coefficient	T-Value	Std. Error	T-Value
Trust in technology -> Intention to participate in a SNC	0.164**	2.857	0.057	0.157	1.815	0.086	0.827
Trust in community -> Intention to participate in a SNC	0.168*	2.334	0.072	0.064	0.634	0.101	10.238***
Hedonic motivation -> Intention to participate in a SNC	0.305***	3.495	0.087	0.534	4.925	0.108	-19.820***
Effort expectancy -> Intention to participate in a SNC	0.110	1.422	0.078	-0.122	1.532	0.079	24.400***
Social influence -> Intention to participate in a SNC	0.161*	2.568	0.063	0.049	0.594	0.082	13.206***
Facilitating conditions -> Intention to participate in a SNC	0.092	1.246	0.074	0.130	1.191	0.109	-3.595***

*= 0.10 significance ** = 0.05 significance, *** = 0.001 significance

[A]The statistical comparison of paths was carried out using the following procedure as suggested byChin et al. (1996) and as shown in Appendix F.

Chapter 16
Identity Design and Identities Exhibited in Social Networks:
A Review Based on Instagram Influencers

Mehmet Ferhat Sönmez
Fırat University, Turkey

ABSTRACT

Identity emerges as a flexible, multidimensional, variable, and slippery concept that cannot be defined through the processes of discussion and understanding. The new construction area of this concept, which is regarded as a process constructed on the social plane, is the social networking platforms. This is because these platforms are the most common communication environments where people and their lifestyles are presented to the outside world, in addition to the cheap and rapid satisfaction of their needs for information and entertainment. Face-to-face communication and language practices are not sufficient enough in the identity presentation anymore. Individuals choose to design and update their identities through social networks and to perform an image-based identity manifestation. This chapter examines how identity was established and manifested through social networks, and analyzes the identities the popular people in these networks designed and exhibited.

INTRODUCTION

As of 2019, 4.3 billion people are Internet users, while 3.4 billion people (about 45% of the world's population) are social media users *(Global Overview Report* https://p.widencdn.net/kqy7ii/Digital2019-Report-en)*.* Even this statistic alone will suffice to determine the position and importance of social media today. These platforms, which have been integrated into everyday life with the information age, have been easily accepted by masses. Even though they do not have a long history, they have been adopted in a short period of time. Every area of social life, from politics to social movements, from entertainment to education, has been influenced by the Internet and social networks.

DOI: 10.4018/978-1-6684-6307-9.ch016

Social Media and Social Networks

Social networking sites are applications that provide information and interaction to users through network technologies (Boyd and Ellison, 2007). In the Merriam-Webster dictionary, social media is defined as "forms of electronic communication (such as websites for social networking and microblogging) through which users create online communities to share information, ideas, personal messages, and other content (such as videos)." According to Mayfield, it is a new type of online media where a high level of sharing occurs and has the following properties (Mayfield, 2008: 5):

- **Participants:** Support and encourage individuals to contribute to the content and provide feedback.
- **Openness:** Social media platforms are open to feedback, they actively allow information sharing, and users can make comments there.
- **Conversation:** They allow bi-directional communication.
- **Community:** They pave the way for the formation of communities in a very short period of time.
- **Connectedness:** They allow links to be created to other pages and media related to topics that interest users.

Unlike traditional media, social media has its own characteristics. These can be summarized as the *determination of the content by the user, lack of time and space limitations, being in an interactive structure and the fact that users are independent of any publisher* (Erkul, 2009: 3). Social networks are the big living spaces within the small "worlds" that people create. People interacting in the Internet environment create a small world of their own. The small-world phenomenon was first discovered by sociologist Stanley Milgram in a mail experiment in 1967. Milgram has proposed a theory claiming that everyone in the world is no more than 6 people away from each other, and he has tested it. According to the classification with six degrees that emerged in the experiment, a person can reach someone he does not know through a maximum of 5 people. Being inspired by this experiment, the first social networking site on the Internet has been called "SixDegrees" (Patch, 2004, p. 4 as cited in Onat ve Alikılıç, 2008, pp. 1116–1117).

Popularity, Popular Culture and Social Media

The etymology of the term "popular" can be traced back to the terms "*populace, population, public,* and *publication*" (Batmaz, 2006, p. 19). The term, which meant "public belonging to the people" in the late medieval period, is used to mean "*loved or chosen by many people*" in the linguistic sense nowadays (Erdoğan & Alemdar, 2005, p. 9). Williams also described the concept as "highly admired by many people and something consciously done to gain appreciation" (Storey, 2009, p. 6). Popular culture is the whole of beliefs, practices and norms that are embraced and shared by a broad circle of people — that is, by almost everyone, if not everyone (Schudson, 1999, p. 169). The middle class, which has changed and thrived through urbanization, has become the strongest bearer of popular culture (Storey, 2009, p. 13). The popular culture, which Rowe (1996, p. 20) considers a leisure practice, prioritizes the elements of entertainment and curiosity. Today, most modern media have also become an entertainment tool, and public events constitute a very insignificant part of media content. Therefore, media has become the primary means in manifesting popular cultural events (Curran, 1997, p. 146).

McQuail has stated that popular cultural content is reflected by the media and that this content is again formatted through the media (McQuail, 1994, p. 40). Popular culture, which is easily accessible to everyone, is unavoidably caught by the radar of the media because of this characteristic of it (Çağan, 2003, p. 77). Social media environments are easily accessible, just like the popular culture, in addition to having an interactive structure. Therefore, a strong flow of information occurs through these environments. Many virtual cultural environments ranging from entertainment to consumption preferences emerge, and popular cultural elements are displayed on this ground created by social networks (Karaduman, 2017, p. 12). Social media, which gathers millions of people in a room, has become a social, cultural and industrial form, not just a technological tool. Social media environments have now evolved into an administrative communication tool that shows, presents and evaluates "what is popular, what is popularized and what is intended to be made popular" (Erdoğan, 2004, p. 15).

Identity, Social Identity and Social Media

Hall defines identity as designs of belonging — continuously established, undertaken and owned by the discourses, conditions and experiences — which are used to address the need for identification and are also formed by different cultural elements (Binark, 2001, p. 75). While the identity phenomenon in the pre-modern period was a concept that was unquestionable and unnegotiable, this situation has changed with modernism, and the concept of identity has become something that is personal, mobile, and open to change and innovation (Karaduman, 2010, p. 2890). According to Kellner, the features of the modern identity are as follows (Kellner, 2001, pp. 195–196):

- The identity has been drawn into the social context and become linked to the "other." And thus, its boundaries have been expanded.
- It has evolved into a selectable, producible and reproducible form.
- In this selection and production process, social norms, social roles and expectations have settled in the position of a reference center.
- Identities now realize that they are in a position to change at any time.

With the "other" becoming prevalent in the identification of identities in the modern period, certain theories concerning the social aspect of identity have been proposed. Names such as Tajfel and Turner (1976, 1978, 1988) have proposed the social identity theory. Gofmann emphasized the identities displayed through daily life. Brewer has proposed that two basic human motives — the need to be unique and the necessity of belonging — are decisive in the formation of social identity, and said that individuals' inclusion and differentiation needs are thus met (Padilla & Perez, 2003, p. 43). Depending on the place of identity on the social plane, individuals distinguish themselves from other groups to raise their positive social judgments and their collective self-esteem. Individuals and groups who do not have satisfactory social identities will try to re-establish/acquire positive identification through "*mobility, assimilation, creativity* or *competition*" (Jenkins, 2016, pp. 125–126). Gofmann has conceptualized this situation as elements such as the highlighting of social category in interpersonal interactions, as well as the image/face that they offer based on their social status. According to Gofmann, the role of a person in the relationship with others will be perceived as an image in the mind of the opposite party (Bilgin, 2007, p. 13). Gofmann concentrates on the concept of "self" and explains how the person reviews and presents himself by updating himself in the event that he encounters the other. He explains to which means the person refers to by using the concept of "self-presentation". The strategy the person develops when making this presentation is bi-directional. On the one hand, he shapes the impressions he desires to give; on the other, he chooses to conceal the impressions that he dislikes and avoids. This situation is described as impression management. This bi-directionality in the presentation of the self is hidden in Goffman's definition of the dual self. According to him, the consensual self — the self that is formed as a result of the practices of both the performer and the observer during an interaction — and the player self implicitly coexist in each individual. This is because the moment an individual gets in touch with another, he actually goes on a stage in front of the other and interacts with the other by transferring some things in this scene, and by covering some things over some other things (Bayad, 2016, p. 83).

With postmodernism, the concept of identity would evolve once again. In the construction of postmodern identity, where unruliness and indeterminateness get to be dominant, slipperiness will prevail and the antecedent paradigm of the modern era, "the other," will be replaced by concepts such as originality, uncertainty, diversity, complexity and relativism (Karaduman, 2010, p. 2894). Bauman, questioning the causes of the need to obtain identity, claims it to be the reason to get rid of the annoying discomfort of the uncertainty of "neither this nor that." This is because the modern social statutes where belongingness is resolved are now inadequate in resolving this need. However, in today's mobility, it also points to the difficulty of identifying someone with something. The identity, described as "a clock to be removed when needed" by Weber, is constructed on the move, planned to be short term and is short-lived, again according to him (Bauman, 2017, p. 38–43).

Social media networks provide the person with a continuous identity development process through the opportunity for global communication and continuity that they offer (Bakıroğlu, 2013, p. 1049). According to Schroeder (1994, pp. 524–525), virtuality circulates the desire of people who wish to re-express themselves/express themselves by renewing.

With online social networks which have evolved with the advancement of communication technologies, the issue of time and space has disappeared, and the room for maneuver has expanded. In these networks, which are open 7/24, people open their everyday lives to the outside world — in every situation they find opportunity — and reflect/build their identities. Individuality that Niedzviecki (2011, p. 18) describes as new conformism sits on a central plane through social networking environments. Again, according to Niedzviecki, the awareness of being individual will be noticeable by being followed by others and by receiving comments (Niedzviecki, 2010, p. 37). Social networks are platforms where an individual escapes from his own reality, finds the freedom to act as he wants to, and experiences his virtual "self" as he desires. He overcomes the negative aspects of his self and the shortcomings he has felt in socialization by using the virtual self he creates and gets away from his true self by being captivated by this virtual reality. Thus, feelings of satisfaction and pleasure are experienced intensely (Akmeşe & Deniz, 2017, p. 28). Goffman's dramaturgical approach was also employed for virtual identities in social media environments. Virtual environments correspond to Goffman's metaphor of the scenes where the self is expressed by wearing a mask (Bayad, 2016, p. 90).

Online social networks allow people to design and consume multiple identities instantaneously. Identities produced on digital platforms are the identities that are intended to be presented to others and have a socially-desirable characteristic. These identities, which cannot fully be exploited in real life, still do not mean that they are not real, and can have a reality effect on the perception of both the identity creator and the person seeing this creation. Identity, which is already a complex concept in the incarnated world, becomes even more complex in the online field (Akgül & Pazarbaşı, 2018, pp. 17–19).

THE STUDY

Purpose and Method

The main objective in this study was to examine the identity exhibitions of the people who were popular in social media environments and analyze how they manifested their identities. In the study, two people who were the most popular and had the greatest number of followers in the Instagram environment were selected for analysis. The reason why Instagram was preferred was primarily for the users of this platform to attach importance to visuality. In addition to this, Instagram is among the popular social networking sites. It was established in 2010 and was soon accepted. The first reason why the application is so popular is that it makes photos look more beautiful through its 11 photo filters. Moreover, users have the opportunity to instantly, practically and quickly share on other social networks the photos they share on Instagram (https://www.brandingturkiye.com/instagram-tarihi-instagram-nedir-nasil-kullanilir-ne-ise-yarar/).

According to TRACKALYTICS data in April 2019, the people who ranked first and second can be seen in Table 1.

Table 1: The accounts of influencers on instagram with the greatest number of followers

Instagram Account of the Influencer	Number of Followers
Cristiano Ronaldo	160,096,599
Ariana Grande	150,042,569

Source: https://www.trackalytics.com/the-most-followed-instagram-profiles/page/1/

This study was centered on Goffman's impression management theory, and netnographic analysis was chosen as the method. Communication ethnography, whose area of study is the daily life of individuals (Kartarı, 2017, p. 216), aims to observe cultural value patterns by receiving supporting from anthropology and to interpret the specific codes of a culture within that culture (Özüdoğru, 2014, p. 266). The adaptation of ethnographic research techniques to online environments is called netnography. Netnographic analysis has recently been used frequently and has become a popular method especially in studies related to social networks (Mansell et al., 2015, p. 292). This method, developed by Kozinets in the 1990s, is a qualitative and interpretative research methodology (Jupp, 2006, p. 193), ensuring both that research environments are examined in more natural forms, as well as reaching richer content (Kozinets, 2002, p. 62; Langer & Beckman, 2005, p. 200).

Findings and Analysis

When the Instagram account of Cristiano Ronaldo, who ranked first in terms of the number of followers, was examined, it was possible to say that he usually shared posts that put forward his "sportsman" identity. The state of "accessible status" (Giddens, 2012, p. 181), which the individual gains by his own efforts, is evident in the posts of C. Ronaldo. C. Ronaldo reflects his sportsmanship as his prominent social identity. He has also strengthened his identity with competitive, ambitious and dominant roles

(Fougère & Moulettes, 2007, p. 17), which coincides with Hofstede's masculinity dimension of the cultural structure. This pronounced image is related to the social context one belongs to. C. Ronaldo perceives to be/feels to be belonging to the football player class and perceived so by those who watch the show. On the other hand, a new type of identity is emerging, with the submission of stationary social structures to today's post modernity. This identity typology, defined by Funk (2007, pp. 7, 12) as a "post-modern self-oriented" personality, has become more prominent at the point of shaping the thinking and action forms of people under the influence of their living conditions and living spaces (İlhan, 2013, p. 240). Again, according to Funk, this personality type is based on a powerful "self" (Funk, 2007, pp. 55–56). The next phase of this construction is the desire and necessity to create a unique and sparkling myth of "self". The individual who cannot fulfill this need and cannot resolve the necessity will not be able to wriggle oneself out of being modern and reach post modernity. The only functional weapon of the person who wants to sculpt his own myth is his visibility. This is because "what is visible is good, and what is good is visible" and in today's world, which Debord described as the society of the spectacle, of course the laws of the show will be decisive (Debord, 1996, p. 16). A person who wants to reach satisfaction by placing his self in the center will present demonstrations supported by his biological and physical characteristics.

Figure 1. His social identity (His modern identity)

Identities exhibited on social media platforms may not always overlap with reality. Posts on personal accounts prioritize the satisfaction of psychological needs such as appreciation, recognition and being noticed. In other words, there may be a mismatch between the image that the person has and the image he wants to reach. However, the identity that a person reveals to his social environment can also be undistorted, reflecting every moment of his life as it is (Sabuncuoğlu, 2015, p. 373).

Another social identity that Cristiano Ronaldo exhibited on stage is having a high-income level, meaning his being "rich." As a status symbol, wealth stands out in the posts of the Instagram influencer. Wealth as a social identity is shared voluntarily and overlaps with reality — considering that he is at the top of the list of sportsmen who earn the most money.

It was to strengthen the self-esteem with these posts where tangible assets were exhibited, and it was aimed to be noticed. Another reason why individuals seek a social identity is to raise self-esteem and get self-respect. According to Scitovsky, it is sometimes not sufficient for an individual to desire to become a member of a particular group. What become a priority in a consumption-centered world is what people have, not who they are (Odabaşı, 1999, p. 95). Tangible assets are assessed according to a social structure that prioritizes power and prestige rather than the necessities that meet vital needs (Sabuncuoğlu, 2015, p. 371). Baudrillard has also stated that the primary purpose of today's people is to pursue the existence through vanity and wealth (Baudrillard, 1997, pp. 193–194). When we take into account that consumption is a way of life, it is possible to say that consumers' search for "drawing attention" is a fundamental need for consumption. This pursuit will be resolved by the exposition of brands and products on virtually any platform (Clark et al., 2007, p. 46, Gökaliler et al., 2011, p. 38). Virtual platforms are the largest of these exhibition halls, and these environments offer an unlimited space for people to show and prove their social identities to the environment (Sözen, 1991, p. 94), liberalizing them at the point of creating exciting identities (Denizci, 2009, p. 59).

Figure 2. His self-oriented identity (His post-modern identity) Sportsman Strong sportsman/invincibility "myth"

Another person who has the highest number of followers on Instagram is the singer and actress Ariana Grande. The first notable feature of the shares of Ariana Grande is that they are the photographs that reflect beauty, aesthetic and physical attraction. These posts triggered by the motivation for appreciation originate from women's feeling that they are under surveillance and that this process becomes a situation that encircles them (Oğuz, 2010: 184). As a matter of fact, according to Berger, a woman's perception of her own existence is complemented by someone else's sense of appreciation of her (Berger, 1990, pp.

46–47). With these shares of her where visual appeal is idealized, A. Grande aims to put her own self into a cognitive comparison process in order to be placed in the category of beautiful/attractive women in the minds of others. In this context, Bocock also highlights that the practice of creating identity through an image and the body is not a simple reflex of consumption, but a process in which desires are embedded (Bocock, 1997, p. 107). Berger conceptualizes this situation through "being watched" (Berger, 1990, p. 447):

Men are however they behave, and women are however they appear. Men watch women. Women watch their being watched. This does not only determine the relationship between men and women, but also the relationship between women and themselves. The observer inside a woman is a male, but the observed is a female. So, the woman turns herself into an object — especially a visual object —, something to be spectated.

When the significance of being watched is combined with the ideal of being beautiful and impeccable, the woman who creates her own mirror and her own myth will internalize being a goddess and put it on stage. If we cite Goffman's (2018, p. 65) quote from Simone de Beauvoir: "... *even the least sophisticated of women does not present herself to observers anymore after she gets dressed. She is a tool that implies a character such as a painting, a sculpture, or an actor on a stage, that is, a character that she represents but not there. What satisfies her is to identify with something that is unreal, unchanging, and perfect such as a novel hero, a portrait or a bust; she strives to identify with this figure, and thereby, to see herself to have stabilized and be legitimized in her own glory.*"

Figure 3. His social identity (his modern identity) rich

Figure 4. His self-oriented identity (post-modern identity) ultra-rich/unreachable myth

Figure 5. Her social identity (her modern identity) being an animal lover

In virtual platforms, the fact that motivations such as desire, being watched and being noticed have become attractive is because these platforms have an untouchable and fictional nature. It is almost impossible to get disappointed in this fictionality. The demonstration scene that is suitable for the irresistible appeal of the satisfaction of desires, the fulfillment of being noticed, and the watching (being watched) is these network environments (Robins, 2013, pp. 40–41).

On Ariana Grande's Instagram posts, we also see pictures taken with animals. Based on this fact, it is possible to say that she has adopted to be an "animal lover" as a social identity and that she is sensitive to animal rights. Grande, who has also preferred veganism, said in an interview related to this topic, "*I am a person who believes in herbal nutrition that prolongs life and will make you a happier person.*" The "exaggeration effect," which is one of the main proposals of social identity theory directly coincides with this situation. It is an undeniable fact that vegan nutrition is essential for health, but the debate continues in the field of medicine as to whether it is the only criterion. Grande has glorified the perception practices of her group when making comparisons between the social group where she belonged/ she had the sense of belonging and other groups, as well as favoring her ingroup. Additionally, Grande's preferring and staging of the animal-lover identity is also related to the elements of compassion, mercy and grace, which are regarded as indicators of the feminine culture.

Figure 6. Her self-oriented identity) her post modern identity) beauty attraction/goddess myth

DISCUSSION AND CONCLUSION

When we carry out a general assessment of the posts of the two people that are popular on Instagram, it is possible to say the following:

- The "sportsman" and "rich" identities that the male influencer chose and exhibited as an identity overlap with the elements of the masculine culture. He tried to prove that he was stronger in nature based on his sportsman identity, and demonstrated his personality that was defiant and aspired to succeed. His family man identity represents masculinity that protects and envelopes. It was seen that he had a desire to be noticed, based on his posts that revealed he had a high-income level.
- The "animal-lower" identity, which was preferred by the female influencer, contains elements such as mercy, soft compassion and mercy, which are the characteristics of the feminine culture.

- In the Instagram posts of both influencers, there was virtually no room for the universal spaces that became symbols and brands. In our opinion, the reason for this situation is due to the photography-based nature of Instagram. As mentioned in Lacan's mirror stage metaphor, the pleasure of seeing and being seen is primarily experienced by the individual himself. (Gündüz et al., 2018, p. 1873). Therefore, the ultimate urge on the basis of the posts is to lure the eyes and attract attention by being attracted to peeking/being peeked.

- Apart from the identities that we analyzed in the Instagram profiles of the both people, we also found posts where they presented their different identities, but these occupied a very small space in the showcase. Goffman suggests that this is due to the assumption that the personality that is reflected covers everything about the person reflecting it because the routine that is staged is perceived to be the only routine or the most important routine (Goffman, 2018, p. 56). According to VanDick, with the emergence of online media, direct experience has been replaced by mediated perception. Thus, an iconic and symbol-based perception form has emerged, and experiencing has been replaced by witnessing (VanDick, 2006, p. 212). When we look from this angle, the posts, which are indicative of the performance identities — that the people who were the subjects of this study prioritized and ranked first — will also be perceived as a holistic reality in the minds of those who watch the scene.

- The posts of the both people were based on self-centered personal content. The subject, rising with post modernism, has come to be both a watchable and observable entity synchronously with the emergence of social networks, and a structure that everyone is watching everyone else has risen (Uluç & Yarcı, 2017, p. 91). What is really important is to demonstrate performances to be applauded while being aware that you are being watched, as well as designing what role to play by watching.

- When we remember that the elements that trigger identity is the need to be unique and to belong to, it is possible to say that the male identity reflects the uniqueness side and the female reflects the belongingness side.

Table 2. Male influencer and female influencer features

MALE INFLUENCER	FEMALE INFLUENCER
Masculine characteristic	Feminine characteristic
Being unique	Being attractive
Desire to be noticed	Desire to draw attention
Defiance of the body	Attractiveness of the body
The myth of invincibility and God	The myth of beauty and Goddess

The reference point for designing both personal and social identities involves psychological motivations such as appreciation, approval and strengthening of self. In essence, there is no major difference between online environment and offline in the construction of identity. The binary structure of identity, based on the self and the internal-external dynamics, is in place but has just transformed into a new form. Users regenerate their offline selves on online platforms, but do not include all of their offline identities in this construction process. Only the appropriate portions of the offline identity, which has many different sorts of content, are manifested. Although it is a matter of debate to reach an induction such as that personal or social identities are to be established with gender codes and that male users will feed on masculine and female users will feed on feminine codes, what is not to be discussed is the fact that "performances" will continue to be exhibited (Morva, 2014, p. 238). Social networks are like black holes that instantly pull every object in their orbit towards them and swallow it with the power of gravity they create. Just as the theory suggests that if an object swallowed by a black hole will not be lost but is assumed to change its dimension, social media environments also have people experience a similar metaphorical situation. The perception/interpretation skills and self-esteem of the person who goes under the influence of social networks will also be transformed — just as black holes change the structure of substances through their force of gravity that is almost infinite. From the moment any person enters social networks, he becomes subject to a mental and cognitive transformation whether he shares any posts or not. The first phenomenon to be influenced by this transformation is the self. This is because the self, that is, the selfhood, is the first station of new quests. The mind that internalizes virtuality will also virtualize the self, and the order of social networks will begin to function.

REFERENCES

Akgül, S. K. ve Pazarbaşı, B. (2018). Küresel Ağlar Odağında Kültür, Kimlik ve Mekan Tartışmaları, Hiperyayın, İstanbul.

Akmeşe, Z. ve Deniz, K. (2017). Stalk, Benliğin İzini Sürmek. *Yeni Düşünceler*, 8, 23–32.

Bakıroğlu, C. T. (2013). *Sosyalleşme ve Kimlik İnşası Ekseninde Sosyal Paylaşım Ağları, Akademik Bilişim, XV*. Akademik Bilişim Konferansı Bildirileri.

Batmaz, V., (1981). Popüler Kültür Üzerine Değişik Kuramsal Yaklaşımlar, İletişim 1981/1, Ankara, Turkey: AGTGA Gazetecilik ve Halkla İlişkiler Yüksek Okulu Yayını No:2, 163-192.

Bauman, Z. (2017). *Kimlik*. Ankara, Turkey: Heretik.

Bayad, A., (2016). Erving Goffman'ın Benlik Kavramı ve İnsan Doğası Yaklaşımı, Psikoloji Çalışmaları / Studies in Psychology, 36-1 (81-93).

Berger, J. (1990). *Görme Biçimleri, Çev.; Salman, Y.* İstanbul, Turkey: Metis.

Bilgin, N. (2007). *Aşina Kitaplar*. İzmir, Turkey.

Binark, M. (2001). Kadının Sesi Radyo Programı ve Kimliği Konumlandırma Stratejisi. In *Toplumbilim, Sayı:14*. Ankara, Turkey: Bağlam Yayınları.

Bocock, R. (1997). *Tüketim, Çev., Kutluk, İ.* Ankara, Turkey: Dost Yay.

Boyd, D. M., & Ellison, N. B. (2007, Oct. 1). Social Network Sites: Definition, History, and Scholarship. *Journal of Computer-Mediated Communication*, *13*(1), 210–230. doi:10.1111/j.1083-6101.2007.00393.x

Çağan, K. (2003). *Popüler Kültür ve Sanat*. Ankara, Turkey: Altınküre.

Curran, J. (1997). Medya ve Demokrasi, 139-197. In Medya, Kültür, Siyaset, (Eds: Süleyman İrvan), Ark Yayınları, Ankara, Turkey.

Demirtaş, H. A. (2003). Sosyal Kimlik Kuramı, Temel Kavram ve Varsayımlar. İletişim Araştırmaları, 1(1), 123-144.

Erdoğan, İ. (2004). Popüler Kültürün Ne Olduğu Üzerine, Bilim ve Aklın Aydınlığında Eğitim Dergisi: Popüler Kültür ve Gençlik. *Sayı, 57,* 7–19.

Erdoğan, İ. ve Alemdar K. (2005). Popüler Kültür ve İletişim, Erk, Ankara.

Erkul, R. E. (2009). Sosyal medya araçlarının (web 2.0) kamu hizmetleri ve uygulamalarında kullanılabilirliği. Türkiye Bilişim Derneği-Bilişim Dergisi (116).

Fougère, M., & Moulettes, A. (2007). The Construction of the Modern West and the Backward Rest: Studying the Discourse of Hofstede's Culture's Consequences. *Journal of Multicultural Discourses,* 2(1), 1–19.

Giddens, A. (2012). *Sosyoloji.* İstanbul, Turkey: Kırmızı Yay.

Goffman, E. (2018). *Gündelik Yaşamda Benliğin Sunumu.* İstanbul, Turkey: Metis.

Gündüz, A., Ertong Attar, G., & Altun, A. (2018). Üniversite Öğrencilerinin Instagram'da Benlik Sunumları. *DTCF Dergisi,* 58(2), 1862–1895. doi:10.33171/dtcfjournal.2018.58.2.32

Jenkins, R. (2016). *Bir Kavramın Anatomisi Sosyal Kimlik.* İstanbul, Turkey: Everest Yay.

Jupp, V. (n.d.). The Sage Dictionary of Social Research Methods. London, UK: Sage.

Karaduman, N. (2017). Popüler Kültürün Oluşmasında ve Aktarılmasında Sosyal Medyanın Rolü, Erciyes Üniversitesi Sosyal Bilimler Enstitüsü Dergisi XLIII, 2017/2, 7-27.

Karaduman, S. (2010). Modernizmden Postmodernizme Kimliğin Yapısal Dönüşümü. *Journal of Yasar University,* 17(5), 2886–2899.

Kartarı, A. (2017). Nitel Düşünce ve Etnografi: Etnografik Yönteme Düşünsel Bir Yaklaşım. Moment Dergi, 4(1), 207-220. Retrieved from http://dergipark.gov.tr/moment/issue/36383/411586

Kellner, D. (2001). Popüler Kültür ve Postmodern Kimliklerin İnşası, Çev: Gülcan Seçkin, Doğu Batı, Sayı: 15.

Kozinets, R. V. (2002). The Field Behind the Screen: Using Netnography for Marketing Research in Online Communities. *JMR, Journal of Marketing Research,* 39(February), 61–72. doi:10.1509/jmkr.39.1.61.18935

Langer, R., & Beckman, S. C. (2005). Sensitive Research Topics: Netnography Revisited. *Qualitative Market Research,* 8(2), 189–203. doi:10.1108/13522750510592454

Mansell, R. vd., (2015), The International Encyclopedia of Digital Communication and Society. UK: Wiley-Blackwell.

Mayfield, A. (2008). What is Social Media. iCrossing. e-book. Retrieved from http://www.icrossing.com/sites/default/files/what-is-socialmedia-uk.pdf

McQuail, D. (1994). *Kitle İletişim Kuramı: Giriş. (Çev. Ahmet Haluk Yüksel).* Eskişehir: Kibele Sanat Merkezi Yayınları.

Mlicki, P. P., & Naomi, E. (1996). Being Different or Being Better? National Stereotypes and Identifications of Polish and Dutch Students. *European Journal of Social Psychology.*

Morva, O. (2014). In S. Çakır (Ed.), *Goffman'ın Dramaturjik Yaklaşımı ve Dijital Ortamda Kimlik Tasarımı: Sosyal Paylaşım Ağı Facebook Üzerine Bir İnceleme, Medya ve Tasarım* (pp. 231–255). İstanbul, Turkey: Urzeni.

Niedzviecki, H. (2010). *Dikizleme Günlüğü, Çev.: Gündüz, G.* İstanbul, Turkey: Ayrıntı.

Niedzviecki, H. (2011). *Ben özelim; Bireylik Nasıl Yeni Konformizm Haline Geldi, Çev.; Erduman, S.* İstanbul, Turkey: Ayrıntı.

Oğuz, G. Y. (2010). Güzellik Kadınlar İçin Nasıl Vaade Dönüşür: Kadın Dergilerindeki Kozmetik Reklamları Üzerine Bir İnceleme, Selçuk iletişim, C.: 6, S.: 3, (184-195).

Onat, F. ve Alikılıç, Ö. A. (2008). Sosyal Ağ Sitelerinin Reklam ve Halkla İlişkiler Ortamları. *Journal of Yaşar University*, 3(9), 1111–1143.

Özüdoğru, Ş. (2014). Nitel Araştırmanın İletişim Araştırmalarında Rol ve Önemi Üzerine Bir Deneme, Global Media Journal, S. 4(8), 260-275.

Padilla, A. M., & Perez, W. (2003, February). Acculturation, Social Identity, and Social Cognition: A New Perspective. *Hispanic Journal of Behavioral Sciences*, 25(1), 35–55. doi:10.1177/0739986303251694

Robins, K. (2013). *İmaj Görmenin Kültür ve Politikası, (N. Türkoğlu, Çev).* İstanbul, Turkey: Ayrıntı Yayınları.

Rowe, D. (1996). *Popüler Kültürler. (Çev. Mehmet Küçük).* İstanbul, Turkey: Ayrıntı Yayınları.

Schroeder, R. (1994). Cyberculture, cyborg post-modernism and the sociology of virtual reality Technologies. *Future*, 26(5), 519–528. doi:10.1016/0016-3287(94)90133-3

Schudson, M. (1999). *Popüler Kültürün Yeni Gerçekliği: Akademik Bilinçlilik ve Duyarlılık, Popüler Kültür ve İktidar, (Derleyen: Nazife Güngör).* Ankara, Turkey: Vadi Yayınları.

Storey, J. (2009). *Cultural Theory and Popular Culture* (5th ed.). Harlow, UK: Pearson.

Tajfel, H. (1982). Social psychology of intergroup relations. *Annual Review of Psychology*, 33(1), 1–39. doi:10.1146/annurev.ps.33.020182.000245

Uluç, G., ve Yarcı, A. (2017), Sosyal Medya Kültürü, Dumlupınar Ünv., Sosyal Bilimler Dergisi, S.: 52, 88-102.

Van Dick, J. (2006). *The Network Society Social Aspects of New Media.* London, UK: Sage.

ADDITIONAL READING

Ellemers, N., Spears, R., & Doosje, B. (2002). Self and Social Identity. *Annual Review of Psychology, 53*(1), 161–186. doi:10.1146/annurev.psych.53.100901.135228 PMID:11752483

Featherstone, M. (2007). *Consumer Culture and Postmodernism*. Sage Publications.

Hall, S. (2000). Who Needs 'Identity. In A. Reader, P. du Gay, J. Evans, & P. Redman (Eds.), *Identity* (pp. 15–30). Sage Publications.

Turkle, S. (1995). *Life on the Screen: Identity in the Age of the Internet*. New York: Simon & Schuster.

KEY TERMS AND DEFINITIONS

Identity: It is a collection of signs, qualities and features that show what a person is as a social being.

Instagram: Instagram, a photo sharing application created by the endeavors of two entrepreneurs at the end of 2010, mainly enables the sharing of photos in mobile devices on social networks.

Masculinity and Femininity: Express roles imposed on genders.

Popular Culture: It can be defined as a type of culture that is based on the pleasures of ordinary people, not a trained elite.

Popularity: It is the state or condition of being liked, admired, or supported by many people.

Postmodern Identities: Postmodernism always envisions how to live if it is felt rather than pre-determined strict rules. Postmodernism considers diversity and differences in identity and diversified identities oppose the monopoly of meta-narrative and teachings.

Self-Presentation: Presenting himself/herself in a way that leaves the desired image in accordance with socially and culturally accepted norms of action and behavior.

Social Media: is an online network that publishes and publishes its own content. Social media is actively used by many people and institutions. In this way, quick access is easier, users can view the contents, articles, news, thoughts, daily events, photos by social media through social media.

This research was previously published in New Media and Visual Communication in Social Networks; pages 192-207, copyright year 2020 by Information Science Reference (an imprint of IGI Global).

Chapter 17
Blogger Mothers as a Transmediatic Narration:
An Examination on Transmediatic Narration Used by Blogger Mothers

Ercan Aktan

Aksaray University, Turkey

ABSTRACT

Individuals are facing message bombardments from many tools. In such a process, trying to reach individuals at any moment using different tools is important for the effectiveness of communication. This requirement led to a new process called transmedia. The transmedia storytelling, which is carried out in order to ensure that the messages planned to be transmitted in transmedia are even more effective, is one of the heavy-duty practices of this new process. This study was carried out in order to reveal how blogger mothers used transmedia storytelling practices, the difference of this use from traditional motherhood, and the role of transmedia storytelling practices in changing form of motherhood. In the study, blogger mothers were found to use transmedia storytelling practices heavily in order to influence their followers. It was also concluded that blogger mothers play the roles of heroines, friends, and dynamic and assistant heroines.

INTRODUCTION

Today, we are in the era of social media in which human relationships depend on digital communication, keyboards and networks. We prefer texting to talking; we prefer to sign in to meeting people; we prefer to watch the smartphone screen to looking around. We just have to look at the "news wall" of our preferred social network in order to know what's happening around us. The real social life is being replaced by the experience of social network and if we know everything about the present day on one side, we know almost nothing about the past on the other side (Dusi etc., 2017, p. 65).

DOI: 10.4018/978-1-6684-6307-9.ch017

This change and difference that has occurred compared to the past has led to the emergence of new processes in many areas of society. Individuals forming society have also had to adapt to this change or have voluntarily participated in this change. This alteration and innovation including many sectors has led to changes in motherhood roles, in maternal practices, or in content of traditional motherhood. "Blogger mothers", which is a new and creative application form of today, and their followers have emerged with this change.

Blogger mothers share their experiences and knowledge about motherhood to future mothers who are their followers or counselee. This sharing leads to the evolution of traditional motherhood actions of followers in modern direction. In other words, it is now possible for future mothers to ask about motherhood to blogger mothers instead of their mothers, who have already experienced motherhood before and even have given birth and raised them, and to apply advices they have posted through blogs. Therefore, this situation opens a door to alteration of the traditional forms of motherhood.

There are a number of underlying reasons why blogger mothers are so influential on their followers. One of the reasons for this is that social media tools are influencing followers by becoming stronger with transmedia applications and storytelling methods. In other words, the stories that blogger mothers will create on their blogs are important. The fact that they are not only included in blog environment but also in other social media tools reaching to followers also supports this increase in importance. The powerful aspects of each of these different tools make it possible for followers to be influenced, thus enabling the blogger to make the desired changes.

This study was revealed based on the idea that social media provides innovative and creative environments for users and content producers. In this regard, the opportunities provided by social media were tried to be examined in the context of new generation motherhood. In this context, 15 active mother blogs followed most in Turkey were examined.

NEW MEDIA, SOCIAL MEDIA AND CREATIVITY

In the last quarter of twentieth century, the digital revolution in information systems and information technologies has made itself evident. Due to these changes, there have been serious differences compared to the past. In addition, new regulations and changes in many areas have been realized with this revolution (Yilmaz, 2011, p. 138).

The change and development in information and communication technologies which has led to relevant digital revolution, has provided an opportunity for different communication methods to emerge. These changes have been resulted with the effects that can be immediately felt in social structures. Nowadays, the new media phenomenon that focuses on digital usage and has the principles of openness, interactivity and innovative connection has become a part of modern human life (Turina etc., 2015, p.174-175; Kocyigit, 2015, p. 331).

Innovations provided with the new media to users include concepts such as Presence, Modification, User-generated content and Social participation. When these concepts are examined, it is seen that 'presence' is the state in which users exist effectively in the environment through their profiles, identities or avatars. If the individual shows an effective presence, it is also expected from him/her to perform actions such as realizing the interaction among the most basic features of the new media, producing content and participating in produced contents. The concept of modification means the fact that an individual move notifications received from both his/her own profile and others, to a new dimension by differentiating them. The fact that the user creates shares in which the content is specified by him/herself, in web environment, according to his/her wishes, indicates a user-active structure, not a sender-active structure. On the other hand, social participation reflects the active role of the user and overall activity that the user has undertaken and developed during the whole process, and it means being in an interaction with others (Baran & Ata, 2013, p. 195).

This process has also opened the way for the emergence of media tools, called social media, created by members of society using new communication technologies. The social media, the whole new communication channels, has brought many innovations and differences that were previously unavailable, to the individual and social life. Mayfield (2008, p. 5) lists the characteristics of social media that provide these innovations as follows:

- **Participation:** It generates courage in everyone involved in social media to contribute to feedback and communication.
- **Openness:** Many social media tools are open for participation and feedback. These tools encourage ranking, commenting, and sharing of information. There may occasionally be obstacles for shares and content reliability is provided through password.
- **Conversation:** The content is a broadcast activity that is transmitted to a viewer by a broadcaster in traditional media, however social media has a structure that allows better two-way communication.
- **Community:** Social media allows an opportunity to communicate effectively and quickly. Thus, for example, communities can share their favorite photos, a political theme, or a favorite television program.
- **Connectedness:** Many types of social media are developing by linking to other sites, resources, or people.

Social media has provided a communication infrastructure that will allow individuals to create their own creative features with these features and technological infrastructure. In other words, individuals are free than ever before to reveal their creative characteristics in the era of social media. Creativity, which can be used freely with social media, is a concept about producing new and useful ideas on products, applications, services, or procedures that are generally both new and potentially useful for the organization (Sigala & Chalkiti, 2015, p. 48). Besides this, creativity expresses the behavior of revealing new and rare things (ideas, emotions, actions, products or services, etc.) different from traditional ones. Especially today, creativity is considered in the context of technological development and progress.

As a result of these technological developments and progresses, the differences in communication area have made social media more visible. In this regard, it can be said that social media infrastructure and social media tools are considerably creative.

The anchor point of social media is the people who use them and their social interactions. The creative aspects of social media are communication, connections, convergence, competition, cooperation, community and creative class (Iasimone & Solla, 2013, p. 303). There are three dimensions of social media. The first one is the "media dimension", which is interpreted as a tool by which communication is transferred to groups or people. The second is the "technology dimension", which is caused by the fact that the infrastructure is created with certain technologies and by using the latest technological infrastructure, and the third dimension is the "user dimension". This dimension can be defined as "the content of the various media types produced by consumer, the end user".

In user dimension, the concept of creative effort formed as a result of common actions of each participant is encountered. It can be said about the creative effort that: "A certain creative effort must be made in the creation of content or in the creation of new content from existing work. In other words, the user must add a value to the content. This creative effort can also be demonstrated through business associations and team work. It can be explained as "Taking a section from any television program and uploading it to a website on the internet does not mean creating user-generated content" (Keskin & Bas, 2015, p. 54). Therefore, social media obtains the power or feature of the creativity from the union of individuals. In other saying, a collective mind and a series of shares have turned social media into a creative channel.

In other words, social media which operates as the ideal communication tool of today (Aktan & Cakmak, 2015, p. 162), is considered as a force supporting creativity since it has an imperialist nature (Killian & McManus, 2015, p. 540), allows millions of people to hear each other's voices (Alikilic, 2011, p.14), has a feature guiding social demands of large masses (Vural & Bat, 2010, p. 3349), includes wide features such as ease of use (Kasemsap, 2015, p. 153), freedom provided to the user (Aktan & Ozüpek, 2015, p. 202). Through these relevant features, social media not only supports individuals in creation, but also has many applications and tools opening the way for creativity. Blogs are among these tools.

BLOG AS A SOCIAL MEDIA TOOL

Blog, which is a combination of the English "Web" and "Log" words (Kathpalia & See, 2016, p. 26), is the best-known and almost the most developed tool among social media tools (Herring etc., 2004, 2010, p. 1; Zarrela, 2010, p.9). The blog, a type of Web 2.0 technology, is a website that allows users (bloggers) to publish posts viewed in reverse chronological order (Ifinedo, 2017, p. 189). "Blog entries combine the ability to enter links and comments on texts, graphics, videos and other web pages. Some blogs address specific art forms such as art (picture diary), photo (photo diary), video (vlog), music (MP3 blog) and audio (podcasting)" (Zeiser, 2015, p. 66).

Blogging has become a popular media that allows people to express themselves, share information, and communicate with each other. Blogs have shown a very rapid increase in numbers recently. This high level growth of blogs can be partially explained by a number of factors such as ease of publication and free hosting services (for example blogspot.com, livejournal.com, and others). Moreover, all these factors have contributed on a large scale to the reduction of costs in the creation and maintenance of spam blogs (or splogs), and this has opened the way for the growth (Zhu, Sun & Choi, 2011, p. 246).

The blogs, which have been thought not to attract great attention during the establishment stage, now have the power to create an agenda (Sezer & Sert, 2013, p. 66). The key transformation has occurred on the significant increase in the number of weblog readers with the growth of the online media (Greer & Pan, 2015, p. 594). Individuals enjoy sharing their own ideas, experiences, positive and negative comments with others (Li & Du, 2017, p. 52). This is perhaps the most important reason for the development of blogs.

Blogs are heavily used and have a strong influence. The main reasons for this can be listed as follows (Mavnacioglu, 2011, p. 26-27):

- Blogs can be created in a very short time compared to websites.
- Blogs can be organized for different sectors and different purposes.

- They can be updated.
- They are usually prepared at no cost or at very low cost.
- There is no need of a large technical information to create blogs like in the creation of websites.
- It is an environment that can be easily formed by every individual who is an internet user.
- The level of interaction is high in accordance with the general characteristics of social media tools.
- They are easily created as an electronic mail account.
- They allow users to transfer and share their experiences, suggestions, requests and complaints.
- Experiential marketing and word of mouth marketing tendencies of internet users are developed by considering opinions and comments of others on the internet before shopping, and blogs allow this process.
- The fact that corporations and brands have noticed the significance of blogs and the fact that blogs have become one of the channels used in communication with the target audience increases the importance of blogs.
- It allows to create categories according to users' hobbies and interests.
- It ensures the sharing of information, suggestions and experiences in the same environment. It is used as a new channel in corporate and in-house communication.

Blogs have four unique features that are social nature, links suggested by blogger to followers (blogroll), trackbacks and cultural ethos (Pang & Goh, 2016, p. 505).

Blogs have become globally popular tools used by practitioners (for example, business, politics, and education) from different areas to create and share knowledge (Ifinedo, 2017, p. 189). In other words, "Blogs have spread in many areas in a short time after they emerged because of their features such as low cost, ease of use and access, free access and free of inspection. They have been begun to be used in a wide range, from individual hobby blogs to corporate promotional blogs, from educational institutions to political campaigns and civil society campaigns" (Ozudogru, 2014, p. 42).

Reaching potential target audiences through the traditional media has been a difficult process and has been actualized in the form of one-way communications (Magno, 2017, p. 142). Blogs, on the other hand, have led to differences in corporate and individual users' communication methods as a powerful tool of two-way communications (Zarrela, 2010, p. 9). This has resulted in the rapid growth of blogs, the large number of usage, the large number of individual and corporate contributions.

Types of Blogs

Blogs are used as a tool to obtain news and information with the number of users increasing each passing day. Blogs offer hundreds of different options for every topic coming to mind such as technology, politics, sports, entertainment, gossip, new trends, fashion, health (Dilmen, 2014, p. 118)

Blogs can be published in various types, depending on usage or users. These blogs can be listed as follows (Mayfield, 2008, p.17):

- **Personal Blogs:** These are blogs focused on hobbies or personal interests. Participants in personal blogs with heavy use are beginning to share information, hobbies, and experiences with others.
- **Political Blogs:** Blogs are written about politics especially in America, and increasingly in the UK. Blogs, which are frequently perceived as a response to media tendency, are the places where analyses of topics are made.

- **Business Blogs:** Today, many professionals and businesses have blogs. These blogs allow businesses to communicate less formally than traditional newsletters, brochures and press products. For individuals in business, a blog can be an effective way of building a network consisted of individuals who are of the same mind, and building up an own rising profile.
- **Thematic Blogs:** They are original content blogs based on a specific theme, topic or a sector. Topics may have a variety of content, such as marketing, communication, entertainment, cars in these blogs. It is observed that thematic bloggers are relevant sector specialists or people who are engaged in similar work with the theme of the blog.
- **Blogs Sponsored by Publishers:** This type of blog is a type of publication that is started by traditional media, meeting readers in addition to existing publications. It is seen that publishers and media organizations pioneer such blogs.
- **Corporate Blogs:** The fact that a group of company employees and executives write articles on behalf of the organization forms the basic principle of corporate blogs. In corporate blogs, first-hand information is transferred to the target audience and feedback can be received from the first hand.

In addition to these blogs there are also types of blogs known as community blogs (Ahumbeyeva & Taalaybekkizi, 2017):

- **Community Blogs:** They are blogs that have a membership system and consist of posts written by these members. Many of these blogs use blog software on their own servers. Historically, they maintain a cultural heritage formed in Live Journal.

STORYTELLING AND NARRATIVE CHARACTERS

Ensuring the impressiveness when story is transferred to target audiences also depends on the characteristics of the characters in the story, and the ability to make an impressive presentation. The fact that followers find out what they are looking for in narrative characters involved in the story, and the ability of the character to direct followers are important for the success of the story.

Narrative character types can be arranged in various forms. "First of these arrangements based on prioritizing the character is as main character(s), secondary character(s), individual(s) who plays (play) the minor role(s), respectively. The other arrangement is based on relative positions of the characters to each other. This arrangement is formed on the difference of the relations between the character A and B, between A and C and between B and C from each other. At the same time, forming pairwise groups such as wife/husband, friend/enemy, and mother/daughter or forming triple groups, such as wife/husband/lover, mother/father/child is another method. In addition, characters can be classified in political, social and occupational groups, in solidarity associations such as love, family, professional organizations, in competition groups emerging in love and business life, and in opposing groups like women/men, single/married and young/old. Besides these general groupings, there are also conceptualizations specific to narrative theorists. This approach dwells on two groups of characters: flat character and round character. The flat character is static and does not change within the story. The round character changes within the story. According to the dialectical narrative model, the axis character and the opposing character play a dominant role. There are also seven character types, including the villain, the dispatcher, the hero, the donor, the helper, the princess, and the false hero besides these differentiations. Apart from these typologies, there is also another differentiation made as confidant character, foil character and chorus character "(Yilmaz, 2014, p. 68-69).

In transmedia storytelling, it can be said that these characters adopted an expression and made efforts to reach their followers with these kinds of characters. This reveals the fact that the character that is the subject of the story can be better understood or the fact that the effectiveness of the story can be increased through the identification of the follower with the character.

BLOGGER MOTHERS AND TRANSMEDIA STORYTELLING

Bloggers write related messages based on relevant events on the internet, and blog service providers keep these messages. The most important feature of the publications is the fact that a group of people who have similar interests and discuss issues of mutual concerns, get together to start a discussion and share their ideas with each other (Chen, 2017, p. 1299). Mother blogs, an example of thematic blogs, refer to a type of blog created by a blogger mother who wants to share her ideas, integratedly with other mothers or future mothers.

In this mother blogs, blogger mothers reveal the ideas they want to share wit their followers by a story in order to ensure effectiveness. Nowadays, blogger mothers get followers through other tools of social media and provide storytelling to those followers through other social media tools, thus trying to spread the effect over a wider area. At this point, the transmedia storytelling emerges.

The term of transmedia storytelling has been suggested by Henry Jenkins with the idea that "each tool makes its own contribution to the emergence of the story" (Gronstedt & Ramos, 2014, p. 5). Transmedia refers to the process in an interactive structure which is created with the story that is added to the narrations formed by a content that exceeds a series of media tools, and in which the audience actively participates (Graves, 2015, p. 38).

According to Jenkins (2006, p. 93), transmedia storytelling develops and strengthens through the contribution of different media tools to the story that is created. For example, a story appears in the cinema, but it can be expanded through television, novels or comics, and can be explored through a play.

The purpose of the transmedia storytelling system is to create a fun alternative for writing-based historical contents. Indeed, because of the importance of visual documents and the need to draw attention of new generations, the system aims to create an innovative form using modern communication technologies (Dusi etc., 2017, p. 67).

In other words, transmedia aiming to divide a story into small pieces spread out multiple channels allows the consumers or followers to move from one channel to another following the pieces. This movement, along with the pattern of the story, does not adversely affect the flow of the story, contrarily ensures that the followers are included in the flow. Thus, followers discover a different direction of the story in every channel they follow and become more willing to be involved in the story. In reality, the story is created by the participants themselves. For example, by the guidance and notifications in advertising message of a brand on television, the audience can also visit the social media tools of that brand, from there to a video sharing site or to a verbal narrative platform such as Ekşi Sözlük. Through this, the audience is able to expand the campaign with their own contribution in any channel (Dönmez & Guler, 2016, p. 157).

It is necessary to present a consistent and combined experience across all platforms where the story is used according to the properties of each platform in a transmedia storytelling process. It is important for each item to operate by its own conditions. However, it is necessary to add something to the story for a larger experience. In other words, giving people something to do while bringing them together is a matter to consider in terms of their experiences. In fact, the design of a transmedia project is built in order to combine social networks, geographical locations and game dynamics in virtual and real dimensions (Ferreira, 2015, p. 22).

Jenkins (2007) has made some explanations about the properties of this type in his report, "Transmedia Storytelling 101". Accordingly, transmedia storytelling has the following properties:

- Transmedia storytelling represents a process in which all elements of a fiction are systematically dispersed into multiple distribution channels in order to create a unified and coordinated entertainment experience.
- Transmedia storytelling reflects the economics of media consolidation or what industry observers call "synergy". In other words, media organizations wish to expand transmedia storytelling horizontally.
- It is a matter that narratives created by transmedia storytelling is based on a complex fictional world composed of many characters related with each other and stories of these characters, rather than individual characters or a certain event pattern.
- In transmedia storytelling, attachments can have different functions.
- Transmedia storytelling can include works for platforms that encourage the participation of different consumer groups in the story.
- Ideally, each episode should be accessible by its own conditions, even if it makes a unique contribution to the narrative system as a whole.
- Since transmedia storytelling requires a high level of cooperation between different media areas spread by the story, it is often seen that successive projects are shaped by a single artist or a person during the propagation of the story in all channels they are transferred, or that different units within a single company cooperate at advanced level.
- Transmedia storytelling is the ideal esthetic form for a collective intelligence era.
- Transmediatic narration does not only disseminate information, but it also presents a number of roles and purposes to consumers in order to be included in their daily lives.
- It can be said that transmedia storytelling texts have an encyclopedic texture.

Transmedia storytelling is different from "multimedia" programs in which the user clicks the same screen to experience video, text and interactivity. In transmedia, various forms of media not only repeat the same story in different forms, but also expand the story with its different elements. The story creates a broadcast that can be enjoyed in both its own and comprehensive way in connection with the story by the power of each tool (Gronstedt & Ramos, 2014, p. 5).

METHODOLOGY

In this study, the best 15 "Mother Blogs" in Turkey were examined. The mother blogs discussed were evaluated based on the ranking at "http://1baba1bebe.com/blog/en-iyi-15-anne-blogger.html". Accordingly, mother blogs examined were arrayed as http://blogcuanne.com/, http://www.slingomom.com/, http://markaanne.com/, http://alternatifanne.com/, http://www.melinasmom.com/, http://guncelanne. com, https://www.obiranne.net/, http://www.balyanaginhikayesi.com/, http://deli-anne.com/, http://www. annekaz.com/, http://www.ozgekopuz.com/, http://gezentianne.com/, http://momsblognote.com/, http:// kokoshanne.com/, http://keyifbebesi.com/, respectively.

It was aimed to reveal the development process of how mother blogs have used the social media as a creative channel providing opportunities through their own life stories and practices; as well as to determine how blogs have given the creative ideas in areas such as motherhood, child care, life, fashion, to the followers of the blog. Besides, it was also aimed to reveal whether there were transmedia storytelling elements in relevant blogs.

The data were obtained by using content analysis and netnography method in the study. The content analysis method analyzes the contents of communication tools at a specific location and time. Moreover, the analysis is made "objectively, systematically and quantitatively" (Severin and Tankard, 1994, p. 41).

In addition, "the increasing use of the internet reveals the need to adapt ethnographic research techniques to virtual environment in order to interpret the behavior of consumers who are increasingly involved in the virtual environment. In this direction, a new research method has been developed that examines the consumer behavior in virtual communities. The method which has a participatory approach to the investigation of online culture and communities is mentioned by names such as "cyber ethnography", "cyber anthropology", "digital ethnography", "online ethnography", "virtual ethnography". However, while these terms are mostly used by sociologists and other researchers, the method is called "netnography" in marketing research. Netnography is the adapted form of the ethnography method to the complexity of today's computer-based social world. While the data are collected through face to face and cultural interactions in ethnography, the data are collected by online communication in netnography" (Ozbölük & Dursun, 2015, p. 232).

While creating the design of the research, the study conducted by Teke (2014), called "A Netnographic Analysis on the Transformation of Motherhood: Blogger Mothers", was benefited (Teke, 2014, p. 34).

In addition, the blogs discussed were evaluated in the framework of transmedia storytelling and social media tools that have been used by bloggers were investigated. Whether the topics discussed in blogs were included in social media tools of bloggers was also included in the research. Moreover, the information of whether followers have participated in the topics about motherhood in social media tools created by bloggers, was included in investigated topics.

Findings and Comments

The mother blogs mentioned above were examined and the data obtained were tried to be assigned to various thematic categories.

Numeric Data Related to Mother Blogs

The contents of the mother blogs that were discussed were tried to be revealed by content analysis method. For this purpose, the numeric data of blogs are presented in tabular form after the coding scheme created (see Table 1).

Table 1. Social media tools used by bloggers

Name of Blog	Social Media Tool Used					
	Facebook	Twitter	Instagram	Google+	Pinterest	YouTube
blogcuanne	+	+	-	-	-	-
slingomom	+	+	+	+	+	+
markaanne	+	+	+	+	-	+
alternatifanne	+	+	+	+	-	-
melinasmom	+	+	+	-	-	-
guncelanne	+	+	+	+	-	+
obiranne	+	-	+	+	-	-
balyanaginhikayesi	+	+	+	+	+	+
deli-anne	+	+	-	-	--	
annekaz	+	+	+	-	-	+
ozgekopuz	+	+	-	-	+	-
gezentianne	+	+	+	-	-	-
momsblognote	+	+	+	-	+	-
kokoshanne	+	+	+	+	+	+
keyifbebesi	+	+	+	-	+	+

As a result of the examination, it was determined that the mother blogs discussed actively used other social media tools besides the blog. These social media tools can be listed as Facebook, Twitter, Instagram, Google+, Pinterest and YouTube. As a result of the examination, the blogs called "slingomom", "balyanaginhikayesi" and "kokoshanne" seem to use all these social media tools. Additionally, it is understood that the blogs called "markaane", "guncelanne" and "keyifbebesi" use five of the social media tools listed. On the other hand, "blogcuanne", "deli-anne", "ozgekopuz" and "gezentianne" blogs are the blogs having the fewest social media tools. Findings reveal that blogger mothers have opportunity to use transmedia (see Table 2).

Another examination of the blogs discussed was about the number of followers on social media tools used by bloggers. According to the results obtained, the highest number followers on Facebook belong to "annekaz" blog with 202,134 followers. Blogs with following highest number of followers on Facebook are "guncelanne" with 87,401 followers, "blogcuanne" with 64,729 followers, "ozgekopuz" with 35,911 followers and "momsblognote" with 35,045 followers. The lowest numbers of followers on Facebook belong to "gezentianne" with 3,487 followers, "markaane" with 3,931 followers, and "balyanaginhikayesi" with 6,868 followers.

The most followed blogs on Twitter are "blogcuanne" with 24,700 followers, "slingomom" with 8,847 followers and "alternatifanne" with 8,481 followers. The lowest numbers of followers on Twitter belong to "deli-anne" with 4 followers and "keyifbebesi" with 52 followers.

It is revealed that the highest numbers of followers on Instagram belonged to "guncelanne" with 119,000 followers, "blogcuanne" with 106,000 followers, "kokoshanne" with 98,000 followers, and "gezentianne" with 95,000 followers, respectively. On the other hand, it is understood that the fewest numbers of followers belong to "obiranne" with 1,769 followers, "keyifbebesi" with 5,812 followers and "markaanne" with 5,943 followers.

Table 2. Number of followers of social media tools that belong to bloggers

Name of Blog	Number of Followers of Social Media Tools					
	Facebook	Twitter	Instagram	Google+	Pinterest	YouTube
blogcuanne	64.729	24,700	106.000	-	-	-
slingomom	7.703	8.847	49.900	20.260	1.033	247
markaanne	3.931	6.120	5.943	370	-	-
alternatifanne	18.147	8.481	8.440	Not Active	-	-
melinasmom	19.547	3.525	7.988	-	-	-
guncelanne	87.401	5.717	119.000	194	-	14
obiranne	1.043	-	1.769	1.033	-	-
balyanaginhikayesi	6.868	4.234	24.800	Not Active	165	376
deli-anne	7.793	4	-	-	-	-
annekaz	202.134	1.948	26.500	-	-	563
ozgekopuz	35.911	3.912	-	-	-	-
gezentianne	3.487	2.386	95.400	-	-	-
momsblognote	35.045	2.600	49.800	-	256	-
kokoshanne	5.563	4.195	98.000	532	127	3.138
keyifbebesi	12.421	52	5.812	-	478	48

On Google+, the highest number of followers is reached with 20,260 followers on the blog called "slingomom", and the fewest number of followers is reached with 194 followers on the blog called "guncelanne". On Pinterest, the blog with the highest number of users is "slingomom" with 1,033 followers, whereas the blog with the lowest number of followers among the users is "kokoshanne" with 127 followers. On YouTube, the situation is positive for "kokoshanne" with 3,138 followers. On the other hand, the number of followers has a negative tendency towards "guncelanne" with 14 followers.

Findings on Innovation and Creativity in Social Media

In child development, family has a very important role, along with other environmental factors. It is generally focused on the role of mother in child's life while it is focused on the role and importance of the family in the development of child. In Turkish society, as in Western societies, mother is the only one who is responsible for the care and education of the child in the majority of families. Especially in the infancy period, which covers the first year of life, the mother who meets all needs of the child is the one who provides all the stimuli that will develop the child (Tezel, 2007, p.767).

Motherhood has undergone various changes over time as a social area. It is clear that it is not necessary to undertake in-depth investigations to observe these changes. Contrarily, this change can be observed even with a simple observation. The difference between the viewpoints of motherhood between today's mothers and their mothers, methods of raising children, how a child is desired to be raised, and the expectation of society from mother and child can be revealed by this simple observation (Teke, 2014, p. 36).

The concept of "social media and innovation", which also constitutes the main topic of the study, becomes clear after this review in a form creating a clear perception. In other words, blogger mothers, who are the writers of the blogs covered, also benefit from their blogs in terms of personal development and angles such as success, income, new job, career, recognition.

From this point of view, it is very important that how and in what way blogger mothers present themselves to their followers. The way blogger mothers introduce themselves on the "About" tab in order to demonstrate this difference, summarizes the situation.

In other saying, these sections are where we can get clues about the way blogger mothers introduce themselves and about their identity designs. Blogger mothers seem to prioritize their personal careers as well as their children who are the reasons for starting a blog. Blogger mothers also express their happiness in their marriages and their children in this section.

For example, blogger mother Elif Doğan tells her story as "Blogger Mother Elif Doğan was born in Mersin. She was graduated from Çankaya Primary School, from which her father was graduated, and from Tarsus American College, from which her uncle was graduated... Even though she was willing to be a teacher, she preferred the quite popular department, department of business, at that time and entered Marmara University... She did not obtain her business license caressively, moreover, she earned a master's degree in business from Baltimore University with the idea of "Maybe I will be an academician". She did not take lessons from this and applied to doctoral program on business. Fortunately, she was rejected and decided to change her way, saying, "I have never liked the business department anyway"... For about five years she worked in various NGOs in America ... "; while another blogger mother Özge Kopuz tells her story as "I could not imagine that I could live the greatest happiness by being the mother of Yade, Asım and Mira, while dreaming myself as a successful young woman of assertive trials since my childhood years... I was eligible to attend Marmara University Faculty of Law as a person who believed in the necessity of working determinedly to achieve her life goals. After a long time studies for midterms and final exams, I was graduated as a lawyer. After a year-long American adventure, when I met new innovations and discovered a new world, I got married with my husband, Ziya, whom I had a great admiration, and opened my own law office... We decided to open a different page with a baby in our life while I was living with the beauty of life..." "gezentianne" blog writer, Özlem Demir gives clues about her career saying "I was graduated from Boğaziçi University, Department of Mechanical Engineering. I have spent 15 years working in a software development department of a bank, and I have visited 46 countries and 162 cities with my husband before and after children, I said goodbye to corporate life in 2015, and I am continuing to travel... ". On the other hand, "kokoshanne" blog writer Meltem Bicioğlu gives details about career saying "After graduation in Turkey and two years of London adventure, I found a job in Turkey, I set in my way, just at that moment I fell in love with my husband who was here for vacation coming from America and moved to San Francisco. I have been trained in digital marketing and project management for 2 years... ".

According to the career clues given by the bloggers mothers who are owners of the blogs covered, in the "About" tab, it is understood that they are composed of highly educated people with different educational backgrounds, who are active in different occupational groups and who have life and work experience abroad. This can be considered as an outcome of the blogger's personal satisfaction element, it may also be a stimulant for career planning of individuals who follow the blog. At the same time, this situation also encourages followers who are active in different fields, to make new professions or applications that can be made internet-based like blogging.

Blogger mothers are individuals who evaluate and use the innovations in alternative professions and interests by their blogs. Blogger mothers, who do not just have the opportunity to write a blog in social media have an active lifestyle, unlike traditional motherhood. In other words, it seems easier for blogger mothers to deal with different things. Blog writer mothers covered have opportunity to deal with income-generating and career-contributor new work such as personal consultancy (sustainable communication, personal motherhood map, social media communication, presentation communication), seminars & workshops (sustainable good parenting, being a mother in Turkish culture, how can I talk with my children to make them listen, 100% organic discipline, what does love have to do with it?, we stop grumbling, Blogger Motherhood: Advantages and Traps), alternative mother activities (we have to talk about this movie, we have to talk about this book).

When the findings are compared to traditional motherhood, there are some advantages of blogger motherhood provided for blogger mothers on creating new business, new action and new source of income. Previously, motherhood had meanings such as especially dealing with children, spending the whole time for children and exerting themselves for their children; the situation has changed in today's blogger mothers.

Blogger mothers also share some posts about education on their blogs. Blogger mothers write articles on topics such as various training methods according to their profession and the necessity of education. For example, one of the blogger mothers presents her ideas saying "We have never thought of it, moreover these concepts were too far away for us. However it is in our life now. Homeschooling, even more Unschooling ... Let's get The Learning Revolution Series started... I was thinking that which one is the right for us? Preferences can vary for every child, every society, for each parent, but for me; Is it Montessori, or Waldorf, or Reggio Emilia, or somebody else, or is the classical system the most comfortable one? The most reasonable one for me, which captivates me most was Homeschooling. But better than that: Unschooling... Of course, it's not easy for us to work with the one which captivates me. This is the reason of all pain, after all!" (deli-anne) and with these ideas she literally changes the educational system which is known and has been applied until today.

Similarly, any blogger mother can compare the education systems of different countries to find the right education system. In one of these comparisons, "gezentianne" discusses education systems in Turkey and England, saying "In England, children start school at the age of 3. It is not the 1st grade, of course. The class of children who are 3 years old is called nursey and the one of children who are 4 years old is called reception and both groups are educated in primary school by wearing the same uniform together with 1st graders and older ones. 1st grade (Year 1, as in the English saying) starts at age 5 and children learn to read and write in the first grade, just like we do. But, compared to their peers in Turkey, they start 1st grade one year earlier.".

In addition, it is also seen that blogger mothers have introduced new and creative educational concepts in addition to traditional education methods, and have organized or have been trained on these subjects. The blogger mother, "momsblognote" tells her followers that she attended the training called "Parent Coaching" with the following words: "Last week, I was on a training course that I enjoyed very much. Nowadays, parents are much more knowledgeable and equipped in every sense. This training was a great opportunity for us who are trying to approach their child in the most correct way... You can benefit from this training which will start on November, 6. Well, what is this parent coaching? It is mentoring parents to make them understand the child's frame of mind, to make them gain coping skills, and to coach them in directing children to the right disciplinary behavior. What does it do? It ensures you to understand your child's frame of mind (communication-interaction style) and it allows you to meet your child's emotional needs. There are four types of frame of mind; Successful, thinker-observer, peaceful and creative-influencing. In this training, you will learn which frame of mind your child has, how and in which conditions you should behave for that and more... ".

The new, different, creative ideas and opinions that blogger mothers have introduced about education, rather than the ideas of traditional motherhood such as sending the child to the school, taking the existing curriculum as it is, completing the education within the framework of formal education methods, may lead to a change in education system, to a change in mothers' opinions about education and to an evolution of educational point of view to new social expectations.

Follower responses to blogger mothers' articles about education can be cited. For example, the follower named İlknur agrees with the ideas such as change of the educational system or education without school, indicating that "The education system we have is unfortunately suggesting that what I read is impossible for me. I have been repeating something in recent days. I say that I will not sacrifice my daughter to this education system, but I find myself studying mathematics with her two days later:(Being happy is the key word, but the education system in Turkey does not allow this, unfortunately. My 1 month-search for school has finally resulted in a school with a gastronomy workshop. I was really impressed. Administrators were the people who say that their goal is not to be a school of children waiting for the break and running away from the class, but to be a school of children saying "I wish the break was over and the course has started". I am still concerned; all these appearances can be of commercial concern and eye wash. I have never thought to change the country. But raising an unhappy child despite success, makes me think of it in recent days. I know it was long, but 15 years ago my neighbor's relative, who has grown in Germany, had made her children graduated from primary school by taking lessons at home without sending to a school in Turkey. I do not know how she did it, but I have found it strange in those years and I have accused that mother of being an asocial. Now I understand and see her purpose better. Most of the mothers would think this option if we had such a chance. I wish you the best, my 'delianne':)".

Blogger mothers attempt to make efforts to guide their followers on their blogs with different and creative ideas. Thus, they strive for both their own and their followers to meet creative ideas and to support followers for involvement in creative actions. Just like "slingomom", saying "On Pinterest, I finally started to search for projects, activities that could be made with children. I try to make some of it, and try to produce newer things by getting inspired with others. We show more attention on pine trees, ornaments and gifts when it comes to new year. Our favorite 'do it yourself' product is the gift box from the toilet paper rolls. It is very easy to make... Some are creating masterpieces with this rolls but for now it is beyond me:)"...

Or like "alternatifanne", saying "Seren, who has not been wearing any chemical-dyed clothes since the day she was born, often gets sick ... Ayşe, who can not even trust her mother with giving care to her son, learns from her doctor that Osman, her son, should start the nursery as soon as possible ... When we see such examples, we question that whether our efforts for our child is meaningless... 'Annelik Haritası' published by Yeni İnsan Publication is an awareness game that can change your definition of "Good Mother" and that will guide you to the path of Sustainable Good Maternity, which can overturn the definition of "Good Mom" in your head ... Determine your route in your map. And see how your child's problems get smaller while your child grows!"...

As can be seen, a mother blogger can send messages to her followers by developing applications such as books, seminar work, and individual work with a creative idea called "maternity map", keeping it out of traditional motherhood patterns. Thus, motherhood goes beyond the traditional forms and becomes modern, innovative and creative.

Findings About Transmedia Storytelling

Blogger mothers seem to be already far away from traditional duties of traditional mothers such as bringing a child to the world, raising, dealing with housework, washing dishes and laundering, cooking, cleaning. At this point, it is also seen that blogger mothers carry out activities that can provide communication between various brands, products or services, businesses with the target audience through their blogs. In other words, blogger mothers, have become the subjects bringing together the target audience with corporations by transmedia applications and storytelling that they have created in transmedia environments.

In this context, there are some posts drawing attention. The title of the blog post which is covered in one of these posts is given as "En Pratik Sling Türkiye'de: Lucky Suppori" (The Best Practical Sling in Turkey: Lucky Suppori). In the content of the article, there are some statements: "I have a new discovery:) You know, I love new and interesting products. Yes, I have an infant carrier. But it is not an easy product to carry around with. If necessary, it already does its job... My new discovery is one of my favorite brands I have discovered recently:) Lucky Mama is the Turkish Official Distributor of Lucky, Japan's oldest baby carrier producer founded in 1934 ..."(keyifbebesi).

After this post shared on "keyifbebesi" blog, which was narrated as a new discovery, for example a follower named Özgecan Sancak on Facebook participated in the process, indicating "Is it possible to publish the photo that you use this product? Previously, Zuhal Kaykaç Messora posted a photo using this product while bathing her child, however, I felt like there was a danger of falling since it seemed uncomfortable without a support. It looks very simple compared to Babasling etc. derivatives. I will keep on following.". It is also remarkable that the follower gives "I will keep on following" message.

On "kokoshanne" blog on the other hand, the content created for the Philips brand is remarkable. In this example, the blogger explains the necessity of hair dryers to her followers based on her child, sharing Alin's choice on hair dryer with a storytelling narrative: "The hair dryer is a product we would all like to have at home. In fact, I do not really like drying my hair but I can not get rid of my neck and back pains because of my wet hair. Therefore, I never go out without drying my hair. Of course, I have a little partner:) Of course, hair of Lady Alin is first covered with cheesecloth, and excess water is eliminated, hair-drying process starts... We both relaxed now thanks to Philips ThermoProtect Ionic Hair dryer... "

On mother blogs covered in the study, not only storytelling for marketing purposes is the subject. At the same time, some stories about prenatal and post-natal periods and delivery, which are the main purposes of stories in mother blogs, one of the thematic blogs, are also the subjects, influencing followers' ideas and attitudes about motherhood. This is the basis of the development of the influence being received from bloggers on future mothers and mothers about pregnancy and pre-pregnancy periods and about raising children after birth.

One of these stories included Ayşenur and Dağhan's story: "I promised myself during the period, in which I was keeping a pregnancy diary, to write all my feelings while they were fresh, my birth story to get a reminder... 2016 was so full of worries, I did not spend one day that I did not feel that burden on my shoulders. I was not able to enjoy the most important moment of my life while I was being squashed under this weight ...I hope that our story would bring light to people who are about to give up... When my head was full, I could not breathe in my nose and I was so scared when I heard the sentence, "birth is coming"... I was relieved when my doctor said that "Whichever way I choose, he will be with me and do whatever it takes," and I got nervous about giving the right decision. Everyone let me to decide and started to wait. How much would I relax if somebody would go out and say, "Well, this is the right way, keep going" ... I was just one of the billions of mothers. Nevertheless, it was the most miraculous moments of our little world, the moment we first met and after that ... My little fighter resisting in the risky pregnancy process, my dear Dağhan... "(blogcuanne).

When the answers given to the story of Ayşenur and Dağhan are examined, it is seen that the mother candidates took lessons and courage about themselves from this sharing. For this reason, the follower named Mavi thanked to the authors of the story via the comment she made, and explained that she was positively affected by their story by saying "I'm really happy to hear about your births, and as soon as I learned that you were on therapy, I immediately looked at your pregnancy diaries. You are a ray of hope for me. 1. My transfer has resulted in a 10-week-low. After despair, I found myself in hospital again with a wish of becoming a mother 3 months later. Your story was the hope for me. Thank you so much for sharing. It is so good that you wrote it." Likewise, another follower named Melike explained that she was impressed by the characters of the story by saying "Do not be unhappy anymore, always be happy with your son, with the people you love... Birth stories have always impressed me deeply; yours have done the same. Best regards."

When we examine the stories created by Blogger mothers, mother candidates or mothers, it is noteworthy that very emotional and impressive narratives are realized. It can be argued that these narratives will affect people with curiosity or concerns about prenatal, natal and postnatal periods; and will lead to some changes in their ideas and practices. In other words, the stories told in the blogs of the blogger mothers can be said to have a very high influence on the surrounding environment.

CONCLUSION

Change is not only observed in communication technology and tools, but also in communication patterns and models in the age of social media. These communication-based changes attract attention in many areas, from the forms of communication that individuals build in their daily lives, to professional and corporate life.

The messages generated do not reach their goals in limited space, limited time and limited form as it used to be, due to the developments occurred. Contrarily, they can be reached with a lot of media use thanks to wide range of tools of today's social media. Efficiency of communication messages are enhanced by integrating these multimedia tools with each other and by benefitting from the specific power of each media tool via the process named transmedia applications.

With the development of transmedia applications, the methods of transmitting the message desired by fictionalizing it around a story have been realized in an extremely effective manner. Thus, the concept of transmedia storytelling comes to light.

This study was conducted to find out how blogs, which are social media tools, are used as a next generation maternity practice and to answer the question of how blogger mothers use transmedia storytelling applications. According to the data obtained from the research, it seems that the blog as a social media tool creates a creative space that can be defined as "blogger motherhood" for the new generation of mothers. It is come to light that blogger mothers put their signature on different projects with the creative substructure that blogging offers them. At the same time, it has been understood that blogger mothers used transmedia storytelling to influence their target audience, expanded their stories with other social media tools, and reached a wide follower network.

However, it has also been revealed that blogger mothers behave in a way appropriate to different character types in different stories created in blogs. It is observed that in the stories created by blogger mothers, blogger mothers are often the main character, and occasionally they give place to other characters in their stories. In the stories created by blogger mothers, bloggers are always seen in the form of a character who is a real friend. At the same time, it seems that they reflect the dynamic character structure of blogger mothers. According to the results obtained from the research, blogger mothers also take the characteristics of heroes and supporting characters.

REFERENCES

AhumbeyevaA.TaalaybekkızıA. (2017). Retrieved from http://ayperia.home.anadolu.edu.tr/egkil.pdf

Aktan, E., & Çakmak, V. (2015). Halkla ilişkiler öğrencilerinin sosyal medyadaki siber zorbalık duyarlılıklarını ölçmeye ilişkin bir araştırma. *Gümüşhane üniversitesi iletişim fakültesi elektronik dergisi, 3*(2), 159-176. Retrieved 09 29.2017, from http://dergipark.gov.tr

Aktan, E., & Özüpek, M. (2015). Corporate advertising at the social media age. In N. Ö. Taşkıran & R. Yılmaz (Eds.), *Handbook research on effective advertising strategies in the social media age* (pp. 197–212). Hershey, PA: IGI Global. doi:10.4018/978-1-4666-8125-5.ch011

Alikılıç, Ö. A. (2011). *Halkla ilişkiler 2.0: Sosyal medyada yeni paydaşlar yeni teknikler.* Ankara: Efil Publications.

Baran, B., & Ata, F. (2013). Üniversite öğrencilerinin web 2.0 teknolojileri kullanma durumları, beceri düzeyleri ve eğitsel olarak faydalanma durumları. *Eğitim ve bilim, 38*(169), 192-208.

Chen, L.-C. (2017). An effective LDA-based time topic model to improve blog search performance. *Information Processing & Management, 53*(6), 1299–1319. doi:10.1016/j.ipm.2017.08.001

Dilmen, N. E. (2014). Yeni medya kavramı çergevesinde ınternet günlükleri-bloglar ve gazeteciliğe yansımaları. *Marmara iletişim dergisi, 12*(12), 113-122.

Dönmez, M., & Güler, Ş. (2016). Transmedya Hikayeceliği "doritos akademi" örneği incelemesi. *Süleyman demirel üniversitesi vizyoner dergisi, 7*(16), 155-175.

Dusi, N., Ferretti, I., & Furini, M. (2017). A transmedia storytelling system to transform recorded film memories into visual history. *Entertainment Computing, 21*, 65–75. doi:10.1016/j.entcom.2017.05.002

Ferreira, S. A. M. (2015). *Location based transmedia storytelling: Enhancing the tourism experience* (Order No. 10593574). Available from ProQuest dissertations & theses global. (1927624254). Retrieved from https://search.proquest.com/docview/1927624254?accountid=38938

Graves, M. (2015). *Lost in a transmedia storytelling franchise: rethinking transmedia engagement* (Doctoral dissertation). University of Kansas.

Greer, J., & Pan, P.-L. (2015). The role of website format, blog use, and information-gathering acquaintance in online message assessment. *Telematics and Informatics, 32*(4), 594–602. doi:10.1016/j.tele.2015.02.001

Gronstedt, A., & Ramos, M. (2014). *Learning through transmedia storytelling*. Alexandria, VA: American Society for Training & Development.

Herring, S. C., Scheidt, L., Bonus, S., & Wright, E. (2004). Bridging the gap: A genre analysis of weblogs. *Proceedings of the 37th hawaii international conference on system sciences*, 1-11. Retrieved from http://ieeexplore.ieee.org

Iasimone, A., & Solla, L. (2013). Sm-Art (social media of art) for the Renaissance of culture on Web. *Procedia Chemistry*, *8*, 302–306. doi:10.1016/j.proche.2013.03.037

Ifinedo, P. (2017). Examining students' intention to continue using blogs for learning: Perspectives from technology acceptance, motivational, and social-cognitive frameworks. *Computers in Human Behavior*, *72*, 189–199. doi:10.1016/j.chb.2016.12.049

Jenkins, H. (2006). *Convergence culture where old and new media collide*. New York, NY: New York University Press.

Jenkins, H. (2007). Retrieved 10.18.2017, from http://henryjenkins.org: http://henryjenkins.org/blog/2007/03/transmedia_storytelling_101.html

Kasemsap, K. (2015). The role of social media in international advertising. In N. Ö. Taşkıran & R. Yılmaz (Eds.), *Handbook research on effective advertising strategies in the social media age* (pp. 171–196). Hershey, PA: IGI Global.

Kathpalia, S. S., & See, E. (2016). Improving argumentation through student blogs. *System*, *58*, 25–36. doi:10.1016/j.system.2016.03.002

Keskin, S., & Baş, M. (2015). Sosyal medyanin tüketici davranişlari üzerine etkisinin belirlenmesi. *Gazi üniversitesi İİBF dergisi, 17*(3), 51-69.

Killian, G., & McManus, K. (2015). A marketing communications approach for the digital era: Managerial guidelines for social media integration. *Business Horizons*, *58*(5), 539–549. doi:10.1016/j.bushor.2015.05.006

Koçyiğit, M. (2015). Sosyal ağ pazarlamasi-marka bağliliği oluşturmada yeni bir pazarlama stratejisi. Konya, Turkey: Eğitim Yayınevi.

Li, F., & Du, T. (2017). Maximizing micro-blog influence in online promotion. *Expert Systems with Applications*, *70*, 52–66. doi:10.1016/j.eswa.2016.10.060

Magno, F. (2017). The influence of cultural blogs on their readers' cultural product choices. *International Journal of Information Management*, *37*(3), 142–149. doi:10.1016/j.ijinfomgt.2017.01.007

Mavnacıoğlu, K. (2011). *Kurumsal iletişimde sosyal medya yönetimi: Kurumsal blog odakli bir inceleme* (Doctoral Dissertation). Available from Council of Higher Education Thesis Center. (No. 303733)

Mayfield, A. (2008). *What is social media*. Retrieved from http://www.icrossing.com

Özbölük, T., & Dursun, Y. (2015). Pazarlama araştirmalarinda paradigmal dönüşüm ve etnografinin dijitale evrimi: netnografi. *Erciyes üniversitesi iktisadi ve idari bilimler fakültesi dergisi*, *46*, 227-249.

Özüdoğru, Ş. (2014). Bir web 2.0 uygulamasi olarak bloglar: Bloglarin dinamikleri ve log alemi. *The Turkish online journal of design, art and communication, 4*(1), 36-50.

Pang, N., & Goh, D. (2016). Can blogs function as rhetorical publics in Asian democracies? An analysis using the case of Singapore. *Telematics and Informatics, 33*(2), 504–513. doi:10.1016/j.tele.2015.08.001

Severin, W. J., & Tankard, J. W. (1994). Kitle iletişim kuramlari kökenleri, yöntem ve kitle iletişim araçlarında kullanımları (A. A. Bir & S. Sever, Trans.). Eskişehir, Turkey: Anadolu Üniversitesi.

Sezer, N., & Sert, N. (2013). Online medya okuryazarliğinin yetişkinler için önemi "online haber sitelerindeki bannerlara yönelik bir inceleme". *Online academic journal of information technology, 4*(13), 63-78.

Sigala, M., & Chalkiti, K. (2015). Knowledge management, social media and employee creativity. *International Journal of Hospitality Management, 45,* 44–58. doi:10.1016/j.ijhm.2014.11.003

Teke, S. G. (2014). Dönüşen anneliğe yönelik netnografik bir analiz: Blogger anneler. *Milli Folklor, 103,* 32–47.

Tezel Şahin, F. (2007). Sosyal değişim sürecinde değişen baba rolü. *International congress of Asian and North African studies. ICANAS 38.*

Turina, J., Lutsenko, E., & Oleynikov, E. (2015). New media in daily life of educational process subjects: A case of khabarovsk higher education institutions. *Social and behavioral sciences, 214,* 174-182.

Vural, Z. B., & Bat, M. (2010). Siyasal seçim kampanyalarinda yeni iletişim teknolojileri ve blog kullanimi: 2008 Amerika başkanlik seçimlerine yönelik karşilaştirmali bir analiz. *Journal of yaşar university, 5*(20), 3348-3382. Retrieved 09.29.2017, from http://www.siyasaliletisim.org

Yılmaz, E. (2011). Yeni medya ve halkla ilişkiler: hedef kitleye ağ üzerinden erişmek. In M. Işık, & M. Akdağ (Eds.), Dünden bugüne halkla ilişkiler (pp. 137-148). Konya, Turkey: Eğitim Yayınevi.

Yılmaz, R. (2014). *Anlatı yoluyla dünyanın zihinsel yeniden kurulumu: "Palto", "Dönüşüm" ve "Hayvan Çiftliği" romanlarının alımlama pratikleri üzerine bir inceleme* (Doctoral Dissertation). Available from Council of Higher Education Thesis Center. (No. 393279)

Zarrela, D. (2010). *The social media marketing book.* O'Reilly Media Inc.

Zeiser, A. (2015). *Transmedia platforms: A creator's guide to media and entertainment.* Waltham, MA: Focal Press.

Zhu, L., Sun, A., & Choi, B. (2011). Detecting spam blogs from blog search results. *Information Processing & Management, 47*(2), 246–262. doi:10.1016/j.ipm.2010.03.006

KEY TERMS AND DEFINITIONS

Blog: The blog, a type of Web 2.0 technology, is a website that allows users (bloggers) to publish posts viewed in reverse chronological order.

Blogger: The blogger concept means blog writer.

Creativity: Creativity is a process based on the ability to produce products.

Mother Blogs: Mother blogs, an example of thematic blogs, refer to a type of blog created by a blogger mother who wants to share her ideas, integratedly with other mothers or future mothers.

Narration: Narration is a process based on the expression of real or designed imaginary events.

Social Media: It is the name given to online platforms where individuals interact with each other.

Transmedia Storytelling: Transmedia storytelling is the sharing and reproduction of a story in different media.

Transmediatic Characters: Transmedia characters are people used in transmedia storytelling.

This research was previously published in the Handbook of Research on Transmedia Storytelling and Narrative Strategies; pages 251-270, copyright year 2019 by Information Science Reference (an imprint of IGI Global).

Chapter 18
A Systematic Review on Self-Construal and Social Network Sites

Soon Li Lee
https://orcid.org/0000-0003-0860-811X
Taylor's University, Lakeside Campus, Malaysia

Cai Lian Tam
Monash University, Malaysia

ABSTRACT

The present research was conducted to systematically review existing research that examined the relationships of the aspects of self-construal and social network sites (SNS) usages. A total of 12 research articles met the inclusion criteria for the present review. The reviewed research articles mainly supported the significant relationship of the interdependent self-construal and SNS-related outcomes. The present review highlighted that the reviewed relationships differed. Some findings supported the direct effect of self-construal on SNS-related outcomes, whereas some supported the indirect effects of intervening variables on these relationships. The reviewed findings supported the influence of self-construal on cognition, emotion, and motivation. Implications of the present systematic review were discussed in the manuscript.

INTRODUCTION

Social network sites (SNS) that function to connect people (e.g. Ellison, Steinfield, & Lampe, 2007) have been tightly integrated into users' daily life. Although these online platforms were initially designed to connect people, SNS have served a range of purposes that include instant distribution of newspaper content (e.g. Ju, Jeong, & Chyi, 2014) and brand advertising (Dehghani & Tumer, 2015). This supports the multifaceted usage of SNS that stemmed from users' exploitation of the features available on these online platforms. Consistent with the intended purposes of SNS to regulate and to maintain connectedness with other users (Boyd & Ellison, 2007), research has supported that the degree of individuality and

DOI: 10.4018/978-1-6684-6307-9.ch018

collectiveness is instrumental in shaping the use of SNS. For instance, the endorsement of individuality and connectedness was linked to the types of connection established through SNS (Chu & Choi, 2010; Choi, Kim, Sung, & Sohn, 2010; Ji et al., 2010; Na, Kosinki, & Stillwell, 2015). Subsequent progression revealed that the assertion of individualism and collectivism affected the underlying attitude and acceptability of SNS (Cho & Park, 2013). Consequently, this endorsement influenced the enacted communication style (Cho & Park, 2013; Park, Jun, & Lee, 2015; Qiu, Lin, Leung, 2013) and self-expression strategies on SNS (Chu & Choi, 2010; DeAndrea, Shaw, & Levine, 2010), motivations (Kim, Sohn, & Choi, 2011; Shin, 2010) and the corresponding levels of engagement on SNS (Chu & Choi, 2011; Jackson & Wang, 2013; Park et al., 2015; Vasalou, Joinson, & Courvoisier, 2010). In this stream of research, endorsement of these self-aspects is known as self-construal (Markus & Kitayama, 1991). Collectively, research findings have supported the significance of self-construal in facilitating SNS usages. Given the importance of self-construal in determining usages of online platforms, the present research aims to systematically review existing research articles that examined the relationships of the aspects of self-construal and SNS related outcomes.

Self-construal is one of the prominent concepts in psychology (Matsumoto, 1999). It refers to the extent to which the self is defined independently of others or interdependently with others (Markus & Kitayama, 1991). The independent aspect of self is known as the independent self-construal, where the self is represented as distinct from others (Markus & Kitayama, 1991; Singelis, 1994). The interdependent aspect of self is known as the interdependent self-construal, where the self is represented as tightly connected to others (Markus & Kitayama, 1991; see also Singelis, 1994). Although these aspects were deemed as mutually exclusive, it was indicated that individuals possess both aspects of self-construal, and the expression of these aspects is dependent on situational context (Markus & Kitayama, 1991, see also Singelis, 1994, Triandis, 1989). The expression of these self-aspects is often consistent with Hofstede's (1980, 2001) cultural dimension of Individualism-Collectivism. The expression of the independent self-construal is more common in individualistic cultures, whereas the expression of the interdependent self-construal is more common in collectivistic cultures (Gudykunst et al., 1996; Markus & Kitayama, 1991; Singelis, 1994). Self-construal was theorized as individual-level of culture-based differences in perception, motivation and behaviour (Markus & Kitayama, 1991). Hence, despite the overlap, the theoretical distinction remained where the cultural dimension of Individualism-Collectivism describes the national cultures, while the aspects of self-construal reflects on individuals' endorsement of individuality and collectiveness (Cross, Hardin, & Gercek-Swing, 2011; Levine et al., 2003).

In the vast literature, self-construal has been used to account for differences in human communication, such as the endorsement of communication strategies (Kim, Shin, & Cai, 1998) and conflict styles (Oetzel, 1998). Empirical research extends the influence of self-construal on human-technology interaction, where the aspects of self-construal dictate the gratifications sought online. To illustrate, individuals with assertion of collectiveness or interdependence reported higher gaming satisfaction with avatar-based video games that promote interactivity (Park & Jin, 2009). When purchasing online products, individuals with high interdependent self-construal are less critical toward reviews written by previous customers (Sia et al., 2009). Additionally, individuals with high interdependent self-construal are less likely to purchase products online due to the absence of human interaction (Frost, Goode, & Hart, 2010). Research also supports that self-construal is conducive of technology acceptance (e.g. Choi & Totten, 2012) and usages (e.g. Hu, Zhang, & Luo, 2016). Thus, researchers have recommended to design online contents such as website design (Kim, Coyle, & Gould, 2009) and corporate pages on SNS (Tsai & Men, 2012) based on these predispositions.

In essence, self-construal is an influential psychological variable that influence human-technology interaction. The purpose of the present research is to systematically review existing research articles that examined the relationships of self-construal and SNS usages. Specifically, the present review will focus on (1) the quantification of self-construal and SNS related outcomes, and (2) the relationship of self-construal and SNS related outcomes. Recommendations from the Preferred Reporting Items for Systematic Reviews and Meta-Analysis Protocols (PRISMA-P; Shamseer et al., 2015) are used as guidelines for the present systematic review.

Figure 1. The flow of the searches and screenings

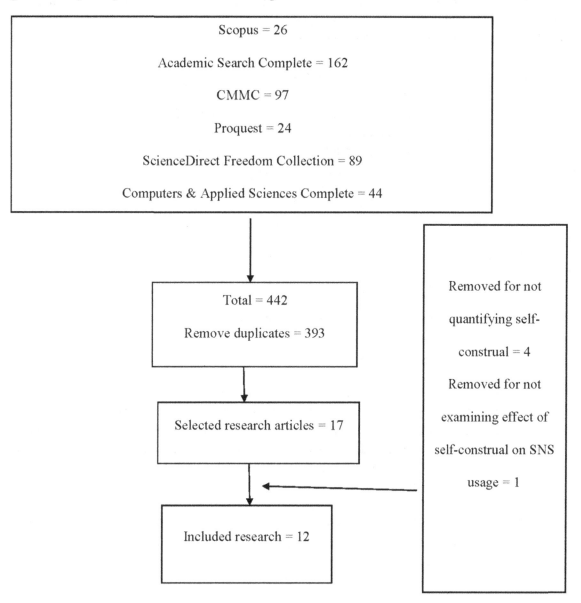

METHOD

Information Sources and Search Strategy

To identify research articles for the present review, a search was conducted with Academic Search Complete, Communication and Mass Media Complete, Scopus, ScienceDirect Freedom Collection, ProQuest databases. Reference lists of included research articles were scanned for additional relevant research articles.

All plausible combinations of the following keywords were used: "social network sites", "social networking sites", "social media", "SNS", "Facebook", "self-construal", "self-construals", "independent self-construal", "interdependent self-construal". No constraint was imposed on the date of publication as an attempt to maximize the search results. Research articles collection was conducted on November 2018. A total of 393 research articles responded to the keywords.

Eligibility Criteria and Selection Process

For the present review, the following eligibility criteria were imposed: (1) original research articles, (2) published in English, (3) quantitative research that manipulates or measures self-construal, and (4) quantitative research that measures SNS related outcomes. Titles and abstracts of the retrieved research articles were screened according to the inclusion criteria. From the initial 393 research articles, 17 research articles were retained for full-text screening. Full-text screening supported the decision to retain 12 research. Figure 1 summarizes the flow of the searches and screenings.

Results

The present research intends to systematically review the relationships of self-construal and SNS related outcomes. A total of 12 research articles met the inclusion criteria and were included in the present review. Table 1 summarizes the characteristics of the included research articles.

Characteristics of Included Research Articles

The included research articles were mainly cross-sectional research, with 1 of the retrieved articles reported a combination of survey design and online experiment (Shim et al., 2016; Study 2), while another 1 research article declared the research as an online experiment (Lee et al., 2012). From the retrieved research articles, the earliest research dated back to 2010 (Kim et al., 2010) and the most recent research is published in 2018 (Kim & Stavrositu, 2018). Two out of the retrieved 12 research articles documented multiple investigations in a single publication (Chang, 2015; Shim et al., 2016).

The sample varied significantly across the retained research articles. Majority of the research articles reported the inclusion of university and college students as research participants, followed by adults. The reported sample size differed across the retrieved research articles. One of the research articles reported a sample of 87 participants (Lee et al., 2016), and the largest sample size reported was 900 (Chang, 2015). Gender ratio was unequal, where female participants exceeded 50% in most of the research articles.

Table 1. Characteristics of the included research articles

Author/s (year)	Aim/s	Sample type	Country	N (female's n)	Age
Bailey & Mimoun (2016)	To investigate the effect of the interdependent self-construal on consumers' view and responses to online social networking.	University students	USA	236 (female = 46%)	75% in the age range of 18 – 24 (M_{age} and SD_{age} not specified)
*Chang (2015)	To investigate the effects of the aspects of self-construal on Facebook activities.	University students	Taiwan	*Study 1* 900 (female = 54.8%) *Study 2* 863 (female = 59.3%)	*Study 1* Age range 19 – 55 (M_{age} = 22.66, SD_{age} = 4.02) *Study 2* Age range 18 – 55 (M_{age} = 22.56, SD_{age} = 4.02)
Chen & Marcus (2012)	To investigate the relationships of the different modes of self-disclosure, personality, and self-construal on SNS	University students	USA	463 (female = 71%)	Age range 18 – 51 (M_{age} = 20.57, SD_{age} = 4.72)
Chu et al. (2015)	To investigate the effects of the two aspects of self-construal on the usage of three social media platforms.	Young adults	USA (n = 306) China (n = 315)	621 (female = 53%)	Age range under 20 and over 21 year (M_{age} and SD_{age} not specified)
*Ferenczi et al. (2017)	To investigate the mediating effects of self-construal and narcissism on the relationships of gender and motives of Facebook usage.	Adults	USA	573 (female = 59%)	Age range not specified (M_{age} = 30.79, SD_{age} = 9.17)
Jiao et al. (2017)	To investigate the effects of the two aspects of self-construal on psychological well-being derived from SNS usage.	Adults	China	437 (female = 47.6%)	Age range 18-46 and above (M_{age} and SD_{age} not specified)
Kim et al. (2010)	To investigate the effects of self-construal on SNS usage and satisfaction	University students	USA	170 (female = 55.3%)	Age range 18 – 23 (M_{age} and SD_{age} not specified)
Kim & Stavrositu (2018)	To investigate the moderating effects of self-construal on the relationships of socially engaging/disengaging emotions on Facebook and well-being.	Adults	USA Korea	USA (n = 320, female = 51.9%) Korea (n = 336, female = 46.7%)	USA Age range not specified (M_{age} = 31.23, SD_{age} = 7.81) Korea Age range not specified (M_{age} = 31.34, SD_{age} = 8.25)
Lee et al. (2012)	To investigate the mediating effects of online community engagement self-efficacy and SNS social outcome expectations on the relationship of self-construal and consumers' electronic word of mouth (eWOM) behaviour.	College students	USA	160 (female = 61.2%)	Age range, M_{age} and SD_{age} not specified.

continues on following page

Table 1. Continued

Author/s, (year)	Aim/s	Sample type	Country	N (female's n)	Age
Lee et al. (2016)	To investigate the effect of the Autonomous-Related self-construal on different SNS usages	University students	Korea China Malaysia	Korea (n = 113, female = 52%) China (n = 87, female = 77%) Malaysia (n = 105, female = 77%)	Korea Age range not specified (M_{age} = 22.27, SD_{age} = 2.18) China Age range not specified (M_{age} = 20.70, SD_{age} = 2.07) Malaysia Age range not specified (M_{age} = 23.22, SD_{age} = 2.59)
Long & Zhang (2014)	To investigate the effects of self-construal on the motives and concerns behind SNS use	Adults	Japan British	Japan (n = 134, female = 58%) British (n = 109, female = 75%)	Japan Age range 16-63 (M_{age} = 30.42, SD_{age} = 10.56) British Age range 16-57, (M_{age} = 22.40, SD_{age} = 7.34)
*Shim et al. (2016)	To investigate the effects of self-construal and public self-consciousness on positive self-presentation on SNS	College students	Korea	Study 1 (n = 137, female = 65%) Study 2 (n = 120, female = 53%)	Study 1 Age range 19 - 27 (M_{age} = 22.77, SD_{age} = 1.79) Study 2 Age range 20 - 32 (M_{age} = 23.70, SD_{age} = 2.95)

The included research articles reported cross-cultural comparisons. There were attempts to examine differences between Western and Asian samples (Chu et al., 2015; Kim & Stavrositu, 2018; Long & Zhang, 2014). One research article uniquely examine differences amongst three Asian countries (Lee et al., 2016).

Appraisal

Consistent with PRISMA-P guidelines (Shamseer et al., 2015), each research article was assessed for risk of bias using NHLBI quality assessment tool (National Heart, Lung, and Blood Institute, 2014). Majority of the research articles have stated clear research objective or research aim, and have utilized suitable measures of self-construal. However, most research articles adapted existing scales to gauge SNS related outcomes without proper screening on their psychometrics. Further screening revealed that gender distribution was unequal for most of the retained research articles. Additionally, there was no clear age restriction for most of the retained research articles. Together, these factors may confound the results. Two online experiments were conducted, where the two aspects of self-construal were manipulated with Trafimow et al.'s (1991) priming procedures (Lee et al., 2012; Shim et al., 2016; Study 2). From these two online experiments, only one reported randomization of the priming conditions (Shim et al., 2016). Both online experiments reported that manipulation check was conducted to ensure the priming was successful. In sum, majority of the retained research articles received poor rating, while only a few received fair rating. Research articles that received a fair rating are distinguished with an asterisk symbol in Table 1.

Self-Construal Measures and Indicators

Table 2 summarizes the measures and procedures used in each respective research articles. The common measure for self-construal is the Self-Construal Scale (Singelis, 1994). However, this measure was utilized inconsistently. From the retained research articles, some utilized the entire scale, whereas some focused on the subscale. In addition, some researchers reduced the items without justification and proper screening on the psychometrics. A research computed the score difference between the subscales for the independent self and the interdependent self to create an index, which higher score indicating for greater orientation towards the independent aspect (Chang, 2015). Other research articles reported the use of other scales to measure the independent and interdependent aspects of self-construal, such as the 4 items from Wagner's (1995) research, the Schwartz's Value Inventory (1992), and the Owe's (2013) self-construal scale from an unpublished thesis. Relatedly, two research articles (Lee et al., 2012; Shim et al., 2016) primed the aspects of self-construal with the procedures outlined by Trafimow et al. (1991). Other aspects of self-construal were measured, which include the relational self-construal that refers the tendency to construe oneself in terms of relationships with significant others (Cross et al., 2000) and the Autonomous-Related self-construal that refers to the balanced state of autonomous and relatedness (Kagitcibasi, 2007).

Table 2. Self-construal measures and indicators

Author/s (year)	Scale/Procedures used	Description	Further remarks
Bailey & Mimoun, 2016; Chang, 2015; Chu et al., 2015; Jiao et al., 2017; Shim et al., 2016	Self-Construal Scale (Singelis, 1994)	This scale consists of 24 items, with 12 items reflecting on the independent self and the remaining 12 reflecting on the interdependent self.	Full items were used in 2 research articles (Chang, 2015, Chu et al., 2015). The remaining research articles reported the use of the shortened scale (12 items, Shim et al., 2016; 9 items, Jiao et al., 2017). One of these articles used the interdependent subscale (Bailey & Mimoun, 2016)
Chen & Marcus (2012)	Four items from Wagner's (1995) research	This scale consists of 4 items, with higher scores indicating greater endorsement of the independent self.	
Kim et al. (2010)	Leung and Kim's (1997) self-construal scale	This scale consists of 29 items that reflect on the independent and the interdependent self-construal.	
Long & Zhang (2014)	Owe's (2013) self-construal scale	This scale consists of 35 items, reflecting on seven dimensions of Self-direction, Self-reliance, Consistency, Inclusion of others in the self, Commitment to others, and Uniqueness.	Long & Zhang (2014) reported the use of 12 items for measuring the independent self, and another 12 items to measure the interdependent self.
Kim & Stavrositu (2018)	Schwartz's Value Inventory (1992)	This scale consists of 56 items that reflect on ten broad dimensions of human values.	Kim & Stavrositu (2018) assessed the independent self with six items, and the interdependent self with another six items.
Ferenczi et al. (2017)	Relational-Interdependent Self-Construal Scale (Cross et al., 2001)	This scale consists of eleven items that reflect on the relational self-construal, which is the tendency to construe the self in relation to connectedness with significant others.	
Lee et al. (2016)	The Autonomy-Relatedness Scale (Kagitcibasi, 2007)	This scale consists of 27 items. It consists of three subscales, each formed by nine items that reflect on the Autonomous self, the Related self, and the Autonomous-Related self (balanced state of independence and interdependence).	The independence and interdependence aspects were discarded due to poor model fit across three countries. Four items from the Autonomous-Related self subscale were removed to improve the fit indices.
Lee et al. (2012); Shim et al.'s (2016) Study 2	Priming procedures used by Trafimov et al. (1991)	One of these procedures requires participants to think of the difference (independent self) and similarity (interdependent self) of themselves in comparison with their significant others. This is used in Shim et al.'s (2016) research. Another procedure requires participants to read a scenario that depicts two different endings to prime the designated self-construal. This was used in Lee et al.'s (2012) research.	Manipulation check was conducted in both research articles (Lee et al., 2012; Shim et al., 2016) by examining the mean difference between the measured independent and interdependent self.

SNS Related Outcomes

Table 3 summarizes the measured usages and aspects of SNS. These measured aspects differed across the reviewed research articles. Due to shortage of valid and reliable scales, four of the reviewed research articles composed measures to reflect on the investigated aspects of SNS (Bailey & Mimoun, 2016; Chang, 2015; Lee et al., 2016; Long & Zhang, 2014). Eight research articles adapted existing scales to reflect on the context of SNS (Chen & Marcus, 2012; Chu et al., 2015; Ferenczi et al., 2017; Jiao et al., 2017; Kim et al., 2010; Kim & Stavrositu, 2018; Lee et al., 2016; Shim et al., 2016). From one of these research articles, the adapted SNS Intensity Scale (Ellison et al., 2007) exhibited good fit indices and the factor structure was interpreted consistently across three Asian samples (Lee et al., 2016).

Secondary Outcomes

Apart from measuring the aspects of self-construal and the usages of SNS, the retrieved research articles also measured other psychological constructs. From Table 4, these secondary outcomes varied as well. These outcomes included personality traits such as narcissism and Extraversion, social orientations, motivations, materialism, active usage of microblogging and the intensity of video sharing, modesty in responding, the degree of satisfaction with life and Facebook, social outcome expectations and public self-consciousness. Most of these outcomes were used as mediators to the relationships of self-construal and the aspects of SNS.

The Relationships of Self-Construal and the Aspects of SNS

Overall, research findings supported the significant effects of the independent and interdependent self-construal on the different aspects of SNS. Table 5 summarizes the main findings. Although both aspects of self-construal were significant predictors of active SNS use, results mainly supported that the interdependent aspect was more influential than the independent aspect (Chu et al., 2015). The reviewed research articles indicated that the relationships examined differed by cultures. In an instance, the measured Autonomous-Related self-construal predicted active use of SNS positively with Malaysian sample, while the same self-construal predicted the same active use of SNS negatively with Korean sample (Lee et al., 2016). In another research article, the amount of motivations significantly predicted by the independent self-construal and the interdependent self-construal differed between British and Japan sample (Long & Zhang, 2014). Findings from these research articles supported the facilitative effect of the interdependent self-construal on the aspects of SNS (Chu et al., 2015; Long & Zhang, 2014).

However, findings indicated that the measured self-construal did not directly predict the aspects of SNS. The measured self-perceptions influence the formation and enactment of certain psychological constructs, which eventually affect the corresponding SNS usages. Two of the reviewed research articles posited the measured aspects of self-construal as mediators (Ferenczi et al., 2017; Kim & Stavrositu, 2018).

Table 3. SNS measures and indicators

Author/s (year)	Scale/s used (α)
Bailey & Mimoun (2016)	Susceptibility to social networking influence scale (α = .92) SNS Social sharing disposition (α = .93) Attitude towards social networking (α = .97) Attitude towards marketers' social networking sites (α = .96) Likelihood to recommend marketers' SNS (α = .93)
Chang et al. (2015)	*Study 1* Time spent online and Facebook, Facebook activities (Responding to others' α = .91, Revealing the self's α = .80) *Study 2* Time spent online and Facebook, Facebook activities (Responding to others' α = .87, Revealing the self's α = .93)
Chen & Marcus (2012)	Intention to self-disclosure online (α = .63) Amount of self-disclosure online (α = .68) Positivity of self-disclosure online (α = .56) Honesty of self-disclosure online (α = .39) Control of self-disclosure online (α = .47) Relevance of self-disclosure online (α = .32)
Chu et al. (2015)	SNS intensity scale (Ellison et al. 2007)
Ferenczi et al. (2017)	Uses of Facebook scale (Facebook prosocial motives' α = .91, Facebook antisocial motives' α = .91)
Jiao et al. (2017)	Social value on SNS (α = .82) Content value on SNS (α = .84) Self-esteem on SNS (α = .80) Flow on SNS (α = .84) Social identity on SNS (α = .79) Psychological well-being derived from SNS (α = .78)
Kim et al. (2010)	Motivations to use Facebook (social motivations' α = .81, nonsocial motivations' α = .79) SNS use per week Number of friends on SNS SNS profile length
Kim & Stavrositu (2018)	Socially engaging/disengaging emotions on Facebook (Positive engagement's α = .88, Positive disengagement's α = .89, Negative engagement's α = .88, Negative disengagement's α = .92) Perceived control on Facebook (α = .78) Perceived relationship harmony on Facebook (α = .89)
Lee et al. (2012)	eWOM intentions on SNS (α = .90) Online community engagement self-efficacy (α = .91) Online brand community type (consumer and marketer generated online brand community)
Lee et al. (2016)	SNS intensity (Malaysia's α = .86, Korea's α = .90, China's α = .87; Ellison et al. 2007) Activities on others' profiles checklist (Increasing contact, Malaysia's α = 0.81, Korea's α = 0.79, China's α = 0.94; Updating, Malaysia's α = 0.86, Korea's α = 0.82, China's α = 0.87) Contact with friends' profiles (Malaysia's α = 0.65, Korea's α = 0.75, China's α = 0.87)
Long & Zhang (2014)	Online self-presentation motives (Image management, Japan's α = .83, British's α = .86; Self-expression, Japan's α = .75, British's α = .88; Maintaining privacy, Japan's α = .79, British's α = .71; Attention seeking, Japan's α = .90, British's α = .57; Modest concern, Japan's α = .75, British's α = .60)
Shim et al. (2016)	*Study 1* Positive self-presentation on Facebook (α = .86) Time spent on Facebook Months of Facebook use *Study 2* Positive self-presentation on Facebook (α = .78)

Table 4. Measures and indicators of secondary outcomes

Author/s (year)	Scale/s used (α)
Chang (2015)	*Study 1* Social orientation (Self-disclosure's α = .95, Social responsiveness' α = .96; adapted from Miller et al., 1983) *Study 2* Social orientation (Self-disclosure's α = .93, Social responsiveness' α = .96) Social goals (Motivation to belong's α = .83; Leary et al., 2007; Motivation to be popular's α = .83; Sanrtor et al., 2000)
Chen & Marcus (2012)	Extraversion (α = .79; Donellan et al., 2006) Self-disclosure (Intent's α = .67, amount's α .70, positivity's α = .64, honesty's α = .58, control's α = .40, relevance's α = .32)
Chu et al. (2015)	Microblogging sites intensity, video sharing sites intensity (adapted from Ellison et al., 2007) Materialism (Richin & Dawson, 1992)
Ferenczi et al. (2017)	Narcissistic Personality Inventory-13 (NP-13; Gentile et al., 2013)
Kim et al. (2010)	Satisfaction towards Facebook (α = .82)
Kim & Stavrositu (2018)	Life satisfaction (α = .89; Diener, 1958)
Lee et al. (2012)	Social outcome expectations (α = .95)
Long & Zhang (2014)	Narcissistic Personality Inventory (Ames et al., 2006; Japan's α = .61, British's α = .76) Modest Responding Scale (Whetstone et al., 2002; Japan's α = .82, British's α = .86)
Shim et al. (2016)	*Study 1* Public self-consciousness (Scheier & Carver, 1985; α = .87) *Study 2* Public self-consciousness (Scheier & Carver, 1985; α = .86)

DISCUSSION

The present research intended to systematically review the relationship of self-construal and SNS related outcomes. Twelve research articles were retrieved and retained for this purpose. To the authors' knowledge, this is the first attempt to systematically review findings on the relationships of the aspects of self-construal and SNS usages. In sum, the reviewed findings supported the significant relationship of self-construal and SNS related outcomes. In particular, the reviewed findings mainly supported the significance of the interdependent self-construal in forming the usages of SNS and other related experiences.

From the reviewed research articles, the diversity in the operationalization and quantification of self-construal is evident. Some of the retained research articles focused on the conventional independent and interdependent self-construal, while some enacted alternative forms of self-construal (Ferenczi et al., 2017; Lee et al., 2016). This demonstrates the complexity of the theoretical constructs of self-construal. Diversity of the operationalization and quantification of the aspects of self-construal hindered systematic appraisal of effect sizes derived from the retrieved research articles. From the reviewed research articles, each of the measured self-construal was treated as unidimensional construct. However, empirical evidences revealed that the aspects of self-construal were multidimensional, that the independent and the interdependent self-construal each respectively consisted of different facets (Hardin, Leong, & Bhagwat, 2004; Hardin, 2006). Measuring the facets of self-construal is vital to the advancement of the conceptual links of self-construal and SNS related aspects since these specific facets tend to produce elaborative results (Hardin, 2006). However, it is unsure if the alternative forms of self-construal, such as the relational self-construal (Cross et al., 2000), are multifaceted. This is an aspect that requires ensuing efforts. The multifaceted perspective of self-construal imposes challenge to the manipulation of self-construal. Although the reviewed research articles supported the effectiveness of the manipulation procedures conducted by examining the differences in the measured self-construal (Lee et al., 2012; Shim et al., 2016), it is still unclear on which facets of the self-construal that has been successfully primed (see Cross et al., 2011). This might have confounded the findings and affected the subsequent interpretation of results.

Table 5. Summary of main findings

Author/s (year)	Main findings
Bailey & Mimoun (2016)	The measured attitude towards SNS and marketers' SNS profile mediated the relationship of the interdependent self-construal and the likelihood to recommend marketers' SNS profile.
Chang (2015)	The interaction orientation mediated the relationships of the interdependent self-construal and the facets of Facebook activities (responding to others, revealing the self). The subsequent research (Study 2) expanded the mediation model, where the interdependent self-construal significantly predicted the measured social goals, which in turn significantly predicted the interaction orientation that relate to the facets of Facebook activities.
Chen & Marcus (2012)	Individuals with high interdependent self-construal, but with low Extraversion, disclosed the least honest and the most audience-relevant information on SNS.
Chu et al. (2015)	The measured aspects of independent and interdependent self-construal positively predicted SNS intensity with Chinese and American users.
Ferenczi et al. (2017)	Male users tend to engage in antisocial use of Facebook due to the higher narcissistic tendencies. Female users tend to engage in prosocial use of Facebook due to their high level of relational self-construal.
Jiao et al. (2017)	The measured social values mediated the relationship of the interdependent self-construal and psychological well-being derived from SNS usage. The independent self-construal predicted content value, which in turn predicted self-esteem that led to psychological well-being.
Kim et al. (2010)	Social motivations of Facebook use mediated the relationship of the interdependent self-construal and the satisfaction with Facebook use.
Kim & Stavrositu (2018)	The experience of socially engaging emotions (both positive and negative) were positively associated with life satisfaction through high level of interdependence. The experience of positive disengaging emotions was positively associated with perceived control on Facebook amongst those with high level of independence.
Lee et al. (2012)	The measured community engagement self-efficacy and their social outcome expectations mediated the relationship of the interdependent self-construal and the consumers' eWOM behavioral intentions.
Lee et al. (2016)	The Autonomous-Related self-construal predicted SNS intensity positively for Malaysians, while negatively predicted SNS intensity for Koreans.
Long & Zhang (2014)	*British sample* The interdependent self-construal positively predict SNS motivations to manage image, to maintain privacy, to seek attention, and the concern for modesty. Analysis also revealed that the independent self-construal negatively predicted the same motivations. *Japanese sample* The interdependent self-construal positively predicted the SNS motivations to concern for modesty, to maintain privacy. The independent self-construal negatively predicted SNS motivations to ensure modesty, to manage image, and to maintain privacy.
Shim et al. (2016)	Public self-consciousness weakened the negative association between interdependent self-construal and positive self-presentation.

Similarly, systematic appraisal of the effect sizes is hindered by the diversity in the operationalization and quantification of SNS related outcomes. Some of the scales used to gauge SNS related outcomes were adapted directly from existing psychological scales, such as psychological well-being on SNS (Jiao et al., 2017) that was based on the construct of psychological well-being outlined by Diener et al. (2009). This has raised a concern on the validity of the measured construct. It is unclear if the existing constructs can be interpreted similarly in the context of SNS. Moreover, there is no clear theoretical or conceptual rationale for these adaptations. Although the FIS (Ellison et al., 2007) is a common scale used among the reviewed research articles (Chu et al., 2015; Lee et al., 2016), there is a lack of evidence to support its validity in measuring SNS engagement (Sigerson & Cheng, 2018). This indicates that the development of scales to gauge SNS related outcomes is still progressing. While it poses limitation to research, it indicates for new research opportunity.

The reviewed relationships differed, where some research articles posited the direct influence of self-construal on SNS related outcomes, whereas some findings unveiled the indirect effect of intervening variables on these relationship. These findings supported that the aspects of self-construal are the sources of cognitive consequences, affective consequences, and motivational consequences that eventually predict tangible behaviours such as SNS usages (Markus & Kitayama, 1991; see also Cross et al., 2011).

The two main cognitive consequences of self-construal are attention to the context or a designated relationship, and the information processing styles (Cross et al., 2011). The reviewed research articles mainly focused on the attentional aspects, which include the attentiveness and willingness to self-disclose (Chang, 2015), the degree of Extraversion (Chen & Marcus, 2012), social value elicited by SNS use (Jiao et al., 2017), and public self-consciousness (Shim et al., 2016). One research article focused on information processing style, which includes the users' self-efficacy to engage online community (Lee et al., 2012). The source of these aspects was the interdependent self-construal, which is consistent with the conceptualization of the heightened self-consciousness amongst individuals with high levels of interdependent self-construal in social setting (Markus & Kitayama, 1991). For the independent self-construal, the content value of SNS, which refers to the perceived benefit gained from SNS usage, determined its relationship with self-esteem that eventually predicted psychological well-being derived from SNS usage (Jiao et al., 2017). This finding posits that individuals with high independent self-construal exploit SNS to enhance their psychological well-being (Jiao et al., 2017), which is in accordance to the conceptualization of the independent self-construal, where social interaction is deemed as a mean to strategically position the self (Markus & Kitayama, 1991).

From the retrieved research articles, only a few investigated the relationships of self-construal and the affective aspects of SNS. The reviewed research articles posited the indirect effect of the measured attitudinal aspect of SNS on the relationship of the interdependent self-construal and the likelihood to recommend marketers' SNS profile (Bailey & Mimoun, 2016). This implicates that self-construal predict certain patterns of SNS usage by influencing users' emotional state, which is consistent with how self-construal was conceptualized to induce emotion (Markus & Kitayama, 1991). Another research posited that self-construal mediated the effects of the experience of engaging and disengaging emotions on life satisfaction. The experience of positive and negative socially engaging emotions predicted greater life satisfaction, mediated by the interdependent self-construal (Kim & Stavrositu, 2018). From the same research article, the experience of positive disengaging emotions positively predicted perceived control on Facebook, mediated by the independent self-construal (Kim & Stavrositu, 2018). These findings supported that emotion can alter behavioural outcomes by stimulating the corresponding self-construal (Markus & Kitayama, 1991).

Lastly, self-construal was theorized to affect individuals' motivations, where individuals with high levels of interdependent self-construal are expected to have salient social motives than those with high levels of independent self-construal (Cross et al., 2011; Markus & Kitayama, 1991). A research article supported the significant relationships of the aspects of self-construal and motivations to use SNS (Long & Zhang, 2014). The independent and interdependent self-construal predicted the motivations in coherent fashion, suggesting for the consistent effects of these self aspects on motivations. The subsequent research article supported the mediating effect of social motivation of Facebook use on the relationship of interdependent self-construal and satisfaction with Facebook (Kim et al., 2010). Additionally, the measured relational self-construal mediated the relationship of gender and the motives of SNS use. Specifically, female users tend to endorse this aspect of self-construal, which contribute to the prosocial use of Facebook (Ferenczi et al., 2017). This finding supports that females emphasize connectedness with their significant others (Cross et al., 2000; Cross et al., 2002), and thus, utilize SNS to consolidate the connection.

From this review, existing findings mainly supported the significance of the interdependent self-construal in predicting SNS related outcomes, justified by the connectedness of SNS (e.g. Ellison et al., 2007) that appeal to users with high levels of this aspect of self. Despite the connectedness of SNS, the independent self-construal that assert on uniqueness and competitiveness (Markus & Kitayama, 1991) can be conceptually linked to SNS usage. The vast literature has supported the link of SNS usage and narcissism (e.g. Buffardi & Campbell, 2008), which is a trait that has been conceptually link with the independent self-construal (Konrath, Bushman, & Grove, 2009). This supports the potential link of the independent self-construal and SNS related outcomes. Despite the connectedness of SNS, individuals with high levels of independent self-construal may benefit from using SNS (Jiao et al., 2017), potentially at the cost of other users due to their self-centredness (Ferenczi et al., 2017). Given that the antisocial usage is contradicting the connectedness of SNS (e.g. Ellison et al., 2007), this could a sign of pathological usage of SNS. In this light, recent findings have supported that narcissism is instrumental to the development of maladaptive features of SNS usage, such as problematic use of SNS (Kircaburun, Demetrovics, & Tosuntaş, 2018; Kircaburun, Jonason, & Griffiths, 2018) and SNS addiction (Andreassen, Pallesen, & Griffiths, 2017; Casale, Fioravanti, & Rugai, 2016). Due to the theoretical overlap of the independent self-construal and narcissism (Konrath et al., 2009), there is a possibility for the independent aspect of the self to facilitate similar problematic aspects of SNS. To illustrate, users that endorsed the independent aspect of the self are actively seeking social affirmation from the features on SNS, which eventually led to satisfaction on these online platforms (Jiao et al., 2017). The tendency to seek affirmation through SNS is similar to narcissistic users (Mehdizadeh, 2010). In this light, there is a clear support that the independent self-construal is a risk factor for maladaptive usages of SNS.

A few practical implications can be derived from this review. The reviewed findings supported that self-construal influence different psychological domains in eliciting the corresponding SNS usages. Therefore, instead of focusing on specific psychological domains that are deemed as impetuses of SNS usages, such as motivations to use SNS (e.g. Long & Zhang, 2014), practising psychologists have the alternative to focus on users' self-construal. Alteration of users' self-construal has the potential to induce changes in the corresponding psychological domains such as emotional state and motivations that directed SNS related outcomes. This can be applicable to managing problematic use of SNS that has been conceptually linked to the independent self-construal. Additionally, results suggested that corporates or business owners can enhance popularity of the maintained SNS profiles by exploiting features on these online platforms to promote climate that appeal to users (Bailey & Mimoun, 2016; Lee et al., 2012). The increased visibility will grant advantages to corporates and business owners to compete in the competitive market. Results supported the effect of the primed self-construal on the usages of SNS (Lee et al., 2012; Shim et al., 2016). This implicates that future research should consider the method of priming for certain psychological tendencies, such as the affective experience towards another's misfortune (Porter, Bhanwer, Woodworth, & Black, 2014), to investigate their effects on SNS usages. This will stimulate initiatives to design experiments, instead of correlational research that is incapable of eliciting causality.

A few limitations are notable in the present review. As an attempt to ensure quality of the reviewed findings, only peer-reviewed research articles were included. This has excluded other materials such as conference proceedings and doctoral dissertations, posing a severe limit on the materials available for the present review. Additionally, there is a lack of standardization in the reviewed research variables of self-construal and SNS related outcomes. Given the small amount of research articles available, it was not feasible to standardize these research variables as this will further reduce the amount of research articles available for review. However, these shortcomings reflect on the growing state of the literature. It is highly recommended for future researchers to replicate similar review with focused SNS related outcomes.

To conclude, the present systematic review has provided a novel elaboration on the relationships of the aspects of self-construal and SNS related outcomes. Despite the inconsistent conceptualization of self-construal and SNS related outcomes, the present systematic review supported the significance of self-construal in predicting SNS related outcomes. Future research is needed to address the methodological flaws identified in the present systematic review.

REFERENCES

Ames, D. R., Rose, P., & Anderson, C. P. (2006). The NPI-16 as a short measure of narcissism. *Journal of Research in Personality, 40*(4), 440–450. doi:10.1016/j.jrp.2005.03.002

Andreassen, C. S., Pallesen, S., & Griffiths, M. D. (2017). The relationship between addictive use of social media, narcissism, and self-esteem: Findings from a large national survey. *Addictive Behaviors, 64*, 287–293. doi:10.1016/j.addbeh.2016.03.006

Bailey, A. A., & Mimoun, M. S. B. (2016). Consumer social orientation-based personality and social media use: An exploration among young US consumers. *International Journal of Internet Marketing and Advertising, 10*(1-2), 1–27. doi:10.1504/IJIMA.2016.076977

Boyd, D. M., & Ellison, N. B. (2007). Social network sites: Definition, history, and scholarship. *Journal of Computer-Mediated Communication, 13*(1), 210–230. doi:10.1111/j.1083-6101.2007.00393.x

Buffardi, L. E., & Campbell, W. K. (2008). Narcissism and social networking web sites. *Personality and Social Psychology Bulletin, 34*(10), 1303–1314. doi:10.1177/0146167208320061

Casale, S., Fioravanti, G., & Rugai, L. (2016). Grandiose and vulnerable narcissists: Who is at higher risk for social networking addiction? *Cyberpsychology, Behavior, and Social Networking, 19*(8), 510515. doi:10.1089/cyber.2016.0189

Chang, C. (2015). Self-construal and Facebook activities: Exploring differences in social interaction orientation. *Computers in Human Behavior, 53*, 91–101. doi:10.1016/j.chb.2015.06.049

Cho, S. E., & Park, H. W. (2013). A qualitative analysis of cross-cultural new media research: SNS use in Asia and the West. *Quality & Quantity, 47*(4), 2319–2330. doi:10.100711135-011-9658-z

Choi, S. M., Kim, Y., Sung, Y., & Sohn, D. (2011). Bridging or bonding? A cross-cultural study of social relationships in social networking sites. *Information Communication and Society, 14*(1), 107–129. doi:10.1080/13691181003792624

Choi, Y. K., & Totten, J. W. (2012). Self-construal's role in mobile TV acceptance: Extension of TAM across cultures. *Journal of Business Research, 65*(11), 1525–1533. doi:10.1016/j.jbusres.2011.02.036

Chu, S. C., & Choi, S. M. (2010). Social capital and self-presentation on social networking sites: A comparative study of Chinese and American young generations. *Chinese Journal of Communication, 3*(4), 402–420. doi:10.1080/17544750.2010.516575

Chu, S. C., & Choi, S. M. (2011). Electronic word-of-mouth in social networking sites: A cross-cultural study of the United States and China. *Journal of Global Marketing, 24*(3), 263–281. doi:10.1080/089 11762.2011.592461

Chu, S. C., Windels, K., & Kamal, S. (2016). The influence of self-construal and materialism on social media intensity: A study of China and the United States. *International Journal of Advertising, 35*(3), 569–588. doi:10.1080/02650487.2015.1068425

Cross, S. E., Bacon, P. L., & Morris, M. L. (2000). The relational-interdependent self-construal and relationships. *Journal of Personality and Social Psychology, 78*(4), 791–808. doi:10.1037/0022-3514.78.4.791

Cross, S. E., Hardin, E. E., & Gercek-Swing, B. (2011). The what, how, why, and where of self-construal. *Personality and Social Psychology Review, 15*(2), 142–179. doi:10.1177/1088868310373752

DeAndrea, D. C., Shaw, A. S., & Levine, T. R. (2010). Online language: The role of culture in self-expression and self-construal on Facebook. *Journal of Language and Social Psychology, 29*(4), 425–442. doi:10.1177/0261927X10377989

Dehghani, M., & Tumer, M. (2015). A research on effectiveness of Facebook advertising on enhancing purchase intention of consumers. *Computers in Human Behavior, 49*, 597–600. doi:10.1016/j.chb.2015.03.051

Diener, E., Wirtz, D., Biswas-Diener, R., Tov, W., Kim-Prieto, C., Choi, D. W., & Oishi, S. (2009). New measures of well-being. In *Assessing well-being* (pp. 247–266). Dordrecht: Springer. doi:10.1007/978-90-481-2354-4_12

Diener, E. D., Emmons, R. A., Larsen, R. J., & Griffin, S. (1985). The satisfaction with life scale. *Journal of Personality Assessment, 49*(1), 71-75. doi: 4901_13 doi:10.1207/s15327752jpa

Donnellan, M. B., Oswald, F. L., Baird, B. M., & Lucas, R. E. (2006). The mini-IPIP scales: Tiny-yet-effective measures of the Big Five factors of personality. *Psychological Assessment, 18*(2), 192–203. doi:10.1037/1040-3590.18.2.192

Ellison, N. B., Steinfield, C., & Lampe, C. (2007). The benefits of Facebook "friends:" Social capital and college students' use of online social network sites. *Journal of Computer-Mediated Communication, 12*(4), 1143–1168. doi:10.1111/j.1083-6101.2007.00367.x

Ferenczi, N., Marshall, T. C., & Bejanyan, K. (2017). Are sex differences in antisocial and prosocial Facebook use explained by narcissism and relational self-construal? *Computers in Human Behavior*, *77*, 25–31. doi:10.1016/j.chb.2017.08.033

Frost, D., Goode, S., & Hart, D. (2010). Individualist and collectivist factors affecting online repurchase intentions. *Internet Research*, *20*(1), 6–28. doi:10.1108/10662241011020815

Gentile, B., Miller, J. D., Hoffman, B. J., Reidy, D. E., Zeichner, A., & Campbell, W. K. (2013). A test of two brief measures of grandiose narcissism: The Narcissistic Personality Inventory-13 and the Narcissistic Personality Inventory-16. *Psychological Assessment*, *25*(4), 1120–1136. doi:10.1037/a0033192

Gudykunst, W. B., Matsumoto, Y., Ting-Toomey, S., Nishida, T., Kim, K., & Heyman, S. (1996). The influence of cultural individualism-collectivism, self construals, and individual values on communication styles across cultures. *Human Communication Research*, *22*(4), 510–543. doi:10.1111/j.1468-2958.1996. tb00377.x

Hardin, E. E. (2006). Convergent evidence for the multidimensionality of self-construal. *Journal of Cross-Cultural Psychology*, *37*(5), 516–521. doi:10.1177/0022022106290475

Hardin, E. E., Leong, F. T., & Bhagwat, A. A. (2004). Factor structure of the self-construal scale revisited: Implications for the multidimensionality of self-construal. *Journal of Cross-Cultural Psychology*, *35*(3), 327–345. doi:10.1177/0022022104264125

Hoffman, D., Novak, T., & Stein, R. (2012, January 22). *Flourishing independents or languishing interdependents: Two paths from self-construal to identification with social media.* Retrieved from https:// papers.ssrn.com/sol3/papers.cfm?abstract_id=1990584

Hofstede, G. (1980). *Culture's consequences: International differences in work-related values.* Thousand Oaks, CA: Sage.

Hofstede, G. (2001). *Culture's consequences: Comparing values, behaviors, institutions, and organizations across nations.* Thousand Oaks, CA: Sage.

Hu, M., Zhang, M., & Luo, N. (2016). Understanding participation on video sharing communities: The role of self-construal and community interactivity. *Computers in Human Behavior*, *62*, 105–115. doi:10.1016/j.chb.2016.03.077

Jackson, L. A., & Wang, J. L. (2013). Cultural differences in social networking site use: A comparative study of China and the United States. *Computers in Human Behavior*, *29*(3), 910–921. doi:10.1016/j. chb.2012.11.024

Ji, Y. G., Hwangbo, H., Yi, J. S., Rau, P. P., Fang, X., & Ling, C. (2010). The influence of cultural differences on the use of social network services and the formation of social capital. *International Journal of Human-Computer Interaction*, *26*(11-12), 1100–1121. doi:10.1080/10447318.2010.516727

Jiao, Y., Jo, M. S., & Sarigöllü, E. (2017). Social value and content value in social media: Two paths to psychological well-being. *Journal of Organizational Computing and Electronic Commerce*, *27*(1), 3–24. doi:10.1080/10919392.2016.1264762

Jin, S. A. A., & Park, N. (2009). Parasocial interaction with my avatar: Effects of interdependent self-construal and the mediating role of self-presence in an avatar-based console game, Wii. *CyberPsychology & Behavior, 12*(6), 723-727. doi: 10.1089=cpb.2008.0289

Ju, A., Jeong, S. H., & Chyi, H. I. (2014). Will social media save newspapers? Examining the effectiveness of Facebook and Twitter as news platforms. *Journalism Practice, 8*(1), 1–17. doi:10.1080/17512 786.2013.794022

Jung, T., Youn, H., & McClung, S. (2007). Motivations and self-presentation strategies on Korean-based "Cyworld" weblog format personal homepages. *Cyberpsychology & Behavior, 10*(1), 24–31. doi:10.1089/cpb.2006.9996

Kagitcibasi, C. (2007). *Family, self, and human development across cultures: Theory and application* (2nd ed.). Mahwah, NJ: Lawrence Erlbaum Associates, Inc.

Kim, H., Coyle, J. R., & Gould, S. J. (2009). Collectivist and individualist influences on website design in South Korea and the US: A cross-cultural content analysis. *Journal of Computer-Mediated Communication, 14*(3), 581–601. doi:10.1111/j.1083-6101.2009.01454.x

Kim, J., & Lee, J. E. R. (2011). The Facebook paths to happiness: Effects of the number of Facebook friends and self-presentation on subjective well-being. *Cyberpsychology, Behavior, and Social Networking, 14*(6), 359–364. doi:10.1089/cyber.2010.0374

Kim, J., & Stavrositu, C. (2018). Feelings on Facebook and their correlates with psychological well-being: The moderating role of culture. *Computers in Human Behavior, 89*, 79–87. doi:10.1016/j.chb.2018.07.024

Kim, J. H., Kim, M. S., & Nam, Y. (2010). An analysis of self-construals, motivations, Facebook use, and user satisfaction. *International Journal of Human-Computer Interaction, 26*(11-12), 1077-1099. do i:10.1080/10447318.2010.516726

Kim, M. S., Shin, H. C., & Cai, D. (1998). Cultural influences on the preferred forms of requesting and re-requesting. *Communication Monographs, 65*(1), 47–66. doi:10.1080/03637759809376434

Kim, Y., Sohn, D., & Choi, S. M. (2011). Cultural difference in motivations for using social network sites: A comparative study of American and Korean college students. *Computers in Human Behavior, 27*(1), 365–372. doi:10.1016/j.chb.2010.08.015

Kircaburun, K., Demetrovics, Z., & Tosuntaş, Ş. B. (2018). Analyzing the links between problematic social media use, Dark Triad traits, and self-esteem. *International Journal of Mental Health and Addiction*, 1–12. doi:10.100711469-018-9900-1

Kircaburun, K., Jonason, P. K., & Griffiths, M. D. (2018). The Dark Tetrad traits and problematic social media use: The mediating role of cyberbullying and cyberstalking. *Personality and Individual Differences, 135*, 264–269. doi:10.1016/j.paid.2018.07.034

Kitayama, S., Markus, H. R., & Kurokawa, M. (2000). Culture, emotion, and well-being: Good feelings in Japan and the United States. *Cognition and Emotion, 14*(1), 93–124. doi:10.1080/026999300379003

Konrath, S., Bushman, B. J., & Grove, T. (2009). Seeing my world in a million little pieces: Narcissism, self-construal, and cognitive-perceptual style. *Journal of Personality, 77*(4), 1197–1228. doi:10.1111/ j.1467-6494.2009.00579.x

Leary, M. R., Kelly, K. M., Cottrell, C. A., & Schreindorfer, L. S. (2007). *Individual differences in the need to belong: Mapping the nomological network.* Unpublished manuscript, Duke University.

Lee, D., Kim, H. S., & Kim, J. K. (2012). The role of self-construal in consumers' electronic word of mouth (eWOM) in social networking sites: A social cognitive approach. *Computers in Human Behavior*, *28*(3), 1054–1062. doi:10.1016/j.chb.2012.01.009

Lee, S. L., Kim, J., Golden, K. J., Kim, J. H., & Park, M. S. A. (2016). A cross-cultural examination of SNS usage intensity and managing interpersonal relationships online: The role of culture and the autonomous-related self-construal. *Frontiers in Psychology*, *7*, 376. doi:10.3389/fpsyg.2016.00376

Leung, T., & Kim, M. S. (1997). *A revised self-construal scale.* Unpublished manuscript, University of Hawaii at Manoa, Honolulu.

Levine, T. R., Bresnahan, M. J., Park, H. S., Lapinski, M. K., Wittenbaum, G. M., Shearman, S. M., ... Ohashi, R. (2003). Self-construal scales lack validity. *Human Communication Research*, *29*(2), 210–252. doi:10.1111/j.1468-2958.2003.tb00837.x

Long, K., & Zhang, X. (2014). The role of self-construal in predicting self-presentational motives for online social network use in the UK and Japan. *Cyberpsychology, Behavior, and Social Networking*, *17*(7), 454–459. doi:10.1089/cyber.2013.0506

Luhtanen, R., & Crocker, J. (1992). A collective self-esteem scale: Self-evaluation of one's social identity. *Personality and Social Psychology Bulletin*, *18*(3), 302–318. doi:10.1177/0146167292183006

Markus, H. R., & Kitayama, S. (1991). Culture and the self: Implications for cognition, emotion, and motivation. *Psychological Review*, *98*(2), 224–253. doi:10.1037/0033-295X.98.2.224

Matsumoto, D. (1999). Culture and self: An empirical assessment of Markus and Kitayama's theory of independent and interdependent self-construals. *Asian Journal of Social Psychology*, *2*(3), 289–310. doi:10.1111/1467-839X.00042

Mehdizadeh, S. (2010). Self-presentation 2.0: Narcissism and self-esteem on Facebook. *Cyberpsychology, Behavior, and Social Networking*, *13*(4), 357–364. doi:10.1089/cyber.2009.0257

Miller, L. C., Berg, J. H., & Archer, R. L. (1983). Openers: Individuals who elicit intimate self-disclosure. *Journal of Personality and Social Psychology*, *44*(6), 1234–1244. doi:10.1037/0022-3514.44.6.1234

Na, J., Kosinski, M., & Stillwell, D. J. (2015). When a new tool is introduced in different cultural contexts: Individualism–collectivism and social network on Facebook. *Journal of Cross-Cultural Psychology*, *46*(3), 355–370. doi:10.1177/0022022114563932

National Heart, Lung, and Blood Institute. (2014). *Quality assessment tool for observational cohort and cross-sectional studies.* Retrieved from: https://www.nhlbi.nih.gov/health- pro/guidelines/in-develop/ cardiovascular-risk-reduction/tools/cohort

Oetzel, J. G. (1998). Explaining individual communication processes in homogeneous and heterogeneous groups through individualism-collectivism and self-construal. *Human Communication Research*, *25*(2), 202–224. doi:10.1111/j.1468-2958.1998.tb00443.x

Owe, E. (2013). *Unpacking cultural orientations: representations of the person and the self* (Doctoral dissertation). University of Sussex.

Palmgreen, P., & Rayburn, J. D. (1985). An expectancy-value approach to media gratifications. In K. E. Rosengren, L. A. Wenner, & P. Palmgreen (Eds.), *Media gratification research: Current perspectives* (pp. 61–72). Beverly Hills, CA: Sage.

Park, C., Jun, J., & Lee, T. (2015). Consumer characteristics and the use of social networking sites: A comparison between Korea and the US. *International Marketing Review, 32*(3/4), 414–437. doi:10.1108/IMR-09-2013-0213

Patwardhan, P. (2004). Exposure, involvement, and satisfaction with online activities: A cross- national comparison of American and Indian Internet users. Gazette. *The International Journal for Communication Studies, 66*, 411–436.

Pearlin, L. I., & Schooler, C. (1978). The structure of coping. *Journal of Health and Social Behavior, 19*(1), 2–21. doi:10.2307/2136319

Porter, S., Bhanwer, A., Woodworth, M., & Black, P. J. (2014). Soldiers of misfortune: An examination of the Dark Triad and the experience of schadenfreude. *Personality and Individual Differences, 67*, 64–68. doi:10.1016/j.paid.2013.11.014

Qiu, L., Lin, H., & Leung, A. K. Y. (2013). Cultural differences and switching of in-group sharing behavior between an American (Facebook) and a Chinese (Renren) social networking site. *Journal of Cross-Cultural Psychology, 44*(1), 106–121. doi:10.1177/0022022111434597

Richins, M. L., & Dawson, S. (1992). A consumer values orientation for materialism and its measurement: Scale development and validation. *The Journal of Consumer Research, 19*(3), 303–316. doi:10.1086/209304

Rosenberg, M. (1965). *Society and the adolescent self-image*. Princeton, NJ: Princeton University Press. doi:10.1515/9781400876136

Santor, D. A., Messervey, D., & Kusumakar, V. (2000). Measuring peer pressure, popularity, and conformity in adolescent boys and girls: Predicting school performance, sexual attitudes, and substance abuse. *Journal of Youth and Adolescence, 29*(2), 163–182. doi:10.1023/A:1005152515264

Scheier, M. F., & Carver, C. S. (1985). The self-consciousness scale: A revised version for use with general populations. *Journal of Applied Social Psychology, 15*(8), 687–699. doi:10.1111/j.1559-1816.1985.tb02268.x

Schwartz, S. H. (1992). Universals in the content and structure of values: Theoretical advances and empirical tests in 20 countries. *Advances in Experimental Social Psychology, 25*, 1–65. doi:10.1016/S0065-2601(08)60281-6

Shamseer, L., Moher, D., Clarke, M., Ghersi, D., Liberati, A., Petticrew, M., ... Stewart, L. A. (2015). Preferred reporting items for systematic review and meta-analysis protocols (PRISMA-P) 2015: Elaboration and explanation. *BMJ (Clinical Research Ed.), 349*(jan02 1), g7647. doi:10.1136/bmj.g7647

Shim, M., Lee-Won, R. J., & Park, S. H. (2016). The self on the Net: The joint effect of self- construal and public self-consciousness on positive self-presentation in online social networking among South Korean college students. *Computers in Human Behavior*, *63*, 530–539. doi:10.1016/j.chb.2016.05.054

Shin, D. H. (2010). Analysis of online social networks: A cross-national study. *Online Information Review*, *34*(3), 473–495. doi:10.1108/14684521011054080

Sia, C. L., Lim, K. H., Leung, K., Lee, M. K., Huang, W. W., & Benbasat, I. (2009). Web strategies to promote internet shopping: Is cultural-customization needed? *Management Information Systems Quarterly*, *33*(3), 491–512. doi:10.2307/20650306

Sigerson, L., & Cheng, C. (2018). Scales for measuring user engagement with social network sites: A systematic review of psychometric properties. *Computers in Human Behavior*, *83*, 87–105. doi:10.1016/j.chb.2018.01.023

Singelis, T. M. (1994). The measurement of independent and interdependent self-construals. *Personality and Social Psychology Bulletin, 20*(5), 580-591. doi: 167294205014 doi:10.1177/0146

Trafimow, D., Triandis, H. C., & Goto, S. G. (1991). Some tests of the distinction between the private self and the collective self. *Journal of Personality and Social Psychology*, *60*(5), 649–655. doi:10.1037/0022-3514.60.5.649

Triandis, H. C. (1989). The self and social behavior in differing cultural contexts. *Psychological Review*, *96*(3), 506–520. doi:10.1037/0033-295X.96.3.506

Tsai, W. H., & Men, L. R. (2012). Cultural values reflected in corporate pages on popular social network sites in China and the United States. *Journal of Research in Interactive Marketing*, *6*(1), 42–58. doi:10.1108/17505931211241369

Vasalou, A., Joinson, A. N., & Courvoisier, D. (2010). Cultural differences, experience with social networks and the nature of "true commitment" in Facebook. *International Journal of Human-Computer Studies*, *68*(10), 719–728. doi:10.1016/j.ijhcs.2010.06.002

Wagner, J. A. (1995). Studies of individualism-collectivism: Effects on cooperation in groups. *Academy of Management Journal*, *38*(1), 152–173. doi:10.5465/256731

Walen, H. R., & Lachman, M. E. (2000). Social support and strain from partner, family, and friends: Costs and benefits for men and women in adulthood. *Journal of Social and Personal Relationships*, *17*(1), 5–30. doi:10.1177/0265407500171001

Wheeless, L. R., & Grotz, J. (1976). Conceptualization and measurement of reported self- disclosure. *Human Communication Research*, *2*(4), 338–346. doi:10.1111/j.1468-2958.1976.tb00494.x

Wheeless, L. R., & Grotz, J. (1977). The measurement of trust and its relationship to self- disclosure. *Human Communication Research*, *3*(3), 250–257. doi:10.1111/j.1468-2958.1977.tb00523.x

This research was previously published in the International Journal of Cyber Behavior, Psychology and Learning (IJCBPL), 10(2); pages 1-18, copyright year 2020 by IGI Publishing (an imprint of IGI Global).

Chapter 19
Depressive Person Detection using Social Asian Elephants' (SAE) Algorithm over Twitter Posts

Hadj Ahmed Bouarara
https://orcid.org/0000-0002-4973-4385
GeCoDe Laboratory, Saida, Algeria

ABSTRACT

With the advent of the web and the explosion of data sources such as opinion sites, blogs and microblogs appeared the need to analyze millions of posts, tweets or opinions in order to find out what thinks the net surfers. The idea was to produce a new algorithm inspired by the social life of Asian elephants to detect a person in depressive situation through the analysis of twitter social network. The proposal algorithm gives better performance compared to data mining and bioinspired techniques such as naive Bayes, decision tree, heart lungs algorithm, social cockroach's algorithm.

INTRODUCTION AND PROBLEMATIC

Depression is an under-diagnosed disease, too often underestimated and yet widespread. It is as common as other major chronic conditions such as cardiovascular disease or diabetes, as evidenced by the fact that more than 20 million of persons each year live a major depressive situation.

According to the World Health Organization (WHO), approximately 11% of people suffer from major depression in their life. It affects young people aged of 15 to 24 years old. According to the WHO, by 2020, depression will become the second leading cause of disability worldwide, after cardiovascular disease. In very simple terms, it can be said that depression results in some way from an imbalance in brain chemistry. When a person is in depression, his body and mind send him warning signals to tell him that something is wrong. Listening to these signals we can provide a quicker diagnosis and put in place remedial measures (Finegold et al., 2013).

DOI: 10.4018/978-1-6684-6307-9.ch019

For example, being sad after losing a loved one or having a feeling of failure in case of problems at work is normal. But when these states of mind return each day for no particular reason or persist for a long time even with an identifiable cause, it can be a depression. Depression is actually a chronic disease, meeting specific diagnostic criteria. In addition to sadness, the depressed person maintains negative and devaluing thoughts: "I am really bad," "I will never succeed", "I hate who I am." She feels worthless and has trouble projecting herself into the future. She no longer has interest in previously popular activities. It is unclear what is the causes of depression, but it is likely a complex disease involving many factors related to heredity, biology, life events, and environment and habits. of life.

In recent years, we are in a digital world where information is available in large quantities and in various forms. 80% of this mass of information was in textual form. For this reason, we need specific tools to access sentiments and meanings hidden in these data, in order to reduce human intervention.

The sentiment analysis is an automatic process of written and spoken discourses by bringing out the different opinions expressed on a specific subject such as a brand, a news or a product. The importance of this paradigm is presented in several areas, namely policy, marketing, reputation management ...ect. It is a part of a broader area of study called NLP for Natural Language Processing with objective is to render a computer program understanding the codes of human language. The content of this chapter discusses the elaboration of new algorithms by the social life of Asian elephants to the problem of detecting depressed person by decision analysis of tweets.

The general structure of the paper will be as follows: we start with a state of the art for presenting the essential works in this topic, after we go on with a section detailing our approach and proposed components then an experimental and comparative study will be carried out for presenting the best results obtained. Finally, we will finish with a conclusion and describing some lines of thought that remain open and that we want to share them with you.

Stat of the Art

The work of Hatzivassiloglou and McKeown in 1997 consists in using the coordinating conjunctions present between a word already classified and an unclassified word, followed by the contributions of researcher Nasukawa and his team in 2003 who proposed a new method for extracting associated concepts from segments and summing the orientations of the opinion vocabulary present in the same segment (Chauan et al., 2017).

In the same year, researchers Yu and Hatzivassiloglou (2003) used the probability of ranking a word to measure the strength of the orientation of the named entities. In 2006, researchers Kanayama and Nasukawa (2006) as well as Ding and Liu in 2008 proposed, for their part, a learning-based approach that uses the coordination conjunctions present between a word already classified and a word unclassified.

The approaches of Pang et al introduced in 2002, and that of Charton and Acuna-Agost published in 2007 consist of classifying the texts according to a global polarity (positive, negative and neutral). These methods were optimized by Wilson and his research team in 2005. However, the difficulty lies in the constitution of these corpora of learning, which is a manual process to perform for each area studied. Finally, Vernier and his team (2009), have relied on a method of detection and categorization of the evaluations locally expressed in a corpus of multi-domain blogs. The second Dictionary-based Approach has had a lot of work. In 2015, Rosenthal and his team built General Inquiry which contains 3596 words labeled positive or negative. In Nakov and al work published in 2016, they use only adjectives for the detection of opinions. They manually build a list of adjectives they use to predict sentence direction and use WordNet to populate the list with synonyms and antonyms of polarity-known adjectives (Mishra et al., 2018).

PROPOSED APPROACH

The Social Life of ASIAN Elephant

Generally, elephants live in family group led by the oldest and experiment female, which coordinate the movements of the herd. She is the matriarch, big sister, mother, aunt, grandmother or great aunt for all group members. The matriarch has the knowledge of the group; she knows the migratory routes, the pace of seasons and important places to find water and vegetation. Herds can be divided temporarily to search for water sources or food while maintaining contact (Poole, 1999).

The Friendships and Communication

The elephants communicate between them directly and discreetly up to 10 KM of distance with an inaudible infrasound for us that are emitted by regular contractions of the muscles of the vocal organ. They are able to hear and emit infrasound which is transmitted over very long distances (less than 20Hz) that our ears do not perceive. Sometimes we look at elephants may seem solitary but they are certainly in communication with others without that we see them or hear them (Bates, 2007). Experiments have shown that elephants have knowledge of individual identities and they are able to recognize and keeps track of their family members (Bates, 2008). They will join the contact calls made by their friends (family member or former group) and especially if the caller elephant has a high index of association with the group. By cons, when elephants hearing appeals from an unknown contact (by elephants where there are no ties of friendship between them) their spatial cohesion increased and they withdrew from the area.

Foraging

The organization of the social life of elephants has a practical advantage: at times when resources are scarce, in case of drought, for example, the links are tightened and friends (group member) distant approach. Some provide the best seats around water points expelling unfamiliar elephants that are in these places.

For us, this tissue of complex relations represents a real social network, which requires important cognitive abilities such as: discussions at long distance by infrasound (very low sounds that propagate away) play an important role in maintaining friendships and also the memory of these giants which is an essential tool for remembering the services rendered or trouble caused by their cronies (McComb et al., 2001). Each elephant in a drought situation search the water points and follows the choice of its congeners. Each elephant when it finds water points it sends signals to inform their friends of the place of water. The elephants retain strong links between them also after a separation of more than one year.

The Scenario

A scenario that summarizes the social phenomenon of Asian elephants in search of food or water points in case of drought is: Initially, a set of elephants are looking for a water point in the space randomly. Elephants do not know where is the water point but they know exactly how far away is and the positions of their elephant friends, then the question that arises: what is the strategy followed to find the water in good conditions? The best solution is to follow the elephants having best position relative to the water point with which have a strong bond of friendship thus to follow the laws of the matriarch who guide the direction of the group.

Passage from Natural to Artificial

This part is dedicated to the passage of the natural life of social Asian elephants to artificial life as shown in Table 1.

Table 1. Passage from social life to artificial life of social Asian elephants' algorithm

Naturel	Artificial
An elephant joins the water point found by his family group	Each user is classified in the most appropriate class (depressive or non-depressive)
Suppose the case where there are only two water points in the search space	Two classes (depressive and no-depressive)
Environment	Search space (twitter)
Elephant	Twitter user
Group of elephants	The user's tweets (corpus)
Matriarch (oldest female)	Represents the message of the person with the highest score in the learning base
Best individual of each elephant group (initialization)	For each class it is the Person who has the best correlation with the centroid (barycenter)
Best individual (in process)	Best fitness function
Friendship link between elephant i and the best individual	α: link between each user and the best individual of each class (depressive or non-depressive)
Friendship link between the elephant I and the matriarch	β: link between each user and the matriarch of each class (depressive or non-depressive)
Communication between the elephant and the best individual	$\left| ME_T^g - E_T^i \right|$
Communication between the elephant i and the matriarch	$\left| PE_T^g - E_T^i \right|$

THE ARTIFICIAL LIFE OF SOCIAL ASIAN ELEPHANTS' (SAE) ALGORITHM

We have imitated the social life of Asian elephants and their water points search phenomenon in case of drought to formulate a new algorithm to detect depressive person by analyzing twitter network.

In our problem we have two classes depressive and no-depressive. The user status will be transformed to vectors. Each user with a velocity V is classified according to a fitness function based on his experience, the experiences of other users, the friendship relation that exists with the users of each class and the directives received by the matriarch of each class. The input of the algorithm is a set of twitter users' vectors (corpus), divided into two parts the learning basis and the test basis. The general process is detailed in Figure 1 and the stages of its operation are discussed later:

Figure 1. General architecture of social Asian elephants (SEA) algorithm for depressive person detection

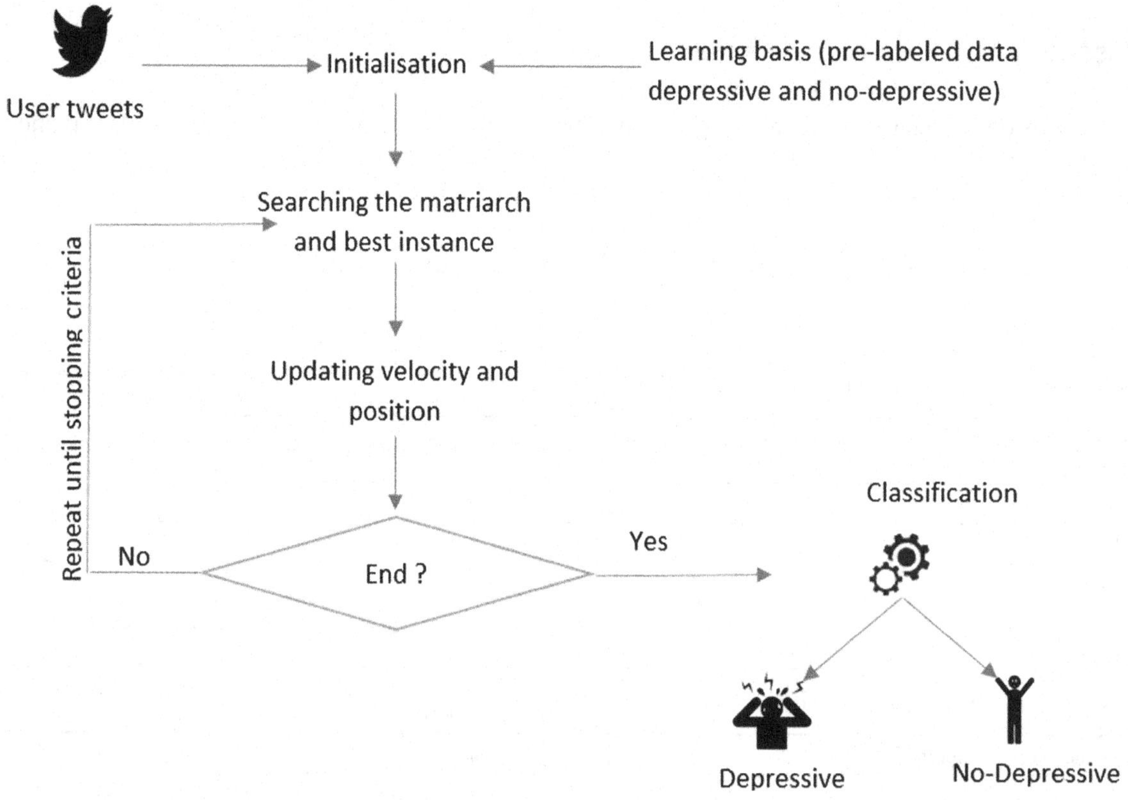

I.A.1. Initialisation

I.A.1. Initialy, the position E_0^i and the velocity V_0^i of each user relative to each class g are calculated by the next equations (1) et (2):

$$VE_0^i = score\left(i\right) \tag{1}$$

$$E_0^i\left(g\right) = \text{the linear correlation between instance i and the centroid of class g} \tag{2}$$

- $VE_0^i\left(g\right)$: The initial movement velocity of the user i.
- $E_0^i\left(g\right)$: The initial position of the instance t relative to the class g.

- *Score(i)*: The weights sum of the component's user vector i.

For the classification of a new instance (of the test database) the following process is launched:

Matriarch

We are looking for the matriarch of each class (depressive or no-depressive) that is the user with the highest score (the elephant female, the oldest and the most experienced).

$$Mt(g) = (\max(score(i)))g \tag{3}$$

- *Mt(g)*: The matriarch user at time t in class g.
- $(\max(score(i)))g$: the user that has the highest score in the class g.

Velocity

The movement velocity of each user changes from time t to t + 1 by the equation (4):

$$VE_{T+1}^{i}(g) = \frac{VE_{T}^{i}}{\alpha\left(\left\|ME_{T}^{g} - E_{T}^{i}\right\|\right) + \beta\left(\left\|PE_{T}^{g} - E_{T}^{i}\right\|\right)} \tag{4}$$

- VE_{T}^{i} : The movement velocity of the user i at time t relative to the class g.
- ME_{T}^{g} : The position of the best user at time t in class g (initially it is the closest user to the centroid of the class).
- E_{T}^{i} : The position of user i at time t relative to the class g.
- PE_{T}^{g} : The position of the matriarch of the class g at the time t.
- α: the friendship relation between the best user and the user i.
- β: the friendship relation between the matriarch and the user i.

The Position (Fitness Function)

This step calculates the new position of each user relative to each class through the equation (5):

$$E_{t+1}^{i}(g) = E_{t}^{i}(g) + VE_{t+1}^{i}(g) \tag{5}$$

- $E_{t}^{i}(g)$: position or fitness function of user i at time T in class g.
- g: has two values depressive or no-depressive.
- $VE_{t+1}^{i}(g)$: velocity of user i at time T + 1 in class g

Evaluation (Classification): Each user is classified in the class (depressive or no-depressive) with the lowest fitness function.

Update: After each iteration the parameters of the algorithm are updated. The same process will be repeated until stopping criterion (number of iteration).

Procedure

The next pseudo code summarizes the functioning of the social elephant algorithm for the detection of depressive people in twitter network.

Social elephants algorithm.

```
1: Elephant: twitter user
2: input:
3:          - corpus (learning basis, test basis)
4:          - Initialisation (E^i_{T=0}, V^i_{T=0})
5: T ← 0
7: while not CD do
8:          for each tweets user to be classified do
9:                  for each class g do
10:                         calculate
11:                         Mt(g) = (max(score(i)))g
12:                         find best user ME: with smaller position E
```

$$13: \quad VE^i_{T+1}(g) = \frac{VE^i_T}{\alpha\left(\left|ME^g_T - E^i_T\right|\right) + \beta\left(\left|PE^g_T - E^i_T\right|\right)}$$

$$14: \quad E^i_{t+1}(g) = E^i_t(g) + VE^i_{t+1}(g)$$

```
15:                  end for
16:                  L'instance(i) ← the class with the smallest fitness func-
tion
17:          end for
18:          update (ME, M, V)
19:          T ← T + 1
20: end while
21: output: the class of each user from the test basis.
```

Vectorization of tweets: for the vectorization of user tweets we use: i) text cleaning by eliminating special characters and numbers. ii) transforming tweets to a set of terms using bag of words, stemming or n-gram characters. ii) coding using TF (Term Frequency) or TF * IDF (term frequency * inversed document frequency).

TWEETS2011 CORPUS (TWEETS)

In our experiments we used the Tweets2011 corpus that was used in information retrieval famous competition called TREC 201. This specialized body built to keywords. The authors of this corpus have used the API to retrieve Twitter4J 649 tweets where they used keywords (politics, cinema, sport, music, war, science). After TREC in 2012 these tweets were classified in two class (depressive tweet, tweet not depressed) (McCreadlie et al., 2012). The following table 2 summarizes the classification of tweets.

Table 2. General statistical dataset Tweets2011

Category	Depressed	not depressed
Cinema	85	62
Policy	49	33
War	64	13
Sport	33	58
Music	119	56
Science	19	58

Validation Measures

The evaluation measures used to evaluate our algorithms are different and each measurement has a usage objective as shown in the following parts.

Confusion Matrix

Table 3 shows the confusion matrix.

Table 3. Confusion matrix

Contingency Matrix		Expert judgment	
		Real	False
Judgment of the algorithm	Real	VP_i	FP_i
	False	FN_i	VN_i
True positive (TP):	The number of instances assigned to a category properly (depressive).		
Negative real (VN):	The number of instances correctly assigned to the class not depressive. (Who does not have to be assigned to a category, and have not been)		
False Positive (FP)	The number of non-depressive and bodies that have been attributed to the depressive class. (Instances attributed to wrong categories)		
false negative (FN):	The number of depressive instances and have been assigned to the class not depressive. (Which should have been assigned to a category but who did not)		

The Tweets Correctly Analyzed

The percentage of people-ranked (as depressive and not-depressive).

Analyzed tweets:

The percentage of misclassified individuals (such as depressive and not-depressive).

kappa Static (K): Assessing the extent of agreement between two or more assessors is common in social sciences, behavioral and medical. Both evaluators are the algorithm and the actual class of the example. Consistency between the two evaluators bed is in the confusion matrix. The value of K is always between -1 and 1.

- K = 1 if the algorithms and expert judgment are the same.

- $K = -1$ if the algorithms and expert judgment are completely different.

$$K = \frac{P_0 - P_C}{1 - P_C}$$

- P_0: Number of people rank well

$$P_C = \frac{\sum_i A_i * R_i}{total^2}$$

- Total: total number of instances in the dataset.
- A_i: Sum of the line items i confusion matrix.
- R_i: Sum of columns in row i of the confusion matrix.

Precision (P): The accuracy measures the ability of an algorithm to return only those depressive. It represents the ratio between the number of individuals correctly classified by the algorithm in the depressive class relative to the total number of people classified by the algorithm in the depressive class.

$$P = \frac{VP_i}{VP_i + FP_i}$$

Recall (R): The recall measures the ability of our system to return-ranked institutions. It represents the ratio between the number of instances correctly classified by our system in deprssive class relative to the total number of documents actually in class c.

$$R = \frac{VP_i}{VP_i + FN_i}$$

f-measure: Used to group in a single number the performance of the algorithm. It is based on the results of the recall and precision.

$$F = \frac{2 * R * P}{R + P}$$

RESULTS AND DISCUSSION

In order to validate the quality of our proposal we have applied an experimental protocol by varying:

- Text representation methods.
- We set the parameters Alpha = 1 and beta = 1.

- Number of iteration.

with objective is to identify the sensitive parameters, we have fixed in each test one parameters and varying the others. We calculate the f-measure, entropy, recall precision kappa static. The best results are illustrated in the following tables.

NB: The boxes colored in blue represent the best results and the boxes colored in red represent the bad results.

Result with Variation of Text Representation

As a result of the different languages that exist in the world, finding the best message representation technique is a very important task. In this part, we set each time the technique of representation of text (N-grams-characters with N of 2 to 5 and bag of words) and we vary the other parameters. The results are shown in the table 4 and figures 2 and 3.

Table 4. The results of analysis using the Asian elephant's algorithm for detecting depressive person in twitter with variation of representation techniques

		Evaluation measures							
		Precision	Recall	f-measure	TS (%)	TE (%)	static kappa	Confusion matrix	
Text representation techniques	Bag of words	0. 724	0. 699	0.7	67.79%	32.21%	0354	258	98
								111	182
	Stemming	0. 786	0617	0.6913	68.72%	31.28%	0386	228	62
								141	218
	2-gram characters	0.819	0.7235	0.769	75.19%	24.81%	0.5038	267	59
								102	221
	3-gram characters	0.86	0.764	0811	79.81	20.19	0.596	282	44
								87	236
	4-gram characters	0.918	0.791	0.854	84.12%	15.86%	0688	292	26
								77	254
	5-gram characters	0844	0.764	0802	78.58	21.42	0.56	282	52
								87	228

By observing the table and the previous figures we found that the technique N-grams characters (the blue boxes) allows to obtain the best results compared to the representation bag of words with a F = 0.85, TS = 84% and kappa static = 0.68. A discussion and interpretation of the different results is detailed below:

The n-gram representation is tolerant to the problems of copy-and-paste technology and especially when copying a tweet from a PDF document, a Word document or from a web page.

Figure 2. Number of tweets depressive and not-depressive obtained by the Asian elephants algorithm classified by categories

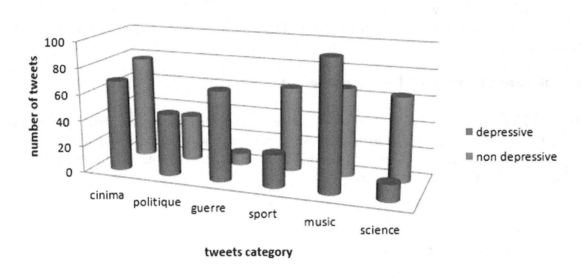

Figure 3. Comparison of text representation techniques results using the Asian elephants algorithm

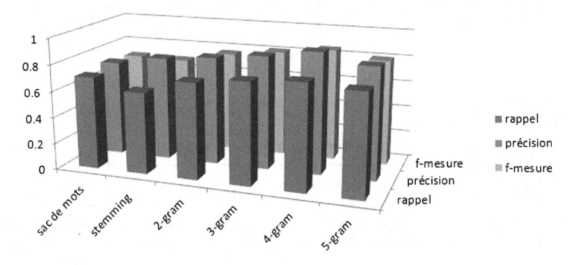

- Some characters of the copied words will be imperfect for example, it is possible that the word "text-mining" is copying "text-ining". A word bag method will have trouble recognizing that it is the word "mining" whereas the technique N-grams characters takes into account other N-grams like 'ini', nin and ing to recognize the word. It can also detect compound words such as "united state" or "data mining", but the word bag method ignores them.
- The bag of word technique requires a semantic and syntactic treatment to remove the ambiguity related to the words and sentences, which is not the case in our work where we have not applied linguistic treatment on the texts because the computer implementation of these procedures is rela-

tively cumbersome. On the other hand, the N-grams technique is independent to the language and makes it possible to treat the tweets of the users in their raw states

- the major drawback of the stemming technique is the loss of complete information on the terms since it is not based on powerful linguistic constraints, which can lead to an amplification of noise and semantic confusions by grouping under the same root words of different meanings. Like the lexical root "port" which groups in the same set the verb "to wear" and the name "port" whereas semantically are very distinct. On the other hand, the technique n-grams is perfectly adapted for texts coming from noisy source and it can lead us to obtain free the roots of the words. For example, the words advance, advance, advance, and advancement automatically have much in common when considered as sets of N-grams. Another advantage is its ability to work with both short and long documents.

- The representation N-grams is dependent on a parameter N and the question which arises: What is the value of N optimal? Analyzing the returned results, we find that N = 4 has spawned the production of relevant terms to allow the Asian elephants algorithm to differentiate between depressive tweets and not-depressive tweets.

Results with variation of iteration number:

Table 5 and Figures 4 and 5 summarize the influence of the parameter iteration number in the obtained results.

The results clearly show that the stopping criterion is a sensitive parameter because the quality of results of the social elephant algorithm change with the variation of the iterations number. The analysis in Table 6 revealed the following observations:

Table 5. The analysis results using the Asian elephants' algorithm and variation of distance measures

		Validation Measures						Confusion matrix	
		Precision	Recall	f-measure	TS (%)	TE (%)	static kappa		
Distances measures	10	0.74	0.59	0.654	65.48%	34.52%	0313	221	76
								148	204
	40	0.918	0.791	0.854	84.12%	15.86%	0688	292	26
								77	254
	80	0.781	0715	0.745	72.41%	27.59%	0.45	264	74
								105	206
	120	0.7217	0674	0.699	66.71	33.29	0347	249	96
								120	184

Figure 4. The results of analysis using the asian elephants algorithm for detecting depressive person in twitter with variation of iterations number

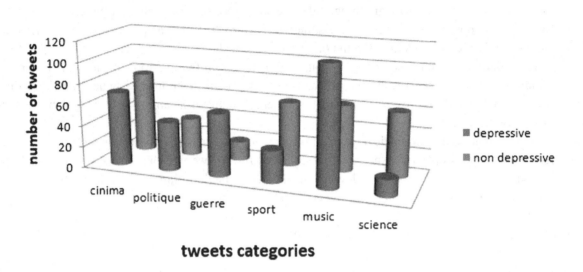

Figure 5. Comparison of distance measurements using Asian elephants

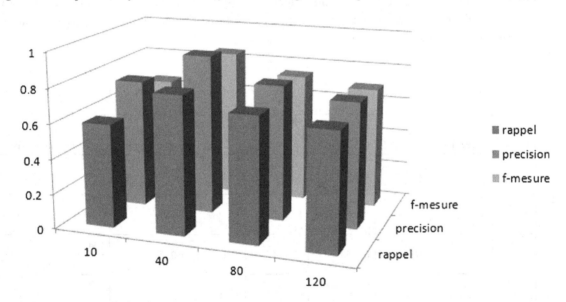

Comparative Study

in order to reference the results of our algorithm we conducted a comparative study with classical techniques (naive bayes, decision tree, KNearest Neighbor) and with bioinspired techniques integrated in the EBIRI tool (machine heart lungs and social cockroaches algorithm (Bouarara et al., 2015)).

Table 6. Comparison results of the social elephant algorithm with other algorithms that exist in the literature for the problem of depressive person detection

		Valuation Measures						Contingency Matrix	
		Precision	Recall	f-measure	TS (%)	Recall (%)	static kappa		
Algorithms	Naive bayes	0.781	0715	0745	72.41%	27.59%	0.45	264	74
								105	206
	Decision tree	0608	0.51	0558	53.62%	46.48%	0.09	190	122
								179	158
	Asian elephants algorithm	0918	0791	0854	84.12%	15.86%	0688	292	26
								77	254
	Algorithm cockroaches	**0.92**	**0.74**	**0.82**	**82.43**	**17.57**	**0.65**	**276**	**21**
								93	**259**
	Heart lung machine	**0.88**	**0.82**	**0848**	**84.28**	**15.72**	**0.68**	**306**	**39**
								63	**241**

The results of this part validate our originally set goal where our algorithm is better than the like algorithms and gives the same performance as the algorithm because our proposal is based on the principle that the solution needs to improve from iteration to another through the intelligence of the group.

CONCLUSION

detecting depressed people is a very difficult task because the feelings of people are not stable and can change from one minute to another and especially based on information shared in virtual world (tweeter). According to our results we notice that Asian elephant's algorithm gives better performances compared to others classical and bioinspired algorithms.

Finally, we propose that Social network owners must add an option to analyze the status of each user to say that a person is in a normal or depressive situation by suggesting those users to:

- Consult a doctor or psychologist because There are many effective treatment modalities against depression, including medications (eg. antidepressants) and psychotherapy.
- Get as much information as possible about depression and how it is treated. This will allow you to understand what is happening to you and make informed decisions.
- Adopt a healthy lifestyle and Work less if necessary, avoid sources of unnecessary stress, allow yourself hours of rest and sleep, and eat well are all measures that can help you get back on your feet quickly.

Future Works

We will apply the algorithm to the problem of suspicious person detection, spam filtering, DNA classification, information retrieval, sentiment analysis in video, plagiarism detection, and all classification problem supervised or unsupervised.

REFERENCES

Artzy, E., Frieder, G., & Herman, G. T. (1981). The theory, design, implementation and evaluation of a three-dimensional surface detection algorithm. *Computer Graphics and Image Processing, 15*(1), 1–24. doi:10.1016/0146-664X(81)90103-9

Bickel, P. J., & Levina, E. (2004). Some theory for Fisher's linear discriminant function, naive Bayes' and Some alternatives When there are many more variables than observations. *Bernoulli, 10*(6), 989–1010. doi:10.3150/bj/1106314847

Bouarara, HA, & Hamou, RM (2017). Bio-Inspired Environment for Information Retrieval (Ebiri): innovations from nature. European academic editions.

Bouarara, H. A., Hamou, R. M., & Amin, A. (2015). Novel Bio-Inspired Technology of Artificial Social Cockroaches (CSA). *International Journal of Organizational and Collective Intelligence, 5*(2), 47–79. doi:10.4018/IJOCI.2015040103

Bouarara, H. A., Hamou, R. M., & Amin, A. (2015). A Novel Bio-Inspired Approach for Multilingual Spam Filtering. *International Journal of Intelligent Information Technologies, 11*(3), 45–87. doi:10.4018/IJIIT.2015070104

Bouarara, H. A., Hamou, R. M., & Amine, A. (2015). New Swarm Intelligence Technique of Artificial Social Cockroaches for Suspicious Person Detection Using N-Gram Pixel with Visual Result Mining. [IJSDS]. *International Journal of Strategic Decision Sciences, 6*(3), 65–91. doi:10.4018/IJSDS.2015070105

Charton, E., & Acuna-Agost, R. (2007). Quel modèle pour détecter une opinion? Trois propositions pour généraliser l'extraction d'une idée dans un corpus. *Actes du troisième DÉfi Fouille de Textes*, 35.

Chauhan, R., Kaur, H., & Chang, V. (2017). Advancement and applicability of classifiers for variant exponential model to optimize the accuracy for deep learning. *Journal of Ambient Intelligence and Humanized Computing*.

Ding, Y., Liu, X., Zheng, Z. R., & Gu, P. F. (2008). Freeform LED lens for uniform illumination. *Optics Express, 16*(17), 12958–12966. doi:10.1364/OE.16.012958 PMID:18711534

Finegold, J. A., Asaria, P., & Francis, D. P. (2013). Mortality from ischaemic heart disease by country, region, and age: Statistics from World Health Organisation and United Nations. *International Journal of Cardiology, 168*(2), 934–945. doi:10.1016/j.ijcard.2012.10.046 PMID:23218570

Hatzivassiloglou, V., & McKeown, K. R. (1997, July). Predicting the semantic orientation of adjectives. In *Proceedings of the 35th annual meeting of the association for computational linguistics and eighth conference of the European chapter of the association for computational linguistics* (pp. 174-181). Association for Computational Linguistics.

Kanayama, H., & Nasukawa, T. (2006, July). Fully automatic lexicon expansion for domain-oriented sentiment analysis. In *Proceedings of the 2006 conference on empirical methods in natural language processing* (pp. 355-363). Association for Computational Linguistics. 10.3115/1610075.1610125

McComb, K., Moss, C., Durant, S. M., Baker, L., & Sayialel, S. (2001). Matriarchs as repositories of social knowledge in African elephants. *Science, 292*(5516), 491–494. doi:10.1126cience.1057895 PMID:11313492

McCreadie, R., Soboroff, I., Lin, J., Macdonald, C., Ounis, I., & McCullough, D. (2012, August). One building has reusable Twitter corpus. In *Proceedings of the 35th International ACM SIGIR conference on Research and development in information retrieval* (pp. 1113-1114). ACM.

Mishra, K. K., Bisht, H., Singh, T., & Chang, V. (2018). A direction aware particle swarm optimization with sensitive swarm leader. *Big data research, 14*, 57-67.

Nakov, P., Ritter, A., Rosenthal, S., Sebastiani, F., & Stoyanov, V. (2016). SemEval-2016 task 4: Sentiment analysis in Twitter. In *Proceedings of the 10th international workshop on semantic evaluation (semeval-2016)* (pp. 1-18). 10.18653/v1/S16-1001

Nasukawa, T., & Yi, J. (2003, October). Sentiment analysis: Capturing favorability using natural language processing. In *Proceedings of the 2nd international conference on Knowledge capture* (pp. 70-77). ACM. 10.1145/945645.945658

Pang, B., Lee, L., & Vaithyanathan, S. (2002, July). Thumbs up?: sentiment classification using machine learning techniques. In *Proceedings of the ACL-02 conference on Empirical methods in natural language processing-Volume 10* (pp. 79-86). Association for Computational Linguistics. 10.3115/1118693.1118704

Poole, J. (1999). Signals and assessment in African elephants: Evidence from playback experiments. *Animal Behaviour, 58*(1), 185–193. doi:10.1006/anbe.1999.1117 PMID:10413556

Rosenthal, S., Nakov, P., Kiritchenko, S., Mohammad, S., Ritter, A., & Stoyanov, V. (2015). Semeval-2015 task 10: Sentiment analysis in twitter. In *Proceedings of the 9th international workshop on semantic evaluation (SemEval 2015)* (pp. 451-463). 10.18653/v1/S15-2078

Vernier, M., Monceaux, L., Daille, B., & Dubreil, E. (2009). Catégorisation des évaluations dans un corpus de blogs multi-domaine. *Revue des nouvelles technologies de l'information*, 45-70.

Wilson, T., Wiebe, J., & Hoffmann, P. (2005, October). Recognizing contextual polarity in phrase-level sentiment analysis. In *Proceedings of the conference on human language technology and empirical methods in natural language processing* (pp. 347-354). Association for Computational Linguistics. 10.3115/1220575.1220619

Yu, H., & Hatzivassiloglou, V. (2003, July). Towards answering opinion questions: Separating facts from opinions and identifying the polarity of opinion sentences. In *Proceedings of the 2003 conference on Empirical methods in natural language processing* (pp. 129-136). Association for Computational Linguistics. 10.3115/1119355.1119372

This research was previously published in the International Journal of Organizational and Collective Intelligence (IJOCI), 9(4); pages 37-51, copyright year 2019 by IGI Publishing (an imprint of IGI Global).

Chapter 20
Users Holding Accounts on Multiple Online Social Networks:
An Extended Conceptual Model of the Portable User Profile

Sarah Bouraga

University of Namur, Belgium

Ivan Jureta

Fonds de la Recherche Scientifique, Belgium & University of Namur, Belgium

Stéphane Faulkner

University of Namur, Belgium

ABSTRACT

The last decade has seen an increasing number of online social network (OSN) users. As they grew more and more popular over the years, OSNs became also more and more profitable. Indeed, users share a considerable amount of personal information on these sites, both intentionally and unintentionally. And thanks to this enormous user base, social networks are able to generate recommendations, attract numerous advertisers, and sell data to companies. This situation has sparked a lot of interest in the research community. Indeed, users grow more uncomfortable with the idea that they do not have full control over their own data. The lack of control can even be amplified when a user holds an account on various OSNs. The data she shares is then spread over multiple platforms. This chapter addresses the notion of portable profile, which could help users to gain more control or more awareness of the data collected about her. In this chapter, the authors discuss the advantages and drawbacks of a portable profile. Secondly, they propose a conceptual model for the data in this unified profile.

DOI: 10.4018/978-1-6684-6307-9.ch020

INTRODUCTION

An area of the Web 2.0 gaining increasing success globally is the Online Social Network (OSN), or Social Networking Site (SNS). OSN refers to, according to Ellison et al. (2007):

Web-based services that allow individuals to (1) construct a public or semi-public profile within a bounded system, (2) articulate a list of other users with whom they share a connection, and (3) view and traverse their list of connections and those made by others within the system. The nature and nomenclature of these connections may vary from site to site."

The last decade has seen an increasing number of OSN users. These systems allow their users to interact with one another. Users set up an account, state relationships with other users, and are then able to communicate with each other, and share content. The most popular OSNs, such as Facebook, Twitter, or LinkedIn count hundreds of millions of members, that is, of users who have registered and thereby can use the features of these OSNs.

The first social network site was introduced in 1997. Called SixDegrees.com, it allowed its members to create a profile, list their Friends and, later to view others' friends lists (Ellison et al., 2007). As they grew more and more popular over the years, OSNs became also more and more profitable. Users share a considerable amount of personal information on these sites, both intentionally and unintentionally. And thanks to this enormous user base, OSNs are able to generate recommendations; attract numerous advertisers; and sell data to interested third parties.

This situation has led to the users' growing reluctance to share information. Users are uncomfortable with the idea that they do not have full control over their own data. In response, most current OSNs offer the possibility to their members to manage their privacy settings; allowing them to control who sees what about them and the content that they shared.

The increasing popularity of the OSN, and the questionable use of the data by the OSN have led to considerable interest in the research community. Many authors, for instance, have addressed the privacy and trust issues (Dwyer et al., 2007; Strater & Lipford, 2008; Madejski et al., 2011).

A way to increase the user trust in OSNs could be the introduction of a portable profile. It would be portable, in the sense that if a user registers on OSN A, she would be able to carry over the content of her profile to OSN B, and choose which of that data and content would appear on OSN B. The portable profile would offer more transparency to users, as they would know what data in some sense defines them on an OSN. This topic about the introduction of an integrated profile has also been mentioned in the literature (Heckmann et al., 2005; Berkovsky et al., 2008; Abel et al., 2011; Kapsammer et al., 2012).

This paper has two objectives and corresponding contributions. Firstly, we aim at listing the advantages and drawbacks of a portable profile, from the perspective of the user and from the perspective of the OSN. We will identify these benefits and limitations via an example. Secondly, we find the content for the portable user profile by looking at the content of user profiles on various existing OSNs, and from there propose a preliminary conceptual model of the portable user profile.

The rest of this article is organized as follows. Related work is introduced in Section 2. In Section 3, we discuss the motivations for a Portable User Profile (PUP). The proposed conceptual model for PUP is presented in Section 4. Finally, we discuss the results and conclude the paper in Sections 5 and 6 respectively.

LITERATURE REVIEW

Online Social Networks

Various aspects of OSNs have been studied. For example, there are studies focusing on the properties of the graph induced by connections between users. Some of the analyzed OSNs include: Flickr, YouTube, LiveJournal and Orkut (Mislove et al., 2007); MySpace and Orkut (Ahn et al., 2007); Sina blogs and Xiaonei SNS, two large Chinese online social networks (Fu et al., 2008); Flickr and Yahoo! 360 (Kumar et al., 2010); and Twitter (Kwak et al., 2010).. For an example of findings, consider Mislove et al. (2008), who found that various OSNs, despite their different purposes, share a number of similar structural features, namely: highly skewed degree distribution, a small diameter, and significant local.

The reasons why people want to use an OSN have also been examined in the literature. Various authors have studied the reasons motivating teenagers (Livingstone, 2008), college students (Park et al., 2009) or young adults (Subrahmanyam et al., 2008) to use an OSN. These reasons range from satisfying a "*friend*" and connection needs to having an additional source of information (Raacke & Bonds-Raacke, 2008; Subrahmanyam et al., 2008).

The privacy issue was examined by several authors. They include the study of privacy on Facebook (Strater & Lipford, 2008; Madejski et al., 2011); as well as the comparison of trust and privacy issues on Facebook and MySpace (Dwyer et al., 2007).

Specific social networks were also studied in more details: MySpace (Caverlee &Webb, 2008); Facebook (Lampe et al., 2006; Pempek et al., 2009); YouTube (Lange, 2007); and Massively Multiplayer Online Games (MMOGs) (Ducheneaut et al., 2006).

User Profile

In the area of OSNs, the topic of the user profile has been researched. Some authors have proposed approaches to compare the profiles of two users, more specifically to measure the distance between two user profiles in an OSN (Rezaee et al., 2012). The similarity between users has been measured based on the information on their Orkut profile (Singh & Tomar, 2009); the correlation between the similarity of two aNobbi (an OSN for book lovers) users' profile and the link between these two users (Aiello et al., 2010). Mislove et al. (2010) also explored the possibility to infer the attributes of some users in an OSN, given the attributes of some users in the same OSN. Our work here is different from these because we are trying to define a generic profile, that would fit any type of OSNs. The cited works here compare user profiles based on their content. We are trying to identify this content before being able to compare two profiles or to execute any kind of manipulations on the user profile.

Other authors have carried out sociological studies based on the user profile. Some researchers studied the popularity of users. More specifically, Lampe et al. (2007) studied the role played by elements of a Facebook user profile in the creation of online connections. They discovered that the more fields a user populates in her profile; the more friends she will have. The factors determining the profile popularity in a professional social network were also examined (Strufe, 2010). Utz (2010) studied how the perceived popularity, communal orientation, and social attractiveness of a user on an OSN (here Hyves) are influenced by the user's extraversion, the extraversion of the user's friends, and the number of friends a user has. Utz et al. (2011) examined the effects of OSN use on romantic relationships. Dunbar et al. (2015) used Facebook and Twitter profiles to create ego-centric social networks. The authors discovered that the structure of OSN mirrors those in the face-to-face networks. Our work here is different from these because we are not interested in the sociological aspect of the user profile. Sociological aspects can have an influence and we investigated that in another work (Bouraga et al., 2015), where we identified factors that can have an influence on the perceived relevance of content. However, for the definition of a generic profile, we are not interested in that area.

The type of information users share on their profile was evaluated by several authors: Nosko et al. (2010) examined the kinds of information Facebook users shared on their profile; Emmanuel et al. (2013) examined the type of information users share on their profile, depending on the context of the social network (the dating OSN and the professional OSN). Silfverberg et al. (2011) explored the effort members of Last.fm (an OSN dedicated to music preferences) invest in the process of maintaining their profile (they called this process "profile work"); that is in the process of controlling their "self-presentation". Chen et al. (2014) modeled profile privacy settings from a game theoretic perspective. Their model shows that users choose for the highest possible privacy if they encounter any risk, regardless of any incentive for profile disclosure. Our work presents some similarities with the cited works here, because the latter identify the types of information shared by users on their profile. However, the difference between the existing work and our work lies in the generality of the models. The cited works define the types of information in a specific context (the information shared on the Facebook profile, the information shared depending on the context of the OSN, the information shared in the context of self-presentation, and in the context of privacy settings management). However, in this paper, we aim to identify generic attributes of a user profile.

Various authors examined the link between the information users share on their profile and the threats they can face as an OSN user. Given the amount of personal information shared on OSN, users are vulnerable to "social engineering attacks". Alim et al. (2011) proposed an automated approach to extract profile data in order to assess the vulnerability of the user. Kontaxis et al. (2011) developed a tool to automatically detect social network profile cloning. Also, My3, a "privacy- aware decentralized OSN", was proposed, enabling its users to have "full access control on their data" (Narendula et al., 2011). Fire et al. (2014) reviewed various threats OSN users can face, such as fake profile or face recognition, and proposed solutions to address these threats, such as fake or cloned profile detection. Before conducting further analysis, this paper aims at the definition of a generic profile. Thus, we are not interested, for now, in the threats a user faces when sharing certain types of information.

Authors are aware that people hold an account on different OSNs. Therefrom, various solutions were proposed to identify the same user on different OSNs. Examples include Nie et al. (2016) who introduced the Dynamic Core Interests Mapping (DCIM) algorithm to match the same user on various OSNs; and Ma et al. (2017) who proposed a solution called MapMe based on both the user profile as well as the user relationship network structures. Komamizu et al. (2017) identified the same users who were both on Github and Stackoverflow. And Zhou et al. (2016) proposed the FRUI algorithm based on friend relationship. The purpose of this article is different from these studies because we are not interested in identifying the same user with a different OSN profiles, rather we want to propose a conceptual model that will gather all the information shared by the user on these various OSNs.

Finally, several researchers have examined the interest of integrating data from various OSN profiles into one user profile. Zhang et al. (2014a, 2014b) addressed the linkage of people having a profile on different OSNs. The difficulty lies in the fact that people may have different usernames on different OSNs. The difference between their work and ours is the motivation behind it. Zhang et al. aimed for a holistic understanding of the OSN user; while we aim to propose a conceptual model of a portable user profile. Heckmann et al. (2005) introduced "GUMO - the General User Model Ontology". The authors used OWL as ontology language to represent "the user model terms and their interrelationships". The motivation for their work is similar to ours, that is, the authors sought "the simplification for exchanging user model data between different user-adaptive systems". However, our work is different from GUMO with regard to two elements. First, we focus here on the OSNs, while GUMO has a larger scope and is meant for intelligent semantic web environments. Secondly, Heckmann et al. developed their ontology for the benefits of the systems; while we take into account the user perspective. Berkovsky et al. (2008) proposed an approach to import and integrate data from several remote RSs to enhance the efficiency of another RS. The recommendations are more accurate thanks to more complete user profiles. The authors call the process of importing and integrating data "the mediating process". More specifically, they define the latter as "mediation of user models is a process of importing the user modeling data collected by other (remote) recommender systems, integrating them and generating an integrated user model for a specific goal within a specific context" (Berkovsky et al., 2008). Abel et al. (2011) examined cross-system user modeling strategies, consisting of the following building blocks: source of user data, semantic enrichment, and weighting scheme. The authors, then, evaluate the strategies' "performance in generating valuable profiles in the context of tag and resource recommendation in Flickr, Twitter, and Delicious". Kapsammer et al. (2012) proposed a "semi-automatic approach to derive social network schemas from social network data". Their process consists of four phases, namely: data extraction, schema extraction, transformation, and integration.

MOTIVATION FOR CENTRALIZED PROFILE

Throughout this Section, we will look at a hypothetical user who is using Facebook, LinkedIn, and Pinterest. We chose these three OSNs because they have different purposes, and the PUP should not be specific to the kind of OSN. Facebook and LinkedIn are network-oriented, that is they put the emphasis on the relationships between users. However, they still differ in purposes. The former is used by people who want to connect with friends; while the latter is used for business contacts. Pinterest is of the knowledge-sharing type, that is the focus is on the content sharing, instead of the relationships (Guo et al., 2009).

To use all three OSNs under the same offline identity, the user has to fill in the same information at all three OSNs, such as name, email, location, gender, profile picture, an "About you" section, and so on. Facebook and LinkedIn also offer the user to share the following elements: her occupation (the school she attends or attended), the job(s) she has (had); her skills (Facebook communicates the languages the user can speak, while LinkedIn introduces the users qualifications, summary, areas of expertise); her interests.

On all three OSNs, the user has to find friends and/or other users to follow. The more active a user is on a social network, the more she can get out of it. The network effect is that the more friends you have, the more valuable the experience can be.

Currently, business models of OSNs aim to make profit by (i) allowing companies to post targeted ads, based on user data; and (ii) selling data about usage to companies. It follows that OSNs do not have incentives to integrate their user data and provide the users with a portable and accessible profile. On the contrary, OSNs are incentivized to keep all the data they gather about their users for themselves, since these data constitute the product they sell to advertisers. Several OSNs allow some connections with other OSNs, to sign in, to share post, and/or find friends. For instance, users of Facebook and LinkedIn can share post across networks, that is they can post simultaneously on both OSNs; also Facebook users can sign in and find friends more easily on Pinterest with their Facebook account. However, this form of collaboration already impairs the collection of user data by social networks; as evidenced by Yahoos decision in March 2014 to discard the use of Facebook and Google to sign in and log into Yahoo services.

Benefits of a Portable User Profile

Several authors in the literature have already put forward some benefits of an "integrated" profile, such as: an enriched user profile (Abel et al., 2010), and improved quality of the recommendations (Berkovsky et al., 2008; Abel et al., 2011; Kapsammer et al., 2012).

Abel et al. (2010) argue that a profile aggregation can lead to an enriched user profile. An aggregated profile offers "significantly more information about the users than individual service profiles can provide". Profile aggregation can be used to improve incomplete profiles. Thus, the user could fill in her profile only once but the information will still be present in every site she uses.

Example 1: Without the PUP: The user has to enter all her personal information on every OSN that she wants to use, here Facebook, Pinterest, and LinkedIn. All three OSNs require an email address and a profile picture. Facebook and Pinterest ask for the name of the user, and offer an "About you" space. Without an integrated or portable profile, the user has to repeatedly provide the same information. Also, the user has to create links on the three OSNs. If she has friends who use the same OSNs as her, she has to create relationships with them on all three OSNs.

Example 2: With the PUP: With a portable profile, the user could share her personal information only once, whether it is on Facebook, Pinterest, or LinkedIn; and this information will be reused by the other OSNs. The user could fill in several fields in her Facebook profile, and this information could then be used by LinkedIn or Pinterest to complete the same users profile. As far as the connections between users are concerned, it would be easier to find friends on different OSNs. For instance, assume that the user is friends with A on Facebook. A decides to set up an account on LinkedIn. Because all the information about the user is stored in an integrated profile, including the links the user has on all the OSNs, the user and A could automatically be linked on LinkedIn. This assumes that the PUP includes the data on relationships the user has on other OSNs.

The PUP leads to another advantage, namely the improved quality of the recommendations (Berkovsky et al., 2008; Abel et al., 2011; Kapsammer et al., 2012).

Because of the enhanced information, the cold start problem is avoided; that is the recommendation algorithms could avoid suffering from data sparsity (Adomavicius & Tuzhilin, 2005). The most common recommendation techniques rely on a large amount of data to generate recommendations. The accuracy of the recommendation depends, thus, on the given data. If the user is new and/or is not active, the recommendations she gets will most likely be of poor quality.

Example 3: Without the PUP: The accuracy of the recommendation varies across OSN. Depending on the activity of the user, the recommendation will be more or less accurate. If the user is very active on Facebook, the recommendations she will get will likely be of high quality. The OSN will make friend suggestions, or will suggest pages to like that correspond to the user profile. However, if the user barely spends any time on Pinterest, then the OSN will probably struggle with the generation of qualitative "pin" (post on Pinterest) or "pinner" (user of Pinterest) recommendations.

Example 4: With the PUP: The accuracy of the recommendation is stable across OSNs. The quality of the recommendations will not depend on the activity of the user on the particular OSN. The user could be more active on Facebook, but it will not impair the quality of the recommendations generated by Pinterest or LinkedIn. The Facebook activity will be stored in the integrated profile and the other OSNs will take advantage of this information to produce recommendations to that user. Furthermore, even if the user were equally active on Facebook and Pinterest, the information gathered by the OSNs would be different. Hence, a portable profile would allow OSNs to have complementary information at their disposal.

A portable profile could also directly benefit the user. The latter would have access to the data OSNs have gathered about her, both explicit data (that is, data the user has explicitly shared with the OSN), and implicit data (that is, data about the user activity). The user could then control and manage the elements present in her integrated profile. This situation could help users accept the recommendations she gets, and it could make the suggestions of items less intrusive.

Example 5: Without the PUP: The user only has control over the data she gives explicitly. The user manages what she posts on Facebook, what she shares on LinkedIn, and what she "pins" on Pinterest. The user can also control the links she creates on all these OSNs. However, the user cannot exactly know what the OSNs gather about her. The user cannot know where the recommendations she gets come from; which could render the latter a little bit intrusive.

Example 6: With the PUP: The user can have control over the data she gives explicitly and the data gathered by the OSNs. The user can manage her activity on Facebook, and can decide if this activity can be used by LinkedIn. The user can figure out why she was recommended a particular job on LinkedIn, or why she was given this particular friend suggestion on Facebook.

Limitations of a Portable User Profile

Abel et al. (2010) identified a "risk of intertwining user profiles, namely that users who deliberately leave out some fields when filling their Twitter profile might not be aware that the corresponding information can be gathered from other sources". A unified profile implies unified information across OSN. Users cannot decide to share more on a OSN, and cannot keep information from being used by a specific OSN.

Example 7: Without the PUP: The user can decide to share more information on a particular OSN. She can decide to be more active on Facebook, for instance; and she does not want LinkedIn or Pinterest to have as many information at their disposal. She can use different profile pictures, or usernames for each OSN. Also, she can decide on the links she wants to create depending on the OSN. She can agree to a friend request on Facebook from a colleague, but she can decide not to share a Pinterest account with that colleague.

Example 8: With the PUP: If the user cannot control which part of the PUP is carried over between OSNs, then she cannot choose which information she wants to share on which OSN. The user has to be more careful about the information she posts on Facebook, because that information can then be used by LinkedIn or Pinterest. For instance, if the user accepts the friend request on Facebook from her colleague; then, if they are both on Pinterest, the link could be automatically created in that OSN. The user cannot separate or compartmentalize her online activity.

Another important issue related to the portable profile is related to privacy. Users post large amount of personal information online. But in a way, the user has more control over what is known about her by each OSN, when she has separate profiles. Indeed, with a portable profile, more information can be discovered by the OSNs. Inferences could be made more accurate because they are based on data coming from various sources. The user is thus more "vulnerable to social engineering attacks" (Alim et al., 2011).

Example 9: Without the PUP: As mentioned above, the user can decide which information she posts on which OSN. We will take the example of the horoscope and the age: "if the age and horoscope signs are present on a profile then it is possible to guess when the birthday is" (Alim et al., 2011). The user can have a board on Pinterest with her horoscope sign, and she can mention her age on Facebook. But the user can decide to keep her exact birthday private. Because the information about her sign, and her age are mentioned on different OSNs, it will be difficult to infer her birth date.

Example 10: With the PUP: The user is more vulnerable; she has less control over what can be known/discovered about her. Indeed, even if she posts her age only on Facebook, and her horoscope sign on Pinterest; that information will be present on the integrated profile. The latter can then be used to infer more personal information about the user, and in our example her exact birthday can be discovered.

PORTABLE USER PROFILE CONCEPTUAL MODEL

Data Used in Facebook, LinkedIn, and Pinterest

Before proposing the PUP conceptual model, we will identify the information that the user gives to the OSNs considered here, namely Facebook, LinkedIn, and Pinterest. We can distinguish three categories of data used by OSNs: the profile data, the relationships information, and the posts. The profile category includes the following pieces of information: her login information, her identity, her occupation, her beliefs, information about her family, her skills, her interests, and a text about herself. Then, the relationships the user creates with other users can also be part of the user profile. These relationships can be categorized in one of two groups: unidirectional relationships, or bidirectional relationships. The former type of relationships is unreciprocated, that is a user likes, or subscribes to a fan page; or follows another user. The latter type of relationships is reciprocated. A friend request is sent by a user to another user, who has to accept or deny the friend request. If she confirms it, then the relationship is created. Otherwise, no link exists between the two users. The third category of profile data is the posts shared by the user, that is the texts, comments, like/repost, tags, media, messages and groups. Those data are not directly and consciously given by the user; rather the OSN gathers this information for every user.

Facebook allows its users to login with their email or phone. It asks the users about their name, birthdate, gender, address, phone number, school, job, family, religious and political views, languages they can speak, favorite quotation, interests, and asks for a profile picture; Facebook also offers an "About you" section. The OSN supports both types of relationships. The user can send and accept/ deny a friend request; and she can also like a page about an artist, a public person, or a company. Facebook supports various types of posts, and hence gathers information about the following user activity: status, notes and links posted by the user; comments on status, or media; like/share; tag of friends on status or media; photos and videos; messages; and groups created or joined by the user.

LinkedIn users can login with their email address. The OSN asks them about their name, title, location, and a profile picture. The OSN also asks about the industry the user works in, and her experience, her qualifications, summary, specialties, specific skills and areas of expertise; her interests; and her personal details and advice for contacting her. LinkedIn supports both types of relationships. Users can ask other users to connect with them; and users can also follow companies' page. LinkedIn can gather information about the activity of the users, that is, their summary, recommendations; comments; like/ share; the connections they tag on status: photos and videos; message; and groups.

Pinterest allows their users to login with their email address or their Facebook, Google, or Twitter account. Pinterest asks for less information than the other two OSNs. Indeed, pinners are asked to provide their name, location, website, gender, and profile picture; and they can also fill in an "About you" section. The relationships in Pinterest are unidirectional. Users follow other users; they do not have to send a friend request to have access to other user's profiles. Pinterest gathers information about the pins posted by users; the comments; the like/repin; tag; photos and videos; messages; and group boards.

This discussion is summarized in Tables 1 and 2.

Table 1. Data Used in Facebook, LinkedIn, and Pinterest - Part 1

	Login	Identity	Occupation	Family/ Beliefs
Facebook	Email, phone	Demographics, picture	School(s), Job(s)	Family, Religious, Political
LinkedIn	Email	Demographics, picture	Industry, Experience	/
Pinterest	Email	Demographics, picture	/	/

Table 2. Data Used in Facebook, LinkedIn, and Pinterest - Part 2

	Skills	Interests	Else	Relationships	Post
Facebook	Languages	V	About me	Bidirectional and Unidirectional	V
LinkedIn	Summary, Expertise	V	Personal details, Contact me	Bidirectional and Unidirectional	V
Pinterest	/	/	About you	Unidirectional	V

Structure of the Data

The user profile is composed of two main categories of data: "Explicit" and "Implicit" data. The first category, the explicit data are the data the user intentionally and directly gives the OSN. The user is fully aware that she gives away that information. That category can be further classified in two groups: the "Profile Information" data and the "Relationships Information" data. The former group consists of: the login information; the identity of the user; her occupation; her beliefs; her skills; her hobbies; and information taking the form of an "About you" section. The latter group, that is the relationships data, consists of information about the links the user creates with other users. In that group, we can find both the bidirectional relationships and the unidirectional relationships.

Thus, two subclasses belong to the class "Explicit" data: Profile and Relationships. Both subclasses can be further specialized. For each subclass, we will identify: (i) the classes specializing the subclass; (ii) the attributes of these classes with their cardinality and their type; and (ii) the potential constraint(s).

We will start by the Profile Information subclass:

- Login information
  - Attributes
    - Email address [0..1], string
    - Phone number [0..1], number
    - Password [1..1], string
  - Constraint
    - The user has at least one value for the email address or the phone number
- Identity, specialized into
  - Identification – Attributes:
- First name [1..1], string
- Last name [1..1], string
- Birthday [0..1], date
- Gender [0..1], string
- Mother language [0..1], string
- Ethnicity [0..1], string
  - Location – Attributes:
- Street [0..1], string
- Home number [0..1], string
- City [0..1], string
- Country [0..1], string
- Time zone [1..1], string
  - Relationship status – Attributes:
- Status [1..1], enumerate: Single, In a relationship, Engaged, Married, In a civil union, In a domestic partnership, In an open relationship, It's complicated, Separated, Divorced, Widowed
- Start date [1..1], date
- End date [0..1], date
- Partner ID [0..1], integer
  - Phone number – Attributes:
- Type [0..1], enumerate: Mobile, Home, Work, Fax
- Number [1..1], number
  - Profile picture – Attributes:
- Photo ID [1..1], integer
- Size [1..1], integer
  - Website – Attributes:
- URL [1..1], string
- Description [0..1], string
  - Occupation information – Attributes:
- Type [0..1], enumerate: School, Job, Industry

- Name [1..1], string
  - ○ Family members – Attributes:
- ID of the family member [1..1], integer
- Relationship [1..1], string
  - ○ Beliefs information – Attributes:
- Type [0..1], enumerate: Religious, Political
- Belief [1..1], string
  - ○ Skills information – Attributes:
- Type [0..1], enumerate: Foreign languages, Qualifications/ Specialties, Area of expertise/Special skills
- Skill [1..1], string
  - ○ Hobbies information – Attributes:
- Type [0..1], enumerate: Interests, Kind of music, Kind of movies, Favorite quote
- Hobby [1..1], string
  - ○ Presentation information – Attributes:
- Type [1..1], enumerate: About you/Describe yourself/ Biography, Advice for contacting me
- Presentation [1..1], string

We will now turn to the Relationship class:

- Unidirectional
  - ○ Attribute
    - ▪ ID of the followed user [1..1], integer
- Bidirectional
  - ○ Attributes
    - ▪ ID of the friend [1..1], integer
    - ▪ Sender of the friend request [1..1], boolean

The second main category is the "Implicit" data, that is the data the user unintentionally gives to the OSN. Similar to the first category, the implicit data can be broken down into two classes, namely the "Posts", and the "Activity". In the posts, one can find all the elements shared by the user with her friends/contacts. This group contains the following elements: text, comment, like/repost, tag, media, message, and group. The activity group consists of the browsing and searching activity conducted by the user when she looks through the OSN.

Similar to the Explicit data, we will go through each concept of the Implicit class, and we will detail the attributes, the attributes' cardinalities, their type, and the potential constraints.

We will start with the Posts class:

- Text information
  - ○ Attributes
    - ▪ Text ID [1..1], integer
    - ▪ Type [1..1], enumerate: Status, Moods, Quotes, Links, Notes
    - ▪ Text [1..1], string

- Comments information
  - ○ Attributes
    - Comment ID [1..1], integer
    - Type [1..1], enumerate: On a profile information, On a text, On a media, On a relationship status
    - Comment [1..1], string
- Like/Repost information
  - ○ Attributes
    - Like/Repost ID [1..1], integer
    - Type [1..1], enumerate: Like a text, Repost a text, Like a media, Repost a media
- Tag information
  - ○ Attributes
    - Tag ID [1..1], integer
    - Type [1..1], enumerate: A friend on a media, A friend on a text, A media, A text
    - Tag [1..1], string
- Media information
  - ○ Attributes
    - Media ID [1..1], integer
    - Type [1..1], enumerate: Photo, Video, Gif
    - Name [1..1], string
    - Size [1..1], integer
- Message information
  - ○ Attributes
    - Message ID [1..1], integer
    - Type [1..1], enumerate: Public message, Private message, Instant chat
    - Content [1..1], string
    - Sender ID [1..1], integer
    - Recipient ID [1..*], integer
  - ○ Constraint
    - A message can be commented, liked, or reblogged if it is of the type "Public message"
- Group information
  - ○ Attributes
    - Group ID [1..1], integer
    - Name of the group [1..1], string
    - Date joined [1..1], date
    - Creator of the group ID [1..1], integer

We will now turn to the Activity class:

- Browse information
  - ○ Attributes
    - Type [1..1], enumerate: User, Media, Text, Comment, Like/ Repost, Tag, Group, Message
    - Timestamp [1..1], date

- Search information
  - Attributes
    - Search ID [1..1], integer
    - Keyword [1..*], string
    - Timestamp [1..1], date

We classified the Profile and the Relationships information in the Explicit category, and we classified the Posts information in the Implicit category for two reasons. Firstly, we believe that the user has to give her profile information, and has to create relationships online, create links with other users before using the OSN. She expects her information to be used by the OSN. However, the posts, and the activity represent the user actually using the OSN; the user may not be aware of the OSN using this type of information. The user shares posts with her friends, and not directly with the OSN. Secondly, today, when the concept of Profile is mentioned, people visualize only the Explicit class; while the OSN takes advantage of both the Explicit and the Implicit classes. By representing the conceptual model with both categories, we can give the user more control and more awareness over her data, that is over the data gathered by the OSN and not only the data explicitly given by the user. The Portable User Profile conceptual model is represented as a UML Class Diagram, in Figure 1.

Figure 1. The Portable User Profile conceptual model

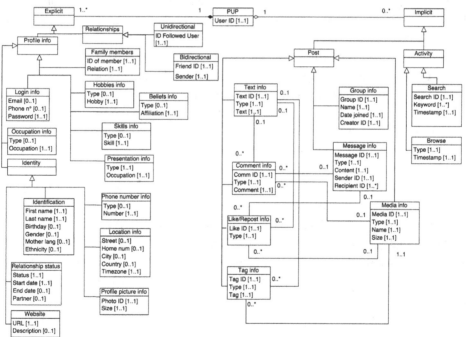

DISUCSSION

Many OSN features allow the user to share content about herself, both directly and indirectly. Directly, by giving, for example, her birth date, marital status, and so on. Indirectly, by performing actions which suggest her preferences; for example, "liking" some specific content on Facebook gives indications about which topics and other users that user may be interested in. The availability of such, so to speak personal content, has led to concerns about, and research on trust and privacy (Dwyer et al., 2007; Strater et al., 2008; Madejski et al., 2011).

It is not possible, we believe, to study OSN features and content without paying particular attention to personal content. Why? Because we expect users to consider more important that personal content over other, and features for manipulating (sharing, hiding, removing, for example) that personal content over those focusing on other, impersonal content. In (Bouraga et al., 2015)], we studied the importance of content for OSN users, generated by other OSN users. More specifically, we address the following question: "How relevant is it to user X to know about some specific event type generated by user Y?". This question can be rephrased into: "How relevant is to user X to know about some specific content in the PUP of a user Y?"

In order to understand how personal content influences users' perception of relevance of other content and features on OSNs, in this paper we have proposed a definition of the personal content, in the form of a conceptual model of the Portable User Profile (PUP). The PUP of a user lists the types of data, and relationships between these types of data, which most well-known OSNs tend to collect. It is portable, in the sense that if it were possible for a user to carry over her personal content from one OSN to another, then the PUP includes data, which it would be relevant to carry over. Put another way, the PUP represents all the information that the user has shared across multiple OSNs.

Also, we believe that the conceptual model is scalable. It is not specific to one particular OSN nor a specific type of OSNs (for instance, for knowledge-sharing OSNs or network-oriented OSNs). If a new OSN arises, it should not be a problem to take into account the information it gathers, we should be able to find a mapping between its features and the proposed class diagram. And it can be easily extended if OSNs propose new features and therefrom, new types of personal content arise. More specifically, the PUP can be updated by adding a class to the conceptual model, accompanied by the potential relationships with other classes.

As mentioned in Section 3, the existence of a Portable User Profile has its benefits as well as its limitations. We will discuss the PUP conceptual model in light of these advantages and limitations.

Firstly, the PUP conceptual model enables the representation and the common understanding of the structure of the data/information in the user profile. The user can share her information only once, and this information will take the form of the conceptual model. Also, if the user is more active on a OSN, for instance, if she uses Facebook daily while she only checks her LinkedIn account once a week; the user can leverage her Facebook activity and take advantage of it on LinkedIn.

The distinction between the explicit and the implicit data is also made clear by the conceptual model: what is implied by "explicit data"? What is implied by "implicit data"? The user can have more control over her information, because she knows what is exactly tracked when she is on the OSN.

However, risks remain. What the user cannot control are the new inferences the OSNs can make (which are not represented in the PUP). The user can identify where the information come from, but cannot control the information that is leveraged from all the various sources. Also, the user cannot choose to share more information on an OSN, and less on another. She cannot hide data from one OSN.

The information at the disposal of the OSN is uniform. The PUP conceptual model does not erase the limitations of an integrated profile, but it makes the user more aware of those risks.

We will now discuss the recommendation topic, in light of the PUP conceptual model. The quality of the recommendations depends on the information it is based on, both in terms of quality and quantity.

Adomavicius & Tuzhilin (2005) distinguish between three recommendation techniques that a Recommendation System (RS) can use, each of which present several shortcomings:

1. Collaborative Filtering (CF), where "the user is recommended items that people with similar tastes and preferences liked in the past";
   a. New user problem: the RS has to learn the user's preferences in order to make reliable recommendations
   b. New item problem: an item has to be rated by a significant amount of users before it can be recommended
   c. The "grey sheep" problem: a user can be classified in more than one group of users
   d. Sparsity: both users and ratings sparsity can cause problems for the generation of accurate recommendations
2. Content-Based (CB), where "the user is recommended items similar to the ones the user preferred in the past";
   a. Limited content analysis: a sufficient set of features per item is required in order to produce recommendations
   b. Over-specialization: the set of recommended items will be very homogeneous
   c. New user problem
3. Hybrid, which is a combination of CF and CB.

A RS could also generate recommendations based on rules. In (Bouraga et al., 2015). we proposed rules for relevant recommendations. We surveyed students of the University of Namur, and based on their preferences, we proposed decision trees for relevant recommendations.

Thus, the more information the RS can use, the more accurate it will be; whether the RS uses CF, a CB, a hybrid, or rules. The information has to be varied as well, and it has to be of good quality. The recommendation will be the most accurate if the user shares all the classes of information found in the PUP conceptual model. More specifically, if she shares her profile information, if she creates relationships online, and if she is active on the OSN that is, if the OSN can gather lots of implicit data. To the contrary, if the user shares only the minimum amount of data, that is her profile information, she will most likely get imprecise recommendations. This discussion is represented in Figure 2. The quality of the recommendation increases as we move towards the external layers. The inner circle depicts the core information we believe is needed to generate recommendations; while the outer circle represents the optional information.

CONCLUSION

In this paper, we proposed the "Portable User Profile" (PUP) conceptual model. This model is meant to gather all the data/information a user shares on every OSN she uses. The PUP should be accessible by both the user, and the OSN.

Figure 2. The PUP conceptual model and the quality of recommendations

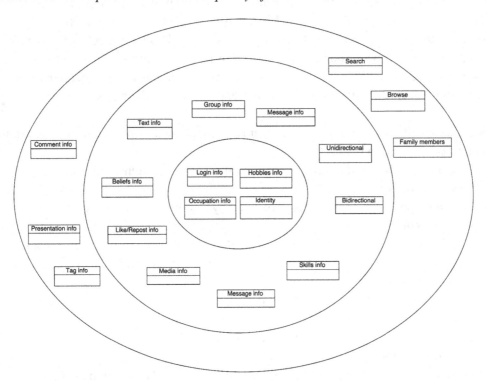

Before introducing the conceptual model, we first discussed the advantages and limitations of such a profile. An integrated profile is richer in terms of information than a single OSN account, and this enriched profile probably leads to better, more accurate recommendations. Also, the user could have access to all the information the OSNs gather about her; and thus the user could have more control over her own data. Nevertheless, with an integrated profile the user cannot choose an OSN where she would be more active, where she would share more information. She is forced to be equally exposed on every OSN she uses. This situation also renders the user more vulnerable. Our PUP conceptual model is composed of two main classes: Explicit and Implicit data. Each of these classes can be specialized into two classes: Profile and Relationship data; and Posts and Activity data respectively. Those four classes are specialized into several other classes. We represented this conceptual model as a UML Class diagram.

The main limitation of this work consists in its research-oriented/ hypothetical nature. We have not validated the proposal. Also, we only took into account three different OSNs; even though, these three different OSNs are different in their approach and objectives. Considering other OSNs would be interesting in order to validate or revise our PUP conceptual model. Another limitation is that we did not consider the information resulting from inference by the OSN or from the collection of information from other sources.

REFERENCES

Abel, F., Araújo, S., Gao, Q., & Houben, G. J. (2011, June). Analyzing cross-system user modeling on the social web. In *International Conference on Web Engineering* (pp. 28-43). Springer. 10.1007/978-3-642-22233-7_3

Abel, F., Henze, N., Herder, E., & Krause, D. (2010). Interweaving public user profiles on the web. *User Modeling, Adaptation, and Personalization*, 16-27.

Adomavicius, G., & Tuzhilin, A. (2005). Toward the next generation of recommender systems: A survey of the state-of-the-art and possible extensions. *IEEE Transactions on Knowledge and Data Engineering*, *17*(6), 734–749. doi:10.1109/TKDE.2005.99

Ahn, Y. Y., Han, S., Kwak, H., Moon, S., & Jeong, H. (2007, May). Analysis of topological characteristics of huge online social networking services. In *Proceedings of the 16th international conference on World Wide Web* (pp. 835-844). ACM. 10.1145/1242572.1242685

Aiello, L. M., Barrat, A., Cattuto, C., Ruffo, G., & Schifanella, R. (2010, August). Link creation and profile alignment in the aNobii social network. In *Social Computing (SocialCom), 2010 IEEE Second International Conference on* (pp. 249-256). IEEE. 10.1109/SocialCom.2010.42

Alim, S., Abdulrahman, R., Neagu, D., & Ridley, M. (2011). Online social network profile data extraction for vulnerability analysis. *International Journal of Internet Technology and Secured Transactions*, *3*(2), 194–209. doi:10.1504/IJITST.2011.039778

Berkovsky, S., Kuflik, T., & Ricci, F. (2008). Mediation of user models for enhanced personalization in recommender systems. *User Modeling and User-Adapted Interaction*, *18*(3), 245–286. doi:10.100711257-007-9042-9

Bouraga, S., Jureta, I., & Faulkner, S. (2015). An empirical study of notifications' importance for online social network users. *Social Network Analysis and Mining*, *5*(1), 51. doi:10.100713278-015-0293-x

Bouraga, S., Jureta, I., & Faulkner, S. (2015), Rules for relevant notification recommendations to online social networks users. In *ASE Eighth International Conference on Social Computing (SocialCom)*. Academic Press.

Chen, J., Kiremire, A. R., Brust, M. R., & Phoha, V. V. (2014). Modeling online social network users' profile attribute disclosure behavior from a game theoretic perspective. *Computer Communications*, *49*, 18–32. doi:10.1016/j.comcom.2014.05.001

Ducheneaut, N., Yee, N., Nickell, E., & Moore, R. J. (2006, April). Alone together?: exploring the social dynamics of massively multiplayer online games. In *Proceedings of the SIGCHI conference on Human Factors in computing systems* (pp. 407-416). ACM. 10.1145/1124772.1124834

Dunbar, R. I., Arnaboldi, V., Conti, M., & Passarella, A. (2015). The structure of online social networks mirrors those in the offline world. *Social Networks*, *43*, 39–47. doi:10.1016/j.socnet.2015.04.005

Dwyer, C., Hiltz, S., & Passerini, K. (2007). Trust and privacy concern within social networking sites: A comparison of Facebook and MySpace. *AMCIS 2007 Proceedings*, 339.

Ellison, N. B. (2007). Social network sites: Definition, history, and scholarship. *Journal of Computer-Mediated Communication, 13*(1), 210–230. doi:10.1111/j.1083-6101.2007.00393.x

Emanuel, L., Bevan, C., & Hodges, D. (2013, April). What does your profile really say about you?: privacy warning systems and self-disclosure in online social network spaces. In CHI'13 Extended Abstracts on Human Factors in Computing Systems (pp. 799-804). ACM.

Fire, M., Goldschmidt, R., & Elovici, Y. (2014). Online social networks: Threats and solutions. *IEEE Communications Surveys and Tutorials, 16*(4), 2019–2036. doi:10.1109/COMST.2014.2321628

Fu, F., Liu, L., & Wang, L. (2008). Empirical analysis of online social networks in the age of Web 2.0. *Physica A, 387*(2), 675–684. doi:10.1016/j.physa.2007.10.006

Guo, L., Tan, E., Chen, S., Zhang, X., & Zhao, Y. E. (2009, June). Analyzing patterns of user content generation in online social networks. In *Proceedings of the 15th ACM SIGKDD international conference on Knowledge discovery and data mining* (pp. 369-378). ACM. 10.1145/1557019.1557064

Heckmann, D., Schwartz, T., Brandherm, B., Schmitz, M., & von Wilamowitz-Moellendorff, M. (2005). GUMO-the general user model ontology. Lecture Notes in Computer Science, 3538, 428.

Kontaxis, G., Polakis, I., Ioannidis, S., & Markatos, E. P. (2011, March). Detecting social network profile cloning. In *Pervasive Computing and Communications Workshops (PERCOM Workshops), 2011 IEEE International Conference on* (pp. 295-300). IEEE. 10.1109/PERCOMW.2011.5766886

Kumar, R., Novak, J., & Tomkins, A. (2010). Structure and evolution of online social networks. In *Link mining: models, algorithms, and applications* (pp. 337–357). Springer New York. doi:10.1007/978-1-4419-6515-8_13

Kwak, H., Lee, C., Park, H., & Moon, S. (2010, April). What is Twitter, a social network or a news media? In *Proceedings of the 19th international conference on World wide web* (pp. 591-600). ACM. 10.1145/1772690.1772751

Lampe, C., Ellison, N., & Steinfield, C. (2006, November). A Face (book) in the crowd: Social searching vs. social browsing. In *Proceedings of the 2006 20th anniversary conference on Computer supported cooperative work* (pp. 167-170). ACM. 10.1145/1180875.1180901

Lampe, C. A., Ellison, N., & Steinfield, C. (2007, April). A familiar face (book): profile elements as signals in an online social network. In *Proceedings of the SIGCHI conference on Human factors in computing systems* (pp. 435-444). ACM. 10.1145/1240624.1240695

Lange, P. G. (2007). Publicly private and privately public: Social networking on YouTube. *Journal of Computer-Mediated Communication, 13*(1), 361–380. doi:10.1111/j.1083-6101.2007.00400.x

Livingstone, S. (2008). Taking risky opportunities in youthful content creation: Teenagers' use of social networking sites for intimacy, privacy and self-expression. *New Media & Society, 10*(3), 393–411. doi:10.1177/1461444808089415

Ma, J., Qiao, Y., Hu, G., Huang, Y., Wang, M., Sangaiah, A. K., ... Wang, Y. (2017). Balancing User Profile and Social Network Structure for Anchor Link Inferring Across Multiple Online Social Networks. *IEEE Access: Practical Innovations, Open Solutions, 5*, 12031–12040. doi:10.1109/ACCESS.2017.2717921

Madejski, M., Johnson, M., & Bellovin, S. M. (2011). *The failure of online social network privacy settings*. Department of Computer Science, Columbia University, Tech. Rep. CUCS-010-11.

Mislove, A., Koppula, H. S., Gummadi, K. P., Druschel, P., & Bhattacharjee, B. (2008, August). Growth of the flickr social network. In *Proceedings of the first workshop on Online social networks* (pp. 25-30). ACM. 10.1145/1397735.1397742

Mislove, A., Marcon, M., Gummadi, K. P., Druschel, P., & Bhattacharjee, B. (2007, October). Measurement and analysis of online social networks. In *Proceedings of the 7th ACM SIGCOMM conference on Internet measurement* (pp. 29-42). ACM. 10.1145/1298306.1298311

Mislove, A., Viswanath, B., Gummadi, K. P., & Druschel, P. (2010, February). You are who you know: inferring user profiles in online social networks. In *Proceedings of the third ACM international conference on Web search and data mining* (pp. 251-260). ACM. 10.1145/1718487.1718519

Narendula, R., Papaioannou, T. G., & Aberer, K. (2011, August). My3: A highly-available P2P-based online social network. In *Peer-to-Peer Computing (P2P), 2011 IEEE International Conference on* (pp. 166-167). IEEE.

Nie, Y., Jia, Y., Li, S., Zhu, X., Li, A., & Zhou, B. (2016). Identifying users across social networks based on dynamic core interests. *Neurocomputing, 210*, 107–115. doi:10.1016/j.neucom.2015.10.147

Nosko, A., Wood, E., & Molema, S. (2010). All about me: Disclosure in online social networking profiles: The case of FACEBOOK. *Computers in Human Behavior, 26*(3), 406–418. doi:10.1016/j.chb.2009.11.012

Park, N., Kee, K. F., & Valenzuela, S. (2009). Being immersed in social networking environment: Facebook groups, uses and gratifications, and social outcomes. *Cyberpsychology & Behavior, 12*(6), 729–733. doi:10.1089/cpb.2009.0003 PMID:19619037

Pempek, T. A., Yermolayeva, Y. A., & Calvert, S. L. (2009). College students' social networking experiences on Facebook. *Journal of Applied Developmental Psychology, 30*(3), 227–238. doi:10.1016/j.appdev.2008.12.010

Raacke, J., & Bonds-Raacke, J. (2008). MySpace and Facebook: Applying the uses and gratifications theory to exploring friend-networking sites. *Cyberpsychology & Behavior, 11*(2), 169–174. doi:10.1089/cpb.2007.0056 PMID:18422409

Rezaee, S., Lavesson, N., & Johnson, H. (2012). E-mail prioritization using online social network profile distance. *Computer Science & Applications, 9*(1), 70–87.

Silfverberg, S., Liikkanen, L. A., & Lampinen, A. (2011, March). I'll press play, but I won't listen: profile work in a music-focused social network service. In *Proceedings of the ACM 2011 conference on Computer supported cooperative work* (pp. 207-216). ACM. 10.1145/1958824.1958855

Singh, R. R., & Tomar, D. S. (2009). *Approaches for user profile investigation in orkut social network*. arXiv preprint arXiv:0912.1008

Strater, K., & Lipford, H. R. (2008, September). Strategies and struggles with privacy in an online social networking community. In *Proceedings of the 22nd British HCI Group Annual Conference on People and Computers: Culture, Creativity, Interaction* (vol. 1, pp. 111-119). British Computer Society.

Strufe, T. (2010, April). Profile popularity in a business-oriented online social network. In *Proceedings of the 3rd workshop on social network systems* (p. 2). ACM. 10.1145/1852658.1852660

Subrahmanyam, K., Reich, S. M., Waechter, N., & Espinoza, G. (2008). Online and offline social networks: Use of social networking sites by emerging adults. *Journal of Applied Developmental Psychology*, 29(6), 420–433. doi:10.1016/j.appdev.2008.07.003

Utz, S. (2010). Show me your friends and I will tell you what type of person you are: How one's profile, number of friends, and type of friends influence impression formation on social network sites. *Journal of Computer-Mediated Communication*, 15(2), 314–335. doi:10.1111/j.1083-6101.2010.01522.x

Utz, S., & Beukeboom, C. J. (2011). The role of social network sites in romantic relationships: Effects on jealousy and relationship happiness. *Journal of Computer-Mediated Communication*, 16(4), 511–527. doi:10.1111/j.1083-6101.2011.01552.x

Wischenbart, M., Mitsch, S., Kapsammer, E., Kusel, A., Pröll, B., Retschitzegger, W., ... Lechner, S. (2012, April). User profile integration made easy: model-driven extraction and transformation of social network schemas. In *Proceedings of the 21st International Conference on World Wide Web* (pp. 939-948). ACM. 10.1145/2187980.2188227

Zhang, H., Kan, M., Liu, Y., & Ma, S. (2014, November). Online social network profile linkage based on cost-sensitive feature acquisition. In *Chinese National Conference on Social Media Processing* (pp. 117-128). Springer Berlin Heidelberg. 10.1007/978-3-662-45558-6_11

Zhang, H., Kan, M. Y., Liu, Y., & Ma, S. (2014, December). Online social network profile linkage. In *Asia Information Retrieval Symposium* (pp. 197-208). Springer.

Zhou, X., Liang, X., Zhang, H., & Ma, Y. (2016). Cross-platform identification of anonymous identical users in multiple social media networks. *IEEE Transactions on Knowledge and Data Engineering*, 28(2), 411–424. doi:10.1109/TKDE.2015.2485222

This research was previously published in Modern Perspectives on Virtual Communications and Social Networking; pages 120-145, copyright year 2019 by Information Science Reference (an imprint of IGI Global).

Chapter 21
At the Mercy of Facebook:
A Meta–Analysis on Impact of Social Networking Sites, Teen Brain on Teenage Pregnancies

Nirupama R. Akella
Wichita State University, USA

ABSTRACT

This chapter is a meta-analysis of teen brain research and social media technology such as Facebook that could result in spiraling rates of teenage pregnancy. The author discusses contemporary theories of brain circuitry including teen brain structure and function as one of the plausible reasons for rising teenage pregnancy rates. The author argues that the challenge is to control the quality and influence of Facebook on teen behaviors, actions, and decisions to minimize the growing influence of social networking sites. In the conclusive section of the chapter, the author focuses on the expansion and extension of instructional and non-instructional physical activities, exergames, and active video games strategies to control the quality and influence of Facebook content by presenting research that advocates use of such activities and games within the Facebook interface. The author ends the chapter by mapping a future research direction of cross-cultural empirical investigation. The author wraps the chapter with a summative conclusion.

INTRODUCTION

"Time and motivation are finite resources… time and motivation spent on social networking sites such as Facebook usually comes at the expense of other activities," stated Wendy Cousins, a researcher at the University of Ulster in the UK. In a recent online survey of 350 high school students and undergraduates, Cousins found that teens spent more than 65% of the day posting and sharing their own pictures', messaging someone, viewing profiles of each other, and commenting on each other's social status. Time that should have spent doing homework, researching future career options, engaging in community activities, talking with friends and family in person, and playing a game (Nauert, 2015). The survey

DOI: 10.4018/978-1-6684-6307-9.ch021

sought to investigate the motivation of daily addictive use of Facebook by teens. Cousins stated that teens experienced a 'high' and a sense of excitement, social approval and thrill when they viewed a 'like' on their Facebook site (Nauert, 2015). The compulsion to replicate the sensation and thrill stated Cousins was one of the chief distinguishing features of teen behavior. Consequences such as becoming pregnant while still in school; engaging in risky behaviors of drinking and drug addiction, pornography do not seem to hold any value (Nauert, 2015). A similar trend has been sweeping across US as Facebook usage was recorded at 73% among teens i.e. adolescents under age of 19 (Madden, Lenhart, Cortesi, Gasser, Duggan, Smith, & Beaton, 2013). According to National Center of Health Statistics [NCHS] researchers, this increase impacted rates of teenage pregnancy significantly with 71.5% teen pregnancies for every 1000 teen girls between ages of 13-19 in 2017 (Landry, Turner, Vyas, & Wood, 2017). Teen girls were more prone to posting and sharing pictures; engaging in risky behavior to experience a 'high' thrill of excitement (Landry et al., 2017). NCHS researchers established a tenuous but direct link between increase in Facebook usage and teenage pregnancy rates with 25% increase in states of Arizona, New Mexico, Nevada, and Texas in 2017 (Madden et al., 2013). More than 26 US states clocked in high rates of teenage pregnancy with more than 72 live birth for every 1000 teen girls aged 15 (Landry et al., 2017). This increase was found to be positively significantly correlated i.e. 49.4% increase in sexual behavior leading to teenage pregnancy due to increased Facebook usage in terms of time and quality i.e. teens were spending maximum time on Facebook posting, sharing provocative pictures, sexting, and real-time sexual activity (Landry et al., 2017). Social networking sites such as Facebook propelled and influenced teens to engage in risky behaviors of gambling, sexual activity whilst in school, sexting, pornographic behavior, and teenage pregnancy (Geidd, 2013).

The chapter, written from a US perspective, maps out how excessive usage in terms of time and misplaced motivation of Facebook leads to irresponsible, harmful and/or risky behavior and action that could result in teenage pregnancy. The author charts an extensive literature review of prevalence of social networking sites focusing primarily on Facebook; theoretical perspectives discussing contemporary neurobiological theories that show why teens use Facebook despite its harmful effects; and plausible methods of controlling the quality and usage of Facebook time and motivation as a means to shape usage of Facebook to control and minimize consequences of teen pregnancy. In her conclusion, the author reiterates her argument that the theoretical meta analyses serves as a foundational launchpad to initiate and further empirical research.

BACKGROUND

The Internet, iPads, Google, Facebook, Instagram, Twitter, Snapchat... have successfully invaded and dominated 20th century society. Youth are sharing more of their personal information on social networking sites than in the past (Gao, 2015). Statistics released by NCHS on teenage attitude, behavior, and action reveal this gradual progression of digital technology over human society (Madden et al, 2013). More than 95% of all people, adult and teenage including adolescents and senior citizens used the Internet and one social networking site almost daily (Lenhart, 2015). In her research, Lenhart stated that usage of the Internet, cell phones, and various social networking sites began as early as ten years in school children and peaked during teenage years at ages ranging from 13-17 (Lenhart, 2015). In 2010, US teens spent an average of 8.5 hours daily interacting with social media technology be it Facebook,

Google, iPad, tablets, or Twitter (Rideout, Foehr, & Roberts, 2010). This number increased to 11.5 hours in 2013 (Geidd, 2013).

In 2015, more than 71% of teens spent an average of 15.8 hours on social media sites or apps (Lenhart, 2015). More than 66% of teens used Facebook, 13% used Instagram, 13% used Google+, and 3% used Snapchat (Lenhart, 2015). The 2010 data from the Kaiser Foundation online survey showed that teens belonging to ages of 13-15 spent more than two-thirds of their day surfing, viewing Facebook posts, following someone on Twitter, chatting with someone online, or commenting on an online pinup board post (Rideout, Foehr, & Roberts, 2010). The researchers stated that these daily consumption habits of teens were extremely beneficial to the digital industry that was inventing new social networking sites and optimizing search engines everyday (Rideout et al., 2010). Researchers at the Pew Research Center said that the number of teens consuming these various digital technology avenues would only increase, and ultimately implode by 2020 (Lenhart, 2015, Gao, 2015).

Teen girls tended to dominate social media with older teens using Facebook to express their social dating skills, friendship requests, identity creation, impression management, and development of self-esteem (Dunne, Lawler, & Rowley, 2010). These reasons for using social networking sites and the Internet have not changed. In her report, Lenhart said teen girls ranging in ages of 15-17 used Facebook 20% more than younger teen girls (Lenhart, 2015). On an average 71% of teen girls used Facebook daily. Teen girls aged 15 used Facebook to create impressions of *'being cool'* and *'popular on the dating scene'* (Gao, 2015, Lenhart, 2015). Each Facebook user had an average of 145 'friends' (Lenhart, 2015). Facebook posts were viewed as a medium to attract and befriend strangers through provocative textual or visual descriptions (Gao, 2015). Older teen girls tended to spend more time, nearly 15%, enhancing their profiles and befriending, inviting persons of the opposite gender to view and comment on their profiles (Geidd, 2013). This trend of posting photographs and pictures of self-doing daily activities in provocative *'cool'* clothing was also identified as the primary reason behind the prevalent use of online pinboard sites such as Pinterest and Polyvore (Lenhart, 2015). Research statistics showed that older teen girls belonging to ages 15-17 used online pinboard sites, namely Pinterest 33% more than young teen girls (Lenhart, 2015). In contrast, only 11% of teen boys used Pinterest. Again, older teen girls ranging in ages of 1 teen behavior 5-17 used online discussion boards such as Reddit and Digg to chat and comment on posted Pinterest or Facebook posted images (Lenhart, 2015). More than 17% of older teen girls constituted major and active consumers of Reddit and Digg online discussion boards (Lenhart, 2015). More than 47% of teen girls use video connections such as Skype, Ovoo, Facetime and Omegle to talk with each other. Older teen girls aged 16 are touted as being more enthusiastic and eager to spend their study time video chatting and calling 'friends' (Lenhart, 2015).

Similarly, older teen girls used the social application of Instagram at an average frequency of 60% (Lenhart, 2015). The social application was primarily used to post and share photographs with each other (Lenhart, 2015). The average typical Instagram user had over 150 followers who shared, commented, and encouraged each other's behavior and action (Lenhart, 2015). The trend of video and photo sharing social application was expanded with the advent of Snapchat. More than 47% of older teen girls used Snapchat to share videos of people, places, and events they liked with each other (Lenhart, 2015). Twitter was another social application that had garnered a niche audience among teen girls (Lenhart, 2015). A third i.e. 33% of female teens used Twitter to develop a network of friends and 'followers' (Lenhart, 2015). Older girl teens used Twitter daily accounting for 49% of its consumers, compared to younger female teens in ages 13 and 14 who used Twitter 31% and 28% respectively (Lenhart, 2015). Vine and Google + were identified as popular social communication applications used mostly by older teen girls to post and share photos (Lenhart, 2015). Vine was used by 27% of older teen girls as a photo and video sharing platform as compared to 20% of older teen boys (Lenhart, 2015). Tumbir was a microblogging social application used by 23% of older teen girls ranging in ages from 15-17, as compared to 5% of older boy teen users (Lenhart, 2015). Tumbir was primarily used by older teen girls to share visual posts of themselves or others. Older teen girls would usually minimize Pinterest images to share on Tumbir and post them on Twitter and Facebook to generate likes, dislikes, and 'followers' (Lenhart, 2015). Tumbir, thus, was used in conjunction with other social networking applications to enhance self-image, garner friendships and become popular (Lenhart, 2015).

Current survey data at the Pew Research Center showed that more than 57% of female teens used more than one social networking site or website to establish friendships, enhance self- image, and create interest about self among members of opposite gender (Lenhart, 2015, Gao, 2015). This introductory section sets the stage highlighting the widespread dominance of all kinds of digital social technology among teen girls. In the next section, the author focuses and traces the reasons behind the emergence and popularity of social networking sites.

Phenomenon of Social Networking Sites

Social networking sites (SNS) such as Facebook, Instagram, and Snapchat were defined as web-based devices that allowed individuals to:

1. Construct and develop a public or semi-public profile within a bounded system
2. Articulate, usually in written format, a list of users with whom they shared a connection. Such approved users were identified as friends on the SNS.
3. View and navigate through their friend list as well as view and share friend networks posted by others (Boyd & Ellison, 2007).

The main feature of SNS was their emphasis on 'networking.' All SNS were primarily social re-lationship sites that fostered sharing of experiences, memories, communication, behavior, and action (Haythornthwaite, 2005). SNSs were developed and based on the premise of relationship creation and maintenance, either with members of an existing known social circle, or connecting users with people who shared similar attitudes and interests (Boyd & Ellison, 2007). SNSs were defined as *"explicit rep-resentation of the relationship between individuals and groups in a community"* (Finn, Ding, Zhou, & Joshi, 2005, p. 419). The SNS community could be real or virtual (Finn et al., 2005). Raacke and col-league elaborated on this concept and explained that SNS were public virtual spaces or platforms where individuals from various levels and sectors of society could interact and share ideas, experiences, and interests with each other (Raacke & Bonds-Raacke, 2008).

The foundational characteristic of SNSs was their ability to allow and enable users to create a profile of themselves (Sunden, 2003). Profiles were described as individualized informative descriptions that usually included visuals, messages, and a list of friends. After logging into a SNS such as Facebook, users had to complete a questionnaire (Sunden, 2003). The completed questionnaire that included de-scriptors of age, location, interests and an 'about me' section was used to generate a basic profile. The profile could be enhanced with visual descriptors of photographs of the user in various poses (Sunden, 2003). Profile pages were unique allowing the user *"to type themselves into being"* (Sunden, 2003, p. 3). Each member was encouraged to upload a personal photograph of self and share a range of varied information such as where they went to school, favorite movie stars, music they liked, information about family, hobbies, and interests. A Facebook user or member had the autonomy and control to share and regulate the content typed into their profile (Sunden, 2003). Users could manipulate information and photographs to show themselves in a favorable, positive, and attractive light (Boyd, 2007). According to recent longitudinal surveys conducted on teens aged 14-17 years, 92% of teens shared their real name on their profile, while 91% posted profile pictures. (Madden, Lenhart, Cortesi, Gasser, Duggan, Smith, & Beaton, 2013, Lenhart, 2015). The survey results as depicted in Table 1, showed that 71% of the users felt comfortable sharing their physical address, while 73% shared their contact information on their profiles (Madden et al., 2013; Lenhart, 2015). Focus group results also showed that older teen girls felt excited and eager to post and share photos of themselves in a towel (Lenhart, 2015).

Table 1. % of Users posting certain profile characteristics on SNS

Profile Characteristic	% of Users
Posted their real name	92%
Posted their photo	91%
Posted their interests, hobbies	84%
Posted their birth date	82%
Posted their school name	71%
Posted the city/ town they currently lived	71%
Posted their real relationship status	62%
Posted their email address	53%
Posted videos of themselves in private poses [in towel]	24%
Posted cell phone number	20%

Source: (Madden, M., Lenhart, A., Cortesi, S., Gasser, U., Duggan, M., Smith, A., & Beaton, M. (2013). Teens, Social Media, and Privacy. http://pewinternet.org/Reports/2013/Teens-Social-Media-And-Privacy .aspx).

After joining a SNS and creating their profile, users were prompted to identify people they wanted to interact with within the system. These interactions were described as virtual relationships (Boyd & Ellison, 2007). The identified individuals were known as 'friends'; 'contacts' or fans' depending on the SNS. An example would be Facebook where a user had the autonomy to identify more than 145 'friends.' It was not necessary for a user to recognize and know his or her users (Boyd & Ellison, 2007). A user could merely initiate contact and identify someone as a 'friend' based on recent posts and messages on Facebook (Boyd & Ellison, 2007). Consequently, a user could have a list of 'friends' who he or she had never met and chatted with face-to-face. Most SNSs were developed on the security and privacy feature of bi-directional confirmation of 'friends' or 'followers.' This kind of dual confirmation meant that an individual could only join a user's 'friends' list if the latter confirmed the friendship request, and vice versa (Boyd & Ellison, 2007). This type of bi-directional confirmation ensured that users had only approved and desired 'friends.' Another integral and crucial component of all SNS was the public display of user established connections or 'friends' (Boyd & Ellison, 2007). This compromised security negating the former feature of bi-directional confirmation allowing any individual with access to log in to Facebook or any SNS to view the user's information and profile. However, advanced security issues allowed users to choose between public and private access. This kind of advanced security protocols allowed user control over their information and communication with 'friends' (Dunne et al., 2010). Older teen girls were more at ease, more than 25% than their male counterparts, in making their profiles public for general navigation and consumption (Lenhart, 2015).

On an average, a user could have ten recognizable friends on a SNS. These friends were identified as the user's classmates; neighbors; family members, or relatives. The bottom line was that these ten friends were people the user knew on a personal or professional basis (Fraser & Dutta, 2008). The remaining 130-140 people on a user's 'friends' list were virtual and not known to the user. This meant that SNS allowed users to establish contact and relationships with a virtual community of people (Fraser & Dutta, 2008). A user did not have to know the 'friend' on a personal basis. Users could have initiated friendship requests by viewing and 'liking' their profile in the public space on a SNS. Hence, SNS provided the means to establish large networks of 'friends' or 'followers.' A user in USA could have 50 'friends' in China—people the user had never seen in his or her personal or professional life (Fraser & Dutta, 2008). Older teen girls had large networks of 'friends' as compared to younger female teens (Madden et al., 2013; Lenhart, 2015). In their path breaking report titled, *'Teens, Social Media, and Privacy'* published for the Pew Research Center, Madden and colleagues noted that older teen girls usually maintained two Facebook accounts – one for the family and one for members of the opposite gender (Madden et al., 2013). The report also stated that older teen girls held multiple SNS accounts to maintain their privacy and *'not to tell their parents everything'* (Madden et. al, 2013). According to the report, 98% of Facebook users were friends with male family members and friends (Madden et al., 2013). The researchers further explained that such Facebook accounts were kept separate from accounts for female friends (Madden et al., 2013). As shown in table 2 below, 33% of teen Facebook users were 'friends' with people whom they had never met (Madden et. al, 2013). According to table 2, 70% of older teen girl Facebook users were 'friends' with their parents (Madden et al., 2013).

Table 2. Type of "friends" by older teen girl Facebook users

% distribution of Facebook users	Type of "friends'
98%	People they know from school
91%	Members of their extended family
89%	People going to a different school
76%	Siblings
70%	Parents
33%	People they have never met
30%	Teachers & Coaches
30%	Celebrities, Musicians, Athletes

Source: (Madden, M., Lenhart, A., Cortesi, S., Gasser, U., Duggan, M., Smith, A., & Beaton, M. (2013). Teens, Social Media, and Privacy. http://pewinternet.org/Reports/2013/Teens-Social-Media-And-Privacy.aspx).

MAIN FOCUS OF THE CHAPTER

Issues, Controversies, Problems

The number of friends was found to be directly and significantly linked to level of sociability, openness, and friendliness of a user (Dunne et al., 2010). In his pioneering research, Dunbar explained this phenomenon with help of human psychology (Dunbar, 1996; Geidd, 2013). The human brain was designed as a social cognitive intuitive brain (Dunbar, 1996). Beginning with the Roman Empire to the number of people on a holiday card list; building, developing social contacts for survival has been a basic primal human instinct (Dunbar, 1996; Geidd, 2013). Humans, thus, had a social perspective combined with survival instinct that compelled them to have many contacts or friends from various corners of society (Dunbar, 1996). This ensured that a person could survive in any kind of environment and society (Dunbar, 1993). Dunbar studied the social communicative and relationship patterns of more than 38 primate species. His data analyses showed that human species needed to have a minimum number of 150 contacts or relationships (Dunbar, 1996; Geidd, 2013). This number of 150 known as 'Dunbar's number' formed the basis of having many friends on a SNS in contemporary society (Geidd, 2013). Twitter users had around 145 followers, while Facebook averaged more than 130. A wider circle of friends on such SNS's also ensured that the teen had less personal knowledge of all 'friends' and was exposing herself to harmful pornographic views publicly (Geidd, 2013).

Researchers from the Pew Research Center stated that Facebook users could shape their profiles to attract members of the opposite gender (Lenhart, 2015). Girl users were more prone to misusing this user control feature by posting pictures of themselves in provocative clothing engaging in risky behaviors of smoking, and gambling (Geidd, 2013). Thus, SNS helped in identity creation and performance, impression management, and enhancement of self-esteem (Fraser & Dutta, 2008; Rubin, 2002). In an exploratory research study using semi-structured interviews, researchers Dunne and colleagues found that teens formed the major consumers of Facebook, which was identified as 'the' popular SNS (Dunne et al., 2010; Spicer & Taehrreport, 2008; Cook & Kaiser, 2004). Teen girls were the predominant drivers of Facebook, 45% more than their male counterparts (Spicer & Taherreport, 2008). The researchers hypothesized that this discrepancy could be attributed to gender and societal bias issues such as girls tended to gossip, communicate more, and engage in widespread activities and hobbies (Spicer & Taherreport, 2008). These teen girls posted positive photographs as well photographs that tended to show them in a favorable light to attract 'friends' of the opposite gender (Dunne et al., 2010). Focus group results revealed that teen girls used Facebook to create and maintain positive and friendly images. They shared experiences and personal stories that revealed their empathetic, sensitive, and fun-loving nature, making their posts and profiles appealing, attractive, and 'cool' to the male member of Facebook (Dunne et al., 2010: 52). Facebook was an extension of offline social interactions- a way to amass many friends, gain social approval and status, and project a positive image to the external world (Madden et al., 2013; Dunne et al. 2010).

A participant aged 14 remarked that "it was a good way of talking to boys and becoming friends with them … saying things without feeling embarrassed or stupid" (Dunne et al., 2010, p. 52).

Results and analyses showed that teen girls posted "cool photos in trendy clothes showing good skin to show how attractive they are…" (Dunne et al., 2010, p. 52).

A participant aged 15 revealed, "you need to pretend on your profile… be something you are not… the more cool you appear… the more likes you get…" (Dunne et al., 2010, p. 53).

The same participant later stated that the prime objective of Facebook posts was to get maximum number of likes (Dunne et al., 2010). Only five-six percent of the teen girls interviewed said that they used Facebook to meet new people and communicate meaningfully about studies, career choices, and school (Dunne et al., 2010). Peer acceptance, social dating, enhanced self-esteem was also identified as some of the uses of Facebook (Dunne et al., 2010). The researchers felt that teen girls tended to use Facebook more than teen boys as their needs and wants were being steadily fulfilled by Facebook (Dunne et al., 2010). Teen girls could befriend anyone on SNS, exchange 'meetup' requests and photos of themselves (Dunne et al., 2010). Basing their research analyses on previous SNS research conducted in 2007 and 1994, the researchers hinted strongly at a uses and gratifications theory (O'Donohoe, 1994; Boyd, 2007; Dunne et al. 2010). The uses and gratifications (U and G) theory holds that people engaged with activities, technologies, and events that satisfied their needs and wants for an extended period (O'Donohoe, 1994). U and G theorists were interested in studying and researching those mediums or avenues that attract and hold audiences to their folds (O'Donohoe, 1994). Boyd translated the U and G theory to SNSs and said that SNS such as Facebook was popular and continued to maintain a strong foothold as it satisfied certain needs and wants of teen girls (Boyd, 2007). The following table lists some of the reported uses and gratifications as reported by participants in the research study.

Table 3. List of U and G of teen girls on Facebook

Uses: Gratifications Sought	Gratifications Obtained
Communication	Portraying one ideal image
Interacting with boys	Social dating
Being friendly	Peer Acceptance
Identity creation and management	Relationship maintenance, enhanced self-esteem
Entertainment, escapism, alleviation of Boredom	Safety from embarrassment and rejection

Source: (Dunne, Lawlor, M. A., & Rowley, J. (2010). Young people's use of online social networking sites: A uses and gratifications perspective. *Journal of Research in Interactive Marketing.* 4 (1), 46-58).

According to the gratifications listed in Table 3, teen girls used Facebook primarily to portray an ideal or positive image and to attract boys for perusal of dating relationships. The anonymity as well as the ease of access afforded by such SNSs could also be another reason behind the regular use of Facebook. The researchers further argued that use of Facebook to develop dating relationships by teens could influence and act as a strong motivator of irresponsible sexual behavior leading to teenage pregnancy (Dunne et al., 2010).

In the following section, exploration and discussion of contemporary neurobiological perspectives explain why teens are compelled to log onto Facebook all the time and engage in risky behaviors and decisions of casual sex and drinking with no fear or care of consequences.

Theoretical Perspectives

In his seminal paper *'Digital Revolution and the Adolescent Brain Evolution,'* renowned M.D. and pioneer of teen brain imaging studies, Dr. Geidd stated that the human teen brain was an active, growing, and adaptive organ (Geidd, 2013). The human teen brain was characterized by key features of:

1. Plasticity or adaptability. Dr. Geidd described the teen brain as remarkably adaptive and flexible to the forces and demands of nature and society such as adapting to different motor and cognitive functions, peer pressure and acceptance, and responding to emotional crises (Geidd, 2013).
2. Increased risk-taking and consequent poor decision-making
3. Increased sensation seeking (Geidd, 2013).

These three characteristics of the developing teen brain combined with the U and G theory make teens highly vulnerable to poor decisions such as casual sex, negative thrills such as drug addiction, and wrongful behavior such as crime and becoming pregnant. The teen brain was described in a constant state of flux wherein growth occurred not in size but structure and depth (Geidd, 2013). Brain growth usually peaked at ages 12 in girls and 14 in boys. Teen brain grew more dense, structured and more social (Geidd, 2013).

Researchers at the UCLA'S Ahmanson-Lovelace Brain Mapping Center stated that teens experienced less cognitive control leading to poor response inhibition (Wolpert, 2016). The researchers conducted a controlled experiment on a random sample of 32 teens aged 13-18, and informed them of their exposure and participation in a small sized SNS, similar to Facebook and Instagram (Wolpert, 2016). The teens saw 148 photographs on a computer screen for 12 minutes out of which 40 photographs were of themselves in various poses and clothes. The study had three conditions of (a) neutral photographs of people engaging in neutral behaviors of reading, walking, and wearing neutral clothing such as pant suits, (b) risky photos showing risky behaviors of frowning, drinking, engaging in casual sex, and wearing provocative clothing such as a two-piece swim suit, and (c) positive photos displaying positive behaviors of smiling, hugging, and wearing positive clothing of dresses and business suits. Brain activity was mapped and analyzed using magnetic resonance imaging (MRI) technique at the three levels.

Lead researcher, Lauren Sherman of the UCLA center reported that the first level of results analyzed showed that all teens responded positively by clicking 'yes' to their own photographs (Wolpert, 2016). This number grew dramatically to encompass the entire sample when teens saw that their photos had generated maximum number of likes. The inverse also occurred as teens responded negatively by clicking 'no' to photos of themselves that had garnered least number of likes (Wolpert, 2016). The reason for this visible behavior was the brain reward circuitry center, known as nucleus accumbens that housed the straitum. Sherman stated that when teens saw a substantial number of likes, they were compelled to respond positively and click 'yes.' But this compulsion slowed when the teens saw photos with least number of likes (Wolpert, 2016). Sherman noted that the nucleus accumbens was known as the 'master planner' that shaped teen behavior and action in the long run. This meant that teen positive behavior of smiling, hugging, participation in community events was due to peaked activity in the brain's master planner (Wolpert, 2016). Activation in the straitum was also strong when risky photos were viewed (Wolpert, 2016). However, little or no activation in the stratium was reported when teens viewed neutral photographs.

The second level of results showed that teens were less likely to click on neutral photos (Wolpert, 2016). Teen brains experienced minimal or less activation in brain regions of dorsal anterior cingulate cortex, bilateral prefrontal cortex, and the lateral parietal cortices (Wolpert, 2016). These three brain regions were responsible for teen cognitive control and response inhibition. Thus, these brain regions were not activated when all teens were exposed to neutral photos (Wolpert, 2016). Teen behavior had no adverse effect when exposed to neutral photos. But, according to MRI scans, these three brain regions reported little or no activation when exposed to the third condition of risky photos (Wolpert, 2016). Sherman stated that at first, level three results meant that teen behavior was not impacted by risky visuals, and this boded well for visual attention (Wolpert, 2016). But detailed analyses of the results showed that minimal or no activation in these brain regions was bad and worrying. When a teen viewed a risky photo in a two-piece swim suit, he or she experienced less cognitive control and reduced response inhibition. Sherman also stated that the three brain regions of the dorsal, prefrontal, and parietal cortex controlled decision-making and consequent actions (Wolpert, 2016). When the teen experienced poor or no response inhibition he or she felt 'compelled' to engage in poor decision-making and indulge in risky behaviors of casual sex without caring for the consequences i.e. becoming pregnant while in school (Wolpert, 2016).

In another similar neuro-imaging study, Young stated that the number of likes or approvals on a SNS such as Facebook increased activation in the brain reward circuitry center (Young, 2017). In the UCLA study, this brain reward circuitry center had been previously identified as being directly correlated to positive, neutral, and risky imagery (Wolpert, 2016; Young, 2017). This strong positive activation also increased the reward trigger in the teen brain (Young, 2017). For instance, if a teen experienced a reward of appreciation on viewing positive imagery and consequently liking and engaging in that positive behavior; the teen would always engage in the positive behavior to keep getting the reward. Reward could embrace many attitudes, actions and behaviors such as social acceptance to support, encouragement and monetary or physical comforts. A teen will be more prone to 'like' and engage in positive imagery of participating in class, eating at the table if such behavior or imagery begets a reward such as good grades, recognition as being academically superior, and appreciation (Young, 2017). On the other side, the inverse also holds true. Propensity to engage in risky behavior increases when such behavior and consequent poor decisions and actions are rewarded (Young, 2017). Teens will be compelled to 'like' risky imagery and behavior and engage in it if they feel such risky behavior is rewarded. For instance, a teen will be more likely to 'like' and engage in casual sex if they envisage a reward in such behavior like being popular with members of the opposite gender. Another example could be when pregnant teens get acceptance and support for their behavior and decision from their school, family and community it simply increases and cements their resolve and conviction of wrongful behavior and decision.

Activation in the brain reward circuitry center also increases the level of the neurotransmitter of dopamine (Geidd, 2013). In his earlier study of video games and addiction, Geidd stated that teens played video games to seek thrills and sensations (Geidd, 2013). Later, he applied the same concept to the issue of teens using SNS. He said that when teens saw risky photos, their brain reward circuitry was activated causing the level of dopamine to peak (Geidd, 2013). This dopamine peak led to profound changes in behavior and cognitive thought such as loss of control and continuation of the risky behavior (Geidd, 2013). This dopamine increase was viewed as a reward as it released 'feel good' and sensation-seeking hormones in the body (Geidd, 2013). Teens viewed and engaged in risky behavior to experience the dopamine rush and seek thrills and sensations (Geidd, 2013).

These neurobiological perspectives when combined with the growing prevalence and influence of SNS's could account for teenage pregnancy (Center for Disease Control [CDC], 2015). Teen girls were compelled to engage in risky behaviors and display thrill and/or sensation seeking attitudes and actions to satisfy brain development processes (CDC, 2015). The challenge, therefore, was to control and influence the quality of SNS impacting teens in contemporary society. According to the Pew Research Center, the control and influence of such SNS's could mitigate their impact on teen behavior and action (Lenhart, 2015, Gao, 2015). In the following section, the author discusses possible ways to restrict the quantity of teen SNS exposure.

SOLUTIONS AND RECOMMENDATIONS

In the *Pew Internet and American Life Project report*, Andersen and colleagues stated that to control the adverse consequences of teen compulsion and addiction to Facebook, and consequently also reduce the rate of teenage pregnancy, schools had to compete with the dopaminergic system of the teen brain (Anderson & Rainie, 2012; Geidd, 2013). Schools and other educational institutions had to ensure that non-instructional physical as well as instructional activities provided teens with equivalent levels of sensation and thrills to produce pleasurable rewards (Geidd, 2013). Continuity of a pleasurable reward system would divert teens from posting, viewing, and engaging in risky behaviors and poor decisions (Geidd, 2013). This meant that instructional and non-instructional activities had to surpass the threshold of dopamine level produced by addictive Facebook (Geidd, 2013).

Non-instructional physical activities meant bodily movement of any type and could also include jumping rope, sport, game, climbing stairs, and group activities of raking leaves, carrying books to a classroom (Castelli, Glowacki, Barcelona, Calvert, & Hwang, 2015). Such physical activities reduced stress, enhanced self-esteem, and social acceptance (Castelli et al., 2015). When teens experienced these external attitudinal changes of social acceptance, self-efficacy, and the consequent reward of popularity and social appreciation; they were more prone to replicate these actions or activities to produce the rewarding behavior. More time and effort spent on instructional and non-instructional physical activities improved cognitive functioning, reduced stress, and the urge to engage in risky behaviors of drinking, gambling, casual sex, and bullying (Castelli et al., 2015). The researchers also suggested competitive team sports and club activities where teens collaborated and communicated with each other in person to discover, invent, develop, publish, or achieve a mutually acceptable and satisfying outcome (Castelli et al., 2015). The occurrence and prevalence of such actions and consequent behaviors would lead teens to spend less time on Facebook. Young and colleagues stated that non-instructional physical activities included after-school programs of playing in a school band, participating in a group club (Young et al., 2017). Such physical activities spurred cognitive and emotional brain growth as the activities required planning, coordination, flexibility, and maturity (Young et al., 2017). Thus, the activities not only led to cognitive functional growth but also enabled teens to distinguish between positive and negative risky behavio. Emotional maturity made it possible for the teen to empathize and be sensitive to other people, situations, and feelings and in the process empowering them to make balanced decisions based on knowledge, and not on thrills and sensations.

Currently, 91% of high schools, and 77% of middle schools offered and conducted physical activity clubs and exercises (Edwards, Bocarro, & Kanters, 2013). In a report released by the Institute of Medicine (IOM), six key guidelines were issued for adoption of instructional and non-instructional activities into mainstream curriculum (Cooper, Greenberg, Castelli, Barton, Martin, Morrow, 2016). According to IOM report stated that time spent in physical activity would reduce but not eliminate time spent on

SNS such as Facebook (Cooper et al., 2016). IOM researchers argued that time spent on Facebook was an innate function of the teen brain and would gradually loose its potency as these teens evolved into adults (Cooper et al, 2016). The six guidelines were coined in the first guideline of a systems approach. A systems approach, as stated in the report and explained by the preceding guidelines, meant that the issue of physical activity should be included in all aspects of the school curriculum (Cooper et al., 2016). Physical activity was to be designated as a key subject as Science and Math. Physical activities could include active commute before school, physical education, physical activity classroom breaks, recess during school, active commute from school, intramurals, and extramural sports (Cooper at al., 2016). The six guidelines in the IOM report were:

1. A systems and whole-school approach to physical activity.
2. The inclusion of instructional and non-instructional activities in school policy decisions.
3. Physical education and consequent activity to be an integral core subject in school curriculum
4. Regular monitoring and evaluation of all school based instructional and non-instructional physical activities by state and federal agencies.
5. Provision to empower and equip all school teachers with knowledge and skills about importance and value of physical activity.
6. Access to physical activity programs by all school-going children (Cooper et al., 2016).

However, more than 82% of schools in US have not implemented these guidelines and even cut funding to develop physical activity programs (Cooper et al., 2016). Schools including administrators and teachers should understand that physical activity programs provide students with mental simulation and perhaps trigger high dopamine levels satisfying sensation and thrill urges in teens and adolescents (Cooper et al., 2016). Revised National Physical Plan initiatives launched in 2015 to meet the challenges of the IOM guidelines called for a stricter practical application of the guidelines (Cooper et al., 2016). The aim of the revised national physical plan initiatives was to increase and enhance physical education activities and curricula across all schools (Cooper et. al, 2016). In a meeting in Washington in December 2015, the National Physical Plan Initiatives Board stated that growth of instructional and non-instructional physical activities could focus student time and motivation to situations and people on the ground and not on Facebook (Cooper et al., 2016). The revised national physical plan initiatives were:

1. Provision of high quality physical activity programs at all levels in all schools.
2. Implementation of instructional and non-instructional physical activity programs in all schools.
3. Implementation of physically based instructional and non-instructional after school programs such as book clubs and team sports
4. Professional and scientific organizations should advocate and sponsor physical activity programs at school and college level (Cooper et al., 2016).

Schools should utilize Facebook to control its addictive influence on teens (CDC, 2015). Facebook posts and messages about challenging physical activity such as team sports and marches should be shared to pique interest and participation (CDC, 2015). Facebook posts could also include positive and neutral photos to elicit positive or no responses. Facebook messages could also be used to disseminate information about the complexity of the activity and inciting teens to respond and perhaps visit the physical activity site on ground.

Another viable option could be the usage of exergames on social networking sites to divert teens from risky behaviors and consequent poor decisions to online physical activity (Staiano & Calvert, 2011). Exergames originally were developed to enhance videogames to have fun and challenging elements that would increase levels of brain activity causing feelings of excitement and pleasure (Peng, Jhi-Hsuan, & Crouse, 2011). This increase in brain activity was identified as the spike in dopamine levels that led to creation of rewards such as pleasure, achievement, and goodwill (Peng et. al, 2011). However, this dopamine spike was due to positive imagery and behavior and not due to risky imagery or behavior. Researchers stated that perhaps exergames could be posted as links on Facebook inviting teens to click on them. Such behavior would reduce and perhaps divert teens towards acceptable and positive beneficial physical activity from the comfort of their SNS (Rudella & Butz, 2015). Teens would spend their time and energy exergaming instead of developing profiles and viewing harmful pictures (Rudella & Butz, 2015). Online exergames that could be posted as links on SNS or mobile apps satisfied the compelling teen brain function to log onto Facebook and connect with people. Exergames could be dance, sports, recreation, social activism, community engagement, and academic exercises. The *Nintendo Wii Sports Boxing* game enabled physical activity as players used their attention, spatial, and visual skills (Fogel, Miltenberger, Graves, & Koehler, 2012). A user clicked the exergame link on the SNS and participated in the boxing game (Fogel et al., 2012). The player could participate individually or collaborate, network with other players to form opposing teams (Fogel et al., 2012). Players had to be quick, with flexible hand-eye coordination utilizing their cognitive and critical thinking skills (Fogel et al., 2012). The exergame was challenging spurring the player or team to achieve more and more hereby leading to a dopamine rush and consequent activation in the brain reward circuitry center (Fogel et al, 2012). Another interactive exergame was *XaviX* that was played in two different formats. The former was the traditional method of purchasing a XaviX port and connecting to a television (Rudella & Butz, 2015). The latter method involved using appropriate links on SNS to participate and play the game. The link would then allow the user to log into the system and choose, subscribe, or purchase a game such as bowling, baseball, golf, J-MAT i.e. running, music and circuit, power boxing, and tennis (Rudella & Butz, 2015). All the games within XaviX were designed to generate enjoyment, camaderie, mental stimulation, and social connectedness among the players (Rudella & Butz, 2015). XaviX games not only increased physical endurance and muscular strength, but also increased cerebral circulation, increased neurotransmitter availability and enhanced neurobiological systems centered around the brain reward circuitry (Rudella & Butz, 2015). Playing XaviX games also increased the executive control function and skills of the teen brain enabling them to choose appropriate positive behaviors and decisions (Rudella & Butz, 2015).

In another dance exergame called *In the Groove*, originally designed for third and fourth graders; it was found that more than 85% of older girl teens who clicked on the appropriate link to play the game had positive self-esteem (Staiano, Terry, Watson, Scanlon, Abraham, & Calvert, 2011). More than 94% of the players stated that they had no time to check their Facebook profiles and view their 'likes and 'dislikes' (Staianno et al., 2011). In the exergame of the *Nintendo WII sports series*, players collaborated, competed, or communicated with each other through their avatars (Rudella & Butz, 2015). The exergame had many physical activities requiring them to be played by two or more than four players. Creation of avatars, and networking among different players increased level of social competence thereby directly impacting self-efficacy levels (Rudella & Butz, 2015). Contemporary exergames could be incorporated into the classroom thus advancing the national physical plan guidelines of a comprehensive systems approach.

In a recent research study involving a purposeful sample of teens ranging in ages 13-18, mobile apps such as smart phones were used to design and develop games with SNSs interfaces (Blackman, Zoellner, You, & Eastabrooks, 2016). In their qualitative exploratory study design using focus groups and interviews, the researchers developed a game that met the expectations of the teens as well as their parents (Blackman et al., 2016). The results generated from the study's three focus groups suggested games that had components of texting, messaging, flirting, challenge, and music. Participants stated that music was an effective means to attract and sustain attention—

music calms me down

music is so relaxing

you can listen to it anytime... anywhere (Blackman et al., 2016).

Parents, on the other hand, were concerned with aspects of privacy, accessibility, and monitoring. More than 70% of parents in their focus groups said that they would welcome mobile app games that could be monitored (Backman et al., 2016). The results in totality segregated the game type into four major categories of (a) recreation, (b) sports with sub-categories of competitive, and cooperative (Blackman et al., 2016). Recreational games such as dance could be competitive or cooperative in nature, and vice-versa.

As shown in Table 4, recreational and sport games were both competitive and cooperative. The categories primarily involved the fostering of social and cognitive skills that challenged players to excel and achieve (Blackman et al., 2016). Winning a game earned participant points that were posted onto their Facebook profiles. Thus, a high score indicated a favorable and positive impression on a Facebook profile (Blackman et al., 2016). This meant that a player was likely to get more 'likes' if he or she participated, played, and scored highly in the game (Blackman et al., 2016). Thus, a higher score produced more 'likes' leading to acceptance of positive game behavior such as achievement, competition, and sportsmanship (Blackman et al., 2016). The study also highlighted the presence and usage of intrinsic motivation as the main reason for engaging in the game. Participants did not feel the need for external motivators of voiceovers or animated agents (Blackman et al., 2016). Intrinsic motivation of high scores propelled teens to engage in gaming behavior of recreation, sports, competition, and cooperation (Blackman, et al., 2016). Intrinsic motivation coupled with high scores led teens to spikes in dopamine levels and an inclination to sustain this elevated level of dopamine at all time. This meant an active and continuous engagement with these mobile app games at all time. This would effectively cut in to time to be spent on Facebook (Blackman et al., 2016).

In a Public Health article on the use of active gaming as a strategy to occupy the time spent on Facebook by teens and adolescents, researchers Barnett and colleagues stated that active videogames had to imitate and assimilate the functionality and process of the Facebook system (Barnett, Bangay, McKenzie, & Ridgers, 2013). Active videogames (AVG) had to be pervasive, continuous, persuasive, challenging, exciting, accumulative, inclusive, and easily accessible to all (Barnett et al., 2013). AVG encouraged physical, social, and higher cognitive functioning wherein users had to exercise their observation, critical and creative thinking, and analytical skills (Barnett et al., 2013). AVG captured and sustained user interest over an extended period (Barnett et al., 2013). AVGs could be accessed by teens and adolescents belonging to low and high socio-economic status. The former accessed AVG on their smartphones with Facebook interface (Kumar, 2013; Barnett et al., 2013). Smartphone AVGs had overlaying synthetic

Table 4. Game types selected by focus groups

GAME	RECREATION	TYPE
Cheer Mania	Similar to dance but cheerleading moves instead	Cooperative
Deer Hunter	Simulates deer hunting	Competitive
Musical Freeze tag	Run around and hide while music plays from the phone and when it stops, everyone has to freeze or stop where they are. The "it" person can see on the phone where the "un-it" persons are and tag them Run around and hide while music plays from the phone and when it stops, everyone has to freeze or stop where they are. The "it" person can see on the phone where the "un-it" persons are and tag them	Competitive
Obstacle Course	Virtual obstacle course where the player jumps, runs and dodges obstacles	Competitive
ZADAT Tag	Music plays when person is tagged or if in the dark, phone lights up. - Team or Individual tag. Music plays when person is tagged or if in the dark, phone lights up.	Cooperative/ Competitive
Funky Chicken	- You can be different colored chickens and you do the funky chicken dance to the funky chicken song	Cooperative
Exercise Twister & Dance	Different types of music are played. The faster you move, the faster the tempo of the music is, the more points you get	Cooperative
Dancing Game	A series of dance moves are displayed and the player has to recreate the moves. Scores are given in points or a letter grade based on accuracy of the dance moves	Competitive
Color Hunt	Pick a color. Use the camera phone to take pictures of the things that are the same cooler as the selected color.	Cooperative
Whack-a-mole	Select a mole. Different moles stick their head out of the ground hole. You get points when you whack your selected mole	Competitive
	SPORTS	
Track/Field	Simulates events done during track like hurdles, discus, running	Competitive
Volleyball	Simulates a volleyball game	Competitive/ Cooperative
Basketball for Dummies	Move around and shoot baskets. More than one basket; Baskets move further away or side to side	Competitive
Softball Mania	Play softball by pitching or if on offense hit the ball and run around bases.	Competitive/ Cooperative
Football/Basketball/NASCAR	Simulates real-life conditions of these activities	Competitive/ Cooperative

Source: (Blackman, C. A. K., Zoellner, J. You, W., & Estabrooks, P.A. (2016). Developing mobile apps for physical activity in low socioeconomic status for youth. *Journal of Mobile Technology in Medicine*. 5 (1), 33-44).

visual content above images of the real world (Kumar, 2013). This kind of augmented reality AVGs were mentally challenging and emotionally satisfying for the teen (Barnett et al., 2013). Augmented reality also included reference images as posters or cards enabling users to navigate through the game. Digital content relative to the reference cards was also displayed urging the player to make sense of the AVG (Kumar, 2013). Thus, augmented reality AVG also shaped teen motivation and perseverance from developing negative or risky imagery to active hands on learning (Barnett et al., 2013). Players had to tap into learnt declarative and procedural knowledge schemas to compete successfully and win. An example of an augmented reality AVG was *'Rolling Dead'* where players had to stake their claim and control a robotic ball through a carnage of digitally overlaid zombies.

The key was using Facebook to make teens participate in such games and physical activities. The challenge lay in not controlling teen addiction to Facebook but using it to influence their motivation, sensation and thrills to a positive level that do not lead to poor decision-making.

FUTURE RESEARCH DIRECTIONS

The author presented a narrow micro perspective on a topical global issue of Facebook and teen age pregnancy linkage. The author outlined the tenuous link between Facebook time and teenage pregnancy rates through theoretical meta-analyses and sparse empirical research. However negligible empirical but strong theoretical research needs to be balanced to provide a comprehensive holistic global outlook. The balance between theory and empirical research would also enable a scholarly-practitioner thrust enabling further debate and discussion on issues of SNS subjects and teen pregnancy challenges. Further, the chapter must embody a macro perspective to make the issue of SNS and teenage pregnancy relevant, topical, current, and global. The thrust of empirical research and study has to shift from the US and European nations to countries such as China, Australia, and Malaysia to become cross-cultural. Issues of prevalence and growth of SNS, type of SNS, and purpose of SNS including the range of users needs to be researched and documented through longitudinal surveys, focus groups exercises, and qualitative case studies. A SNS dashboard needs to be constructed that would house all this data and research enabling causal analysis and correlational research with local teenage pregnancy data. The research would also enable identification and development of methods to combat the influence of SNS on teenage pregnancy. Further it would also allow academicians and research practitioners to compare SNS and teenage pregnancy rates between different countries, and focus on a common cause such as culture, race, or gender, and solution driving use of SNS and consequent impact on teenage pregnancy. Some issues that could be investigated include the underlying influence of culture and gender on use of SNS.

CONCLUSION

The chapter endeavored to strengthen the link between Facebook usage and teenage pregnancy rates and show that an increase in Facebook time impacted teenage pregnancy. The author based her analyses on a robust foundation of theoretical meta-analyses research. The chapter could be divided into three main sections of background as evidenced by the exhaustive literature review discussing the varied use of Facebook and other social networks by teens, and a description and analysis of Facebook. Chapter analysis also reflected on the reasons for the usage of Facebook, namely the Uses and Gratifications (U and G) theory. Neurobiological research highlighted the fact that teens were driven to use Facebook, view and post risky imagery and engage in risky behavior of casual sex, and take poor decisions such as becoming a teen mother. But research also focused on the undeniable truth that Facebook systems could not be controlled. In the third section of her chapter, the author dwelt on this issue of quality control of Facebook. The author mapped out the need and benefits of diverse instructional and non-instructional physical activities including exergames and active video gaming. The bottom line was to combine physical activity and video games within Facebook systems. This meant that even though teens continued to spent time on Facebook, they did it for a different reason i.e. of playing a game. Teens continued to experience a dopamine rush and spike but instead for risky imagery the spike occurred for a positive reason with consequent positive rewards. Hence, the compulsion to view, post, engage in risky behaviors of casual sex, and make poor decisions of becoming a mother while still in school were reduced but not eliminated. However, presence of overwhelming theoretical research does not satisfy a scholarly-practitioner perspective of tangible physical research evidence combined with theory. National and international empirical evidence is needed to support the tenuous link between Facebook usage and teenage pregnancy rates.

REFERENCES

Anderson, J., & Rainie, L. (2012). *Millennials will benefit and suffer due to their hyperconnected lives.* Washington, DC: Pew Research Center.

Barnett, L. M., Bangay, S., McKenzie, S., & Ridgers, N. D. (2013). Active gaming as a mechanism to promote physical activity and fundamental movement skill in children. *Frontiers in Public Health*, 1. PMID:24400301

Blackman, K. C., Zoellner, J., McCrickard, D. S., Harlow, J., Winchester, W. W. III, Hill, J. L., ... Estabrooks, P. A. (2016). Developing Mobile Apps for Physical Activity in Low Socioeconomic Status Youth. *Journal of Mobile Technology in Medicine*, *5*(1), 33–44. doi:10.7309/jmtm.5.1.6

Boyd, D. (2007). Why youth (heart) social network sites: The role of networked publics in teenage social life. *MacArthur foundation series on digital learning–Youth, identity, and digital media volume*, 119-142.

Boyd, D., & Ellison, N. (2007). Social network sites: Definition, history, and scholarship. *Journal of Computer-Mediated Communication*, *13*(1), 1–11. doi:10.1111/j.1083-6101.2007.00393.x

Castelli, D. M., Glowacki, E., Barcelona, J. M., Calvert, H. G., & Hwang, J. (2015). Active education: Growing evidence on physical activity and academic performance. *Active Living Research*, 1-5.

Centers for Disease Control and Prevention. (2015a). *Results from the School Health Policies and Practices Study 2014.* Atlanta, GA: Author. Retrieved from http://www.cdc.gov/ healthyyouth/data/shpps/ pdf/shpps-508-final_101315.pdf

Cook, D. T., & Kaiser, S. B. (2004). Betwixt and between: Age ambiguity and the sexualization of the female consuming subject. *Journal of Consumer Culture*, *4*(2), 203–227. doi:10.1177/1469540504043682

Cooper, K. H., Greenberg, J. D., Castelli, D. M., Barton, M., Martin, S. B., & Morrow, J. R. Jr. (2016). Implementing policies to enhance physical education and physical activities in schools. *Research Quarterly for Exercise and Sport*, *87*(2), 133–140. doi:10.1080/02701367.2016.1164009 PMID:27100264

Dunbar, R. (1996). *Gossip, grooming and the evolution of language*. Cambridge, MA: Harvard UP.

Dunbar, R. I. (1993). Coevolution of neocortical size, group size and language in humans. *Behavioral and Brain Sciences, 16*(4), 681–694. doi:10.1017/S0140525X00032325

Dunne, Á., Lawlor, M. A., & Rowley, J. (2010). Young people's use of online social networking sites–a uses and gratifications perspective. *Journal of Research in Interactive Marketing, 4*(1), 46–58. doi:10.1108/17505931011033551

Edwards, M. B., Bocarro, J. N., & Kanters, M. A. (2013). Place disparities in supportive environments for extracurricular physical activity in North Carolina middle schools. *Youth & Society, 45*(2), 265–285. doi:10.1177/0044118X11416677

Finin, T., Ding, L., Zhou, L., & Joshi, A. (2005). Social networking on the semantic web. *The Learning Organization, 12*(5), 418–435. doi:10.1108/09696470510611384

Fogel, V. A., Miltenberger, R. G., Graves, R., & Koehler, S. (2010). The effects of exergaming on physical activity among inactive children in a physical education classroom. *Journal of Applied Behavior Analysis, 43*(4), 591–600. doi:10.1901/jaba.2010.43-591 PMID:21541146

Fraser, M., & Dutta, S. (2010). *Throwing sheep in the boardroom: How online social networking will transform your life, work and world*. John Wiley & Sons.

Gao, G. (2015). *15 Striking Findings from 2015. Pew Research Center.* Available from http://www.pewresearch.org/fact-tank/2015/12/22/15-striking-findings-from-2015/

Giedd, J. N. (2013). The digital revolution and adolescent brain evolution. *The Journal of Adolescent Health, 51*(2), 101–105. doi:10.1016/j.jadohealth.2012.06.002 PMID:22824439

Greenfield, P. M. (2009). Technology and informal education: What is taught, what is learned. *Science, 323*(5910), 69–71. doi:10.1126cience.1167190 PMID:19119220

Haythornthwaite, C. (2005). Social networks and Internet connectivity effects. *Information Communication and Society, 8*(2), 125–147. doi:10.1080/13691180500146185

Kohl, H. W. III, & Cook, H. D. (Eds.). (2013). *Educating the student body: Taking physical activity and physical education to school*. National Academies Press.

Kumar, J. (2013, July). Gamification at work: Designing engaging business software. In *International Conference of Design, User Experience, and Usability* (pp. 528-537). Springer. 10.1007/978-3-642-39241-2_58

Landry, M., Turner, M., Vyas, A., & Wood, S. (2017). Social Media and Sexual Behavior Among Adolescents: Is there a link? *JMIR Public Health and Surveillance, 3*(2), e28. doi:10.2196/publichealth.7149 PMID:28526670

Lenhart, A. (2015). *Teens, social media and technology overview 2015*. Pew Research Center Internet & Technology. Retrieved from http://wikiurls.com/?http://www.pewinternet.org/2015/04/09/teens-social-media-technology-2015/ on September 3, 2017.

Lyons, E. (2009). *Criticisms of exergaming*. Presentation at the *annual meeting of Games for Health*, Boston, MA.

Madden, M., Lenhart, A., Cortesi, S., Gasser, U., Duggan, M., Smith, A., & Beaton, M. (2013). Teens, social media, and privacy. *Pew Research Center*, *21*, 2–86.

Nauert, R. (2015). Does Social Networking Limit Physical Activity? *Psych Central*. Retrieved on October 6, 2017, from https://psychcentral.com/news/2012/09/11/does-social-networking-limit-physical-activity/44412.html

O'Donohoe, S. (1994). Advertising uses and gratifications. *European Journal of Marketing*, *28*(8/9), 52–75.

Parker-Pope, T. (2005). The PlayStation workout: Videogames that get kids to jump, kick and sweat. *Wall Street Journal*, p. 4.

Peng, W., Lin, J. H., & Crouse, J. (2011). Is playing exergames really exercising? A meta-analysis of energy expenditure in active video games. *Cyberpsychology, Behavior, and Social Networking*, *14*(11), 681–688. doi:10.1089/cyber.2010.0578 PMID:21668370

Raacke, J., & Bonds-Raacke, J. (2008). MySpace and Facebook: Applying the uses and gratifications theory to exploring friend-networking sites. *Cyberpsychology & Behavior*, *11*(2), 169–174. doi:10.1089/cpb.2007.0056 PMID:18422409

Rideout, V. J., Foehr, U. G., & Roberts, D. F. (2010). *Generation M [superscript 2]: Media in the Lives of 8-to 18-Year-Olds*. Henry J. Kaiser Family Foundation.

Rubin, A. M. (2002). The Uses-and-Gratifications Perspective of Media Effects. In Media effects (2nd ed.; pp. 535-558). Routledge.

Rudella, J. L., & Butz, J. V. (2015). Exergames: Increasing physical activity through effective instruction. *Journal of Physical Education, Recreation & Dance*, *86*(6), 8–15. doi:10.1080/07303084.2015.1022672

Spicer, K., & Taherreport, A. (2008, March 9). Girls and young women are now the most prolific web users. *The Sunday Times*.

Staiano, A. E., & Calvert, S. L. (2011). Exergames for physical education courses: Physical, social, and cognitive benefits. *Child Development Perspectives*, *5*(2), 93–98. doi:10.1111/j.1750-8606.2011.00162.x PMID:22563349

Staiano, A. E., Terry, A., Watson, K., Scanlon, P., Abraham, A., & Calvert, S. L. (2011). *Physical activity intervention for weight loss in overweight and obese adolescents*. In Poster presented at the biennial meeting of the Society for Research in Child Development, Montreal, Canada.

Sundén, J. (2003). *Material Virtualities*. New York: Peter Lang.

Wolpert, S. (2016). *The teenage brain on social media*. UCLA Health. Retrieved from: https://www.uclahealth.org/body.cfm?id=1397&action=detail&ref=2807&fr=true

Young, D. R., Felton, G. M., Grieser, M., Elder, J. P., Johnson, C., Lee, J. S., & Kubik, M. Y. (2007). Policies and opportunities for physical activity in middle school environments. *The Journal of School Health, 77*(1), 41–47. doi:10.1111/j.1746-1561.2007.00161.x PMID:17212759

Young, K. (2017). *Social media and the teen brain- How to make it work for them.* Retrieved from http://www.heysigmund.com/the-teen-brain-on-social-media/

ADDITIONAL READING

Acharya, D. R., Bhattarai, R., Poobalan, A., Teijlingen, V. E., & Chapman, G. (2014). Factors associated with teenage pregnancy in South Asia.

Bonell, C. (2004). Why is teenage pregnancy conceptualized as a social problem? A review of quantitative research from the USA and UK. *Culture, Health & Sexuality, 6*(3), 255–272. doi:10.1080/136910 50310001643025 PMID:21972877

Lara, D., Decker, M. J., & Brindis, C. D. (2016). Exploring how residential mobility and migration influences teenage pregnancy in five rural communities in California: Youth and adult perceptions. *Culture, Health & Sexuality, 18*(9), 980–995. doi:10.1080/13691058.2016.1150514 PMID:27439657

Meier, E. P., & Gray, J. (2014). Facebook photo activity associated with body image disturbance in adolescent girls. *Cyberpsychology, Behavior, and Social Networking, 17*(4), 199–206. doi:10.1089/cyber.2013.0305 PMID:24237288

Sercombe, H. (2014). Risk, adaptation and the functional teenage brain. *Brain and Cognition, 89,* 61–69. doi:10.1016/j.bandc.2014.01.001 PMID:24468052

Shapiro, L. A. S., & Margolin, G. (2014). Growing up wired: Social networking sites and adolescent psychosocial development. *Clinical Child and Family Psychology Review, 17*(1), 1–18. doi:10.100710567-013-0135-1 PMID:23645343

Valente, T. W. (2014). Peer influences: The impact of online and offline friendship networks on adolescent smoking and alcohol use. *The Journal of Adolescent Health, 54*(5), 508–514. doi:10.1016/j.jadohealth.2013.07.001 PMID:24012065

Young, S. D., & Jordan, A. H. (2013). The influence of social networking photos on social norms and sexual health behaviors. *Cyberpsychology, Behavior, and Social Networking, 16*(4), 243–247. doi:10.1089/cyber.2012.0080 PMID:23438268

KEY TERMS AND DEFINITIONS

Brain Plasticity: The brain's ability to change throughout life. The human brain has the amazing ability to reorganize itself by forming new connections between brain cells.

Dopamine: A neurotransmitter, a chemical responsible for sending messages between the brain and different nerve cells of the body. It affects bodily functions, such as movement, memory, sleep, mood, pleasurable reward, behavior, and cognition.

Dorsal Cortex: A component of the prefrontal cortex of the brain of humans and non-human primates. It is one of the most recently evolved parts of the human brain. It undergoes a prolonged period of maturation which lasts until adulthood.

Nucleus Accumbens: A critical component of the basal forebrain controlling major neurotransmitter levels, reward circuits or neurons, and basic human functions of hunger and sex.

Parietal Cortex: One of the four major lobes of the cerebral cortex in the brain of all mammals. It controls sensation, perception, and cognition.

Prefrontal Cortex: The gray matter of the anterior part of the frontal lobe of the brain that is highly developed in humans and plays a role in the regulation of complex cognitive, emotional, and behavioral functioning.

Social Networking Site: A website that enables users to create public profiles within that web site and form relationships with other users of the same web site who access their profile.

This research was previously published in Socio-Cultural Influences on Teenage Pregnancy and Contemporary Prevention Measures; pages 129-149, copyright year 2019 by Information Science Reference (an imprint of IGI Global).

Index

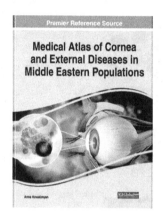
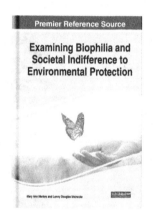
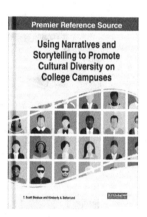

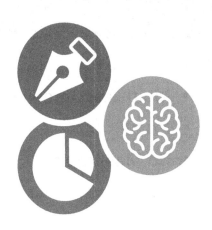

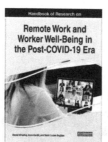

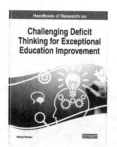

Have Your Work Published and Freely Accessible
Open Access Publishing

With the industry shifting from the more traditional publication models to an open access (OA) publication model, publishers are finding that OA publishing has many benefits that are awarded to authors and editors of published work.

Freely Share Your Research

Higher Discoverability & Citation Impact

Rigorous & Expedited Publishing Process

Increased Advancement & Collaboration

Acquire & Open

When your library acquires an IGI Global e-Book and/or e-Journal Collection, your faculty's published work will be considered for immediate conversion to Open Access *(CC BY License)*, at no additional cost to the library or its faculty *(cost only applies to the e-Collection content being acquired)*, through our popular **Transformative Open Access (Read & Publish) Initiative**.

Provide Up To **100%** OA APC or CPC Funding

Funding to Convert or Start a Journal to **Platinum OA**

Support for Funding an **OA Reference Book**

IGI Global publications are found in a number of prestigious indices, including Web of Science™, Scopus®, Compendex, and PsycINFO®. The selection criteria is very strict and to ensure that journals and books are accepted into the major indexes, IGI Global closely monitors publications against the criteria that the indexes provide to publishers.